W9-AOG-026

Workplace Diversity

Issues and Perspectives

Edited by

Alfrieda Daly

NASW PRESS
National Association of Social Workers
Washington, DC

Josephine A.V. Allen, PhD, ACSW, *President*
Josephine Nieves, MSW, PhD, *Executive Director*

Jane Browning, *Executive Editor*

Christina A. Davis, *Senior Editor*

Christine Cotting, UpperCase Publication Services, *Project Manager*

Cinci Stowell, *Copy Editor*

Caroline Polk, *Proofreader*

Bernice Eisen, *Indexer*

Chanté Lampton, *Acquisitions Associate*

Heather Peters, *Editorial Secretary*

Library of Congress Cataloging-in-Publication Data

Workplace diversity : issues and perspectives / edited by Alfrieda
   Daly.
      p.   cm.
   Includes bibliographical references and index.
   ISBN 0-87101-281-2 (pbk. : alk. paper)
      1. Diversity in the workplace—United States.   2. Human services—
   United States—Management.   I. Daly, Alfrieda.
   HF5549.5.M5W674   1998
   331.13′3—dc21   98-12180
                                                            CIP

Printed in the United States of America

To **Henry J. Meyer**

Professor Emeritus, University of Michigan,
who understood what it took to affirm diversity
in the workplace, as well as in training and
education, before the term "workplace diversity"
entered the lexicon!

Contents

Preface   xi
Alfrieda Daly

Introduction   xiii

PART I: Construction of Diversity Paradigms   1

1   **A Group Psychological Perspective on Multiculturalism: What Will It Take for the High Priests and Priestesses to Change Their Minds?**   3
Clayton P. Alderfer

PART II: Origins of Diversity and Its Influence in the Workplace   19

2   **Diversity and Challenges of New Immigrants in the Changing American Workplace**   21
Richard A. English and Fariyal Ross-Sheriff

3   **Supervision and Management of American Indian Social and Human Services Workers**   36
Joyce Z. White

4   **Latinos in the Work Force: A Systemic Overview of Potentials and Barriers to Access**   45
Yolanda Mayo-Quiñones

5   **Organizational and Social Barriers Confronting People with Disabilities in the Workplace**   56
Dawn Howard

6   **Some Common Misperceptions about Deafness in the Workplace: Attitudinal Barriers Resistant to Change**   61
Michael Schwartz

PART III: Policy Issues   67

7   **Historical Review of U.S. Policy on Diversity**   70
Ernest F. Dunn

8   **Social Issues, Social Policy, and Workplace Diversity**   88
John E. Tropman

 9   **Working It Out: What Managers Should Know**   103
      about Gay Men, Lesbians, and Bisexual People
      and Their Employment Issues
      Beth D. Kivel and Joel W. Wells

10   **The Americans with Disabilities Act and**   116
      Inclusive Personnel and Employment Policy
      Richard O. Salsgiver

11   **Linguistic Diversity and Organizational**   132
      Communication Policy
      Ovetta H. Harris

      PART IV: Organizational Structure and   141
              Communication

12   **Ethnicity, Gender, Earnings, Occupational**   144
      Rank, and Job Satisfaction in the Public
      Social Services: What Do Workers Say?
      R. L. McNeely, Marty Sapp, and Alfrieda Daly

13   **African American Women in Academic**   166
      Leadership
      Jeanette Jennings, Ruth R. Martin, and
      Phyllis Ivory Vroom

14   **Conflict, Cooperation, and Institutional Goal**   176
      Attainment in Diversity: Improving
      Relationships between Urban Organizations
      and Neighborhood Residents
      R. L. McNeely, Marty Sapp, and Henry J. Meyer

15   **Multicultural Communication in Human**   191
      Services Organizations
      Joyce O. Beckett and Delores Dungee-Anderson

16   **Latino Diversity in Communication in the**   215
      Workplace
      Humberto Fabelo-Alcover and Karen M. Sowers

      PART V: Organizational Development Efforts   229
              as Change Processes

17   **Implications of the Americans with Disabilities**   231
      Act for Institutions with Student Teaching,
      Practicum, and Internship Requirements
      Sue Schmitt

18   **Managing Biculturalism at the Workplace:**   243
      A Group Approach
      Nan Van Den Bergh

19 The Consultation Circle: A Model for Team   253
    Consultation
    Carol F. Kuechler

20 White Racial Identity: Theory, Research, and   265
    Implications for Organizational Contexts
    Caryn J. Block and Robert T. Carter

21 Mentoring and Diversity in Organizations: 281
    Importance of Race and Gender in
    Work Relationships
    David A. Thomas

    PART VI: Emerging Issues in the Workplace   293

22 Workers' Use of Supportive Workplace   297
    Policies: Variations by Gender, Race, and
    Class-Related Characteristics
    Susan J. Lambert

23 Concerns of Employed Women: Issues for   314
    Employee Assistance Programs
    Glenda Dewberry Rooney

24 African American Entrepreneurship and Work   331
    Force Diversity
    James I. Herbert

25 The Afrocentric Paradigm and Workplace   341
    Diversity
    Jerome H. Schiele

26 Diversity in the Workplace: Issues and   354
    Concerns of Africans and Asians
    Letha A. See

27 Creating Fair Workplaces for Asian American   373
    Women: A Joint-Constructional Approach
    Gui-Young Hong

28 Hawaiian Health, Native Healing, and   385
    Medical Hegemony
    Lana Ka'opua

    Afterword   399

    Index   403

    About the Editor   415

    About the Contributors   417

Preface

A few years ago I had a discussion with several colleagues about how little investigative and intellectual attention is given to the notion of diversity as an organizational change process and to organizational efforts to encourage diversity. We expressed concern about the lack of research and substantive scholarship that could provide a basic framework for addressing the problems of increasing diversity now emerging from formal organizations. We observed that there is no integrative framework for conceptualizing the effects of diversity on the variables that organizational management uses in strategic planning and prediction.

The change process we envisioned would involve the following steps: (1) learn about the history and cultural experiences and attributes of various groups, (2) identify areas of need and address these areas with supportive workplace policies and procedures, (3) examine organizational structure and processes to find barriers to inclusion and identify interpersonal supports for communication, information processing, and feedback, and (4) identify organizational development needs and implement change to supply those needs. Realizing change as ongoing, steps 3 and 4 should contain information feedback mechanisms so that policies can be adapted to address emerging needs as they become apparent.

Open systems theory posits change and conflict as inevitable in organizations: Change in any part of a system eventually will affect all of its parts. It follows, therefore, that any organizational change that develops more staff diversity will alter many organizational variables. We need paradigms to lead us to fresh understandings of diversity and its dynamic interactions with those variables.

My colleagues and I discussed the need for a book comprising a series of frameworks that might be useful in managing the range of issues that emerge in contemporary organizations and the environments in which these organizations operate. Because my particular interest is in human services organizations and the delivery of services in dynamic environments, those interests are reflected throughout this book.

Workplace Diversity: Issues and Perspectives presents state-of-the-art theory, research, and practical guidance generated by some of the brightest scholars in the United States. Each chapter provides context for understanding workplace diversity as a change process. Taken together, the chapters yield a perspective on diversity viewed through a wide-angle lens that suggests the range and complexity of the issues diversity raises. Overall, the book contributes to an understanding of the dynamics of change as organizations move toward more inclusive systems.

ACKNOWLEDGMENTS

This book is a reality because of the support and encouragement of many people. With Glenda Dewberry Rooney of the Department of Social Work at Augsburg University, Minneapolis; Katherine Giscombe, research director for Catalyst, New York City; and Sylvia Bittle, doctoral candidate in organizational psychology at the University of Maryland and cofounder and codirector of the Center for Strategic Community Development, Charlotte, NC, I discussed the need to look beyond diversity training in making the workplace truly supportive of diversity.

Clayton P. Alderfer of the Graduate School of Applied and Professional Psychology at Rutgers, R. L. McNeely of the School of Social Welfare at the University of Wisconsin–Milwaukee, Nan Van Den Bergh of Humboldt State University, and Lee See of the School of Social Work at the University of Georgia encouraged me in many ways. R. B. Leashore of Hunter College provided not only wise counsel but also that most precious commodity—time; he was unfailingly affirming in more ways than I can count.

I am particularly grateful to each of the expert contributors. Many had arduous situations to manage—births, weddings, reconstructive surgery, and submissions of tenure packages—and each saw the project as significant and persevered in completing their chapters. Their expertise is awesome.

For me, Murphy's Law applied during the last nine or 10 months of this project. Everything that could go wrong did—several times. I want to recognize as my birth coach Chanté Lampton, acquisitions associate for NASW Press. She saw me through the difficult beginning of a very hard labor, and I am grateful for her focus and quiet assurances. Senior editor Christina A. Davis and project manager Christine Cotting were prodigious in providing gentle guidance through the major work of bringing the book to completion. I thank them both for working through numerous problems and always teaching me as they did. I am very grateful for the skills of copy editor Cinci Stowell, proofreader Caroline Polk, and indexer Bernice Eisen. I also thank Linda Beebe and Nancy Winchester, former executive editors at NASW Press, for their guidance and capable assistance.

I am also deeply grateful for the many excellent mentors I have known, particularly Dr. Henry J. Meyer. He can take pride in the accomplishments of all the people of color who completed the joint doctoral program in social work and social sciences at the University of Michigan, because he encouraged, guided, and supported us in so many ways. He is a peerless mentor.

—Alfrieda Daly

Introduction

Diversity issues have spawned many diversity management programs and initiatives—not all of which are effective. Some workshops have actually resulted in more serious problems than they solved (Murray, 1993; Swisher, 1995). An oversimplification or lack of understanding of diversity's complexity can intensify pre-existing problems (Murray, 1993). The lack of an integrative framework derived through theoretical arguments and epistemological discussions around diversity's effects on organizational variables means few consistent guidelines exist for implementing diversity programs. Little attention has focused on structural responses to efforts to promote a climate more supportive of diversity.[1]

Systems changes affect all parts of a system—frequently in unanticipated ways. To better foresee diversity's effects, organizations need an enhanced understanding of workplace processes that occur in response to diversity. This understanding is particularly crucial for public and volunteer institutions whose major endeavor is the delivery of services to a larger system. How will diversity and its challenges affect organizational practices and services delivery? How are organizational members affected by the confluence of cultural and diversity issues in the larger system from which they come? Unlike the private sector, outcomes for human services are frequently ambiguous and value driven, and core technologies are indeterminate—cause-and-effect relationships between intervention and outcome are not reliable. Thus, studying the processes and effectiveness of diversity efforts in human services can be difficult.

A change process that can lead to organizational systems truly inclusive of diverse groups is needed. Three underlying assumptions are identified for any organization looking for an effective response to diversity: (1) Diversity should be approached as a change process that requires investment of resources and time, (2) any diversity intervention should focus on the context for the needed change, and (3) the intervention plan should be based on an assessment of the particular situation in the target system.

Why is workplace diversity an issue now? Among the reasons for a growing interest in it are immigration and global migration patterns, the increasing presence of women in the workplace, and extension of

---

[1]As we define it here, *diversity* is inclusive of all who are defined as "other" or outside of the hegemony and may include those people who are marginalized by age, sexual and affectional orientation, or language concerns as well as people of color and people living with disabilities.

civil rights to people living with disabilities and equal rights to gay men, lesbians, and bisexual people. These external factors prompt an organizational response because diversity in staffing and related issues affects organizational practices. These factors will become issues in human services organizations because social issues shape public policy. For example, societal concern gave rise to the 1990 Americans with Disabilities Act and to changes in affirmative action legislation in Texas and California. Public policy affects internal organizational policy related to managing diversity. Communication and interpersonal relationships are vital contributors to successful, supportive management of diversity in the workplace. Organizations have to assess workplace factors that hinder or promote diversity goals to ensure that reporting and communication structures are clear. Organizations also must develop policies and reward systems that support the integration of diverse groups into the organizational culture.

Research literature about racial, ethnic, and gender effects on organizational variables is scarce and narrowly focused. Methodologic flaws, such as the assumption of race or gender neutrality in organizations, have led to faulty and inappropriate generalizations. Why would objective scientists perpetrate what Nkomo (1993) called "noninclusive universalism"? In his seminal work, *The Structure of Scientific Revolution,* Kuhn (1970) defined a core reason: Problem selection and methods used to search for answers are influenced by the social and political conditions of the times. There is considerable evidence of a prevailing hegemony of white males in the workplace, and they are in the majority in positions with legitimate authority and decision-making responsibility. Organizational members who are not white males are generally members of marginalized groups (such as women or people of color) and research into these nondominant groups has been of little interest in terms of organizational needs.

Furthermore, philosophical underpinnings of Western thought have resulted in an axiology that seeks order to end chaos and uncertainty, suppress contradictions, and find the one perfect truth. Organizational research has, for example, shied away from questions that might reveal privileges enjoyed by dominant members or the oppression of the other members (Nkomo, 1993; Scott, 1992).

Before 1990, few journal articles addressed diversity issues, and the few that did were tightly focused on such matters as racial demographics and performance appraisals (Cox & Nkomo, 1990). Overall, there is a paucity of published theory from which to derive integrative frameworks for implementing organizational diversity. Among the issues we discuss in this book are the factors that shape the social and cultural terrain of diversity, the perspectives of some subjugated voices who point to their strengths and needs, and the centrality of communication and information processing throughout an organization for any successful resolution of diversity problems in the workplace.

Traditional paradigms for addressing organizational dynamics focus on uncovering the one correct or most efficient way to achieve goals, but the thrust of contemporary organizational research suggests those paradigms are too rigid to respond appropriately to new dynamic demands. For that reason, this book looks to alternative paradigms for implementing workplace diversity.

THEORETICAL UNDERPINNINGS

Postmodernism

For a deeper understanding of the present reality and meaning of diversity we turn to postmodern theory. This framework emphasizes the social role in the development of knowledge. It is interdisciplinary in its approach to examining social theory. It crosses the fields of anthropology, history, philosophy, women's studies, and sociology. Postmodern theory concerns the reconceptualization of theory to reveal false knowledge that serves reality poorly. Foucault (1980) identified the development and institutionalization of "global unitary knowledges" that subjugate and disqualify whole sets of knowledge as beneath the required level of validity. More recently, he identified two aspects of subjugated knowledge: (1) historical contents that have been buried and disguised in a systematic way and (2) an entire set of knowledges that have been disqualified as inadequate to the task, insufficiently elaborated, or naive (Foucault, 1994). As those who carry this subjugated knowledge work to reclaim the validity of their history and knowledge, Foucault (1994) perceived this as "an insurrection of subjugated knowledge" (p. 41). In this book, chapters 5, 6, 13, and 28 are among several chapters that are clearly examples of this insurrection of knowledge.

Embeddedness

"Embeddedness" is a term used to conceptualize the notion of attitudes and behaviors as fixed within a culture. That is, many of our ideas and responses to "others" derive from the culture by which we are surrounded; many responses are not cognitively derived. This concept comes out of intergroup theory (Alderfer, 1987).

There has been a propensity for viewing race dichotomously—as a black and white issue. Before the 1990s, research on race was predominantly about black people in white America (Cox & Nkomo, 1990). This partialized thinking can be attributed largely to the enslavement of African people. The striking physical and immutable differences combined with vastly different cultural perspectives served as justification for the enslavement and the dehumanizing treatment of slaves. To a large extent, immutable physical and cultural differences resulted in other marginalized groups and other peoples of color facing varying degrees of dehumanization as well. People with immutable differences continue both to experience differential treatment and to differ in what they expect from interpersonal interactions in the workplace. Even when immutable differences are minimal or not immediately apparent, any number of messages are perceived differently among various groups, and these contribute to problems in many subtle ways. For example, no one is identified as black on a U.S. passport except native-born African Americans. Because whiteness is the standard in the United States, this status can be psychologically confusing to all people of color and can reinforce the status of "otherness" among African Americans.

These issues move the discussion to intergroup theory, the discipline most concerned with otherness and thus thought to be most appropriate for cross-level analysis. Alderfer (1987) has suggested that some theories in this area are shaped more by national ideology than by good conceptual thinking because the national ideology pits individuals against the group. He offers a conceptualization of embeddedness to explain cultural and demographic factors that operate on individuals and affect what those people bring into a group interaction. There also is an organizational level of embeddedness that operates through structure and other variables. These attitudes and responses may be so embedded in the culture of the individual or the organization that they are not cognitively perceived. Thus, one needs to become aware of how individual *and* group factors (for example, gender relations or socioeconomic status differences) may interact in a diverse work group.

Another important issue in the matter of embeddedness is the power differential among organizational members in their work groups. When one discusses diversity among members, particularly when there are demographic differences, power differences among members are assumed. Even if people do not differ on underlying attributes, members from dominant groups are vested with more power than are those members from nondominant groups. Dominant-group members are more likely to have greater access to resources that symbolically represent power, and thereby are more likely to have greater influence on decisions. Values and professional ethics are most likely to be those of the dominant group, and privileges they hold and exercise are unlikely to be a part of any real discourse. Communication patterns and procedural norms help sustain power with the dominant-culture members. Most often, privileges are perceived as earned or inherited, and cultural dynamics at play are denied or are attributed to inherently negative attributes of the "other." Thus, power dynamics are deeply embedded in the processes of incorporating diversity.

Brain Structures

The actual structure of the brain depends in part on environmental input. For example, an enriched environment will affect neurotransmitters and certain neural pathways to form more connections with the cortex so that more complex thought can be achieved. Brain structures also can be influenced by the schema the brain forms. Schema are integrated patterns of knowledge stored in memory; they guide the acquisition of new information. Schema make perception more efficient. The way in which a person from one culture comprehends and remembers a story from another reflects the schema used by that person, and this may differ greatly among cultures.

Finally, language affects brain structure. The French /r/, Hebrew /ch/, and South African "click" sounds are difficult to learn as an adult because enhancing our neural machinery is difficult. Chinese is a tonal language in which the pitch of a spoken word defines the word. In the West, speech is a function of the right-brain hemisphere, but for Chinese people some functions of speech shift to the left hemisphere. These examples of the effects of cultural environment on the morphology of the brain are further evidence of the embeddedness of culture and why change can be so difficult. Although this is not presently codified as theory, it has a place in a paradigmatic approach to understanding diversity in an organizational system. The retraining of thinking patterns can occur with effort and with motivation to participate in a pleasant and supportive workplace.

HOW THIS BOOK IS ORGANIZED

The book is divided into six parts. Part I, "Construction of Diversity Paradigms," explores explicit and tacit theories in their historical and current contexts. Examples illustrate how adherence to a particular paradigm, which may be subjected to cultural and political influences, can frustrate adaptive responses and progress. Implications of new approaches and perspectives for intergroup relationships are presented.

Part II, "Origins of Diversity and Its Influence in the Workplace," examines a range of factors that have contributed to increasingly intense diversity issues in the workplace (for example, wars causing major emigration from Asia and Africa and issues of American Indians and people living with disabilities).

Part III, "Policy Issues," looks at emergent changes in society and how they influence policy toward diversity. One focus is on identifying the organizational policies that intergird programs that support diversity effectively.

Part IV, "Organizational Structure and Communication," looks at structural arrangements in organizations and their implications for managing diversity. We approach interpersonal structure and its effect on organizational variables when diversity is an issue by looking at multicultural communication and culturally derived linguistic variations among Latino groups. We also address adaptive structure, which facilitates the interactions among an organization and the diverse groups in a community.

Part V, "Organizational Development Efforts as Change Processes," presents several models of organizational development that enhance support for diversity. These models include structural supports and the use of racial identity scales in assessment and intervention. This section also covers the use of mentoring to support diversity.

Part VI, "Emerging Issues in the Workplace," presents several concerns that will require attention as present trends continue to unfold.

Women's issues and family concerns are among the unresolved workplace issues that are driven by changing demographics and public policies. The last four chapters address issues emerging from people of color and involve power shifts in organizational practices. These chapters do not exhaust the changes that will emerge from a more diverse work force in which formerly disadvantaged groups gain self-esteem as they find their voices in the changing workplace.

REFERENCES

Alderfer, C. P. (1987). An intergroup perspective on group dynamics. In J. Lorsch (Ed.), *Handbook on organizational behavior* (pp. 190–222). Englewood Cliffs, NJ: Prentice Hall.

Cox, T., Jr., & Nkomo, S. M. (1990). Invisible men and women: A status report on race as a variable in organizational behavior research. *Journal of Organizational Behavior, 11,* 419–431.

Foucault, M. (1980). *Power/knowledge: Selected interviews and other writings.* New York: Pantheon Press.

Foucault, M. (1994). Geneology and social criticism. In S. Seiman (Ed.), *The postmodern turn: New perspectives on social theory* (pp. 39–45). New York: Oxford Press.

Kuhn, T. S. (1970). *The structure of scientific revolution* (2nd ed.). Chicago: University of Chicago.

Murray, K. (1993, August 1). The unfortunate side effects of "diversity training." *New York Times,* p. D-1.

Nkomo, S. M. (1993). The emperor has no clothes: Rewriting "race in organizations." *Academy of Management Review, 17,* 487–513.

Scott, W. R. (1992). *Organizations: Rational natural and open systems* (3rd ed.). Englewood Cliffs, NJ: Prentice Hall.

Swisher, K. (1995, February 5). Diversity's learning curve: Multicultural training's challenges include undoing its own mistakes. *Washington Post,* pp. H-1, H-4.

Part I

CONSTRUCTION OF
DIVERSITY PARADIGMS

In the past 10 to 15 years, diversity has become a significant topic for organizational theorists and researchers, largely in response to environmental factors. Classical, traditional paradigms for research and scholarship developed under conditions arising from large migrations of uneducated and unskilled laborers into European cities and the concurrent migration of skilled and unskilled workers to the Americas in search of the jobs generated by the Industrial Revolution.

In the traditional paradigm, also referred to as Western or Eurocentric, several assumptions guided the development of knowledge. Positivism, sometimes called "empiricism," focused both on the belief that knowledge is gained through objective observation and on the assumption that we come to "know" through the senses. The knowledge gathered is validated only by trained people observing or experiencing the same event in the same way, so all aspects of an event must be reproducible. To accomplish that, research must be conducted in controlled circumstances so that relationships among hypothetical propositions can be systematically observed. Thus, empirical evidence is derived in support of a hypothesis. Objectivity is crucial in traditional paradigms, ensuring that empirical findings are fair and impartial. Furthermore, the traditional paradigm uses quantitative methods on the assumption that appropriate and precise measurement permits generalizations. Other facets of these paradigms reflect the hegemony of authority relationships that existed at the time and in the culture in which they developed, and they are paternalistic. Any cultural diversity in the 18th and 19th centuries was subsumed by strong and embedded authority relationships and a class system that evolved into the hierarchical structure of organizations.

Paradigms that can accommodate contemporary cultural diversity must approach knowledge building differently. They must accommodate various "ways of knowing" and allow such differences to be interpreted contextually. They have to be sensitive to the direct and indirect effects of diversity on organizational variables, and they must recognize where values and beliefs diverge and where they converge, even if they are expressed differently.

Useful alternative research and scholarship paradigms have four interrelated dimensions: interpretive, intuitive, subjective, and qualitative. Together they form the process and products of the alternative worldviews that concern us here.

Interpretive knowledge uses methods common to studies in the humanities, paying attention to language and the role of descriptors in interpretation. Studying the interpretation and phrasing of knowledge helps us understand differences among groups of people. Deconstructing social identities of subjugated or marginalized individuals and groups is a powerful tool. Dismantling false, oppressive, and biased constructions of identity helps reveal the clearer reality of truth. A contextualized analysis that interprets the broader issues involved can lead to a reframing of what once may have been perceived negatively.

Intuitive knowledge derives from direct and nonintellectual bases in which an expanded state of awareness exists. This kind of knowledge is often synthesizing and nonlinear; it sees the "big picture." Subjective knowledge respects the personal experience as valuable. Qualitative methods of knowledge building identify the ways in which people who share similar experiences process and give meanings to these experiences. Neither the subjective nor qualitative dimensions support the traditional practice of generalizing across varied contextual situations. Taken together, these four dimensions are flexible and adaptive for sensing cultural differences in values and responses to phenomena.

Chapter 1, by Alderfer, uses a group relations perspective to show how underlying sociopolitical issues and theory affect two historical and two contemporary events. The vignettes reveal the struggles involved in the presently emerging system of accommodating diversity and multiculturalism and illustrate processes that help explain the product or outcome of an event. Beginning with this chapter enables the reader to see the embeddedness of culture and the struggles involved in resolving cognitive dissonance and deconstructing stereotypes through scholarly discourse.

I thank Joseph M. Schriver for describing with great clarity his thinking on alternative paradigms and paradigm building in his book Human Behavior and the Social Environment: Shifting Paradigms in Essential Knowledge for Social Work Practice. *It helped focus my thinking about paradigms and diversity.*

A Group Psychological Perspective on Multiculturalism:
What Will It Take for the High Priests and Priestesses to Change Their Minds?

Clayton P. Alderfer

Theories about human behavior matter. In reference to happenings involving people, who does not ask, "Why did these events occur?" "Will certain (desired or feared) outcomes take place?" "What would it take to create this particular condition?" or "What is the meaning of these happenings?" No matter what the answers are to questions such as these, some mode of abstract thinking lies behind them (Kaplan, 1964). All of us—not just social scientists, historians, and journalists—have ways of being theorists about human behavior.

But as important as theories are, they are not always explicit; sometimes they are tacit (Polanyi, 1958). Theories are tacit whenever theorists are unaware that they bring a conceptual position when they understand, explain, predict, and intervene. In fact, we all are probably at least partially unaware of the theoretical constructs we use.

This chapter explores several aspects of the explicit and tacit theories we use to deal with multiculturalism. The key issues include whether or not we have an explicit conception of groups and, if so, what that conception is; how, if at all, we think of that conception as applying to ourselves; when we use explicit and when we use tacit theories; and what implications our conception of groups has for how we think and act in relation to multiculturalism.

The analysis involves two potential pitfalls. First, we sometimes think that whether we have a conception of groups in our theory is a function of the culture, that is, the groups to which we belong. According to some theorists (for example, Triandis, Kurowski, & Gelfand, 1994), the choice of "individualism" or "collectivism" as a way to explain social phenomena is a function of our ethnic or national culture—*not of one's theory.* A group relations perspective, on the other hand, argues that our choice of theory about groups—including how we understand individualism and collectivism—is in part an expression of our relationship to our own group memberships, including ethnic, racial, and national groups (Alderfer, 1987). The Triandis et al. (1994) view implies that they believe, perhaps

This chapter was originally delivered as a keynote address at the A. K. Rice Scientific Meetings, May 1993, Los Angeles, Edward B. Klein, Chair.

tacitly, that a person is *either* an independent individual *or* a group member in good standing, but not both. This view derives from their perhaps tacit assumption about possible relationships between individuals and groups. That view does not include the possibility that groups (for example, families, work groups, and racial groups) can be supportive of individuals, but rather that groups inevitably call on individuals to give up crucial aspects of themselves in order to be group members in good standing (Smith & Berg, 1987).

Second, the very existence of talk about multiculturalism suggests that a major conceptual reorientation may be occurring. Either an accelerated struggle among differing schools of thought is occurring, or a paradigm shift among social scientists is about to take place (Kuhn, 1970). We observe writers referring to themselves and to others with terms such as "Afrocentric" or "Eurocentric." These terms imply an awareness of conceptual systems having been shaped by group forces present in regions and cultures. Taken to its logical conclusion, this line of reasoning, perhaps tacitly, implies that intellectual products and exchanges inevitably are shaped by the groups and intergroup relationships of the scholars who participate. How else would we explain the use of terms like "Afrocentric" and "Eurocentric" (whether they are applied to our own or to others' groups)? The alternative view is that there is a single set of standards (*the* canon) against which all are to be judged. But the argument for a single canon (as compared to multiple canons) is so obviously ethnocentric as to be indefensible in the long run.

However, this interpretation of the behavior about multiculturalism is the product of a known conceptual position. Only from a group relations viewpoint are the explanations offered here inevitable (Alderfer, 1987; Rice, 1969; Smith & Berg, 1987; Wells, 1980). Other conceptual perspectives offer different interpretations.

BACKGROUND

The ideas contained in this chapter follow from perspectives on depth psychology, both group and individual. To those theoretical bases, I bring three decades of experience as an organizational consultant on race relations, leadership, and organizational change. The consultation work has been particularly influential in my developing an embedded intergroup relations perspective for understanding organizations (Alderfer, 1987).

A key event in my professional development was participation during the early 1970s in an interdisciplinary seminar on groups, that was based at the Connecticut Mental Health Center and involved faculty from Yale University's Department of Psychiatry and School of Organization and Management. The person most responsible for introducing me to the Tavistock group relations perspective was Edward B. Klein. He encouraged me to read the works of Wilfred Bion (1961) and A. K. Rice (1969) and to learn through direct experience about the Tavistock way of thinking about groups and organizations.

From my association with the Tavistock culture, I have learned how important our personal psychoanalysis can be. It matters who analyzed our analyst, along what theoretical lines our analyst traces her or his development, and with which pioneer of psychoanalytic thought those ideas originated. For this reason, I feel somewhat obliged to reveal my background—in no small measure because it is Jungian, not Freudian, and Freud's concepts are at the roots of Tavistock theory. My experience includes work with male and female Jungian analysts, at least one of whose origins go to Esther Harding, a close associate of Jung himself.

Those familiar with analytic history know that Freud and Jung once were close friends and colleagues, but not after 1913. As a result, there were times when it was unsafe to be Jungian in a Freudian group—and perhaps vice versa—although Jung claimed not to believe in groups. Even today, however, when those tensions are less severe than they once were, as a Jungian of sorts, I feel obliged to reveal this potentially traitorous aspect of my history when discussing group relations theory that has an intellectual debt to Freud.

It sometimes has been observed that people choose professions that allow them to work on their basic conflicts. In fact, Jung (1931) meant something like that when he observed, "The serious problems in life, however, are never fully solved. If ever they should appear to be so, it is a sure sign that something has been lost. The meaning and purpose of a problem seem to lie not in its solution but in our working at it incessantly. This alone preserves us from stultification and petrification"(p. 21). Thus, we see lawyers who are corrupt, business executives who receive millions when their corporations lose money, physicians who abuse drugs, and psychotherapists who have sex with their patients. In my case, I acknowledge that there is no small paradox in my claiming expertise on groups and organizations, in part based on my experience with an analytic psychology that focuses primarily, if not exclusively, on the individual.

As a matter of fact, the fundamental insight for this chapter is derived from Jungian theory. The terms "priests" and "priestesses" in the title are meant to be understood as archetypes. Used in this sense, the words may not always refer to representatives of institutionalized religion. As archetypes, the terms refer to individuals with roles and unconscious interpretations of those roles, which authorize them to determine accepted dogma about groups and the relations among cultures. In the sections that follow, the concrete use of the terms refers both to representatives from institutionalized religions and from other organizations.

PURPOSES

The four objectives of this work are (1) to describe four specific historical events; (2) to frame those events in group relations terms; (3) to relate those concepts to the struggles we as a society are experiencing with multiculturalism; and (4) to place those difficulties within the context of struggles about alternative theories of group relations. I shall pursue these aims by examining the four episodes in some detail. Two are historical, and two are contemporary. Two concern physical science, and two pertain to social science. The events have in common several properties. First, as they have become known, they include strong effects from group and intergroup processes. Second, they are intrinsically struggles about whose authority will prevail—an existing establishment bent on maintaining the status quo or an alternative perspective aimed at bringing about change. Third, the struggles are fundamentally or in substantial part about how human beings view themselves in relation to the world; they are about humankind's conception of itself. Finally, the contending ideas have practical implications; which ideas prevail affect many people's lives.

EPISODE 1: SHAPE OF THE EARTH

For this first example I draw on Daniel Boorstin's 1983 work, *The Discoverers*. In reading this book, I was especially affected by his account of the changing views about whether the earth was flat or spherical—mainly because it so altered what I recall being taught about that subject in courses on world history. To a student of group relations, the Boorstin account provides a rich example of group and organizational forces shaping beliefs about scientific theory and the nature of physical reality.

The world history that I recall being taught located this debate in the 15th century, around the time Christopher Columbus set sail in a westerly direction to arrive in the east. The Italian navigator sailing under a Spanish flag was portrayed as undertaking a great experiment. If the earth was flat, as was widely believed at that time, then sailing west would result in falling off the face of the earth. If the earth was spherical, as he believed, then westward travel would eventually lead to the Far East. As we all know, the westward trip supported the spherical theory even though it did not lead as immediately to East Asia as Columbus expected.

What the Boorstin history told me for the first time was that the debate about the shape of the earth was not at all new in 1492. Rather, the dispute was nearly 2,000 years old when Columbus undertook his great adventure. The time during which Columbus lived witnessed a reopening of minds to theory and data pertaining to the shape of the earth that previously had been suppressed by dogma from the Christian Church for more than a millennium.

Indeed, historians named the period during which the spherical theory of the earth was suppressed the "Great Interruption." Readers attuned to the unconscious sexual meanings of word choice will probably take additional information from the historical terms. What comes to mind when you hear the words "great interruption"? A variety of historical facts also give conscious rational meaning to the development of knowledge that was being interrupted by the church's insistence on holding onto an apparently more secure construction of reality.

- As early as the fifth century B.C., Greek scholars thought the earth was a globe. Both Plato and Aristotle affirmed those beliefs. Plato argued for the spherical theory on aesthetic grounds, but Aristotle made his case with physical evidence from the movement of falling bodies and the phenomena of lunar eclipses.
- Eratosthenes, who lived between approximately 276 and 195 B.C., developed a remarkably accurate technique for measuring the circumference of the earth. He estimated the earth was 28,700 miles around—an approximation that was only about 15 percent too high.
- Hipparchus, perhaps the greatest Greek astronomer, took the next natural step by developing a system of horizontal and vertical coordinates that permitted location of any place on earth.
- Ptolemy, best known for his erroneous astronomy, was a systematic recorder of the advances made by the ancient Greeks. According to Arab legend, he lived during the second century A.D., after which his work survived the Great Interruption and served as a primary source for Christopher Columbus.

Historians do not know how or why the Great Interruption occurred. Boorstin (1983) wrote,

> It is easier to recount what happened than to explain satisfactorily how it happened or why. After the death of Ptolemy, Christianity conquered the Roman Empire and most of Europe. Then we observe a Europe-wide phenomenon of scholarly amnesia, which afflicted the continent from A.D. 300 to at least 1300. During those centuries, Christian faith and dogma suppressed the useful image of the world that had been so slowly, so painfully, and so scrupulously drawn by ancient geographers. (p. 100)

There is no lack of records about what the medieval Christian geographers thought. More than 600 maps of the world from this period survive, and there is remarkable consistency among them. The maps were designed to show what orthodox Christians were expected to believe—not to record knowledge of the physical world. The classic defense of this view of the earth was provided by Cosmas, a sixth-century monk, who wrote a 12-volume treatise demolishing what he called the "pagan" view and supporting the Christian conception.

Instead of relying on carefully collected and systematically organized facts, as the Greek scholars had done, the dogmatic Christian view replaced concrete physical data with fantasies. As sea travel developed again during the 14th century, a need once again arose for geography based on observable facts. Mariners needed charts on which they could rely, and Christian geography was no help. But the mere accumulation of new facts by mariners and cartographers was not enough (Boorstin, 1983); a better theory also was needed.

It was to the need for a better theory that Ptolemy's previously suppressed work responded. Somewhat mysteriously, it was brought forth to influence European civilization again in 1400, after being cared for by Byzantine and Arabic scholars for 1,000 years. Because the theory worked in practice despite its numerous defects, Ptolemy's work regained its former favorable reputation.

The loss and recovery of the spherical theory of the earth by Western European scholars was a remarkable phenomenon. Distinguished historian Boorstin confessed his lack of understanding about how and why these events occurred. It was not just the effects of Christian dogma, that is, of ideas alone, that this embarrassment to European intellectual thought took place. It was through an organized human institution—the Roman Catholic Church. The reigning spiritual powers of the Christian Middle Ages were able to develop a social consensus that replaced a more valid with a less valid theory. In this case, real priests and archetypal priests were one and the same.

EPISODE 2: MOVEMENT OF THE EARTH AROUND THE SUN

On October 31, 1992, the *New York Times,* on page A1, carried a story titled "After 350 Years, Vatican Says Galileo Was Right: It Moves." The story marked the end of a 13-year investigation by the Roman Catholic Church's Pontifical Academy of Sciences into the condemnation of Galileo in 1633. At that time, Galileo was forced to recant his empirical findings and his interpretation of them as "abjured, cursed and detested." The renunciation caused him great personal anguish, according to the *Times,* but it allowed him to live for eight more years under house arrest rather than being burned at the stake. He died at age 77 in 1642. The Vatican's announcement acknowledged that the church had made an error, that Galileo had been wrongfully condemned by the Inquisition, and that he had been correct in his scientific conclusions. What had the Italian astronomer and physicist done that so disturbed the church?

Galileo built a telescope that allowed him to develop empirical observations that favored the Copernican theory of the solar system over a literal interpretation of the scriptures. In 1543, Nicolaus Copernicus, a Polish astronomer, had published a theory stating that the earth revolved around the sun. The Copernican view was declared heretical in 1616, because it refuted the biblical view that "God had fixed the earth upon its foundation, not to be moved forever." Before the Italian astronomer obtained the data, arguments between the two theories had been made only on logical or theological grounds. Galileo's telescope, however, allowed him to observe the four largest moons of Jupiter revolving around that planet. These data refuted the notion that all heavenly bodies must orbit the Earth, as attributed to scripture.

In 1632, Galileo published his findings as part of the *Dialogue Concerning the Two Chief World Systems*. His argument presented the new data within a framework that favored the Copernican theory over papal doctrine. For this, he was summoned to Rome, where church authorities refused to accept his defense that Christian faith could be separated from scientific research. Already suffering from the effects of aging, Galileo recanted rather than endure additional torture. His book was banned by the church until 1757.

As told in the *Times* and in most other places, the Galileo story is not formulated in group relations terms (Reston, 1994). I want to reframe the Galileo story from that perspective. The *Times* and other sources frame the Galileo story in terms of the conflict between reason and religious dogma, or between science and faith.

The reason-versus-religion formulation, like any conceptualization, may serve a defensive function. It can suggest that what happened to Galileo is a thing of the past—a phenomenon from a time when religious prejudice ruled over scientific reason. In the literal sense, that phenomenon clearly no longer exists today. Physicists and astronomers do not have to contend with theologians and church leaders to conduct research or to publish findings. What happened to Galileo, according to this line of thought, could not happen today. Western European civilization no longer persecutes scientific leaders for using physical concepts that challenge church doctrine.

A group relations formulation, however, may have different implications for the present. According to this view, Galileo and Copernicus become representatives of a new group—physicist–astronomers who believed in a revolutionary theory and who developed a method (Galileo's telescope) that produced data favoring the revolutionary theory over the more established view. Moreover, these physicist–astronomers published and taught about their preferred theory. The physicist–astronomer group was experienced as deeply threatening by the most powerful authorities of their day (that is, the Roman Catholic Church). With threats of torture and death, the authorities demanded that the revolutionary thinkers recant their beliefs. More than three centuries passed before the authorities corrected their error. Even then the press expressed surprise at the change. The *Times'* reporter observed, "The Vatican's formal acknowledgement of an error...is a rarity" (p. A1).

Was it an accident that the man who was pope at the time of the rare acknowledgment was by identity group Polish and by organization group Italian—the same groups represented by Copernicus and Galileo? This group relations interpretation—unlike the reason-versus-faith argument—is as appropriate for contemporary events as for happenings in 1633. A philosopher of science who understood and believed in the group relations theory might say this conceptual system was more elegant than the reason-versus-faith perspective because the newer theory can explain both contemporary and historical phenomena.

EPISODE 3: ACADEMIC CRITICISM OF MULTICULTURALISM

During the summer of 1992, *The Disuniting of America: Reflections on a Multicultural Society*, written by Arthur M. Schlesinger, Jr., appeared on the *New York Times* bestseller list. Schlesinger is one of the more respected liberal historians in the United States today. He once was a faculty member in the Harvard University history department and then a special advisor to President John F. Kennedy. Having written several highly regarded books about the Kennedy brothers, he currently is a faculty member at the City University of New York.

Schlesinger became so concerned about what he believed to be the fragmenting effects of racial and ethnic consciousness in the United States that he wrote a book warning the American people of the danger he believes we face. Well written and in touch with the thoughts and feelings of our populace, the book remained on the bestseller list for several weeks. In the text we find Schlesinger's tacit theory of group dynamics. Quotations that follow reveal key elements of that framework.

> The eruption of ethnicity had many good consequences . . . shamefully overdue recognition to the achievements of minorities . . . acknowledge[ment] of the great swirling world beyond Europe . . . our children try[ing] to imagine the arrival of Columbus from the point of those who met him as well as those who sent him. . . . (p. 15)

> * * *

> But pressed too far, the cult of ethnicity has had bad consequences, too. The new ethnic gospel [note the religious metaphor] rejects the unifying vision of individuals from all nations melted into a new race. Its underlying philosophy is that America is not a nation of individuals at all but a nation of groups. . . . Instead of a transformative nation with an identity all its own, America in this new light is seen as a preservative of diverse alien identities. . . . The multiethnic dogma abandons historic purposes, replacing assimilation by fragmentation, integration by separation. It belittles *unum* and glorifies *pluribus*. (p. 16)

> * * *

> But the burden to unify the country does not fall exclusively on the minorities. . . . Not only must they want assimilation and integration; we must want assimilation and integration, too. (p. 19)

Schlesinger's normative view is complex. He recognizes the power of racism in our country's history, he accepts the distortions in American history that currently are being corrected as a result of a greater ethnic and racial consciousness, and he criticizes the "noble lies" of what he calls Afrocentrists' revisions of history and sometimes of other ethnic groups as well. In fact, his criticisms are most severe when directed toward African and African American writers. In taking this direction, he repeatedly uses group-level concepts in referring to writers by their racial and ethnic group memberships. He also refers to individual writers and cites the works of particular persons. Thus, his *theory-in-use* employs individual *and* group concepts, whereas his *espoused theory* argues for individual *versus* group concepts.

Especially noteworthy about Schlesinger is his assertion that European culture is superior to other forms. The key quotation states

> Whatever the particular crimes of Europe, that continent is also the source—the *unique* [italics his] source of those liberating ideas of individual liberty, political democracy, the rule of law, human rights, and cultural freedom that constitute our most precious legacy and to which most of the world today aspires. These are *European* [italics his] ideas, not Asian, nor African, nor Middle Eastern ideas, except by adoption. (p. 127)

I find this a remarkable assertion. To make it, Schlesinger must assume that he knows all there is to know about all those cultures that he states have access to European values only by adoption and that no new discoveries will ever occur that might alter what he thinks he knows. Until I read those words, I might not have imagined that a man of his political persuasion and intellectual interests would make such a statement. His assertion of the superiority of European culture is significant, because it takes the quest for better understanding of these matters out of the realm of a simple liberal–conservative dichotomy. Schlesinger is a self-identified liberal whose assertions reflect a tacit theory of group dynamics that does not differ from the perspective of many thoughtful—and some not so thoughtful—conservatives. The fundamental question, therefore, is not one of liberal versus conservative, but rather one of a particular theory of group dynamics versus another.

Examining Schlesinger's assertion about the superiority of European culture and observing his criticisms of Afrocentric perspectives from the point of view of depth psychology and group relations, one is led to believe that his tacit theory of group dynamics does not include the concepts of projection and ethnocentrism applied to himself and to members of his own groups.

Is criticizing Schlesinger's tacit theory of group dynamics unfair? He is, after all, a historian, who might not be expected to understand group relations. Yet he uses group and individual concepts freely with professed authority. Moreover, his book was a bestseller—a fact that may be interpreted to indicate that his tacit theory was in accord with those of many Americans during the summer of 1992. Perhaps even more telling is the fact that echoes of Schlesinger's tacit theory of groups and individuals can be found in the work of Nathan Glazer

(1983), a Harvard sociologist who has spent much of his life studying racial and ethnic group relations, and in the writings of Cynthia Fuchs Epstein, whose interpretation of "gender and sex as deceptive distinctions" was published in 1988 by Yale University Press. If criticized for not having an adequate theory of group dynamics to use in *The Disuniting of America,* Schlesinger could reply that his views were in accord with those of some of the most prominent white female and male social scientists of our times—and he would be correct! The difference does not turn on his disciplinary identification as a historian in comparison with others as social scientists. Schlesinger's concepts reflect consensual views on matters of group dynamics in contemporary culture.

EPISODE 4: NEW YORK CITY SCHOOLS CHANCELLOR VERSUS THE BOARD OF EDUCATION

The fourth episode also comes from the front page of the *New York Times.* The February 11, 1993, lead headline read "Board Removes Fernandez as New York Schools Chief after Stormy 3-Year Term: Social Issues Cited: 4-to-3 Decision Points to Painful Divisions in School System." The text of the article states, "The board clashed with the Chancellor over AIDS education. . . . And when Mr. Fernandez chose to suspend a local school board because it refused to accept a controversial multicultural curriculum, the board overturned his decision" (p. A1).

On the matter of firing Fernandez, the *Times* was not neutral. Their news pages gave the matter extensive coverage, and their lead editorial of that day was "Fire the Board of Education." The board fired the chancellor, and the *Times* wanted to fire the board. Events like these give new meaning to the bumper sticker "[Stuff] happens!" Moreover, despite the conflict over who should be fired, there seemed to be some agreement that the firing of Fernandez was damaging to New York City public schools and even more consensus about what should be done to prevent repetition of that problem in the future.

The *Times* editorial espoused fixing the problem by giving the mayor additional powers to control a majority of the appointments to the school board. In subsequent statements, the *Times'* view was echoed by then–New York City Mayor David Dinkins and by former New York City school board president Robert Wagner, Jr. The unspoken assumption in this solution seemed to be that the real conflict that led to the firing of Fernandez was between the mayor and his political rivals. The proposed solution seemed to imply that if the power to control the board rested more fully with the mayor, then the dynamics set into motion around Fernandez could be prevented in the future. For purposes of this discussion, I shall call this the "political–legal" model and shall contrast it with a group relations perspective.

The group relations perspective raises questions about whether the deeper problems of future chancellor–board conflict could be prevented simply by giving the mayor greater legal authority to appoint a majority of the board. Indeed, the political–legal model, when examined from a group relations perspective, not only may fail to solve the problems it is designed to address but also may create additional, equally severe difficulties. How would a group relations perspective address board–chancellor conflict?

We might begin by asking, "What is the primary purpose of the board–chancellor relationship?" My answer is to establish the best possible conditions to ensure high-quality public education for New York City school children. The work of the board is to select the chancellor, to work with the chancellor to establish educational policy for the city's schools, to assess competently and fairly the chancellor's performance in implementing that policy, and to remove the chancellor when sound evidence indicates that doing so would better serve the educational needs of New York City school children than would keeping the chancellor in office.

In the chancellor–board relationship, inevitable tensions exist. The board, for example, can exceed its policy-setting role and interfere with the chancellor's leadership and management duties. The board can attempt to micromanage the chancellor, and there was evidence that it had done so in the New York City case. But the chancellor also may not follow the policy established by the board; board members suggested that this had happened to Fernandez. In fact, a dispute may have occurred between Fernandez and the board over exactly what was the policy.

In the *Times* article photography suggested that race, ethnicity, and gender played a substantial role in the board's action. But there was no explicit talk about the effects of these factors. The article made explicit statements that the chancellor's personality and leadership style were matters of concern to some board members. Do boards of any organizations generally deal fully and professionally with these kinds of issues? Certainly, many examples suggest that it is by no means obvious that they do.

After the firing and in response to a newsperson's question, Fernandez said he thought that the best way to prevent future problems of the kind he faced was to be sure that the chancellor and the board were working on the same agenda. He did not say that giving a majority of the school board appointments to the mayor was the answer. Fernandez's answer on how to solve the problems he faced was more in accord with a group relations perspective than with the political–legal model.

From a group relations perspective, the key question is, Given the nature of chief executive and board relations and the relevance of racial, ethnic, gender, and religious group differences, what is the best way to design the relationship between chancellor and board to maximize the likelihood of having that relationship serve the educational needs of New York City school children? Certainly the process of determining who will be board members is relevant. But the issues surrounding potential appointees are less about to whom they are politically loyal—the practical answer should be to New York

City's public school children—and more about what educational objectives they are able and willing to support and toward what behavior are they inclined when faced with the predictable conflicts they will encounter as board members. With those issues clear, then the design questions become, What kind of appointing authority is most likely to select appropriately qualified board members? and What kinds of structures and processes might be put into place to increase the likelihood that the board will operate effectively as a group and in the several intergroup relationships with the chancellor? To someone with a group relations perspective, these questions suggest the use of group consultation—with the board of education appointing authority, with the board of education, and in the relationship between the chancellor and the board of education—to work toward answers.

How unlikely does such an idea seem? Why do the relevant public officials not call for group relations consultation to assist with such matters, instead of relying on the political–legal model, which so frequently has demonstrated its ineffectiveness for all to see? Do you know of any board of education that is not inclined toward the sort of outbreak of irrationality that characterized the New York City group? Do you believe that there are individuals and groups with the capabilities to take on such a consultation assignment? What criteria do you use when you think about this question? When, if ever, do you believe there will be a social consensus such that problems of the kind that faced the chancellor and New York City school board will result in requests for the services of the best of group and organizational consultants? How do you understand the fact that a search for such services is not automatic under conditions like those described in this case? What kinds of changes will be required in society and in the social work profession for such a response to become more natural?

CONCLUSION

The four examples presented in this chapter relate directly to the objectives stated at the outset. First, the current debate about multiculturalism is as important for our time as the disputes about the shape and movement of the earth were in the 14th and 15th centuries. The priests and priestesses of our times are more likely to be found in political bodies, in corporations, and in universities than in religious institutions. For society and its institutions to cope more effectively with how cultures come together, the priests and priestesses must change their minds about how they conceive of group-level events.

Second, at its core, the debate about multiculturalism is a debate about theories. Even though parties with diverse views sometimes frame their arguments in moral terms—an observation no less true of those who prefer change than of those who prefer to remain the same—I do not believe the fundamental questions turn on religious or ethical values. Indeed, the presence of religious metaphor can be interpreted as evidence about the severity of the intergroup conflict among proponents of different theories. Conceptual systems are in conflict, and it matters greatly whether change occurs and around which theory a new social consensus forms. To continue to frame the debate in moral or ethical terms rather than in intellectual terms is to maintain the status quo.

Third, group relations theory in the form I know best represents a fundamental—even revolutionary—alternative to the view of group dynamics around which there is currently a social consensus within established academic and professional circles (Alderfer, 1987). On these matters, the priests and priestesses of our times have not yet changed their minds. Glazer (1983) and Epstein (1988) represent those priests and priestesses.

Five key components of the alternative theory are as follows:

1. Do not think in terms of individual *versus* the group, but rather frame the relationships as about individuals *and* groups.
2. Take groups as whole entities in their own rights, that is, as significantly different from merely the sum of their individual members.
3. Imply that, regardless of role, individuals do not leave behind their identity-group affiliations—namely, that we all are influenced as individuals intrapsychically and as group representatives by our several group memberships, including race, ethnicity, gender, generation, and family.
4. Indicate that we are less objective in the traditional sense when we ignore or deny these effects than when we accept and embrace them.
5. Base knowledge of group and intergroup relations in part on taking account of unconscious processes in individuals, in groups, and between groups. People whose actions are influenced by these theoretical assumptions behave differently than those who hold the established view of groups.

In identifying these components, I do not mean to imply that everyone who takes a group relations perspective agrees with all of them. Undoubtedly differences exist among people who have group relations perspectives on which of these propositions they accept as their own and on which ones directly affect their behavior. However, I do believe these statements differentiate an embedded intergroup relations perspective from the political–legal theory of group dynamics represented by the social consensus of our times.

The group dynamics theories of sociology; of politics, law, and journalism; and of establishment historians in our times are similar to the flat-earth and earth-centered cosmologies of the Middle Ages. In part those theories are out of date because they both consciously and unconsciously keep "us" and "our group" too much at the center of how we think about human beings in the world. Moreover, holders of these explicit and tacit theories about groups generally do not think of themselves as being explained by the theories they hold. They thus tacitly place themselves as outside the laws of human behavior.

Fourth, we are living at a time of significant intellectual and social convulsion—not unlike the era following the breakup of the Roman Empire. The theory of groups we hold—whether as a layperson or as a professional, whether explicit or tacit—affects how we understand and act in relation to the widespread problems with authority and multiculturalism we all face. We also live at a time in which society as a whole largely resists and rejects what is known about the depth psychology of individuals and groups. The resistance, however, is not total. Organizations such as the A. K. Rice Institute and the N.T.L. Institute continue to exist outside the mainstream. There is struggle, and signs of change coexist along with the resistance. Indeed, some believe that the resistance is greatest just before irreversible change occurs.

For example, within the past decade, the president and the corporation of Yale University dismissed without review an entire group of faculty because they were believed to be contaminating the minds of professional management students by teaching effectively a group relations perspective (Berg, 1993). Yale did not succeed in suppressing the story in the years following the original episode, and eventually the public became aware of the mass dismissals (Sedgwick, 1994; Steinberg, 1994).

The group dynamics of Galileo's age are not gone. Today, however, the agents of repression and the protesters against repression are less often representatives of institutional religions than of corporate, political, and educational organizations in our society (Reston, 1994). The priest and priestess archetype appears outside of institutionalized religion.

If conceptual change about group dynamics does occur, the revolution will be as fundamental to how we view ourselves as people and as peoples as were the Ptolemaic and Copernican revolutions for how we view this Earth and solar system. All disciplines that deal with the human condition—including history—will be affected. How we think about important matters of authority and multicultural relations will be altered.

As to whether the conceptual change will occur, I am uncertain. Signs of the potential for another great interruption in the development of these ideas are among us, as the events at Yale University and the popularity of the Schlesinger (1992) book show. Yet, alternative conceptions also remain alive for those who are prepared to consider them. Another great interruption has not yet taken a singular direction. I do not know whether it will.

REFERENCES

After 350 years, Vatican says Galileo was right: It moves. (1992, October 31). *New York Times*, pp. A1, A22.

Alderfer, C. P. (1987). An intergroup perspective on group dynamics. In J. Lorsch (Ed.), *Handbook of organizational behavior* (pp. 190–222). Englewood Cliffs, NJ: Prentice Hall.

Berg, D. N. (1993). *Keeping the faith: The clinical tradition in organizational behavior at Yale, 1962–1988.* Woodbridge, CT: Berg Group.

Bion, W. (1961). *Experiences in groups.* New York: Basic Books.

Board removes Fernandez as New York schools chief after stormy 3-year term: Social issues cited: 4-to-3 decision points to painful divisions in school system. (1993, February 11). *New York Times*, pp. A1, A6.

Boorstin, D. J. (1983). *The discoverers: A history of man's search to know his world and himself.* New York: Random House.

Epstein, C. F. (1988). *Deceptive distinctions: Sex, gender, and the social order.* New Haven, CT: Yale University Press.

Glazer, N. (1983). *Ethnic dilemmas, 1964–1982.* Cambridge, MA: Harvard University Press.

Jung, C. G. (1931). The stages of life. In J. Campbell (Ed.), *The portable Jung* (pp. 3–22). New York: Viking Press.

Kaplan, A. (1964). *The conduct of inquiry.* San Francisco: Chandler.

Kuhn, T. S. (1970). *The structure of scientific revolutions* (2nd ed., enlarged). Chicago: University of Chicago Press.

Polanyi, M. (1958). *Personal knowledge: Towards a post-critical philosophy.* New York: Harper & Row.

Reston, J., Jr. (1994). *Galileo: A life.* New York: HarperCollins.

Rice, A. K. (1969). Individual, group, and intergroup processes. *Human Relations, 22,* 565–584.

Schlesinger, A. M., Jr. (1992). *The disuniting of America: Reflections on a multicultural society.* New York: W. W. Norton.

Sedgwick, J. (1994). The death of Yale. *GQ, 64*(4), 182.

Smith, K. K., & Berg, D. N. (1987). *Paradoxes of group life.* San Francisco: Jossey-Bass.

Steinberg, J. (1994, December 12). Is Western civilization worth $20 million? Yale struggles with itself over a gift from Lee M. Bass for Western studies only. *New York Times*, p. B1.

Triandis, H. C., Kurowski, L. L., & Gelfand, M. J. (1994). Workplace diversity. In H. C. Triandis, M. D. Dunnette, & L. M. Hough (Eds.), *Handbook of industrial and organizational psychology* (2nd ed., Vol. 4, pp. 769–827). Palo Alto, CA: Consulting Psychologists Press.

Wells, L., Jr. (1980). The group-as-a-whole: A systemic socioanalytic perspective on interpersonal and group relations. In C. P. Alderfer & C. L. Cooper (Eds.), *Advances in experiential social processes* (Vol. 2, pp. 165–200). New York: John Wiley & Sons.

Part II

ORIGINS OF DIVERSITY AND ITS INFLUENCE IN THE WORKPLACE

This part examines some sources of diversity in the workplace within the context of currently emerging factors. Chapters included here address the range and complexity of issues that are present within groups that we will call the "other"—groups socially and culturally distant from the dominant culture. Each group faces a set of factors that contextualizes their members' present circumstances and affects their experience within a workplace. These factors include environmental factors and geographic location (for example, access to transportation and availability of jobs); resources (in the form of finances, skills, and training); history or patterns of past behaviors (for example, embedded cultural patterns and past relations with the hegemony within the workplace); and strategies or stream of decisions about use of resources (for example, social and political support and structure of decision making concerning matters relevant to the group within the context of history).

The five chapters in this part do not exhaust the spectrum of diversity that is transforming the American workplace, but issues and concerns presented herein are similar to those experienced by other groups that have been marginalized or whose voices have been subordinated. We address the issues presented here at policy and macro levels and at the micro level regarding people living with physical or sensory challenges.

Chapter 2 describes domestic and public policies on immigration and how those policies have affected acculturation of immigrant groups. English and Ross-Sheriff present a review of key immigration policies and events that have helped shape present patterns of immigration and the impact of the "new" immigrants on the workplace. The chapter brings perspective to the effect on the American workplace of the immigrants, who are largely people of color, often with immutable physical characteristics.

Human services institutions have long recognized the need to have served populations represented on staff and, sometimes, on boards. In chapter 3, White describes some of the issues that surround the integration of American Indian workers in human services agencies. American Indians are not a monolithic group. Among the important factors that shape this variability are physical presence within a tribal group, in the mainstream, or in transition between the two and the history of past relations and encounters of a particular American

Indian nation with the dominant culture. White includes suggestions that can not only develop good working relationships that enable American Indian workers to contribute from their full human potential but also aid groups with a history of marginalization.

In chapter 4, Mayo-Quiñones examines the political–economic factors that shaped immigration patterns of the Latino population. The marginalization of Latino men has had a devastating impact for many, because these men often lack language skills as well as the education and occupational skills needed to be upwardly mobile. These problems confine many Latinos to low-paying and temporary positions. Mayo-Quiñones argues for social action within the political–economic sector, in which public policy tends to sustain this exploitation.

The passage of the Americans with Disabilities Act (ADA) of 1990 created statutory requirements that protect the civil rights of people with disabilities in employment. Although policy has shifted from separation and institutionalization for people living with disabilities to one of inclusion, too often the dominant culture perceives people living with disabilities, particularly those with visible differences, as without value or worth. Cultural belief systems shape much of the response to people with disabilities; thus, even professionals who provide care and education may be culturally blind or defend rejection behaviors by projecting cause to the person with the disability. In chapter 5, Howard shares her journey in living with a mild form of cerebral palsy. Her poignant narrative makes the need for ADA and its provisions clear.

The last chapter in this part further illustrates how too many organizations circumvent the issue of hiring people living with disabilities. In chapter 6, Schwartz contrasts a needs-based system for distributing wealth to people with disabilities with a work-based system for the abled norm; together, the two systems encourage dependency of people who are differently abled while relieving the guilt of abled professionals. Schwartz also presents an overview of the Deaf community, its major issues, and the debate about deafness as disability within the community.

Taken together, these chapters identify sources and complexity of issues within and among nontraditional groups in the workplace. Current and projected demographic information on racial–ethnic immigration patterns in the United States, along with socioeconomic variations within these groups, suggest that workplaces will continue to be affected by external factors as well as by internal processes. A first step in planning for adaptation generated by this new cultural context is to gain knowledge about factors that shape their emergence as a concern for the workplace. Factors include the extent of congruence of relevant aspects of Western culture generally and of the United States specifically, the perception of the status of a group in the hegemony of the workplace, the extent to which physical differences are mutable or immutable, social supports for the group, and how a particular group may be affected by public policy and social status within the larger society.

2

Diversity and Challenges of New Immigrants in the Changing American Workplace

Richard A. English and Fariyal Ross-Sheriff

The social transformation of the American workplace is one of the remarkable changes occurring in the latter part of this century. The American workplace transformed is more diverse than ever before. Changes created by this transformation have been aided by three critical factors: people, public policy, and technology. The combination of technology and public policy changes and innovations have facilitated the entry of greater numbers of racial and ethnic groups and women into the labor force. These changes also have opened opportunities for new immigrants to the United States, many of whom have entered the labor force. In this chapter we are concerned about the latter group—new immigrants. First, we describe and document the diversity that is transforming the American work force. Second, we identify key immigration policies affecting immigration flows to the United States. Third, we describe the newcomers. Fourth, we describe and characterize workplaces where the newcomers are located, the work they do, and their impact on the workplace. We also discuss employment and wages of native workers and present some evidence about how they find their jobs. Last, we identify some challenges arising from the presence of newcomers in the workplace. Exogenous factors, including the changing demography of the U.S. population, economic expansion and change, and employment expansion also have significantly affected the labor market. These changes are acknowledged as critical to the workplace but are not discussed.

TRANSFORMATION OF THE AMERICAN WORKPLACE: RISING DIVERSITY

The transformation of the American workplace in the latter part of the 20th century has been fueled by two types of public policy. The two categories are (1) those dealing with domestic issues and (2) those addressing immigration matters. Domestic policies helped increase the numbers of racial and ethnic group members, women, and people with disabilities in the workplace. By the early 1970s significant increases in the number of African Americans in businesses and industries with previously low levels of participation by members of nondominant cultures had begun to occur. These changes were precipitated by the passage of the Civil Rights Act of 1964, in which the provisions of Title VII, Equal Employment Opportunity, prohibited discrimination against any person on the basis of race, color, religion, sex, or national origin. The act outlawed discrimination against members of nondominant cultures and women in employment.

The Civil Rights Act positively affected the position of black people in the workplace; however, increases in their educational attainment also had a positive influence (Beller, 1974). Other domestic policies affecting the workplace include the Vietnam Era Veterans' Readjustment Assistance Act of 1972, the 1978 Pregnancy Disability Amendment to Title VII of 1978, the Age Discrimination in Employment Act of 1967, and the Americans with Disabilities Act of 1990 (Gardenswartz & Rowe, 1993). These laws forbid discrimination in the workplace on the basis of sex, color, race, religion, pregnancy, national origin, age, and physical ability. They have fundamentally changed the people in the workplace to represent the broadly diverse faces of America: black, brown, yellow, and white; young, middle-aged, and old; women and men; those with physical challenges; and newcomers to America.

The passage of key federal legislation dealing with immigration matters also significantly influenced the social transformation of the American workplace. Foremost among these is the 1965 Immigration and Nationality Act, the Refugee Act of 1980, the Immigration Reform and Control Act of 1986, and the Immigration Act of 1990 (U.S. Immigration and Naturalization Service, 1993). Starting in 1965, these changes in immigration policy facilitated the entry of unprecedented numbers of immigrants to the United States from Asia, Latin America, and the Caribbean Islands. By 1992, the presence of new immigrants in the workplace had taken hold. These newcomers had enhanced the cultural diversity of the American workplace.

The combination of globalization and technological changes also have aided diversity in the workplace. The globalization of the world's economy has significantly changed the workplace not only in the United States but also in many parts of the world. In Europe, for example, much of the work force by the next millennium is predicted to be composed substantially of people of color (Johnston, 1991). Similarly, nearly half of all net additions to the U.S. labor force by the end of the 20th century are expected to be people of color (largely first-generation immigrants from Asian and Latin American countries) and women (Fullerton, 1987).

The role of technology in these vast and far-reaching changes has been critical. Modern transportation and computers have eased both travel and communications. People are able to traverse large distances by various means of travel and communicate with each other through high-speed computers and other telecommunications devices. As the push to leave one's native land has affected countless people, the ability to leave has been aided greatly by modern technology. Again, the enactment of federal legislation has played a pivotal role in these circumstances.

Although the doors of opportunity have been greatly widened by federal legislation, allowing many more Americans from diverse cultures and women to enter the work force, diversity has not been achieved without conflict and adversity. The "glass ceiling" in many corporations has been a barrier to promotion and upward mobility for women and people from nondominant cultures. Discrimination and racism continue as major impediments in hiring and promotion at all levels in organizations (Neuberne, 1996).

The impact of new immigrants in the American work force compounds the effects of the existing diversity created by domestic policies. Furthermore, the new immigrants will have far-reaching consequences on public opinion, public policy, and outcomes in the workplace.

The public policy debate over immigration provides a critical backdrop for considering workplace issues. The immigration controversy has continued unabated throughout the 1990s and reflects serious political and social tensions about immigration throughout all levels of American society. The impact on immigration is seen not only in the workplace, but also in local communities and neighborhoods and in institutional life, including schools, places of worship, and political and social organizations (Bach, 1993; Ungar, 1995). This debate has been fueled by the increasing numbers of both legal and undocumented immigrants entering the country and by questions as to whether or not they contribute to the overall quality of society. It has not gone unnoticed that the proportion of nonwhite people among the new immigrants has continued to rise since the 1970s and far exceeds the number of white immigrants (Branign, 1997). The passage of the 1996 welfare reform legislation that restricts immigrant access to welfare benefits is further indicative of public opinion and the strong anti-immigrant sentiment in the country.

Recent immigrant flows have included substantial numbers of foreign-born individuals who are more likely to live in poverty, to be unemployed, and to have less than a high school education (Branign, 1997). Although these data may be foreboding, for successful resettlement and job placement of immigrants, research shows that immigrants who live in the United States longer tend to recover from their initial economic disadvantage and fare better in the long run (Meisenheimer, 1992; Schwartz, 1996). Thus, although the workplace may be bleak for these immigrants in the short run, evidence suggests that within two decades they will catch up economically with U.S. natives.

KEY POLICIES AFFECTING IMMIGRATION FLOWS TO THE UNITED STATES

Since 1965 changes in U.S. immigration policies have altered the numbers, origins, and characteristics of new immigrants. Before that time, American immigration was guided by a national-origin quota system of the Immigration Act of 1924 that was revised in the 1952 Immigration and Nationality Act. These policies produced a system of selective immigration by giving a quota preference to skilled workers from Western Europe (whose services were needed in the United States) and to relatives of U.S. citizens and aliens who were predominantly from Western European countries. The 1965 Immigration and Nationality Act abolished the national-origin quota system and eliminated national origin, race, or ancestry as a basis for immigration to the United States. The amendments established two categories of immigrants not subject to numerical restrictions. Family reunification was the main objective of the new policy. It allowed immediate relatives (spouses, children, and parents) of U.S. citizens to emigrate. The second category was designated "special immigrants" and included certain ministers of religion, former employees of the U.S. government abroad, and others (U.S. Immigration and Naturalization Service, 1993, 1996). The 1965 act was intended to increase the number of immigrants from Eastern European countries to the United States. However, economic conditions in Western Europe were a greater pull. Lifting restrictions on immigration changed the national-origin mix of immigrants in the country. By 1980 the increases in immigration from Latin America and Asia approached 50 percent (Borjas & Freeman, 1992).

In 1980 Congress passed the Refugee Act, which created the first permanent and systematic procedure for admission and resettlement of refugees in U.S. history. The act facilitated the entry of vast numbers of newcomers to America, including Cubans, Haitians, Vietnamese, Russians, and others from Africa, Eastern Europe, and Latin America and the Caribbean Islands (U.S. Immigration and Naturalization Service, 1993).

The Immigration Reform and Control Act of 1986 gave amnesty to more than 3 million undocumented people and authorized their legalization. The Immigration Act of 1990 amended the preference system and replaced it with a family-sponsored and employment-based immigration system. A "diversity" category allows for the entry of people from countries that have sent few immigrants to the United States since 1963. This provision is intended to benefit people from Europe and Africa (Borjas & Freeman, 1992). Collectively, this body of immigration law has allowed a much broader range of individual immigrants, refugees, and their families to come to the United States.

PROFILE OF THE NEWCOMERS

Unlike most of the previous immigrants with European ancestry, large numbers of recent immigrants have come from Asia, South America, Mexico, and the Caribbean Islands since the passage of the 1965 Immigration and Nationality Act. The newcomers look different, sound different, often dress differently and eat different foods, listen to different types of music, and follow many different faiths (Ungar, 1995); many are unlikely to assimilate with ease into the American "melting pot" (Furuto, Biswas, Chung, Murase, & Ross-Sheriff, 1992; Meemeduma, 1987). Like immigrants and refugees from earlier periods, these diverse groups of newcomers have come to America in search of better opportunities and safety and security for themselves and their families. They have come for financial self-sufficiency, economic success, participation in a civil society, and control over their own destinies. They desire to live peacefully and respectfully and share in the American dream (Farley & Allen, 1987; Furuto et al., 1992; Li, 1993).

Immigration flows to America decreased between the end of World War I and the 1960s; during these years, there were tight constraints on immigration. The 1924 Immigration Act effectively prohibited Asian immigration. Not until the 1952 Immigration and Nationality Act did the exclusion of Asian immigrants officially end.

For much of the century, America remained an industrialized society with concerns largely about its own markets. There was little or no competition from abroad. The Vietnam War helped change the nation's focus, and the 1965 Immigration and Nationality Act ushered in a new era for immigration in the U.S. labor market. By the 1980s, immigration had become a national issue, causing public debates in Congress, in state legislatures, in public-interest groups, and among advocates for and against immigration. The nation was changing. America was entering a new age of globalization; competition from overseas was threatening traditional and dominant American markets, such as those for the automobile, steel production, and garment industries. New relations with foreign governments were emerging after the Cold War ended. The newcomers were being re-evaluated as either contributors to the culture and society or social and economic burdens.

By the 1990s the debate continued to rage as to how the nation should deal with these immigrants and others who desire to come to America. How wide should the doors stay open and should the doors be closed altogether were common questions (Bean, Vernez, & Keely, 1989). There were concerns as well about people who had come illegally and were not documented. But the doors were open sufficiently to allow one of the two largest waves of immigrants ever admitted to the United States. The first wave came between 1905 and 1914 and the second from 1986 to 1995 (Figure 2-1 and Table 2-1).

In the wave between 1905 and 1914, immigrants to the United States were largely from Western Europe, in contrast to the origins of the modern newcomers. Unlike any other period in American history, immigrants have come in large numbers from Asia and Latin and South America (Tables 2-1 and 2-2). Between 1961 and 1970 and between 1991 and 1995, immigration from Europe declined from 34 percent to 15 percent, whereas immigration from Asia rose from a low of 13 percent in the 1961–1970 period to a high of 37 percent in the 1981–1990 period (Table 2-3). China, Korea, the Philippines, and Vietnam were contributors to the increase in Asian immigrants. Immigration to the United States from North America remained relatively high between these two periods. The shift in U.S. immigration from 45 percent in the 1961–1970 period to 51 percent in the 1991–1995

Figure 2-1
Legal Immigrants to the United States, 1901–1995

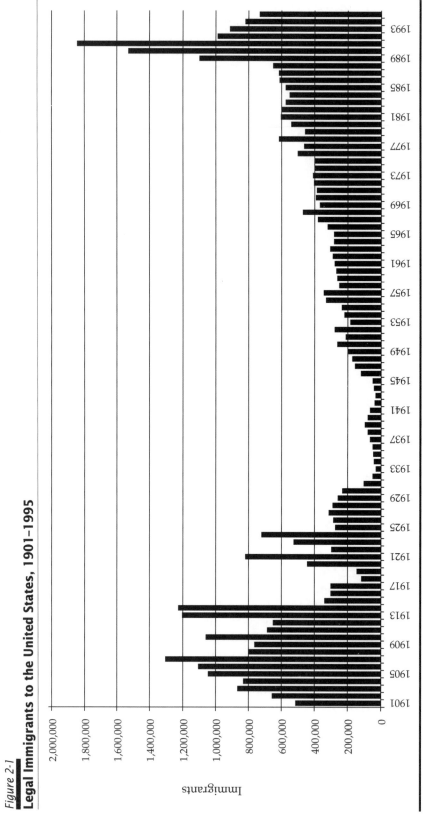

SOURCE: U.S. Immigration and Naturalization Service. (1996). *Statistical yearbook of the Immigration and Naturalization Service, 1995.* Washington, DC: U.S. Government Printing Office.

Table 2-1

Two Decades with the Highest Number of Immigrants to the United States during the 20th Century

Year	No. of Immigrants	Year	No. of Immigrants
1905	1,026,499	1986	601,708
1906	1,100,735	1987	601,516
1907	1,285,349	1988	643,025
1908	782,870	1989	1,090,024
1909	751,786	1990	1,536,483
1910	1,041,570	1991	1,827,167
1911	878,587	1992	973,977
1912	838,172	1993	904,292
1913	1,197,892	1994	804,416
1914	1,218,480	1995	720,461

SOURCES: U.S. Immigration and Naturalization Service. (1993). *Statistical yearbook of the Immigration and Naturalization Service, 1992.* Washington, DC: U.S. Government Printing Office. U.S. Immigration and Naturalization Service. (1995). *Statistical yearbook of the Immigration and Naturalization Service, 1994.* Washington, DC: U.S. Government Printing Office.

period was largely the result of immigration from Mexico and the Caribbean (Tables 2-2 and 2-3).

Among the newcomers were refugees from Vietnam, Cambodia, Laos, Sudan, Cuba, Ethiopia, and El Salvador. Between 1975 and 1989 a million refugees entered the United States from Cambodia, Laos, and Vietnam (Tollefson, 1989). Another large group of newcomers were undocumented migrants, for whom there are no official numbers. The estimated number of undocumented migrants in 1992 was 3.4 million people. Schwartz (1996) reported that 200,000 to 500,000 undocumented people enter the United States each year.

When long-term immigrants elect to get naturalized, they become citizens, pledge allegiance to the United States, and renounce allegiance to their countries of origin. Naturalization is an indication of a long-term commitment to a country. Naturalization rates of people from Asian countries steadily increased from 13 percent in the 1960s to 49 percent in the 1990s. Simultaneously, the naturalization rates of people from Europe declined steadily from 62 percent in the 1960s to 12 percent in the 1990s (Table 2-4). The largest group of immigrants continues to come from North America and shows a steady increase (Table 2-3).

The two largest groups of recent immigrants and naturalized citizens, those from Asia and North America, are not homogenous. Within each category, there are people with diverse languages, cultures, and religions. The immigrants from North America come from Mexico, the Caribbean Islands, Cuba, the Dominican Republic, Haiti, and Jamaica (Table 2-2). From Asia come large populations of Filipinos, Koreans, Indians, Vietnamese, and Chinese. All these groups are further distinguished by their representation of some of the world's great religions. They are Buddhists, Confucianists, Hindus, Muslims, and Sikhs. Like previous immigrants to America, these newcomers are likely to maintain their religious and cultural identities. Many reside in large ethnic enclaves (Li, 1993; Meemeduma, 1987).

Table 2-2

Number of Immigrants from Major North American and Asian Countries and Regions, by Decade

Country/Region of Origin	1951–1960	1961–1970	1971–1980	1981–1990	1991–1994
North American countries					
Canada and Newfoundland	377,952	413,310	169,939	156,938	84,613
Mexico	299,811	459,937	640,294	1,655,843	1,400,108
Cuba	78,948	208,536	264,863	144,578	47,556
Dominican Republic	9,897	93,292	148,143	252,035	180,055
Haiti	4,442	34,499	56,335	138,379	80,867
Jamaica	8,869	74,906	137,577	20,474	71,927
Other Caribbean	20,935	58,980	134,216	128,911	56,066
El Salvador	5,895	14,992	34,436	213,539	117,463
Other Central American	38,856	86,338	100,204	254,549	150,128
Asian countries					
China	9,657	34,764	124,326	346,747	170,191
Hong Kong	15,541	75,007	113,467	98,215	58,676
India	1,973	27,189	164,134	250,786	149,374
Korea	6,231	34,526	267,638	333,746	76,901
Philippines	19,307	98,376	354,987	548,764	248,466
Vietnam	335	4,340	172,820	280,782	110,300
Total immigration	2,515,479	3,321,677	4,493,314	7,338,062	4,509,852

SOURCE: U.S. Immigration and Naturalization Service. (1995). *Statistical yearbook of the Immigration and Naturalization Service, 1994.* Washington, DC: U.S. Government Printing Office.

Table 2-3

Legal Immigration to the United States between 1961 and 1994, by Region of Last Residence

Region of Last Residence	1961–1970		1971–1980		1981–1990		1991–1994	
	No.	%	No.	%	No.	%	No.	%
Europe	1,123,492	34	800,368	18	761,550	10	760,106	15
North America	1,478,078	45	1,687,989	38	3,153,836	43	2,654,860	51
South America	257,940	8	295,741	7	461,847	6	23,281	5
Asia	427,642	13	1,588,178	35	2,738,157	37	1,582,764	30
Africa	28,954	1	80,779	2	176,893	2	151,101	3
Other	25,215	1	41,254	1	46,237	1	29,727	1

SOURCES: U.S. Immigration and Naturalization Service. (1993). *Statistical yearbook of the Immigration and Naturalization Service, 1992.* Washington, DC: U.S. Government Printing Office. U.S. Immigration and Naturalization Service. (1995). *Statistical yearbook of the Immigration and Naturalization Service, 1994.* Washington, DC: U.S. Government Printing Office.

Table 2-4

Percentage of Naturalized Citizens by Region of Birth and by Decade of Naturalization

Region of Birth	1961–1970	1971–1980	1981–1990	1991–1994
Europe	62	31	15	12
North America	21	28	26	27
South America	2	5	7	8
Asia	13	34	49	49
Other	2	2	3	4
Total	100	100	100	100

SOURCE: U.S. Immigration and Naturalization Service. (1995). *Statistical yearbook of the Immigration and Naturalization Service, 1994.* Washington, DC: U.S. Government Printing Office.

THE TRANSFORMED WORKPLACE

Increased numbers of immigrants, largely from third world countries, along with women, people from diverse cultures, and an aging work force, are changing the workplace. A need for people with higher levels of education and skills is changing the workplace as well. It is difficult to describe fully and precisely what micro changes have occurred in the full range of workplaces because a serious gap exists in the empirical research.

An important exception is the research of Lamphere, Stepick, and Grenier (1994) in five urban areas—Miami, Los Angeles, Chicago, Philadelphia, and Houston—and a small community in Garden City, Kansas. Their study was part of a larger study on newcomers and residents funded by the Ford Foundation (Bach, 1993). Lamphere and associates analyzed several workplaces, including a beef-processing plant; the construction, garment, hotel, and restaurant industries; and a lightbulb fixture plant.

The research literature on workplaces where a majority of new immigrants are found does help in addressing several issues. It tells us about where the newcomers are working, about the types of work they do, and about other public concerns, including those related to established residents in the workplace.

Immigrants labor in a variety of workplaces in diverse positions. Borjas and Freeman (1992) noted that by 1988, more than 9 percent of the U.S. labor force was foreign born and that the representation of immigrants in the labor force will increase through the beginning of the 21st century. Recent immigrants are joining the work force at a time of restructuring of the U.S. economy—of deindustrialization and the search for inexpensive labor—and in a period in which there are more women and ethnically and racially diverse groups in the work force than before.

The research literature reveals that differences remain between men and women and among ethnic and racial groups in rate of pay (Butcher, 1994; Hughey, 1990; Long & Gill, 1989; Petras, 1992; Stier,

1991; Yamanaka & McClelland, 1994) and division of labor. The meat-packing industry, which has been described as "the most hazardous industry in America" (Lamphere et al., 1994, p. 29; Stull, 1994), remains largely male dominated. Young, single, male immigrants are easy recruits for these industries, which have relocated to the South and Southwest (Lamphere et al., 1994).

The garment industry employs women almost exclusively (Petras, 1992). Inexpensive female immigrant labor from Asia and Latin America provides a steady supply of workers for this industry. The evidence suggests that these shops employ underage workers, have dangerous working conditions, and require 12-hour workdays. There is no career ladder for women garment workers, and they remain at the bottom of the industry. Women immigrants and refugees face the additional difficulties of obtaining social support, child care services, and health care (Louie, 1992; Shepherd, 1987).

There is a widely held perception that immigrants and refugees—some highly skilled, some with financial resources, and many unskilled—are taking jobs from native-born workers, particularly people of color (Wilson, 1996). This perception arises partially because of the concentration of immigrants in certain low-income jobs and professions in which ethnic groups have created a niche and are visible, and partially because of the restructuring of the U.S. economy, especially in those occupations in which immigrants are most likely to be employed.

Sorensen, Bean, Ku, and Zimmermann (1992) explored the effects of immigrants on native employment and wages and found little overall impact. However, there was a differential impact based on the specific category of immigrants and native-born populations. For example, immigrants entering the United States under the family-preference category had "no negative effects on the earnings or employment opportunities of native male workers" (Sorensen et al., 1992, p. 4). On the other hand, employment-preference immigrants appeared to exert a small negative effect on white native-born males. Other legal immigrants had insignificant effects on the labor market outcomes of native-born workers. Similarly, undocumented immigrants had no significant effect on native-born workers.

Specifically, it is alleged that recent immigrants—mainly Asians and Hispanics—have fewer skills, depress wages, are less likely to assimilate into the American work force, and therefore will be a burden to society. Research evidence shows the contrary. Using census data and current population survey samples, La Londe and Topel (1991); Simon, Moore, and Sullivan (1993); and Chiswick, Cohen, and Zach (1997) found that although the average earnings of recent immigrants were much lower than those of comparable native-born populations, immigrant earnings over a decade caught up with the natives with similar ethnic backgrounds and national origins. These results indicate assimilation of immigrants in the labor force, even though their earnings do not reach levels comparable to those of white workers.

In general, comparisons of immigrants and U.S. natives in the work force indicated little difference in labor force participation rates of men under age 55; that is, the proportion of each of the four groups of men (ages 16–24, 25–34, 35–44, and 45–54) in the employed or seeking-employment categories were similar (Meisenheimer, 1992). However, immigrant men who had lived in the United States for less than three years and recent immigrant women in all age groups had lower labor force participation rates and weekly earnings. Labor force participation rates of immigrant men who had resided in the United States three to eight years and eight to 15 years were similar to those of the native-born men. Length of time in the United States, level of formal education, and English language skills explain work force participation rates and income for immigrant men. As new immigrants gain more information and understanding about the U.S. labor market, establish contacts, and gain English language competency, their participation rates increase over time and their earnings eventually equal, and in certain occupational categories overtake, earnings of similar nonimmigrants (Borjas & Freeman, 1992).

In contrast, Borjas and Freeman (1992) reported that immigrant women in all age groups had lower rates of labor force participation. Their participation varied by length of residence and age cohorts. Using age cohorts similar to those for men (16–24, 25–34, 35–44, and 45–54), these investigators found that immigrant women ages 35–44 had the highest rate of participation. Their rates increased slowly and took much longer to reach parity with native-born women. For example, immigrant women in the 35–44 age group who had lived in the United States for less than three years had a 49 percent participation rate, those with three to eight years of residency had a 65 percent participation rate, and those with eight to 15 years had a 71 percent rate. It took 30 years for women who had emigrated as children to reach a 77 percent participation rate—the same as native-born women (Meisenheimer, 1992). Borjas and Freeman (1992) noted that immigrant earnings reach parity with those of their ethnic counterparts but not with the typical native-born worker. People who emigrate as adults do not experience economic "assimilation," as indicated by their wages. However, those who come to the United States as children do eventually reach parity with the native-born population.

Although the literature reveals that the new immigrants enter the work force in greater numbers at the lowest levels than do established residents, Asians show some variation in their occupational distribution. Asians, which are the dominant group among the new immigrants (Asia accounted for 40 percent of total legal immigrants to the United States through 1990), are reported to have the highest proportions of professionals. Kanjanapan (1995) analyzed Immigration and Naturalization Service data for fiscal years 1988–1990 on the total immigration of professionals to the United States. Asians contributed to the largest component. Kanjanapan restricted his analysis to engineering, the sciences, and health. The five leading Asian countries sending professionals to the United States are the

Philippines, Vietnam, Republic of Korea, People's Republic of China, and India.

How do the newcomers find their jobs? Established immigrants generally help newer immigrants from their countries or localities of origin find employment. Similarly, they share their knowledge of job skills with family members and friends. Ungar (1995) described how "Ethiopians in business here prefer to hire their own compatriots in part because there is a natural tribal identification and an affinity for their own people" (p. 226). They share language and cultural backgrounds that create comfort and reduce tensions and hostility. In an assessment of the economic adaptation of Eastern European, Afghan, and Ethiopian refugees, Gozdziak (1989) noted that a large proportion of refugees found their jobs through informal referrals from extended family members and conationals. As a result of such referral and employment patterns, over a period of time many immigrants and refugees from the same countries of origin enter the same industries or ownership of the same types of businesses (Lamphere et al., 1994). The consequence of these informal practices is that many low-paying workplaces are homogeneous in terms of worker background and country of origin.

Recent ethnographic studies (Cohen, 1994; Erickson, 1994; Goode, 1994a, 1994b; Ninivaggi, 1994; Ungar, 1995) reported that many of these immigrants work long hours, work several jobs, or establish cooperative ventures with family or friends to set up their own businesses. These immigrants include large numbers of Indian, Pakistani, Ethiopian, and Korean small business owners who have established a specific small business niche. Increasingly, small hotels and motels in the United States are owned or managed by Indian or Pakistani immigrants, taxi cab businesses by Ethiopians, dry cleaning businesses by Koreans and Indians, and "mom-and-pop" stores by Koreans (Ungar, 1995). Several of these business owners have come with high levels of education or skills from their countries of origin but are unable to find jobs because there is no market for their skills or they do not have appropriate American experience or English language skills.

CHALLENGES

The United States has a rich history of immigrant labor involvement in building the infrastructure of the country. Chinese laborers helped build the railroads and Irish immigrants helped construct the vast complex of highways. Also, a huge number of Africans were enslaved, brought to the country, and used as laborers in agriculture and employed as freedmen in the steel, automobile, and other assembly-line industries. Many African American workers in low-paying jobs today feel left out and pushed out by the new immigrant workers. In addition, conflicts have been reported between all categories of new immigrants and established residents. Yet, as a Ford Foundation study (Bach, 1993) reveals, when the new immigrants and the established

residents work together, they can bring about social change beneficial to all groups and to the larger society.

Many people in America today have defined immigration as a major national problem. Studies reviewed in this chapter support the
point of view that the new immigrants working in the most undesirable jobs have sustained these workplaces and contributed to the
economic welfare of the country.

REFERENCES

Age Discrimination in Employment Act of 1967, P.L. 90-202, 81 Stat. 602.

Americans with Disabilities Act of 1990, P.L. 101-336, 104 Stat. 327.

Bach, R. (1993). *Changing relations: Newcomers and established residents in U.S. communities* (Report to the Ford Foundation by the National Board of the Changing Relations Project). New York: Ford Foundation.

Bean, F. D., Vernez, G., & Keely, C. B. (1989). *Opening and closing doors: Evaluating immigration reform and control.* Washington, DC: Urban Institute.

Beller, A. (1974). *The effects of Title VII of the Civil Rights Act of 1964 on the economic position of minorities.* Doctoral dissertation, Columbia University, New York.

Borjas, G. J., & Freeman, R. B. (1992). *Immigration and the work force: Economic consequences for the United States and source areas.* Chicago: University of Chicago Press.

Branign, W. (1997, April 9). Nearly 1 in 10 in U.S. is foreign born, census says. *Washington Post,* p. A18.

Butcher, K. F. (1994, January). Black immigrants in the United States: A comparison
with native blacks and other immigrants. *Industrial and Labor Relations Review, 47,*
265–284.

Chiswick, G., Cohen, Y., & Zach, T. (1997). The labor market status of immigrants:
Effects of the unemployment rate at arrival and duration of residence. *Industrial
and Labor Relations Review, 50,* 289–303.

Civil Rights Act of 1964, P.L. 88-352, 78 Stat. 241.

Cohen, C. (1994). Facing job loss: Changing relationships in a multicultural urban
factory. In L. Lamphere, A. Stepick, & G. Grenier (Eds.), *Newcomers in the workplace: Immigrants and the restructuring of the U.S. economy* (pp. 231–250). Philadelphia: Temple University Press.

Erickson, R. (1994). Guys in white hats: Short-term participant observation among
beef processing workers and managers. In L. Lamphere, A. Stepick, & G. Grenier
(Eds.), *Newcomers in the workplace: Immigrants and the restructuring of the U.S. economy* (pp. 78–98). Philadelphia: Temple University Press.

Farley, R., & Allen, W. (1987). *The color line and the quality of life in America.* New
York: Russell Sage Foundation.

Fullerton, H. (1987, September). Labor force projections: 1986 to 2000. *Monthly Labor
Review,* pp. 19–29.

Furuto, S., Biswas, R., Chung, D., Murase, K., & Ross-Sheriff, F. (1992). *Social work
practice with Asian Americans.* Newbury Park, CA: Sage Publications.

Gardenswartz, L., & Rowe, A. (1993). *Managing diversity.* San Diego: Pfeiffer.

Goode, J. (1994a). Encounters over the counter: Bosses, workers and customers on a
changing shopping strip. In L. Lamphere, A. Stepick, & G. Grenier (Eds.), *Newcomers in the workplace: Immigrants and the restructuring of the U.S. economy* (pp.
251–280). Philadelphia: Temple University Press.

Goode, J. (1994b). Polishing the Rust Belt: Immigrants enter a restructuring Philadel-
phia. In L. Lamphere, A. Stepick, & G. Grenier (Eds.), *Newcomers in the workplace:
Immigrants and the restructuring of the U.S. economy* (pp. 199–230). Philadelphia:
Temple University Press.

Gozdziak, E. G. (1989, December). *New Americans: The economic adaptation of Eastern
European, Afghan and Ethiopian refugees.* Washington, DC: Refugee Policy Group.

Hughey, A. M. (1990, June). The incomes of recent female immigrants to the United
States. *Social Science Quarterly, 71,* 383–390.

Immigration Act, ch. 190, 43 Stat. 153 (May 26, 1924).

Immigration Act of 1990, P.L. 101-649, 104 Stat. 4978.

Immigration and Nationality Act, ch. 477, 66 Stat. 163 (June 27, 1952).

Immigration and Nationality Act, P.L. 89-236, 79 Stat. 911 to 920 (1965).

Immigration Reform and Control Act of 1986, P.L. 99-603, 101 Stat. 3359.

Johnston, W. (1991, March–April). Global work force 2000: The new world labor market. *Harvard Business Review,* pp. 115–127.

Kanjanapan, W. (1995). The immigration of Asian professionals to the United States. *International Migration Review, 29*(1), 7–26.

La Londe, R., & Topel, R. (1991, May). Immigrants in the American labor market: Quality, assimilation, and distributional effects. *AEA Papers and Proceedings,* pp. 297–302.

Lamphere, L., Stepick, A., & Grenier, G. (Eds.). (1994). *Newcomers in the workplace: Immigrants and the restructuring of the U.S. economy.* Philadelphia: Temple University Press.

Li, S-H. (1993). *Initial adaptation experiences of Chinese American immigrants.* Doctoral dissertation, Howard University, Washington, DC.

Long, S., & Gill, A. (1989). The gender gap in the wages of illegal aliens. *Social Science Journal, 26*(1), 65–74.

Louie, M. C. (1992). Immigrant Asian women in Bay Area garment sweatshops: After sewing, laundry, cleaning and cooking I have no breath left to sing. *Amerasia Journal, 18*(1), 1–26.

Meemeduma, P. (1987). *The support networks of Sri Lankan women living in the United States: A study of settlement and adaptation.* Doctoral dissertation, Howard University, Washington, DC.

Meisenheimer, J., II. (1992). How do immigrants fare in the U.S. labor market? *Monthly Labor Review, 115*(12), 3–18.

Neuberne, E. (1996, November 25). Divisionality trumps diversity. *USA Today,* p. 3B.

Ninivaggi, C. (1994). Poverty and politics: Practice and ideology among small business owners in an urban enterprise zone. In L. Lamphere, A. Stepick, & G. Grenier (Eds.), *Newcomers in the workplace: Immigrants and the restructuring of the U.S. economy* (pp. 281–301). Philadelphia: Temple University Press.

Petras, E. M. (1992). The shirt on your back: Immigrant workers and the reorganization of the garment industry. *Social Justice, 19*(1), 76–114.

Pregnancy Disability Amendment to Title VII of 1978, P.L. 95-555, 92 Stat. 2076.

Refugee Act of 1980, P.L. 96-212, 94 Stat. 102.

Schwartz, J. (1996, March–April). Coming to America. *Forecast, 4*(2), 19–26.

Shepherd, J. (1987). *Social Development Issues, 11*(2), 72–86.

Simon, J. L., Moore, S., & Sullivan, R. (1993, Summer). The effect of immigration on aggregate native unemployment: An across-city estimation. *Journal of Labor Research, 14,* 299–316.

Sorensen, E., Bean, F., Ku, L., & Zimmermann, W. (1992). *Immigrant categories and the U.S. job market: Do they make a difference?* (Urban Institute Report 92-1). Washington, DC: Urban Institute Press.

Stier, H. (1991, March). Immigrant women go to work: Analysis of immigrant wives' labor supply for six Asian groups. *Social Science Quarterly, 72*(1), 67–82.

Stull, D. (1994). Knock 'em dead: Work on the killfloor of a modern beefpacking plant. In L. Lamphere, A. Stepick, & G. Grenier (Eds.), *Newcomers in the workplace: Immigrants and the restructuring of the U.S. economy* (pp. 44–77). Philadelphia: Temple University Press.

Tollefson, J. (1989). *Alien winds: The re-education of America's Indochinese refugees.* New York: Praeger.

Ungar, S. J. (1995). *Fresh blood: The new American immigrants.* New York: Simon & Schuster.

U.S. Immigration and Naturalization Service. (1993). *Statistical yearbook of the Immigration and Naturalization Service, 1992.* Washington, DC: U.S. Government Printing Office.

U.S. Immigration and Naturalization Service. (1995). *Statistical yearbook of the Immigration and Naturalization Service, 1994.* Washington, DC: U.S. Government Printing Office.

U.S. Immigration and Naturalization Service. (1996). *Statistical yearbook of the Immigration and Naturalization Service, 1995.* Washington, DC: U.S. Government Printing Office.

Vietnam Era Veterans' Readjustment Assistance Act of 1972, P.L. 92-540, 86 Stat. 1074.

Wilson, W. J. (1996). *When work disappears: The world of the new urban poor.* New York: Alfred A. Knopf.

Yamanaka, K., & McClelland, K. (1994, January). Earning the model-minority image: Diverse strategies of economic adaptation by Asian-American women. *Ethnic and Racial Studies, 17,* 79–114.

Supervision and Management of American Indian Social and Human Services Workers

Joyce Z. White

Workplace diversity is a fact of life. Van Den Bergh (1991) discussed the need for the employer to address ways in which workers from diverse backgrounds can become "fully contributing" members of an organization and be socialized into the workplace culture, "which for the most part will reflect mainstream values and beliefs." Failure in mutual accommodation and adaptation can lead, for workers from nondominant cultures, to sociocultural dissonance, the "stress, strain and incongruence which can occur for an individual attempting to belong to different cultures." The worker is faced with "maintenance of core beliefs, values, and behavioral styles" while simultaneously adopting "new and potentially conflictual attitudes and values" (p. 72).

Managers must ensure equity, create harmony, develop their workers, and draw on the strengths of diversity. This is no small task, even for managers who are themselves members of nondominant-culture groups. Unfortunately, top management often assumes that once they have hired a person from a different culture, the problems of workplace diversity are resolved. Managers who recruit, supervise, and evaluate American Indian social work and human services staff must possess appropriate knowledge, attitudes, and skills to do so. There is little in the social work supervisory literature to guide the manager. This article is an initial effort to address some of the deficits.

There are many similarities among First Nations. The term "First Nations" was used originally in Canada to refer to recognized groups and is used more inclusively in the United States for both recognized and nonrecognized indigenous peoples. There is a growing pan-Indian movement, but with more than 500 groups in the mainland United States alone, there are vast differences among the nations. No other ethnic group's identity is determined by federal and state government regulations. Members of no other group are asked to produce documentation to prove their ethnic, cultural, or racial status. The federal government and most states recognize only tribally enrolled people as "Indian" or "Native American." The most common determination of eligibility for enrollment is direct descent from people living on a reservation at the time rolls were first prepared; a blood quantum must be met, usually half to one-eighth.

36

After meeting this criterion, the individual is assigned another ethnic–racial status, usually white. First Nations people, including those who live within their culture and traditions and who speak their native language, are denied federal recognition. Some were encouraged to give up their native status in return for land, training, or relocation to urban areas. Others had their native status arbitrarily terminated by government policy. These policies exist in both Canada and the United States. As a result of these and similar policies, the number of unrecognized people may exceed that of recognized people. The resultant skewing of data toward underrepresentation has a profound impact on social and human services delivery.

First Nations people with whom human services agencies come in contact and from among whom personnel are hired can be categorized as traditional, urban/transitional, and assimilated/nonrecognized. Workers who have grown up in reservation settings are likely to have close ties to history, culture, and kindred. Their knowledge of their culture may be learned in school, but more likely it is learned through oral tradition and observation. DuBray, a Lakota woman, noted that orientation to time, success, and values may differ markedly from that of the majority culture (DuBray, 1992). They often lived much of their lives in marginal economic situations with high unemployment and problems traditionally associated with poverty —alcoholism, apathy, large school dropout rates, family violence, and child abuse. These workers may be especially at risk as they enter the majority culture. Special challenges face those who are from a reserve and have returned to work among their own friends and families.

TRADITIONAL FIRST NATIONS PEOPLE

Among risk factors for those raised in the traditional manner or on the reserve are

- lack of fluency in standard English
- poor educational preparation
- lack of knowledge and skills necessary for success in the majority culture
- unfamiliarity or discomfort with competitive styles of interaction
- beliefs that formal schooling makes one different from one's family and kindred
- family commitments placed before other commitments
- differing time orientation.

Tensions are high for workers caught between traditional lifestyles and demands of the industrial workplace. Much of this tension arises from bridging two worlds. How does the employee explain the need for a leave for urgent spiritual or medical reasons to a supervisor who has a secular orientation or, worse, who regards native practices as pagan or primitive? Workers with strong ties to tradition and extended family may need to return home to participate in traditional healing ceremonies, feasts, giveaways, and other important community occasions. In some instances, healing of the patient cannot take place without members of the family present. These trips may require long-distance travel and great expense for gifts; ceremonies may require four or more days to complete properly. These needs arise from a profound spirituality, from knowledge that the world offers a difficult journey, and from awareness that spiritual needs cannot be truncated to fit demands of school or workplace. The manager can recognize the traditional person's obligation to family and community and can work with the employee to meet the needs of both workplace and worker. The goal is flexibility that will benefit the organization and all its employees.

Although many First Nations people have adopted the lifestyles and religions of the majority, others have not. Those who adhere to traditional practices may not discuss them, but employers can be sensitive to the fact that the wearing of braids, men not cutting their hair, and the avoidance of certain colors, objects, or foods may be related to religious beliefs and practices. The native person may not welcome intrusive or persistent questioning about traditional beliefs and practices. Such information is given slowly over a long period of time to initiates who are considered ready for it. Readiness is judged by the way one lives one's life—by actions; rarely is it based on words. Those who are knowledgeable are cautioned not to share powerful spiritual wisdom with those who might misuse it.

Some traditional people are uncomfortable with intense scrutiny by others, extended questioning about personal matters, or being expected to speak just for the sake of speaking. Traditional people may regard undue curiosity as a breach of privacy, good manners, or respect. Silence does not mean the individual has failed to observe or understand what is happening or being said. Observation, learning by experience, and respect for authority are taught from childhood. Advice is seldom given directly. When it is given, it is often in the form of a story or an observation about something that happened to someone else.

Silence has great value in small and closely knit communities. It maintains harmony, recognizes the autonomy of others, avoids judgment of the decisions or words of another, creates inward peace, and allows time for reflection. Non-natives may feel uncomfortable or believe the person does not like them, that they are not "relating." Silence for the non-native may be associated with anger, withdrawal, or lack of interest. However, one has only to sit in a talking circle to observe the benefits of waiting one's turn. Talk goes around the circle; each person has a chance to state his or her opinion or thoughts as long as he or she wishes; the process may go around several times. It is rude to interrupt the speaker or speak out of turn. Many traditional people are able to process and hold in their minds complex sequences of thought for long periods of time as a result of early training and adherence to cultural norms. Their recall of events and what is said is precise.

Employers can assist by being aware of the meaning of silence among traditional peoples. They can help other workers understand that interactional styles differ. They can give the employee time to ponder. They can allow the employee more time to respond to questions or more time in discussions, for example. They can recognize that although the worker may appear disinterested, she or he is paying close attention to actions and body language as well as words and is likely to have accurate recollection of the total meeting or encounter. A supervisor in the Northwest was able to capitalize on the aural skills of his First Nations employee during intense and hostile interrogation by partisan county commissioners who provided significant funding to the agency. The worker's excellent powers of observation and ability to recall what was said were invaluable in preparing for the next round. The program was funded.

The employee who has come from a rural or reservation setting may feel isolated in an unfamiliar organizational or urban environment. Employers and colleagues can help through friendly support, such as an invitation to join others at lunch or for coffee. Opportunities to discover mutual hobbies, sports interests, television shows, information about families, and the like are welcome and help to build rapport. Some may view First Nations people as exotic or possessing special powers or knowledge. The reality is that First Nations people are more like other Americans than not—they enjoy the same television shows, music, foods, and sports. They live in the same homes. Their children want the same bicycles, compact discs, and Barbie dolls as other children.

URBAN/TRANSITIONAL FIRST NATIONS PEOPLE

"Urban/transitional" refers to people with tribal membership or affiliation who have moved to an urban setting, generally in search of employment and better educational opportunities for their children. It also includes their descendants who have remained in the urban setting but who maintain ties to their community or family of origin and possibly to some traditions, customs, foods, child-rearing practices, and healing practices. They may return to the reserve when funds and work permit. It is common to return at times of childbearing, family crises, illness, weddings, funerals, and ceremonial occasions such as giveaways, namings, or sings. Elderly people may return to the reserve as they approach the end of their lives, and children may be sent to or from the reserve to live with family members.

In the city or town, extended family members, close relatives, and friends from the tribe may live nearby or share housing and form a close and supportive network. People from other Indian nations may be included in this network. Because most First Nations communities value generosity and hospitality, the sharing of food, clothing, child care, and other resources is common and permits survival in a difficult environment. These systems also may be sources of stress and serve to maintain dysfunctional behavior and relationships.

Sharing of material possessions is becoming less common, and this may be a source of conflict between family members or between old-timers and new arrivals.

In the workplace, urban/transitional people may present an appearance of adaptation that belies a very real bewilderment and unfamiliarity with Anglo customs, sense of time, placement of priorities, and so forth. Retreat to familiar behaviors may appear, such as withdrawal from conflict. First Nations people may be seen as apathetic by those accustomed to confrontation and to open—often aggressive—assertion of rights.

First Nations workers may have difficulty learning to use the social, economic, and political systems of the city as well as the organization. They may experience delay in moving upward in the organization as a result of their lack of knowledge of corporate culture. For example, modesty and humility are honored traditional values, but these values may keep the individual from mentioning accomplishments. Supervisors used to the self-promotion of employees in a corporate structure may not recognize the contributions of the First Nations employee. Mentors and supervisors can help aspiring and new workers to understand organizational structure, rules, and processes and can alert them to the need to promote their accomplishments. They also can help by allowing the workers to discuss the dilemmas they may experience, such as feeling pulled between differing value systems or norms.

Supervisors can recognize the difficulties of bicultural or transitional lifestyles as the worker and family move from reservation into the unfamiliar world beyond. Old support systems may not exist; new support systems may be needed. Contacts with others in similar situations may be of help. Contacts with native associations can be encouraged, as can involvement in local tribal centers or festivals or in pan-Indian associations. Opportunities to attend workshops or talk with First Nations professionals can help new employees function within the larger structure while remaining true to their own values.

Supervisors can make suitable mentors available to First Nations workers. These mentors need not have the same background, but they should be sensitive people willing to help the workers develop a sense of trust and familiarity with the mentor and the workplace. Mentors can introduce workers to other employees, offer suggestions and guidance, link them to resources, and help them understand the work environment.

ASSIMILATED FIRST NATIONS PEOPLE

Assimilated First Nations people are no different from other employees. They have grown up in or learned to function comfortably and easily within the dominant culture. First Nations people from assimilated homes often have educated, affluent parents; have attended good schools; and are in every way prepared for work in an organizational or bureaucratic structure.

Employers need to be aware that people who are recruited from native communities and return to their home community have unique issues. Boundaries between professional and personal life are more blurred in these communities than in other social work and human services settings. Family and friends may remember when the social worker was young or recall youthful misdeeds; they may not view the new worker as an authority or professional. Friends and relatives may expect special consideration or favors; for example, elders may ask to borrow an agency car or expect the worker to run an errand for them.

Isolation is a problem for those who work in remote communities. Workers need to get away from the setting and share concerns and experiences with others in similar circumstances. Social work education programs do not prepare new workers for this situation and, in fact, compound the difficulty for them by insisting such relationships are unprofessional and anti-therapeutic.

EFFECTIVE SERVICES DELIVERY TO FIRST NATIONS PEOPLE

Managers can work more effectively with First Nations employees if they draw on fundamental social work values—tolerance, nonjudgmental acceptance of difference, and acknowledgment of strengths the individual or group brings to the workplace. The 11 suggestions that follow will help managers develop a mutually beneficial rapport with their First Nations employees.

1. **Approach First Nations employees with respect and acceptance.** Avoid barraging new employees with questions about family, beliefs, or appearance. Do not ask about blood quantum for evidence of tribal enrollment unless it is a legitimate requirement for the job. Do not make comments about weight, appearance, cheekbones, hair texture, or skin color as evidence of being truly "Indian." Do not single out the First Nations employee as "our Indian social worker" or someone different from other employees.
2. **Do not ask for details of religious and spiritual beliefs or practices.** The employees may not be able to or may not wish to share those with you. Work with the employees to develop a plan to meet job responsibilities and personal and family needs, if such needs arise. The agency should not have different policies on absenteeism for First Nations employees; in fact, it is unwise to do so. The agency, however, can be flexible in meeting the needs of all employees when family emergencies, illness, and rites of passage demand their presence.
3. **Be aware of the important role that elders and spiritual leaders play in the traditional community.** "Elder" does not mean any older person but rather a person who has been singled out by the community for his or her leadership, wisdom, common sense, and spiritual qualities. Few projects will go forward without their approval. Elders are the living repositories of

knowledge for the nation and possess profound knowledge not only of the traditions and history of the community but also of human nature.

4. **Do not expect instant rapport or bonding, particularly with elders and traditional people.** Remember that the history of native peoples is one of invasion, oppression, and genocide that continues today in numerous subtle ways. Because of native reticence and aversion to complaining, your sympathy is best expressed not in words but through respectful behavior. Your concern about current oppression and discrimination is best expressed not in words but in righting that which is wrong.

5. **Use observation and silence to learn about culture.** You will learn little from the media about the culture of the people with whom you are working. Much of what is in books and on film is erroneous and misleading. However, keen observation and silence are excellent educational tools. You will learn what you need to know as trust develops. Let the First Nations people take the lead and disclose themselves and their world to you at their pace. Remember that trust takes time and patience is a virtue. Remember that First Nations people have many reasons not to trust you.

6. **Help new employees by offering mentoring by a sympathetic, mature person.** The mentor need not be a native person or even a member of the nondominant culture. The ideal mentor is accepting, tactful, and knowledgeable about the agency. Above all, he or she should be interested and willing to provide encouragement and guidance.

7. **Provide opportunities for all employees to develop cultural competence.** Help employees and supervisors recognize that cultural competence is not the gathering of information but the use of a process that involves acceptance, respect, and willingness to learn. Each group brings strengths to the workplace. Help employees discover the contributions each member gives to the whole.

Workshops are only one of many ways to develop cultural competence. Activities such as home and community visits, shared recreation, and invitations to meals and social gatherings for families provide chances to know one another better. Realize, however, that some First Nations staff may be slow to invite others into their homes; some may feel unsure or uncomfortable with entertaining outside the family. Encourage employees to take an active role in the life of the First Nations community. This helps the workers develop important support systems. Offering leave for community meetings and celebrations or asking the employees if they would like to represent the agency at such gatherings can help the employees and assist the agency in outreach and linkage with native communities. Be aware of the stresses faced by people who are leaving the reservation or are in transition to or living in urban settings, even when they have been away at school, and be aware of the possible loss of supports they experience in making their transition.

8. **Increase the pool of First Nations applicants by developing native professionals in their own communities.** Agencies should consider recruiting and training employees in lower-rank positions as well as encouraging young people in middle and high school to consider social and human services. Personal outreach and word-of-mouth recruitment have special appeal for First Nations people.

   Licensing and credentialing requirements have acted to hold back First Nations workers who may have excellent skills and knowledge of their communities but who lack a BSW or MSW. Agencies and schools of social work can explore alternative routes to the degree, including onsite and extension programs that make it possible for workers to remain on the job and obtain needed training and degrees. Most adults cannot leave home, family, and employment to attend training programs miles from home. Creative use of technologies that permit distance learning and credit for life experience are other options. Satellite, computer, and video technology can meet the needs of people in underserved and remote areas. For example, a school in the West flew faculty more than 300 miles on alternating weekends to train child welfare workers. Students who do leave the community for training need relevant educational experiences; financial and other supports, including support of native peers; and mentoring. Faculty can be aware that higher education can make the students feel "different" or that they may be regarded by family and friends as having "sold out" or as being "white" or an "apple" (red outside, white inside).

9. **Don't assume that any First Nations person can do the job.** The most essential skill an employee needs to work with diverse populations, including his or her own, is cultural competence. Group membership alone does not guarantee knowledge and skills to work with that group. Cultural competence involves an attitude toward differences in others, use of a process approach, respect, sensitivity, and experience.

   Be cognizant of tribal and national rivalries and politics. Agency administrators need to educate themselves on the local political situation before hiring personnel for key positions. Intra- and intertribal differences are real and long standing; just any "native" person may not be accepted.

10. **Provide mechanisms by which employees can develop and upgrade skills.** Some may need help in upgrading language skills, using computers and technology, learning organizational culture, or conforming to corporate time strictures or dress. All employees can benefit from training in coping with stressors such as family problems, marital dysfunction, domestic violence, and parenting issues and in developing support systems. Well-designed employee assistance programs can do more than

provide referral or counseling to health and mental health services. Workshops on wellness, lifestyle, etiquette, and corporate
dress have long been offered by businesses for their employees;
social and human services organizations can offer the same.

11. **Have a plan for recognizing and using the strengths of diversity.** First Nations people may bring to the workplace experiences, characteristics, or needs that differ from those of majority-culture employees. The shrewd manager or supervisor will have a plan of action for introducing the new employee to the agency, strategies to encourage acceptance and support of the new worker, and a commitment to recognizing and using the strengths of diversity.

REFERENCES

DuBray, W. H. (1992). *Human services and American Indians.* St. Paul: West.
Van Den Bergh, N. (1991). Managing biculturalism at the workplace: A group approach. In K. L. Chau (Ed.), *Emerging perspectives of social group work* (pp. 71–85). Binghamton, NY: Haworth Press.

Latinos in the Work Force:
A Systemic Overview of Potentials and Barriers to Access

Yolanda Mayo-Quiñones

The past and present history of Latino men in the American work force is the story of the invisible man once again told. Although their presence is strongly felt in this system, they remain limitedly acknowledged, caught in a world of gray, between the white and black extremes of the American world of work. Because of Latino invisibility, work-related issues and their importance among Latinos have been rarely explored by human services. As part of the popular view, Latino men remain the subject of myths and stereotypes, linked to a world of poverty and public aid, facing systemic and cultural barriers that, for the most part, prevent their access to mainstream society.

This chapter provides an overview of Latino male employment from a sociocultural and a systemic perspective (Meyer & Mattaini, 1995). It discusses the history of Latinos and the conceptual meaning of work for their self-identity, with implications for family mental health (Mayo-Quiñones, 1993). Accordingly, it highlights the need for Latinos to maintain their self-worth and manhood (their *machismo*) as well as their self-esteem in relation to a traditional family system in a world culturally perceived as hierarchically and ascriptically structured (Wells, 1968). The goal is both to show the link between barriers that impede motivation and opportunity for access to work for the larger number of Latinos living in the United States and to encourage professional aid in enhancing the group's continued productivity and participation in the labor force. The Puerto Rican experience, past and present, highlights the understanding of the world of work of poor Latino immigrants now entering the United States in record numbers; their unique situation presents a model for men of color of varied backgrounds in the American work force.

Although Hispanic men are the focus of this chapter, I have selected "Latinos" as the descriptive term for two reasons. First, the term has been described in the literature as inclusive, depicting people from Latin America who not only reflect Spanish language ties but also include the bicultural, ethnic, and racial cultures that have blended with the "conquistadors"—among them African and other Mediterranean, Middle Eastern, and European groups adopted by the "Americas." Second, the term increasingly has become the popular

term for Spanish-speaking and Spanish-derived populations residing in the United States (Mayo-Quiñones, 1993; Shorris, 1992).

A DEMOGRAPHIC VIEW

For the most part, Latinos in the labor force, both historically and in
the present day, tend to have high rates of unemployment and underemployment (Borjas & Tienda, 1982; DeFreitas, 1991; Institute for
Puerto Rican Policy, 1995). Mexican Americans and Puerto Ricans,
who at the turn of the century were recruited in large numbers in the
eastern, southern, and western parts of the United States as agricultural workers, have been prominent in the labor movement (Centro
de Estudios Puertorriquenos [CENTRO], 1979; Gonzalez, 1995). The
post–World War II years have seen a greater variety of Latinos entering the United States as documented and undocumented workers.
Yet, their participation in the work force remains largely in service
occupations, farming (migrant workers), and unskilled labor. For example, although the Latino white-collar work force has increased
from 35 percent to almost 40 percent since 1980, Latinos are less likely to be found in managerial or professional occupations (Schick &
Schick, 1991). In addition, the blue-collar population among Latinos
decreased from 45 percent to 37 percent during this same period.
This fact notwithstanding, the bulk of the Latino work force continues to grow in agricultural and unskilled labor, areas that lack potential for meeting the basic human needs for survival, such as stability,
benefits, health, housing, and education (Garza, 1977; Schick &
Schick, 1991). The link between national economics and the need for
workers cannot be disassociated from the average laborer. Likewise,
1994 census reports continue to show a high unemployment rate for
Latinos in comparison with the rest of the population (Social Security Administration, 1997). This same report notes some improvement
in managerial or professional occupations (highest for Cubans, 22.6
percent, and lowest for Mexicans, 8.8 percent); however, operators
and laborers are still the areas of greatest employment, particularly
for Puerto Ricans (25.9 percent) and for Mexicans (31.7 percent). The
competition among Latino groups for work remains at the unskilled
level. In a world of expanding technology, the lack of technological
skills becomes a serious limitation for Latinos entering the labor
market.

A LATINO PERSPECTIVE

An understanding of Latinos in the work force cannot be considered
in isolation from United States national politics, immigration policy,
and economic trends. Nor can Latinos be seen as totally separate
from other ethnic groups with a past historical presence or from
those now entering the United States as documented and undocumented immigrants. Viewed in this light, the relationship of immigrants and work extends from a national concern to one that ultimately reaches a global perspective.

In addition to language, Latinos bring together a variety of diverse ethnic, cultural, historical, and racial variables as a unifying force (Shorris, 1992). This population originates in varied geographical areas of the "new world" and presents different national, individual, and group attitudes and behaviors (Williams, 1984). They are thus not a homogeneous group of people. Latinos include people from the more European-focused South American countries such as Argentina, Chile, and Uruguay; those identified by a predominantly Andean culture, such as Bolivia and Peru; and those bordering the northern part of the continent, such as Colombia and Venezuela. The Latin American world includes Central America, the Caribbean region, and Mexico, a North American country. To add to the understanding of the complexity of the Latino population in the United States, additional groups may be included, such as those people who trace their origins to early Spanish colonization beginning in the 16th century, which included Sephardic Jews in their exodus from Spain (de Varona, 1996; "Exploring Our Lost Century," 1988; Shorris, 1992).

From the above diversity, this chapter focuses on Latinos who have emigrated to the United States mainly during the latter part of the 20th century, seeking economic opportunity and political stability. Much like their early European counterparts, they are a poor, unskilled population with low educational achievement (De La Cancela, 1991). But unlike their earlier immigrant predecessors, the current Latino population, based on skin tone and poverty, faces the restrictions of biased immigration policy that discriminates against people of color seeking to enter the United States. Opportunity to enter the country and participate in the "American Dream" has thus been limited and favorable to those who can afford the high cost of entry visas and who have desirable professions or national backgrounds, namely, Western Europeans (See, 1986). Unlike most of the Latino immigrants, a selected and, for the most part, small group of citizens from various Latin American countries, often well educated and highly skilled, has been able to fit into the middle and upper-middle classes. These immigrants have not posed a threat to the status quo or to American workers and thus have faced easier transition into the American mainstream.

Latin American groups with qualities considered to be positive by the dominant culture—namely, Western European values and traits, including race—generally have been seen as contributors to the economy and to U.S. society (Devore & Schlesinger, 1991). The remaining immigrant population from Latin America, indirectly tracked by class and race, occupy lower socioeconomic status by virtue of the unskilled, low-paid jobs of its members. Three Latino groups merit a special note for their differences in the informal tracking process of class and race. Cubans, Mexicans, and Puerto Ricans, by virtue of their distinctive histories (the Mexican–American War in 1848 and the Spanish–American War in 1898), have maintained different relationships with the continental United States. It is thus not coincidental that these groups are more prominently represented in the American labor force and the demographic literature (CENTRO, 1979).

IMMIGRATION POLICY AND ECONOMICS

Immigration policy (or rather, the lack thereof) as well as its unevenness, has been closely linked to an American preference for some groups and the exclusion of others. In fact, it is noted by historians that, in 1797, 21 years after U.S. independence was declared, a member of Congress argued for stopping all immigration. The rationale was that immigration suited the needs of the country while it was unsettled but not after it reached maturity (See, 1986). Early immigration favored English and Irish settlers (Teutonic and Celtic), later expanding to settlers from Germany, the Netherlands, France, Canada, and Switzerland (See, 1986).

The link between immigration and economic opportunity is perhaps best seen after the depression of 1837, when the Irish were the first group to meet with overt hostility between 1820 and 1849. Anti-immigration sentiment increased after the 1840s, spurred by poor harvests, famines, political conflicts, and revolutions in Europe. See (1986) noted that in the absence of federal laws, the states exercised their prerogative in this area and instituted programs to attract low-cost labor as early as the late 1800s. A new precedent for obtaining inexpensive labor in the absence of slavery was initiated: "Capitalists in the United States reached for, and imported ethnically, cheap and tractable labor that resulted in their realizing huge profits" (p. 45). These programs set a pattern for Puerto Rican participation in the American labor force in 1898 and helped bridge national economic needs for workers with a pool of men who needed to work (Gonzalez, 1995; Maldonado-Denis, 1980).

PUERTO RICANS: MIGRANTS, IMMIGRANTS

Addressing the multitudes of ethnic, national, and cultural groups encompassed by the term "Latino" presents a complex dilemma. A historical overview of Puerto Ricans in Puerto Rico and in the United States is a logical beginning for understanding the totality of the Latino population as a work force. As migrants coming from a U.S. territory and as immigrants coming from a different geographical location with a different language, culture, and values, Puerto Ricans present a unique case of Latinos in America. Their citizenship status and their more recent commonwealth system of government, instituted in 1952, have allowed them to be pacesetters for other Latino groups entering the country. A review of the history of Puerto Ricans as part of the U.S. labor force also shows a pattern that has been followed by other economic immigrants who enter the country with poor language, academic, and work skills, automatically becoming a part of the lowest-paid work force. Taking the only jobs available, in which abuses in the workplace are common, has been among the more negative experiences of the poor masses entering as economic immigrants (Maldonado-Denis, 1980). The type of work available and a positive motivation for work are still evident among a sample of poor Puerto Rican men in New York City's South Bronx, an area well known for its extreme poverty. Of 50 men in the sample, 37 reported employment and 39 reported that they did not receive public assistance (Mayo-Quiñones, 1993). Of interest is how the reality of this population regarding work may be markedly different from both national statistics, which report Puerto Ricans at the lowest strata of social dysfunction, and from public perception, which tends to perceive the bulk of the Puerto Rican male population to be on public assistance.

Puerto Ricans saw their island shift to a one-crop economy at the turn of the 20th century and into the post–World War II years, as dictated by large corporate monopolies that formed following the Spanish–American War in 1898. The designated crop became sugar, a decision not too different from what became economic policy for Cuba and other Caribbean islands. Not only did large corporations control large tracts of land and dictate what was to be grown, they also simultaneously controlled the work potential of a totally agrarian society. Large numbers of small landowners were displaced as they lost their land, and they moved to the cities in search of work to support themselves and their families. Many of those who remained on the land they previously owned became workers for the corporations that now owned it (Maldonado-Denis, 1980; Steiner, 1974). Those who moved in search of work contributed to the rise of the infamous San Juan slums, which began to develop as the numbers of the unemployed and the now-poor urban dwellers grew.

An additional aftermath of the imposed economic change was the institutionalization of *el tiempo muerto* (the dead time). The sugar cane industry devoted six months of the year to the harvest and the next six months to planting and waiting. Farmers had to subsist on company-store credit to survive the six months of waiting until the crop became ready for harvest. With the family's debts growing, a vicious cycle of poverty became rooted and institutionalized in the Puerto Rican economy. This scenario is being duplicated in the misery of U.S. migrant farmers, many of whom are Mexican Americans. Planned depopulation of Puerto Rico became governmental policy for dealing with unemployment (Marques, 1969; Morales-Carrion, 1983).

In the years before World War II, potential employers and corporations recruited Puerto Rican workers on the island for farm work and for the development of new industries throughout the United States, such as the garment industry in New York City. The Puerto Rican work force dispersed as men were recruited for such new industries as manufacturing in Ohio; farmwork in Louisiana, Arizona, and California; and the pineapple industry in Hawaii. The advertising for workers on the island, with promises of a living wage and opportunity for bettering their living conditions, created a unique economic diaspora of men seeking work to survive and set a precedent for removing unemployed people from their homeland (Maldonado-Denis, 1980; Silen, 1971).

Similarly, the promise of a land of plenty continues to lure men to the United States to this day. Most, particularly Latinos, are not only responsible for their own survival in a hostile and markedly different environment, but also for the survival of families and even communities left in their native land. The money that these immigrants send home often constitutes the only income available in many towns of Latin America. The needs of extended families of immigrants in two geographical locations often must be met by those least able to meet them. The close association between migration and economics has been further expanded to such unlikely places as the border between the United States and North Mexico, with the *maquiladora* economy that has given rise to new communities of workers. Changes in the work force–economy relationship also are evident with the Dominican population in recent decades. American manufacturing has changed the face of that Caribbean nation as well as that of Haiti, Guatemala, and border towns in northern Mexico (Gonzalez, 1995).

Little demographic information shows Puerto Ricans as doing better after these periods of planned work migration. Continuing unemployment and poverty, as well as the unavailability of work, led to massive governmental aid programs on the island. This situation ultimately led to the creation of *El Banco de Fomento Industrial* (Bank for Industrial Development), which in turn developed the tax-exempt systems for corporations that would take manufacturing to the island. Lending money through a newly developed bank, this system helped create an insecure middle class; there emerged an expanded world of poverty in which the poor became poorer and totally dependent on government aid for survival (Williams, 1984). For Puerto Ricans, dependence on government subsidy has been institutionalized with its own descriptive terminology, known popularly as *mantengo*. This pattern of patchwork and block-grant aid is not too far removed from that of inner-city poor communities in the United States, in which welfare, food stamps, and government subsidies have become the norm for much of the population. It also should be noted that present-day welfare reforms are based on the assumption that jobs are available for those who would work. Reality, nonetheless, suggests that even the lowest-paid menial jobs have become competitive in our inner cities, where youths, women, and unskilled men vie for the poorly paid, no-benefits work, often in fast-food establishments (Alter, 1997). Another result of this "economic boost" was a second exodus of Puerto Ricans in the 1945–1959 period, primarily led by women who found ready work in New York City's garment industry. The men who followed were relegated, for the most part, to service positions, the only readily available opportunity in a system in which race and language determined a man's potential as well as his opportunity to work. Again, there is a similarity to present-day inner-city poverty in the United States, most visible in communities of color, where work and welfare programs are developed to meet specific needs or private interests without assessment or understanding of the individual population. This situation undoubtedly constitutes a source of stress for Latinos.

Other Latino populations entering the country in the 1990s face a situation similar to that of Puerto Ricans before the 1970s. An additional, commonly overlooked source of stress emerges as men begin to realize that women are their greatest competitors. Women, who are paid less and find more openings as child care and health workers and who are less able to advocate for themselves, tend to find more readily available sources of employment than men. The Latino economic migrant, as well as the immigrant, documented or not, still faces the discrimination of language and culture as well as the legacy of third world status—poor education and health and a history of socioeconomic oppression. Although this legacy and the ensuing abuses brought about by these limitations did not begin in the United States, they have been exacerbated by the limited opportunities, culture clash, and institutionalized racism and discrimination prevalent in the country. The tendency not to explore access to mainstream society in a holistic manner (that is, not to look at past strengths, the present situation, and potential future contributors) and the continuing economic and immigration patchwork policies have become major barriers for Latinos and failures of American society.

WORK ETHICS AND THE FAMILY

The professional literature on Latinos in the United States focuses on the traditional family structure, but there is a dearth of literature that addresses the psychosocial dynamics and national differences of Latinos. The father's role, in particular, bears special attention. In the traditional extended family system, the man is not only the undisputed head of the household but also the designated breadwinner. As the expected family provider and symbolic decision maker, the concept of work for Latino males fits into a culture-bound system that enables them to meet their families' requirements of food, shelter, and other human needs. As such, work takes on special meaning. It follows that the head of the family must meet the expectations of both the extended family and society if he is to maintain his self-esteem, or *respeto*, as well as his *machismo*. *Respeto* (respect), a term best described as the culture-appropriate view of self-respect, self-love, and dignity for oneself and others, is at the core of Latino male identity (Mayo-Quiñones, 1993; Wells, 1968). A man's "manhood," encompassing all culturally appropriate gender and social role expectations, popularly known in American culture as *machismo*, is taken from him when society deprives him of his potential for work and the means to support his family with *dignidad* (dignity). Thus, for the Latino male, being deprived of work attacks the very core of his virility by limiting his potential for meeting cultural and family expectations. The Spanish-language idiomatic definition of manhood as *un hombre cabal y responsable en su trabajo* (a trustworthy and responsible man in his job) designates him among his family and community as the epitome of male achievement and success. The retention of traditional values, where the man can find strength in meeting cultural expectations, often averting social castration and undermining of his strengths, is of great importance to Latinos.

The work role reversal in the United States, where women have easier access to employment, albeit low-paid, presents Latino men with yet another energy-depleting situation and reason for loss of *dignidad* and *respeto*, with the reversal cited as a major contributor to the problem of substance abuse, specifically alcohol abuse, among Latinos (Laureano & Poliandro, 1991). Similarly, changing trends in the economy continue to show women balancing two roles: that of traditional wives and mothers and that of full-time employees. Thus, stress in reference to work is not limited to men because Latinas also pay a hefty price—most often, the deterioration of their mental and physical health, as noted in the escalating incidence of depression and anxiety syndromes as well as cardiovascular problems (Olmedo & Walker, 1990).

Likewise, within the family, where they cannot adjust to the impact and demands of role reversal and culture–value clash, men often withdraw to the variety of behaviors that begin to tear the family apart—alcohol and drug abuse and other traditional ways of male socialization, such as hanging out in the *bodega* (local grocery store). These behaviors can be viewed as attempts to save face and compensate for the loss of self-esteem caused by unemployment and underemployment. Stress on the family structure and functioning also is felt by the children, who see parenting and extended family boundaries not only reversed, but often at odds with each other. When compared with American culture, which emphasizes individualism and doing for one's self, as well as with the changing role of women in society, Latino men are increasingly losing ground and becoming marginalized not only in society but also within their own families.

CONCLUSION

What lessons can social scientists and American society learn about the role of work and Latino men? A look at men as consumers in the world of work suggests that avoiding cultural misunderstanding and misinterpretation is critical for them (Fitzpatrick, 1971). As men internalize the absence of opportunities in work and education, they realize that limited access to upward mobility through employment is available to people of color in an advanced technological society. As reality sets in, they begin to see themselves manipulated for the good of the few and devalued as individuals. As noted by Maldonado-Denis (1980), they become people "who are part of American capitalism's industrial reserve army. When there is a labor shortage, employers hire from this pool of cheap labor. When production is cut back and layoffs occur, these workers are an easily identified layer and are among those fired first, with the acquiescence of many white workers" (p. 29).

Unless there is social and professional intervention, a major portion of Latinos in unskilled jobs may see themselves as ineffective as well as less able and productive workers in a society whose values and attitudes reinforce negative traits and stereotypes. They can feel overwhelmed by conflicting messages from a society that seeks them out as a cheap source of labor yet cuts them off from the rewards available to others. In this light, it is not surprising that Latinos have the highest school dropout rates and a disproportionately high rate of unemployment and substance abuse (Olmedo & Walker, 1990). Also, Latino men can fall further into the depths of self-deprecation, adding to the loss of self-esteem, when they are compared in national statistics that pit one group of Latinos against another. When lack of understanding of sociocultural history and institutional racism result in comparisons such as those among Chicanos, Cubans, and Puerto Ricans, Latinos may see these associations as divisive tactics that further dehumanize them. The epitome of success, defined as the attainment of a college education and a high-technology job, is out of their reach. Of note is the overlooked difficulty of the move from a traditional agrarian society to an advanced technological one (Mayo-Quiñones & Resnick, 1996). Survival, in the case of Latino workers, requires both inordinate persistence to succeed and unflinching motivation to maintain their cultural work ethic.

Mainstream society in America has its own tools of oppression, as seen in the control of opportunity through policy formulation that limits immigration to those groups considered desirable and restricts access to education, employment, shelter, and food, all of which are common human needs as described in the professional ethics of social work (Towle, 1965). When these needs are viewed in the context of the institutionalized racism and discrimination that permeates the country, there is a stark division in American society between black and white. Latino males, comprising shades of gray, can therefore be said to feel not only the nebulousness of anonymity, but also the impact of multiple forces of external social and economic oppression. These forces, in addition to their own internal cultural dynamics and expectations as dictated by traditional values, turn their world into a dysfunctional one when the men are transplanted to the United States.

It thus falls on the human services professions, in their opportunity for intervention and in accord with their stated mission and commitment to the person-in-environment and to individual rights, to view the Latino male worker in light of the social stress and the generated internal stress that he faces. Also, given the marginal existence of men who, for the most part, work in menial and thankless jobs and the serious deficits they face in English-language and academic skills, human services must see a critical need to stress the strengths of the group and avoid further blaming of the victims. Demographic information suggests that migrant farmers, undocumented people, and even those who engage in steady but back- and spirit-breaking jobs pay an immense price in the deterioration of their physical and mental health and their family life.

This chapter has focused on historical and present issues facing Latinos in the American work force. Among the human and other services systems that work with this population, care must be taken not to continue to lump Latinos into a world of nebulous diversity in which individual and group needs are overlooked in the interest of a very general common good and the needs of a capitalist economy. Although all groups share common needs, the historical, sociocultural, and, at times, even biological differences of Latinos demand differential assessments and an individualized road to empowerment. Manufacturing and production in a capitalist economy also have a stake here. Worker satisfaction leads to greater productivity and ultimately is cost effective and profitable. Ideally, the variety of systems involving workers, the production of goods, and individual and corporate economic gain at national and international levels develop cooperative relationships toward a common global goal. Work is a human need that cuts across national boundaries and moves us into global cooperation.

Work force diversity needs to be explored at the macro and micro levels because of the importance of diversity in the total population. This exploration is critical as more diverse groups enter the United States. Because of differences in culture, language, skin color, and educational attainment, these groups have less opportunity to achieve the American dream. Both society and the helping professions have contributed directly and, at times, indirectly to maintaining the status quo among Latino and other workers of color. Change requires the combined efforts of human services and economic interests, as well as adherence to professional ethics, in a firm belief that human beings have a right to work. Policy formulation must address the lack of opportunities available to individuals, communities, and groups within communities of color, who have remained marginalized even in the face of affirmative action programs. Thus, communities of color must be addressed through an understanding of the socio-historical, religious, cultural, ethnic, and racial differences and in recognition of their right to earn a decent living. Opportunities to work and opportunities for training and learning are major factors in the empowerment of Latino men. In the words of a well-known Spanish idiom, *Permiteme Señor ganarme el pan de cada día"* (allow me, Oh Lord, the opportunity to earn my daily bread).

REFERENCES

Alter, J. (1997, August 25). A real piece of work: Welfare reform's progress. *Newsweek*, p. V130.

Borjas, G. J., & Tienda, M. (Eds.). (1982). *Hispanics in the U.S. economy*. Orlando, FL: Academic Press.

Centro de Estudios Puertorriquenos. (1979). *Labor migration under capitalism: The Puerto Rican experience* (Research Foundation of the City of New York). New York: Monthly Review Press.

DeFreitas, G. (1991). *Inequality at work: Hispanics in the labor force.* New York: Oxford University Press.

De La Cancela, V. (1991). Progressive counseling with Latino refugees and families. *Journal of Progressive Human Services, 2*(2), 19–24.

de Varona, F. (1996). *Latino literacy: The complete guide to our Hispanic history and culture.* New York: Henry Holt.

Devore, W., & Schlesinger, E. G. (1991). *Ethnic sensitive social work practice.* New York: Macmillan.

Exploring our lost century. (1988, March). *National Geographic,* p. 364.

Fitzpatrick, J. (1971). *Puerto Rican Americans: The meaning of migration to the mainland.* Englewood Cliffs, NJ: Prentice Hall.

Garza, C. (Ed.). (1977). *Puerto Ricans in the U.S.* New York: Pathfinder Press.

Gonzalez, J. (1995). *Roll down your window: Stories of a forgotten America.* London: Verso Press.

Institute for Puerto Rican Policy. (1995, August). *Datanote,* p. 17.

Laureano, M., & Poliandro, E. (1991). Understanding cultural values of Latino male alcoholics and their families: A culture sensitive model. *Journal of Chemical Dependency, 4,* 137–155.

Maldonado-Denis, M. (1980). *The emigration dialectic: Puerto Rico and the U.S.A.* New York: International Publishers.

Marques, R. (1969). *The oxcart.* New York: Charles Scribner's Sons.

Mayo-Quiñones, Y. (1993). *The utilization of mental health services, acculturation and machismo among Puerto Rican men.* Unpublished doctoral dissertation, Adelphi University, Garden City, NY.

Mayo-Quiñones, Y., & Resnick, R. P. (1996). The impact of machismo on Hispanic women. *Affilia, 11,* 257–277.

Meyer, C. H., & Mattaini, M. A. (Eds.). (1995). *The foundations of social work practice.* Washington, DC: NASW Press.

Morales-Carrion, A. (Ed.). (1983). *Puerto Rico: A political and cultural history.* New York: W. W. Norton.

Olmedo, E. L., & Walker, V. R. (Eds.). (1990). *Hispanics in the United States: Abstracts of the psychological and behavioral literature, 1980–1989.* Washington, DC: American Psychological Association.

Schick, F. L., & Schick, R. (1991). *Statistical handbook on U.S. Hispanics.* Phoenix: Oryx Press.

See, L. A. (1986). *Tensions and tangles between Afro-Americans and Southeast Asian refugees.* Atlanta: Wright.

Shorris, E. (1992). *Latinos: A biography of the people.* New York: W. W. Norton.

Silen, A. S. (1971). *We the Puerto Rican people: A story of oppression and persistence.* New York: Monthly Review Press.

Social Security Administration, Office of Research, Evaluation and Statistics. (1997, August). *Earnings and employment data for workers covered under social security, by state and county, 1994* (SSA Publication No. 13-11784). Washington, DC: Author.

Steiner, S. (1974). *The worlds of the Puerto Ricans.* New York: Harper & Row.

Towle, C. (1965). *Common human needs.* Washington, DC: NASW Press.

Wells, H. (1968). *The modernization of Puerto Rico: A political study of changing values and institutions.* Cambridge, MA: Harvard University Press.

Williams, E. (1984). *From Columbus to Castro: The history of the Caribbean.* New York: Vintage Books.

Organizational and Social Barriers Confronting People with Disabilities in the Workplace

Dawn Howard

One out of every 12 Americans ages 16 to 64 (13,400,000 people) reports a work-related disability. More than 200 million people have speech impairments, and 2 million people have a form of epilepsy. One million people use wheelchairs. Adults with disabilities are almost four times as likely as nondisabled adults to have less than a ninth-grade education. Yet 31.6 percent of people with disabilities either are employed or actively seeking work, compared with 78.6 percent of people without disabilities who are employed.

The Americans with Disabilities Act of 1990 (ADA) provides people with disabilities protections similar to those that other groups received under the Civil Rights Act of 1964. It prohibits private-sector employers, businesses, and service organizations from discriminating. Section 504 of the Rehabilitation Act of 1973 prohibited discrimination in any organization, school, or agency that received federal funding. The ADA strongly affects employment. Employers with 25 or more workers cannot discriminate based on disabilities. In 1994, this provision in the law was extended to employers with 15 or more workers.

The ADA requires that employers look beyond disability when interviewing applicants for positions. It uses and defines specific language to enable employers to apply the law effectively. A "qualified person" is one who meets the educational or skill requirements of a given job. A person also must be able to perform the "essential functions" of a given position. Two defining characteristics of essential functions are

1. Can an employee in the position actually perform the function with or without reasonable accommodations?
2. Would removing a particular function fundamentally change the job?

Accommodations may involve making existing facilities more readily accessible to or usable by a person with a disability; restructuring a job; modifying work schedules; acquiring or modifying equipment; providing qualified readers or interpreters; or appropriately modifying examinations, training, or other programs. More than three-quarters of accommodations for employees cost less than $1,000.

Employers must first understand the requirements of the ADA if they are to establish policies that encourage its implementation. The implementation of the rules and the spirit of the ADA can benefit both employer and employee.

There are many examples of people with disabilities who have made and continue to make significant contributions to society. Franklin D. Roosevelt, president of the United States from 1932 until his death in 1944, used a wheelchair because of poliomyelitis. Stephen Hawking, one of the world's foremost theoretical physicists, has amyotrophic lateral sclerosis, which leaves him unable to walk, talk, or breathe without sophisticated technology. However, he continues to pursue his profession and makes presentations in his field. Arthur John Callahany, author of *Don't Worry, He Won't Get Far on Foot*, has quadriplegia. Actress Marlee Matlin, who is deaf, has won an Academy Award. Many other people living with disabilities are contributing members of society.

LIVING WITH CEREBRAL PALSY

"Cerebral" refers to the brain, and "palsy" refers to muscle weakness or poor control of muscles. "Cerebral palsy" refers to a group of chronic, nonprogressive conditions caused by damage to the brain before, during, and shortly after birth (before age 2). The effects can range from weak ankles to an inability to move or speak without assistance. A half-million adults and children have cerebral palsy in the United States.

I have ataxic cerebral palsy. This diagnosis means I have difficulties with balance (I need the support of a railing to descend stairs) and with general smoothness in my motor activities. I have a tremor when I do activities needing fine motor control, such as writing. I also have speech articulation difficulties, which have improved with extensive speech therapy over an extended time. I was educated with my nondisabled peers from preschool through graduate studies and benefited from the experience by learning to adapt and be resourceful in how I did assignments. I also learned how to relate to my peers. Although I did not struggle academically, I struggled with finding friends. I also had many teachers who did not understand the importance of adapting assignments for me.

Throughout school, teachers sometimes did not understand that requests to reduce the amount of written work or have me evaluated in other ways were not attempts to avoid work. I write about five words a minute, which is approximately three times slower than a nondisabled person writes. I had no access to a computer until I was a high school senior. Throughout school, I took my own notes and spent hours doing homework and taking essay exams, because my small, private high school provided limited support services. It helped tremendously in college to have note takers and scribes to write answers on exams. Not only did appropriate supports help me academically, but they also enabled me to be a leader in two campus groups and still have time to spend with friends. Growing up, I focused much of my time on either therapy or homework. Although I did participate in some activities and had a few friends in high school, my social network expanded greatly during college. This wider network allowed me not only to work more effectively but also to resolve issues of separation and individuation that are normally resolved in adolescence.

Some people have assumed that I have cognitive disabilities simply because my speech has a unique pattern. Four years ago, I was at a mall with a friend who did have a cognitive disability. My friend had a seizure. I was familiar with her seizures and knew what she needed. Two people came over to assist and promptly took over. An ambulance was called over my protests. Because I was not my friend's guardian, we had to wait before she could receive care. Finally, one of the paramedics talked to me and understood I was professionally trained and capable of handling the situation. However, on the way to the hospital, I heard the other paramedic, who had not spoken to me, indicate to the hospital that both my friend and I were cognitively disabled. The paramedic later apologized. After a few hours, one of my colleagues came to give me relief because my friend's guardian had not arrived. My colleague was treated with much more deference than had been accorded to me. She was allowed to wait in the waiting room and was offered other amenities that had not been extended to me.

BECOMING AN OCCUPATIONAL THERAPIST

In ninth grade, I volunteered in a classroom for children with severe disabilities whose ages were seven to 14. The classroom was led by a speech therapist and an occupational therapist. At the end of the summer program, when the teachers recognized my interest in becoming an occupational therapist, I was advised not to go into the field because of my difficulty with lifting and feeding children. I could not resist a challenge. From then on, my goal was to become a registered occupational therapist (OTR).

In 1990, I earned a bachelor of science degree in occupational therapy. A requirement of the program was to do at least 960 hours of clinical work. For the first portion of my clinical experience, I was placed at a Day Treatment Center for people with chronic mental illness. The second clinical portion was at a nursing home that had a long-term rehabilitation component. Before I started the clinical work, I asked my university fieldwork coordinator to advise my clinical supervisors of two adaptations I needed: (1) Because my handwriting is slow and laborious, I needed to do documentation on a computer; and (2) because my balance is slightly impaired, I should not be required to transfer people (assist them in moving from a wheelchair to another surface, such as an exercise mat or a bed) independently. Neither of these activities were essential functions as defined by the

1990 ADA law. With those two adaptations, I successfully completed my 960 hours of clinical work.

I was very interested in pediatric occupational therapy, and I chose to do an additional three months of clinical work in the area. I interviewed at a children's hospital. I assumed that my fieldwork coordinator would have conveyed the two adaptations I needed and I did not bring them up in the interview. To my delight, I was accepted. As I began this internship at the beginning of 1991, I was surprised when one of the people assigned to me was a nonambulatory teenager who needed to be transferred. My supervisor quickly saw the problem and did the transferring. Other problems arose. I was not coordinated enough to perform the neurodevelopmental treatment used with many children, which involved guiding a child's movement in a controlled and smooth way. My supervisors kept assuring me that we would work together to solve the problems. One day, without notice, one of my supervisors told me that the previous day a meeting had been held that included my fieldwork coordinator from my university and that it had been decided that my clinical work at the hospital was over. I should have been included in the meeting that they held to assess my ability to complete the internship. At the very least I should had been given the opportunity to give input into the process. My ability to be an occupational therapist was questioned.

Because my pediatric clinical experience ended so abruptly, I had not secured employment. Fortunately, I had passed the national exam and was fully qualified to work as an OTR. I interviewed for 15 to 20 positions, once even having a third interview, without being hired. I learned that potential employers heard that I could not transfer independently and that this was a reason I was not hired.

I think there was another factor that contributed to my difficulties in finding a position. It may be difficult for some professionals to move from working with people with disabilities to accepting them as colleagues. My cerebral palsy is slightly evident in how I move and speak. I needed people to overlook my disabilities and see my professional skills. Instead, I think I made people feel uncomfortable.

While I looked for full-time employment, I worked on call as OTR at a local hospital. I used aides to help me transfer people, an arrangement that allowed me to focus on teaching patients the skills they needed, such as using a reacher (a device that allows people to obtain objects out of their reach) and dressing themselves without bending after having a hip replaced. I also evaluated patients' safety practices as they prepared food while using a walker. I effectively work as an OTR when reasonable and inexpensive accommodations are made. At least one employer was able to see that I was a "qualified person" and that I could perform the "essential functions" of being an on-call OTR. The employer determined that my inability to transfer people did not fundamentally change the job. The arrangement benefited both me (in that I was working) and my employer (in having a qualified employee). A full-time position, however, did not become available at the hospital during my tenure there.

After a seven-month search, I found employment in a facility that provided service and education to people with head injuries and profound disabilities. I was hired as a certified occupational therapist assistant (COTA). A COTA has a two-year degree, compared with the four-year degree I held. I was also paid a COTA salary—two-thirds of what an OTR would be paid. I received no salary increase during the year I worked at the facility. I was bothered by the arrangement, but I was glad to be working in the field. I left this employment after a year because of concerns about my personal safety. Because this employment was from 1991 to early 1993, and provisions of the ADA did not go into effect until July 1992, I was not protected by its provisions.

The hospital that had hired me as an on-call OTR illustrates how making a reasonable accommodation allowed me to share both my professional knowledge and the creative problem-solving skills I have learned from my own disability. The use of aides to transfer people allowed me to work. The same accommodation could have been made at any of the other facilities at which I interviewed. At the children's hospital where I interned, several accommodations could have been made. I could have been trained to be a consultant rather than assigned so many patients needing direct, hands-on care, which was physically challenging to me. Also, I could have been assisted in exploring other environments within the hospital where I could practice. (A current trend in the occupational therapy field is to work with people in the community, helping them engage in useful, everyday activities—not just work on skills in a clinical setting.) I recognize, also, that I could have been more assertive in self-advocacy.

I presently have an appointment to a statewide council that oversees services to families with infants and toddlers with disabilities. As a council member, I am involved in establishing and implementing policies for people with disabilities in Colorado. I also have worked on a federal grant that assists adolescents with disabilities in developing increased self-determination and leading richer lives in their communities. A strength I bring to the work is the insight from the perspective of a person living with disabilities and all the life experiences I have gained.

REFERENCES

Americans with Disabilities Act of 1990, P.L. 101-336, 104 Stat. 327.
Civil Rights Act of 1964, P.L. 88-352, 78 Stat. 241.
Rehabilitation Act of 1973, P.L. 93-112, 87 Stat. 355.

6 Some Common Misperceptions about Deafness in the Workplace:
Attitudinal Barriers Resistant to Change

Michael Schwartz

About two months shy of the effective date of the Americans with Disabilities Act (ADA) in January 1992, I sent a résumé and cover letter to more than 135 law firms and corporate law departments seeking employment as an attorney. My résumé reflected the career moves of a young up-and-coming lawyer who had broad ambitions: a BA in English with cum laude honors from Brandeis University; an MA in Theater Arts from Northwestern University; a JD from New York University School of Law; a clerkship with a federal judge in the U.S. District Court for the Southern District of New York; a 7½-year stint as an assistant district attorney for the New York County District Attorney's Office; and a position as a trial attorney for the Employment Litigation Section of the Civil Rights Division of the U.S. Department of Justice in Washington, DC. One would think that kind of résumé would open doors at least for an interview.

I included in my cover letter the fact that I am Deaf. (I use "D" to reflect my view that Deaf people, like African Americans, Latinos, and other members of nondominant groups, constitute a specific cultural group and, as such, require denotation as a proper noun; see Crenshaw, 1988.) I felt that professional courtesy required disclosure of that information. In my view, it would not have reflected well on me to walk in without having told the potential employer in advance that I had a disability. To me, nondisclosure was not honest. By disclosing my disability, I wanted to avoid embarrassment or an awkward moment. I felt the interviewer should have a chance to be prepared for the interview. I also explained that I had excellent speech and lip-reading skills. However, I received a rejection letter from every one of the firms I contacted in my quest for a job. No firm wanted to talk to me. No one wanted me to come in. No one wanted to take a look at whether I would be able to handle the work. No one had any curiosity about whether a Deaf attorney would add diversity to the work force as well as to the client base.

I set up my own practice instead.

ABLEISM AND OTHER BELIEFS

This experience with rejection, I suspect, has its roots in the common societal perception, presumably shared by these law firms, of Deafness. The feeling that the "other" is not worthy of hiring or of fair treatment is pervasive and entrenched in our culture—a culture soaked in racism, sexism, and "ableism" (discrimination based on disability). Just as the pervasive "white" perspective, described by Harris (1993), marginalizes and devalues people of color, so too does an "ableist" perspective ascribe superior worth to health, fitness, and beauty. People with physical or mental disabilities need not apply and are encouraged instead to stay at home and out of sight. This stigmatization of people with disabilities was documented in the 1986 Louis Harris and Associates survey that led to the passage of the ADA. The survey showed that two-thirds of all Americans with disabilities between ages 16 and 64 were not working, only one in four worked full-time, and another 10 percent worked part-time (no other demographic group younger than 65 had such a small proportion working, including young African Americans). The survey also found that 66 percent of working-age people with disabilities who were not working said they would like to be employed. The majority of the people who were not working and were out of the labor force depended on insurance payments or government benefits for support. The survey also found that Americans with disabilities were less educated and poorer than Americans without disabilities.

In *The Disabled State*, Stone (1984) posited two systems of wealth distribution side by side: (1) a work-based system (the workplace) and (2) a needs-based system (for example, disability insurance programs, welfare, and unemployment benefits). Workers who, for one reason or another, cannot maintain their position in the work-based system can transfer to the needs-based system for sustenance and support. That system supplements the work-based system, which remains the primary system for millions of workers, most of whom happen not to have disabilities. Once a worker is disabled, there is pressure to leave the work-based system and enter the needs-based system, which distributes less of the economic pie. The irony, however, is that many people with disabilities can and are willing to work if the proper accommodation is made for their disability.

Many barriers, however, stand in the way of full and equal employment for workers with disabilities, particularly Deaf workers, in the American work force. These barriers are not only physical but also attitudinal. Disability evokes a fear among people who are not disabled, a fear that they, too, will one day become disabled. America's obsession with health and fitness, youth, and beauty leaves people with disabilities rarely portrayed positively in films or advertising; disability is seen as marginal, ugly, undesirable, sad, disgusting, and evil (the Nazi biomedical vision of the "Deutsch Volk," the Aryan race, rested on this "fear and loathing" of disability and led to the mass extermination of people with disabilities as "useless eaters"; Lifton, 1986). This fear of people with disabilities is subtle, often cloaked by paternalism and pity, reactions that the ADA says have no place in the workplace.

THE DEAF COMMUNITY

Unlike ambulatory or mental disabilities, Deafness is a communication-based disability. Because Deaf people cannot hear, a language based on signs serves as a rich, vibrant, complex visual communication mode that nurtures the life of the Deaf community. TTYs (teletype-writer devices that enable Deaf people to use the telephone); visual alarms for fire, smoke, or other emergencies; assistive listening devices; closed-captioned decoders (devices that subtitle television programs); and interpreters (both sign language and oral) have all contributed to a sense of culture and a sense of identity that instills pride in Deaf people. Indeed, many people in the Deaf community simply regard themselves not as disabled but as members of a cultural and linguistic minority. Their mastery of American Sign Language (ASL), along with the provision of sign language interpreters skilled in ASL, yields a competent and productive work force of Deaf workers capable of performing many jobs in the American economy. Unfortunately, employers have little education about this culture, particularly about how to use skilled interpreters to maximize the productivity of these workers.

Deafness cuts across race, class, age, gender, sexual identity, and every other human classification. In this sense, there is no one Deaf community in the United States. There are as many Deaf communities as there are categories of people: African Americans, European Americans, Latinos, Jews, elderly people, young people, gay men and lesbians, and so forth. This fact offers a partial explanation of why the task of unifying and articulating a Deaf voice in American life is so difficult. Indeed, there is precious little unity among Deaf members of the working class. Who can speak for such a multifarious, multicolored community?

The political fragmentation of the Deaf community also has been exacerbated by a long-running controversy over how to educate Deaf children, with two basic schools of thought: the Manualists versus the Oralists. The Manualists believe that ASL should be the primary language used to educate Deaf children; the Oralists argue that speech-reading and lip-reading skills are of paramount importance in Deaf education. Many Manualists argue that society's attitudes toward Deafness (with a "D") constitute the real barrier, whereas others, including some Oralists, argue that deafness (with a "d") is a medical disability to be overcome with audiology and speech training. Of course, many people feel that the method of educating a Deaf child should fit the child's needs.

BARRIERS TO WORK

For years, Deaf workers have encountered significant barriers on the job. Until the late 1970s, accommodations such as interpreters, closed-captioned decoders, TTYs, and visual alarms for emergencies were not made available to create an accessible working environment. Deaf workers were, and still are, often last hired and first fired. They had, and still have, far fewer promotions and smaller pay increases. It was not until the enactment of the Rehabilitation Act of 1973 that employers who received federal financial assistance were required by law to remedy some of these inequities, and it was not until 1977 that regulations were implemented to enforce the law. Yet, even the passage of the 1973 law failed to measurably improve the lot of Deaf workers; many Deaf people worked for companies that did not come within the purview of the law, or the companies covered by the law refused to comply.

The enactment of the ADA in 1990 finally brought privately owned companies with more than 15 employees within the antidiscrimination orbit. Like all laws, however, the ADA is a piece of paper, and without aggressive and comprehensive enforcement, it does not do much for Deaf workers. As the Civil Rights Act of 1964 teaches us, no law can be completely successful in combating discrimination based on attitude; African Americans and women know well that although de jure segregation may be a relic of the past, de facto segregation stubbornly persists in all arenas of American life, including employment, education, and housing. So it is with Deaf workers: The barriers to full and gainful employment are very slow in coming down. Indeed, the jury is still out on how effective the ADA and the Rehabilitation Act of 1973 have been in bringing more Deaf workers into the workplace.

Another major barrier to fuller integration of Deaf workers in the workplace lies in the quality of education for Deaf children. The deficiencies and drawbacks of education for Deaf children have been well documented elsewhere (Lane, 1984). Because they cannot hear spoken English, Deaf children need to learn to read and write by "seeing" how the rules of English grammar and language work in everyday speech and writing. This need requires a very small teacher–student ratio, through either a small class or one-on-one training, something most schools, public or private, are ill equipped to do. Thus, Deaf children are handicapped by the poor quality of education made available to them, and many graduate from high school with a third- or fourth-grade reading level. This leaves them unable to compete fairly and aggressively for jobs held by hearing people. Obviously, although Deaf children and adults may have mastery of ASL, often poor mastery of written English is a difficult obstacle to advancement in the working world, particularly in the corporate culture and academia. By not directly addressing the problems of Deaf education, the ADA does little to aid Deaf people in their search for more satisfying work.

A major problem facing Deaf workers on the job has always been the biases, fears, and erroneous assumptions of hearing supervisory personnel and other workers toward Deaf workers (Goffman, 1963). Many hearing people fear and pity Deaf people as "dumb" or "mute." On meeting a Deaf person, a hearing person immediately assumes that the Deaf person is incapable of speaking or understanding the hearing person. They simply do not know that some, if not many, Deaf people have speech- and lip-reading skills. Hearing people have no inkling that ASL is a living, complex, and vibrant language; that TTYs and closed-captioned decoders make the outside world accessible to Deaf people; and that Deaf people are productive, satisfied, healthy human beings. Indeed, instead of a heterogeneous community reflecting the prevalence of Deafness in all walks of life (rich and poor, young and old, or Deaf and hard of hearing), the Deaf community is perceived as monolithic. These biases, fears, and erroneous assumptions about Deaf people resonate in the workplace, raising difficult obstacles for Deaf workers. Instead of crafting reasonable accommodations that are based on a proper and realistic analysis of the factual circumstances surrounding the Deaf worker's needs and abilities, the employer often acts on irrational assumptions that have no relation to these circumstances. Indeed, these biases, fears, and erroneous assumptions underlie much of discriminatory behavior that the ADA seeks to reach and change.

Many employers do not understand the role and function of the sign language interpreter. Whereas they see interpreters as a function of money, Deaf workers see interpreters as a function of workplace accessibility. Also, employers tend to think that the interpreter is the Deaf worker's interpreter, instead of regarding the interpreter as a communication link, a bridge available to both hearing and Deaf people. Many employers do not understand that the interpreter is a skilled professional who has had years of training to be in a position to interpret for both hearing people who do not sign and Deaf people who do not speak.

According to a post-ADA study conducted by the Job Accommodations Network (1998), based in Morgantown, West Virginia, the cost of a reasonable accommodation is far lower than the expectations of most employers. Over 50 percent of accommodations cost less than $50, and the Internal Revenue Service allows a deduction for access-related expenses. Under the law, employers are encouraged to consult with the disabled employee about the appropriate accommodation, and often creative thinking and consultation will result in cost savings. Yet, when faced with the prospect of dealing with a Deaf applicant or employee, many employers do not understand or know how to best communicate with the Deaf person so as to acquire useful information on crafting the appropriate accommodation. Discrimination based on an employer's fear of uncontrolled, spiraling costs needs to be countered with the facts; employers need to understand that creative thinking by both parties can go a long way in crafting an economical and functional accommodation.

CONCLUSION

Aggressive enforcement and monitoring of the ADA is a necessity to preserve and protect the legal rights of Deaf workers, but an equally aggressive campaign must be undertaken to educate employers about Deafness, the culture, and the complex community that makes up Deaf America. An understanding of TTYs, closed captioning, interpreter services, and accessible written material, along with an exposure to Deaf culture, will go a long way in breaking down the attitudinal barriers that frustrate Deaf workers. History teaches us that a dual-pronged campaign of legal and educational pressure is a long-term struggle with many small victories guiding us in the right direction.

Maybe I would not have found an attorney's position with any one of the 135 law firms, but I should have been given a chance to show what I can do as a lawyer.

REFERENCES

Americans with Disabilities Act of 1990, P.L. 101-336, 104 Stat. 327.

Civil Rights Act of 1964, P.L. 88-352, 78 Stat. 241.

Crenshaw, K. (1988). Race, reform, and retrenchment: Transformation and legitimization in antidiscrimination law. *Harvard Law Review, 101,* 1331, 1332, note 2.

Goffman, E. (1963). *Stigma: Notes on the management of spoiled identity.* New York: Simon & Schuster.

Harris, C. (1993). Whiteness as property. *Harvard Law Review, 106,* 1709.

Job Accommodations Network, President's Committee on Employment of People with Disabilities. (1998). [Online]. http://www.jan.wvu.edu/english/accfacts.htm.

Lane, H. (1984). *When the mind hears: A history of the deaf.* New York: Random House.

Lifton, R. J. (1986). *The Nazi doctors: Medical killing and the psychology of genocide.* New York: Basic Books.

Louis Harris and Associates. (1986). *The ICD survey of disabled Americans: Bringing disabled Americans into the mainstream.* New York: Author.

Rehabilitation Act of 1973, P.L. 93-112, 87 Stat. 355.

Stone, D. (1984). *The disabled state.* Philadelphia: Temple University Press.

Part III

Policy Issues

This section focuses on emergent changes in society for marginalized groups and how these changes challenge traditional organizational policy. The development of organizational policy and its role in shaping structure and process in the workplace is an integrating thread. The term "emergent" refers to the notion of cultural and social phenomena that emerge or evolve from interaction and transaction among people in a social system. Interactions can involve roles, shared experiences and training, and accommodating values. From diverse perspectives, the emergence of new norms that orient system members to the norms' adaptations is an example of emergent changes. To have a flexible internal climate that truly accepts diversity, one needs to be knowledgeable about the history of policies that may not have been consistent with this goal as well as of those that reinforce and reward behaviors supporting goal achievement. By looking at the history of public policies on diversity in the United States, we see not only patterns of behavior but also variation in the social construction of diverse groups as they become acculturated. After examining numerous factors affected by an accelerating rate of environmental and organizational change, we address diversity and its challenges regarding differences in gender, physical abilities, affective orientations, and linguistic patterns as they interact with policies that support or circumvent diversity.

In chapter 7, Dunn discusses the evolution of public policies regarding integration of people with mutable and immutable differences. This chapter presents a reconstruction of history to reveal the changing social construction of the "other." He describes a range of models for handling diversity, from ethnic cleansing to integrative pluralism, in relation to assimilation dynamics. Finally, he presents a process for managing diversity in the workplace.

Tropman addresses the obverse of workplace diversity in chapter 8. He argues that diversity is central to organizations facing an environment that is itself diverse, multifaceted, and multidimensional. His focus is on general and specific factors that serve as "independent variables." He examines how these factors generate pressures within nonprofit human services organizations and how internal value conflicts can complicate resolution to some problems.

To consider more specifically some factors that shape the focus of policies addressing diversity in the workplace, we present three examples: (1) people whose affectional orientation is toward the same sex, (2) people living with different physical or cognitive abilities, and (3) people with linguistic diversity. Each group has experienced some form of marginalization and oppression. These differences can be perceived by some as deviant and as indicators of inferiority. Thus, policies that lead to a deconstruction of the stigma attached to differences, address isolating behaviors, and support these groups within the workplace promote positive inclusion. Knowledge, particularly that which comes from these subordinated voices, is an essential element in building a more accurate and humanizing social construction of people with gender or affectional variations, different physical abilities, and linguistic differences, releasing these people to fulfill their potential.

In chapter 9, Kivel and Wells describe the process of sexual identity formation and define four types of homophobia. They describe interpersonal issues with which people who identify as lesbian, gay, or bisexual may have to negotiate in the formal and informal workplace environment. The chapter discusses organizational policies and civil rights concerns and protections that facilitate understanding of issues from the perspective of lesbian, gay, and bisexual employees. The chapter ends with recommendations to employers as well as to lesbian, gay, and bisexual employees for integrating issues into policies that accommodate their concerns.

Salsgiver presents in chapter 10 a blueprint for an inclusive policy for supporting underrepresented groups in an organization. He begins with a review of the legislation that extends civil rights to people living with disabilities, and he succinctly presents a history of how this society has traditionally viewed disability before the evolution of the independent-living movement. This chapter describes a process for organizational accommodation of people living with disabilities. He explains appropriate recruiting procedures, including the application and interviewing processes. He then examines reasonable accommodations for people with various disabilities in the workplace and addresses health benefits that do not discriminate against people with disabilities. He concludes by raising issues that involve keeping this policy current and responsive to new concerns.

A relatively new issue in the diversity discourse is cultural and linguistic diversity. In chapter 11, Harris notes that linguistic diversity will intensify in response to changing population demographics as we go into the 21st century and that linguistic diversity will be reflected in organizational communication policies. She provides background knowledge on communication diversity and its significance in work systems. Differences in dialect, creolization, augmentative and alternative communication, as well as American Sign Language, are defined; the myth of standard English is deconstructed. Black English, or "ebonics," is used to illustrate how dialects are governed by rules. Harris discusses the impact of technology on communication and other support needed in the workplace as a result of the Americans with Disabilities Act. Cultural competency is crucial for professionals involved with developing support and providing other communication services to diverse groups.

This is not an exhaustive coverage of workplace policies; however, chapters provide perspectives and guidelines for addressing other issues about workplace policies. Knowledge about the culture of a new group to be included is critical to the process of developing supportive policies. Policies need to be clear about encouraging diversity in workplace environments. Policies that support and reward input from and acceptance of marginalized groups include education and career development programs, integration of informal networks through mechanisms that support sharing communication (for example, social events), and a reward system that supports diversity goals.

7 Historical Review of U.S. Policy on Diversity

Ernest F. Dunn

Picture to yourself a society which comprises all the nations of the world—English, French, German: people differing in language. . . . beliefs. . . . openness; a society possessing no common ideas, no national character. . . . What is the connecting link between these so different elements? How are they welded into one people?

—Alexis de Tocqueville, 1835

AMERICA'S ATTEMPTS AT ASSIMILATION

A prevailing cultural mythology has been sustained by the belief that America, from its inception, was a culturally homogeneous society. As people from Europe emigrated to these shores, they were immersed in a "melting pot" that assimilated them into what was considered "characteristically American" (Sollars, 1986). This process of assimilation contained a common impulse of passion united by the common aggregate interests of the emerging community. However, America has always been and now was becoming even more a multiracial, ethnically diverse society. And although we would point with a hint of pride at some acculturation, basically society continued to exclude people of color. The leaders of the founding colonies recognized from the outset that differences—cultural diversity—would inevitably lead to factionalism and disunity. Accordingly, American statesman James Madison, in one of his essays penned for inclusion in *The Federalist Papers,* argued that the zeal for differing opinions in religion, government, and economics ultimately divides humankind, inflames them "in mutual animosity" (Hamilton, Madison, & Jay, 1788/1961, p. 79). Madison went on to assert that if cultural assimilation did not naturally solve the problem, there were two alternative methods. The first was to curb the liberty that would promulgate such diversity. Should that fail, then cultural assimilation should be enforced by demanding that each person accept "the same opinions, the same passions, and the same interests" (p. 70).

The mythology notwithstanding, Parrillo (1996) contended that since its commencement, even from the colonial cradle, cultural diversity has been an ongoing reality in America. Diversity was not simply the result of European immigration. Europeans came to a land that already was peopled by a diverse group of Native Americans. Furthermore, the slaves brought from Africa represented a diversity Europeans failed to appreciate.

Assuming there is some truth in Parrillo's assertion, one must return to the questions about the connecting links among diverse peoples posed by 19th-century statesman Alexis de Tocqueville to slightly modify and expand on them. A valid question is, What were the connecting links? The second question must be modified and posed in this manner: What attempts were made to weld Americans into one people—*e pluribus unum?* How successful were these attempts? What barriers stood in the way or were erected to inhibit the creation of an assimilated society?

When the American essayist Jean de Crèvecoeur (1787/1957) defined the new race of men emerging from the American melting pot, there were three problems readily discernible in his definition. First, he omitted Africans and Native Americans. These ethnic groups were not to share in the American dream, to participate as empowered equals in the emerging society. Second, he assumed that the people who emerged as Americans had, by the refining "heat of the pot," been stripped of their cultural heritage. Finally, as did all other 18th-century men, he failed to recognize the existence of women. It was not difficult for Crèvecoeur to exclude diversity from his definition because he also failed to appreciate the cultural diversity among European Americans (Parrillo, 1996).

The American people, as defined by Crèvecoeur, included well-to-do white men. Excluded were women, poor white people, certain European ethnic groups, Native Americans, and African Americans. In spite of these exclusions, he was still able to pontificate that individuals of all nations were miraculously being melted and forged into a new race. *E pluribus unum* was being transformed from a motto into a reality.

To his credit, Ralph Waldo Emerson envisioned a "smelting pot" that would include not only a few selected European groups, but all European tribes, Africans, and Polynesians. Emerson proposed that America should become an asylum for all nationalities (Parrillo, 1996). His notion sounded the call for an American renaissance, in which the destiny of this new nation would draw strength out of its contradictory composition (Sollars, 1986). Interestingly, Emerson did not include Native Americans in this new amalgamated society. However, while Emerson was attempting to present this glorious image of the emerging nation, de Tocqueville presented an opposing scenario. His image of racial diversity in America was as bleak as Emerson's was hopeful. Admittedly, Emerson's vision was more future oriented, whereas de Tocqueville was analyzing the present conditions. Nevertheless, de Tocqueville (1835/1960) was convinced that racial prejudice in America was increasing, and he foresaw that African Americans and Native Americans, in particular, would perish in isolation.

Poesche and Goepp (1853), perhaps influenced and motivated by Emerson's vision of the rebirth of a future-oriented, new, superior America, were hopeful that this vision would become a reality. They wrote "the American republic is destined to possess the continent of which it bears the name, and to share it, by absorption with the inhabitants of all the lands of the earth. America is the crucible in which European, Asiatic, and African nationalities and peculiarities are smelted into one" (p. 47). To evoke such a manifest destiny, they concluded that along with a spiritual fusion, there also would have to be an accompanying physical fusion. They developed a theory that promoted the cohabitation of white males and black females. A kind of racial homogenization would result from the racially blended offspring produced.

Although some limited efforts were made during the 19th century to assimilate Native Americans into the dominant society, such was not the situation with African Americans. From the time of the framing of the Constitution to the Emancipation Proclamation, conferences were held to address the "Negro problem." The consistent outcomes of such conferences were the reinforcing of the belief that European Americans and African Americans could not and should not coexist amicably in American society. Such diversity was impossible, or at least it was deemed unacceptable. Regarding this matter, de Tocqueville (1835/1960) wrote "in the United States . . . the prejudice which repels the Negro seems to increase in proportion as they are emancipated, and inequality is sanctioned by the manners while it is effaced from the laws of the country" (pp. 359–360).

Thus, the Americanization process, whether using the notion of the melting pot or some other metaphorical reference to assimilation, served primarily to define a new ethnic people in contradiction to a general American identity. The rhetoric in support of American group cohesion and consensus also could be used "to forge divergent and dissenting ethnic groupings" (Sollars, 1986, p. 49).

W.E.B. DuBois (1903/1964), in his apologia *The Souls of Black Folks*, metaphorically envisioned that a veil had fallen on American society that separated black from white America. Although they did not have DuBois's imagery available to them at the time, certainly Richard Allen, Absalom Jones, and the other founders of the Free African Society recognized the wide gulf of divisiveness that existed racially in America during the time of the framing of the Constitution. Black people were considered separate and distinct from the general American society (Bennett, 1982).

In the mid-1880s, when blatant racism was reaching a new zenith in its development and persuasion, for a brief moment interracial cooperation held out the hopeful promise for a new era of racial harmony. Poor white people and black people worked together, united by such organizations as the Knights of Labor and the Farmers Alliance. There was a serious attempt at racial fusion. But with the defeat of the Populist Party, embittered white people turned against their black allies. They became eager converts to the most malicious forms of racial supremacy ever devised (Parrillo, 1996).

At the close of the 19th century, not only were African Americans and Native Americans excluded from the mainstream "in-group," but also some European groups were excluded—the Dutch, Swiss,

Scandinavians, French, and Irish. Therefore, in spite of the allusions to the melting pot, America remained a "patchwork quilt of cultural diversity" (Parrillo, 1996, p. 150).

At the dawn of the 20th century, strong support remained for the theory of the melting pot. But the theory, as portrayed in Israel Zangwill's (1921) play of the same name, retained its exclusivity. The melting pot was to be understood strictly as a white phenomenon. To be an American was to be a white person, and often that notion was refined to designate white people of British ancestry. As more immigrants came from northern and western Europe, they were able somewhat to redefine mainstream America so as to include themselves.

The notion of the melting pot as a means for dealing with cultural diversity in America was doomed to failure from the outset, because it was simply a limited call to assimilation of a predetermined nature. Emerson, in explaining his theory of the smelting pot, pointed out that when you mix a number of differing metals, their fusion results in a new compound. The metals do not assimilate themselves into what has been predesignated as the most valuable or viable metal. You cannot blend gold, silver, lead, and zinc and expect the mixture to emerge as pure gold. Similarly, he explained that when placing all the ethnic groups in a smelting pot, if they were successfully fused, an unpredictable group would emerge. The New American would be an amalgamation of all the ethnic energies and components that went into the mix. In spite of any rhetoric to the contrary, however well intentioned, America was not prepared to envision an ethnically harmonious society composed of people possessing such amalgamated qualities (Parrillo, 1996).

Furthermore, questions were posed as to whether this was the best way to achieve cultural unity and, more important, whether it was possible or necessary. Was the eradication of ethnic identification essential? Certainly, for a host of reasons, America in no way resembled a nation approaching anything close to full assimilation, nor was there a groundswell of public sentiment for it to become so.

Horace Kallen (1924), an immigrant from Eastern Europe and an early proponent of multiculturalism in the 20th century, wrote rather metaphorically when he referred to an "orchestration of mankind" to suggest how the multiplicity of ethnic groups in America should interact in a pluralistic society. He offered that "in an orchestra every... instrument has its specific timber... as every type has its... theme and melody in the whole symphony, so... each ethnic group may be the natural instrument... and the harmony and dissonances and discords of them all make the symphony of civilization" (pp. 124–125). On the surface, Kallen seemed to be advocating an abandonment of the melting pot and the acceptance of pluralism—cultural diversity. But a thoughtful analysis of his concept exposed his "orchestra" as being essentially a Eurocentric vision of reality. People of color were mentioned only incidentally and were not to be allowed to sit with, let alone play in, the orchestra (Parrillo, 1996).

During the middle decades of the 20th century, for myriad reasons, some in direct conflict with each other, America was mainly influenced by the melting-pot theorists, who maintained that it was possible for all marginalized groups on the fringes of the dominant society to be assimilated into that culture—not only white ethnic groups, but those of color as well. Robert Park (1950), a sociologist who preferred assimilation to pluralism, proposed that it was not only possible but probable. Park and those who subscribed to this theory were convinced that ethnic diversity was ephemeral, merely a stopping point on the way to nationalism. Some even argued that absorption would be most beneficial for marginalized groups, because they would move from an inferior to a superior culture, one more civilized and more advanced.

Park (1950) went on to advocate that the process of assimilation in America was "progressive and irreversible." This process involved three stages. First, there would have to be contact, interaction between those on the inside and those on the outside looking in. Second, there would be accommodation, the adjustments necessary for the new inclusivity. Finally, there would be assimilation. Such assimilation would not require total obliteration of ethnic values. It would only require what Park labeled "superficial uniformity."

It was not essential for marginalized groups to abandon their cultural legacies, but such assimilation would require some movement away from ethnic identity, cultural roots, values, and behaviors, especially those values and behaviors in conflict with those of the dominant culture. Some conformity to the mores and behaviors of the accepting society, simultaneously shedding some of those ethnic differences that tend to distinguish and divide, would certainly facilitate acceptance and hasten the progress toward assimilation. This view is reminiscent of the French concept of assimilation: Whatever your ethnic persuasion, if you speak French, gesture in French, dream in French, and aspire to be French, you will become French and be accepted as French. Similarly, in America, were you to act, think, and acquire the same values and aspirations as those of the "in-group," you would soon be admitted and accepted.

It appears that the price for superficial uniformity requires more than a modicum of conformity by those ethnic groups seeking inclusion. Although it may not reverberate with the same stringency as Madison's enforced assimilation, there is a disconcerting echo of familiarity. Of course, one striking difference was that assimilationists during this era were hoping for voluntary compliance, a willingness by ethnic groups to pay the price for acceptance. Certainly it would have been to their advantage.

Assuming that some were willing to pay the price for acceptance into the general society following the mandates laid down by Park and others, and although some may have gained admittance through this process, there have always been those who remained on the outside. In fact, it has been suggested that for every group that was accepted, a new group was created that was deemed unacceptable. The process is not progressive and irreversible.

Park (1950), adamant in his position, also embraced the notion espoused earlier by Poesche and Goepp (1853) that this progressive assimilation would progress more rapidly with the acceptance and promotion of racial amalgamation. Some scholars in support of this concept alluded to Brazil as a model of how well racial amalgamation was bringing about assimilation and racial harmony. Amalgamation hopefully would produce mirrored results in America.

Assimilation was and will remain an unrealistic assumption, according to Glazer and Moynihan (1963)—unrealistic not only because racism was so deeply ingrained in American society, evoking glaring contradictions and crippling efforts at positive racial interaction, but also because, historically, assimilation had remained only partial, incomplete even among white Americans. A pattern of ethnic distinction and separation was seemingly more in keeping with American social values than assimilation.

This truth was evident not only in America, but also, according to Smith (1980), even in countries where "the dissolution of ethnicity, the transcendence of nationalism, the internalization of culture" (p. 1) had long been the aspirations. In spite of great expectations, in practically every situation, failure was the result. The people were left "confounded and disappointed."

In the late 1960s and early 1970s, there was a concerted effort to bring all European Americans into the fold of mainstream America, engendered and motivated by an "us against them" mentality. This movement was fueled by two phenomena. First, there was what Steinberg (1981) labeled "ethnic fever" (p. 3). Spurred on by the "black revolution"—a renewed interest in black nationalism and cultural pride—other racial groups, including Chicanos, Puerto Ricans, and Native Americans, sought to rediscover their ethnic heritage—to make a spiritual return to their cultural past and then posit it as a reality to guide their present as it unfolded into the future. More than a "fever," it was in reality an ethnic revival.

Second, by 1970, immigrants from third world countries and people of color outnumbered immigrants from European countries. This change did not seriously threaten the white racial majority, but it was thought that a continuation of this pattern could lead in time to the "browning of America."

In spite of the proclaimed threat and the call to unite, acculturation and assimilation among white people remained incomplete. In fact, some white ethnic groups seem to have been infected by the "ethnic fever" bug.

As a consequence of all these factors, although it did not desire this to be the situation, America was forced to be more cognizant of the ethnic diversity that existed. It was much too obvious to be glossed over with platitudes proclaiming unity. If there is to be a candid realization of America's cultural diversity, and if we are to confront what must be done to provide some harmony, stability, and racial unity in this continually developing multicultural society, we must discover new models of ethnic cooperation that offer viable procedures. Until we do, there are several existing procedural models vying for adherents to their banners.

MODELS OF ETHNIC COOPERATION

Ethnic Cleansing

I hope that few Americans subscribe to this doctrine as a solution for dealing with ethnic diversity. Nevertheless, there are those who believe that ethnic cleansing is the answer to the problems posed by the present multicultural society. Ethnic cleansing may be accomplished in a variety of ways, but the basic goal of each method is to limit and ultimately destroy ethnocultural diversity. One popular approach that has been considered many times in America's past as a way of dealing with the "Negro problem" was forcible removal to some distant location. Central America was the favorite site. Today, white supremacist hate groups advocate a forceful emigration of all African Americans back to Africa.

A second approach encourages secession and fragmentation (Kymlicka, 1995). Unwanted groups would be granted a section of the country where they would live. The borders separating them from the dominant culture would be bilaterally closed. There would be no cultural, social, political, or economic interaction. In essence, this would accomplish the same purpose as forced separation, but in this manner it would be argued that the separation, a kind of ethnic segregation, was voluntary and acceptable to all concerned.

A third approach, although it may not appear as radical as the two just described, has the potential for being more severe in forcing acculturation and assimilation. In its most extreme form, supporters of this approach would adhere to the dictates of 19th-century Marxist social scientist Friedrich Engels, who frowned on cultural diversity. According to Kymlicka (1995), Engels "endorsed the concept that minority cultures and languages should be suppressed with iron ruthlessness" (p. 9). Depending on the level of resistance, ruthless suppression could result in genocide or other serious measures of oppression. Least offensively, this approach could simply use a policy of "benign neglect" of nondominant cultures, assuming that in time such neglect would result in their demise.

None of these alternatives are viable options for dealing with ethnocultural diversity in America. Suppression of diversity, however one may attempt to accomplish it, is inimical to the principles of a democratic society. This approach, in its various manifestations, further fails to appreciate the fact that ethnic-group identity can be very important to the well-being of its members.

Formal Racial–Ethnic Separation

Most Americans decry and disavow formal separation and its obvious racist philosophy, suggesting that advocates marching under this banner are, for the most part, disenfranchised white people who contend that mainstream America has "sold them out." Advocates of this approach appeal to the "right of self-determination," proclaiming that racial and ethnic separation is absolutely essential for their preservation.

Although paramilitary groups, skinhead movements, and separatist groups such as the Ku Klux Klan attract attention to themselves with their poisonous racist rhetoric, one can only speculate as to how large the following is for this approach and the true nature of its constituency. If the history of racist persuasion holds true to form in this instance, then surely there are advocates from mainstream America who are loyal to this movement, which in one shape or another has been present for centuries.

The basic tenet, the driving force for this approach, is a white America separate and totally distinct from all other ethnic groups. Any interethnic cooperation would result in contamination of white ethnic purity. In addition to the virulent racism endemic to this approach, there are several false assumptions underlying its principles. There is, for example, the assumption that if a separate white nation were established, it would not have to deal with the problem of cultural diversity. However, given that white society has not achieved total assimilation, the problem of diversity would still be there demanding to be resolved.

Given the ongoing diversity among white people, the best that such hate groups can hope to accomplish, if they were able to secede successfully, would simply be the creation of new subgroups of white people, separate and distinct from the dominant white society that supposedly betrayed them. More important, the creation of borders inside the borders of this country would inevitably lead to conflict and clashes across them.

Assimilation

A substantial number of people still cling to the notion of ethnic assimilation, some variation of the melting-pot theory. Subscribers to this approach believe that we must eliminate cultural differences, because such differences are divisive and focus attention more on that which separates than on that which unites. Supporters of this approach hold to the Madisonian principle, proposed two centuries ago, that we, as American people, should speak the same language and cherish the same values and other attributes of the mainstream. Strength derives not from diversity, they would assert, but from harmonious unity. Rather than seeking to establish various ethnic identities, we should be striving for a common identity. Allegiance to a particular racial or ethnic group is nonproductive; it should be eliminated. Focus must be on our common humanity, the acceptance of a shared national identity. If we all work together toward this common goal, we will hasten the dawn of total assimilation.

What proponents of this approach have always failed to comprehend is that many people who reject their theories are not simultaneously rejecting or denying the idea of a common culture, a single society. What they continue to oppose is the Anglocentric cultural focus that is purported to be our common heritage—white middle-class Protestant America. Anti-assimilationists argue that supporters of assimilation fail to realize that America's great strength lies in its capacity to forge unity, to create and maintain a nation of people who represent diverse racial, linguistic, and ethnic origins.

Furthermore, opponents of assimilation reject the Madisonian intolerance for differences, advocating rather that America should be an open society based on mutual respect for individuals and tolerance for ethnic and racial differences. This nation simply cannot continue to be preserved, as it has been historically and culturally, strictly on an Anglo-Saxon base. If we are to have a common culture, they argue, let it be multicultural.

Inclusion

Somewhat akin to the philosophy espoused by the assimilationists is that of the inclusionists. Similarly, they would have America seek and be bound by a common culture but, in contrast to the assimilationists, they assert that we must incorporate the contributions and values of all racial and ethnic groups. Ethnic and racial parity should exist from the outset. Inclusionists are one of the groups that proclaim that our common culture must be multicultural. Our common culture and identity should be an amalgamation, the sum total of all the values that would go into the mix. This kind of blending is reminiscent of that suggested by Emerson in his smelting-pot theory. The basic assumption of this group is that allegiance to a common humanity and shared national identity would not only supersede but also eliminate allegiance to a specific racial or ethnic group.

Diane Ravitch (1990), a social scientist and one of the most eloquent voices advocating a common culture in the 1990s, argued that the time has come to recognize and accept the diversity that is America and to recognize the contributions that all members of this diversity have made to the many aspects of American culture. We should let differences remain; we should be free to choose who we are ethnically and otherwise. But most important, we must continue to strive for unifying ideals. To that end, we must work together to inhibit those things that escalate into antagonism and hatred.

Inclusionists believe in the full membership of all racial and ethnic groups. As Americans, we do not stand apart; rather, we "all share one multicolored umbrella whose strength and character reflect the diverse backgrounds but singular cause of those standing under it together" (Parrillo, 1996, p. 159).

The question that must be posed is whether the dominant society is prepared, first of all, to recognize the legitimacy of the contributions of all ethnic groups that should go into the mix. Is mainstream America convinced that such inclusion will not only dilute, but also contaminate what it means to be an American?

Separative Pluralism

According to Parrillo (1996), separative pluralists generate the most controversy; he labeled them proponents of "minority nationalism" (p. 159). Followers of this approach are the Afro-, Anglo-, Euro-, Etcetero-centrics (each ethnic group provides the appropriate constructive designation). Given the history of racial and ethnic groups in America, supporters of separative pluralism do not feel it is possible for Americans to use their diversity as a catalyst for pursuing a common bond of identity. Their goal, rather, is to build strong and separate group identities.

To achieve their goals, Parrillo further contended, such ethnocentrics seek to create a positive group identity for themselves, yet at the same time refuse to acknowledge the positives of the dominant-culture mores. In some instances, he asserted, they attempt to denigrate dominant-culture customs, deriding them as aberrational derivations of a particular subordinate culture.

Cultural separatists, unlike the formal separatists, seek to coexist but wish to stand apart and alone. Schlesinger (1992) argued that such groups are promoting "a cult of ethnicity" (p. 15). When pushed far enough, this promotion leads to bad consequences. The new ethnicity being proclaimed is "that America is not a nation of individuals at all but a nation of groups, that ethnicity is the defining experience for most Americans, that ethnic ties are permanent and indelible, and that division into ethnic communities establishes the basic structure of American society and the basic meaning of American history" (p. 15). Furthermore, Schlesinger maintains that such ethnic revival tends to lack any real substance or organic unity. The cultural symbols they so proudly espouse exist in limbo. There is a crisis of authenticity, and ethnocentrism is built without structural roots. Ethnocentrism is divisive and therefore threatens the fabric of American society as it drives "even deeper the awful wedges between the races by its exaggeration of ethnic distinctions" (p. 58). In belittling *unum* and glorifying *pluribus*, the ethnic separatists "nourish prejudices, magnify differences and stir antagonisms" (p. 117). Even if we all tread the same path and attempt to weather the same storm, these separatists insist that we find shelter with our own kind (Parrillo, 1996).

It appears that both Parrillo and Schlesinger have targeted Afrocentrics as the chief proponents of cultural separation. Although there may be some limited legitimacy to the objections raised by Parrillo and Schlesinger, especially when referring to what has been labeled "militant ethnicity," some Afrocentric proponents do not want to drive wedges of division. These proponents argue that developing pride in one's ethnic roots is necessary for building bridges of understanding among the ethnic groups of this nation. Reinforcing pride in one's cultural ties enables groups to interact with each other, assured that they each, in turn, have contributions to offer for viable societal linking. This is certainly not simply a matter of raising self-esteem and sanitizing history, as Schlesinger (1991) suggests. I wholeheartedly agree with him that "the purpose of history is to promote ... understanding of the world and the past, dispassionate analysis, judgment, and perspective, respect for divergent cultures and traditions, and unflinching protection for those unifying ideas of tolerance, democracy and human rights" (p. 99). However, it is not a creation of nonexistent history to assert that in the recognition of past and present contributions to American society, historians in the main have not been "dispassionate" in their analysis. Schlesinger displays his own disregard for the contributions of ethnic subcultures when he arrogantly stated that "if they had genuine vitality, [they] would be sufficiently instilled in children by family, church and community" (p. 90).

To Schlesinger's "passionate" analysis, some Afrocentrics would respond that there is genuine vitality, and it is instilled by many facets of the African American community. But, in turn, it is bombarded by sentiment deriding and denying its genuineness. Pride and inspiration must be internally as well as externally reinforced. If you ask African Americans to abandon the pride generated from within, you ask them to come to the multicultural conference table and place themselves at the mercy of a society that has been reluctant to recognize them as contributors to our common American culture.

Integrative Pluralism

Integrative pluralists, as do the separative pluralists, envision a multiculture of distinct umbrellas, each sheltering a different group. But, in contrast, they would have us see that "the umbrella's edges are attached to each other so that collectively they cover everyone" (Parrillo, 1996, p. 161). These pluralists would move Kallen's (1924) idea of an effective process of functional integration beyond his Eurocentric vision. Diverse groups would not only be invited to perform in the orchestra, they also would have some of their compositions included as a part of the musical repertoire. According to Triandis (1976) and Graff (1992), including the viewpoints and contributions of the diverse subcultures constituting America would result in cultural enrichment. Triandis supported the notion that the essence of what he called "additive pluralism" is to develop an appreciation for people from other cultures and to seek to discover skills that enhance intimate interaction. All Americans, whatever their ethnicity, need to expand their minds to greater cultural diversity.

The time has come to be aware that America does not, should not, must not belong to a privileged group operating from a position of power. We must forge a new common identity based on greater cross-cultural understanding and appreciation of varying viewpoints. This new common identity, the resulting cohesiveness, and the establishment of superordinate goals need not come at the expense of individual ethnic identity. Parrillo (1996) argued that "guided equally by the many handles of the interconnected umbrellas, one can see where another group is coming from within the framework of the whole" (pp. 161–162).

It would appear that this procedural model offers the best of all possible worlds. It allows for unity while retaining diversity—diversity with parity. Parrillo, Triandis, Graff, and others would have us believe that it is the flagship in which we may navigate the perilous seas of cultural diversity. Aboard, there will be no upper-deck vis-à-vis lower-deck passengers—no notable differences in status.

Before we set sail, however, at least one nagging point begs for clarification. Triandis and Graff, for example, recognized that we cannot have a hierarchy of power with any one group at the seat of control. Yet Triandis (1976) suggested that through the cultural enrichment that will come from the interaction of diverse cultures, "the majority can be enriched" (p. 181). Borrowing Emerson's notion of the smelting pot, I trust Triandis et al. are not proposing that the majority culture is the base metal and that the cultural additives are merely alloys that make the base metal stronger, more malleable, more resistant to rust, and shinier, and yet, in the final analysis, do not significantly alter the composition of the base.

A colleague suggested that given the reality of racial and ethnic relations in America, this is the proper way to effect cultural diversity. He did, however, introduce an important caveat. Translating his comments into the context of the metal analogy, his formula for success requires that a little alloy of ethnic diversity be added at a time, appearing not to change the base. It is important that any change not occur too rapidly or too radically. However, he claims that as more and more small additions are made, more alloy is added to the base without any great social upheaval, the composition of the base metal is altered, and a new "Corinthian gold" emerges.

If his recommended formula is successful and a new metal is forged and a multicultural society emerges, the question of composition must still be posed. Straining the analogy just a little further, one must ask, If the new metal is, shall we say, 70 percent base metal and 30 percent alloys, will the new metal react differently than if the percentages are reversed, demonstrating a greater equity of inclusion? Given that the base metal is still dominant, in spite of change, will this dominance not find expression in some fashion?

Having raised the issue, I trust that I am simply "splitting semantic hairs," that Triandis and those who support this form of diversity are truly committed to an open society. Of course, this approach will be difficult, for as Schlesinger (1992) stated, "The question America confronts as a pluralistic society is how to vindicate cherished cultures and traditions without breaking the bonds of cohesion—common ideals, common political institutions, common language, common culture, common fate—that hold the republic together" (p. 138).

One also must wonder if the task will be made more difficult by the fact that people or groups in positions of dominance, those who have been, at least in their own eyes, the keepers and preservers of the cherished traditions, will be reluctant to sacrifice their position of dominance and privilege even for the noble goal of cultural diversity. Is the best that we can hope for in our quest for greater unification truly an enriched majority culture? If such is the reality, then marginalized groups seeking full participation would be required to relinquish many of their cultural attributes to adapt themselves to—yes, assimilate themselves to—the attributes of the new enhanced culture. Those in the majority would make small adjustments, whereas those in the minority would have to make radical ones. That situation is certainly not parity.

If the essence of pluralism is the development of an appreciation for the viewpoint and values of all people and ethnic groups contributing to a society, can such pluralism prove effective if there is a disparity in the levels of appreciation? That question is somewhat rhetorical as, it is hoped, all would agree the answer is no. The critical question is, Can remove the disparities and move toward equitable appreciation? Some people would argue that given the present racial and ethnic climate in America, the answer to this question echoes with a resounding no. The mood of the majority in America is to regard any "enhancement" to the dominant culture from any subordinate culture as something that will either downgrade or replace some cherished value already present. This mood is set in a quantitative mode. In the context of Kallen's analogy of the orchestra, the argument would be that if you add a new violin player in the string section from a nondominant-culture group, given a fixed number of positions, you must displace a violinist already there. Ethnic enhancement is viewed as a win–lose situation, with the majority standing on the right side of the dash. Any seeming increase in power or presence of any nondominant-culture group can come only with an accompanying disadvantage for the dominant society. Therefore, such enhancements, such increases, whatever their nature, should be opposed and rejected.

BRINGING INTEGRATIVE PLURALISM INTO AMERICA

In spite of the objections raised and the nagging reservations, integrative pluralism seems to pose the best hope for overcoming the "disunity of America." As the nation stands on the threshold of a new millennium, all of its people, whatever their ethnic identification, must recognize that America's strength does lie in its diversity. If we are to invoke unity; to proclaim the ideas of democracy, freedom, and human rights; and to scale the walls of ethnic and racial separation, we must first deal with the real problem producing disunity—racial discrimination, both personal and institutional. Our rich tradition of pluralism has never been the barrier to harmony and unity; the real enemy is systemic racism (Parrillo, 1996).

Hacker (1992) agreed with Parrillo. Hacker stated that racial separation in America remains pervasive and penetrating; it easily surpasses gender "in intensity and subordination" (p. 3). America has its own version of apartheid, lacking only the overt legal trappings that such a system once enjoyed in the land of its invention. It is evident that, in recent years, Americans have felt freer to vent their feelings of racial animosity—feelings that a decade earlier they might have attempted to repress. "Race has become a national staple for private and public controversy" (Parrillo, 1996, p. 4). Racism perpetuates the fear that, if granted full participation, racial and ethnic subgroups will somehow contaminate the rest of society (Parrillo, 1996).

The paradox of race in America, West (1994) argued, "is that our common destiny is more pronounced and imperiled precisely when our divisions are deeper" (p. 8). This nation is interracially interdependent, and failure to come to terms with this fact will doom us "to collective paranoia and hysteria—the unmaking of any democratic order" (p. 8). As determined as some may be to deny it, we live in a culturally diverse country; we live in a culturally diverse world. No amount of glossing over can hide this reality. Nor is "flight" to some insulated suburb "quite as simple and certain to guarantee escape from the conflict of ethnic and racial intermingling" (Graff, 1992, p. 141).

So what can we do? How can we harness the spirit and the vision of inclusive pluralism to confront the challenge of cultural diversity, racial animosity, and all the cultural chaos that leads to fragmentation and disunity? West (1994) suggested that we begin with a three-phase approach. First, we must acknowledge that our power and most valuable resources consist of ourselves and our common destiny. Second, we must draw our attention to the common good that undergirds our national and global destinies. Finally, we must generate new leadership by electing courageous leaders who will be willing to jettison older, ineffective frameworks and to search for viable new ones that will enable us to deal with the problems and crises threatening to rush us headlong into an abyss of hopelessness and powerlessness (West, 1994). "Our ideals of freedom, democracy, and equality must be invoked to invigorate all of us" (p. 13).

Graff (1992) wrote of cultural diversity in the context of the university and cultural wars that have been fought over curriculum development. However, he made a suggestion that is applicable beyond the halls of academia: "Cultural diversity implies dialogue and debate rather than isolation and marginalization" (p. 142). But over the past several years, we have squandered several grand opportunities for substantive discussions about race, ethnicity, and cultural diversion. This pattern must be eliminated. We must begin to develop the courage, the hope, the integrity, and the vision to deal meaningfully with the racial and ethnic divides. We must decide whether we wish to perpetuate the ideas and ideals that have led us spiraling downward into division and distrust, or whether we would rather enter a new century in open dialogue and debate, discussing mutually and honestly ways that will enable us to challenge and overcome the forces that have long divided us, created inequality, and fomented racism. To opt for the latter, as West (1994) pointed out, is not to profess the belief that a social utopia or a political paradise is capable of descending on America, nor to hope that we can fulfill the dreams of the founding fathers to establish at last a theocracy reminiscent of St. Augustine's *The City of God* (1610/1957). It is rather to recognize that each one of us has a social responsibility, in fact a civic duty, to confront and overcome the poverty, the hatred, the despair, the paranoia, the divisions, and the distrust that have haunted and taunted us for all the centuries of America's unfolding.

With such social responsibility in mind, New Jersey convened a diversity summit during the summer of 1995. With the commitment from a number of corporations in the state, the intent of the summit was to capitalize on the state's cultural diversity, hoping as a by-product of the process to discourage bias and discrimination in the marketplace. The summit reconvened in September 1996, and at the close of the final plenary session issued a "declaration of diversity," pledging adherence to the above-stated goals. The declaration was signed by 41 of the state's major employers ("Multiculturalism Advances," 1996).

This declaration represents a significant step forward. It is hoped that corporations in other states will emulate New Jersey's bold initiative by promulgating similar declarations to which they will pledge allegiance. The times and the circumstances mandate that more declarations be issued and followed in the workplace: The work force in the United States and in many nations around the globe is becoming increasingly more diverse in gender, race, and ethnicity (Fullerton, 1987; Johnston, 1991). According to Cox (1991), about 45 percent of all new additions to the labor force during the remainder of this decade will be nonwhite. Blank and Slipp (1994) suggested that this ethnic reconfiguration, along with gender initiatives, will result in a work force that soon will be dominated by women, people of color, and immigrants from the third world. By the year 2000, 85 percent of the entering work force will be female, African American, Asian American, Latino, new immigrants, or some combination of these traits. These groups will bring different expectations, work styles, needs, and values.

Given the changes indicated by this ethnic and gender shift, which may be mind boggling to some employers, it is imperative that employers begin now to prepare for leadership that will "understand the effects of this diversity on human behavior in the workplace" (Cox, 1994, p. 5). Cox (1991) proposed that a top priority for organizations in the workplace should be to develop a process for managing diversity, planning, and implementing organizational systems in a way that will maximize the potential advantages of cultural diversity and exceed any potential disadvantage. This is an opportune time, he contended, for employers in the marketplace to dispense with the erroneous assumption that an increase in cultural diversity will automatically engender certain dysfunctional outcomes such as miscommunication and lower group cohesion.

At the same time employers should begin to incorporate the kinds of procedures that will enhance cultural diversity, such as encouraging tolerance for ethnic, racial, and gender differences; promoting fairness; providing equal access to advancement; and outlawing discriminatory practices and procedures (Cox, 1991). Management should seek to expand the "comfort zone" to make diversity a means for improving worker productivity and bettering working relationships among these diverse groups.

We may wish for quick-fix solutions in the marketplace and in the other arenas of human interaction, but such outcomes will not be found. Illnesses and problems that we have allowed to fester for centuries cannot be eliminated instantly. Solutions will require time which, in turn, will require patience, but not the kind of patience that traditionally has been a smokescreen for failure to address the problem. Solutions will require vision and courage, tolerance and respect, love and compassion, humor and imagination, and intelligence and analysis. The critical questions posed by West (1994) are whether we possess these essential qualities in sufficient measure and whether we are willing to commit to putting them into practice to achieve a common destiny.

That common destiny that should have been ours, whether the country's founders envisioned or intended it from the start, is the ongoing development of a multicultural society. If we are to establish the motto *e pluribus unum* as a reality, then we must learn to translate cultural diversity into unity. We must cease to equate differences with deficiencies or assume that differences will automatically lead to division and animosity. We must exhaust all our resources in our quest. We must be prepared for a healthy infusion of various ethnic values and ideas that will affect and change "all aspects of American life—our politics, our music, our painting, our movies, our cuisine, our customs, [even] our dreams" (Schlesinger, 1992, p. 135).

If there is one point on which I am in agreement with Schlesinger (1992), it is his contention that the American creed should not be viewed statically as "an imperious, final, and complacent orthodoxy intolerant of deviation and dissent." Rather, it should be perceived dynamically as "an ever-evolving philosophy, fulfilling its ideals through debate, self-criticism, protest, disrespect and irreverence; a tradition in which all have rights of heterodoxy and opportunities for self-assertion" (p. 136).

The ever unfolding of such a creed, in Schlesinger's (1992) opinion, will allow for movement from exclusion to inclusion, facilitated by the appeal "from the actual to the ideal" (p. 136). I contend that the converse, from the ideal to the actual, would be more effective. In its attempt to deal with diversity, by combining diverse ethnic groups into a single culture, progress has been thwarted because the actual too often has fallen short of the ideal. As the poet T. S. Eliot (1952, p. 58) poignantly phrased it,

> Between the idea
> And the reality
> Between the motion
> And the act
> Falls the Shadow.

Certainly in the history of America's dealings with cultural diversity, many times the shadow has fallen between the ideal and the reality. Under the cover of those shadows, we have groped in noncommitment or used the shadows as a shield to hide malignant neglect.

If we are to realize the dream of the American creed, if we are to manage ethnic diversity successfully, we must first make the ideal actual. It is in those rare yet profound moments in which we try to actualize the ideal that we provoke the great movements that combat racism, promote tolerance, defend freedom of expression, and enhance human rights.

REFERENCES

Augustine, St. (1957). *The city of God* (John Healey, Trans.). New York: E. P. Dutton. Originally published 1610.

Bennett, L., Jr. (1982). *Before the Mayflower.* New York: Penguin Books.

Blank, R., & Slipp, S. (1994). *Voices of diversity.* New York: Anacom.

Cox, T., Jr. (1991). The multicultural organization. *Executive, 5*(2), 34–47.

Cox, T., Jr. (1994). *Cultural diversity in organizations: Theory, research and practice.* San Francisco: Barrett Koehler.

de Crèvecoeur, M.G.J. (1957). *Letters from an American farmer.* New York: E. P. Dutton. Originally published 1787.

de Tocqueville, A. (1960). *Democracy in America* (Phillip S. Bradley, Ed.). New York: Knopf Press. Originally published 1835.

DuBois, W.E.B. (1964). *The souls of black folk.* New York: Fawcett Books. Originally published 1903.

Eliot, T. S. (1952). "The hollow men." *The complete poems and plays.* San Diego: Harcourt Brace Jovanovich.

Fullerton, H. N. (1987, September) Labor force projections: 1986–2000. *Monthly Labor Review,* pp. 19–29.

Glazer, N., & Moynihan, D. P. (1963). *Beyond the melting pot: The Negroes, Puerto Ricans, Jews, Italians and Irish of New York City.* Cambridge, MA: MIT Press.

Graff, G. (1992). *Beyond cultural wars.* New York: W. W. Norton.

Hacker, A. (1992). *Two nations: Black and white, separate, hostile, unequal.* New York: Charles Scribner's Sons.

Hamilton, A., Madison, J., & Jay, J. (1961). *The Federalist papers* (Clinton Rossiter, Ed.). New York: New American Library. Originally published 1788.

Johnston, W. (1991). Global work force 2000: The new world labor market. *Harvard Business Review, 69,* 115–127.

Kallen, H. M. (1924). *Culture and democracy in the United States: Studies in the group psychology of the American people.* New York: Boni and Liverwright.

Kymlicka, W. (Ed.). (1995). *The rights of minority cultures.* New York: Oxford University Press.

Multiculturalism advances in the workplace. (1996, October 3). *Star Ledger,* Union County Edition, p. 15.

Park, R. (1950). *Race and culture.* New York: Free Press.

Parrillo, V. N. (1996). *Diversity in America.* Thousand Oaks, CA: Pine Forge Press.

Poesche, T., & Goepp, C. (1853). *The new Rome, or the United States of the world.* New York: G. P. Putnam.

Ravitch, D. (1990). Multiculturalism: E pluribus plures. *American Scholar, 59,* 337–354.

Schlesinger, A. M., Jr. (1992). *The disuniting of America.* New York: W. W. Norton.

Smith, A. D. (1980). *The ethnic revival.* Cambridge, England: Cambridge University Press.

Sollars, W. (1986). *Beyond ethnicity: Consent and descent in American culture.* New York: Oxford University Press.

Steinberg, S. (1981). *The ethnic myth.* New York: Atheneum.

Triandis, H. (1976). The future of pluralism. *Journal of Social Issues, 32,* 179–208.

West, C. (1994). *Race matters.* New York: Random House.

Zangwill, I. (1921). *The melting pot: Drama in four acts.* New York: Macmillan Press.

8 Social Issues, Social Policy, and Workplace Diversity

John E. Tropman

In a workplace setting, the concept of diversity points us in the direction of difference, heterogeneity, variety, and multiplicity. I define *diversity* as multidimensional heterogeneity. The modern organization needs diversity because of the complexity, uncertainty, and rapidly changing nature of the tasks it confronts.

The term "diversity" is often used to refer to the currently popular dimensions of ethnicity, racial origin, sexual orientation, and gender. However, religion, region of origin, and educational status are important. Height, eye and hair color, and weight are differentiating variables as well.

As a word, "diversity" is often a code for ideas that we do not want to express directly. When someone says "Our workplace needs to be more diverse" and that workplace is made up of white males, it is reasonable to conclude that the person really wants to say "We need more women and black people here" but feels uncomfortable in speaking directly.

From my perspective, diversity used as a code misses the concept's rich multidimensionality. Worse, it locates movement toward diversity in some kind of social policy lagoon, seen by managers as "nice" but not central to the success of their organization. I argue the reverse: Diversity is central to organizations because the environment of organizations is diverse.[1]

As Alfrieda Daly suggests in her introduction to this book, workplaces are becoming more diverse than ever before. A number of general and specific factors account for this diversity. Those factors are the contextual elements that serve as "independent variables"—the variables that push toward greater diversity within that workplace. Although factors also limit and constrain diversity, from my

---

[1]There is one approach to diversity—the social justice approach—that I am not taking here. I am not supporting diversity in this chapter because it provides opportunity to groups that have been denied opportunity in the past. I support such an initiative, but that is not the fulcrum of the argument. One example of this social justice argument can be found in the diversity statement of the Sigma Xi research society. After some discussion of issues of women and people of color in science, the society argued that "Sigma Xi members should be willing to provide women and persons of color with that mentoring needed by all to succeed in science and engineering" (Hollingsworth, 1995, p. 390).

perspective the overwhelming thrust of sociological pressure is to expand diversity.

In this chapter, I will examine general pressures that are moving organizations toward diversity enhancement. Then I will look at pressures that generate within and focus most strongly on the non-profit human services sector. That discussion looks at diversity in more detail in the workplace context. I will conclude with an examination of the value conflicts that affect internal diversity.

ORGANIZATIONAL IMPETUS: PRESSURES FOR DIVERSITY ENHANCEMENT

One can look at organizations as a collection of entities that are individually and as a group responding to their environments—trying to make themselves more competitive, more adaptable, and more sustainable. In the contemporary context, a number of changes are occurring to those organizations that have direct and indirect effects on diversity within human services organizations. Although there are many more changes affecting modern organizations in the last decade of the 20th century, the ones I have outlined capture many of the key changes. These changes work toward increasing organizational diversity when diversity is broadly understood to include that of customers, of products, of input, of ideas, of approaches, of decision-making centers, and so on. The contemporary literature suggests 12 such changes that are relevant for the discussion here.

Many Ideas: From Money-Centered to Idea-Centered Organizations

Organizations once competed on the "bottom line"; anything that contributed to profits was okay, and anything that detracted from profits was not okay. Organizations were money centered. A crude phrase—"Money talks; BS walks"—captures the essence of the money-obsessed organization. In these organizations, statements such as "If I need an idea from you, I'll give you one" have been the norm.

Newer organizations do not, of course, ignore money, but they realize, paradoxically, that money is a by-product of "right organizational living." In particular, organizations are now competing on ideas—who has the newest product ideas; who has the best ideas for getting products to market; and who can provide services more efficiently and effectively, less expensively, and with higher quality. Organizations are looking for a greater range of ideas. Occasionally, ideas will emerge fully formed. Most of the time, however, new ideas require a diversity of input, different perspectives, and different people to make them whole.

Many Approaches: From Means Control to Ends Control

Older organizations were convinced that if they structured the means properly, the desired ends would follow. Malinowski (1948) discussed this idea in *Magic, Science and Religion*. If he were writing the book to-day, he would probably call it *Magic, Science, Religion, and Business*, because in all four cases "means exactitude" is the sine qua non for desired results. If the process is performed correctly, the results are never in doubt. In social work practice, this idea would emerge as "if we use the right techniques, the client *will* get well."

As true as this idea may be in theory, it is sadly limited in practice. For one thing, it is difficult to control means so precisely. That effort can lead to what Merton (1957) called "means ritualism," which occurs when old means are used regardless of their appropriateness. Also, means regularity assumes sameness of input. For example, a system set up to process one kind of marital problem does not work so well on another kind of marital problem. Means control, therefore, restricts input to that which the organization can actually deal with.

The newer organization needs just the opposite approach. It specifies ends and lets the workplace and people in that workplace configure the means to those ends, depending on a variety of factors including local setting, skills of the workers, client specifications, and so on. Variations in means may produce identical ends. Hence, organizations are looking for a range of "diversities," such as methods diversity, approach diversity, skills bank diversity, and skills set diversity, to move them toward the desired ends.

Many Workers: From Thing-Centered to People-Centered Organizations

In the past, organizations were driven by the things in their environment—products, machines, forms. Consistent with ends control, organizations of the future will be driven by people. Organizations are recognizing that it is people who make them run. The mechanical or nonhuman elements of the organization are being returned to their appropriate support role. This change is forcing organizations to look for human diversity within the organization to help solve business problems.

Many Decision Centers: From Fixed Structures to Burrows, Spiderwebs, and Lattices

The structure of organizations is changing. Older organizational forms were relatively fixed. A triangle was used frequently to describe the fixed structure. The boss was at the top, with fixed positions below the boss, fixed positions below that level, and so on. This organizational chart is still driven by concepts such as "span of control" and "reporting relationships."

Newer forms of organizations are more fluid. As the burrow, spiderweb, or lattice suggests, they are not without structure, but they have a different structure—a multicentric structure. Burrows and spiderwebs are networks, and lattices have many intersections. A variety of intersections rather than a string of reporting relationships characterize new organizations.

Many Decision Makers: From Office-Centered to Decision-Centered Organizations

In the older, more rigid organizations, decision makers were people who were officially authorized to make decisions. Whether they knew anything about the issue or were the right person to make the decision was irrelevant.

Contemporary organizations start with a set of decisions that need to be made and then find the people best able to provide useful input into these decisions. Cohen, March, and Olsen (1972) argued that the right people to involve in decision making must include problem knowers, problem solvers, and resource controllers, a group I call "annointers." Decisions, not rank, are the focus. Nobody in today's organization mistakes compliance for good judgment. This emphasis on good judgment brings to the surface not only a plurality of decision points but also a plurality of decision makers.

Many Sizes and Distances: From Boxes to Bubbles

The old boxlike organization—emphasized in the organizational chart mentioned before—had fixed faces, both vertically and horizontally. Vice presidents were a certain distance from the chief executive officer and from each other. Boxlike charts did not communicate any interaction, any mutuality, or any cooperation. In fact, many organizations were driven by the pictures in their heads and on their charts. The people in those boxes did not interact. They jealously guarded their own boxes—their own turf—and tried to get people in other boxes to report to them.

Today an organization's departments need to work together. The image of "organizational bubbles" depicts the dynamism and merging, then separating, that occurs. Like bubbles emerging from an airpipe, people flow together in large groups, then sometimes separate, breaking apart and floating away on their own, only to join other bubbles. An advantage of such a metaphor is that it may actually produce what it represents, in the same way that the box metaphor tended to produce what it suggested.

Many Tasks at the Same Time: From One at a Time to All at Once

Organizations of the past focused on doing, making, or accomplishing one thing after another. The phrase "one day at a time" communicates this idea well. The assembly line is an example of this serial approach. For example, step H could not be completed before step G and had to be completed before step I, and so on.

Today's organizations thrive on simultaneity. If B, H, I, and K can be done today, then "Let's do it." The fact that K may need to await the completion of J for final assembly is okay. The organization is taking advantage of capturing previously lost opportunity. Simultaneity is diversity in time, and it is an important presence in today's organization.

Many Perspectives: From Photograph to Kaleidoscope

Organizations of the past had a "photograph" culture. There was one picture—one way to view things—and it was captured in the photo. Today's organizations have a "kaleidoscope" culture. They may have the same basic components, but a twist here and a twist there create diverse combinations. Many views exist about what the organization is, might be, does, and could do. It is from this kaleidoscope that "pictures of our disposition" are assembled.

Many Identities: From Self versus Community of Work to Self in Community of Work

The workplace can be viewed as a community in which people come together and have unity around common tasks or goals. Historically, as represented by labor–management conflict, the worker was viewed as opposed to management. Implicit in this view was the idea that the work community was a place in which one had to protect oneself. In the case of management, one could protect oneself through politics, flattery, and the like. In the case of workers, organizing or threatening to go to another organization was a way to produce a pay raise. The workplace was a coliseum, and the "lion managers" and the "Christian workers" contested daily. And the score always seemed to be lions 28, Christians 0. It is no wonder that the workers sought communal solace elsewhere—in the bowling alley, in the saloon, and in ethnic and other enclaves where "people like them" could share support.

The new organization seeks to break down these barriers and emphasize partnership—to emphasize that the competition is with those outside, not with those inside. So bloody is the organizational history here that it might be a long time, if ever, before a majority of organizations achieve the communal status that more successful organizations seem to have constructed. All that is required is the development of common goals and a willingness to truly share the product—the results of common energy being applied to those common goals. In this case, the diversity of community previously excluded from the organization is brought into the organization, structured, and harnessed around a common focus.

Many Energies: From Either–Or to the Sprint–Pause Cycle

It used to be that in organizations, one was either working or was not—work and nonwork. This mindset led to busywork (appearing to be working), face time (showing up so the boss can see you and think you are working), and self-promoting work (being busy on your computer doing your résumé for your next job). Perhaps these working behaviors are captured in this joke from the Eastern bloc countries: "We'll pretend to work, and you'll pretend to pay us."

The more flexible organizations of today recognize what might be called the "sprint–pause cycle." Most organizations are not on or off;

they merely adjust the pace. The sprint pace often occurs when a contract is near deadline or a product approaches launch, and all talents must roll up their sleeves and work together. Here diversity blends into uniformity, as distinctions are dropped, subcultures set aside, idiosyncrasies interdicted, and everybody works to get the product out on time. In the pause cycle, diversity flourishes again in more apparent ways. The pace slows; people are working, but not as frenetically as in the sprint cycle. Everybody relaxes a bit, does more of their own thing, but that "thing" is still linked to the organization. In time, the sprint will come again.

Many Rewards: From Enervation to Energizing

The older workplace, given the characteristics of rigidity, means-ritualism, anti-self, and social distance, tended to be an enervating place. It was not a place that one really looked forward to going. To paraphrase the poet Robert Frost (1971), it was the place you went because you worked there and they had to let you in.[2] The new workplace is designed to provide, in addition to cash compensation, a measure of psychic income, an environment to which one actually wants to go, a setting in which one draws energy rather than loses it.

Many Worlds: From Local to Cosmopolitan

The last change pushing against organizations is perhaps the one that most directly deals with the diversity issue—the change from local points of reference to more cosmopolitan ones. Cosmopolitanism comes to organizations in many ways. Obviously, heterogeneity of the work force is one way, but given the global links required to put together today's complicated products, other kinds of diversity include, for example, linking with workers in Canada, Mexico, Hong Kong, Singapore, Poland, and London as well as with customers in those same countries. The idea that global emphasis is the prerogative of only large organizations is not true. Small organizations are experiencing similar kinds of connections and context. With the Internet and the World Wide Web developing quickly, contact with the rest of the world is easy.

HUMAN SERVICES SYSTEMS AND DIVERSITY: PRESSURES FOR DIVERSITY CONSTRICTION

A number of changes in the social welfare system will affect human services organizations. I have scoured the social welfare sector to find the changes that seem most pressing as well as the ones that have the most to say to people with diversity interests. In this section, I will emphasize the problems that lack of diversity has created.

---

[2]The original expression dealt with going home. In "The Hired Man," Frost (1971) says, "Home is the place where, when you go there, they have got to take you in!" (p. 156).

Public Welfare's Success (and Our Failure to Reinvent)

Public welfare came into being when President Franklin Roosevelt signed the Social Security Act in 1935. By 1995, public welfare had achieved astronomical success—that is, its main goals had been accepted, its programs had proliferated, and its personnel and budget had grown huge. Unfortunately, the mindset of much of the human services profession was still that of beleaguerement. The profession itself, internally, was not able to see the successful steps it had taken. It was also unable to see that this very success was generating opposition—present all along—that would eventually permit President Bill Clinton to "end welfare as we know it."

The public welfare system suffered from a lack of diversity of ideas. It suffered from many of the same organizational flaws that I discussed earlier. This is not to say it was bad, and anyone tempted to bristle at these mild criticisms is, in many respects, part of the problem. Public welfare established what Argyris (1985) called "defensive routines." Certain things are not discussable, and their nondiscussability is not discussable. For that reason, public welfare became the classic "boiled frog"—no one saw the water slowly heating up until they spotted the dead frog. Organizationally, this phenomenon is known as the "just-noticeable difference"—the change in the environment is small enough that adaptation never seems necessary until it is too late.

More Visible Social Problems (and Our Failure to Address Them Energetically and Honestly)

The success of public welfare is really success of an organizational rather than a programmatic or results sort. Despite large staffs and budgets, the problems that programs were supposed to be addressing never seemed to go away. In some respects, they grew worse, or at least more visible. Cities continued to decline, education continued to be problematic, and so on. From the perspective of the society as a whole, huge sums were being spent with little "bang for the buck" in solving social problems. This suggests an absence of goal diversity.

Welfare State in Eclipse (and Our Failure to Take Corrective Action)

Many European countries, which are often more "welfare-statish" than the United States, are reconsidering what should be provided as entitlements and how. We often characterize them from our perspective as "vacillating" or "giving up"—negative, judgmental terms that permitted us the expensive luxury of failing to engage the global welfare state marketplace, assess what was happening there, and ask honestly what events might mean for us.

Need for Evaluation and Accountability (and Our Failure to Engage This Necessity Effectively)

Increasingly in recent years, organizations have been pressed to evaluate their services. Has the program, product, or service satisfied customers and made an impact? Total quality management has made an impact throughout the organizational world, but human services organizations, for a variety of reasons, have ignored it. Lack of diversity seems to be the reason. The human services profession tends to be clannish (for a discussion of clan subculture, see Quinn, 1989); we like to emphasize the differences between "us" and "them" ("them" referring to business organizations). In fact, we often say "if *they* are doing *it,* whatever it is, *we* should certainly avoid it. It would probably be inappropriate." We choose to misperceive demands for accountability and evaluation, interpreting them as criticisms rather than as honest requests. Thus, replying to them as criticisms, we tend to invoke denial ("there's nothing wrong with us") or some kind of attack ("they just don't understand"). For these reasons, we fail to adapt or even use the best practices that others might have been able to teach us.

Growth of the Voluntary Sector (and Our Failure to Understand and Move on from This Success)

Historically, American society was made up of first the private sector (businesses) and then the public sector (government). Everyone knew there were churches, volunteer hospitals, the Red Cross, and the United Way, but until the work of Lester Solomon, a distinguished scholar and researcher at Johns Hopkins University, few realized that the voluntary sector was a $200 billion enterprise (in 1983 dollars), with more than 900,000 organizations having one or more paid staff (probably more than 1 million today) (for an amalgam of Solomon's findings, see Tropman and Tropman, 1987). It is understandable that government or business might have missed this large growth, but that we in the human services field missed it shows a lack of diversity of information and an inability to grasp the basic demographics of our own field. We had more of a photographic than a kaleidoscopic culture.

Failure of the Business Model (and Our Failure to Understand and Incorporate This Knowledge)

The lack of diversity in the business model is obvious. Throughout the 1950s and, to some extent, the 1960s and 1970s, business was golden. We had not experienced large-scale business failures. We had not experienced the severe market incursions of Japanese cars and the shocking picture they presented to us of the quality of U.S. manufacturing. Fishing tackle, musical instruments, and consumer electronics were still dominated by the American juggernaut. Then all of that changed. Businesses proved to be as unable to adapt, as fallible and, frankly, as stupid as any other organizational form. Our view, however, perhaps drummed into us by status differences between sectors, was that businesspeople knew best. Boards of human services organizations were dominated by businesspeople. During the War on Poverty, we had to fight to get "maximum feasible participation of the poor," which often was the minimal representation of the customer (Moynihan, 1968). Lack of perspective diversity was a factor in causing us not to understand that failure was all around us.

Status Inversion (and Our Failure to Include the "Customer")

The example of "maximum feasible participation of the poor" is an interesting one because its phraseology predates status inversion (those at the bottom—clients—rising to the top as customers). For most organizations, poor people are our "customers," and the voice of the customer should influence how we do business. It is paradoxical in the human services field that despite our language of inclusion and diversity, often along racial and gender lines, we rarely think to include the customer. In fact, we seldom use the term "customers"; "clients" creates a comfortable social distance. However, distance and diversity are not a good mix.

Tentative Acceptance of the Helping Profession (and Our Failure to Accept and Move On)

Social work, for a variety of reasons, seems to many to be a "second-class profession." In this context, "second class" means, sadly, "a woman's profession." That designation means that the pay is low and the jobs are demanding. In addition, most of social work deals with "second-class citizens"—people with disabilities, people with illnesses, elderly people, and children—people about whom society gives lip service but does not really care too much. Furthermore, social work deals with people society "really" hates—the poor population, those threatening individuals who remind us that status that goes up can also come down.[3] We might not go as far as to kill the messenger of bad stratification news, but we certainly have gone as far as hating that messenger. Greater diversity within the profession might have helped us to understand how successful we really are, and to accept and deal with those successes instead of always being defensive (Tropman, in press).

Change in Recruiting Patterns (and Our Failure, Again, to Recognize and Adjust)

Through the 1960s, social work was, in many ways, a woman's profession. Gockel (1966), in his study of 1961 college graduates who went into professional studies, called his work *Silk Stockings and Blue Collars*. What he wanted to convey was his sense that women who went into the social work profession were largely middle class and were, in effect, treading occupational water, whereas the "men of

---

[3]Poor hate, like anti-Semitism, is always there, seldom acknowledged, and corrosive. Who are "the poor"? People who have a correlation of deficits—little money, little power, poor or no jobs, low education, and low status—are the "status poor." People at the end of the life cycle—elderly people—are the "life-cycle poor." See Tropman, in press.

their dreams" went to law, medical, business, or engineering school or got a PhD. The men who went into the social work profession were largely of blue-collar origin and had a different view of the social work profession. For them, it was a way to break into the lower professional rungs. They feared, rightly or wrongly, that they could not be accepted in the professions mentioned above, but they could get into social work and perhaps work themselves up into some managerial capacity, thus becoming a social work executive.

In the 1970s, the employment outlook for women began to change. Previously "closed" professions opened up, and by 1996, women were substantially represented (in the 35-percent range) in medicine, law, business, and other fields. Social work lost its access to highly qualified women. It was a long time, however, before the schools recognized that their applicant pools were somewhat different—perhaps less appealing and less qualified—and began to act. Diversity in the field would have helped us recognize what was happening and adjust.

The Importance of Management (and Our Failure to Recognize It)

Diversity deficiency hurt social work in the management department. In human services, management has been considered unimportant. Few schools of social work train human services managers, although the numbers of schools that do is increasing. Promotions of people with clinical backgrounds and failure to provide them with managerial training is routine. The problem is not our failure to use business models (they were failing, too) but our failure to use sensible management models (something that many businesses also failed to do).

New Structures and Old Values (and Our Failure to Change)

The perplexing policy paradox confronting human services organizations at the turn of the millennium can be better understood through inspecting the two sets of forces—general and specific. On the large-scale organizational side, many changes are creating pressure for increasing diversity. This diversity is essential to the coping ability of organizations, generally speaking, and to their developing capability and competence.

In the human services field, changes are occurring, too. Regrettably, for a variety of reasons, including a lack of diversity in staff, perspectives, ideas, approaches, and cultures, we failed to see the need to change. As a result, changes in many ways have been forced on us (see the discussion of chaos below and Figure 8-1).

Human services values formed in a cauldron of conflict in the 1920s and 1930s have passed the point of serviceability and are now in a state of "cultural lag." We are in a situation of new structures and old values. We modeled the old values, but they do not serve us well. Even the discussion of diversity itself is uncommonly narrow, focusing as it often does on issues of race and ethnicity only.

WHY DIVERSITY IS A PROBLEM FOR HUMAN SERVICES ORGANIZATIONS

Many people ask why diversity achievement is a problem in organizations and why it is a particular problem for human services organizations. There are a number of answers.

Cloning Is Easier

Diversity management takes skill and energy; it is easier to "clone" than to "combine." It is easier to hire somebody like yourself and to feel good about that decision than to hire somebody different from yourself and then deal with the differences.

Differing Views Are Considered Critical Views

Diversity challenges our own explanations. Somebody who says "We're not doing things right around here" can be perceived as critical (they probably are critical). Our view about, for example, what kinds of treatment couples need, how best to help children from the ghetto to read, and so on is thus scrutinized, and in a society heavy with personal responsibility, a first impulse may be to save our own perspective at all costs. This impulse may not even be conscious. It may be the same kind of reaction that Johnny has when he is standing on the kitchen stool, his hand in the cookie jar, when his mother walks in and asks, "What are you doing?" His deniability is zero, his guilt is 100-percent clear, there's nowhere to run, and he still says, "Nothing." Diversity is, therefore, embarrassing because it may call our own actions into question.

Diversity Requires New Skills

Diversity is a problem because it requires skills we do not have— more people to talk to means more styles to accommodate. It is easier to talk when everybody speaks the same language.

VALUES OF DIVERSITY

We resist diversity for a number of reasons, behavior which leads to the question, "If it's hard to accomplish and live with, why do we need it?" The most popular answer is that diversity is an "opportunity enhancer." Sometimes "diversity" is used as a code word for paying special attention to particular groups that have experienced suffering and lack opportunities (or at least the rate of opportunities) available to others. In that usage, "diversity" becomes the code word for "hiring women or ethnic minorities" when nobody wants to use those words. It becomes a cover for plain speaking and acting. There is nothing wrong with this use of the word, except that its proxy nature prevents us from looking at broader and more important definitions of diversity and considering the importance that these others might have.

If one comes to a definition of *diversity* as multidimensional heterogeneity, then gender, ethnicity, different abilities, and race would be factors to consider in any workplace. However, many other kinds of heterogeneity could be considered under the multidimensional approach. For example, one could consider age—seeking younger and newer employees as well as older employees. Similarly linked might be sector experience. Obviously, social agencies want and need people with experience in doing what they are doing. On the other hand, people without much experience may have a lot to contribute.

Similarly, conceptual diversity and point-of-view represent a vital but usually ignored dimension. Some people start with the forest and then see the trees. Other people start with the trees and then see the forest. Some always stay in the shrubbery. Differing ways of looking at a problem reveal different elements and aspects of that problem and are thus vital for organizational problem solving and decision making.

Also, different learning and teaching styles might be a diversity element. Some people are talkers who like to express their ideas first verbally and then go to a written text. Others are readers who like to read the text first and then go to an oral discussion. Some people like to present ideas visually through pictures, slides, and overheads. Still others like to present in writing. Different learning and teaching styles, as well as the ways in which we prefer to absorb information, are key.

Extending the concept of learning styles, one might think of a representation of intelligences in the sense that Gardner (1983) talked about it in his *Frames of the Mind: The Theory of Multiple Intelligences.* Most often, we think of two kinds of intelligence: (1) verbal intelligence (facility with and use of words) and (2) an analytical, math–music intelligence. Gardner argued that instead of two, there are seven. He retains verbal intelligence; divides math and music into two; and adds spatial intelligence (people who always know where they are and can find their way around any physical space—sculptors), kinesthetic intelligence (people who have body control—athletes and musicians), interpersonal intelligence (people who can understand how others are feeling and thinking), and intrapersonal intelligence (people who can understand how they themselves are feeling and thinking). People strong in any one of these intelligences can make a contribution that others cannot. Further, each intelligence supplements the others.

Diversity, then—thought of as multidimensional heterogeneity—has a wide range of dimensions along which it can be explored. Regrettably, the proxy use of "diversity" as a code word for adding women and people of color placed conceptual blinders on the rich range of possibilities for diversity that an organization might, through policy and action, wish to achieve. Given that this rich range exists, why is diversity important? As noted before, the decision to make an effort to create viable opportunity structures for those whom the society has subordinated is a laudable effort and should be continued. However, the purpose of that diversity initiative has a different kind of organizational health in mind—a "representation" of different identified groups. Although representation contributes to overall organizational health, the basic proposition I would like to advance is that an even more fundamental diversity is vital if organizations are to survive and prosper. I further suggest that this point of view must logically come before the opportunity enhancement point of view, because if the agency goes out of business, it will not have any opportunities to offer. Therefore, diversity is fundamental, in my view, to the health of the organization, because organizations exist in complicated, turbulent, rapidly changing environments. In those environments, change is essential. Diversity is essential for change to occur.

Change comes in two speeds—fast and really fast—and in two magnitudes—big and really big. Slow and small changes can be dealt with (but, remembering the boiled frog, they have their own problems). These dimensions allow construction of the fourfold matrix in Figure 8-1. If change is big and fast, innovation—improvements in what the organization is now doing—will help. If speed or magnitude ratchets up so that the organization is in the off-diagonal cells, then more fundamental change is needed—reinvention, re-engineering, or transformation. Work in each of the three cells is essential if slippage into the fourth cell—chaos—is to be avoided. An organization in chaos is at the mercy of others.

Environmental complexity and velocity, then, are the key reasons why diversity is vital. We do not have good rules for creating organizational shapes, forms, structures, and behaviors that ensure success in such an environment. Many thousands of organizations die each month because they cannot think fast enough, cannot move fast enough, or do not know how to reorganize to deal with a today that is not very much like yesterday and will not be like tomorrow at all.

Figure 8-1

The Speed and Magnitude of Change

IMPACT \ SPEED	Fast	Really fast
Big	Innovation	Re-engineering Transformation Reinvention
Really big	Re-engineering Transformation Reinvention	Chaos *Avoid this cell!*

Organizations, therefore, need to repeatedly undergo a process of deep change. Agencies that do not undergo deep change will die. Small organizations experience fast death. Large organizations may experience slow death, which occurs as the organization drops from viability, continues to hang on, engages in low-order repositioning, loses more employees, loses more market share, and finally collapses. Lassen (1996) captured this process well when discussing the D'Amico Brothers, restaurant food consultants who became disillusioned with their clients' unwillingness to change: "People would hire us based on our innovation and creativity, and when you get there they don't really want innovation and creativity. They decide what they really need is a gourmet hot dog" (p. 36).

The antidote to fast or slow death is to have a staff sufficiently diversified in the many dimensions discussed in this chapter so that the organization can determine what it needs to do and has the array of skills to repair and even transform itself. Organizational analysts often make presentations like "Organizational Transformation: Repairing a Plane in Flight" or, for the really adventurous, "Organizational Re-engineering: Building a Plane in Flight." As humorous (or foolish) as these phrases appear, they contain much truth. Much of the recrafting of contemporary organizations must occur in the background of the organizational setting while in the foreground the organization is going about its business. Only fundamental, multidimensional diversity can provide the social capital needed to undertake those kinds of tasks.

CONCLUSION

Diversity, then, is essential for organizational health and prosperity. A "some-of-these-and-some-of-those" approach will not address the fundamental issues. Although there are great contextual pressures in the direction of diversity enhancement, the human services system has power pressures toward diversity reduction. These pressures have created a situation in which human services organizations do not change as fast as they need to; they are entering a period of slow death. Because we do not know exactly what to prepare for in the future, we need to prepare for the unexpected. Diversity is an important tool for that preparation.

REFERENCES

Argyris, C. (1985). *Strategy, change, and defensive routines.* Boston: Pittman.

Cohen, M., March, J., & Olsen, J. (1972, March). A garbage can model of organizational choice. *Administrative Science Quarterly,* pp. 1–25.

Frost, R. (1971). *The road not taken.* New York: Holt, Rinehart & Winston.

Gardner, H. (1983). *Frames of the mind: The theory of multiple intelligences.* New York: Basic Books.

Gockel, G. (1966). *Silk stockings and blue collars: Social work as a career choice of America's 1961 college graduates.* Chicago: National Opinion Research Center.

Hollingsworth, P. (1995, July–August). The Sigma Xi approach to diversity. *American Scientist,* p. 390.

Lassen, T. (1996, October). Savoring success. *Northwest World Traveler*, pp. 33–38.

Malinowski, B. (1948). *Magic, science and religion, and other essays.* Boston: Beacon Press.

Merton, R. (1957). *Social structure and social process* (rev. ed.). New York: Free Press.

Moynihan, D. P. (1968). *Maximum feasible misunderstanding: Community action in the War on Poverty.* New York: Free Press.

Quinn, R. (1989). *Beyond rational management.* San Francisco: Jossey-Bass.

Tropman, J. E. (in press). *Do Americans hate the poor?* Westport, CT: Greenwood Press.

Tropman, E. J., & Tropman, J. E. (1987). Voluntary organizations. In A. Minahan (Ed.-in-Chief), *Encyclopedia of social work* (18th ed., Vol. 2, pp. 825–842). Silver Spring, MD: National Association of Social Workers.

Special thanks to Laura Rojo for her careful reading and thoughtful comments on this chapter.

Working It Out:

What Managers Should Know about Gay Men, Lesbians, and Bisexual People and Their Employment Issues

Beth D. Kivel and Joel W. Wells

> *We need to examine the space neither in nor out of the closet, but rather the space in between which allows for possibilities.*
>
> —Sedgewick, 1990

A variety of factors (such as social, emotional, cognitive, and physical) and contexts (such as family, religious institutions, and community) influence our development as individuals. Although we have some control over these factors and contexts, there is at least one context in which most of us (women and men) have a compulsory obligation to participate—the context of work outside the home. Indeed, by the year 2000, more than 61 percent of women will be employed outside the home (Seck, Finch, Mor-Barak, & Poverny, 1993).

From a very young age, children, as a result of media and through their play and interactions with adults, are socialized into believing that they will become teachers, doctors, lawyers, nurses, or engineers. Children are, at the same time, being socialized into acceptable gender and sexual identities. Given the societal norms and mores about gender and sexual identity which, as Herdt and Boxer (1993) explained, are ingrained in children as young as age 3, it seems inevitable that those who stray from these roles would be at risk of violating one of our most basic and cherished cultural norms—that "'good' girls are inherently feminine, that 'good' boys are inherently masculine and that when they grow up they will be 'good' heterosexuals" (Kivel, 1996, p. 8). Children are taught to believe that girls and boys behave in certain ways that are different from one another and that they will grow up, meet someone of the opposite sex, get married, and have children.

So what happens to people who, as they develop their social identity, begin to question their gender or sexual identity, and how does this questioning intersect with the development of their work identity? How do people negotiate the development of a stigmatized "private" self within the public context of paid employment? Moreover, what happens within the context of work for people who are gay, lesbian, or bisexual and who may or may not want to reveal this aspect of identity in the workplace? To what extent do stereotypes about gay, lesbian, and bisexual people affect coworkers' attitudes about and behaviors toward those who may or may not be gay, lesbian, or bisexual? Finally, why should managers and human resources workers be concerned about issues that affect gay, lesbian, and bisexual people in the workplace? The purpose of this chapter is twofold: (1) to identify and explore workplace issues that affect gay, lesbian, and bisexual people, and (2) to examine the role that organizational managers and planners can play in affecting attitudes, knowledge, and behaviors concerning gay men, lesbians, and bisexual people in the workplace.

GAY, LESBIAN, AND BISEXUAL PEOPLE IN THE WORKPLACE

About 20 million people in the United States are gay, lesbian, or bisexual (Seck et al., 1993) and that a large proportion of those eligible to be employed work outside the home. Thus, it seems likely that almost everyone in the United States works directly or indirectly with gay, lesbian, or bisexual people, either as colleagues, bosses, coworkers' relatives, clients, or customers. Indeed, it is highly unlikely that people come into no direct or indirect contact with gay, lesbian, or bisexual people in the workplace. The reality, which parallels the situation of gay men and lesbians in the armed forces, is that gay, lesbian, and bisexual people have always been and will continue to be employed outside the home in public contexts of work. A 1992 survey of gay men and lesbians indicated that 47 percent of gay men and 40 percent of lesbians were employed in professional or managerial jobs (Overlooked Opinions, 1992). Moreover, a 1996 *Newsweek* poll indicated that "nearly 84 percent of Americans who voted last year also support equal rights for gay Americans in the workplace" (Kaplan & Klaidman, 1996, p. 24).

Yet, despite the fact that gay, lesbian, and bisexual people are such an integral part of public workplace contexts and despite widespread American support for their right to participate in the workplace, they are, at the least, rendered invisible by policies that fail to include them individually or as part of a familial relationship. Worse yet, sometimes they are harassed verbally and, in extreme instances, are the targets of physical violence.

ATTITUDES TOWARD GAY MEN, LESBIANS, AND BISEXUAL PEOPLE

Why should one aspect of an individual's identity—sexual identity—be a catalyst for a wide variety of behaviors ranging from ostracism and antilocutions (the rhetoric of prejudice) to physical violence? Perhaps one reason is the continued perception that homosexuality is "abnormal"—such a perception contributes to a culture of sanctioned intolerance and hatred toward people who are lesbian and gay. Children receive a variety of messages from the media, family members, and teachers that tell them that it is not okay for someone to be gay or lesbian. In fact, teachers often remain silent when students taunt other students with antigay remarks (Dennis & Harlow, 1986). Children in kindergarten use words like "fag" and "queer" to tease other children. Within the context of sports, when a female or male does not conform to gender-appropriate behaviors, that person is harassed with such slurs as "dyke," "lezzie," "fag," and "queer."

Adults also display a range of attitudes and behaviors toward gay, lesbian, and bisexual people that range from being inwardly hostile and outwardly tolerant to inwardly and outwardly hostile to outwardly hostile but inwardly questioning one's own sexual identity. Researchers from a variety of disciplines who study gay men, lesbians, and bisexual people do so "almost exclusively within the areas of deviance, gender or sexuality" (Stein & Plummer, 1994, p. 180), and they have, perhaps unwittingly, also contributed to a culture in which homosexuality is perceived as "other" and "less than."

Sexual Identity Formation

Although researchers study how heterosexual people behave and interact with one another, few spend their time pondering the question, Why are people heterosexual? Because heterosexuality is considered the "norm," there is little support (financial and otherwise) for examining this question. Yet numerous researchers from across disciplines—medicine, psychology, genetics, sociology, and nursing—spend a great deal of time trying to understand the "causes" of homosexuality.[1] Indeed, one of the most notable of these researchers is Simon LeVay, whose 1993 book *The Sexual Brain* examined differences between gay and nongay men that can be traced to the brain. Few researchers, however, talk about the social construction of identity or about the social, economic, and political factors that shape their research and influence their funding. Stein and Plummer (1994) explained that in sociology, the study of gay, lesbian, and bisexual issues and people can be divided into two categories: "The first is primarily empirical; the second tends to be more theoretically oriented. The first tends to accept sexual categories; the second often problematizes these categories. . . . Useful as they can be, empirical studies have tended to be unreflective about the nature of sexuality as a social category" (p. 179).

Understanding the use of categories to organize our culture, especially in terms of sexuality, can be illuminating in discussions about gay, lesbian, and bisexual issues in the workplace. Among the numerous questions typically raised is whether being gay, lesbian, or bisexual is the result of biology or society (nature or nurture). Herdt and Boxer (1993) provided a response to this question that reflects

---

[1]Although Freud (1905/1962) studied homosexuality and those who were "polymorphously perverse," Bem (1996) noted that Freud also believed that heterosexuality should be studied. Bem cited Freud as suggesting that "[Heterosexuality] is also a problem that needs elucidation and is not a self-evident fact based upon an attraction that is ultimately of a chemical nature" (p. 320).

"the nature of sexuality as a category" and at the same time provides some empirical support for the origins of (sexual) desire:

> Sexual identity is more fundamentally concerned with the defini-
> tion of social and psychological reality. Identity is the culturally
> informed process of expressing desires in a social role and with
> socially shared cultural practices within a social context. We view
> sexual identity development as an interlocking and overlapping
> set of processes embedded in historical cultural contexts. These
> processes begin, we think, with a given, perhaps a biologically
> grounded form of "desire.".... Desires, we believe, originate from
> within the nature of the person; however, desires interact with
> cultural experiences and social learning to achieve particular set
> goals or end points. Desire is not a timeless universal either; both
> form and content are historically, culturally and psychologically
> negotiated throughout life.... it is fruitless to venture to search for
> "nature/nurture" dichotomies here. (p. 179)

Stein and Plummer (1994) provided some questions that might help us read and think critically about the current literature on gay, lesbian, and bisexual issues. However, it is also important to review some of the empirical literature about sexual identity. Several researchers in the past 16 years have written about lesbian and gay identity formation (Cass, 1979; Sophie, 1985; Troiden, 1989) and suggested that gay, lesbian, and bisexual identity formation is a developmental process. Typically, this process includes some variation of four stages: (1) self-awareness, which involves an acceptance or rejection of this aspect of identity; (2) a "coming-out" process (acknowledging this identity internally and externally to others); (3) an integration of this aspect of self (both in terms of personal and social identity); and, for some, (4) a connection to a larger, broader community in terms of activism, volunteer work, or involvement in gay-, lesbian-, or bisexual-identified activities (such as social groups, religious institutions, and sports groups). Clearly, not everyone follows this developmental process in the same way, but this process is typical. Because heterosexuality is the dominant sexual identity in this culture, anyone who is not heterosexual typically engages in some variation of a coming-out process. Not only must gay, lesbian, and bisexual people engage in a coming-out process, but many of their parents, friends, and family members must also experience a coming out. Taking it one step further, Winfield and Spielman (1995) asserted that companies, too, engage in a coming-out process in terms of gay, lesbian, and bisexual employee issues.

Homophobia, Invisibility, and Discrimination

Perhaps the most insidious issue that gay, lesbian, and bisexual people face in the context of work is invisibility. Herek (1996) referred to the lack of recognition of gay men and lesbians as *psychological heterosexism*—an attitude that not only are most people heterosexual but also that heterosexuality is preferable. Such attitudes and beliefs manifest themselves within individuals and within institutions through *homophobia*—an irrational fear and hatred of homosexual people. Winfield and Spielman (1995) suggested four types of homophobia:

1. *Personal homophobia* [involves the belief that] gay people are sick, immoral, inferior to straights or incomplete as men or women. . . . When people believe the image they project does not satisfy that of a "real man" or a "real woman" (whatever those terms mean to those particular individuals) and that they might be labeled "gay" because of it, this makes them defensive and leads to homophobic behavior. (p. 18, italics added)
2. *Interpersonal homophobia* [is] the fear, dislike, or hatred of people believed to be gay. . . . It is likely to show itself in the form of name-calling, verbal and physical harassment, or widespread acts of discrimination. (p. 18, italics added)
3. *Institutional homophobia* manifests itself in terms of policies, [and] resources. . . . Not explicitly listing sexual orientation in non-discrimination policies is homophobic. . . . Not giving equal access to benefits and resources of the organization to (same-sex) domestic partners is homophobic. Not using inclusive language such as "partner" or including the unmarried significant (same-sex) others in invitations to corporate events is homophobic. (p. 21, italics added)
4. *Cultural homophobia* . . . is the largely unstated but prevalent belief that everyone is straight or ought to be ("heterosexism" is another term for cultural homophobia). This standard is reinforced in almost every TV show or print advertisement, where virtually every character is straight and every sexual relationship involves a man and a woman. In the workplace, heterosexism is at the root of many of the molehills that become mountains in the minds of people who think that progressive policies toward their gay employees will be detrimental to the organization. (pp. 21–22, italics added)

Thus, homophobia is tied to culturally appropriate and culturally sanctioned gender and sexual identities. Regardless of whether one's sexual identity is made public, even the perception that one is "different" (that is, not blatantly heterosexual or not obviously a woman or a man) vis-à-vis gender and one's sexual identity is enough to provoke a variety of negative behaviors ranging from derogatory comments to murder.[2] Therefore, anyone who violates these culturally sanctioned norms relative to gender and sexual identity may be at risk for some form of harassment.

The workplace setting is a primary context for most, if not all, of the four forms of homophobia. Crude and derogatory references to gay men and lesbians are told as jokes in public and private gatherings, with all those present being assumed to be heterosexual. Moreover, negative attitudes toward gay men and lesbians have consistently been found to be more prevalent in the business world than in any other workplace environment. In their groundbreaking book, Friskopp and Silverstein (1995) interviewed more than 100 graduates from the Harvard Business School, their partners, and other family members between 1991 and 1994. Their book chronicles hundreds of

---

[2]The bulk of violence perpetrated against lesbian, gay, and bisexual people is committed by white males between ages 15 and 28 (Berrill, 1992).

firsthand descriptive and narrative accounts of comments, jokes, and behaviors that gay, lesbian, and bisexual people experienced at a variety of workplace contexts, the majority of which were upper-level management positions.

> The most commonly reported form of discrimination by far that gay professionals reported took the form of a hostile atmosphere created by antigay jokes or comments. Dorothy, who is highly closeted at work, said, "You know, being antigay is the last prejudice that it's OK to have. It's politically incorrect to do all sorts of things, but it's OK to bash gays." (p. 116)

The attitude that "it's okay to bash gays" takes many forms—antigay remarks made by teachers to their students in elementary and secondary school classrooms, antigay remarks heard on the playground as children call each other "queer" and "fag," antigay rhetoric used at armed services boot camps to humiliate new recruits who do not perform as well as they should, and antigay remarks heard in locker rooms used to shore up a conviction of masculinity. It addition, the subtle and sometimes not-so-subtle messages conveyed in this culture about gay men, lesbians, and men and women who are bisexual are primarily negative and based on stereotypes. Even images in popular culture are stereotypical, portraying gay men as effeminate and lesbians as masculine. Such homophobic attitudes not only negatively affect gay, lesbian, and bisexual employees in the workplace, but these attitudes also can contribute to a hostile work environment that affects every employee (Winfield & Spielman, 1995). Winfield and Spielman have suggested that homophobia

- Inhibits the ability of straight people to form close relationships with people of their own sex for fear of being labeled gay.
- Locks people into rigid gender-based roles that squelch creativity and self-expression.
- Compromises human integrity by pressuring people to treat others badly, actions that are contrary to their basic humanity.
- Combined with AIDS-phobia, . . . results in the lack of forthright sex education in business and in schools. These phobias are killing people.
- Prevents some gay people from developing an authentic self-identity and adds to the pressure to marry, which in turn places undue stress and trauma on themselves, their spouses and their children.
- Inhibits appreciation for other types of diversity, making it unsafe for everyone who has a unique trait not considered mainstream or dominant. (pp. 17–18)

Within the context of paid employment, satisfaction with one's work and workplace is an important predictor of success on the job. Perhaps even more salient to job satisfaction and success are the "perceptions" that one develops and brings to the workplace—perceptions about social interaction; support from colleagues and those in authority; and acceptance of the public self and, in some instances, of the private self as well. Satisfaction in the workplace affects other areas of one's life, and one's life affects one's satisfaction with work and the workplace. If acceptance at one's workplace is conditional, that is, based on socially acceptable norms of sexual and gender identity, then people who are gay, lesbian, or bisexual might feel the need to conceal part of their identity because of the fear that they might lose their jobs, that they might not be promoted, or that their coworkers would reject them. If gay, lesbian, or bisexual people do not feel safe (both emotionally and physically) in the workplace, if they have to be concerned about others' perceptions and the possibility that they might be harassed, how can they be expected to be "themselves," to be honest about who they are, and to be honest in their interactions with coworkers? The ramifications for concealing one's identity are twofold:

1. Psychological adjustment and feelings of well-being for people who are gay, lesbian, or bisexual are associated with being able to be honest about one's sexual identity; having to hide can be psychologically damaging and can, in turn, affect one's performance on the job.
2. The ability to be honest about one's sexual identity is often related to greater job satisfaction and, ultimately, to greater individual and perhaps even collective productivity. Ellis and Riggle (1995) found that gay men and lesbians working for companies with nondiscrimination policies that include sexual orientation were more satisfied with their jobs.

Work environments are typically divided along formal and informal lines. The formal environment of the workplace is dictated by policies that explicitly identify behaviors that are acceptable and not acceptable in the workplace (for example, no sexual harassment). The informal environment is governed by a set of culturally sanctioned norms that are implicitly conveyed through interactions with coworkers (for example, what people choose to share about themselves, their relationships, and their families); through comments about items in the news (such as gays in the military); and through signs and symbols that are conveyed in their workspace (for example, pictures, postcards, and cartoons). How many of us stop to think that the pictures we display on our desks or bulletin boards at work represent personal and political contexts? How many of us make the connection between the antigay rhetoric we espoused as children and the public sanctions that either directly or indirectly are imposed on people who are gay, lesbian, or bisexual?

For gay men, lesbians, and bisexual men and women, workplace discrimination takes a variety of forms: invisibility in the underlying assumption that everyone is heterosexual; fear of intimidation and of loss of one's job; silencing through the inability to share in discussions about one's personal life; the creation and implementation of policies that do not represent or include nonheterosexual marriages or relationships; and fear for one's personal safety as a result of physical threats of violence. These forms of discrimination can be exacerbated by other identity issues such as gender, race, HIV status, disability, and ethnicity. For example, women, people of color, and people with disabilities may experience multiple layers of discrimination beyond their sexual identities. If there is either blatant or tacit acceptance of antigay attitudes and behaviors, then it is probable that other forms of prejudice also are part of the informal workplace environment.

EMPLOYER RESPONSES TO GAY, LESBIAN, AND BISEXUAL ISSUES IN THE WORKPLACE

Although legal protection for gay, lesbian, and bisexual people from discrimination in the workplace has been enacted in nine states (California, Connecticut, Hawaii, Massachusetts, New Jersey, New York, Rhode Island, Vermont, and Wisconsin), a 1997 attempt to pass legislation at the federal level failed by a Senate vote of 49 to 50. The bipartisan Employment Non-Discrimination Act would have made it illegal for employers with more than 15 workers to discriminate against gay men, lesbians, and bisexual people in hiring, firing, promotion, and compensation policies and practices. One detractor of the bill, Robert Knight of the Family Research Council, argued that "under this bill, a man could come to work one day in a dress and high heels and say that his transvestism is an integral part of his sexual orientation" (cited in Reynolds, 1994, p. 8). Such comments illustrate the blurred boundaries between gender identity and sexual identity and the sanctions that are imposed against those who violate gender expectations. His comments also reveal the idea that certain attributes and behaviors are divided along gender lines. Warren Phillips, former chair of Dow Jones & Company, spoke the beliefs of the bill's proponents when he explained that, contrary to the opposition's main argument that such a bill would give gay men, lesbians, and bisexual people "special rights," the bill "is the right thing to do; it is the sensible thing to do; and it's the business-like thing to do" (cited in Reynolds, 1994, p. 8).

In addition to the personal costs associated with discrimination, there also are economic costs. Kovach (1995) suggested that

> as businesses face greater competition, both domestically and globally, companies will have to ensure that they're recruiting the most qualified candidates available.... It's self-defeating for a company to deliberately cut itself off from a particular talent pool just because of misgivings about that group's lifestyle.... [Another argument against discrimination] is based on the costs of discrimination on taxpayers, consumers and corporations. Taxpayers and corporations bear the cost for discrimination in that an estimated 42,000 gay workers are dismissed each year due to sexual orientation. This translates into a $47 million loss in terms of training expenditures and unemployment benefits. (p. 49)

About 25 percent of *Fortune* 1,000 corporations have some official personnel policy that prohibits discrimination against gay and lesbian workers. A variety of companies and organizations—Adolph Coors, Walt Disney, Sun Microsystems, IBM, Lotus, Microsoft, Times-Mirror,

Knight-Ridder, and many universities (for example, University of Iowa, University of Minnesota, Harvard University, and Brown University)—have implemented nondiscrimination policies. Many of these organizations also provide benefits for domestic partners. In some instances, the gay, lesbian, or bisexual domestic partners must sign affidavits that attest to their being in a primary relationship, to jointly owning a house or other property, and to having been together in a monogamous relationship for at least one year. Conversely, heterosexual couples who are at least 18 years old (in some states even younger) and who have known each other for only a day (or even less) can get married; they will automatically be entitled to their spouse's health, death, and social security benefits; and they typically do not have to provide proof of their marriage when they complete benefits paperwork. This type of discrepancy is just one of many ways that gay men, lesbians, and bisexual people experience discrimination in the workplace.

Some employers, recognizing that policies are not enough, now offer diversity training to their employees. Knight-Ridder "is running 'sexual orientation in the workplace' seminars at all its newspapers. There are no exceptions" (Fitzgerald, 1996, p. 12). Sun Microsystems provides in-house training programs on diversity, and the company sponsors focus groups for African Americans, Hispanics, people with disabilities, women, and gay men and lesbians. "The focus groups, working with their friends and support organizations outside the company, take a proactive role in bringing minority applicants to hiring managers who, at this point, are no longer exclusively white males. The focus groups are proactive on issues within the company once the minorities are hired" (Major, 1993, p. 13). These are only a few examples of companies and organizations that are taking a proactive role in changing the workplace environment and workplace attitudes toward people who are gay, lesbian, or bisexual.[3]

HOW ORGANIZATION LEADERS CAN IMPROVE THE WORKPLACE ENVIRONMENT

Managers and human resources professionals can make significant contributions in influencing knowledge, attitudes, and behaviors concerning gay men, lesbians, and bisexual people. Social work administrators, as one example, can assume a variety of roles—direct service provider, educator, administrator, advocate, colleague, friend and ally—all of which can directly or indirectly influence how people perceive and interact with those who are gay, lesbian, or bisexual. However, before raising awareness within the organization, managers and human resources professionals must assess their own knowledge, attitudes, and behaviors concerning these employees. They have to

---

[3]Yet, as one human resources manager at Xerox Corporation noted, "No matter how the company as a whole treats you, it's the idiot in the cube next to you who will make your life hell" (Swisher, 1996, p. 53).

ask themselves difficult questions and be able to accept that the answers may not be what they expect—that they are perhaps more or less open-minded than they thought (see Figure 9-1).

The purpose of the exercise in Figure 9-1 is not to have one internalize guilt because he or she has some "politically incorrect" feelings and attitudes; rather, it is to help one understand how he or she feels and thinks. Having stereotypes and negative feelings is not an indictment of one as a person—indeed, given the level of antigay sentiment and homophobia in this culture, it seems highly unlikely that anyone could be immune to the rhetoric heard in school, in religious institutions, at home, and in the media. The real issue, having examined your own feelings, is honestly deciding if you can and want to work with people who are gay, lesbian, or bisexual. If you decide that you cannot (that is, that you cannot be a supportive, nurturing manager, advocate, or ally), for whatever reasons, then you should make it clear to your colleagues that you do not want to be in these roles. If you want to work with gay, lesbian, or bisexual clients but have some concerns (for example, you are not sure how to be an advocate or ally), seek support from other colleagues or friends who have such experience.

In the role of a human resources and employee assistance professional, one can provide support, counseling, and referrals around a variety of issues. These issues include coming out to oneself, family members, and friends; dealing with harassment and homophobia on the street and in the workplace; managing a dual identity; and finding or enhancing one's voice to ask for nondiscrimination policies in the work such as domestic partner benefits. In addition to counseling

Figure 9-1

Understanding Feelings and Attitudes about Gay Men, Lesbians, and Bisexual People

Read the following questions, and give your honest response to each.

1. What are your thoughts and feelings about working with gay men, lesbians, or bisexual people?
2. What are your thoughts and feelings about seeing gay men, lesbians, or bisexual people being affectionate with one another?
3. What are your thoughts about gay men, lesbians, and bisexual people and issues of mental illness?
4. What are your thoughts about lesbians, gay men, and bisexual people and issues of morality?
5. What are your thoughts and feelings about teachers in elementary and junior high school who are openly gay, lesbian, or bisexual?
6. What are your thoughts about gay men, lesbians, and bisexual people as parents, adoptive parents, or foster parents?
7. What are your thoughts about working with 13- and 14-year-olds who self-identify as gay, lesbian, or bisexual or who are questioning their sexual identity?

and referrals, you can be available as an ally or can provide a safe space for gay, lesbian, and bisexual people by displaying signs or symbols in your workspace (a rainbow sticker or flag; a lambda symbol; a pink triangle; or information about gay, lesbian, bisexual, and other inclusive organizations).

Managers and administrators can take a proactive role in changing the workplace environment by developing and lobbying for policies that include gay men, lesbians, and bisexual people (for example, nondiscrimination policies and domestic partner benefits). You can also develop policies that lead to a workplace environment free of antigay jokes and slurs. In addition to changing the workplace environment, you can strive to change attitudes and behaviors concerning gay men, lesbians, and bisexual people by providing in-service diversity training as an integral part of a broad-based continuing education program for service providers and administrators. This training should focus on how to work with and be responsive to the needs of a variety of gay, lesbian, and bisexual people. Topics should include coming out; parenting (foster, adoptive, and natural); issues affecting elderly gay, lesbian, and bisexual people; working with gay, lesbian, and bisexual youths; issues relevant to people of color who are gay, lesbian, or bisexual; and issues surrounding HIV/AIDS prevention and intervention strategies.

Education is essential. Managers and human resources professionals should know about current issues affecting gay, lesbian, and bisexual people, for instance, the status of nondiscrimination legislation; legal precedents for gay, lesbian, and bisexual single- and two-parent adoptions; and the laws relating to emancipated minors as they affect gay, lesbian, and bisexual youths. In addition, managers and human resources professionals should become familiar with a variety of national organizations: Parents and Friends of Lesbians and Gays, the Human Rights Campaign, the National Gay and Lesbian Task Force, Lambda Legal Defense and Education Fund, the National Center for Lesbian Rights, and state and local organizations. Resources can be found in local libraries and on the World Wide Web, which has many sites about gay, lesbian, and bisexual issues generally and about work-related issues specifically. Workers familiar with these issues should tell colleagues that they are a resource for information and referrals concerning gay, lesbian, and bisexual issues. In the role of educator, managers and human resources professionals should teach others to think critically and to question commonly held beliefs about gender and sexual identity; challenge stereotypes and myths about gay, lesbian, and bisexual people; and ask why society perpetuates and reinforces rigid categories of gender and sexuality.

Perhaps the most important role that managers and human resources professionals can play is that of an advocate. Advocates work on both the personal–private and political–public levels to effect change. At the personal–private level, you can provide counseling, support, and referrals; at the public–political level, you can dispel myths and stereotypes and offer accurate information. An advocate can perhaps assist those who need to prepare testimony for hearings or help with ongoing emotional support and legal referrals.

CONCLUSION

Our purpose in this chapter has been to identify and address the workplace issues and concerns of gay men, lesbians, and bisexual people and the ways in which social workers can become aware of and responsive to these issues. Social workers, through the different roles that they can assume, can make a difference in the lives of people who are gay, lesbian, or bisexual. For most of us, work requires such a large commitment of time and is such an integral part of our lives that it seems critically important for workplace managers and professionals to assume a proactive role in changing the workplace environment and in changing attitudes about and behaviors toward people whose sexual–affectional orientation is not heterosexual. Gay, lesbian, and bisexual people should be able to take for granted that they work in an environment free of harassment and discrimination, that they can speak freely about their partner or how they spent their weekend, that they can display photographs of their partner on their desk, and that benefits will be extended to their partner without requiring proof of their relationship. Such an environment will only materialize when attitudes and behaviors change and when policies support a workplace environment that is visibly supportive and inclusive of gay, lesbian, and bisexual people.

REFERENCES

Bem, D. J. (1996). Exotic becomes erotic: A developmental theory of sexual orientation. *Psychological Review, 103*, 320–335.

Berrill, K. T. (1992). Anti-gay violence and victimization in the United States: An overview. In G. M. Herek & K. T. Berrill (Eds.), *Hate crimes: Confronting violence against lesbians and gay men* (pp. 19–45). Newbury Park, CA: Sage Publications.

Cass, V. (1979). Homosexual identity formation: A theoretical model. *Journal of Homosexuality, 4*, 219–235.

Dennis, D. L., & Harlow, R. E. (1986). Gay youth and the right to education. *Yale Law & Policy Review, 4*, 447–478.

Ellis, A. L., & Riggle, E.D.B. (1995). The relation of job satisfaction and degree of openness about one's sexual orientation for lesbians and gay men. *Journal of Homosexuality, 30*, 75–85.

Fitzgerald, M. (1996, October 12). Workplace "out"-reach. *Editor and Publisher*, pp. 12–13, 52.

Friskopp, A., & Silverstein, S. (1995). *Straight jobs, gay lives: Gay and lesbian professionals, the Harvard Business School, and the American workplace.* New York: Charles Scribner's Sons.

Freud, S. (1962). *Three essays on the theory of sexuality.* New York: Basic Books. Original work published 1905

Herdt, G., & Boxer, A. (1993). *Children of horizons: How gay and lesbian teens are leading a new way out of the closet.* Boston: Beacon Press.

Herek, G. (1996). Psychological heterosexism in the United States. In A. D'Augelli & C. Patterson (Eds.), *Lesbian, gay and bisexual identities over the life span* (pp. 321–346). New York: Oxford University Press.

Kaplan, D. A., & Klaidman, D. (1996, June 3). Gays: Winning a battle, not a war. *Newsweek*, p. 24.

Kivel, B. D. (1996). *In on the outside, out on the inside: Lesbian, gay, and bisexual youth, identity and leisure.* Unpublished doctoral dissertation, University of Georgia, Athens.

Kovach, K. A. (1995, August). ENDA promises to ban employment discrimination for gays. *Personnel Journal*, pp. 42–55.

LeVay, S. (1993). *The sexual brain.* Cambridge, MA: MIT Press.

Major, M. J. (1993). Sun sets pace in work force diversity. *Public Relations Journal, 49*(6), 12, 13, 32.

Overlooked Opinions. (1992). *Gay Market Report, 3.* Chicago: Author.

Reynolds, L. (1994). Proposed bill would ban workplace discrimination based on sexual orientation. *HR Focus, 71*(10), 1, 8.

Seck, E. T., Finch, W. A., Mor-Barak, M. E., & Poverny, L. M. (1993). Managing a diverse workforce. *Administration in Social Work, 17*(2), 67–79.

Sedgewick, E. K. (1990). *Epistemology of the closet.* Berkeley: University of California Press.

Sophie, J. (1985). A critical examination of stage theories of lesbian identity development. *Journal of Homosexuality, 12,* 39–51.

Stein, A., & Plummer, K. (1994). "I can't even think straight": Queer theory and the missing sexual revolution in sociology. *Sociological Theory, 12,* 178–187.

Swisher, K. (1996, July–August). Coming out in corporate America. *Working Woman,* pp. 50–53, 78–80.

Troiden, R. (1989). The formation of homosexual identities. In G. Herdt (Ed.), *Gay and lesbian youth* (pp. 43–74). London: Harrington Park Press.

Winfield, L., & Spielman, S. (1995). *Straight talk about gays in the workplace: Creating an inclusive, productive environment for everyone in your organization.* New York: American Management Association.

10 The Americans with Disabilities Act and Inclusive Personnel and Employment Policy

Richard O. Salsgiver

The Americans with Disabilities Act (ADA) of 1990 is considered one of the most comprehensive pieces of civil rights legislation in U.S. history. With the passage of the ADA, Congress acknowledged that over 43 million Americans with disabilities have been subjected to serious and pervasive discrimination in employment and services provision.

The ADA has five parts. Title I addresses issues of discrimination in employment; it deals with the definition of disability, outlines reasonable accommodation in the workplace, provides guidelines for undue hardship criteria for an employer not providing accommodation, and defines essential functions of the job. Title II applies the ADA to public entities, including public transportation. Title III brings the Civil Rights Act of 1964 and the Rehabilitation Act of 1973 into the private sector for people with disabilities. Title III makes discrimination against people with disabilities illegal in public accommodations and in commercial facilities. If services are provided, they must be accessible and equal. Title IV mandates the establishment of telecommunications relay services. Title V contains several miscellaneous provisions and exclusions (Jarrow, 1992). Title I has the most direct bearing on employment issues.

Shapiro (1993) traced the passage of the ADA directly to the civil rights movement of people with disabilities. The independent living movement, a cornerstone of the disability civil rights movement and a product of the turmoil of the 1960s, challenged the two historical models of conceptualizing disability: the moral and the medical model. Both models feed the stereotyping and social prejudice around disability. The moral model is the oldest way of viewing disability. The moral model is the belief that disability is directly linked to sin and evil. Longmore (1993) showed that the moral paradigm of understanding disability views people with disabilities as incongruous with the spiritual order of the universe. Albrecht (1992) indicated that the origin of the moral model can be found with early Neolithic tribes, who thought members of the tribe with physical, mental, or social attributes not considered normal were possessed by spirits. They freed the evil spirits by drilling holes in their skulls. The moral model still remains well entrenched in the United States.

Out of the European Enlightenment came the perspective that all humans could be perfected—even humans with disabilities. Longmore (1993) pointed out that although on the surface this medical model appears benevolent, it is in reality insidious. In the medical model, people with disabilities are presented with the dilemma of being measured against biological perfection, even though it is an impossible objective. Thus, people with disabilities inevitably never measure up and require constant supervision by medical professionals.

The independent living movement offered a constructive alternative to the traditional models of viewing people with disabilities. The paradigm of independent living views the locus of the problems of people with disabilities not with the person but with the social and environmental structure of society. Fine and Asch (1988) stressed that the behavior, self-concept, educational achievement, and economic success of people with disabilities can be understood only by looking at people with disabilities as a marginalized group that is subjected to the discrimination found in social environments. This framework finds its logical conclusion in the ADA, which stated under its Findings and Purposes that

> Individuals with disabilities are a discrete and insular minority who have been faced with restrictions and limitations, subjected to a history of purposeful unequal treatment, and relegated to a position of political powerlessness in our society, based on characteristics that are beyond the control of such individuals and resulting from stereotypic assumptions not truly indicative of the individual ability of such individuals to participate in, and contribute to, society. (Section 2)

In framing a personnel policy inclusive of people with disabilities, administrators and managers should take into account both the history of disability and the ADA. Within that synthesis, seven components of a personnel policy should be addressed: recruitment, application, interviewing, reasonable accommodation, grievance procedure, promotion and advancement, and health benefits.

RECRUITMENT

Announcements of job openings should be developed with the ADA in mind. Announcements should be supported by relevant job descriptions; if a person currently in the position does not in fact perform the essential functions described in the vacancy announcement, if he or she performs them infrequently, or if the position is significantly different from the one described in the announcement, then the outdated description can be a detriment in proving compliance with the ADA. If the job announcement clearly reflects the essential functions of the job, then men and women with disabilities can accurately assess whether they are truly qualified for the position. This saves the employer the time and money for interviewing what appear to be qualified candidates who, in reality, cannot perform the work.

Job announcements should be available in a variety of media, including recorded form, enlarged print, and Braille for people who are blind or visually impaired. Job announcements should include a nondiscrimination statement including people with disabilities, a statement concerning willingness to provide reasonable accommodation if requested, and a TDD (telecommunication device for the deaf; increasingly called a TT or text telephone) number to allow deaf people to make inquiries about the position (Lee, 1995).

Good personnel policy seeks to hold recruitment activities in accessible facilities. Employers holding recruitment fairs or having recruitment days need to ensure that prospective employees with disabilities can be present; for example, working elevators should give access to the area if the event is held in a multilevel facility and restrooms must be wheelchair accessible. Material presented should be in a variety of media for different disabilities. A certified American Sign Language (ASL) interpreter should be present for presentations, and videocassette-recorded materials should be closed captioned for people who are deaf or hard of hearing.

A proactive personnel or employment policy seeks people with disabilities in the recruitment process. There are hundreds of organizations across the United States that have access to qualified people with disabilities; many can be found through the Internet or in the myriad publications from the federal government on the ADA and the employment of people with disabilities. Each state has a department of vocational rehabilitation that can provide not only skilled and qualified people with disabilities as candidates for positions but also linkages to other organizations that may have pools of qualified people with disabilities. At a minimum, employers should send job announcements to their local state department of rehabilitation, and ideally, employers should maintain an ongoing relationship with this department.

APPLICATION

A comprehensive personnel policy inclusive of people with disabilities as well as the ADA requires that employers make the job application process accessible (Equal Employment Opportunity Commission [EEOC] & U.S. Department of Justice [DOJ], 1991). Accessibility may require assisting people who have visual, learning, or cognitive disabilities to fill out application forms. In the job announcement, the employer should provide information about the application form and process so that applicants with disabilities can request accommodation as needed.

As detailed in the ADA handbook (EEOC & DOJ, 1991), the employer cannot ask on an employment application

- whether the applicant has been treated for particular conditions or diseases
- whether the applicant has ever been hospitalized

- whether the applicant has been treated for any psychiatric or mental condition or has ever seen a psychiatrist or psychologist
- about any health-related condition or physical defects that would prohibit or interfere with the candidate's ability to perform the job
- for any information on the number of absences from work that the candidate has had in previous employments
- whether the applicant is taking any prescribed drugs or has been treated for drug addiction or alcoholism
- whether the candidate has filed for worker's compensation insurance.

There is one exception to the pre-employment inquiry prohibition required by the ADA: An employer can ask a person who has requested accommodation for a hidden disability to provide documentation of the disability and the need for accommodation (Nester, 1994).

Aside from the standard background information on work experience, address and telephone, and education, the employer can ask whether and how the candidate can perform specific job functions. If the employer has an affirmative action policy including people with disabilities, then it is appropriate to invite these individuals to identify themselves on a separate form or other method to satisfy an affirmative action policy or requirement. This information must remain confidential and not be tied in any way to the applicant or his or her application.

If the application process requires testing, policy should incorporate several points. All tests, whether they measure aptitude, physical agility, intelligence, or specific skills, must test for essential functions of the position. They must be accurate predictors of the candidate's ability to perform the job. Examination policy must avoid tests that screen out certain classes of people with disabilities, such as those with learning or physical disabilities. If tests, by their nature and that of the essential functions they are testing, do screen out certain disabilities, the employer must show that these relate directly to the essential functions of the job (Nester, 1994).

Just as with the process of filling out applications, testing procedures should contain a reasonable accommodation component. For example, if an applicant has a learning disability that affects his or her ability to read, then the test should be given orally. Some people with disabilities may require extra time to complete the test. If the test requires hearing and the applicant, before the test, has requested accommodation, then policy should allow the hiring of an ASL-certified interpreter. Policy should prohibit testing in areas with inaccessible environments (Nester, 1994).

The ADA prohibits medical testing before an offer of employment and establishes standards for its use in other ways (EEOC & DOJ, 1991). Everyone applying for the position must be required to take the exam. All medical information obtained in the exam must be held in confidence; it must be kept in a separate medical file and cannot be a part of the candidate's application or personnel file. If the candidate is hired, the information ascertained from the medical exam can be shared with the employee's supervisor to establish accommodation, if needed, and with public safety personnel. Employers also may share this information with insurance personnel in the process of administering health insurance plans (Nester, 1994).

INTERVIEWING

Because of the history of how society views disability and people who have disabilities, interviewers' conscious or unconscious views about such individuals may result in important information being overlooked in the interviewing process. Fear, apprehension, and paternalism often are telegraphed through body language. These attitudes and feelings prevent the employer from completing the primary task of interviewing, which is to determine the best qualified person for the position. All professionals interacting with people with disabilities need to examine their own feelings and attitudes regarding people with disabilities (Mackelprang & Salsgiver, 1996).

Some guidelines in the interviewing process are helpful in creating the interactive bridges important in gathering data for making good employment decisions. Morrissey (1991) established six rules of etiquette in interviewing people who have disabilities:

1. When interviewing a person with a disability, look directly at him or her. This is not only a sign of respect; avoiding eye contact increases tension. Eye contact also should be used with people who are blind.
2. If it is apparent that communication may be difficult, ask the person with the disability the best way of communicating with him or her. Usually the person is comfortable and willing to explain the most appropriate way.
3. If the person with a disability is accompanied by a helper or an interpreter, speak directly to the person with the disability and not to the helper or interpreter.
4. Do not assume that a person with a disability needs assistance. If it looks like the candidate needs help with, for example, opening a door, ask if you can be of assistance. Most people with disabilities have mastered mobility tasks; in fact, an unsolicited interference by another person may result in the person not being able to accomplish the task or, worse yet, in an accident.
5. Avoid telling an applicant that you "admire his or her courage" or that you are "sorry" that this "horrible" thing has happened. Most people with disabilities simply wish to live like everyone else. They do not consider their lives particularly heroic or tragic, but do what they must to accomplish personal and career goals.
6. Do not avoid asking certain interview questions because you assume that the candidate is too sensitive or fragile. All pertinent interview questions should be asked in a straightforward manner.

How does the interviewer walk this apparently perilous tightrope? An example may be helpful. A manager must interview a person who has the use of one arm for a job that requires driving a car. The interviewer can ask if the person has a valid driver's license, the status of the person's accident record, and how the candidate would perform any special aspects of driving that are required with or without accommodation. The interviewer cannot ask about the loss of the one arm or how the person can drive with just one arm.

As another example, a manager must interview a person who uses a wheelchair for the position of mail room clerk. The job description states that the employee is responsible for receiving and sorting mail and for distributing it by cart to many buildings several blocks apart. The employee must receive incoming boxes that weigh up to 50 pounds, and these must be placed on shelves up to six feet high. The interviewer cannot ask whether a wheelchair user can get the mail to the various buildings and lift the boxes onto the shelves. The interviewer can ask whether or not the person can perform the tasks with or without accommodation and exactly how he or she would go about it.

Managers responsible for interviewing need to be aware of communication guidelines related to specific disabilities. In interviewing people who are deaf or hard of hearing, always look directly at the candidate. For a person who can read lips, speak slowly and distinctly and avoid gesturing around the face. If the person uses a sign language interpreter, the interpreter should be positioned next to the person doing the interviewing so that the candidate can shift back and forth between the interpreter and the interviewer. Always avoid the term "deaf and dumb"; it is inaccurate and offensive. It is not necessary to avoid using the word "hear" with a candidate who is deaf. It is appropriate to tap the person on the shoulder or to wave a hand to get visual contact. Speaking loudly around a person who is deaf or hard of hearing is not helpful.

For applicants who are blind you may extend an arm to help guide the candidate to a chair. Introduce everyone involved in the interview, because a person who is blind may not be aware of all those present. In the introduction, indicate where other participants are sitting in the room. As with candidates who are deaf, people who are blind have little need for you to speak in a loud voice.

Do not assume that an applicant with a mobility disability needs help. Provide assistance only if the candidate requests it, but do tell the candidate the location of elevators, ramps, and accessible restrooms.

If while interviewing a person who has a speech impairment you do not understand a response to a question, ask the candidate to repeat the answer. Do not hesitate to follow up on an answer that does not make sense or seems confusing. Usually, if you can relax while listening, you will become more accustomed to the sound and pattern of the candidate's speech (Morrissey, 1991).

It is important for both the employer and the candidate that an honest appraisal takes place in the interview process. The employer needs to know that the candidate can perform the job; the candidate needs to know whether the job will allow success. Paternalism is as much a part of discrimination against people with disabilities as other actions. Pity is never productive for either the employer or the candidate.

REASONABLE ACCOMMODATION

A comprehensive personnel policy that includes people with disabilities must have a reasonable accommodation component; certain ADA requirements apply. Reasonable accommodation encompasses all aspects of employment; therefore, policies must include the application and interview process, hiring, retention, and promotion. The limits on reasonable accommodation are dictated by the concept of undue hardship, which involves an accommodation that is too expensive or significantly difficult for the employer to provide (EEOC & DOJ, 1991). Several studies (Lee, 1995), however, have shown that more than half of the accommodations made by employers cost nothing, and about 15 percent cost less than $500. Further, tax credits are available to employers who eliminate environmental obstacles in the workplace; provide assistive devices and other accommodations, including interpreters for people who are deaf; and seek to employ people with disabilities. In addition, the worker has the right to pay for all or part of an accommodation if the employer finds it to be an undue hardship. As part of a sound policy, employers should develop accommodation guidelines in terms of cost and difficulty based on their budget, the number of employees, and the impact on the daily operation of the business or agency.

Policy needs to be developed that will determine how an employee receives reasonable accommodation. What exams will be required? Who in the company will make the decision? What type of accommodation will be provided? How will the position be evaluated to determine which essential functions will be accommodated? Input from the employee with the disability is crucial in determining the nature of any accommodation. Conferring with the employee is the most significant component in implementing accommodation policy (Johnson, 1992).

Accommodating Workers with Musculoskeletal Disabilities

In general, musculoskeletal disabilities encompass significant impairment to muscles, bones, joints, or supporting connective tissue that resulted from disease or injury. Musculoskeletal disabilities usually require some mobility adaptation, such as crutches or a wheelchair.

Workplace accommodation for people with musculoskeletal disabilities can be of two types: (1) environmental–architectural and (2) job restructuring. Environmental–architectural accommodations can include redesigning the employee's work area, redesigning equipment or tools, or increasing access to and within the building in which the employee works. Job restructuring might include the assignment of other employees to assist the worker with the disability, the reassignment of the worker with a disability to a vacant position with a different and more compatible job description, or offering a flexible work schedule. Job restructuring also might include allowing the worker to accomplish part of the essential function of the job within his or her home (Morosky, 1994).

Accommodating Workers Who Are Blind or Visually Impaired

Accommodation for people who are blind or visually impaired in the application and interviewing process can include a variety of components. On initial contact, the employer should ask the applicant how he or she would prefer accomplishing the necessary application tasks. Does the applicant want the application mailed? Does the applicant wish to come to the office for assistance in completing the application form? In setting up the interview, the employer should ask if the applicant needs directions to the office. If the applicant will be using public transportation, the employer should inform the applicant of the nearest stop and the directions to the office from there. When the applicant arrives, the interviewer should offer assistance in moving to the interview room by asking whether the applicant would like to take the interviewer's arm. If the applicant needs assistance, he or she will lightly grasp the interviewer's arm just above the elbow and will follow one step behind. If the applicant uses a guide dog, the dog will follow (the interviewer should avoid petting the dog or distracting it in any way). When the applicant and the interviewer get to the interview room, the interviewer should place the person's hand on the back of the appropriate chair.

Accommodation on the job for people who are blind or visually impaired may be relatively simple and low tech or can include sophisticated computer hardware and software. Low-tech examples of accommodation include Velcro fasteners on protective clothing. A dot of silicon adhesive on switches or control knobs that need constant monitoring permits a person who is blind or visually impaired to use electronic machines with controls. Enlarged print or Braille labels make file folders readable and soft drink selection at the vending machine possible. Stripping codes using masking tape can help identify parts on shelves.

High-tech accommodation involves mostly computers. Hardware and software accommodation can include enlarged print on an enlarged screen, voice synthesizers, and Braille tactile boards. An optical scanner along with a voice synthesizer makes reading of regular print possible. Currently, most access technology is in the DOS operating format, and cost varies from $500 to $15,000. Most computer vendors have access to accommodating hardware and software (Dickson, 1994).

Accommodating Workers with a Cognitive Disability

People with a cognitive disability have difficulty learning new things, making generalizations from past events, picking up social cues, or expressing themselves in speech or writing. They generally have difficulty working with numbers. In the application process, people with cognitive disabilities may need a simplified version of the application and assistance in completing it. In the interviewing process, communication must be direct and simple. The applicant may need to see others performing the job. The interview should be as short as possible and in an environment with minimal distractions.

Accommodation on the job can take a variety of forms. Most likely, workers with a cognitive disability will require extra assistance in learning the various components of the job. Accommodation will require that the supervisor take extra time in job training. Training will require that the overall job be broken down to clearly discernible and easily understood pieces; these pieces need to be placed in an easily understood sequence resulting in successful job performance. Language used to instruct about job duties must be clear and direct. Special labeling may be helpful. An important aspect of accommodation for cognitively disabled employees is the involvement of coworkers in giving support. Assistance probably will be required to help the person with a cognitive disability fit into the worker milieu, including the worker socialization process (Bruyere & Golden, 1994).

Accommodating Workers Who Are Deaf or Hard of Hearing

In the application and interview process, accommodation for people who are deaf or hearing impaired takes several forms. Because many people who are deaf are fluent in ASL and not English, reading and comprehending applications may be difficult. Accommodation could include allowing the person to take the application from the office to find assistance in its completion. More time than the standard could be allowed for its completion. An ASL interpreter could be provided to answer any questions the applicant may have. In the interviewing process, the nature of accommodation will depend on the nature of the disability. For an applicant who is hard of hearing, a quiet, well-lighted interviewing room is adequate. The applicant may have a listening device that must be used in the interview.

Accommodation in the work environment need not be expensive but will take knowledge and concern. The working environment should be well-lighted, and environmental noise should be kept at a minimum. The work space can be arranged in such a way that the worker can easily see someone entering the area. The employer should have access to the use of an ASL interpreter when needed. Supervisors and coworkers should be supported in learning sign language, and the employer could offer onsite training classes at minimal expense. The employer needs to ensure that TDDs or TTs are available. In some areas, social services agencies serving people who are deaf or hard of hearing can help in obtaining these at little or no cost. Employers should be knowledgeable about state telecommunication relay services and should train employees in its use (the 800 number for this service is listed in local telephone directories). The employer should consider using e-mail or fax machines for office communication. As part of an emergency plan, the employer should provide visual and auditory mechanisms on telephones and fire alarm systems that alert workers to dangers (University of Arkansas, 1994).

Accommodating Workers with a Psychiatric Disability

Accommodating workers with psychiatric disabilities centers on fairness, balance, consistency, and open communication, all of which can be accomplished with good management and supervision. Supervision must support strengths and abilities. Criticism must be balanced with positive feedback. Performance expectations must be presented clearly and precisely. Supervisors must be accessible. In addition to good supervision, accommodation can include a flexible work schedule and breaks; time off for medical appointments; and environmental changes that result in a quieter, more comfortable working environment (Mancuso, 1994).

Accommodating Workers with Learning Disabilities

Learning disabilities and attention deficit hyperactivity disorder (ADHD) are neurologically based. Workers with learning disabilities have difficulty receiving information from the senses, processing the information, and communicating knowledge to others. Usually, people who are learning disabled will have problems with reading, writing, or doing math. A worker with ADHD will find it difficult to stay in one place and put full attention on a task.

People with learning disabilities may require alternative methods of reading. Using computers with a voice synthesizer or recorded tapes may be helpful. Workers who read slowly can be allowed extra time to do so. Workers with auditory perception problems require an environment with minimal background noise. A supervisor should take extra time to make eye contact when conveying instructions. The worker should be asked to repeat the instructions to ensure that he or she has processed the information correctly.

If the worker has difficulty spelling, spell-checking computer software or a handheld spell-checker accommodates this problem. Software that corrects grammar also is available. Auditory alarms, such as buzzers, and computer software with calendar reminders help workers who have difficulty managing time. A worker with ADHD may need a work environment relatively free of noise and distraction. Allowing a flexible schedule to work in the evening or at home may be a reasonable accommodation. Hyperactivity may require frequent short breaks (Brown, 1994).

GRIEVANCE PROCEDURE

Title II of the ADA states that "a public entity that employs 50 or more people shall adopt and publish grievance procedures" to resolve complaints around alleged prohibitions of the ADA law (Regulation Section 35.107). This requirement is not extended to employers in the private sector, but sound personnel policy dictates that an employer have a grievance procedure to address alleged discrimination against individuals with disabilities in the workplace.

Grievance procedures can vary greatly. For disability issues, the process should begin with the immediate supervisor. If the issue is not resolved at that level, the problem is generally presented to a higher level of administration. If the problem remains, a committee of representatives from management and workers may review the problem. If the employee remains unsatisfied, the next step would be for the employee to file an EEOC administrative grievance.

Most public- and private-sector employers who have unions have a contract-based grievance procedure. In most cases this procedure can be modified to deal with alleged issues of work problems or discrimination against employees with disabilities. The union and the employer may create a joint committee of representatives from management and labor to deal with ADA complaints and other personnel issues concerning workers with disabilities. In addition, the committee may function as part of the mechanism by which reasonable accommodation is decided. The committee could research available accommodations and how these would affect other workers. An additional duty may include reviewing job descriptions to ensure that the essential functions presented are clear and pertinent (Johnston, 1994).

PROMOTION AND ADVANCEMENT

Both sound management and the ADA dictate that personnel policy include workers with disabilities in the process of job advancement and promotion. This translates into accessibility. The pillars of promotion are the skills and knowledge acquired in experience and training. For a person with a disability to take advantage of training, it must be accessible. Making training accessible may include rewriting training curricula to simplify formats. All training rooms, whether within the employer's facility or at another location, should be wheelchair accessible. The ADA prohibits the contracting of services by the employer that are inaccessible to people with disabilities; this certainly applies to training. Alternatives to printed materials, such as Braille or tape recordings, should be available. Sign language interpreters should be available to deaf workers participating in the training. All videotaped materials should be captioned. Training should occur in an irritant-free environment.

Many seminal writers on organizational theory and practice, including Drucker (1985), Etzioni (1975), and Simon (1976), stressed the importance of the normative socialization component in the work arena. An important variable in promotion is the ability to network. Networking depends to a large degree on socialization. For workers with disabilities, accessibility to the places that colleagues and supervisors congregate is important. Therefore, the company cafeteria and employer-sponsored social events must be accessible. Company trips should include accessible transportation and lodging. A comprehensive personnel policy inclusive of employees with disabilities recognizes all the arenas that make up a successful work experience. Performance appraisal criteria should reward managers and supervisors for their accommodation of workers with disabilities in these social arenas.

HEALTH BENEFITS

The ADA prohibits discrimination in hiring based on a disability and also prohibits employers from making contractual arrangements with an organization providing services that discriminates against people with disabilities. These restrictions can manifest in personnel policy in two ways. First, personnel decisions regarding people with disabilities cannot be made based on whether they would be covered by an existing health plan. An employer's decision on whether to hire a person with a disability or a person who has a family member with a disability cannot be based on the impact on the employer's health insurance costs. Second, the law and a sound personnel policy requires that people with disabilities have equal access to health insurance. Health insurance companies cannot screen out coverage of certain classes of disability. Insurers and health maintenance organizations can make health-related distinctions based on actuarial data, risk assessment, and claims data. The burden of proof and legal obligation lies with the employer (EEOC, 1993).

QUESTIONS THAT EMPLOYERS MUST ANSWER

An employer interested in creating and implementing a comprehensive personnel policy that includes people with disabilities and also complies with the ADA must answer several questions. First, have job descriptions been reviewed in the past year? Do descriptions exist for each type or class of position? Do descriptions reflect the essential functions of the job?

Second, have procedures used in recruiting, advertising for, and selecting employees been reviewed in the past year for disability inclusion? Are job advertisements accessible to people with hearing or vision impairments? Do advertisements include a TDD/TT number? Are recruitment offices accessible for people with disabilities? Are announcements, advertisements, and other recruitment notices located and available in alternative formats? Is there a set of procedures in place that can handle requests for reasonable accommodation specific to the application and interview process, and is it advertised?

Third, have application forms been reviewed in the past year? Are application procedures and interview processes available in accessible formats? Are accommodation procedures in place for applicants with disabilities? Have questions about disability been removed from applications? Have questions concerning a history or record of a medical condition been removed? Have questions asking about drug addiction or alcoholism been removed? Have questions concerning worker's compensation claims been removed? Is affirmative action data assured confidentiality?

Fourth, in the past year, have interview procedures been reviewed for disability awareness and inclusion? Are interview personnel trained in disability etiquette? Are the same interview questions asked of all job applicants for similar positions? Do the interview questions reflect the essential functions of the job and how the applicant would perform them?

Fifth, have employment tests and exams been reviewed in the past year for disability inclusion? Are identical qualification standards, employment tests, or other selection criteria used for all applicants for a job or class of jobs? Are alternative formats provided? Do the tests accurately reflect the skills and aptitude necessary for performing the essential functions of the position? Do the test results accurately reflect the ability of the applicant to perform the essential functions of the position?

Sixth, have all written employment and personnel policies been reviewed in the past year for disability inclusion? Do all written policies reflect appropriate terminology concerning people with disabilities? Are policies free from discriminatory treatment of nondisabled applicants or employees who have family members, associates, or friends with a disability? Do employment practices avoid limiting, segregating, or classifying job applicants or employees in ways that adversely affect their opportunities or status because of a disability? Do employment policies refrain from adversely affecting or limiting the advancement or promotion of people with disabilities? Do payroll and personnel policies avoid negatively affecting rates of pay or other forms of compensation of job applicants or employees with disabilities? Are people with disabilities portrayed appropriately on forms, reports, personnel manuals, and other employment-related documents?

Seventh, are a reasonable accommodation policy and procedure in place for employees who self-identify with disabilities? Has an entity, whether person or committee, been identified for keeping records, evaluating, approving, or denying requests for reasonable accommodation? Are the policy and procedures regarding reasonable accommodation provided in alternative formats? How are decisions to approve or deny reasonable accommodation documented? Are funds set aside to facilitate meeting reasonable accommodation requests?

CONCLUSION

Statcher and Hendren (1992) indicated that employers have at best a tacit agreement with the ADA. In some cases, employers are becoming vocally more resistant to the ADA. Weaver (1993), writing for the

Milken Institute for Job and Capital Formation, described the ADA as "a costly and ineffective means of enhancing the well-being of people with disabilities" (p. 1). There are signs that employers are slow to comply with the ADA ("Numbers of ADA Charges," 1993). Employment figures for people with disabilities indicate that the ADA is not fulfilling its promise of increasing their employment (Mathews, 1995).

On the other hand, positive signs exist that the ADA has begun to imprint its message on Americans and U.S. business. A poll commissioned by the National Organization on Disability and conducted by Louis Harris and Associates in June 1993 showed clearly that Americans see people with disabilities as part of the work force. Harris found that "fully 92% of the public favors efforts to increase the number of people with disabilities in paid jobs" ("New Survey," 1993, p. 1). The ADA is working for people with disabilities. Data from the U.S. Bureau of the Census indicate that 800,000 more individuals with severe disabilities became part of the work force in 1994 than did in 1991, a 27 percent increase ("ADA Wins Praise," 1996). Erlich (1993) pointed out that in the computer business corporations see that ADA adaptation makes job performance more effective for everyone. Lord (1992) saw corporations in the fast-food industry welcoming the ADA as reinforcement of their experience that people with disabilities make excellent employees.

Whether or not business as a whole agrees with the ADA, comprehensive employment and personnel policies that include people with disabilities make good sense for an employer. Discrimination against these men and women in employment is illegal. A sound personnel policy ensures compliance and a minimal risk of potential litigation. An inclusive personnel policy promotes getting the best person for the job. Many people with disabilities are the top people in their fields; many bring myriad talents to the work world. A prejudicial and discriminatory personnel policy and procedure prevents employers from reaping the benefits of the talents and skills possessed by many people with disabilities. Finally, employers live in a diverse world. Each day markets reflect more and more an ethnically and culturally rich world. Those of us with disabilities are part of those markets and part of that world.

REFERENCES

ADA wins praise as census data show job gains of people with disabilities. (1996, July 31). *Fair Employment Report*, p. 124.

Albrecht, G. (1992). *The disability business: Rehabilitation in America*. Newbury Park, CA: Sage Publications.

Americans with Disabilities Act of 1990, P.L. 101-336, 104 Stat. 327.

Brown, D. S. (1994). *Working effectively with people who have learning disabilities and attention deficit hyperactivity disorder*. Ithaca, NY: Cornell University, Program of Employment and Disability, New York School of Industrial and Labor Relations. [http://www.ilr.cornell.edu/PED/ADA]

Bruyere, S. M., & Golden, T. P. (1994). *Working effectively with persons who have cognitive disabilities*. Ithaca, NY: Cornell University, Program of Employment and

Disability, New York School of Industrial and Labor Relations.
[http://www.ilr.cornell.edu/PED/ADA]

Civil Rights Act of 1964, P.L. 88-352, 78 Stat. 241.

Dickson, M. B. (1994). *Working effectively with people who are blind or visually impaired.*
Ithaca, NY: Cornell University, Program of Employment and Disability, New
York School of Industrial and Labor Relations.
[http://www.ilr.cornell.edu/PED/ADA]

Drucker, P. (1985). *Management: Tasks, responsibilities, practices.* New York: Harper
Colophon Books.

Equal Employment Opportunity Commission (1993, June). EEOC issues interim enforcement guidance on the application of the ADA to disability-based provisions
of employer-provided heath insurance. *EEOC News,* pp. 1–16.

Equal Employment Opportunity Commission, & U.S. Department of Justice. (1991).
Americans with Disabilities Act handbook. Washington, DC: U.S. Government Printing Office.

Erlich, R. (1993, May 5). Managers and employees benefit from disabilities act.
MacWeek News, pp. 20, 23.

Etzioni, A. (1975). *A comparative analysis of complex organizations.* New York: Free
Press.

Fine, M., & Asch, A. (1988). Disability beyond stigma: Social interaction, discrimination, and activism. In M. Nagler (Ed.), *Perspectives in disability* (pp. 61–74). Palo
Alto, CA: Health Markets Research.

Jarrow, J. E. (1992). *Title by title: The ADA's impact on postsecondary education.* Columbus, OH: Association on Higher Education and Disability.

Johnson, M. (Ed.). (1992). *People with disabilities explain it all for you: Your guide to the
public accommodations requirements of the Americans with Disabilities Act.* Louisville,
KY: Advocate Press.

Johnston, L. M. (1994). *The ADA and collective bargaining issues.* Ithaca, NY: Cornell
University, New York School of Industrial and Labor Relations, Program of Employment and Disability. [http://www.ilr.cornell.edu/PED/ADA]

Lee, B. A. (1995). *Reasonable accommodation under the Americans with Disabilities Act.*
Horsham, PA: LRP Publications. [http://www.ilr.cornell.edu/PED/ADA]

Longmore, P. K. (1993, October). *History of the disability rights movement and disability
culture.* Address to the California Disability Leadership Summit, Anaheim.

Lord, M. (1992, July, 20). Away with barriers: Employers can satisfy the new disabilities act without spending a mint. Here's a guide. *U.S. News & World Report,* pp.
60–63.

Mackelprang, R. W., & Salsgiver, R. O. (1996). People with disabilities and social
work: Historical and contemporary issues. *Social Work, 41,* 7–14.

Mancuso, L. L. (1994). *Employing and accommodating workers with psychiatric disabilities.* Ithaca, NY: Cornell University, New York School of Industrial and Labor Relations, Program of Employment and Disability.
[http://www.ilr.cornell.edu/PED/ADA]

Mathews, J. (1995, April 16). Disability act failing to achieve workplace goals: Land-
mark law rarely helps disabled people seeking jobs. *Washington Post,* pp. A1, A18.

Morosky, F. N. (1994). *Workplace accommodations for persons with musculo-skeletal disorders.* Ithaca, NY: Cornell University, New York School of Industrial and Labor Relations, Program of Employment and Disability.
[http://www.ilr.cornell.edu/PED/ADA]

Morrissey, P. (1991). *Disability etiquette in the workplace.* Washington, DC: Employment Policy Foundation.

Nester, M. A. (1994). *Pre-employment testing and the ADA.* Horsham, PA: LRP Publications. [http://www.ilr.cornell.edu/PED/ADA]

New survey shows people with disabilities not well informed on ADA. (1993, Summer). *National Organization on Disability Report,* pp. 1, 3.

Numbers of ADA charges rising rapidly. (1993, December 6). *CUPA News,* p. 1.

Rehabilitation Act of 1973, P.L. 93-112, 87 Stat. 355.

Shapiro, J. P. (1993). *No pity: People with disabilities, forging a new civil rights movement.* New York: Times Books.

Simon, H. A. (1976). *Administrative behavior: A study of decision-making process in administrative organization.* New York: Free Press.

Statcher, J., & Hendren, G. R. (1992). Employer agreement with the Americans with Disabilities Act of 1990: Implications for rehabilitation counseling. *Journal of Rehabilitation, 58*(3), 13–17.

University of Arkansas Research and Training Center for Persons Who Are Deaf and Hard of Hearing. (1994). *Working effectively with persons who are deaf or hard of hearing.* Ithaca, NY: Cornell University, New York School of Industrial and Labor Relations, Program of Employment and Disability.
[http://www.ilr.cornell.edu/PED/ADA]

Weaver, C. L. (1993). The Americans with Disabilities Act: A costly way to increase employment. *Jobs & Capital, 2*(1), 1–9.

Linguistic Diversity and Organizational Communication Policy

Ovetta H. Harris

ultural and linguistic diversity has always been a part of U.S. life
because people from various parts of the world came to this
country bringing their native languages, dialects, and ways of
communicating. Communication diversity is a reality in contemporary life, because multilingual populations continue to enter the country. Current trends indicate that linguistic diversity will intensify during the remainder of this century and into the next because of the
changing population demographics. These demographics will be reflected in the work force.

Organizational communication policies are becoming more inclusive of diverse populations, including people who are culturally, linguistically, and physically diverse. The purpose of this chapter is
twofold: (1) to provide a general background of communication diversity and (2) to discuss the significance of communication diversity in work systems.

COMMUNICATION DIVERSITY

Much attention during recent years has been given to accommodating diversity, including linguistic diversity. *Linguistic diversity* refers
to variation in language use. People who understand, speak, or are
literate in languages other than English or use various dialects of
English are said to be linguistically diverse. For example, a person
who speaks primarily Spanish in the United States is considered linguistically diverse. A person who can speak or write fluently in two
or more languages or dialects is linguistically diverse. Linguistic diversity also includes manual sign languages, such as American Sign
Language (ASL). Many manual sign languages are considered languages separate from English because the linguistic components of
sign language—semantics, syntax, morphology, and pragmatics—
differ from those of spoken English.

The Standard-English Myth

Many residents of the United States take it for granted that English is
the official language of this country and assume that every American
speaks it fluently. In reality, the U.S. government has never formally

declared an official language; thus, there is no legislated standard language. Some countries have declared a standard language. For example, France maintains the Institute of French to regulate the correct pronunciations and grammatical structures of the language. The United States not only has refrained from declaring an official language, but historically also has allowed various agencies and organizations to function without using English at all. For example, before World War I many children living in parts of the Midwest were taught in schools in which German was used for instruction. In Rhode Island at the end of the 19th century, many fishing-industry workers spoke only Portuguese.

Presently, non-English speakers live in all 50 states. In at least two states—New Mexico, with its large population of Mexican Americans and Native Americans, and Hawaii, with its large proportion of Asian Americans—more than 25 percent of the population are non-English speakers. In Florida, California, Arizona, Texas, Louisiana, New Jersey, Connecticut, Rhode Island, Massachusetts, New York, and North Dakota, 16 percent to 25 percent of the residents claim a non-English-speaking background. In the 25 largest U.S. cities, the non-English-language population constitutes at least 10 percent of the total population.

Dialectal Diversity

Every major language spoken in the world has evolved variations; these occur across all the component parts of language, including semantics, or vocabulary use; syntax, or the rules for organizing words; pragmatics, or the functions of language; and phonology, or the rules for organizing sounds that compose words. Variations within a language are called "dialects." Dialect users are considered diverse communicators when they are in a setting in which their dialect of English is used infrequently or if their dialect is not used outside a particular geographic area. Many dialects are spoken in the United States, such as creole-English, Boston dialect, New York dialect, and Southern dialect.

Dialects are rule governed; thus, one can describe the rules and understand the uses of language for any particular dialect. For example, people who prolong vowel sounds, produce final consonant reductions, speak with a nasal quality, and substitute the sound /f/ for voiceless /th/ as in "bath = baf" are said to speak with a Southern dialect. Some of these features are present in other dialects as well, such as vernacular black English, also known as "ebonics." For example, speakers of the vernacular black English also will produce final consonant reductions (see Table 11-1). Dialects are delineated by variations in the frequency of occurrence of various linguistic features.

Any discussion of dialects must be grounded in correlations with social variables, or the behavioral factors that determine the linguistic diversity that forms social dialects. Dialects are inherently social because language is used in social settings for particular social purposes,

Table 11-1

Linguistic Features of Black English

Feature	Explanation	Rules and Examples
Phonological	How sounds are formed and used to construct words	Deletion of /R/ as in "sista" vs. "sister"
Prosodic	Syllable stress	Stress on beginning of two-syllable words, as in "PO-lice," "HO-tel," "DEE-troit"
Morphosyntactical	How words and sentences are formed to carry meaning	Reduction of progressive suffix (-ing), as in "He jumpin" or "whoopin"
Semantic	Word meaning	Words with multiple meanings, as in "kitchen," which refers to the lower back hairline
Pragmatic	How language is used in social contexts	Turn taking; beginning statements before the conversational partner has finished speaking

whether business or pleasure. Because dialects are socially based, some dialects are considered more acceptable than others. Unpopular dialects are usually so not because of the dialect itself but because of the population that uses it. Social value is not ascribed to any group of linguistic rules but to the social status of the speaker.

The social variables that relate to dialects are numerous and include age, sex, ethnicity, region, status, and style. To limit this discussion, I will not include the interplay of these variables with each other (however, it is the interaction of many social variables that accounts for linguistic diversity). I will discuss how geographic region and ethnicity operate and influence linguistic variables of dialect.

Geographic Region. A reality of social dialects is that they exist in the context of regional variation. One of the primary reasons most often cited for the emergence of regional dialects in the United States is settlement patterns of immigrants entering the country. Two phenomena exist in the dialects of the early settlers. First, settlers came from different parts of Europe, bringing their dialects with them. For example, Europeans from England sound very different from those from Scotland, who also speak English. Second, the development of regional varieties of English occurred in the pattern of population movement, generally from east to west. Thus, dialect boundaries of mainstream speakers of English run more horizontally than vertically across the country. Vertical dialectal patterns often are more multifaceted than horizontal dialectical patterns.

Regional dialects are influenced greatly by physical boundaries such as rivers, mountains, and other natural barriers. Relic areas, or areas isolated by natural boundaries such as islands or mountain ranges, produce dialects that relate to older forms of English or a mixing of English and another language (creolization). The Sea Islands off the coast of South Carolina have produced a dialect called "Gullah," which is a mixture of English and several West African languages. Many people living in the Appalachian Mountains use a dialect of English that has elements of Old English.

In contrast to relic areas, focal areas serve as regional centers from which dialects spread outward. For example, Boston is a focal area. One can see the influence of Bostonian speech (the deletion of the post-vocalic /r/, as in "ca" for "car") in areas far outside of the city and into neighboring states.

Ethnicity. Within cities a great deal of dialectal variation exists among members of various ethnicities. A positive correlation exists between ethnicity and the social distance between particular ethnic groups. Dialectal variations exist within as well as among ethnic groups. African Americans are an example of an ethnic group that presents extreme dialectal variation. However, about 80 percent of African Americans in the United States speak or understand vernacular black English, a dialect that blends grammatical and phonological features from West African languages with English. Vernacular black English has historically been and is presently the most studied dialect in the United States.

African Americans developed their dialect of English, to some degree, because of social isolation from the mainstream population. The members of any ethnic group who are isolated from the dominant society generally produce more dialectal features. Every ethnic group in the United States includes people who are more assimilated than others into the dominant society. The people who have most contact with mainstream America can code-switch (change from one dialect to another) more easily than individuals who do not tend to travel outside of their linguistic communities. For example, African Americans commonly greet each other with a phrase such as "what's up." An African American who is greeting a person from outside his or her culture may use the more mainstream greeting of "Hello. How are you?" In business and private settings, African Americans generally speak differently when they are in a homogenous group from when in the company of members of other ethnicities. This ability to code-switch between two or more dialects is common among most people who speak dialects of English.

Communication using one's dialect may be preferred in particular settings for particular purposes. Speakers may use a dialect to capture the attention of nondialect speakers. Use of a dialect can infuse emphasis into a conversation. Dialects, like idioms, often can be understood only by people familiar with the culture of origin. Similar to idioms, figurative phrases, or other languages, dialectal phrases can be fun to learn and use.

Augmentative and Alternative Communicators. Another type of communication diversity is augmentative or alternative communication (AAC). AAC involves the use of any augmentation to natural speech. Most AAC users are nonspeakers because of neurological damage, degenerative conditions, congenital conditions, acquired conditions, or temporary conditions. This population may include those with cerebral palsy, hearing impairment, developmental apraxia, spinal cord injury, cerebral vascular accident, closed-head injury, laryngectomy, multiple sclerosis, muscular dystrophy, Parkinson's disease, amyotrophic lateral sclerosis, or AIDS. People who use this type of communication can communicate only through use of manual signs or technological assistance such as electronic communication devices with voice synthesizers, digitized voice output, or written message output. Some augmentative and alternative communicators use low-technology aids, such as communication boards.

Many people who live with disabling conditions can be found in work environments and in fact have made tremendous contributions to their disciplines. For example, Stephen Hawking, Nobel Prize recipient in science, uses an augmentative communication device because of a neural degenerative disorder that affects the speech musculature. Hawking uses his communication technology to give lectures, consult with colleagues, write research papers, and in other ways to meet the communication demands of his profession.

AAC is an area of clinical practice that attempts to compensate (either temporarily or permanently) for the impairment and disability patterns of people with severe expressive communication disorders (Beukelman & Mirenda, 1992). AAC services must use a person's communication to its fullest capacity, including the use of gestures, sign language, high-technology and low-technology tools, voice, or combinations of these. The American Speech-Language-Hearing Association (ASHA, 1991) reported that about 8 percent of the U.S. population, or 2 million people, may need AAC services.

During the past decade there has been a rapid increase in the quality and quantity of services available to people in need of AAC services. Technological advances in the fields of speech–language–hearing pathology and education have provided access to sophisticated communication strategies and systems for nonspeaking people. Speech–language pathologists usually have been the professionals responsible for assessing, designing, and implementing AAC programs; however, a multidisciplinary diagnostic and intervention team is necessary for appropriate service delivery. An AAC team of specialists should consist of a speech–language pathologist, a social worker, a psychologist, special educators, occupational and physical therapists, rehabilitation engineers, a vocational specialist, and a primary physician. These specialists play a vital role in providing educational adaptations geared toward classroom inclusion, employment transition, and employment referral for nonspeaking people. Each specialist can make changes or modifications in the AAC system to fit the educational and life experience needs of the user as well as provide technical and training assistance.

Manual Sign Users

The majority of people who are born deaf use nonspeech methods of communicating and are considered augmentative communicators. There are several manual sign systems, such as Cued Speech, Ame-Ind, Sign Exact English, as well as many natural sign languages. Most Americans who are deaf use ASL to communicate; ASL is the third most-used language in the United States. ASL is considered a separate language because its linguistic attributes do not resemble spoken language. For example, an ASL user who wants to invite a friend to sit beside him or her may sign a phrase that can be interpreted literally in English as "welcome sit," whereas in spoken English one would say "please come sit beside me." Thus, ASL users may be considered bilingual because most users understand English and can use ASL as their expressive language system.

People who are deaf and bilingual are similar to hearing bilingual people in several ways. People who are deaf and bilingual tend to be diverse in their knowledge and use of language because they are able to use and understand the languages used in educational, occupational, and social settings. Similar to hearing people, deaf people tend to use less-formal language when in casual social peer groups than in formal settings, such as the classroom.

Although there are many similarities between deaf and hearing bilingual people, some striking differences also exist. First, deaf people have just recently been recognized as being bilingual. Historically, deaf people have been seen as being monolingual in English. Second, because many deaf people will never become hearing individuals, they may always have to be bilingual and not transition to the sole use of one language. Deaf people may continue to use sign language throughout life, whereas hearing bilingual people may transfer from their native language to the dominant language. Third, because of their hearing loss, some deaf people may find it challenging to demonstrate full competency or learn specific skills of the dominant language. When one uses a nonwritten language system as the main mode of expressive communication, it can be difficult to remember all of the rules for correct written language. Although deaf people are able to shift from one language to another, they spend more time using the monolingual sign language because they are usually grouped together in educational and social settings.

Deaf Culture. Increasingly, people who are deaf perceive themselves more as members of a cultural subgroup than as disabled people. They and others feel that the deaf culture consists of many of the same variables as other cultures, given their distinct language and their tendency for in-group marriage. Local, regional, state, national, and international organizations serve deaf people. There are cultural events, athletic competitions, and even a Miss Deaf America pageant. A person may be diagnosed as deaf by an audiometric assessment of hearing loss, but identifying with the deaf community or culture takes a certain attitude, a mind-set of cultural values and ways of behaving.

The deaf culture developed as many cultures do—through isolation of a group of people from the mainstream. Historically in the United States, many deaf people were sent to special schools. It was during this period of isolation that present-day deaf culture developed. Johns Hopkins University and Michigan State University have developed programs of study in deaf culture.

People gain bicultural status by adapting in some degree to two cultures as a result of having lived in both cultures and blending aspects of the two cultures (Davis, 1989). This definition of biculturalism fits deaf people, who live in at least two cultures: the deaf community and the hearing community of their family, friends, coworkers, and colleagues. Deaf people must operate within the hearing world to get basic needs met, such as going to the grocery store, to restaurants, or to sports events. Thus, deaf people must adapt in some degree to the hearing world as a result of the contact that they have with hearing people.

The degree of a deaf person's acculturation to the hearing world varies. Factors such as degree of deafness, number of other deaf family members, type of education, and educational or work setting all contribute to variability in levels of acculturation. Some deaf people have fewer contacts with the hearing world and are less acculturated than other deaf people; thus, bicultural dominance can differ. The case for biculturalism also is applicable to hearing people who have close contact with deaf people, such as hearing children of deaf parents and friends who have developed strong ties with the deaf community. Many deaf people are culturally competent in both hearing and nonhearing communities. Many of them, however, choose to be predominantly members of the hearing world and are successfully working in the hearing world. Among deaf people with visibility in the hearing world are Heather Whitestone, Miss America 1994, and Academy Award winner Marlee Matlin. Because of improved technology, improved social sensitivity, and awareness of the abilities of deaf people and improved educational techniques, many more deaf people are working in public and corporate positions than was previously the case.

Deaf African Americans. There are about 2 million African Americans with some hearing impairment in the United States, 22,000 of whom are profoundly hearing impaired. African American deaf people are mainstreamed into the larger society at a much slower rate than deaf Americans who are not African American. They miss many social, economic, and political opportunities because their communication style differs from that of more mainstream deaf Americans.

Many deaf African Americans use gestures, facial expressions, and signs that some interpreters and deaf people from the dominant culture do not understand. Thus, interpreters sometimes have difficulty communicating with them (Callaway & Tucker, 1986). Deaf Americans from the dominant culture often reject the communication style of deaf African Americans because of these differences.

Unique expressions in signing used by African Americans who are deaf arise because, historically, African American families could not afford or did not have access to formal rehabilitation services that teach standard communication skills. Furthermore, when training is provided, many resist change because it does not incorporate the communication style already developed with their friends and family, even when this style is used by other African American members of the deaf community. These deaf people are sometimes asked to denounce their style of communicating and thus risk a communication breakdown in their primary group.

Many deaf African Americans are isolated from mainstream socialization or experiences. Social activities established for deaf people typically do not include a focus on meeting the needs of African American participants (Callaway & Tucker, 1986). Activities often are held in locations that are distant from African American communities, which limits opportunities for African Americans to communicate with other deaf people and slows their communication growth. This phenomenon occurs in other non-mainstream ethnic groups as well.

As young children, many deaf African Americans were placed in academic and vocational classes for mentally disabled people. This placement leads to inadequate education and low self-esteem and limits these students' potential for success in the work force. African American students develop little positive identification with their teachers, because the teachers are usually culturally, educationally, and racially different. Educators of deaf people, like speech–language pathologists, are overwhelmingly members of the mainstream hearing culture.

Although many needs of deaf African Americans differ from those of mainstream deaf people, similarities also exist. Over the past decade, society has recognized the need to provide better educational services and job opportunities to all deaf Americans.

LINGUISTIC DIVERSITY IN ORGANIZATIONAL SETTINGS

Culture affects communication patterns, methods of conveying messages, and the comprehension of information. Cultural elements of communication that are not integrated into the daily experiences of culturally diverse people may alienate them. Similarly, the populations of non-English, limited-English, bidialectal, and augmentative communicators are at higher risk of being denied access to culturally appropriate ways of obtaining information. For example, in India people use small shakes of the head from side to side to signify yes in the same way that people in the United States signal no. This culturally based communication gesture will be misinterpreted by an Indian in the United States as a negative response when the communicator really means yes.

Professionals such as speech–language pathologists, linguists, or bilingual educators working with linguistically and culturally diverse individuals may be the primary facilitators in developing cultural–communicative competence (Light, 1989). AAC users are most often initially dependent on professionals to assist them in creating a formal communication system. Most professionals, including those who specialize in areas of linguistic diversity, are members of the dominant or mainstream culture (Blackstone, 1993). According to ASHA (1995), only 4 percent of its members belong to ethnic subcultures. Without multicultural awareness, professionals cannot begin to adequately serve linguistically diverse people from diverse racial and ethnic backgrounds (see, for example, Anderson, 1992; Cole, 1986; Taylor, 1986a, 1986b; Taylor & Clarke, 1994).

REFERENCES

American Speech–Language–Hearing Association. (1991). Position statement on non-speech communication. *ASHA, 23*, 577–587.

American Speech–Language–Hearing Association. (1995). *Demographic profile of the ASHA membership and affiliation for the period January 1, 1994 through December 31, 1994.* Rockville, MD: Author.

Anderson, J. A. (1992, November). *Enhancing learning styles of diverse populations in the university classroom.* Miniseminar presented at the annual convention of the American Speech–Language–Hearing Association, San Antonio, TX.

Blackstone, S. (1993). Cultural sensitivity and AAC services. *Augmentative Communication News, 6*(2), 3–5.

Beukelman, D. R., & Mirenda, P. (1992). *Augmentative and alternative communication: Management of severe communication disorders in children and adults.* Baltimore: Paul H. Brookes.

Callaway, T., & Tucker, C. (1986). *Rehabilitation of deaf black individuals: Problems and intervention strategies.* Available online 1997.

Cole, P. (1986). The social responsibility of the researcher. *ASHA Reports, 16*, 26–29.

Davis, D. (1989). The effects of sign characteristics on sign acquisition and retention: An integrative review of the literature. *Augmentative and Alternative Communication, 5*, 69–74.

Light, J. (1989). Toward a definition of communication competence for individuals using augmentative and alternative communication systems. *Augmentative and Alternative Communication, 5*, 137–144.

Taylor, O. L. (1986a). *Nature of communication disorders in culturally and linguistically diverse populations.* Austin, TX: Pro-Ed.

Taylor, O. L. (1986b). *Treatment of communication disorders in culturally and linguistically diverse populations.* Boston: College-Hill Press.

Taylor, O. L., & Clarke, M. G. (1994). Culture and communication disorders: A theoretical framework. *Seminars in Speech and Language, 15*, 103–113.

Part IV

ORGANIZATIONAL STRUCTURE AND COMMUNICATION

This section departs from the usual perspective on *organizational structure*, defined as authority and reporting relationships, to focus on interpersonal relationships and communication processes in structure. *Power*, usually defined as the ability to influence or control the behavior of another, is not explicated as such at this point, largely because it is too often conceptualized as a tool of control rather than as a dynamic process. This notion of power is based largely on dependence on the "other" for rewards for acquiescing to another's influence. A subtext in the discourse about diversity in the workplace is about shifts in power and in the ways it is exercised. Power in interpersonal relationships can be relational (for example, legitimate authority or social hegemony), situational (for example, rising to the occasion or a seniority relationship), or mutual (for example, horizontal decision-making structure). It is this conceptualization of power that is threaded through the five chapters in this section. The purpose is to observe sources of power in multicultural and diversity situations as power is exercised. Such observations can suggest research questions for exploration concerning the exercise of power in dynamic exchanges in which values that affect responses vary greatly. This example demonstrates the importance of communication for diverse groups in the workplace.

The chapters in this part address differences in styles of communication and actual language usage and patterns. They discuss the potent effect of communication on organizational functioning, and they provide recommendations for more-inclusive and effective communication.

In chapter 12, McNeely, Sapp, and Daly explore factors associated with job satisfaction among organizational members employed in public social services in five metropolitan counties. More than two-thirds of all organizational members in public assistance agencies are women, and a fifth of all employees are people of color. The effect of perceived racial and gender inequities on job satisfaction, which research generally supports as an indicator of productivity, has been an underresearched area. Chapter 12 examines quantitative data as well as material from interviews to gain empirical understanding of differential predictors of job satisfaction among diverse groups of employees. These reflect cultural and some gender differences regarding factors associated with job satisfaction, differences that can be addressed through informed management and communication structures.

Chapter 13, by Jennings, Martin, and Vroom, addresses the bicultural stresses frequently experienced by administrators. The chapter views African American women as a subsystem of black culture. Interestingly, postmodernists and postfeminists often view these women as a subculture within the women's movement (Collins, 1990; Rothenberg, 1990). The chapter addresses racism and sexism as sources of stress in the workplace and how they affect mentoring relationships and informal networks. The issue of credibility is a constant challenge to the stereotypes of African Americans, women, and African American women. Although enduring isolation and challenges to their values, African American women gain coping strategies and rewards.

As institutions deliver human services in urban communities experiencing demographic changes, they face the challenge of how to reduce the social distance that often exists between organizational members, older residents, and newcomers to the neighborhood. This issue is addressed in chapter 14, by McNeely, Sapp, and Meyer. Organizational members are mostly middle class, but newcomers to urban neighborhoods are frequently poor or near-poor members of diverse racial and ethnic groups. This diversity may lead to social estrangement that can adversely affect an institution's ability to achieve its goals. This chapter uses Litwak and Meyer's balance theory (1974), a model for retaining organizational vitality and optimally achieving organizational goals when a community has undergone significant demographic change.

Organizational communication and information processing are as essential to organizations facing dynamic and diverse environments as blood and the circulatory system are to a living organism. When we analyze structure, a key element in that analysis is "who talks to whom" and how well that information is processed and used. In chapter 15, Beckett and Dungee-Anderson present a process model for structuring communication in culturally diverse workplaces. These authors identify two types of communication errors: (1) *Type I errors,* defined as interpersonal relationship errors among and between organizational levels, and (2) *Type II errors,* defined as incorrect interpretation and application of multicultural knowledge that can lead to faulty strategies. Beckett and Dungee-Anderson present an eight-step process to recognize and prevent these errors. A case example illustrates the usefulness of the model in addressing multicultural and diversity concerns in human services organizations.

Fabelo-Alcover and Sowers discuss another significant issue regarding communication with diverse organization members and clients in chapter 16. This chapter addresses diversity within racial–ethnic groups by looking at Latino culture. Latinos can be described, as can Asians, African descendants, and Europeans, as encompassing many subcultures. Although Mexicans, Puerto Ricans, Cubans, and Central and South Americans share Spanish as their common language, variations in customs, beliefs, and practices can result in different definitions for the same word, making communication treacherous. The authors point out subcultural communication preferences and present strategies to promote effective communication in the workplace.

The chapters in this part illustrate power sharing, even in the midst of interpersonal conflict. Full communication and input from all staff members reduce the perception of dominance and hegemonic oppression and at the same time reduce stress and a sense of identity loss. Some form of conflict in work groups is inevitable and even healthy, as long as the groups try to resolve the conflict rather than deny it exists. If structure encourages broad input from all staff levels and across constituencies, power and diversity issues can be approached as opportunities for education or creative problem solving.

REFERENCES

Collins, P. H. (1990). *Black feminist thought: Knowledge, consciousness, and the politics of empowerment.* Boston: Unwin Hyman.

Litwak, E., & Meyer, H. J. (1974). *School, family, and neighborhood: The theory and practice of school–community relations.* New York: Columbia University Press.

Rothenberg, P. (1990). The construction, deconstruction, and reconstruction of difference. *Hypatia, 5*(1), 42–57.

12

Ethnicity, Gender, Earnings, Occupational Rank, and Job Satisfaction in the Public Social Services:

What Do Workers Say?

R. L. McNeely, Marty Sapp, and Alfrieda Daly

Threading the topic of job satisfaction is not important merely because dissatisfied human services workers provide inferior services; the health, mental health, and social functioning of workers can be affected substantially by their level of job satisfaction (Daly, 1990, 1994; McNeely, 1978, 1979). Therefore, it is important to examine factors related to job satisfaction not only because of the relationship of these factors to worker productivity but also because of their relationship to the physical and emotional health of workers. Although a number of factors related to job satisfaction are common to all workers, some studies have found others to be related most strongly to workers' race and ethnicity, gender, and occupational rank (McNeely, 1987b, 1988e, 1989c, 1992). Hence, human services managers may need not only to recognize the possibility that factors affecting the job productivity, health, and mental health of their subordinates are as diversified as the racial, ethnic, and gender groups under their supervision but also devise managerial practices that are sensitive to these differences.

Human services managers also need to know about job satisfaction determinants peculiar to women and members of numerically nondominant racial and ethnic groups, given their disproportionately high representation in human services employment. More than 65 percent of all welfare workers are women, and about 20 percent are members of numerically nondominant ethnic groups (Dressel, 1987). Also, women and members of racial and ethnic groups, along with immigrants, constitute the fastest growing segment of a shrinking U.S. labor force (Johnston & Packer, 1987). Women and members of racial and ethnic groups also constitute a disproportionate share of clients receiving public welfare services. Although some question it (Sullivan, 1989), these demographics forecast increasing pressure on the human services to promote women and ethnic group members into positions of prominence and leadership.

A review of the literature on human services job satisfaction reveals that little attention has been given to issues related to gender, race, and ethnicity. Even within the broader job satisfaction literature, insufficient work has been done to answer definitively a number of basic questions, including whether consistent job satisfaction differences exist between the genders and among the races. In addition, few studies have addressed the issue of whether there are race and gender inequities in human services employment. Most job satisfaction research has focused on private-sector corporations. Even fewer studies have examined whether a relationship exists among such inequities and the satisfaction levels and performance of workers (Dressel, 1987; Martin & Chernesky, 1989).

These and other deficits in the literature argue for a need to examine race and ethnicity and gender issues specifically within the human services. Studies seeking to examine these deficits should focus on workers who operate under similar conditions, such as workers employed in the public social services. Otherwise, the results of studies examining human services workers may be confounded by wide variations in the working conditions found in human services employment, such as significant differences in organizational size and bureaucratization of working conditions. Researchers also should use a uniform methodology with a variety of work sites, because some discrepant findings reported in the job satisfaction literature undoubtedly result from the vast array of methodological approaches used in job satisfaction research. Even among human services workers within the same field, conditions are likely to vary from site to site, as would be the case if members of nondominant racial and ethnic groups or women in some welfare departments perceived more intense discrimination than did those employed elsewhere. Single-site studies are less capable of examining these sorts of differences, again leading to the reporting of discrepant findings.

The purpose of this chapter is to provide insight into the job satisfaction of women and ethnic group members. To achieve this objective, we discuss factors found by some studies to be associated with the job satisfaction of public social services workers by race and ethnicity and gender, we examine income and occupational rank by race and ethnicity and gender, and we include the extemporaneous comments of workers who participated in a longitudinal, multisite job satisfaction study to elucidate points under discussion.

Following a review of this chapter, readers should have an improved grasp of factors affecting the job satisfaction of public welfare workers, the nature of satisfaction among these workers, and factors peculiar to the gender and predominant racial and ethnic groups employed in the public social services. Three questions raised are (1) What, if any, *consistent* factors related to race and ethnicity or to gender are associated with the job satisfaction of public welfare workers? (2) Are there inequities in occupational rank and income by race and ethnicity and by gender in the public social services and if so, are they explained by differences in educational levels and length of employment? and (3) Presuming that there are differences in factors predictive of job satisfaction by race and ethnicity and gender, what measures can be suggested to administrators to enhance the job satisfaction levels of these groups?

PURPOSE AND METHOD OF THE STUDY

Driven by the wish to know more about the job satisfaction of workers employed in public social services, an ongoing multisite study involving county human services departments located in geographically disparate areas of the nation was begun in 1979. Data were collected from six county welfare departments. Longitudinal data were collected during 1979 and 1981 from Racine County (Racine, Wisconsin); retrospective data for 1977 also were collected from this county in 1979. Data were collected in 1983 from Dade County (Miami), in 1984 from Genesee (Flint, Michigan) and Sacramento (Sacramento, California) counties, in 1986 from El Paso County (Colorado Springs, Colorado), and in 1987 from Fulton County (Atlanta). A mail survey was used to collect information. The study generated 2,198 returned usable questionnaires. The response rate was 52.2 percent.

Demographic information focused on race, gender, age, length of employment, education, occupational status, and annual earnings before taxes. An instrument designed to yield information on respondents' attitudes about specific working conditions was embedded in the questionnaire, and two measures of job satisfaction were included.

The Science Research Associates Attitudes Survey was used to capture the attitudes of respondents about a wide range of working conditions including but not limited to job dullness/monotony, supervisory and managerial fairness, adequacy of fringe benefits, fairness of pay and promotions, and excessiveness of workloads (Miller, 1977). The Index of Job Satisfaction focuses on subjective assessments that yield a measure of overall job satisfaction (Miller, 1977). The four-item intrinsic satisfaction subscale of the Morse Index (Miller, 1977) was used to determine intrinsic satisfaction levels. Intrinsic job factors refer to a job's inherent features, such as its capacity to confer on workers a sense of challenge, achievement, responsibility, and accomplishment; extrinsic factors focus on features that are external to the job itself, such as the convenience of working hours, cleanliness of the work environment, and fringe benefits (Herzberg, 1959).

Respondents participating in the study were able to give additional information by penning extemporaneous comments onto the reverse side of the questionnaire's final page. Although limited for purposes of this chapter to five counties (Dade, El Paso, Fulton, Genesee, and Sacramento), an analysis of those comments was performed to yield a rank ordering, reported elsewhere, of the concerns expressed (McNeely, 1992). More detailed accounts of the study's methods also may be found elsewhere (McNeely, 1988a, 1990).

FINDINGS BY GENDER

> I have had many jobs, most of which require less work and re-sponsibility than what is required of a welfare eligibility worker. They all paid much better because of the fact that men usually performed them. *(Native American female eligibility worker, age 29, Sacramento County)*

> Compared to a man working the assembly line at General Motors, we [women] make two dollars less per hour, they get more time off, and their benefits are twice as good. *(European American female assistance payments worker, age 38, Genesee County)*

Contrary to popular perception, few European American women expressed concerns about discrimination against women in the award-ing of salaries. There were virtually no assertions that women were segregated occupationally in the human services work force despite, the comments cited here. For example, only six women of the entire sample voiced non-race-related dissatisfactions about the failure of their organizations to implement comparable-worth policies. This finding is inconsistent with the frustrations expressed by women in many other employment sectors. A large number of European Ameri-can men, on the other hand, expressed their perceptions that they were being victimized unfairly by affirmative action policies.

> White males are never going to get promoted again in the county scheme of things. They are becoming an acceptable target of bias, without any legal rights or defense. *(European American male health services counselor, age 52, Dade County)*

> A man, especially a white man, has no chance to expand. On the other hand, a woman, white or black, can write her own ticket. *(European American male supervisor, age 36, Genesee County)*

When the affirmative action concerns of European American men were subjected to empirical analysis, however, these men were found as a group to have little about which to complain. Although these men comprised 15.7 percent of the total study group, they oc-cupied 40 percent of all the administrative positions, and their earn-ings were significantly higher than every other race and gender co-hort (McNeely, Blakemore, & Washington, 1993).

Job Satisfaction

Although one publication emerging from this study reported that fe-male human services workers were significantly more satisfied than their male counterparts (McNeely, 1984), it was based on an analysis of data from a single site. Findings generated by an examination of the study's six sites indicate no consistent differences between the genders on either overall or intrinsic job satisfaction levels. The dis-crepant findings (as well as other discrepant findings and reversals in findings reported later in this chapter) have implications that are discussed in the "Conclusion."

The satisfaction of human services workers, like that of other work-ers (Doering, Rhodes, & Schuster, 1983), increases with age (McNeely,

1988a). Both older women and older men were significantly more satisfied than younger workers. Presuming the data reflect career-cycle
changes rather than differences among generations of workers, young
human services workers can expect increased satisfaction as they
look to the decades ahead.

Job Dullness/Monotony

> Most of the middle managers have relatively high longevity,
> which is a cause of ennui and boredom. *(Native American division
> chief, age 59, Sacramento County)*

> My job is very fulfilling, especially during the busy times. *(African
> American female office manager, age 39, Genesee County)*

A consistent finding among both women and men is the salience of
job dullness/monotony as a predictor of satisfaction. When multisite
analyses were performed, this predictor generally emerged as the single best predictor of satisfaction for both genders, regardless of age,
occupational rank, or income. These findings are similar to those reported in a national study of human services workers conducted by
Jayaratne and Chess (1982–1983, 1983) in which job challenge was the
best predictor of satisfaction for both men and women. In light of
these findings, the reader may wish to contemplate present-day pressures for human services departments to adopt highly routinized
methods and procedures and the likely long-term effects on workers
of such routinization.

Use of Abilities

> When I first began working as a caseworker and for several years
> after, I found the job to be tremendous. The opportunity to learn
> seemed endless . . . as my skills increased. . . . I loved my job. . . .
> [But] as the years went on I found I learned less and my role of in-
> tervention became more routine. . . . I believe I am currently facing
> burnout. *(European American female foster care social worker, age 35,
> El Paso County)*

> I think a job development program would be very useful. I don't
> know where I can go from here with my special skills and educa-
> tion. *(European American female legal transcriber, age 45, Sacramento
> County)*

Another consistent finding was the comparative importance in predicting women's satisfaction with the extent to which jobs provide
workers with opportunities to use their abilities. Data generated indicated this predictor to be much more pervasive across occupational categories among women, with dissatisfied women, regardless of rank,
significantly more likely than men to report that "I have little opportunity to use my abilities in this organization." Other studies examining
women two to three decades ago documented the importance of skill
underutilization in predicting their satisfaction (Andrisani & Shapiro,
1978). Authors of more recent studies of the human services have suggested that despite proper training, sexism militates against the

placement of women in managerial positions and maintains their exclusion from important informal networks (Kravetz & Austin, 1984).

Speaking more broadly, Miller (1980) offers an additional explanation. With no reference to discrimination, she found that men more than women tend to be placed in jobs that are compatible with the skills they possess. To some extent this happens because women, particularly European American women, are more likely to have punctuated work histories and to engage in voluntary part-time work (Nardone, 1986). Both tendencies militate against opportunities for promotion and, particularly for college-educated women, placement into jobs that are commensurate with their academic qualifications, resulting in a poorer "fit" among women between the skills they possess and the tasks required by their jobs.

Based on these findings, it appears desirable for human services executives, working with unions, to launch investigations to determine the degree of job–person fit among women, particularly those in paraprofessional positions. Similarly, investigations should examine gender bias in promotional patterns and women's access to informal professional networks inside organizations. Results of such investigations can provide an objective, rather than pro forma, affirmative action basis within organizations for assigning jobs commensurate with women's skills. Appropriate use of those results also may increase satisfaction levels as well as use an organization's human resources more efficiently.

Excessive Pressure and Expectations

> I am yelled at, sworn at, called names, and threatened. I see approximately one person per minute. While on this specific job, my children say I have had an abrupt attitude change. . . . I am also overeducated for my position. *(European American female receptionist, age 39, Genesee County)*

> There have been times of unbearable pressure. There are times when the paperwork makes me want to scream. *(European American female social services worker, age 42, Sacramento County)*

Examined in the aggregate, the satisfaction of women was affected much more than that of men by perceptions of excessive on-the-job pressure (for example, long working hours, lack of office cleanliness, and degree to which jobs are tiring) and of excessive job performance expectations. Subsequent analysis revealed that concerns about job pressures and performance expectations were most salient for middle-aged (ages 30–54) women. As such, it was assumed that middle-aged women were most likely to be experiencing work–family conflict resulting from child rearing and other life-cycle changes.[1]

---

[1]A younger middle-aged woman, for example, is likely to be engaged in balancing work with child-rearing demands, whereas an older middle-aged woman may be confronted simultaneously with children leaving home, parental caretaking, the death or imminent death of a parent, the onset of menopause, and a husband experiencing mid-career crisis.

At some sites, however, the strength of these predictors was most strongly tied to the satisfaction of female administrators and supervisors, whereas at other sites it was tied most strongly to the satisfaction of female paraprofessionals. If work–family conflict is the most compelling explanation, one would expect professional and managerial women to be consistently less likely than more poorly paid women to report excessive pressure associated with work–family conflicts because of their greater access to child care and other resources that foster smoother interfacing of work and family roles (Burris, 1991). Because this was not the case, perhaps a better explanation is that situational factors associated with the different sites account for the inconsistencies observed in the study.

Whatever the explanation, data obtained for the study indicate a clear gender discrepancy, with female satisfaction, regardless of occupational status, affected far more than male satisfaction by perceptions of excessive pressure and expectations. These findings are consistent with those reported by Jayaratne and Chess (1983) for human services workers and by Miller's (1980) examination of women more representative of the nation.

Supervisors, Managers, and Promotional Opportunities

All we really need is to be respected and supported and understood by management! When this is done, difficult clients become a challenge, and the job is OK. (*European American female eligibility worker, age 52, Sacramento County*)

Top management parks next to the building. (*European American male welfare services specialist, age 32, Genesee County*)

[Your] questionnaire seems to target supervisors and managers. Are there no questions such as "Do you have troublesome prima donna subordinates?" (*European American male health services counselor, age 52, Dade County*)

Supervision is a no-win job. No one is ever happy. (*European American female eligibility supervisor, age 51, Sacramento County*)

I have worked with middle- and upper-management. I have always been impressed with the thought and care that goes into decision making. I wish line employees could be exposed to this process. (*European American female secretary, age 32, El Paso County*)

There is no career ladder to speak of. Recently, our bureau chief told us that two positions had disappeared. Apparently, they were lost, like someone loses a wallet. (*European American female social services worker, age 39, Sacramento County*)

Promotions are just handled by favoritism, race, or political affiliation. (*Latino male social worker, age 31, Dade County*)

One report emerging from this study indicated that male satisfaction is affected more than female satisfaction by perceptions of administrative supervisors (McNeely, 1984). An examination of data obtained from all of the study's sites, however, indicates no clear gender differences in the importance of these perceptions. Perceptions about competence, fairness, the concern of supervisors for subordinates, and the willingness of executives to communicate with staff are important for both genders. Men, on the other hand, appear to be more affected than women by the closeness of supervision they experience, by the extent to which they perceive promotional opportunities, and by whether they have the ability to exercise judgment on the job. These findings were consistent with Miller's (1980) report that men are much more satisfied when in decision-making jobs of positional authority allowing the exercise of leadership. Whether supervision was so "close" as to militate against autonomy (use of initiative, thought, and independent judgment) was central in predicting male satisfaction, whereas the quality of supervisory exchanges was more important to women.

Jayaratne and Chess (1983) also found limited promotional opportunities to be more important in predicting turnover decisions for men, but the finding was reversed when they examined (1982–1983) a more occupationally diverse group of human services workers, with women being affected most by promotional opportunities.

Pay and Fringe Benefits

> I find it annoying that I have to pay $159.20 every month for health insurance and have no dental or eye coverage. *(African American female assistance payments worker, age 42, Genesee County)*

> The benefits program is great. . . . I have not had to pay a medical bill in a year. . . . I love my job. *(European American female assistance payments worker, age 34, Genesee County)*

Examined in the aggregate, concerns about income and fringe benefits were more salient predictors of women's satisfaction. Among women, however, the importance of these predictors diminished as occupational rank increased, and they were most strongly associated with the satisfaction levels of younger women (younger than age 30). These findings appear to support the notion, advanced in numerous studies (Loscocco, 1989; Shapiro, 1977), that the job characteristics of women (and ethnic groups) encourage greater focus on extrinsic factors, because low-ranking women and younger women tend to earn less than other workers. Nonetheless, the absolute importance of concerns about pay issues was weak, and actual income differences among respondents were not predictive of their satisfaction levels (McNeely, 1988c).

Other Factors

African American women were the most satisfied, both on overall and intrinsic satisfaction, followed, respectively, by Latino and European American women. As reported by other studies documenting racial differences among female human services workers (Wright, Wesley-King, & Berg, 1985), married European American women were more satisfied with their jobs than were other European American women, but marital status was not predictive of satisfaction for African American or Latino women (McNeely, 1987b). When rank and income were examined, women were found to earn less and be disproportionately placed in lower-status positions, even when educational background and employment longevity were taken into account. In some cases such discrepancies were slight, however, as occurred in an examination restricted to human services workers who were at least age 40. The study revealed that gender accounted for only 2 percent of the variance in income among these workers (McNeely, 1989a). Finally, differences observed between the genders diminished when examinations were restricted to those of high occupational rank. Men and women occupying these positions (administrators, supervisors) appeared to become similar in the extent to which their satisfaction was predicted by perceptions of managerial competence, fairness, ability to facilitate "smooth running" of the organization, and so forth.

FINDINGS BY RACE AND ETHNICITY

African Americans

Examined in the aggregate, African American human services workers were significantly more satisfied than European American workers on both overall and intrinsic satisfaction, regardless of occupational rank (McNeely, 1989c). Subsequent analyses indicated that racial differences in satisfaction levels were attributable to the county locations of respondents rather than to the race of the respondents, with satisfaction between the races within the human services departments patterned differently. Efforts to interpret these findings suggested that situational factors peculiar to the various employment sites offered the most reasonable explanations. One explanation focused on the degree to which respondents perceived that they had been victimized by racism within their departments. For example, the least-satisfied African Americans were located in a site within which significant racial strife had occurred recently regarding layoffs, with employees of color feeling that they had been targeted unfairly (McNeely, 1988e).

A second explanation is consistent with Fox and Lefkowitz's (1974) suggestion that some race-linked job satisfaction differences may be related to the racial status of those in chief executive roles, given reports that employees of color experience more stress in organizations that are run by European Americans (Bush, 1977). Thus, it should not be surprising that the present study of human services workers found African Americans employed in departments headed by African Americans to be significantly more satisfied than other African American workers. In contrast, European Americans' satisfaction appeared unrelated to the racial status of the executive director. The pattern of their satisfaction corresponded to the degree to which their employment sites had experienced funding cuts, with those in departments experiencing the harshest cuts the most dissatisfied (McNeely, 1988e).

Although similar to other workers in the importance of job dullness as a predictor of satisfaction, the satisfaction of African Americans (particularly women) was predicted strongly by the degree to which they felt affiliated with their work organizations. Similarly, the degree to which supervisors solicited their input and evidenced that the input was valued tended to be stronger predictors for African Americans than for other employees. These findings were consistent with those of other studies indicating that African Americans experiencing workplace social exclusion from other races reported less satisfaction. Specifically, African Americans in segregated work groups are less satisfied (Moch, 1980), although Konar (1981) suggested that factors responsible for the segregation (on-the-job discrimination) rather than the physical segregation itself is the most likely explanation for depressed satisfaction levels. African Americans who provide accounts of work experience have emphasized repeatedly the adverse effects of race-linked isolation on the job (Jones, 1973) and of race-linked exclusion from informal social groups that fraternize and network away from the office (Taylor, 1982). In addition, both men and women were affected strongly by their perception of the fairness of promotional patterns and the extent to which they felt jobs would be available for them to fulfill career aspirations.

Taken in sum, the factors identified thus far (organizational strife related to race, "belongingness" to the organization, promotional fairness) suggest the salience of perceived discrimination as key in predicting the satisfaction of African Americans. Other robust predictors were consistent with literature previously reviewed: The satisfaction of African American women was predicted strongly by whether they regarded job expectations as being excessive, and satisfaction of men was predicted strongly by the degree to which they felt able to exercise judgment.

Contrary to much of the job satisfaction literature (a great deal of which is based on individual examinations of single sites that cannot determine differences among sites), these findings suggested that factors associated with individual workplaces might be more salient in determining satisfaction levels than other factors, such as having race-related frames of reference that anticipated on-the-job discrimination, thereby causing African Americans (and women) to expect less from their employment and to be satisfied with less (Brenner & Fernsten, 1984; Varca, Shaffer, & McCauley, 1983). Implications to those in executive positions suggested that African American satisfaction can be modified according to the race relations climate of the employment setting. Moch (1980) suggested that particular attention should be paid to manipulating work assignments to ensure proportional racial representation in work groups.

African American human services workers earned less than European American workers, even when occupational status, education, and length of employment were taken into account. Among all human services workers, African American and other women of color were the most poorly paid, and they experienced disproportional representation in lesser-status positions, even when years of schooling and employment tenure are controlled.

Asian Americans

Following a review that revealed no references to Asian Americans in the human services job satisfaction literature, the senior author of this chapter was prompted to disaggregate the sample so that Asian Americans could be examined (McNeely, 1987a). Unfortunately, the limited number ($N = 68$) of Asian Americans in the study group did not permit separate analyses for ethnicity. Separate examinations of Chinese, Japanese, and Koreans might have revealed important intergroup differences.

Results indicated no significant differences in the job satisfaction of Asian American workers compared to other workers. This finding was surprising because studies of some Asians, notably Japanese and Japanese Americans, have been consistent in demonstrating these workers to have lower job satisfaction levels than either non-Asian Americans or Europeans, arguably (Lincoln, Hanada, & Olson, 1981) because they expect more from their work organizations than the latter groups (Cole, 1979). Thus, the differential frame-of-reference assumption, which suggests that workers of color will have high satisfaction levels because they expect less, was not supported by these data.

The pattern of variables that were predictive of Asian American satisfaction, however, were different. The best predictor for Asian Americans, a variable that was virtually unrelated to the satisfaction of other workers, was whether they perceived that "Most of the 'higher-ups' are friendly toward employees." This finding mirrors other research conducted on Asians (native Asians and Asian Americans) wherein it has been reported that Asian cultural values (particularly Japanese values) lead these workers to expect, value, and have more job satisfaction when there are paternalistic personal ties between supervisors and subordinates (Cole, 1979; Lincoln et al., 1981). Unlike other workers, personal ties and job satisfaction increase for Asian workers as hierarchical differentiation (tall status hierarchies) and organizational size increase. As noted by Lincoln and colleagues (1981), these findings have important implications for commonly held Western assumptions that tend to emphasize the universal desirability of "egalitarian" (horizontally differentiated) organizational forms. (Although Japanese organizations tend to be highly differentiated vertically, they nonetheless are characterized by substantial informal participation in decision making, limited role differentiation and task specialization in the division of labor, and personalized interpersonal relations; Cole, 1979). Executives of human services departments need to be sensitive to the possibility that Asian American workers expect demonstrable personal concern from their supervisors.

As with other human services workers, the satisfaction of Asian Americans was predicted strongly by whether they perceived their jobs as being dull and monotonous and whether they felt able to use their abilities in their jobs. These workers, however, were less affected by perceptions of excessive pressure and expectations, a finding consistent with that of other studies reporting some Asian groups to prefer supervisors who make heavy demands as long as they evidence personal interest in employees (Marsh & Mannari, 1976, p. 194). Other findings indicated that Asian Americans earned less and were represented disproportionately in nonprofessional human services positions, despite having attained more years of schooling and longer employment tenure than their non-Asian counterparts. These findings are consistent with national norms, however, wherein Asian Americans have higher educational attainment, have longer service to the employer, work more hours per week, work more weeks per year, and yet still earn less than European Americans (Sandefur & Pahari, 1989; Takaki, 1985).

Latinos

Another group about which little is known in human services work is Latinos. Unlike Asian Americans, a sample of Latinos ($N = 124$), composed of nearly equal percentages of Cubans and Mexican Americans, were found to have significantly higher job satisfaction levels than non-Latinos on both overall and intrinsic satisfaction (McNeely, 1989b). In their study of Latino workers, Hawkes, Guagnano, Accredolo, and Helmick (1984) reported that, in contrast to the average European American, who measures his or her status primarily in terms of attained or potential income, the job satisfaction of Latinos is predicted more strongly by the degree to which an occupation is held in high esteem regardless of job income. Noted as a dramatic finding, they reported that job satisfaction was highest among Latinos when occupational status was high and income status low. Within Latino communities, having full-time nonseasonal employment with fringe benefits in a relatively clean professional setting may be more likely to generate respect, perhaps accounting for the high satisfaction levels of Latino employees engaged in comparatively low-paying public welfare work.

Similar trends were observed in the pattern of variables predictive of satisfaction for Latinos and non-Latinos. Both groups were affected most substantially by perceptions of job dullness, both were influenced by assessments of the extent to which they were able to use their abilities in the job, and both were affected by perceptions of on-the-job pressure. Compared with non-Latinos, Latino satisfaction was influenced to a greater degree by perceptions of managerial competence, whereas non-Latino satisfaction was predicted more strongly by the extent to which non-Latinos felt affiliated with their workplaces.

The most discrepant comparisons between the two groups were observed for upper-echelon (administrative, supervisory, professional) Latino and non-Latino women. Whereas predictors of satisfaction for non-Latino women conformed generally to the patterns reported in this chapter, the satisfaction of Latino women was affected most by whether their supervisors were able to get employees to work together as a team and whether they felt free to talk with supervisors when they had complaints (McNeely, 1987b).

The relationship to job satisfaction of these variables for similarly employed African American and European American women was low, suggesting that Latino women may be a distinctive subgroup of the larger group of women occupying professional, supervisory, and administrative positions. Alternatively, these findings might be attributable to an artifact of the sample that appeared to be consistent with national norms in public welfare work. Among high-echelon women, Latinos had served the fewest years within their departments. McIlwee (1982) has shown that female newcomers in nontraditional positions (in this case, professional and higher positions) were especially appreciative of coworker cooperation. Thus, executive directors are urged to consider the historical representation within their departments of employees of color in high-echelon positions. Executives should make special efforts to foster cooperation among workers employed in departments within which employees of color are perceived, or perceive themselves, as comparative newcomers to positions of high rank.

As was the case with other ethnic groups, Latinos were disproportionately placed in positions of low rank and earned less than non-Latinos. However, after controlling for education, occupational rank, and length of employment, statistically significant income differences applied primarily to those who were more highly educated and most recently employed; that is, the greatest income discrepancies between Latinos and their European American counterparts were experienced by recently employed professional Latinos (McNeely, 1989b).

RACE AND ETHNICITY, GENDER, EARNINGS, AND OCCUPATIONAL RANK

As noted previously, differences in status and income by race and ethnicity and gender are evident in the public social services. Chi-square (χ^2) and Cramer's V (CV) analyses were performed to determine whether the differences with respect to race and ethnicity, gender, and occupational status were statistically significant.[2] The analysis was achieved by combining the race and ethnicity and gender groups. African American women, for example, constituted one group, followed, respectively, by the remaining individual groups:

[2]For a discussion of the importance of using a measure of association such as Cramer's V with chi-square when analyzing data generated from large samples, see McNeely et al. (1993).

Table 12-1

Race and Ethnicity, Gender, and Occupational Status Controlling for Education and Length of Employment

Analysis	N	χ^2	df	p	CV	p
Race and ethnicity and gender by occupational status	1,917	261.18	20	≤0.001	0.165	≤0.001
Controlling for education	1,916					
Less than college degree	801	133.44	20	≤0.001	0.182	≤0.001
College degree	1,115	96.29	20	≤0.001	0.131	≤0.001
Controlling for education and length of employment	1,902					
No degree, less than 6 years	326	78.97	20	≤0.001	0.220	≤0.001
No degree, more than 6 years	467	73.95	20	≤0.001	0.178	≤0.001
Degree, less than 6 years	430	50.37	20	≤0.002	0.153	≤0.001
Degree, more than 6 years	679	58.22	16	≤0.001	0.141	≤0.001

NOTE: Excludes Racine County employees.

African American men, European American women, European American men, other women, and other men. There were 232 "others," of whom 70 were Asian and 127 were Latino. Occupational status ranged from servicers (for example, building maintenance workers and storeroom keepers) to administrators. The relationship among race and ethnicity, gender, and occupational status was statistically significant ($\chi^2 = 261.18$, $p \le 0.001$, CV = 0.165, $p \le 0.001$) (Table 12-1).

A question left unanswered is whether the relationship among race and ethnicity, gender, and occupational status was explained by differences in educational attainment and employment length. Multidimensional chi-square analyses were performed to answer the question. To achieve the analysis, the sample was disaggregated for education and employment length. Educational attainment was dichotomized, with one group having at least a college degree and the other having less than a college degree. Similarly, employment length was dichotomized, with one group including those who had been employed in their human services departments for at least six years and the other including those with fewer than six years of service.

Controlling for education does not reduce the strength of the relationship between race and ethnicity, gender, and occupational status to statistical insignificance. Although the association (0.165) indicated by CV was reduced somewhat for one educational group (0.131), it was higher (0.182) for the other group. Thus, educational attainment does not explain race and gender discrepancies in occupational rank.

After controlling for educational attainment and employment tenure, the associations remained statistically significant, and no dramatic reductions in the strength of these associations were evident. Consequently, the disproportionate representations in occupational rank by race and ethnicity and gender were not explained by educational attainment or employment seniority. At the same time, readers should note the actual CV values. Although all of the values were statistically significant, the highest value reported is 0.220; this value does not denote a particularly robust relationship, indicating that, at best, the capability of race and ethnicity and gender in predicting occupational status was no more than merely moderate.

In addition, the association among race and ethnicity, gender, and occupational status steadily attenuates as education and seniority increase. The greatest disparities related to race and ethnicity and gender and occurred for those who had the fewest years of schooling and years of service to their agencies. These people earned the least and occupied the lowest positions compared with their similarly educated and tenured European American counterparts.

European American men earned the highest incomes. Whereas African American men had the next-highest incomes, the standard deviation for this group was larger than that for any other group, suggesting that although some of these workers were faring well, others were faring poorly. Although the table does not report data disaggregated for education, length of employment, and occupational rank, significant income discrepancies remained even when these variables were taken into account, and patterns evident in Table 12-2 remain the same (McNeely et al., 1993). As noted previously, European American men occupied 40 percent of all administrative positions and occupied 21 percent of all supervisory positions, even though they comprised only 15.7 percent of the sample. In reference to women, some social work writers have suggested that the profession and schools of social work have deliberately developed men for (higher-paying) leadership positions to legitimize social services agencies to members of powerful external publics, many of whom regard women as ill suited to management (Patti, 1984).

Both European American men and women were more likely than their same-sex counterparts to hold high-ranking jobs, and African American men were less likely than either European American or other men to hold high-ranking jobs. Those experiencing the harshest conditions in public welfare work were African American and other women; they earned the least and were least likely to occupy professional or higher-status positions, even when education and employment length were controlled (observed differences significant at $p < 0.002$ for all employee groups stratified by education and employment length).

DO THESE DATA PROVE DISCRIMINATION?

It is possible that a number of factors other than discrimination may be converging to explain the disproportionalities observed with respect to status and earnings. Two explanations, for example, have been offered recently to explain the low earnings of other-race (Latino and Asian American) human services workers. For Latinos, a lack of

Table 12-2

Race, Gender, and Income for All Occupational Groups

Population Group	N	M	SD	Scheffe Contrasts[a]	F	Significance of F Value
Total	1,914[b]					
1. African American women	435	20,143	6,305.7			
2. African American men	75	24,278	10,142.3	1,5		
3. European American women	870	22,673[c]	6,363.6	1,5	46.01	≤ 0.001
4. European American men	302	27,356	8,827.3	1,2,3,5,6		
5. Other women	160	19,686	6,527.9			
6. Other men	72	21,124	5,857.6			

NOTE: Reported income figures are based on computations converting grouped data into dollar figures according to Blalock's (1960) recommended procedure. Dollar figures are presented to aid readers in interpreting data. *F* tests and Scheffe contrasts are based on analyses of grouped data. Thus, the procedure used yielded the most conservative estimates of income differences.

[a]Scheffe contrasts (Kachigan, 1986) denote pairs of groups significantly different at $p \leq 0.05$. For example, the numbers 1 and 5 are reported for African American men. This indicates that the mean income of these men is significantly different from that of groups 1 (African American women) and 5 (other women).

[b]Excludes Racine County employees for whom income data were not collected.

[c]The earnings data reported understate the true income of European American women because a much higher percentage of these workers, compared with other workers, were employed voluntarily in part-time jobs.

"fluid" bilingualism among some workers was suggested (McNeely, 1989b) as a reason. Recent immigrant status, inexperience in the norms of American society, and a lack of fluent bilingualism have been suggested to explain the lower earnings of Asian American human services workers (McNeely, 1987a). These factors might be converging to explain the lower earnings of other races. It also is possible that the lower earnings reflect discriminatory treatment in the awarding of salaries.

European American men, African American men, and European American women tended to be paid the highest incomes, whereas other-race women, African American women, and other-race men tended to be paid the lowest incomes. Yet these data do not offer unequivocal support to those asserting discrimination related to race and ethnicity and gender in social welfare work. The more meager salaries of women, for example, might be related to the tendency of women in social welfare to select, or succumb to encouragement to select, career paths that lead to lower-paying clinical work rather than to higher-paying administrative work. In addition, the proclivity of European American women to self-select into part-time employment (Nardone, 1986) may explain why, as a group, they earn less than do African American men. Readers should also remember that part-time employment does not merely deflate income because of the fewer hours part-timers work; income also is deflated for part-timers because departmental executives are less likely to select part-timers, regardless of gender, for promotion and less likely to select them for training opportunities designed to impart administrative or other technical skills that lead to positional authority and higher income. Unfortunately, whether a participant was working part time could not be taken into account by this study.

CONCLUSION

Not adequately captured in the preceding comments of this chapter is the fact that many human services workers, despite the variety of problems they encounter, truly enjoy their jobs, feeling that they are challenging and rewarding and allow them to do something of genuine value for other people.

> I have been a dedicated nurse for over 25 years. This work will never become dull and noninteresting. *(African American licensed practical nurse, age 53, Dade County)*

> Compared to other jobs, this one has the potential for a greater sense of accomplishment. *(European American female welfare eligibility worker, age 35, Sacramento County)*

> I am happier in this position than any other I have had in the past, in spite of the emotional drain that it entails. *(European American female medical secretary, age 44, Dade County)*

> It is good to feel necessary and useful. *(European American recreation therapist, age 62, Dade County)*

As is the case in any employment setting, the morale of those less satisfied can be improved by instituting effective policies and programs (McNeely, 1988b; McNeely & Fogarty, 1988), and because many departments continue to experience diminished resources, it is refreshing to know that job satisfaction may be restored in a relatively short period following budget cuts (McNeely, Feyerherm, & Johnson, 1986).

Regardless of race and ethnicity or gender, a key morale-enhancing factor is for workers to have meaningful opportunities to participate in decision making, or at least have their input seriously considered.

> It would be wonderful if bosses would ask our opinion on what changes need to be made. After all, we deal with it all the time and know how to get better results. *(European American female assistance payments worker, age 39, Genesee County)*

Participative decision making in itself can help address the boredom that appears pervasive among human services workers who are dissatisfied. Although participation in decision making conveys to most workers a sense that their opinions and, therefore, they themselves are of value to the organization, a particular form of participation is associated with the performance of high-quality work, whereas other forms are not related to positive organizational outcomes (Bacharach, Bamberger, & Conley, 1990; Cotton, Vollrath, Lengnick-Hall, & Froggatt, 1988; Leana, Locke, & Schweiger, 1990). Workers allowed discretion in the execution of their jobs are more likely than those participating in policy development to perform high-quality work (Whiddon & Martin, 1989), and participative decision making tends to work best with employees who have high growth needs (Hackman & Oldham, 1980).

Also evident is the importance of situational factors—factors peculiar to the sites within which workers are employed—in predicting satisfaction. Efforts to address factors peculiar to a work site may be more important in raising morale than other efforts focused on factors that characterize the race and ethnicity or gender groups in the aggregate, although executives must be sensitive to any influences that appear to be generally common to the race and ethnicity and gender cohorts. At the same time, it is important to recognize that findings reported for aggregated groups of workers, even when restricted to specific race and ethnicity and gender subgroups, mask important individual differences in motivation and life-cycle changes.

An implication of contradictions and reversals in findings reported previously also must be considered. To some extent these reversals and contradictions result from noncomparable instruments and methods used by different researchers examining job satisfaction. However, they also result from numerous factors that often vary in unknown ways across different sampling frames. For example, Martin and Hanson (1985) have shown that primary wage-earning women are more concerned about extrinsic rewards, whereas secondary earners are more concerned about intrinsic satisfaction, more likely to seek jobs that provide comfort and convenience, and more inclined to eschew jobs high in material rewards (Martin & Shehan, 1989). Sampling frames composed disproportionately of one of these groups, therefore, will generate findings that contradict those obtained from a sample with disproportionate representation from the other group.

Although these comments may help explain the many contradictions and reversals found in the work satisfaction literature, of greater importance is their implication for those who are stewards in the public social services. The implication is that effective administrators will not need merely to be knowledgeable of conditions peculiar to their organizations, and factors associated broadly with the aggregated race and ethnicity and gender groups, they also must be sensitive to differences in the motivational characteristics (such as whether a woman is a primary or secondary wage earner) and life-cycle stages of workers (such as whether an employee is engaged in balancing work with child rearing). Generally speaking, women appear to be affected substantially by opportunities to use their perceived abilities, African Americans appear to be affected substantially by their sense of "belongingness" to an organization and by their perceptions of discrimination within an organization, and Asian

Americans appear affected most by perceptions of their affiliations with administrative supervisors. As Hasenfeld (1984) has emphasized, employees are the most important resource of human services agencies, and administrators should strive to be sensitive to apparent intergroup differences such as these.

Such sensitivity also should enable executives and others seeking to improve satisfaction to recognize and appropriately act on the needs of individual workers as those needs unfold and change over time. Among other things, workers should be provided with choices within the organization in the conditions of their employment. As noted by two respondents:

> I work half-time, so I enjoy my job more because of this. I was working full-time until one month ago. I appreciate the fact that I was allowed to work half-time, although it took me 3 months to convert. *(European American female welfare eligibility worker, age 28, Sacramento County)*

> Management talks about improving morale, but how can you build morale when any small benefits, such as flex working hours or the four-day workweek, are not utilized? *(African American casework senior, age 32, Fulton County)*

Organizations that do not allow for part-time employment possibilities, job sharing, flexible scheduling, flexible benefits, and the like (McNeely, 1988d) are not likely to be regarded by employees as positively as those that do. Finally, executives and others wishing to improve satisfaction must be aware that restoring and maintaining satisfaction requires recurring efforts. Such efforts should be regarded as a dynamic rather than static organizational process.

REFERENCES

Andrisani, P., & Shapiro, M. (1978). Women's attitudes toward their jobs: Some longitudinal data on a national sample. *Personnel Psychology, 31,* 15–34.

Bacharach, S., Bamberger, P., & Conley, J. (1990). Work processes, role conflict, and role overload. *Sociology of Work and Organizations, 17,* 199–228.

Blalock, H. (1960). *Social statistics.* New York: McGraw-Hill.

Brenner, O., & Fernsten, J. (1984). Racial differences in perceived job fulfillment of white-collar workers. *Perceptual and Motor Skills, 58,* 643–646.

Burris, B. (1991). Employed mothers: The impact of class and marital status on the prioritizing of family and work. *Social Science Quarterly, 72,* 50–66.

Bush, J. (1977). The minority administrator: Implications for social work education. *Journal of Education for Social Work, 13,* 15–22.

Cole, R. E. (1979). *Work, mobility, and participation: A comparative study of American and Japanese industry.* Los Angeles: University of California Press.

Cotton, J., Vollrath, D., Lengnick-Hall, M., & Froggatt, K. (1988). Employee participation. *Academy of Management Journal, 13,* 8–22.

Daly, A. (1990). *Perception of influence and job satisfaction.* Unpublished manuscript, School of Social Work, Rutgers University, New Brunswick, NJ.

Daly, A. (1994). African American and white managers: A comparison in one agency. *Journal of Community Practice, 1*(1), 57–79.

Doering, M., Rhodes, S., & Schuster, M. (1983). *The aging worker: Research and recommendations.* Beverly Hills, CA: Sage Publications.

Dressel, P. (1987). Patriarchy and social welfare work. *Social Problems, 34,* 294–309.

Fox, H., & Lefkowitz, J. (1974). Differential validity: Ethnic groups as a moderator in predicting job performance. *Personnel Psychology, 27,* 209–223

Hackman, R., & Oldham, G. (1980). *Work redesign.* Reading, MA: Addison-Wesley.

Hasenfeld, Y. (1984). The changing context of human services administration. *Social Work, 29,* 522–529.

Hawkes, G. R., Guagnano, G., Accredolo, C., & Helmick, S. (1984). Status inconsistency and job satisfaction: General population and Mexican-American subpopulation analyses. *Sociology and Social Research, 68,* 378–387.

Herzberg, F. (1959). *The motivation to work.* New York: John Wiley & Sons.

Jayaratne, S., & Chess, W. (1982–1983). Some correlates of job satisfaction among social workers. *Journal of Applied Social Sciences, 7,* 1–17.

Jayaratne, S., & Chess, W. (1983). Job satisfaction and turnover among social work administrators. A national survey. *Administration in Social Work, 7,* 11–22.

Johnston, W., & Packer, A. (1987). *Workforce 2000: Work and workers for the twenty-first century.* Indianapolis: Hudson Institute.

Jones, E. (1973). What is it like to be a black manager? *Harvard Business Review, 51,* 108–116.

Konar, E. (1981). Explaining racial differences in job satisfaction. *Journal of Applied Sociology, 66,* 522–524.

Kravetz, D., & Austin, C. (1984). Women's issues in social service administration. *Administration in Social Work, 8*(4), 25–38.

Leana, C., Locke, E., & Schweiger, D. (1990). Fact and fiction in analyzing research on participative decision making: A critique of Cotton, Vollrath, Froggatt, Lengnick-Hall, and Jennings. *Academy of Management Review, 15*(1), 137–146.

Lincoln, J., Hanada, M., & Olson, J. (1981). Cultural orientations and individual reactions to organizations: A study of employees of Japanese-owned firms. *Administrative Science Quarterly, 26*(1), 93–115.

Loscocco, K. (1989). The instrumentally oriented factory worker: Myth or reality? *Work and Occupations, 16,* 3–25.

Marsh, R. & Mannari, H. (1976). *Modernization and the Japanese factory.* Princeton, NJ: Princeton University Press.

Martin, J., & Hanson, S. (1985). Sex, family wage earning status and satisfaction with work. *Work and Occupations, 12,* 91–109.

Martin, J., & Shehan, C. (1989). Education and job satisfaction: The influence of gender, wage-earning status, and job values. *Work and Occupations, 16,* 184–198.

Martin, P. Y., & Chernesky, R. H. (1989). Women's prospects for leadership in social welfare: A political economy perspective. *Administration in Social Work, 13*(3–4), 117–143.

McIlwee, J. (1982). Work satisfaction among women in nontraditional occupations. *Sociology of Work and Occupations, 9,* 299–355.

McNeely, R. L. (1978). Life satisfaction, job attitudes, and involvement among men in humanistic versus rationalistic work environments. *Social Development Issues, 2,* 70–88.

McNeely, R. L. (1979). Sources of alienation at work and household violence within middle-class families: A theoretical perspective. *Social Development Issues, 3,* 12–34.

McNeely, R. L. (1984). Occupation, gender and work satisfaction in a comprehensive human services department. *Administration in Social Work, 8,* 35–47.

McNeely, R. L. (1987a). Job satisfaction and other characteristics of Asian American human service workers. *Social Work Research & Abstracts, 23*(4), 7–9.

McNeely, R. L. (1987b). Predictors of job satisfaction among three racial/ethnic groups of professional female human service workers. *Journal of Sociology and Social Welfare, 14,* 115–136.

McNeely, R. L. (1988a). Age and job satisfaction in human service employment. *Gerontologist, 21,* 163–168.

McNeely, R. L. (1988b). Five morale-enhancing innovations for human service settings. *Social Casework, 69,* 204–214.

McNeely, R. L. (1988c). Job satisfaction differences among three age groups of female human service workers. *Journal of Aging Studies, 2,* 109–120.

McNeely, R. L. (1988d). Managing work and family demands: Strengths, weaknesses and barriers to implementing twenty innovative programs. *Social Work Papers, 21,* 1–15.

McNeely, R. L. (1988e). Recisions, organizational conditions and job satisfaction among black and white human service workers: A research note. *Journal of Sociology and Social Welfare, 15,* 125–134.

McNeely, R. L. (1989a). Gender, job satisfaction, earnings, and other characteristics of human service workers during and after midlife. *Administration in Social Work, 13,* 99–115.

McNeely, R. L. (1989b). Job satisfaction and other characteristics among Hispanic American human services workers. *Social Casework, 70,* 237–242.

McNeely, R. L. (1989c). Race and job satisfaction in human service employment. *Administration in Social Work, 13,* 75–93.

McNeely, R. L. (1990). Do respondents who pen comments onto mail surveys differ from other respondents? A research note on the human services job satisfaction literature. *Journal of Sociology and Social Welfare, 17,* 123–137.

McNeely, R. L. (1992). Job satisfaction in the public social services: Perspectives on structure, situational factors, gender, and ethnicity. In Y. Hasenfeld (Ed.), *Human services as complex organizations* (pp. 224–255). Newbury Park, CA: Sage Publications.

McNeely, R. L., Blakemore, J. L., & Washington, R. O. (1993). Race, gender, occupational status, and income in county human service employment. *Journal of Sociology and Social Welfare, 20,* 47–70.

McNeely, R. L., Feyerherm, W., & Johnson, R. E. (1986). Services integration and job satisfaction reactions in a comprehensive human resource agency. *Administration in Social Work, 10,* 39–53.

McNeely, R. L., & Fogarty, B. (1988). Balancing parenthood and employment: Company receptiveness to innovations. *Family Relations, 37,* 189–195.

Miller, D. C. (1977). *Handbook of research design and social measurement.* New York: David McKay.

Miller, J. (1980). Individual and occupational determinants of job satisfaction: A focus on gender differences. *Sociology of Work and Occupations, 7,* 337–366.

Moch, M. (1980). Racial differences in job satisfaction: Testing four common explanations. *Journal of Applied Psychology, 56,* 299–306.

Nardone, T. J. (1986). Part-time workers: Who are they? *Monthly Labor Review, 109,* 13–19.

Patti, R. (1984). Who leads the human services? *Administration in Social Work, 8,* 17–29.

Sandefur, G., & Pahari, A. (1989). Racial and ethnic inequality in earnings and educational attainment. *Social Service Review, 63,* 199–221.

Shapiro, E. (1977). Racial differences in the value of job rewards. *Social Forces, 56,* 21–30.

Sullivan, T. (1989). Women and minority workers in the new economy. *Work and Occupations, 16,* 393–415.

Takaki, R. (1985). Is race insurmountable? In W. Van Horne (Ed.), *Ethnicity and the workforce* (pp. 208–222). Milwaukee: University of Wisconsin–Milwaukee, Urban Corridor Consortium.

Taylor, A. (1982, December 6). The myth of the black executive. *Time,* p. 53.

Varca, P. E., Shaffer, G., & McCauley, C. D. (1983). Sex differences in job satisfaction revisited. *Academy of Management Journal, 26,* 348–353.

Whiddon, B., & Martin, P. Y. (1989). Organizational democracy and work quality in a state welfare agency. *Social Science Quarterly, 23,* 254–271.

Wright, R., Wesley-King, S., & Berg, W. E. (1985). Job satisfaction in the workplace: A study of black females in management positions. *Journal of Social Service Research, 8*(3), 65–79.

The senior author expresses his appreciation to all the county human services employees who participated in the study described in this chapter.

13 African American Women in Academic Leadership

Jeanette Jennings, Ruth R. Martin, and
Phyllis Ivory Vroom

Biculturalism—the experience of living simultaneously in two cultures—has been one of the most compelling conceptualizations used to frame the experience of African Americans in white society (Chestang, 1972) and in predominantly white organizations (Bell, 1990). More than 20 years ago, Chestang (1972) observed "the black man is not a marginal man but a bicultural man. He does not live on the fringes of the larger society, he lives in both the larger society and the black society" (p. 46). Chestang continued by describing two styles of coping—transcendent and depreciated—that black people must keep in balance to deal effectively with this dual perspective. Similarly, concluding that the African American women in her study lived a bicultural existence that required balancing this dualism, Bell (1990) described the perceived tensions, challenges, rewards, and coping strategies used to balance their dualism. Many of the elements described by Chestang and Bell characterize the experiences set forth in this chapter.

This chapter assesses the bicultural situation of African American women associate deans in social work education. It illustrates the challenges and rewards of being African American women in leadership positions and the dual and interacting challenges of gender and race. The challenges include isolation; finding mentors; maintaining credibility, integrity, and values; and negotiating the unwritten organizational rules. Both intrinsic and extrinsic rewards are assayed, and coping strategies are explored relative to gender, race, and leadership positions of African American women in higher educational institutions headed predominantly by white men. The bicultural framework will be used because the culture of African American women will be viewed as a subsystem of the black culture. This viewpoint serves to underscore the diversity within the African American community, and yet it preserves the complex picture of the black woman as *boundary spanner*—one who serves at the boundary of as well as in two systems or cultures—and identifies with an additional subsystem. These realities may limit or preclude alliances with men of color and white women, both of whom are likely to move into leadership positions earlier than African American women. This reality will be discussed in the section on mentoring.

LITERATURE REVIEW

In the past two decades there have been an increasing number of studies of women and African Americans in the workplace. In many ways the experiences of African American women parallel those of white women and African American men. However, differences exist between African American women and those groups. Women in the workplace have issues that are grounded in historical traditions that include the socialization of women, devaluation of women's work, and the employment of women in traditionally undervalued female work. Similarly, African Americans were almost entirely denied entry into the labor markets and were thus confined to certain employment opportunities.

Studies of African Americans address the issues of the entire ethnic group and do not address the unique issues of African American women (Davis & Watson, 1982; Dickens & Dickens, 1982). The assumption that "what is true for African American men is true for African American women" does not present a true representation of African American women. African American women's work experiences are different, primarily because they are members of two groups—women and African Americans—to which low status as well as limited employment opportunities are ascribed. In addition, the labor market is simultaneously structured on the basis of race and gender, which work together and separately. Thus, for African American women the interaction of race and gender makes the experiences of African American women different.

Racism and sexism tend to heighten the stresses of African American women in the workplace. Gilkes's (1982) conceptualization of a "web" is an appropriate characterization; he stated that the African American woman "is caught in a possible conflicting web of expectations which are far more complex than those of simply being a professional, being a woman or being black" (p. 290). The complexity of the roles is evident in higher education as well as in the corporate world.

Nearly two decades have passed since Martin (1980) studied minority women administrators' perception of barriers in higher education, which included structural, internal, external, and racial barriers. Bell (1994) and Atwater (1995) are among recent authors whose research indicated that these barriers have not weakened significantly. In fact, the outlook for the year 2000 and beyond is bleak because of an expected shortage of people of color in higher education and fewer than today in the academic pipeline because many are entering other professions (Tack & Patita, 1992). Women in higher education are disproportionately concentrated in untenured and nontenurable ranks, underpaid by all institutions in all fields and at all ranks, and overloaded with introductory courses. Women face problems in the areas of salaries, academic rank and tenure, and the extent of administrative responsibilities and decision making. Men of color hold higher academic ranks, are tenured more often (Davis & Watson, 1982) and have higher publication rates (Schiele, 1991, 1992a, 1992b) than do women of color. Demographic data from Gill and Showell's (1991) research document sexual and racial barriers that prevent African American women from obtaining top leadership roles in higher education.

ROLE OF ASSOCIATE DEANS

Associate deans are appointed by the dean of the school to share in the leadership and management functions (see Hellriegel, Slocum, & Woodman, 1992; Katz & Kahn, 1978). Leadership functions are the primary tasks of the deanery and include determining the need for and promoting organizational change; creating a vision and setting the direction of the organizational change; and aligning faculty and staff with the vision, mission, goals, and objectives. Generally, associate deans are delegated leadership and managerial responsibilities focused on the academic affairs of the school: chairing major committees or task forces as assigned by the dean; establishing faculty workloads; establishing the schedule of classes and assigning full-time and part-time faculty to teach them; handling problems related to faculty and student performance, including the procedures for student grievances, academic termination, and reinstatement; and handling emotional and behavioral problems of students. In addition, most associate deans have responsibility for coordinating the activities and handling the diverse problems of the school's offices of admission, student services, and field education.

As the chief executive officer, deans have the managerial responsibilities of planning, budgeting, organizing, and coordinating staff activities and promulgating and enforcing the rules of the university and the school (Hellriegel et al., 1992). Although deans attend to the myriad responsibilities and complexities of planning and budgeting and to organizational–environmental relations including fundraising, associate deans are responsible for the day-to-day operation of the school. To implement their duties and responsibilities, five sources of power are delegated differentially to the associate dean:

1. *Legitimate power*—The right to request faculty and staff perform tasks and responsibilities by virtue of the position.
2. *Reward power*—The limited ability to provide something desired by the faculty and staff in exchange for desired behavior.
3. *Coercive power*—The ability, through the use of force (although rarely used), to achieve desired performance.
4. *Referent power*—The ability to achieve desired behavior, based on the admiration, liking, or desire to receive approval of the associate dean.
5. *Expert power*—The ability to achieve desired behavior because of the perceived expertise of the associate dean (French & Raven, 1968, cited in Hellriegel et al., 1992).

The impact of race and gender on the exercise of each of these sources of power embodies the challenges described in subsequent sections. Harper (1990) described the perceptions of powerlessness of female administrators on each of the five dimensions of power compared with the greater sense of power of their male counterparts. Perhaps these perceptions are grounded in the persistent and grinding daily hassles of women, particularly African American women, in higher education. Barriers notwithstanding, they push on inexorably in their leadership roles in the face of challenges such as isolation, need for mentoring, maintaining credibility and values, and sparse intraorganizational networks and support.

CHALLENGES

Race and Gender

According to Lerner (1972), African American women "have historically carried the dual burden of Jim Crow and Jane Crow. We have not always carried it graciously, but we have carried it effectively" (p. 592). This duality means that, unlike for African American men, the identity of African American women is not based on gender; unlike white women, their identity is not based on color. Thus, two important characteristics of identification are not available to African American women. These sources of identity have implications for the success of African American women in leadership positions. The lack of a reference group based either on gender or race and the paucity of African American women in leadership roles result in her isolation. She has no one with whom to consult or serve as a confidant, no support system, and no one to help her negotiate the system or difficult situations. In addition, African American women must always assess whether an incident is based on race or gender. The continuous weighing of these factors may be the source of psychological stress.

The position of African American women is different because they have a different organizational reality. They are confronted with all the issues that women confront as well as with those that confront African American men and those that are unique to African American women. Even though African American women share the experiences of white women and African American men, they differ from these groups because of the socialization, orientation, and responses of the larger society to African American women.

A case could be made for describing the experience of African American women in higher education as a multicultural experience. African American women span three cultures: (1) the larger society, (2) the African American community, and (3) the community of black women. African American women share with African American men the experiences of injustice, oppression, and exclusion and share with white women the effects of sexism, discrimination, and the glass ceiling. Still, African American women must confront all of the stereotypes attributed to their race and gender and often carve out uncharted professional roles while confronting these stereotypes (Bell, 1990; Denton, 1990).

The new styles of doing business have implications for and demand adjustments for women as well as for those with whom they work. The dual burden of race and gender translates into a series of factors that affect African American women in higher education administration. One of the most prominent is isolation.

Isolation

"Black women feel isolated because they are isolated" (Jackson, 1972, cited in Carroll, 1973). In most institutions, African Americans are a small minority of the administrators. Carroll provided the following description of the professional loneliness African American women experience:

> There is no one with whom to share experiences and gain support, no one with whom to identify, no one on whom a black woman can model herself. It takes a great deal of psychological strength "just to get through the day," the endless lunches, and meetings in which one is always "different." The feeling is much like the exhaustion a foreigner speaking an alien tongue feels at the end of the day. (p. 179)

Tidball (1974) noted that the structure of most colleges and university environments is relatively nonsupportive of women faculty and students. It is probably not just getting the job done, but the sense of belonging on the job and the recognition one receives from the position that is most important. Perhaps the lack of informal signs of belonging and recognition bother the academic women the most—not having someone with whom to have lunch, take coffee breaks, or share research interests.

Mentoring

Because of the isolation, many African American women do not reap all of the benefits that mentoring offers. Mentoring is crucial for people who want to advance in an organization. It is important to have a mentor who can provide the psychosocial functions—role modeling, acceptance and confirmation, counseling, and friendships—as well as the career functions—sponsorship, coaching, protecting, and making the protégé known to others (Kram, 1985). Women appear to have a more difficult time finding a mentor than do men (Noe, 1988).

Mentor relationships with men can be harder to manage and may provide a narrower range of benefits for women than for men (Noe, 1988). Male mentors may fail to consider the different effects of organizational practices on women. Furthermore, sexual harassment and sexual relationships can occur and have a negative impact. Similarly, mentoring across racial lines has inhibitions as well, among which are lack of access to information networks, tokenism, stereotyping, and socialization practices. According to Thomas (1990), same-race relationships were found to provide significantly more psychosocial support than cross-race relationships. In addition, "black men and women identified significant proportions of their sponsors as being of their own racial or gender groups or both" (p. 488).

African American women have the same difficulties as white women and African American men face in finding mentors. Mentoring tends to be homogeneous—people form relationships with others like themselves—so African American women may be excluded because there is often no natural affinity between them and African American or white men, or with white women.

Because of her awareness of stereotypes of African American women as aggressive, controlling, authoritarian, militant, and hostile, the African American woman may hesitate to approach someone to serve as a mentor. These same stereotypes may prevent people in the organization from coming forth to serve as a mentor to the African American woman. Without the opportunity to work closely with African American women, these stereotypes will persist.

Affirmative action has increased the critical mass of white women in social work education (Lennon, 1994, 1995). Following the principle of homogeneity, white men and women have their informal networks for conducting business and relaxing, excluding African American men and women from their processes (Bell, 1990; Swiss, 1996). The bonding of white men and white women in their separate groups signals to African American women that they remain outsiders and excludes them from informal and sometimes important channels of communication (Swiss, 1996). Moreover, exclusive networks can deprive women in leadership roles of important alliances and important feedback about their performance that white men or white women might feel comfortable giving to their "buddy" (Swiss, 1996).

Credibility

Establishing and maintaining credibility is a challenge in higher education and even more so for African American women. African American administrators are constantly pushed to prove, even to the lowest person on the totem pole, that they are competent and know the job. For example, when the associate dean enforces a policy, often students will go to a higher authority—the dean—for confirmation. In addition, often students go to a faculty member or a staff member to find out if the information given by the associate dean is correct.

Many faculty members will perform an "end run" around the associate dean to the dean for perceived gains. These gains may include self-promotion ("I thought you might be interested in what I'm doing relative to. . . ." or "For this reason, I really need an exception to the travel policy for. . . ."); to circumvent an unpopular decision ("My assignment to teach [undergraduate course, extension course, early morning, evening course] has interfered with my scholarship"); to seek a highly visible assignment ("We've been wondering who you might select to chair. . . ." or "You know, I've had an enduring interest in. . . ."); to make their input into a process more visible;

to change a previous decision ("We really should not. . . ."); or to "ex-pose" the lack of knowledge of the associate dean about an event, is-sue, or office gossip that might be viewed as strategic information. When students, faculty, or staff question the authority or knowledge of the associate dean, it is important for those in higher positions to convey that their behavior is inappropriate.

Not only are the associate dean's veracity and knowledge ques-tioned, but often her education and achievements are questioned as well. Sometimes the challenges to her authority, expertise, and legiti-macy result from the desire to view her as a token appointment to ap-pease affirmative action requirements. In this instance, the associate dean must give a measured response: She must acknowledge firmly and nondefensively that she is "an opportunity that was waiting to happen." That is, her current appointment and her presence in acad-eme is a result of the civil rights movement and the agitation of the African American community and students, the women's movement, and her readiness and preparedness to benefit from their advocacy.

For African American women interested in leadership positions in higher education, the pathway to the associate dean position often in-volves the decision to eschew the "special" (Pouissant, 1974) posi-tions created for people of color and women, including dean of mi-nority students, vice president for minority affairs, and coordinator of women's studies. Women's and minority positions in higher educa-tion often result in the position holders being permanently ensconced in them, precluding the opportunity for these women to have a broader impact on curriculum, organizational policy, and practices. Unless this track is what is desired, following the special track can end an upward career trajectory and might result in positions and roles of substantially less influence than that of associate dean.

Values

The experience of African American women in leadership positions can cause them to examine the efficacy of following the values extant in the black community. These values include selflessness and trust-worthiness, "standing by your word," "standing for something," holding "sacred" the reputations and secrets of others, eschewing self-promotion, focusing on collective as well as individual welfare, and being fair and judicious in the exercise of power. Often these values are challenged with a vengeance. One associate dean de-scribed the experience of being told an organizational secret with the admonishment, "Don't you dare tell," only to find later that almost everyone in the school knew the secret. One associate dean has seen members of her organization exercise the power of informal networks and alliances to mount a campaign to promote and tenure a faculty member whose talents were seriously mismatched with the needs of the organization. Each of the associate deans has witnessed the un-folding of a hidden agenda in meetings in which all of those present protested that no such agenda existed. However, it was evident from the nature of the interactions, including nonverbal communication patterns and the options presented, that much planning had gone into setting the hidden agenda. Each of these examples involved white faculty members acting in opposition to the counsel and confidence of the associate dean. In these instances, there is often no confidant with whom to discuss these issues, leaving the associate dean to take counsel with her own values to maintain ethical behavior.

Coping strategies needed to counter these and other assaults on values and integrity relate to Chestang's (1972) transcendent and depreciated characters. Rather than succumb to bitterness and cynicism that could result from many episodes like these examples, one balances hopefulness, optimism, and belief in the self-worth of others with a strong dose, where appropriate, of wariness and watchfulness, best characterized by the oxymoron "healthy paranoia."

Organizational Unwritten Rules

Swiss (1996) documented the unwritten rules that present barriers to women in corporate America. These and other barriers are experienced by African American women in higher education. All organizations have unwritten rules. However, as noted by Katz and Kahn (1978), it is impossible to codify all of the rules of any organization. For example, most organizations have unwritten rules about the appropriate time for new members to begin speaking and being visible. New members who break this rule by "talking too much too soon" at faculty meetings are often politely told to observe and listen a while longer before speaking. In many academic organizations, there is an unwritten rule about how soon one may seek tenure. For this reason, most neophytes need socialization through the formal and informal channels in the organization, including one or more mentors to help them with these unwritten rules.

Many unwritten rules present barriers to women and to African American women, such as the "old boys' network" and, increasingly, the "old girls' network" in social work education. The unwritten rule is that much informal and important communication and decision making and many hidden agendas are developed in these networks.

CONCLUSION

In addition to the balancing described by Chestang (1972), a variety of coping strategies exist to mitigate the effects of isolation, exclusion, and assaults on integrity and credibility. Many of these coping strategies result from the bicultural nature of African American women in academe.

For example, African American women might select as mentors African American men and women, including African American or white deans, who may be internal or external to their institution (Denton, 1990). African American women can find support by forming collegial relationships with counterparts in other schools and colleges in the university. For many women, coping strategies include maintaining strong connections with sustaining organizations in the African American community, including churches, sororities, and business and professional organizations (Bell, 1990; Daly, Jennings, Beckett, & Leashore, 1995; Denton, 1990). One successful coping strategy used by African American women in corporate roles involves successful compartmentalization of work, family, and other interpersonal and spiritual roles (Bell, 1990). Swiss (1996) described the use of this strategy by the white women in her sample. Developmental and psychological gains have resulted from women helping women instrumentally and emotionally (Bell, 1990; Denton, 1990; Swiss, 1996).

As noted, the successful use of resources in both cultures and the African American female subculture serves to sustain African American women in leadership and managerial roles, such as that of associate dean. Perhaps for these reasons, associate deans are able to identify some rewards of being African American women in largely uncharted territory. Some of the rewards are intrinsic: the pleasure derived from developing roles heretofore undeveloped; the joy of being sought and serving as mentor to African American and female students and faculty; some opportunity to influence the institution's response to African Americans; the freshness resulting from the ever-changing demands and challenges; and the growth and development of one's decision making, human relations, communication, and technical skills. Other rewards are extrinsic: opportunities to influence curriculum and policy, access to information and professionally challenging assignments, and the financial reward. However, these rewards come at a high price. For African American women in higher education, the glass ceiling is perceived as a steel vault, sealing them from ready access to the resources and rewards for which they are personally and professionally prepared.

REFERENCES

Atwater, M. (1995). Administrative support in initiating transformations: A perspective of an African American female administrator. *Journal of Innovative Higher Education, 1,* 277–286.

Bell, D. (1994). *Confronting authority: Reflections of an ardent protester.* Boston: Beacon Press.

Bell, E. L. (1990). The bicultural life experiences of career-oriented black women. *Journal of Organizational Behavior, 11,* 459–477.

Carroll, C. (1973). Three's a crowd: The dilemma of the black woman in higher education. In A. Rossi & A. Calderwood (Eds.), *Academic women on the move* (pp. 173–186). New York: Russell Sage Foundation.

Chestang, L. W. (1972). Character development in a hostile environment (University of Chicago, School of Social Service Administration, Occasional Paper No. 3). In M. Bloom (Ed.), *Readings in human growth and development* (pp. 40–50). New York: Macmillan.

Daly, A., Jennings, J., Beckett, J., & Leashore, B. (1995). Effective coping strategies of African Americans. *Social Work, 40,* 240–248.

Davis, G., & Watson, G. (1982). *Black life in corporate America: Swimming in the mainstream.* New York: Doubleday.

Denton, T. (1990). Bonding and supportive relationships among black professional women: Rituals of restoration. *Journal of Organizational Behavior, 11*, 447–457.

Dickens, F., & Dickens, J. B. (1982). *The black manager: Making it in the corporate world.* New York: AMACOM.

Gilkes, C. T. (1982). Successful rebellious professionals: The black woman's professional identity and community commitment. *Psychology of Women Quarterly, 6,* 289–311.

Gill, W. E., & Showell, D. R. (1991). *The Cinderella concept of the black female in higher education.* Bowie, MD: Bowie State University.

Harper, K. V. (1990). Power and gender issues in academic administration: A study of directors of BSW programs. *Affilia, 5,* 81–93.

Hellriegel, D., Slocum, J. W., Jr., & Woodman, R. W. (1992). *Organizational behavior* (6th ed.). St. Paul: West.

Katz, D., & Kahn, R. L. (1978). *The social psychology of organizations* (2nd ed.). New York: John Wiley & Sons.

Kram, K. (1985). *Mentoring at work.* Springfield, IL: Scott Foresman.

Lennon, T. M. (1994). *Statistics on social work education in the United States, 1993.* Alexandria, VA: Council on Social Work Education.

Lennon, T. M. (1995). *Statistics on social work education in the United States, 1994.* Alexandria, VA: Council on Social Work Education.

Lerner, G. (1972). *Black women in white America: A documentary history.* New York: Pantheon Books.

Martin, R.V.R. (1980). *Minority women administrators' perceptions of barriers in higher education.* Unpublished dissertation, University of Connecticut, West Hartford.

Noe, R. A. (1988). Women and mentoring: A review and research agenda. *Academy of Management Review, 13*(1), 65–78.

Pouissant, A. (1974, September). The black administrator in the white university. *Black Scholar,* pp. 8–14.

Schiele, J. H. (1991). Publication productivity of African American social work faculty. *Journal of Social Work Education 27,* 125–134.

Schiele, J. H. (1992a). Disparities between African American women and men on social work faculty. *Affilia, 7*(3), 44–56.

Schiele, J. H. (1992b). Scholarly productivity and social work doctorates: African Americans. *Journal of Multicultural Social Work, 2*(4), 75–90.

Swiss, D. J. (1996). *Women breaking through: Overcoming the final 10 obstacles at work.* Princeton, NJ: Peterson.

Thomas, A. D. (1990). The impact of race on manager's experiences of developmental relationships (mentoring and sponsorship): An intra-organizational study. *Journal of Organizational Behavior, 11*(6), 479–492.

Tack, M.W.S., & Patita, C. L. (1992). *Faculty job satisfaction: Women and minorities in peril* (ERIC Digest). Washington, DC: ERIC Clearinghouse on Higher Education.

Tidball, M. E. (1974). *Women role models in education in graduate and professional education of women* (Proceedings of American Association of University Women Conference). Washington, DC: American Association of University Women.

14

Conflict, Cooperation, and Institutional Goal Attainment in Diversity:
Improving Relationships between Urban Organizations and Neighborhood Residents

R. L. McNeely, Marty Sapp, and Henry J. Meyer

The following case account details a reasonably commonplace scenario in which a major service-delivering institution encounters problems as it tries to operate effectively in a racially or ethnically changing urban environment.

Decision makers in a metropolitan area are contemplating the possibility of changing the structure of the area's health care delivery system. Previously, the city had been noted for the richness of its educational medical institutions and hospitals and for the level of care provided to the city's indigent residents. However, financial crises occurring during the past two decades have led to severe funding cutbacks, resulting in diminished resources for services and to a growing intolerance by the area's middle-class residents toward groups dependent on social and medical services that largely are incapable of paying for them. The intolerance manifested by some residents of the metropolitan area also is reflected in the attitudes of some of the middle-class staff at a particular hospital. Over the years, they have witnessed a change in the hospital's surrounding neighborhood, with indigent and working-poor African Americans and Hispanic Americans replacing the area's formerly lower-middle-class, blue-collar European American residents. Sensing this intolerance, some of the neighborhood's recently arrived adolescents have trashed the hospital periodically with hostile graffiti, and incidents of interpersonal hostility between caregivers and recipients have been increasing.

City administrators, arguing that the private sector operates more efficiently, have pushed to close the hospital and several others located in the city's poorest areas that serve mostly people of color and members of marginalized populations. Some human services professionals, including caseworkers, neighborhood organizers, and social planners, argue that private hospitals are not accessible to working poor people without job-related fringe benefits or to those who are indigent. They argue—ironically in light of growing disenchantment between many hospital staff and neighborhood residents—that the municipal hospital affords an environment more capable of forming family-like relationships with people suffering chronic problems and that such relationships are

> a viable and valuable part of the delivery system that would be
> very difficult to establish in a private facility. Although operating
> with diminished resources, no one anticipates that the hospital's
> expenses will exceed its revenues. Members of the hospital's exec-
> utive management team remain committed to providing services
> at the level of excellence for which the hospital has been recog-
> nized, and to keeping the hospital in its present location, despite
> growing budgetary retrenchment, and they remain committed to
> providing service to residents of the neighborhood.

The hospital's executive management staff is faced with a problem similar to those confronting other institutions operating under like conditions, such as public schools and police departments situated in racially changing neighborhoods. One key element of this problem is growing estrangement (alienation) of the diverse people these institutions now serve and the adverse effects this estrangement will have on the ability of the institutions to achieve their organizational goals. Moreover, the bureaucratic nature of institutions such as police departments, public schools, and hospitals (particularly those serving large numbers of poor or near-poor people) tends to militate against formation of the family-like relationships argued in the case account as being crucial to maintaining the hospital's goal of continuing to provide excellent care.

Similarly, increasing estrangement between recently arrived, culturally diverse poor and near-poor residents and neighborhood institutions works against institutional goal attainment, because these institutions need the cooperation of the neighborhood's residents to attain their goals. For example, consider how a police department's effectiveness can be increased when neighborhood residents regularly report witnessed criminal activities and suspicious events occurring in the neighborhood. Consider how a public school's effectiveness is enhanced when parents reinforce educational goals in the home and when such goals are reinforced by a neighborhood's volunteer associations. Similarly, when alienation spills over to caregivers and patients in a hospital setting or when hospital staff must operate in a hostile environment, such conditions ultimately erode the climate of the workplace and impede the delivery of quality health care. Also, the health, mental health, and social functioning of hospital staff working under such conditions may suffer because the conditions exacerbate the stress of the work these people perform. The same may be said of public school teachers and staff seeking to attain educational goals in a hostile neighborhood environment or in a school workplace where there is episodic violence or other forms of conflict between students and teachers.

Fortunately, guidelines to improve cooperation between bureaucracies and primary groups (that is, informally organized social entities such as families and neighborhood associations) are available. These guidelines can help create an environment in which primary groups reinforce institutional goals and can help foster a workplace climate that promotes goal attainment. These guidelines, developed by Litwak and Meyer (1966, 1974a, 1974b) and discussed by McNeely (1983a), were used originally during the middle 1960s in Detroit, where substantial estrangement occurred between a predominantly middle-class public school teaching faculty and recently arrived southern Appalachians recruited to work in Detroit's automobile factories. The migrants often brought with them fundamentalist Baptist religious convictions and practices, including "speaking in tongues" at religious ceremonies. They tended to concentrate residentially in specific Detroit neighborhoods, and their school-age children frequently regarded the public schools as alien environments. The parents found little in common with the teachers, most of whom were solidly middle-class in outlook and values, and they saw little use in what they perceived to be the educational mission of neighborhood schools. Many parents threatened to remove their children from the public schools when Detroit's Board of Education announced that it was considering implementing sex education coursework in elementary schools. Litwak and Meyer's (1966) ideas in their publication "A Balance Theory of Coordination between Bureaucratic Organizations and Community Primary Groups" were used to reduce tensions between these newcomers and the schools. The balance theory emphasizes how bureaucracies and community primary groups operate, noting especially that they tend to operate on the basis of antithetical principles.

BALANCE, BUREAUCRACIES, AND PRIMARY GROUPS

The notion of *balance* refers to a condition in which the social distance between a bureaucratized institution and its pertinent primary groups is neither too great nor too intimate. Social distance that is out of balance in either direction militates against optimal attainment of bureaucratic goals, such as the provision of quality medical care in a hospital setting, effective crime detection and prevention by the police, or the education and socialization of children in a public school. When social distance is too intimate, satisfactory reinforcement of institutional goals also is impeded, as is the case when teachers assess student performance based on their personal friendships with community members. When social distance is too great, bureaucracies and primary groups do not mutually reinforce common goals, such as when parents fail to support the educational mission of their children's schools by refusing to attend consultative meetings with teachers regarded as alien. It is the latter balance problem with which we are concerned in this chapter; namely, one in which there is estrangement between primary group and bureaucracy (Moore & Kelly, 1996; Soderfeldt, Soderfeldt, & Muntaner, 1996).

Achieving the proper balance between bureaucracies and primary groups can be difficult because both subscribe to antithetical organizing principles. Bureaucracies, for example, tend to operate on the principles of merit, transitory membership, the use of rules, and impersonal interpersonal relationships. Primary groups, by contrast, tend to operate on the opposite values of nepotism, permanence of membership, internalized values, and personalized face-to-face contact. The antithetical cultures created by adherence to these contrasting principles require bureaucracies to make certain accommodations in organizational structure and to implement certain mechanisms to create a balanced linkage with their pertinent primary groups, if desirable social goals are to be reinforced mutually and attained optimally (Fong & Gibbs, 1995; Litwak & Meyer, 1961, 1974b; Shera & Page, 1995).

ORGANIZATIONAL STRUCTURE

Consider what occurs when neighborhood residents, motivated to report crimes or suspicious events in the neighborhood, are confronted with an impersonal front-desk sergeant and a mountain of paperwork to be filled out at the neighborhood precinct station. The desk sergeant is likely to engage in structured, routinized, oral questioning. One result is that, in time, the motivation of the interested resident will wane because of irritation with the impersonal and formalized routine of police station intake procedure. This reaction occurs because members of primary groups prefer operating on the basis of personalized face-to-face interaction, whereas staff in bureaucracies tend to operate in depersonalized fashion and to be guided in handling the public by formalized a priori rules of procedure (for example, policy manuals).

Thus, people entering a precinct station to report criminal activity are confronted with a preset standardized procedure that will govern how their information is to be obtained. Because it results, ultimately, in diminishing the motivation of neighborhood members to report suspicious activities, the routinized intake procedure works at cross-purposes with developing a milieu in which primary group members, such as neighborhood residents, and bureaucracies, such as precinct stations, work together in achieving desirable social goals (such as giving tips to the police that help in crime abatement). As experienced by the formerly motivated neighborhood resident, the depersonalized and routinized manner of submitting information creates a sense of being present in an unfriendly atmosphere, one in which the resident comes to feel estranged from or, in extreme cases, even alienated from the institution.

Such an outcome need not occur. Accommodations in bureaucratic organizational structure can establish conditions that facilitate mutual reinforcement rather than working against such cooperation. Such accommodations have been referred to by Litwak and Meyer (1974a, 1974b) as "human relations" organizational conditions. These conditions contrast with the typical "rationalistic" conditions of bureaucratic organizational structure and, taken together, constitute a polar opposite but equally structured style of formal organization. In fact, the term "bureaucracy," as used henceforth in this chapter, refers to a specific style of formal organizational structure, which may be known

Table 14-1

Administrative Styles as Defined by Organizational Structure

Dimensions of Organizational Structure	Administrative Styles	
	Rationalistic	Human Relations
Authority structure	Hierarchical	Collegial
Division of labor	Specialist	Generalist
Interpersonal relations	Impersonal	Personal
Performance guides	A priori rules	Internalized goals

SOURCE: From *School, Family, and Neighborhood* by E. Litwak and H. J. Meyer. Copyright ©1974 by Columbia University Press. Reprinted with permission of the publisher.

also as the "rationalistic model of organizational structure" or as "the Weberian model" (so named to honor sociologist Max Weber, who first described this organizational style). Its polar-opposite style, the human relations model, is no less valid a model of organizational style, but it accommodates cooperation with primary groups with much less conflict than the rationalistic model (see Table 14-1).

According to the theory underlying these models, the key factor in applying the appropriate style to an organization is the nature of tasks performed by members (McNeely, 1975). If the tasks members must perform to accomplish the organization's mission can be routinized, as is the case with the repetitive work of a factory assembly line, the theory, despite compelling contrary evidence (McNeely, 1983b), suggests that a rationalistic structure is most appropriate. The human relations style is more appropriate when ambiguous tasks must be performed.

Organizations dealing with human beings (rather than with the raw material of factory production), for example, are likely to find the tasks that must be performed to be ambiguous in nature (Tucker, Baum, & Singh, 1992). Dealing with distressed patients in a hospital, for example, is not by nature a routine event because human beings bring different needs and emotional states to the hospital treatment room. Diagnosing complicated health problems is by no means a routine event, often requiring physicians to collaborate before finalizing a diagnosis. Similarly, dealing with distressed individuals at a crime scene is not a routine event, because different people bring to such a situation an infinite variety of reactions and present-moment needs.

Public school employees can attest to the fact that there is no single best way of teaching students—of routinizing the dissemination of educational content—because different students learn at different paces, in different ways (deductively or anecdotally, for example), and with different motivational levels for learning. Nonetheless, each of the institutions mentioned tends to operate as though organizational missions are pursued best by structuring organizational conditions in accord with the rationalistic model. Such structuring conflicts with the theory that underlies appropriate application of organizational style (thereby exacerbating the normal stress imposed on these workers), so the staffs of these organizations (police officers, nurses, public school teachers) tend to suffer unusually high rates of burnout (Glisson, 1978; Glisson & Martin, 1980; Hasenfeld & Gidron, 1993; Kraus & Pillsbury, 1994; McNeely, 1982, 1983a, 1983b, 1983c; Woodward, 1994) and other stress-related maladies (hypertension, alcoholism) associated with the working environment (Gardell, 1971, 1972; Kornhauser, 1965; Roman & Trice, 1969; Susser, 1967; Theorell & Rahe, 1972).

These same conditions also militate against the sort of atmosphere that encourages cooperation between members of a primary group and staff of a bureaucracy. For example, a horizontal structure in which people deal with each other as colleagues, with an accompanying emphasis on the decision-making input of each person as being of value, is perceived by primary group members as being more "open" and "warm" than an organizational structure emphasizing hierarchical rank and decision making.

As used in Table 14-1, the term "specialist" refers to specialization of task and function rather than to occupational specialty. It connotes a situation in which the worker performs virtually the same tasks throughout the working day or repetitively performs the same series of tasks. This is routinized work, requiring a worker to treat the human beings encountered on the job (patients, crime victims, pupils) as though they were routine objects.

"Generalists," by contrast, are people who have the requisite training to perform a wide variety of tasks and are expected by the organization to have diffuse duties associated with solving ambiguous problems. A social worker employed under these conditions might, for example, be involved in individual advocacy, crisis intervention, proposal writing, and program evaluation, all within a span of several days.

The result is that generalists have a good deal more flexibility in determining how to respond to the problems a person seeking services requires, compared with "specialists," who must try to fit the person into a specific routinized procedure. Thus, people seeking to interact with a human relations–style organization are less likely to encounter "red tape" and less likely to "fall through the cracks" of preset procedures and processes. This outcome, too, is perceived more favorably by primary group members.

Similarly perceived as more open and warm is the emphasis in human relations organizations on personalized interaction and collegial decision making. "Personalized" interfacing, as used here, is not meant to suggest that nepotism within an organization is encouraged. Rather, the emphasis is on staff having an ability to interact with other staff without constraints based on differences in occupational rank. When organizational members, for example, do not have to fear retaliation from higher-ranking members of the organization, they can more easily pursue collegially supported decision-making efforts to solve ambiguous problems.

The emphasis on collegial decision making is based on the recognition that single decision makers trying alone to solve a recurring mélange of ambiguous problems are more likely to burn out than are those engaged in collegial decision making. Collegial decision making helps diffuse stressors associated with trying to make consistently the best decisions about complex and ambiguous problems. Improving police–community or hospital–community relations in a given locale, for example, is likely to require personalized professional sharing if the person charged with such a responsibility is not to suffer unduly under the weight of these ambiguous tasks.

Personalized interfacing is likely to enhance decision making because it allows participants to ventilate their concerns and uncertainties comfortably. Simply put, when a single decision maker is confronted with a recurring assortment of ambiguous problems for which the best decisions constantly must be made, the quality of decision making, in the long run, is likely to suffer, with the decision maker ultimately breaking down, unless the stress of such decision making is shared with others. Also, organizational conditions encouraging personalized relations are more likely than would be the case in a rationalistically structured organization to create an organizational atmosphere that fosters solicitation of input from selected community primary group members; this atmosphere has obvious benefits in reducing social distance between the organization and its pertinent primary groups.

Non-policy-setting staff in rationalistically structured organizations are guided in their decision making by a priori rules, that is, by policy manuals or some similar device. Rules can be set before the problem occurs if the problem can be anticipated. When work is a series of repetitive and routine events, solutions to anticipated problems may be decided on before the problems occur and recorded in policy manuals. Thus, one can construct a policy manual to cover all of the problems that might occur on an assembly line, because one can anticipate all of the problematic events associated with assembly-line production methods. Such manuals are effective problem-solving tools because they divorce decision making from on-the-spot human judgment error.

But the problems human beings bring to organizations are not routine. Thus, rationalistically structured organizations trying to deliver services to humans inevitably have large numbers of people "falling through the cracks." To deal effectively with the ambiguous problems brought by people seeking services from an organization or by community primary groups seeking to align with an institution to promote desirable social goals often requires the flexibility of on-the-spot professional decision making. If a primary group wishes to align with the organization to pursue a mutual goal, the organization must socialize its staff by means of in-service seminars and staff retreats, for example, so that staff internalize the mission of the organization and can provide non-policy-manual, on-the-spot decisions consistent with the organization's mission and goals.

An obvious result of staff empowered to make decisions without being restricted to a policy manual is greater flexibility, which is a requirement for organizations wishing improved relations with community primary groups. Flexibility also is a prerequisite of organizational responsiveness to a changing environment (Schmid, 1992). Without flexibility, conditions tend to be spawned that increase the social distance between institutions and newcomer primary groups, especially those evidencing significant ecosystem distrust. As used here, *ecosystem distrust* means a tendency to trust neither institutions nor other people, a condition often associated with poverty, particularly with respect to people of color. Institutions wishing to improve relations with lower-class or culturally dissimilar neighborhood newcomers must pierce through such distrust or endure continued graffiti trashing, commonplace interactional hostility, and episodic violence (Hasenfeld & Gidron, 1993).

Overall, the human relations model of organizational structure is much friendlier to primary group members. However, institutions are not likely to change their rationalistic administrative structures. They can, however, improve relations by creating human relations–oriented satellites in their surrounding neighborhoods, such as police storefronts in a precinct area. Bureaucracies also can create, within the organization, departments that are human relations oriented in character. Such departments need to be physically segregated from the rest of the bureaucracy, because the organizational culture that results from the more open structure is so different from the rest of the organization. Staff working in such departments also should report to an administration that is separate from the rest of the (rationalistically styled) organization.

Let us return to the situation in Detroit to illustrate the latter point. In seeking to improve relations with the fundamentalist Baptist Appalachians migrating to manufacturing jobs, the Detroit Board of Education situated staff known as "school–community agents" in certain public schools (Deshler & Erlich, 1974; Myrtle & Wilber, 1994). These staff operated offices structured according to human relations principles, thereby easing the interface with the culturally dissimilar neighborhood newcomers. These offices always were distantly located from school administration offices because the administration tended to operate more rationalistically and closer proximity likely would have resulted in conflict between the competing organizational styles.

Similarly, because traditional school administrations operate more rationalistically, a separate administrative structure was created to which school–community agents reported. (Also, a separate structure was necessary because agents, to maintain or establish their credibility, periodically led demonstrations against policies espoused by school principals.) This separate administrative structure operated in a more human relations fashion. Decision making was more collegial. Thus, with offices that were physically segregated and with an administrative structure separate from traditional school management, school–community agents were imbued with the flexibility needed to work effectively with estranged, often alienated, community members.

The overarching point of this section is that to be effective in reducing social distance between a bureaucracy and its pertinent primary groups, the institution will have to create conditions that are more favorable to the principles by which primary groups operate, particularly lower-class primary groups.[1] Schools can achieve favorable conditions either by locating human relations–style satellite offices off the school campus or by physically segregating such offices within the school. However, more than this will be required to achieve the balanced linkage that optimizes goal attainment (Golden, 1990).

MECHANISMS OF LINKAGE

Litwak and Meyer (1966, 1974a, 1974b) have detailed several mechanisms of linkage, some of which serve to increase distance when relations are too intimate between bureaucracies and primary groups and others of which serve to decrease social distance when relations are estranged. This chapter concerns the sort of distance often encountered with culturally and ethnically diverse lower-class newcomers to an urban community, so only the latter mechanisms will be discussed. These mechanisms include detached experts, settlement houses, voluntary associations, delegated function, and opinion leaders.

Detached Experts

Detached experts are professionals who have skills that can be generalized to diverse situations. The customary mode of operation is to achieve credibility by becoming trusted members of the primary group with whom they interact, thereby overcoming ecosystem distrust. Because the development and maintenance of credibility requires detached experts to respond quickly to requests by primary

---

[1]The salience of low socioeconomic status with respect to this comment arises from the fact that middle-class European Americans are more likely than lower-class people, regardless of race, to experience less conflict when dealing with bureaucratic organizations. Their higher class status, for one thing, is likely to introduce an intensity to interfacing that reduces obstinate adherence to inflexible rules by bureaucratic officials. For another thing, they are more likely to accept bureaucratically sanctioned authority because they are more likely than lower-class people to defer to authority and tend more often to give credit (legitimacy) to a person's bureaucratic office and rank. Lower-class individuals, particularly lower-class African Americans, are far more likely to display ecosystem distrust, tending therefore to distrust institutions, European Americans, and even other African Americans. Such distrust often functions positively for African Americans as a healthy survival tactic in an often hostile world, and organizations seeking improved relations with this population must implement mechanisms designed to stem distrust (Kochman, 1974; McNeely & Badami, 1984; Triandis, 1976).

group members for assistance, they must act with relative autonomy. Much of their involvement with primary group members occurs within the context of face-to-face interaction, and staff working hours should be flexible enough to accommodate community concerns.

Foot-patrol officers in some crime-ridden urban areas are examples of how detached experts work. Where estrangement with community residents is common, a foot-patrol officer, able to exercise the discretion common to police officers on the street, is likely to develop credibility superior to that possible for officers cruising the neighborhood in police cars. Through the face-to-face interaction of common discourse and assistance, occurring in circumstances not involving official intervention following criminal incidents, an officer's personal credibility in the neighborhood is likely to develop, thereby reducing social distance between the police bureaucracy and neighborhood residents. Similarly, Detroit's school–community agents are detached experts, deployed to the external homes and associations of neighborhood residents, as are nurses serving as outreach workers to residents benefiting from in-home nursing assistance.

Settlement Houses

Settlement houses provide a physical milieu in which spontaneous discourse, the interchange of ideas, and planned neighborhood or institution–neighborhood meetings can occur. It is easily conceptualized as a community center approach, either housed within the institution or in an offsite location. Settlement houses should be structured according to human relations principles.

Storefront police stations capture the idea of a settlement house. Operating less rationalistically than the precinct station, storefronts are perceived by neighborhood residents as friendlier places and often result in improved neighborhood cooperation with the police. Neighborhood residents are less likely to encounter a mass of paperwork or routinized interaction when entering a police storefront, and they are more likely to have easy discourse and interaction with staff deployed there. Satellite outpatient health care–providing sites can be developed in much the same way.

One example of the settlement house approach occurred in Seattle's Ballard area, where an offsite facility was used to provide recreational and counseling services to the community's middle and high school truants, kickouts, and dropouts. Located off the campus of any school to avoid stigmatizing people entering its premises, the settlement house afforded recreational activities such as basketball, pool, and ping-pong. It was staffed by youthful-appearing and youthfully attired professional social workers (detached experts), whose credibility developed as they played basketball and other games, thereby providing a basis for subsequent professional counseling and other intervention efforts with these students. These students typically were too disenchanted to respond favorably to other, more traditional efforts to initiate counseling.

Interestingly, the Ballard area, at the time this settlement house was operating, was almost exclusively a middle-class, European American (Scandinavian) community. The settlement house was so successful in reducing truancy that it closed operations in less than four years. It exemplifies how the settlement house and detached-expert forms of linkage can be used effectively in tandem. Yet, one disadvantage of this approach is that it relies on the initiative of community members to visit the premises. If primary group members are too estranged from the institution, detached experts may have to be deployed first to the homes of neighborhood residents and to meetings of their voluntary associations.

Voluntary Associations

Voluntary associations create a structure within which members of a bureaucracy can interact and communicate with primary group members. The ideal form, for balance theory purposes, is a voluntary association that seeks to wed bureaucratic staff and members of pertinent primary groups, such as parent–teacher associations, public-housing tenant councils (if staffed by housing authority workers), guilds, and auxiliaries. An ultimate purpose of a voluntary association is to bring together at scheduled times bureaucratic officials, staff, and involved community members. This form of linkage seems especially pertinent to the hospital situated in a demographically changing urban neighborhood described at the beginning of this chapter. If ecosystem distrust is too pronounced, however, the deployment of detached experts to pierce community suspicions will need to precede formation of an association (Mordock, 1989).

Delegated Function

Delegated function occurs when one organization acts through another organization, with the latter organization having better access, greater expertise, more appropriate facilities, or greater legitimacy in society. Churches are used frequently for delegated-function purposes. An example is speakers sent by a local United Way to a church to communicate to members the good use to which their United Way contributions are being put. Fire departments, police departments, and local safety councils use public schools in this fashion; they disseminate information to community residents through their school-age children (Tambor, 1996).

Delegated function, operating in tandem with voluntary associations, seems especially pertinent to hospitals. Hospitals are likely to have the types of facilities that encourage interaction, such as comfortable roundtable meeting rooms and auditorium or quasi-auditorium meeting areas that can be served by the hospital's cafeteria. Such facilities provide an ideal location for meetings of voluntary associations the hospital itself has established with community members and for meetings of voluntary associations operating autonomously in the hospital's immediate service area.

Located in Milwaukee's racially changing Sherman Park neighborhood (McNeely & Padgett, 1996; Saltman, 1990), St. John's Hospital[2] has experienced a significant influx of lower-income ethnic group residents, primarily African Americans, within the past decade. With this influx has come some drug and gang activity, but none of it has spilled over to the hospital: There is no graffiti on hospital exterior walls or indoor restrooms, and the institution has no reputation for episodic violence occurring between staff and hospital invitees (patients or others present because of hospital business).

St. John's operates in a culturally diverse community. The Sherman Park community, home to an increasingly African American population on its eastern perimeter, includes a significant population of Jewish residents, including Orthodox Jews. Also, particularly on the western side, there are significant numbers of European American Protestants and Catholics. St. John's Hospital serves all these diverse groups. Illustrating how the mechanisms of delegated function and voluntary association can work in tandem, within a recent three-week span, St. John's hosted two community forums: (1) "Our Orthodox Jewish Neighbors" and (2) "Where Does Sherman Park Go from Here?" Hospital parking was made available to community residents attending the forums, which were open to the public. The hospital worked with local rabbis and members of the board of directors of Sherman Park's Yeshiva Elementary School to put on the first event. Kosher food was available for program participants, and the forum was moderated by St. John's congregational nurse (detached expert), who was hired in part to serve the neighborhood's Orthodox Jewish community. The second event was sponsored by the Sherman Park Community Association, a nonprofit organization devoted to community development and interracial harmony.

St. John's also is visible in the Sherman Park area through its detached experts' participation in community development activities designed to maintain the area's quality of life. As a result, area residents perceive the hospital as a positive force in the neighborhood and embrace its staff. Also, the hospital's working environment has remained an attractive place for health care professionals to work, and the hospital continues to deliver quality health care services to those in need.

Opinion Leaders

Opinion leaders are community residents who are "natural" leaders—people recognized by others in the neighborhood as unusually wise, astute, or experienced and to whom people go for advice. Ministers, priests, and rabbis, for example, are likely to be opinion leaders in their communities. Thus, recalling Milwaukee, the approach

---

[2]"St. John's Hospital" is a fictionalized name. The policies and programs ascribed in this chapter to that institution are being executed by a large hospital located in the Sherman Park neighborhood of Milwaukee, Wisconsin.

used by St. John's Hospital to improve community relations and achieve organizational goals involved the use of delegated-function, voluntary association, detached-expert, and opinion leader forms of linkage. Regardless of other forms of linkage appropriate to a given situation, use of opinion leaders is highly advisable.

A CAVEAT

The preceding discussion can serve as a basis for spawning innovations by bureaucratic institutions seeking to improve relations with pertinent primary groups operating within their immediate physical environments. This discussion has emphasized the need to balance and coordinate relations between bureaucracies and primary groups to foster optimal achievement of organizational goals. Organizations should be mindful, however, that some studies have shown a tendency for them, especially human services organizations, to displace other organizational goals as they pursue improved institution–community relations (Campbell, 1986; Hasenfeld, 1985; Kang & Chaan, 1995; Rothman, 1974; Rothman, Erlich, & Teresa, 1976). Goal displacement would be an ironic and unfortunate outcome to implementing guidelines discussed in this chapter that, at their heart, seek to enhance goal attainment.

CONCLUSION

Some urban institutions may choose to ignore changing neighborhood demographics, thereby increasing the possibility of adversity. Changing demographics may simply "sneak up" on other institutions that either are not vigilant or are impervious to the reality of change occurring around them. Because attainment of an organization's mission is affected by the environment in which it operates, institutions in changing urban areas cannot afford to be so cavalier. Adjustments have to be made. Handling organizational change may be unsettling to bureaucracies, however; it requires organizational members to confront their own personal thoughts with respect to the daunting reality of what poverty brings physically, emotionally, and spiritually. Personal safety may be threatened. It is not easy for some staff to look at faces at the "bottom of the well." The institution may have little vested interest in the community. But for institutions that are committed to the areas in which they are located, effective modes of organizational adjustment and effective mechanisms of linkage can retain organizational vitality and help attain organizational goals.

This chapter has offered guidelines to organizational leaders who remain committed to the areas in which they operate, despite the onset of "white flight" and despite the influx, most likely, of poorer and more diverse community residents, who often bring with them values, norms, and folkways different from those of the institution's staff. Although not supported by numerous empirical studies, happily, the guidelines presented in this discussion have proven their effectiveness to those who have used them.

REFERENCES

Campbell, A. K. (1986). Private delivery of public services: Sorting out the policy and management issues. *Public Management, 68,* 3–5.

Deshler, B., & Erlich, J. L. (1974). A new intervention approach: The school–community agent. In F. Cox, J. Erlich, J. Rothman, & J. Tropman (Eds.), *Strategies of community organization* (pp. 381–391). Itasca, IL: F. E. Peacock.

Fong, L. G., & Gibbs, J. T. (1995). Facilitating services to multicultural communities in a dominant cultural setting: An organizational perspective. *Administration in Social Work, 19*(2), 1–24.

Gardell, B. (1971). Alienation and mental health in the modern industrial environment. In L. Levi (Ed.), *Society, stress, and disease* (Vol. 1, pp. 148–180). New York: Oxford University Press.

Gardell, B. (1972). Health and the work-setting—A sociological perspective. *Psychologist News, 7*(18), 12–14.

Glisson, C. A. (1978). Dependence of technological routinization on structural variables in human service organizations. *Administrative Science Quarterly, 23,* 383–395.

Glisson, C. A., & Martin, P. Y. (1980). Productivity and efficiency in human service organizations as related to structure, size, and age. *Academy of Management Journal, 23*(1), 21–27.

Golden, O. (1990). Innovation in public sector service programs: The implications of innovation by "groping along." *Journal of Policy Analysis and Management, 9,* 219–248.

Hasenfeld, Y. (1985). The administration of human services. *Annals of the American Academy of Political and Social Science, 479,* 67–81.

Hasenfeld, Y., & Gidron, B. (1993). Self-help groups and human service organizations: An interorganizational perspective. *Social Service Review, 63,* 217–236.

Kang, C. H., & Chaan, R. A. (1995). New findings on large human service organization boards of trustees. *Administration in Social Work, 19*(3), 17–44.

Kochman, T. (1974). Orality and literacy as factors of "black" and "white" communicative behavior. *International Journal of the Sociology of Language, 3,* 91–115.

Kornhauser, A. (1965). *Mental health of the industrial worker.* New York: John Wiley & Sons.

Kraus, A., & Pillsbury, J. B. (1994). Streamlining intake and eligibility systems: Agencies find ways to simplify the process for both clients and staff. *Public Welfare, 52,* 9–21.

Litwak, E., & Meyer, H. J. (1961). Models of bureaucracy which permit conflict. *American Journal of Sociology, 57,* 177–184.

Litwak, E., & Meyer, H. J. (1966). A balance theory of coordination between bureaucratic organizations and community primary groups. *Administrative Science Quarterly, 11,* 31–58.

Litwak, E., & Meyer, H. J. (1974a). The administrative style of the school and organizational tasks. In F. Cox, J. Erlich, J. Rothman, & J. Tropman (Eds.), *Strategies of community organization* (pp. 82–95). Itasca, IL: F. E. Peacock.

Litwak, E., & Meyer, H. J. (1974b). *School, family, and neighborhood: The theory and practice of school–community relations.* New York: Columbia University Press.

McNeely, R. L. (1975). *An examination of the relationship of work satisfaction correlates to the worker's conception of the organizational style of the work setting.* Doctoral dissertation, Brandeis University, Florence Heller Graduate School for Advanced Studies in Social Welfare, Waltham, MA. Ann Arbor, MI: University Microfilms.

McNeely, R. L. (1982). Organizational patterns for pragmatic humanism in public schools. *Educational Review, 34*(1), 35–46.

McNeely, R. L. (1983a). Conceptualizing models of linkage for community involvement in educational desegregation. *Urban Review, 15,* 165–176.

McNeely, R. L. (1983b). Organizational patterns and work satisfaction in a comprehensive human service agency: An empirical test. *Human Relations, 36,* 957–972.

McNeely, R. L. (1983c). Organizational patterns, work, and burnout in the public school. *Urban Education, 18*(1), 82–97.

McNeely, R. L. & Badami, M. K. (1984). Interracial communication in school social work. *Social Work, 29*, 22–26.

McNeely, R. L., & Padgett, D. L. (1996). *The structure of neighborhood improvement in an urban community: Why and how community practitioners help community organizations to incorporate.* Milwaukee: University of Wisconsin, School of Social Welfare, Center for Advanced Studies in Social Welfare.

Moore, S. T., & Kelly, J. (1996). Quality now: Moving human service organizations toward a consumer orientation to service quality. *Social Work, 41*, 33–40.

Mordock, J. B. (1989). Organizational adaptation to policy and funding shifts: The road to survival. *Child Welfare, 68*, 589–603.

Myrtle, R. C., & Wilber, K. H. (1994). Designing service delivery systems: Lessons from the development of community-based systems of care for the elderly. *Public Administration Review, 54*, 345–352.

Roman, P. M., & Trice, H. M. (1969). The development of deviant drinking behavior. *Archives of Environmental Health, 19*.

Rothman, J. (1974). *Planning and organizing for social change.* New York: Columbia University Press.

Rothman, J., Erlich, J. L., & Teresa, J. G. (1976). *Promoting innovation and change in organizations and communities.* New York: John Wiley & Sons.

Saltman, J. (1990). *A fragile movement: The struggle for neighborhood stabilization.* Westport, CT: Greenwood Press.

Schmid, H. (1992). Executive leadership in human service organizations. In Y. Hasenfeld (Ed.), *Human services as complex organizations* (pp. 98–117). Newbury Park, CA: Sage Publications.

Shera, W., & Page, J. (1995). Creating more effective human service organizations through strategies of empowerment. *Administration in Social Work, 19*(4), 1–15.

Soderfeldt, B., Soderfeldt, M., & Muntaner, C. (1996). Psychosocial work environment in human service organizations: A conceptual analysis and development of the demand–control model. *Social Science and Medicine, 42*, 1217–1226.

Susser, M. (1967). Causes of peptic ulcer. *Journal of Chronic Diseases, 20*.

Tambor, M. (1996). Employment-at-will or just cause: The right choice. *Administration in Social Work, 19*(3), 45–57.

Theorell, T., & Rahe, R. (1972). Behavior and life satisfaction characteristics of Swedish subjects with myocardial infarction. *Journal of Chronic Diseases, 25*, 139–147.

Triandis, H. C. (Ed.). (1976). *Variations in black and white perceptions of the social environment.* Champaign: University of Illinois Press.

Tucker, D. J., Baum, J.A.C., & Singh, J. V. (1992). The institutional ecology of human service organizations. In Y. Hasenfeld (Ed.), *Human services as complex organizations* (pp. 47–72). Newbury Park, CA: Sage Publications.

Woodward, K. L. (1994). Packing effective community service delivery: The utility of mandates and contracts in obtaining administrative cooperation. *Administration in Social Work, 18*(2), 17–43.

15 Multicultural Communication in Human Services Organizations

Joyce O. Beckett and Delores Dungee-Anderson

Communication is the basic and necessary medium for effective interaction and achievement of organizational goals. This chapter presents a model that can be used to increase the effectiveness of communication processes in human services organizations. The model focuses on communication between people and groups that differ in one or more ways. Traditionally, the literature on communication differences in the workplace has looked largely at racial differences and, more recently, at gender as factors that help explain individual and group cultural variations. This chapter expands the definition of *difference* to include other important variables such as social class; gender preference; ethnicity; religion; disability; nationality; age; place of residence; and social, educational, and economic status.

Each characteristic is an important determinant of individual identity, values, beliefs, and communication styles. All are viewed as factors that contribute to the shaping of individual uniqueness within and among different cultural groups. As human services agencies shift to meet expanding and more complex societal needs, the human services work force and the client populations served increasingly reflect the growing variations in types of diversity. This reality drives the need for human services organizations to adopt a formal focus on the development of proficient communication with people who are different in more than the traditionally recognized ways. We refer to this focus as "multicultural communication," a term that includes organizational communication exchanges among people and groups characterized by a broad range of cultural differences.

Another factor related to communication and an important determinant of organizational efficiency and effectiveness is *workplace climate,* defined as the emotional life of employees in the workplace. It is strongly influenced by accuracy, consistency, and the types of communication customary in the organization. It is measured by the collective *predominant* affective experiences of employees with each other and within the larger organization.

From a broad range of possible workplace experiences, feelings of respect for others and their unique differences, positive regard, mutuality, valuing others combined with reasonable expectations of trust, and loyalty among all organizational employees are believed to be among the factors most expected by employees and most highly regarded as positive. Conversely, the cumulative absence of these factors is likely to differentiate a workplace climate that severely re-strains effective communication and, consequently, limits the ability of the organization to achieve its desired goals and objectives. This chapter presents the common barriers to multicultural communication and a process model to overcome these barriers. Identifying and overcoming multicultural communication barriers results in increased proficiency in both worker and organizational communication effectiveness in the human services workplace.

IMPORTANCE OF MULTICULTURAL COMMUNICATION

Current and projected demographic changes underlie the increasing need for multicultural communication in human services organizations. Planning and delivery of human services must include the principal challenges of the 21st century. Many of these challenges emanate from emerging demographic trends that affect the demand for and provision of services. In general, the American population is changing in ethnicity, gender, age, sexual orientation, and disability. The population and workplace are becoming more diverse. People of color, women, and people with disabilities are increasing their ranks in the workplace. For example, Johnston and Packer (1987) predicted that 84 percent of new entrants into the work force would be men and women of color, white women, and immigrants.

Passage of the Americans with Disabilities Act of 1990 provided people with disabilities a legal recourse for workplace and other types of discrimination. Similarly, an increasing percentage of the gay and lesbian populations is openly identifying sexual orientation and requesting equitable employment benefits. Following similar trends, the "55-and-older" population is expanding and is expected soon to mushroom as each year more baby boomers reach that age. We expect, then, that the populations of disabled, gay, lesbian, bisexual, transgender, and elderly people will increase the ranks of both human services employees and consumers of these services (Jensen & Katz, 1996).

These trends were discussed in the 1987 Hudson Institute publication *Work Force 2000* (Johnston & Packer, 1987). More current U.S. projections indicate that these changes are occurring faster than the Hudson predictions. For example, Rand Corporation (1996) predicted that, in California by the year 2000, no ethnic or racial group will constitute a statistical majority; each will be less than 50 percent of the population. In the entire American population, women will outnumber men in the work force by the turn of the century (Swisher, 1995). These changes suggest not only a more diverse workplace but also a more varied client pool for human services organizations. All of these trends point to the need for having multiculturally competent employees in human services organizations.

Diversity and, consequently, multicultural communication are possibly the most important considerations for human services organizations in the upcoming century (Griggs & Louw, 1995; Jamieson &

O'Mara, 1991). Unfortunately, these topics are neglected in public administration and management literature. For example, White and Rice (1996) reported that between 1979 and 1994, on average, fewer than 2 percent of the articles per year from 121 journals related to these fields discussed racial issues. To meet the challenges that the projected demographic changes will bring, human services agencies must prepare to develop more inclusive work environments. This requires that organizations expand their understanding of the many ways people can be different from each other and from the organization's traditional employees and service consumers. For organizations to survive and thrive in the 21st century, they must give thoughtful attention to a host of multicultural differences, such as race, ethnicity, age, gender, disability, sexual orientation, and religion, and promote effective communication processes among people with these diverse characteristics. The differences are complex because in addition to those between groups, differences also exist among people within groups. The difference between one middle-class Asian American and another may be as great or greater than the difference between middle-class Asian Americans and middle-class Latinos.

Dimensions of Culture

Culture is tightly woven into a person's life and continually pervades thinking, behavior, and communication patterns. Beliefs about the world influence both perceptions and interactions. To understand similarities and differences in communication across cultures, it is helpful to consider how cultures can vary, because these variations provide a basis for describing and explaining multicultural communication. Kluckhohn and Strodtbeck (1961) and Ibrahim (1985) suggested that cultures vary on the following five dimensions of values and beliefs: (1) person-to-nature relationship, (2) time orientation, (3) relations with people, (4) preferred mode of activity, and (5) the nature of person (see Table 15-1 and Table 15-2).

Person-to-Nature Relationship. This dimension describes the relationship of people with their physical environment. As a cultural group, European Americans value control and mastery of nature. They believe people have a responsibility to overcome obstacles in nature. In contrast, people of color emphasize harmony with nature, in which human life, nature, and the supernatural are only extensions of each other. For example, the Asian Confucian system concentrates on the quest for spiritual fulfillment as a means of achieving harmony with the world. Native Americans see themselves as part of a greater whole, believing that plants and animals have souls and should be treated as humanely as possible (Keyes, 1977; Lum, 1992). African Americans become "centered" in the world or harmonious with nature through spirituality or religion (Clark, 1972; Ho, 1987; Pinderhughes, 1989).

Table 15-1
Dimensions of Worldviews

Dimension		Value Organization	
Time orientation What is the temporal focus of human life?	Past The past is important. Learn from history.	Present The present moment is everything. Don't worry about tomorrow.	Future Plan for the future. Sacrifice today for a better tomorrow.
Preferred mode of activity What is the modality of human activity?	Being It's enough just to be.	Being-in-becoming Our purpose in life is to develop our inner self	Doing Be active. Work hard and your efforts will be rewarded.
Relations with people How are human relationships defined?	Linear Relationships are vertical. There are leaders and followers.	Collateral We should consult with friends and family when problems arise.	Individualistic Individual autonomy is important. We control our destiny.
Person-to-nature relationship What is the relationship of people to nature?	Subjugation to nature Life is largely determined by external forces (God, fate, genetics).	Harmony with nature People and nature coexist in harmony.	Mastery over nature Our challenge is to conquer and control nature.
Nature of person What is the innate character of people?	Bad People must work very hard to overcome bad impulses.	Neutral People are socialized by their environments, but they have choices in life.	Good People are basically good. When they make "wrong" choices, they experience guilt and anxiety.

SOURCE: Adapted from Ibrahim, F. A. (1985). Effective cross-cultural counseling and psychotherapy: A framework. *Counseling Psychologist, 13*, 625–638. Copyright © 1985 by Sage Publications. Used by permission of Sage Publications, Inc.

Table 15-2
Cultural Value Preferences of Middle-Class European Americans and Ethnic People of Color

Area of Relationships	Middle-Class White Americans	Asian and Pacific Americans	American Indians and Alaskan Natives	African Americans	Hispanic Americans
Person-to-nature relationship	Mastery over	Harmony with	Harmony with	Harmony with	Harmony with
Time orientation	Future	Past–present	Present	Present	Past–present
Relations with people	Individual	Collateral	Collateral	Collateral	Collateral
Preferred mode of activity	Doing	Doing	Being-in-becoming	Doing	Being-in-becoming
Nature of person	Good and bad	Good	Good	Good and bad	Good

SOURCES: Adapted from Ho, M. K. (1987). *Family therapy with ethnic minorities* (p. 71). Newbury Park, CA: Sage Publications, and Kluckhohn, R., & Strodtbeck, F. (1961). *Variations in value orientations.* New York: Harper & Row.

Time Orientation. Time focus determines whether in their daily interactions and current involvements with each other groups have a predominant focus on the past, present, or future. Groups with a past orientation value tradition and regard the past as important to current philosophies about life. Present-oriented groups believe that one need not worry about tomorrow because the "present moment is everything" (Ibrahim, 1985). Future-oriented groups believe that current sacrifices should be made to ensure a better future (Ibrahim, 1985; Lum, 1992).

People of color are largely past *and* present oriented. For example, Asian Americans worship their ancestors and accent past historical events. Death dates rather than birth dates are more likely to be honored. Similarly, although the strong hierarchical sense of Hispanic Americans ties them to the past, their value of "personalism" makes any present encounter a spontaneous activity (Ho, 1987). Native Americans conceive of time as circular and believe that linear schedules are disruptive to natural patterns, whereas African Americans are more likely to have interest in present problems and their immediate solutions. European Americans are future oriented. They tend to worship youthfulness, have abstract philosophical goals, and believe that sacrifices today make a better tomorrow (Ho, 1987; Pinderhughes, 1989). In addition, people of color have a tendency to do several things at once and favor the involvement or participation of other people. They are more likely to focus on interpersonal transactions rather than on tasks, schedules, and procedures, which are important to European Americans (Ibrahim, 1985).

Relations with People. This dimension describes human relationships. Groups that value linear relations believe that relationships are vertical or characterized by leaders and followers. European Americans usually prefer linear relations and value individual autonomy, independence, and competition at all points in interpersonal interactions. People of color value collateral social relations and believe that family and friends are of primary importance and should be consulted when problems arise. Among people of color, family may include the extended family and "fictive" kin, or people who perform family roles but are *not* biological kin. Unlike European Americans, people of color tend to seek formal community help as a last resort for problem solving (Beckett & Dungee-Anderson, 1992). Some European Americans may mistakenly describe people of color as unmotivated, lazy, or unproductive because they do not adhere to the values of competition and immediate use of formal organizations (Billingsley, 1992; Ho, 1987; Pinderhughes, 1989). Table 15-2 compares the family value preferences of European Americans and people of color.

Preferred Mode of Activity. Activity is a cultural dimension that describes how groups most frequently and consistently behave. Three frequently occurring values of human activity are (1) being, (2) being-in-becoming, and (3) doing. Groups with a being orientation believe that the value of life is in life itself, whereas groups that value being-in-becoming treasure life for what opportunities it offers for development of the inner self. Groups most focused on doing tend to be active and hard workers who believe that rewards in life come from hard work and that if one does not receive adequate rewards, one has only oneself to blame (Ibrahim, 1985).

The doing orientation is basic to the style of European Americans and includes a demand for activity, which results in accomplishments that are measurable by some standard. Asian and African Americans also share the doing orientation, but they demonstrate it differently. Asian Americans show such behaviors as stoicism, self-discipline, and control of feelings. African Americans endure suffering and view education as an essential path to combat discrimination and succeed in life (Ho, 1987). Hispanic Americans and Native Americans prefer a being-in-becoming mode of activity. The focus is on striving for an integrated self rather than accomplishments. For both Native Americans and Asian Americans, respect for the right for self-determinism and noninterference by others is of fundamental significance (Ho, 1987).

Nature of Person. This dimension considers cultural significance for the innate character of people. European Americans view people as a product of the physical and nurturing environment. African Americans view people as potentially having both good and bad qualities and also accept that the environment can influence people. They therefore tend to be more receptive to environmental sources for change and improvement. Asian Americans and Native Americans perceive that people are basically good. They value the characteristics of compassion, respect for life, moderation in behavior, and selflessness. Asian Americans believe the best solutions to problems are found within the family and not from outside sources. Similarly, Native Americans believe that if a person is left alone with caring people in a nurturing environment, goodness in character will outweigh any evil (Ho, 1987; National Indian Council on Aging, 1986).

Culture and Organizational Behavior

Culture and its defining values influence not only the perceptions, beliefs, and behavior of people but also management styles within an organization and organizational behavior. In the relatively scarce research literature on the effects of race, ethnicity, and gender on management values and behavior, startling differences in managers' work values, styles of management, management objectives, and problem-solving approaches have been observed. For example, Blazini and Greenhaus (1988, as reported by Wooldridge, 1996) found that African American male and female managers scored higher than European American male and female managers on three dimensions of management values and behavior. Both African American male and female managers placed greater emphasis on extrinsic work values,

values of independence, and intrinsic work values than did European American male and female managers.

In considering gender differences, Segal (1991) found that women tended to be more cooperative, whereas men were more competitive; the organizational structure that men developed tended to be vertical and hierarchical, whereas that of women was horizontal and egalitarian. Segal further found that a basic objective of men was "to win," in contrast to women, whose basic objective was to produce a quality product; men were more likely to use a rational and objective approach, whereas women relied on a more intuitive and subjective approach to management behavior and values. Bowman and French (1992) reported that even when men and women have the same values, their behaviors may differ. Although the majority of both genders valued the concept of teamwork, women were more likely to actually work collectively and to believe that this type of work had a cumulative effect. It is especially interesting that both the gender of the manager and the employees' expectations of the manager influence the employees' evaluation of the manager. In a study that compared perceptions about male and female managers who used either an authoritarian or a participative leadership style, employees viewed more positively the managers whose leadership style was typical of and consistent with their gender (Griffin, 1992).

Some research has underscored the complexity of the relationships among ethnicity, gender, values, and workplace dynamics. As early as 1973, Sue and Wagner discussed intragroup and intergroup differences. In their summary of organizational research on Asian Americans, they reported that Asian American men showed less need for dominance, aggressiveness, exhibitionism, autonomy, and heterosexuality than did white men. Asian American women were found to be more deferent, nurturing, and achievement oriented than were white women. It is interesting to note that Asian women were both more nurturing and more achievement oriented than white women, because many European Americans view these two characteristics as mutually exclusive.

Research on Mexican Americans indicates the importance of job level as a mediating variable in attitudes toward the work environment and job satisfaction (Rubaii-Barrett, Beck, & Lillibridge, 1993). From a sample of local government workers, three groups of Mexican American workers (front-line employees, supervisors, and managers) were more satisfied with personnel policies and less satisfied with employee competence than their white counterparts. The data also showed that the higher the job level, the fewer the items of dissatisfaction. Consistent with the correlation among culture, job level, and attitudes, Mexican American front-line employees were less satisfied than white front-line employees on five items, supervisors on three items, and managers on two items (Rubaii-Barrett et al., 1993).

Cox, Lobel, and McLeod's (1991) work demonstrates both direct and indirect links among values, ethnic heritage, and work behavior. They found that attitudes, values, and norms of people of different ethnic heritage reflect their cultural heritage. For example, carryover of ethnic traditions of "individualism–collectivism" (p. 829) exists among the ethnic groups in the American work force. Specifically, Asian Americans, African Americans, and Hispanic Americans had a more collectivist–cooperative orientation to a task than did European Americans. They also found empirical evidence that ethnic group differences influence at least some aspects of behavior in work task groups. Hofstede's work (1980a, 1980b, 1991, 1994) showed that countries, like people, differ in work-related values. He developed five dimensions of these values—power, uncertainty avoidance (need for structure), individualism–collectivism, femininity–masculinity, and long-term–short-term orientation—on which he rated several countries (see Table 15-3). For example, the United States and European countries are high on individualism and more short-term focused than Hispanic, Asian, or African countries. Asian countries rank highest on the long-term dimension. Chile, West Africa, and Indonesia are the only countries that score less than 50 on masculinity. These results suggest that knowledge about cultural differences can positively influence the selection of appropriate management theories and styles in human services organizational settings. For example, Hofstede (1980b) concluded that theories that advocate subordinate participation in management decision making would produce effective results in the United States but would not work well in France, because French people have different beliefs about intraorganizational boundaries.

Although research in this area is relatively sparse, studies have demonstrated the relationships among culture, values, attitudes, and organizational behavior and suggest important similarities and

Table 15-3

Hofstede's Five Dimensions of Work-Related Cultures

Country	Power	Uncertainty	Individualism	Masculinity	Long-Term
Chile	63	86	23	28	—
Germany	35	65	67	66	31
Hong Kong	68	29	25	57	96
India	77	40	48	56	61
Indonesia	78	48	14	46	—
Ireland	28	35	70	68	—
Italy	50	75	76	70	—
Japan	54	92	46	95	80
Mexico	81	82	30	69	—
Philippines	94	44	32	64	19
United States	40	46	91	62	29
West Africa	77	54	20	46	16

SOURCE: From B. Wooldridge, Work force diversity, identity groups, and management theory, in M. Rice (Ed.), *Diversity and public organizations.* Copyright 1996 by Kendall/Hunt Publishing Company. Used with permission.

differences among and within groups from different cultures. There are, however, some obvious omissions in the research. Other important societal groups, such as people with disabilities, gay men and lesbians, and people who practice various religions are not represented. Also, none of the reported literature compared oppressed groups. As members of oppressed groups increasingly find employment in the work force, it is becoming essential to study similarities and differences from a multicultural perspective as defined in this discussion. For example, how do African Americans and Hispanic Americans, or people with disabilities and gay and lesbian populations, or Jewish and Protestant groups differ? In what ways are they similar? How can such data help support effective individual and organizational functioning in human services settings?

Culture and Communication

Much of the difficulty found within and among human services organizations correlates strongly with breakdowns in communication processes. In the context of our society, one cannot avoid communication. Everyone communicates either intentionally or inadvertently. The communication process may be inadvertent, but it is still interpersonal and requires at least two people for messages to be sent and received. What message the sender sends and what interpretations the receiver makes depend on an elaborate set of factors. As noted earlier in this discussion, individual characteristics such as age, gender, race, social class, physical ability, and education all help determine communication processes, including the particular words used and the specific situations in which they are used. Influencing these differences also are the types of relationships the communicators have with each other. Colleagues, for example, communicate differently in formal meetings than at lunch or sports events. In these same events, different levels of deference may be demonstrated in communication exchanges between an individual and a superior, a coworker, or a subordinate.

Ineffective communication and miscommunication often pose interactional problems when people are similar but become more complex and present greater obstacles when communicating across cultures. Yet more difficult is the challenge to communicate across cultures about differences. Topics such as disabilities, sexual orientation, and race pose particular obstacles to effective communication because they tend to be emotionally charged and promote caution around finding the "correct" words. For example, how does one refer to a person who is physically disabled? Is "disabled" too harsh? Is "physically challenged" euphemistic? Because such questions are often left unasked, responses and opinions about these topics are not discussed, causing the potential for frequent misunderstandings in multicultural organizations.

Even if people share many characteristics, they are still unique in a variety of ways. Remember that no cultural group is homogeneous and that each contains great diversity. Thus, communication styles, which include what, how, and the conditions under which language is used or not used, vary widely within the same cultural group. Consider ethnicity, for example. There are more than 2,000 Native American tribes. Asian Americans include people from 33 Asian Pacific nations. Hispanic Americans have roots in countries as different as Cuba, Puerto Rico, Mexico, Brazil, and Spain (Griggs & Louw, 1987). African Americans may have roots in African countries such as Ghana, Nigeria, and Liberia, or they may be from South America or Russia. Because as much diversity exists within cultural groups as among groups, human services professionals must be sensitive to the cultural values of groups while simultaneously recognizing and respecting individual differences to achieve the goals of the organization and provide the most effective services to all groups of people.

When knowledge of another's culture is diminished or absent, no appropriate referent script exists for effective interaction. The only basis that then may be established for communication is the other person's membership group (male, homosexual, or professional, for example). This basis is often accompanied by stereotypical information that is either unrecognized or erroneous. Either situation provides negative expectations and judgments and causes overt attempts to avoid interactions with others who are different.

BARRIERS TO MULTICULTURAL COMMUNICATION

In human services organizations, workplace productivity depends on several intervening factors that directly affect individual employees. Significant to organizational efficiency are workplace climate and the accuracy and consistency of communication that describes workplace expectations, responsibilities, and evaluations of performance measures. Because human services organizations are often as diverse as the populations they serve, a careful assessment of intraorganizational communication barriers likely to adversely influence the workplace climate and impede proficient services delivery is important.

Types of Communication Errors

Two types of communication errors—type 1 and type 2, as conceptualized by Dungee-Anderson and Beckett (1995)—can impede internal organizational functioning and the efficacy of organizational services delivery. *Type 1 errors* are defined as interpersonal relationship errors among and between all levels of employees in the organizational structure. They can occur at all junctures of communication exchanges across the entire workplace. They originate from employee interactions and are caused by a lack of self-awareness or sensitivity to one's own blind spots or general biases. Type 1 errors include communication-sabotaging behavior such as engaging in power struggles with lateral or line colleagues, indiscriminately offering opinions and positions that are judgmental and that lower workplace morale (for example, one's own personal "shoulds" and "should nots"), and inadvertently attributing one's own negative feelings and attitudes to others. The reasons for such failures in self-awareness are as diverse as the workers who hold them; however, their impact on organizational functioning is clear. Type 1 errors obscure and merge personal and professional boundaries in the workplace. They promote contentiousness, cynicism, and workplace paranoia. They encourage negative interactional patterns and adverse processes that establish hostile and lethal communication feedback loops within the organization. Type 1 errors prevent clear multicultural communication, the development of effective working relationships, and competent functioning of the organization, and they promote workplace divisiveness.

Type 2 errors are defined as incorrect interpretation and application of multicultural knowledge. Type 2 errors result in faulty organizational strategies designed to help achieve organizational goals but found to be ineffective for promoting organizational growth. Upon examination, these strategies are formulated on inadequate multicultural knowledge that causes misguided and erroneous application of multicultural communication principles. One common example is the defining of the aggregate of group differences solely by the apparent and distinct characteristics of its members. In human services organizations, type 2 errors most often occur in services delivery systems when human services workers develop intervention plans for diverse client populations but have little or only stereotypical information about differences among and within cultural groups. The same type of type 2 error occurs intraorganizationally when individual employees or employee groups define the sum of coworker differences solely by the apparent and distinct characteristics observed. The case example at the end of this chapter illustrates both types of multicultural communication errors and the organizational difficulties that they create.

Improving Multicultural Communication

Overcoming the barriers and increasing proficiency in multicultural communication cannot occur with a specific one-time strategy but rather is an active process that continually occurs and recurs over time in the life of the organization. Many steps constitute the process, and although some may seem unrelated to communication, each is an important dimension of the communication process (Beckett, 1994).

Acknowledge Cultural Differences. Understanding that different cultures have different communication styles is essential knowledge and also an essential step in improving multicultural communication. It is appropriate and desirable to observe differences among people. As Thiederman (1991) proposed, "Just because we are equal does not mean we are the same" (p. 11). Differences determine individual and group uniqueness. Difficulty in seeing and recognizing differences, or cultural blindness, poses insurmountable barriers to effective multicultural communication. Cultural blindness negates individuality and disregards the significance of many of the cherished values and behaviors of others different from ourselves. The acknowledgment of differences facilitates learning from other cultures and decreases interpersonal and organizational miscommunication. Acknowledging differences does not promote racism or other types of oppressive interactions. It neither prevents the recognition of commonalities nor perpetuates stereotypes.

A common communication error that can originate from both type 1 and type 2 errors is believing that there is a single set of individual or formal organizational rules that applies to communication exchanges. For example, the absence of eye contact or the presence of social personal conversation in formal organizational exchanges cannot always be interpreted in the same manner in multicultural situations. Understanding and acknowledging that cultural differences often determine different but not inferior or inept communication styles permit sensitive and effective adjustments. In workplace situations in which these differences are not understood or are ignored, inordinate amounts of energy often are used to formulate and maintain negative and uninformed judgments. Thoughts or comments such as "he has poor social skills," or "she is not leadership material" or judgments that flow from a more aggressive perspective such as "he is illogical, irrational, or self-centered" command exhausting amounts of emotional energy. Understanding and acknowledging cultural differences can free this energy for investment in positive communication, such as clarifying, seeking additional information, or speaking with others in ways they are able to understand and make themselves understood.

Know Yourself. An essential step in the multicultural communication process is achieving individual cultural self-awareness. *Self-awareness* is the conscious awareness of beliefs and values one holds and the clear recognition that they are products of one's own culture. Thus, as people become culturally self-aware, they also recognize that they are culture bound. Becoming culturally aware is accompanied by a number of challenges. A particular one is that all people belong to a number of cultural groups. There are occupational cultures, regional and neighborhood cultures, gender cultures, and cultures associated with hobbies and avocations. Just about any group designation one can describe shares some values, etiquette, rules of behavior, and an agreed-on set of rules for living that constitute a culture. The process of achieving cultural awareness requires focused attention to these multiple cultures. The conscious awareness of one's own cultural characteristics helps prevent distortions in perceptions of other groups. A lack of self-awareness often causes unconscious projection of erroneous or negative positions onto other people. Learning about ourselves, then, enhances sensitivity to other cultures and prepares for learning about others.

An example may help clarify this concept. Assume that your supervisor is a Cambodian woman. As you begin to speak, she drops her eyes and keeps them down during the entire conversation. It is likely that you will have some reaction to this behavior that you do not readily understand. The important question is, What information will you use when trying to comprehend this behavior? Most likely, you will use knowledge most readily available to you—your own cultural assumption about what lack of eye contact means. If you are European American, you attribute the European American view that lack of eye contact means shyness, distraction, disinterest, or dishonesty. Further complicating your understanding of this behavior might be gender, age, or socioeconomic status. The conscious awareness that your assumptions flow from your own beliefs and values about this type of exchange will then permit you to entertain other reasons for your supervisor's behavior. Actually, the supervisor's behavioral "deference" (a European American view) is interpreted in Cambodian culture as respectful, socially appropriate, and mannerly.

Know Other Cultures. Learning about other cultures prevents projection of one's own cultural meanings onto situations with people of different cultures. Gaining knowledge about other cultures does not mean that we have to become anthropologists or learn all the behavioral specifics that characterize various cultures. What we do learn, however, are some of the cultural values and patterns that motivate behaviors. This knowledge will offer the insights necessary to substitute the correct, culturally aware interpretation for the old habit of projecting meanings from one's own culture onto the situation.

Identify and Value Differences. Human services workers must consciously look for and identify cultural differences between themselves and others. This is often a difficult task, because it conflicts with at least two values internalized during socialization processes that hinder multicultural communication. First, many people have been socialized to treat every person alike—to become color, gender, and culture blind. Expressions such as "Race does not matter," "all people are just people," or "When I look at her, I do not see a woman —I see an individual" are statements that indicate a dismissal of unique individual differences that are crucial to each person's identity and behavior. Further, if all people are indeed alike, which actual differences in individual characteristics determine the norm to which everyone conforms? Discomfort about open and direct discussions of race, gender, age, and other differences inhibits effective interpersonal and organizational communication and prevents constructive interaction.

Second, some people are socialized to observe differences but quickly ignore them or relegate them to a position of minor importance during multicultural exchanges. Many people in this category believe that acknowledging differences is racist or sexist or a reflection of other discriminatory positions. People who do recognize such differences are quick to label them as bad or good. In reality, differences are not good or bad but are simply differences.

Identification and positive valuation of differences facilitate important changes in the human services workplace. If employees demonstrate the determination to identify, respect, and value differences among themselves and the populations they serve, accepting one's own culture as only one of many cultures permits attitudinal shifts and defines a new workplace culture of openness and flexibility. Until recently, health and mental health systems did not consider the effects of gender differences in services delivery to multicultural populations. One consequence was that women were not included in medication trials and were prescribed dosages of medications identical to men's. Group advocacy and questioning of such practices have led to a beginning sensitivity and changes in practices around these issues. For example, a local hospital ran the following one-page newspaper advertisement: "This area's most remarkable new medical facility will view women's health from the unique perspective of how being a woman influences everything from diagnosis to recovery. How does a woman react differently to pain? Should your medication be administered differently than a man's? How do a woman's health needs change over the course of her life?" ("Advertisement," June 6, 1993, p. C8).

The same considerations are needed for other cultural groups. We know, for example, that medication dosages differ for older people other adults and that certain illnesses are more prevalent in some cultural groups than in others. African American women, for instance, are at much higher risk for sickle cell anemia and fibroid uterine tumors than are other women. Identification of these issues of difference at the organizational level can provide data from which value-based human services can be offered.

Identify and Avoid Stereotypes. Each of us has preconceived notions about groups of people. When we have inflexible views of people based on prejudgments, we are using stereotypes. Stereotypes assume that everyone from a group has certain characteristics and do not allow for individual differences. They distort the truth. Some examples are "all Native Americans do not make eye contact," "all African Americans are athletic," "all Japanese Americans are technically skilled," "all Hispanic Americans are 'party people,'" and "women are not good with mathematics." Stereotypes may be positive or negative, but each type has the same result—the distortion of reality about other people and groups.

Stereotypes result in cases of "mistaken identity" (Thiederman, 1991) and are barriers to reality. They negate the person and minimize the possibility that people will be valued for the characteristics they truly possess. Stereotypes must not be confused with descriptive knowledge-based information about groups of people. For example, it is credible to say that people of Japanese descent generally place great value on personal honor. In this case, the descriptive statement is based on general facts about a group, but such a fact is in no way an indication that *every* person of Japanese descent places great value on personal honor. This type of descriptive information provides general knowledge-based guidelines for considering group characteristics but at the same time provides latitude for consideration of individual differences.

To eliminate stereotypes, people must first become aware of and identify the preconceived notions they accept about other people and groups. Second, a valid process must be selected that can reliably separate knowledge about particular groups from the inflexible beliefs that influenced earlier feelings and behavior. Third, the person must be willing to discard the faulty beliefs and accept the new information as valid, with accompanying changes in feelings and behavior. It is important to point out that these steps comprise a process that is repeated many times as people study and engage in exchanges to nullify stereotypical beliefs.

Another effective method that helps eliminate stereotypes is to have multiple experiences with culturally different groups. This immersion approach is interactionally based and can be successful. However, a primary consideration is that the multiple experiences with other groups must be based on a strategy called "matching." Contact with others who are different in many ways is more likely to be perceived as positive if identification can occur around one or more shared variables. It is more difficult to stereotype people with whom there is extensive contact about shared interests. Connecting with others around areas of mutual interest and similarities creates a structure for observations, dialogue, and challenges to stereotypes. Often, these multiple experiences lead to interest in acquiring in-depth knowledge about other groups, to increases in multicultural sensitivity, and to reductions in stereotyping incidents.

Empathize with People from Other Cultures. Empathy involves the ability of a person to shift frame of reference to better understand others' specific experiences. Empathy is different from sympathy, in which a person imagines how he or she would feel in the same situation. Empathy requires more than the capacity for sympathy. Whereas sympathizing requires one step—the shift in circumstance of placing oneself in another's position—empathizing is a two-step process. Not only must one put oneself in the other's position, but one also must be able to experience the situation *as though* she or he were the other person. This, then, is a shift in both circumstance and frame of reference. Empathy acknowledges cultural differences and respects these differences by the willingness to temporarily give up one's own worldview to experience that of the other. Sympathy is an ethnocentric process, whereas empathy is an ethnorelative process and requires knowledge of the other person.

Adapt Rather than Adopt. Adapt behaviors to cross- or multicultural interactions rather than adopt the values and behaviors of others.

Multicultural exchanges require adjustments and compromises in interactions rather than a necessary change in one's own values, beliefs, or behaviors. Relinquishing one's cherished values or adopting behaviors that are insincere is not required and can be detrimental in efforts to communicate in multicultural settings. For example, in the earlier situation of the Cambodian woman who does not make eye contact, it is not necessary for the worker to cease eye contact, nor is there a need to mirror the behaviors for effective communication to occur between the parties. One only needs to give thoughtful and informed consideration and, if they are indicated, nonjudgmental responses to the unfamiliar behavior to demonstrate acceptance of such differences.

Acquire Recovery Skills. Human services workers skilled in multicultural communication differ from the novice not necessarily by the number of errors made, but by the demonstrated ability to recover from these mistakes with each other and with the clients they serve. If skilled workers do not report making errors or questioning interactions in multicultural exchanges, they may not be taking the required qualitative risks for successful multicultural communication—or a type 1 error may be occurring.

Type 1 errors do occur with workers skilled in multicultural communication processes. Because these errors flow from a person's blind spots or from a lack of cultural self-awareness, a human services worker may have a plethora of knowledge about specific cultural groups but fail at some juncture in a multicultural exchange to see an unconscious assumption he or she may have made about the other person. The point is that not every person will participate in error-free multicultural exchanges, but that the capacity to recover also requires the capacity for accurate and continual assessment of communication processes. The worker who feels more competent about recovery from multicultural exchanges is less likely to experience excessive anxiety about miscommunications than is the worker who doubts his or her recovery skills.

At the organizational level, opportunities for recovery from multicultural miscommunications must be built into organizational structure and processes. Policies and procedures must exist that not only explain the organization's sensitivity to multicultural differences but also consistently address goals of multicultural communication competency through both internal and external processes. Training, other types of staff involvement, and evaluations of performance and processes within and across all levels of organizational structure can help demonstrate the organization's commitment to competent multicultural communication processes. Organizations that illustrate this level of commitment to addressing issues of diversity tend to function with a higher degree of flexibility and more adaptive skills for recovery than organizations without structural recovery processes. They are readily able to implement recovery strategies when organizational errors in multicultural exchanges occur.

CASE EXAMPLE

The following case example illustrates a lack of attention to multicultural differences and chronicles the ripple effect that occurs throughout the agency. Both type 1 and type 2 communication errors occur.

Agency and Staff

Charlene Morris Services (CMS) is a well-established, medium-sized, private nonprofit agency located in the northeastern corridor of the United States. It is funded primarily with state-allocated services grants. It is one of several human services agency sites that operate under the umbrella of the parent organization, Charlene Morris Services, Inc.

CMS has a total staff of 35 people, who represent a broad range of cultural differences. Mr. Kain, age 50, is European American and has been agency director for eight years. Mr. Kain has three executive assistants, all of whom are women. Two are European Americans between ages 33 and 35. One is employed full-time and the other occupies a well-paid part-time position. The third, Mrs. Austin, is African American. She is in her early 50s and has been employed at CMS longer than most of the other staff. Mrs. Newman, age 46, is European American and is assistant director of CMS. She was promoted six months ago from program coordinator to her current position. She has an assistant, Mrs. Ivan, age 34, who is European American. The agency accountant, Ms. Baker, is 43 years old and European American. She is assisted by Ms. Washington, age 26, an African American.

Five agency programs are each administered by women ranging in age from 47 to 60. Three of these women are Protestant, one is Jewish, and one is Mormon. There are 27 professional staff employed across all five programs. Included are two African American men ages 51 and 54, four African American women ages 40 to 54, seven European American women ages 37 to 58, two Latino men ages 34 to 40, and one Native American woman age 42. The remaining staff comprises one Asian American woman and 10 European American men, all of whose ages range from 34 to 73. Included in the professional staff are five people with same-sex orientation, two with bisexual orientation, and 20 with opposite-sex orientation. Eight people are Jewish, five are Catholic, three are Mormon, and the rest are Protestant. Three people have identified disabilities. Staff originate from all sections of the United States and, in most instances, each has family residing in his or her respective home areas. Finally, there is a clerical support staff of one Asian American, one Native American, and four African American women who range in age from 23 to 54. Each year, the agency serves more than 700 clients representing most ethnic and other cultural groups, but the majority of clients are middle-class European Americans.

The staff group meets the criteria for designation as multicultural by virtue of the broad spectrum of areas on which people differ. Communication within and across programs and administration therefore qualifies as multicultural communication exchanges as defined in this chapter. The following situation occurred in the agency, and produced seismic reverberations in two of the agency's largest programs.

Multicultural Interactions

Ms. Goings, age 47 and European American, manages the largest program at CMS. At the beginning of the previous year, she hired Ms. Harris, age 56 and Native American, as her administrative secretary for the program. Ms. Harris has been successfully employed in several clerical capacities at CMS for 26 years. She has close and long-standing relationships with other clerical employees as well as other long-term relationships with human services professional staff within the agency. Ms. Harris is an efficient and skilled employee but has become a somewhat bitter and mistrustful worker over the past six years. The agency has undergone several reorganizations, and she was reassigned to three programs during that period with various levels of decreasing autonomy. Ms. Goings was aware of Ms. Harris's efficiency as well as her bitterness. She believed that hiring Ms. Harris would be a strategic move for her program and that, at the same time, she might also help reduce Ms. Harris's bitterness and enhance her loyalty to CMS. Ms. Goings believed that a strategy of "inclusiveness" with Ms. Harris would help achieve both objectives. She defined inclusiveness as immersion, that is, teaching Ms. Harris about her program, describing its objectives and functions, and explaining how it fit within the agency's overall service delivery programming. Also, she believed that consistent reinforcement of Ms. Harris's considerable clerical skills by all staff might help elicit more friendly exchange from Ms. Harris with the staff.

Over a period of eight months, Ms. Goings began to believe her relationship with Ms. Harris was becoming a very strong manager–employee alliance. She was pleased to see that Ms. Harris was increasingly offering suggestions for more efficient program procedures and sharing informal and confidential observations with her about program staff work habits and performance. Based on her assessment of Ms. Harris's growing openness and confidences, Ms. Goings commented to another program manager that she "could see a change" in Ms. Harris's level of comfort and that her relationship with Ms. Harris seemed to be based on trust and growing employer–employee intimacy. Ms. Goings expressed her sincere belief that she had largely accomplished her goals of helping Ms. Harris become invested in CMS, become more loyal to the program, and become strongly loyal to her as program manager by using management strategies of inclusion and positive reinforcement.

Several months later, when a professional staff vacancy occurred in Ms. Goings's program, she hired Ms. Bluewater, a newly credentialed 52-year-old Native American. Ms. Bluewater had worked in various positions as a human services professional since earning her master's degree at age 27 and had returned to school at age 49 for advanced professional certification. On completion, she applied for the position at CMS and was hired.

Previously, Ms. Bluewater had worked exclusively in human services agencies that were largely administered by European American managers of both genders, that employed a statistical majority of European American professional staff, and that provided services to populations largely comprising other ethnic groups and people with a range of cultural differences. Consequently, when Ms. Bluewater was hired at CMS, newly certified and with a wealth of previous experience, knowledge, and professional achievements in her field, she accepted the position as a permanent move until her eventual retirement. She came to CMS with the anticipated new-employee "jitters" but felt confident in her capacity to make the adjustment to the new workplace. Around this same time, Ms. Bluewater also had become interested in learning more about her cultural background and the customs she had abandoned while seeking professional achievements in a society and profession defined primarily by European American customs and values. Her renewed interest in Native American customs led her to research her tribal culture. She searched for and found several items of tribal attire, which she began wearing to her workplace two days each workweek.

Because Ms. Goings's office was adjacent to Ms. Harris's, Ms. Goings had observed Ms. Bluewater's visits to Ms. Harris's office sometimes during lunch breaks or on other brief occasions at various times. She had also noticed the changes Ms. Bluewater had made in dress—the wearing of Native American clothes, jewelry, and hairstyles—and had begun experiencing some personal discomfort about the Native American braided and adorned hairstyle as well as some of the clothing Ms. Bluewater wore. She did not feel Ms. Bluewater was inappropriately dressed in native apparel, but that she was not *professionally* attired. Ms. Goings believed that Ms. Bluewater's dress was "out of place" for a professional employed in a human services agency and was concerned that her appearance might detract from her ability to work effectively with the clients that the agency served.

As a result, Ms. Goings decided to speak "privately and confidentially" with Ms. Harris, her administrative secretary, who was Native American, and someone with whom Ms. Goings increasingly felt she shared a "close and personal relationship." Ms. Goings commented to Ms. Harris that she had noticed Ms. Bluewater's braided and adorned hairstyle and wondered what Ms. Harris's "impression" was of Ms. Bluewater's ethnic hairstyle in a professional agency? She also remarked that she realized Ms. Bluewater was new to the agency and that at times she appeared anxious as new employees often tend to be. Ms. Goings went on to ask whether Ms. Harris had heard any feedback from other staff or clients that Ms. Bluewater's dress was "unbecoming for a professional." Ms. Goings further shared that, as program manager, she appreciated diversity and had been excited about, supportive of, and sensitive to Ms. Harris's own increasing interest in her Native American customs. Ms. Goings added, however, she believed that Ms. Harris had been "tasteful and professional" in her choices of attire and that her hairstyle had not drawn negative attention. Ms. Goings concluded her exchange with Ms. Harris by saying she did not feel Ms. Bluewater was as "discriminating" as was Ms. Harris in her choices of cultural dress.

Ms. Harris's response to Ms. Goings is much less important than are the events that followed. Within the week, Ms. Harris went to Ms. Bluewater's office and closed the door. She recounted her entire interaction with Ms. Goings and ended by saying, "I just wanted you to know so you can watch out and be careful of what you say and do around Ms. Goings. I don't like to carry tales, but I had to tell you because we are 'sisters.' I just can't believe Ms. Goings would say something like this to me and not think I would tell you!" Ms. Bluewater was devastated. She felt that Ms. Goings had acted in a discriminatory, judgmental, and unprofessional manner and made every effort to avoid her in the workplace. Ms. Bluewater also shared this situation with two colleagues, one of whom was Ms. Bluewater's informal staff ombudsman. As a result, Ms. Goings was confronted with her behavior, and other staff learned of the situation, causing a wave of disbelief among CMS employees. Mr. Kain, the executive director, attributed Ms. Goings's "indiscretion" to gender characteristics. He believed that male managers had the foresight not to engage in "gossipy interactions" in the workplace. He believed Ms. Goings's poor judgment resulted from her need, as a woman, "to help others" and to try and form close relationships with others, wrongly, in the office.

Case Analysis

Ms. Goings committed grave multicultural communication errors. There were many type 1 errors. She wrongly believed that her interpersonal interactions with Ms. Harris extended beyond the internal hierarchical levels and personnel boundary lines characteristic in organizational structures (Drucker, 1974). Ms. Goings saw Ms. Harris's friendliness and workplace intimacy as symbols of personal friendship. In this situation, Ms. Goings had inaccurately assumed a different type of interpersonal intimacy with Ms. Harris than had Ms. Harris with her supervisor. Ms. Goings's assumptions flowed from her intuition and were based on her belief of having cultivated positive ethnic workplace interactions with her Native American administrative secretary. She was not aware of obvious cues that might have alerted her to her mistaken assumptions. For example, Ms. Harris did not share personal information about herself beyond the level of the friendliness and politeness she believed to be required for an employer–employee relationship. Nor did Ms. Goings grasp that she had shared far more substantive personal information with Ms. Harris than Ms. Harris had shared with her. She also was totally insensitive to the possibility that shared cultural values between Ms.

Harris and Ms. Bluewater might promote a connectedness that she could not share.

As a result of the type 1 errors, Ms. Goings blindly stumbled into type 2 errors. She entered into a value-based competitive multicultural exchange with Ms. Harris when she privately and confidentially approached her assistant with the intent of forming an "alliance" with her—in support of Ms. Harris's own ethnic dress and in judgment of Ms. Bluewater's choices of dress. Ms. Goings's lack of knowledge about Native American cultural values and her inability to identify differences between her own value-based assumptions and the cultural beliefs Ms. Harris and Ms. Bluewater shared caused an organizational rift that was difficult to mend, and she herself was deeply "wounded" and resentful that Ms. Harris had betrayed their relationship and broken a personal confidence.

Ms. Goings's lack of self-awareness (type 1 error), cultural blindness (type 2 error), and related defensive responses to this incident initially prevented her from using more effective multicultural communication and behaviors. She had failed to respect the differences in cultural dress and had negatively judged Ms. Bluewater's hairstyle from her own cultural perspective. Insensitive to the significance of the shared cultural values between Ms. Harris and Ms. Bluewater, Ms. Goings further projected her own negative cultural assessment of professional dress onto Ms. Bluewater. She buttressed her behavior by rationalizing that she was protecting the clients from differences they would not accept.

Finally, during a later discussion with Ms. Harris about this incident, Ms. Bluewater learned that, as she had suspected, Ms. Harris had indeed shared Ms. Goings's remarks with her from a strong sense of cultural connectedness—their "sisterhood." However, Ms. Bluewater was also surprised to discover that Ms. Harris's primary reason for sharing the remarks came from her position as a long-term agency employee. Derived from her own experiences as a clerical employee, Ms. Harris stated she understood the sometimes-invisible "pecking order" at CMS. She did not wish Ms. Bluewater to inadvertently "bump into" these vertical boundaries at CMS as she herself had in earlier years. Thus, the series of interactions that occurred were not primarily precipitated by ethnic differences, as initially seemed to be the case. As Ms. Harris noted, as a long-time CMS employee, her behavior was largely based on her need to protect an uninitiated "newcomer" from the "wolves" in the organizational setting. She believed her longevity and agency experiences had sensitized her to potentially dangerous situations, and she felt she owed the benefit of her experience to younger and newer employees. "Sisterhood," however, allowed her to cross the hierarchical boundaries of social class and job status.

CONCLUSION

The unexpected twist to this case illustrates the multilayered complexity of organizational multicultural communication exchanges and the many types of diversity that influence them. One might assess the multicultural communication exchanges from many perspectives in this case and in any organization. The interactions, as presented at CMS, strongly underscore the necessity for developing effective agency multicultural communication processes. These processes must include strategies designed to provide continual opportunities for promoting staff self-awareness skills and teaching comprehensive multicultural content and appropriate interactional behaviors to all agency employees. The method we find most effective in imparting this information is the multicultural communication model presented in this chapter. Staff sufficiently armed with appropriate multicultural communication skills and behaviors will provide the necessary ingredient to meet organizational goals.

REFERENCES

Americans with Disabilities Act of 1990, P.L. 101-336, 104 Stat. 327.

Advertisement. (1993, June 6). *Richmond Times-Dispatch*, p. C8.

Beckett, J. (1994, May). *Multicultural communication in health and mental health settings.* Galt Scholar Lecture given at the Department of Mental Health, Mental Retardation and Substance Abuse Services, Richmond, VA.

Beckett, J., & Dungee-Anderson, D. (1992). Older minorities: Asian, Black, Hispanic, and Native Americans. In R. Schneider & N. Kropf (Eds.), *Gerontological social work* (pp. 277–322). Chicago: Nelson-Hall.

Billingsley, A. (1992). *Climbing Jacob's ladder: The enduring legacy of African American families.* New York: Simon & Schuster.

Bowman, J., & French, B. (1992). Quality improvement in a state agency revisited. *Public Productivity and Management Review, 16,* 53–64.

Clark, C. (1972). Black studies, or the study of black people. In R. Jones (Ed.), *Black psychology* (pp. 125–133). New York: Harper & Row.

Cox, T., Lobel, S., & McLeod, P. (1991). Effects of ethnic group cultural differences on cooperative and competitive behavior on a group task. *Academy of Management Journal, 34,* 827–847.

Drucker, P. (1974). *Management tasks, responsibilities, and practices.* New York: Harper & Row.

Dungee-Anderson, E., & Beckett, J. (1995). A process model for multicultural social work practice. *Families in Society, 76,* 459–466.

Griggs, L., & Louw, L. (1987). *Valuing diversity: Communicating across cultures.* San Francisco: Copeland Griggs Productions.

Griggs, L., & Louw, L. (Eds.). (1995). *Valuing diversity: New tools for a new reality.* New York: McGraw-Hill.

Griffin, B. (1992, March). *Perceptions of managers: Effects of leadership style and gender.* Paper presented at the Annual Meeting of the Southeastern Psychological Association, Knoxville, Tennessee.

Ho, M. K. (1987). *Family therapy with ethnic minorities.* Newbury Park, CA: Sage Publications.

Hofstede, G. (1980a). *Culture's consequences: International differences in work-related values.* Beverly Hills, CA: Sage Publications.

Hofstede, G. (1980b, Summer). Motivation, leadership and organization: Do American theories apply abroad? *Organizational Dynamics,* pp. 42–63.

Hofstede, G. (1991). *Culture and organizations: Software of the minds.* New York: McGraw-Hill.

Hofstede, G. (1994). Management scientists are human. *Management Science, 40,* 4–12.

Ibrahim, F. (1985). Effective cross-cultural counseling and psychotherapy: A framework. *Counseling Psychologist, 13,* 625–638.

Jamieson, D., & O'Mara, J. (1991). *Managing workforce 2000: Gaining the diversity advantage.* San Francisco: Jossey-Bass.

Jensen, M., & Katz, J. (1996). Downsizing and diversity: Navigating the path between trauma and opportunity. *Journal of Public Management and Policy, 2,* 22–31.

Johnston, W., & Packer, A. (1987). *Workforce 2000: Work and worker for the 21st century.* Indianapolis: Hudson Institute.

Keyes, C. (1977). *The golden peninsula.* New York: Macmillan.

Kluckhohn, F., & Strodtbeck, F. (1961). *Variations in value orientations.* New York: Harper & Row.

Lum, D. (1992). *Social work practice and people of color* (2nd ed.). Monterey, CA: Brooks/Cole.

National Indian Council on Aging. (1986). *Research project to derive and disseminate information on the health, housing and safety status of Indian elders.* Albuquerque, NM: Office of Human Development Services.

Pinderhughes, E. (1989). *Understanding race, ethnicity and power: The key to efficacy in clinical practice.* New York: Free Press.

Rand Corporation. (1996, October 23). Census predicts California will grow 56% by 2025. *USA Today,* p. A7.

Rubaii-Barrett, N., Beck, A., & Lillibridge, L. (1993). Minorities in the majority: Implications for managing cultural diversity. *Public Personnel Management, 22,* 503–521.

Segal, J. (1991). Women on the verge of . . . equality. *H R Magazine, 36,* 117–123.

Sue, S., & Wagner, N. (1973). *Asian Americans: Psychological perspectives.* Palo Alto, CA: Science and Behavior Books.

Swisher, K. (1995, February 5). Diversity's learning curve: Multicultural training's challenges include undoing its own mistakes. *Washington Post,* pp. H1, H4.

Thiederman, S. (1991). *Bridging cultural barriers for corporate success.* New York: Macmillan.

White, H., & Rice, M. (1996). The multiple dimensions of diversity. In M. Rice (Ed.), *Diversity and public organizations* (pp. 1–3). Dubuque, IA: Kendall/Hunt.

Wooldridge, B. (1996). Workforce diversity, identity groups and management theory. In M. Rice (Ed.), *Diversity and public organizations* (pp. 35–49). Dubuque, IA: Kendall/Hunt.

16 Latino Diversity in Communication in the Workplace

Humberto Fabelo-Alcover and
Karen M. Sowers

Worldwide, business organizations have discovered that intercultural communication is important. In addition to many organizations having to deal increasingly with "foreigners," the work force of the future is growing increasingly diverse, both ethnically and culturally (Limaye & Victor, 1991). Coping with greater diversity in the workplace is one of the urgent matters with which managers will have to deal in the future (Wagel & Levine, 1990).

Communication plays a crucial role in international management. Yet emphasis on cultural variables is only beginning to be felt (for example, Adler, 1991; Hofstede, 1980; Jackofsky, Slocum, & McQuaid, 1988). People bring their cultural values into the work environment, including such dimensions as power distance and individualism versus collectivism (Bochner & Hesketh, 1994), and bring these values and different meanings, assumptions, and discourse styles into the workplace conversation. Such differences can lead to misunderstandings and breakdowns in communication and can threaten a common orientation to organizational goals (Fine, 1991). Even people who speak the same language may have difficulty communicating with each other because of different racial and cultural backgrounds. Interactions between people from different cultures are affected by structural and contextual factors in their organizations. Moreover, in terms of numbers and significance, cross-cultural interactions are occurring more frequently in business and other organizational settings. It is within these settings that cultural differences present the greatest difficulties (Albert, 1992).

Although past immigration to the United States has been primarily European, this situation is no longer the case. Latinos are one of the fastest growing segments of the U.S. population. Currently, Latinos make up 8.5 percent of the total U.S. population. By 2050, demographers predict that one of every six Americans will be Latino. Latinos will constitute the largest and youngest ethnic group in the United States (Harper & Lantz, 1996). Employers that ignore this phenomenon will shut themselves off from a pool of talented employees at a time when skilled labor is expected to be increasingly hard to find (Matthes, 1992).

DIVERSITY AMONG LATINO GROUPS

The term "Latino" encompasses many subgroups—Mexican, Puerto Rican, Cuban, Central and South American, and other Spanish-speaking cultures—that have different customs, beliefs, and practices. Many employers do not realize that a wide range of diversity exists among Latino people. Latino groups share general characteristics: In language, philosophy of life, and family structure, there are probably more similarities than differences (Bernal, 1982). For example, in most Latin American countries rich and poor people are fixed in their socioeconomic status with little chance for mobility. Focusing on inner qualities, therefore, allows a person to experience self-worth, regardless of worldly success or failure. This form of individualism is referred to as "personalism." This form clearly contrasts to European American individualism which values achievement above all else. Thus, for example, Puerto Ricans define self-worth in terms of those inner qualities that give them self-respect and earn them the respect of others.

Although several similarities exist, employers must realize that different customs, beliefs, and practices exist among the Latino subgroups. Throughout U.S. history, Latinos have emigrated from different countries at different times and for different reasons and have settled in different parts of the country. Broad cultural generalizations do not do justice to regional, generational, socioeconomic, and idiosyncratic variations in lifestyles. Cultural values and communication styles evolve as part of a process of change linked to the stage of acculturation of the Latino group or person.

Mexican Americans

Mexican Americans were the first Spanish-speaking population to become an ethnic group in the United States (Harper & Lantz, 1996). The population began to grow rapidly in the early 1900s when thousands fled the violence of the Mexican Revolution of 1910. Many Mexican workers were recruited by American railroads, mining companies, and farm owners. Because of the severe unemployment of the Great Depression, thousands of Mexican immigrants were deported or were pressured by the U.S. government to return to Mexico. During World War II a new wave of Mexicans came to the United States. Many were farm workers who had been issued temporary work permits. Many Mexicans continue to enter the United States daily in search of better economic opportunities. Most immigrants come from the northern bordering states and central rural areas of Mexico.

It is estimated that well over 6.5 million Mexican Americans live in the United States, making them the second largest nondominant ethnic group in the country. A large majority of Mexican Americans specify Spanish as their native tongue or the language that was spoken in their homes when they were children. The Mexican man or woman newly arrived in the United States differs in many areas of life from the Mexican American man or woman who has lived in this country for a decade or more and from the Chicano man or woman who was born in this country. In spite of inevitable acculturation, there is evidence that Mexican American families who have resided in the United States for several generations preserve many identifiable threads of their original culture. Even families who are upwardly mobile become acculturated but not assimilated and many retain their language and ethnic identity (Gordon, 1964; Teske & Nelson, 1976).

Cuban Americans

Since 1959, well over a million Cubans have emigrated to the United States. In the late 1960s and early 1970s, a major influx of immigrants entered the country after political and economic structures disrupted their social system (Szapocznik & Hernandez, 1988). This immigration had unique characteristics that distinguish it from other Hispanic or Latino groups. The suddenness of the Cuban emigration, its size within relatively brief periods, and its predominant middle- and upper-class composition, particularly during the early waves, seemed to magnify its impact and set up a special situation in relation to other Latinos in the United States. The impact of Cubans has been greatest in the major metropolitan areas, such as Miami, New York and New Jersey, Chicago and, to a lesser degree, Los Angeles.

Many Cuban refugees began their U.S. careers in lower-skilled jobs and in positions far less prestigious than those they had in Cuba. Over the years, however, a remarkably large proportion of Cuban Americans climbed up the occupational hierarchy. Early on, they formed strong and cohesive communities, developing business ties among extended families and friends and systems of mutual support and financial assistance.

Puerto Rican Americans

Puerto Rican culture has been influenced by several races and ethnic groups. A present-day Puerto Rican family may consist of a mother who is white, a father who is black, and children who are various shades of color. Their cultural ancestry may be a mixture of African, Taino, Corsican, and Spanish, although their ethnic identification is Puerto Rican (Garcia-Preto, 1982). Because Puerto Ricans did not solidify as an ethnic group until the 1800s, the definition of their cultural patterns is probably less fixed than that of many other groups.

Puerto Rican Americans came to the United States as naturalized citizens beginning in the early 1900s. They came primarily to the northern cities of the United States in search of jobs and education. After the U.S. occupation of Puerto Rico, industrialization rapidly affected all segments of the Puerto Rican population; town and urban centers grew in size, and the populations became differentiated into classes or sociocultural groups. One important development was the growth of a middle class of people having varied occupations and incomes. They represented a new trend, a new set of values that ascribed major importance to the symbols of personal achievement and wealth. Middle-class people exhibit less group identity and emphasize competition and upward mobility. The U.S. pattern of feminine independence has influenced middle-class Puerto Rican women. Women in this group usually work, and many have professions (Papa-John & Spiegel, 1975).

Central and South Americans

With origins in 15 countries covering a vast geographical area, Central and South Americans make up a heterogeneous group. Most Central and South American immigrants arrived in the United States over the past few decades. As thousands escaped wars in El Salvador, Nicaragua, and Guatemala in the 1970s and 1980s, Central American communities grew rapidly in many parts of the United States. The largest group of South American immigrants is from Colombia, which accounts for more than one of every four South Americans who legally emigrated during the 1980s. The Central and South American labor force is about equally distributed across the country's northern, southern, and western regions. A disproportionate share of both Central and South Americans live in the Washington, DC, metropolitan area.

ORGANIZATIONAL COMMUNICATION AND DIVERSITY

In the field of communication, culture often has been ignored (Limaye & Victor, 1991). Theories about communicating in organizations most often have been based on the assumption of homogeneity. Because white men have dominated corporate life, organizational theories have been developed based on their experiences (Fine, 1991; Kanter, 1977). However, the words that are used in business communications can set up barriers that hold back nontraditional work force members. How business leaders choose to refer to diverse groups of people can set the tone for an organization's entire diversity effort.

The issue of perceived differences is complex. Studies have suggested that women and men in organizations do not share similar perceptions of their own and others' communication (Infante & Gordon, 1979; Staley & Shockley-Zalabak, 1986). Just as women and men experience the organization through different cultural assumptions (Belenky, Clinchy, Goldberger, & Tarule, 1986; Gilligan, 1982; Johnson, 1989), so do people of other culturally diverse groups (Fine, Johnson, & Ryan, 1990; Greenhaus, Parasuraman, & Wormley, 1990). For example, Brazilian corporations have far fewer meetings, have fewer hierarchical levels, and give greater autonomy to executives than do their American or European counterparts. This results in more flexibility and enables Brazilian managers to function more effectively in a rapidly changing economic environment. In another example, a manager in Peru is likely to be more directive, formal, and authoritarian than a manager in the United States when communicating with subordinates (Albert, 1992). In addition, a common misperception is that Mexican men have difficulties accepting a woman in the authority role. Professionalism among women is more widespread in Latin

America than in the United States and, in general, Mexican people who have had very limited access to educational opportunities value the knowledge and manners of an educated person regardless of gender.

Understanding multicultural communication in organizations should begin with a theoretical position that confronts difference directly, recognizing the "assumption of difference" rather than the "assumption of homogeneity" as the organizational norm (Fine, 1991; Jandt, 1995). By recognizing and valuing differences among diverse cultures, the organization can anticipate ways in which differing languages and norms will affect communication in the workplace (Jandt, 1995). Awareness of cultural differences can enhance views of others because cultural knowledge brings forth a more informed context of perception in interpreting people's behavior.

COMMON ISSUES IN THE CULTURALLY DIVERSE WORKPLACE

Communication is an integral part of an organization. Through communication, roles of people, goals, and tasks are explicitly and implicitly defined. In the culturally diverse workplace, barriers to accurate communication can impede organizational initiatives. Awareness of the differences in verbal and nonverbal communication can help the organization initiate plans to promote effective communication in a multicultural and diverse work setting.

Language Barriers

Language, a set of symbols shared by a community to communicate meaning and experience, is the primary and most complex issue facing corporate America and those who manage foreign-born workers. The language one speaks has a direct relationship to one's culture (Jandt, 1995). There are more than 140 languages and dialects spoken in the United States, and about 11 percent of the population speaks a language other than English at home.

Even people who speak the same language can have difficulty communicating with each other because of their different cultural backgrounds and different definitions of words (Castillo & Bond, 1972; Diccionarios A–Z, 1974). For example, in Colombia *ahorita* means "later" or "in a while." In Cuba, *ahorita* means "this instant." When conversing, miscommunication can occur between these two subgroups. Imagine the difficulties that may occur if a Cuban supervisor asks an Colombian employee to do something *ahorita* (this instant) and the employee does not immediately tend to the task because his or her interpretation of the supervisor's request meant that he or she should do the task later. The supervisor may well assume the employee to be insubordinate or intentionally defiant. In turn, the employee may be surprised to find the supervisor unsupportive, despite his or her hard work and attention to work demands. It is likely that such a scenario of miscommunication and misunderstanding may never be openly addressed. In fact, language diversity in the workplace often is not addressed adequately (Solomon, 1993), possibly leading to poor work relations and undermining a common orientation to the organization's goals.

English Proficiency

One major difficulty among ethnic groups and immigrants is a lack of basic skills in the English language. Businesses are finding it increasingly difficult to hire employees who are proficient in English (Fine, 1991). One impediment that has hindered some groups in adopting new skills is the fear of losing their cultural identities, especially among older people (National Commission for Employment Policy, 1991). A lack of proficiency in English is common among Mexican Americans (Falicov, 1982). Island-born Puerto Ricans are more likely to have difficulty communicating in English than those born in the continental United States (Garcia-Preto, 1982).

Interactive Style Elements

Three elements can affect the quality of interactions in the workplace: (1) conversational norms, (2) degree of eye contact during interaction, and (3) speaking style. These elements reflect individual culture and are potential sources of cultural miscues that can lead to conflict (Waters, 1992).

Conversational Norms. Cultural differences can manifest themselves in the area of conversational norms (Kochman, 1983); that is, the way one shows attention in a conversational setting is different among racial and ethnic groups (Hall, 1976). For European Americans, paying attention in a conversation usually involves several distinct behaviors. Typically, European American listeners will demonstrate attention by looking at the speaker, nodding occasionally (generally a sign of agreement), and making little noises that indicate they are paying attention. In other cultures, these typical conversational feedback mechanisms may be completely absent and misunderstood by others; that is, people do not particularly feel the need to look at one another while conversing. Further, the use of the conversational nod can indicate something different in Latino conversation (Asante & Davis, 1985). For instance, it is not uncommon for a Cuban administrator to find head-nodding and other nonverbal movements to be distracting and a sign of inattentiveness bordering on rudeness. Thus, an employee, thinking he or she is communicating agreement and interest, may in fact be presenting an opposite impression.

It is not at all difficult to imagine the problems that can occur when culturally diverse social actors with different conversational styles interact. To the extent there is incongruity in terms of what is considered standard, conflict will occur.

Eye Contact. The degree of eye contact a social actor maintains in conversation is both reflective of culture and a potential source of conflict. From the perspective of European Americans, it is desirable to maintain frequent eye contact while engaged in face-to-face conversation (Asante & Davis, 1985). Eye contact is seen to be intimately related to a person's level of trustworthiness, masculinity, sincerity, and directness; people who do not maintain eye contact are people whose trustworthiness and sincerity are suspect (Waters, 1992). For other cultures, however, there are different rules of eye contact (Adler, Doktor, & Redding, 1986). For example, many Puerto Ricans believe that it is unacceptable to make eye contact with strangers, especially women and children (Garcia-Preto, 1982). Eye contact may be interpreted mistakenly as disinterest or rudeness when, in fact, it is intended as a gesture of respect. A new female boss could easily assume that a Puerto Rican employee is intentionally ignoring her or indicating disrespect when, in fact, just the opposite is the case.

Speaking Style. Speaking style is seen to be both culturally reflective and a source of cultural miscues leading to potential conflicts. Normally regulated speech styles can strongly affect observers' assumptions about the background and values of the speaker (McKirnan, Smith, & Hamayan, 1983). The notion of speaking style is related to the belief similarity paradigm indicating the importance of language to intergroup behavior (Giles & Powseland, 1975). Language exerts its influence by being normatively regulated (McKirnan & Hamayan, 1980); the extent to which one's language is seen as conforming to the norm dictates the extent to which one is seen as being an in-group or out-group member. This phenomenon occurs because language and language similarity are used as markers of social group membership (Waters, 1992). The connection between speech style and conflict is subtle and indirect (Waters, 1992). Conflict can occur as each person reacts to the heightened sense of discomfort because both people more than likely would be aware of the linguistic dissimilarity, and they would be unable to avoid communicating their discomfort to each other.

The discourse style of many members of less-powerful groups is often judged in light of the privileged discourse of white men. Thus, poor, rural Puerto Rican women, who tend to be soft-spoken, polite, and deliberate in their speech, often feel compelled to speak more loudly than they would otherwise. Whereas European American male assertiveness and aggressiveness may be valued in the corporation, Puerto Rican men tend to value an appearance of outward dignity and calm, even at the expense of the expression of their own needs (Garcia-Preto, 1982). Cuban Americans tend to use humor or *choteo* and an exaggerated self-criticism, styles that often involve exaggerating things totally out of proportion (Manach, 1955). This conversation style may appear to European Americans as taking matters too lightheartedly when, in fact, it is an attempt to modify situations through jokes or satirical expressions or gestures (Rubenstein, 1976).

Variations in Social and Power Distance

There are significant variations among cultures in the styles of communication among strangers (Hall, 1959, 1976). One can study how variations in power distance affects communication in business organizations (Brislin, Lonner, & Thorndike, 1973; Strodtbeck, 1964; Triandis, 1980). *Power distance* is the perceived degree of inequality between subordinates and superiors in an organization. In most cultures, a decrease in distance means either a proposition to increase intimacy or a threat depending on other information conveyed in the communicational package. A code of meanings is built on the basis of relative rather than absolute distances; that is, what is a normal distance for one given purpose in a culture may be normal distance for a different purpose in another culture (Goffman, 1955, 1966). A person raised in a country in which the Latino culture prevails, for example, defines a neutral, safe, and formal face-to-face distance shorter than the one defined as such by a person raised in a non-Latino culture (Felipe & Sommer, 1966; Garfinkel, 1964; Hall, 1959). Therefore, the distance a Latino will consider "safe" and "neutral" will be labeled as close—and loaded with the corresponding meaning—by the non-Latino. This is the starting point of a self-perpetuating misunderstanding.

With Mexican Americans, initial encounters tend to be formal, polite, and reserved. However, once a relationship is established, hugging or touching and impromptu visiting are common, and over time friendships tend to assume the quality of kinship. European Americans, in contrast, are generally casual and friendly, often using first names from the time of introduction. Yet, when closer working relationships do develop (usually after a considerable amount of time), European Americans customarily continue to maintain a certain distance. Mexican American subordinates are likely to feel a greater degree of power distance between themselves and their European American managers than European American subordinates would. One would expect that this greater power distance, in turn, would affect the kinds of interactions and communication the Mexican Americans would consider appropriate and desirable.

Cuban Americans are likely to use an informal form of addressing others. Rather than using the polite or formal *usted* (you), Cubans have a tendency to use *tu* in many interpersonal situations as a means of diminishing distance and establishing familiarity (Bernal, 1982). Alternatively, although most Colombians normally use *usted* in addressing others, Colombians from Bogota and the Coast use *tu* among equals and reserve the use of *usted* for communicating only with people who are socioeconomically significantly lower or higher than they are. Failure to understand these differences could create misunderstandings and conflicts (Albert, 1983, 1986). For instance, a Colombian manager may address a supervisee as *usted*. The Cuban or Colombian supervisee from Bogota may interpret this as a means of establishing distance and superiority while classifying the supervisee as significantly lower in rank and status. Feeling slighted and perhaps humiliated, the supervisee may lose regard and respect for the manager, thus damaging the manager–worker relationship.

STRATEGIES TO PROMOTE EFFECTIVE COMMUNICATION

Because of the growing awareness of the powerful role language can play in reinforcing stereotypes, effective communication in diverse organizations requires more sensitivity and skill than ever before (Louden & Rosener, 1991). "When employees develop collaborative ways of interacting with people from different cultures and ethnic groups, with people of the opposite sex, and with people they view as different, there is increased potential for organizational productivity" (Wagel & Levine, 1990, p. 19). The following strategies can be helpful in promoting effective communication in a multicultural and diverse work setting:

- Communicate an organizational policy that honors all forms of discourse (Anderson, 1993). Cross-cultural communication presupposes the interplay of alternative realities; it rejects the actual or potential domination of one reality over another (Adler, 1991). Refrain from comparing the communication styles of one group with those of another or providing privilege to one over another (Fine, 1991; Petrini, 1993).
- Use words that are all-inclusive. For example, the term "people of color" is preferable to "minority," and "differently abled" is preferred to "handicapped" (Fine, 1991; Petrini, 1993).
- Do not use adjectives that suggest exceptions such as "Hispanic engineer" or "Puerto Rican doctor" (Fine, 1991). Avoid us–them dichotomies; these can lead to people believing that "we are good and deserving, and they are wrong and undeserving" (Henderson, 1994).
- Do not avoid the issue of diversity (Henderson, 1994). Encourage managers and employees to ask for explanations when they are unclear about the meaning of words or phrases. Learn to be flexible in using different styles and avenues of communication (Hill & Scott, 1992). Remember that the meaning of your statement is based not only on your intended message but also on how the listener responds to it (Charlston & Huey, 1992). Surface meaning can often be misleading. Probing what was meant can help clarify the message (London & McMillen, 1992). Stop to clarify the message and the response if there is any discrepancy between the two.
- Learn about how different groups use eye contact or the lack of it during supervisor–subordinate interactions as well as what meaning is attached to raising one's voice or using much gesturing with hands and arms (Charlston & Huey, 1992). This approach recognizes that not everyone is familiar with all the jargon and idioms present in language and will help avoid misunderstandings (Fine, 1991). Refrain from allowing others to "explain

what was really meant" by another's discourse (Gallagan, 1993; Hill & Scott, 1992).

- Encourage language workshops and informal peer education in each other's languages to help employees become comfortable hearing a variety of languages (Hill & Scott, 1992; Mobley & Payne, 1992). This also can help employees identify important similarities in their cultural and ethnic backgrounds, thus minimizing the potential negative of significant differences (Hill & Scott, 1992).
- Use periodic prejudice reduction workshops for managers to help reduce decision making based on stereotypes and false assumptions, as well as to prevent conflicts based on inaccurate information (Charlston & Huey, 1992; Hill & Scott, 1992).
- Learn how different needs are expressed by different groups. For example, almost all groups have ways of demonstrating the need for respect, time, space, and rewards (Gordon, 1982).
- Promote cultural diversity as a valuable and positive aspect of the work environment. The use of newsletters that call attention to specific cultural celebrations and holidays important to members of the staff is one way to accomplish this (Hill & Scott, 1992).

CONCLUSION

Scholars and practitioners are becoming increasingly aware that cultural factors heavily influence management practices (Adler, 1983; Child, 1981; Hofstede, 1980; Laurent, 1983; Maruyama, 1984; Triandis, 1982). A similar awakening has occurred in the field of business communication (Haworth & Savage, 1989; Kilpatrick, 1984). As the work force becomes increasingly diverse, the failure to manage differences will mean a substantial loss of valuable human resources. Organizations must go beyond mere tolerance or acceptance of non-Western modes of thinking, values, and communication practices; acceptance alone is not enough. Most successful managers have found that there is no substitute for the nose-to-nose hard work of understanding and managing people (Coleman, 1990). To promote productivity and success, managers and organizations must become sensitive to and appreciate the differences brought to the workplace by their workers. This change requires a great deal of self-awareness, sensitivity, and skill. It also requires a thoughtful application of standard practices as well as the flexibility to change current policies, systems, and behaviors to adapt to the needs of the diverse work force.

REFERENCES

Adler, N. J. (1983). Cross-cultural management research: The ostrich and the trend. *Academy of Management Review, 8,* 226–232.

Adler, N. J. (1991). *International dimensions of organization behavior* (2nd ed.). Boston: PWS-Kent.

Adler, N. J., Doktor, R., & Redding, S. G. (1986). From the Atlantic to the Pacific century: Cross-cultural management reviewed. *Journal of Management, 12,* 295–318.

Albert, R. D. (1983). Mexican American children in educational settings: Research on children's and teachers' perceptions and interpretations of behavior. In E. E. Garcia (Ed.), *The Mexican American child: Language, cognition and social development* (pp. 183–194). Tempe: Arizona State University.

Albert, R. D. (1986). Communication and attributional differences between Hispanics and Anglo Americans. *International and Intercultural Communication Annual, 10,* 41–59.

Albert, R. D. (1992). Polycultural perspectives on organizational communication. *Management Communication Quarterly, 6,* 74–84.

Anderson, J. A. (1993, April). Thinking about diversity. *Training and Development,* pp. 59–60.

Asante, M., & Davis, A. (1985). Black and white communication: Analyzing work place encounters. *Journal of Black Studies, 16,* 77–93.

Belenky, M. F., Clinchy, B. M., Goldberger, N. R., & Tarule, J. M. (1986). *Women's ways of knowing: The development of self, voice, and mind.* New York: Basic Books.

Bernal, G. (1982). Cuban families. In M. McGoldrick, J. K. Pearce, & J. Giordano (Eds.), *Ethnicity and family therapy* (pp. 187–207). New York: Guilford Press.

Bochner, S., & Hesketh, B. (1994). Power distance, individualism/collectivism, and job-related attitudes in a culturally diverse work group. *Journal of Cross Cultural Psychology, 25,* 233–257.

Brislin, R. W., Lonner, W. J., & Thorndike, R. M. (1973). *Cross-cultural research methods.* New York: John Wiley & Sons.

Castillo, C., & Bond, O. (1972). *The University of Chicago Spanish–English English–Spanish dictionary* (rev. ed.). New York: Pocket Books.

Charlston, A., & Huey, J. (1992). Breaking cultural barriers: Cultural diversity in the workplace. *Quality Progress, 25,* 47–50.

Child, J. (1981). Culture, contingency and capitalism in the cross-national study of organizations. In L. L. Cummings & B. M. Staw (Eds.), *Research in organizational behavior,* (Vol. 3, pp. 303–356). Greenwich, CT: JAI Press.

Coleman, T. (1990). Managing diversity at work: The new American dilemma. *Public Management, 72*(9), 2–5.

Diccionarios A–Z. (1974). *Diccionario manual de la lengua Espanola.* Barcelona, Spain: Editorial Vosgos.

Falicov, C. J. (1982). Mexican families. In M. McGoldrick, J. K. Pearce, & J. Giordano (Eds.), *Ethnicity and family therapy* (pp. 134–163). New York: Guilford Press.

Felipe, N. J., & Sommer, R. (1966). Invasions of personal space. *Social Problems, 14,* 206–214.

Fine, M. G. (1991). Multicultural communication. *Journal of Business Communication, 23,* 259–275.

Fine, M. G., Johnson, F. L., & Ryan, M. S. (1990). Cultural diversity in the workplace. *Public Personnel Management, 19,* 305–319.

Gallagan, P. A. (1993). Trading places at Monsanto. *Training and Development, 47,* 45–49.

Garcia-Preto, N. (1982). Puerto Rican families. In M. McGoldrick, J. K. Pearce, & J. Gordano (Eds.), *Ethnicity and family therapy* (pp. 164–186). New York: Guilford Press.

Garfinkel, H. (1964). Studies of the routine grounds of every-day activities. *Social Problems, 11,* 225–250.

Giles, H., & Powseland, P. F. (1975). *Speech style and social evaluation.* San Diego: Academic Press.

Gilligan, C. (1982). *In a different voice.* Cambridge, MA: Harvard University Press.

Goffman, E. (1955). On face work. *Psychiatry, 18,* 213–231.

Goffman, E. (1966). *Behavior in public places.* New York: Free Press.

Gordon, G. (1982). This man knows what diversity is. *International Association of Business Communicators, 9,* 8–14.

Gordon, M. (1964). *Assimilation in American life: The role of race, religion and national origin.* New York: Oxford University Press.

Greenhaus, J. H., Parasuraman, S., & Wormley, W. M. (1990). Effects of race on orga-
     nizational experiences, job performance evaluations, and career outcomes.
     Academy of Management Journal, 33, 64–86.
Hall, E. T. (1959). *The silent language.* Garden City, NY: Doubleday.
Hall, E. T. (1976). How cultures collide. *Psychology Today, 10,* 66–74.
Harper, K. V., & Lantz, J. (1996). *Cross-cultural practice: Social work with diverse popula-
     tions.* Chicago: Lyceum Books.
Haworth, D. A., & Savage, G. T. (1989). A channel-ratio model of intercultural com-
     munication. *Journal of Business Communication, 26,* 231–254.
Henderson, G. (1994). *Cultural diversity in the workplace: Issues and strategies.* West-
     port, CT: Quorum Books.
Hill, A., & Scott, J. (1992). Ten strategies for managers in a multicultural workforce.
     HR Focus, 69, 6.
Hofstede, G. (1980). *Culture's consequences.* Beverly Hills, CA: Sage Publications.
Infante, D. A., & Gordon, W. I. (1979). Subordinate and superior perceptions of self
     and one another: Relations, accuracy, and reciprocity of liking. *Western Journal of
     Speech Communication,* 212–223.
Jackofsky, E. F., Slocum, J. W., & McQuaid, S. J. (1988). Cultural values and the CEO:
     Alluring companions? *Academy of Management Executive, 2,* 39–50.
Jandt, F. E. (1995). *Intercultural communication: An introduction.* Newbury Park, CA:
     Sage Publications.
Johnson, F. L. (1989). Women's culture and communication: An analytical perspec-
     tive. In C. M. Lont & S. A. Friedley (Eds.), *Beyond boundaries: Sex and gender diver-
     sity in communication* (pp. 301–316). Fairfax, VA: George Mason University Press.
Kanter, R. M. (1977). *Men and women of the corporation.* New York: Basic Books.
Kilpatrick, R. (1984). International business communication practices. *Journal of Busi-
     ness Communication, 21,* 33–43.
Kochman, T. (1983). *Black and white styles in conflict.* Chicago: University of Chicago
     Press.
Laurent, A. (1983). The cultural diversity of Western conceptions of management. *In-
     ternational Studies of Management and Organizations, 13,* 75–96.
Limaye, M., & Victor, D. A. (1991). Cross cultural business communication. *Journal of
     Business Communication, 28,* 277–299.
London, A., & McMillan, M. (1992). Discovering social issues: Organizational devel-
     opment in a multicultural community. *Journal of Applied Behavioral Science, 28,*
     556–560.
Louden, M., & Rosener, J. B. (1991). *Workforce America! Managing employee diversity as
     a vital resource.* Homewood, IL: Business One/Irwin.
Manach, J. (1955). *Indagacion del choteo.* Havana: Editorial Libro Cubano.
Maruyama, M. (1984). Alternative concepts of management: Insights from Asia and
     Africa. *Asia Pacific Journal of Management, 1,* 100–111.
Matthes, K. (1992). Attracting and retaining Hispanic employees. *Human Relations
     Focus, 69,* 7.
McKirnan, D. J., & Hamayan, E. V. (1980). Language norms and perceptions of ethno-
     linguistic diversity. In H. Giles (Ed.), *Language: Social psychological perspectives* (pp.
     161–169). Tarrytown, NY: Pergamon Press.
McKirnan, D. J., Smith, C. E., & Hamayan, E. V. (1983). A socio-linguistic approach
     to the belief–similarity model of racial attitudes. *Journal of Experimental Social Psy-
     chology, 19,* 434–447.
Mobley, M., & Payne, T. (1992). Backlash! The challenge to diversity training. *Train-
     ing & Development, 47,* 35.
National Commission for Employment Policy. (1991). Fishing for the best employ-
     ees. *Small Business Reports, 16,* 27.
Papa-John, J., & Spiegel, J. (1975). *Transactions in families.* San Francisco: Jossey-Bass.
Petrini, C. (1993). The language of diversity. *Training and Development, 47,* 35–37.
Rubenstein, D. (1976). Beyond the cultural barriers: Observations of emotional dis-
     orders among Cuban immigrants. *International Journal of Mental Health, 5,* 69–79.
Solomon, C. M. (1993). Managing today's immigrants. *Personnel Journal, 72,* 56.

Staley, C., & Shockley-Zalabak, C. (1986). Gender and communication research: Deliberations, dilemmas, and directions. *Pennsylvania Speech Communication Annual,* *27,* 29–35.

Strodtbeck, F. L. (1964). Considerations of meta-method in cross-cultural studies. *American Anthropologist, 66,* 223–229.

Szapocznik, J., & Hernandez, R. (1988). The Cuban American family. In C. Mindel, R. Habenstein, & R. Wright (Eds.), *Ethnic families in America: Patterns and variations* (pp. 160–172). New York: Elsevier North-Holland.

Teske, R. H., & Nelson, B. H. (1976). An analysis of differential assimilation rates among middle class Mexican Americans. *Sociological Quarterly, 17,* 218–235.

Triandis, H. C. (1980). Introduction. In H. C. Triandis & W. W. Lambert (Eds.), *Handbook of cross-cultural psychology* (Vol. 1, pp. 1–14). Boston: Allyn & Bacon.

Triandis, H. C. (1982). Dimensions of cultural variations as parameters of organizational theories. *International Studies of Management and Organization, 12,* 139–169.

Wagel, W., & Levine, H. (1990). HR'90: Challenges and opportunities. *Personnel, 67,* 18–42.

Waters, H. (1992). Race, culture and interpersonal conflict. *International Journal of Intercultural Relations, 16,* 437–454.

Part V

Organizational Development Efforts as Change Processes

This section presents examples of interventions for increasing the inclusion of diverse staff. Although the emergence from a postindustrial society into a more technological, information-dependent society has resulted in more adaptive organizational approaches in many instances, change is always difficult. Human services organizations are under pressure to respond to environmental demands, shrinking resources, and the need to train and update needed skills of employees to meet challenges from internal and external diversity. Knowledge and information systems are crucial in preparing for challenges that emerge with little historical precedent to provide some direction for resolution. Each chapter in this section presents an approach that can enable an organization to respond adaptively and innovatively to challenges of diversity.

The first change effort addresses the important dual task of meeting the needs of students living with disabilities in educational programs requiring a practicum or internship and at the same time meeting the requirements of the Americans with Disabilities Act of 1990. Schmitt draws on her vast experience in academic administration and in rehabilitative and human services to address key issues in chapter 17. Educators have to negotiate their individual paradigm shifts from viewing people with disabilities as clients to whom services were provided to preparing these women and men to become professionals in their field. The author uses vignettes to capture the lost potential of people and professions when people living with disabilities did not have legislation to support their efforts to negotiate institutional barriers in pursuit of the training they desired. Schmitt provides guidance for negotiating with training sites to accommodate students' needs and enable them to fulfill educational requirements.

In chapter 18, Van Den Bergh addresses ways to promote the integration of diverse organizational members in the process of developing a bicultural identity. Her model includes competing forces and sociocultural dissonance within the family to maintain core beliefs, values, and behavioral styles while helping the employee adapt to different expectations in the workplace. Four group approaches are presented with examples that have been useful in workplaces to increase bicultural employees' sense of belonging to the organization.

Kuechler's model in chapter 19 is particularly suited to human services agencies that have interdisciplinary professionals as well as diversity among staff and clients. This group process model has a structure for inclusion of all participants. The structure whereby each participant listens and then asks questions is a particular strength of the model, ensuring a nonjudgmental environment for exchanging information. The model can be particularly useful when a professional colleague suggests a new approach to try, when multiple observations are needed, or when sensitive and value-laden issues (such as transracial adoption) need to be addressed.

One issue surfacing in the literature on diversity is the notion of white people as having race. In chapter 20, Block and Carter point out that most of the current approaches to understanding diversity in the workplace focus on nonwhite people. The authors apply white racial identity attitude theory to understand individual differences in identification with white racial group membership and to understand how the workplace is affected by white identity. Block and Carter use their research to explicate the usefulness of white racial identity theory in predicting evolution of organizational culture as well as policies, procedures, hiring, and promotion decisions associated with it.

In chapter 21, Thomas investigates the dynamics of race in developmental relationships. Two types of developmental relationships are sponsor–protégé relationships, which involve career support exclusively for the junior member; and mentor–protégé relationships, which offer both career and psychological support. The author used survey data to explore the formation of developmental relationships and the effects of race and gender on the pattern, location, and type of support that emerged. Analyses of experiences of both same-race and mixed-race dyads revealed that race had significant effects on, for example, the type and duration of the relationship. Thomas identified four variations of development models based on a preference for open engagement versus suppression of race-related matters in the relationship and complementary versus noncomplementary racial perspectives. These salient findings have enormous potential for managerial support in career development among women and people of color in leadership as well for developing organizational policies and structures to support the development of leadership in all organizational members.

These chapters illustrate four approaches to organizational development strategies that promote an organizational environment that supports diversity and full use of human potential: (1) a strategy that involves some structural approach, (2) the use of models grounded in research, (3) a strategy making white people the subject of a change, and (4) use of developing relationships for effective mentoring.

17 Implications of the Americans with Disabilities Act for Institutions with Student Teaching, Practicum, and Internship Requirements

Sue Schmitt

The Americans with Disabilities Act (ADA) of 1990 will have a significant impact on professional programs, specifically those in education, allied health services, and human services. Educational institutions, programs, students, and practicum and intern sites will be influenced by more than the legal mandates of the act. More important, implementation will be shaped by personal beliefs and biases, knowledge about specific disabilities, previous legislation that either protected or failed to protect people with disabilities and the role that the professions have traditionally played in the lives of people with disabilities. The mere passage of legislation will not ensure that people with disabilities will be given equal access to or rights in society. Full empowerment takes a commitment far greater than adherence to the letter of the law. For professionals it also requires that we embrace people with disabilities as colleagues as well as recipients of services.

ATTITUDES AND BIASES

Educators and professionals in education, allied health services, and human services are subject to the same range of attitudes and biases as the general public. Today, efforts are made to address tolerance and diversity issues. However, this situation has not always been the case. For decades educators, as well as allied health and human services professionals, viewed people with disabilities as patients or clients and not as potential colleagues. The primary role played by these professionals was that of caregiver or provider. With the passage of the Rehabilitation Act of 1973 and, more recently, the ADA, these same professionals are now asked to prepare people with disabilities to be professionals in their fields.

The materials provided in this chapter are not meant to serve as a legal interpretation of the implementation of the Americans with Disabilities Act. Rather, they are intended to stimulate discussions of and preplanning for the inclusion of students with disabilities. Readers with specific questions about ADA implementation should consult the appropriate offices and legal sources.

To better understand the impact of the ADA, one must consider the following three factors: (1) the effects of stereotypes and beliefs, (2) the lack of protection against discrimination for people with disabilities before the 1970s, and (3) the impact of the Rehabilitation Act of 1973 and the Education for All Handicapped Children Act of 1975.

STEREOTYPES

Membership in the group known as "people with disabilities" is open to everyone. Disability membership welcomes men and women, as well as people of all races, creeds, and colors. Disability does not care about sexual orientation; whether one is married, widowed, single, or has children; whether one is young or old, or if one already has a disability. Disability does not allow one to prepare for it. There may be a warning that something is seriously wrong; at other times disability happens as quick as an oncoming car, a dive into shallow water, a stroke, or an embolism.

People with disabilities often are labeled with multiple stereotypes. A woman who is blind lives in a world filled with biases and stereotypes about gender as well as disability. As she ages, she then must cope with the stereotypes and biases regarding age. Add to membership in these three stigmatized groups the distinction of being Hispanic, and this woman is now open to all the biases and stereotypes attached to that group as well. When this woman seeks education, employment, or social opportunities and meets resistance, she must determine which of the many biases and stereotypes are primary contributors to her inability to achieve her goals. Given the multiple effect of membership in several subgroups, it is little wonder that older women who are disabled and members of a nondominant group are among the least educated and most likely to be unemployed.

People with invisible disabilities are not subject to the same biases faced by those whose disabilities are observable. However, people with epilepsy, hearing problems, respiratory ailments, mental illness, and cognitive disorders are sometimes seen as being unable to learn or as having drug or other behavioral problems. These assumptions often lead society to limit the roles these members can play.

HISTORY OF DISCRIMINATION

People with disabilities have the distinction of being one of the last groups to gain any type of equal rights protection. Before the mid-1970s with the passage of legislation such as Section 504 of the Rehabilitation Act of 1973 and the Education for All Handicapped Children Act (now the Individuals with Disabilities Education Act, or IDEA), there was no protection for people with disabilities in education, housing, employment, medical care, transportation, or social services. With the passage of these acts, people with disabilities gained protection only in areas that involved the use of federal dollars. What did this lack of protection prior to the 1970s mean for people with disabilities? Consider the following case studies.

In 1969, Beth Ann, a 20-year-old nursing student, was involved in a car accident while returning to school from Christmas break. As a person having paraplegia, Beth Ann found that the university would no longer allow her to continue in her nursing program. The university dorms, cafeteria, and classrooms were not accessible. After applying to several other universities, Beth Ann found that none of the state or private universities in her state were accessible. Moreover, they were not willing to make any accommodations such as installing ramps, relocating classes to accessible rooms, widening doors, or creating accessible parking or bathrooms. Eventually, a private university in another state was willing to make the needed physical accommodations if Beth Ann's family would cover the costs. The university, however, would not allow Beth Ann to continue in nursing and required her to pick a major outside of the health field.

It is 1968, and Harry, age 53 and profoundly deaf, wakes at 3:00 a.m. with severe chest pains. He cannot call an ambulance because the hospital is not required to have a telecommunications device for deaf people. As a result, Harry dresses and drives himself to the emergency room. An hour later, Harry dies of a massive heart attack. Would the result have been the same if it had been 1980 and the hospital had been required to have a telecommunications device?

In 1971, Gene, legally blind, completed a degree in social work and applied for a position in a major hospital. Although Gene graduated at the top of his class, the hospital would not hire him because they did not feel he could perform adequately. The hospital also was concerned that patients would not relate well to someone who is blind. Gene had no recourse and no protection under the law. Unable to find employment and without an employment history, he was forced to accept social security income benefits.

If Beth Ann had been paralyzed after the passage of Section 504, would she be a nurse today? Would Harry be alive? Would Gene be a social worker? We will never know.

What we do know is that even if they had access to education, employment, and hospital services, they still would have had no protection in the private sector. Unless state laws mandated protection, hotels, restaurants, apartments, and retail stores would still not be required to make any accommodations for these people. Only entities that received public funding were covered under Section 504 of the Rehabilitation Act of 1973. How unfortunate that the largest subgroup in society should go without any civil rights protection until the 1990s, when the ADA was passed.

IMPACT OF THE REHABILITATION ACT OF 1973

Many of the issues covered in the ADA are the same as those addressed by the Rehabilitation Act of 1973. However, remedies for the lack of equal physical and programmatic access to education, social services, health facilities, housing, transportation, and recreation were still being sought 30 years after the passage of Sections 503 and 504 of the Rehabilitation Act.

As the private sector was gearing up to address the requirements of the ADA, public universities, health facilities, social services agencies, and recreation facilities were re-examining their progress in providing for physical and programmatic access to people with disabilities. New self-evaluations and implementation plans had to be drafted. This time the stakes were higher because, unlike Section 504, the ADA carried fiscal penalties for noncompliance that potentially were much higher.

BRIEF OVERVIEW OF THE ADA

The ADA provides the first broad-based federal legal recourse against discrimination for people with disabilities. A person with a disability is defined as someone who has a physical or mental impairment that limits one or more life activities. The act extends coverage to people who have a history of such an impairment or who are regarded as having such impairments.

In many ways, the ADA does not differ in substance from the Rehabilitation Act of 1973 on which it was based. It does, however, differ in two important ways: (1) It covers private and public entities whether or not they do business with the government, and (2) it provides for civil legal action. The court may grant the following four remedies depending on the title involved: (1) provision of an auxiliary aid or service, policy, practice, or procedure modification; (2) requirement to make facilities accessible; (3) monetary damages to the plaintiff; and (4) civil penalties of up to $50,000 for the first violation and $100,000 for subsequent violations. ADA legislation covers a much broader group of providers than does the Rehabilitation Act of 1973 and has real monetary implications for violations. The following sections are based on the text of the ADA.

The act consists of five parts: (1) employment, (2) public services, (3) public accommodations and services operated by private entities, (4) telecommunications, and (5) miscellaneous. The text of the ADA should be consulted for more details on the five sections. The focus of this discussion will be on Title III, which deals with public accommodations and services operated by private entities. A few of the many entities covered by this title are nursery, elementary, secondary, undergraduate, and postgraduate private schools or other places of education; day care and senior citizen centers; homeless shelters; food banks; adoption agencies and other social services centers; professional offices of health care providers; and hospitals and other service establishments.

Discrimination

The ADA prohibits both outright and exclusionary discrimination. Outright discrimination can include architectural, transportation, and communication barriers as well as rules and policies that are discriminatory. Exclusionary discriminatory policies include those pertaining to qualifications; standards and criteria; segregation; and lesser services, programs, activities, benefits, and jobs. It is critical that professions clearly define the essentials of their training and education or potential employment, particularly as they relate to charges of exclusionary discrimination.

Discrimination can take many forms, including criteria that screen out on the basis of disability; discriminatory polices, practices, and procedures; architectural, communication, and transportation barriers; and failure to seek alternative methods of delivering services when barrier removal is not readily achievable. Eligibility criteria that screen out on the basis of disability cannot be used unless it can be shown that they are necessary for the provision of the "goods, services, facilities, privileges, advantages, or accommodations being offered."

Modifications and Accommodations

Two terms usually associated with the ADA are "readily achievable" and "reasonable modifications." The term "readily achievable" is used as a guideline for the types of accommodations that must be provided. To be considered readily achievable, the accommodations must be easily accomplished and be carried out without much difficulty or expense. There are no dollar amounts attached to this term. When determining whether an accommodation is readily achievable, a number of items are considered, including the nature and cost of the action, the financial resources of the facility, the number of people employed, the effect on expenses and resources or the operation of the facility, the type of operations, the geographic separateness, and the administrative or fiscal relationship of the facility in question to the covered entity (for other examples, consult Section 301 of the ADA).

Reasonable modifications of policies, practices, or procedures must be made unless such "modification would fundamentally alter the nature of such goods, services, facilities, privileges, advantages, or accommodations." People with disabilities may be excluded, denied services, segregated, or otherwise treated differently because of the absence of auxiliary aids and services when the entity demonstrates that such steps would "fundamentally alter the nature of the good, service, facility, privilege, and advantage, or accommodation being offered or would result in an undue burden." When removal of architectural, communication, and transportation barriers in existing vehicles is not readily achievable, alternative methods must be used if they can be accomplished swiftly.

Section 309 is of particular interest to universities with professional programs. It requires that "examinations and courses related to applications, licensing, certification, or credentialing for secondary or post-secondary education, professional, or trade purposes shall offer such examinations or courses in a place and manner accessible to persons with disabilities or offer alternative accessible arrangements for such individuals." Courses covered by this section include internships and practicums, which are often offered at sites off campus.

Auxiliary aids and services, as well as structural modifications, may be needed by people with hearing, visual, physical, and cognitive losses. Structural modifications, such as those involving parking, ramps, door widths, signage, bathrooms, and elevators, are somewhat standard and regulated by specific criteria. No one aid or service, however, is appropriate for all people with disabilities. People with disabilities have developed a number of ways of interacting with their environment and are often the best source of information on the best types of aids and services.

Making materials that are aurally accessible for people with hearing impairment is one type of accommodation. The exact accommodation depends on the person. For some people with hearing impairments, a qualified interpreter is needed. Other accommodations could include providing a room with minimal noise distractions; providing captioning; facing the person when speaking; writing notes; making notes, tests, or office hours available by computer; and allowing additional time on written tasks. Structural accommodations include visual safety alarms and visual indicators on some types of equipment.

People with visual impairments require materials and services provided in accessible ways, including in auditory or tactile form. Numerous options are available to achieve this goal, including taped texts, large-print and color-contrast print items, tactile graphics, voiceover adaptations to the computer, and Braille printers and materials. People with visual disabilities also may have individualized devices such as Braillers, opticons, and paperless Braille. Knowledgeable rehabilitation professionals may assist people in selecting appropriate types of aids if they are not already aware of them. Tactile and auditory signage within facilities is a critical issue for all people with visual impairments. Adjustable lighting is important because some people find less or more light helpful. Equally important is avoiding placement of protruding objects into the commonly used pathways in the facility and on pathways leading up to the facility.

Adaptations for people who are physically disabled are numerous and, with the exception of structural modifications, are specific to the person. Generally, parking, access to and ingress within the facility, door widths, placement of telephones, elevators, and bathroom facilities are the structural issues that face all people with physical restrictions. Other adaptations can include raising or lowering work surfaces, adapting or providing alternatives to file cabinets, offering computer peripherals such as modified keyboards or scanners, or reducing the amount of movement between work areas. Adaptive aids that increase the person's ability to reach, bend, lift and grasp objects (or that decrease the need for such actions) are readily available but are specific to each person. Numerous mobility aids are available to people with ambulatory or fatigability restrictions. Often the person with the disability has these individual adaptations. Other times, consultation with knowledgeable rehabilitation professionals can provide access to as well as funding for these devices.

People with cognitive impairments or learning disabilities also may need auxiliary aids or services. Services may include additional time when orienting the individual to the tasks, qualified note takers and tutors, additional test time, and access to a computer with spelling and grammar checkers. For the most part, the accommodations to the physical environment are not needed. However, services must be individualized and the strengths of the individual maximized.

IMPACT OF THE ADA ON CLINICAL SITES

What does the ADA mean for faculty and administrators preparing students for careers in health and human services? The issues that needed to be addressed ethically before the passage of Section 504— the same issues that section of the law required to be addressed— still need attention today. With the passage of the ADA, these issues are more apparent than ever, as consumers with disabilities arrive on campus more aware of their rights to physical and programmatic access. To better understand how the ADA may impact clinical programs and sites, consider the following five case studies.

Case Study 1

June, who uses a wheelchair for mobility, has completed all of the coursework needed before her first field experience. Her program allows students to select up to three sites for each field. June's first site will not accept her because she is in a wheelchair. The second site will accept her, but there are steps into the building and the bathroom door is too narrow. They will accept June only if the university will pay for the physical accommodations. The third site will accept June, but because of distance, June would require special transportation. Can the first site refuse to accept June because she is in a wheelchair? Can the second site require the university to cover the costs of the accommodations? Is the university liable for the extra costs incurred if June is required to go to the third site, which requires special transportation? What will happen to the relationship between the university and the clinical site if the university pushes the issue of access based on the ADA?

Whether a site can refuse to accept June would depend on a number of factors. Would the modifications be readily achievable, and what would be the fiscal impact of these changes on the entity as a whole? On the other hand, if the facility is covered by the ADA, then it will need to address these issues sooner or later. The placement of the student may provide an opportunity for the university to assist the facility in exploring ways in which it can meet the ADA standards. What might have been a difficult discussion may turn out to be a meeting of mutual benefit.

Although the university is offering the program, it is most likely not responsible for the cost of the accommodations. The university is, however, responsible for providing June with a practicum or intern site that is equal to that available to other students. The site does not have to be a specific facility, but the experience must be equal in breadth to that afforded other students. It would not be appropriate for the university to have a large number of choices available to other students and limit all people with disabilities to one site.

The range of sites available and how students are treated in the site assignment process should be addressed in the program policy. The same process for site selection should apply equally to all students.

The question of who pays for the transportation needs to be addressed as it relates to how other students are treated. If all other students are provided transportation by the institution, then June's transportation need also must be addressed. Minimally, the university needs to work with June to identify alternative forms of transportation. If the site is on or close to campus and accessible transit is available to students with disabilities, it may be possible for June to use this transportation system. If mass transit is available, there may be lift-equipped buses serving the site. June may wish to contact the city or county transit provider that serves the elderly population and people with disabilities to determine the criteria for use of the service. Discussions with the site may result in a schedule that allows longer times on site rather than several shorter sessions, thereby reducing the number of trips needed. Other students with appropriate vehicles may be doing clinical work in the same area and may offer to share transportation with June.

Case Study 2

Gail has applied for admission to the MSW program. The interviewer has knowledge, not provided by the student, that Gail has a history of mental illness. Can this information be revealed by the interviewer during the interview? Is it relevant to admission? If Gail has not shared the information and not identified herself as disabled under Section 504 of the Rehabilitation Act of 1973 or the ADA, must the program provide any accommodations?

Whether information about an applicant's mental health history can be shared depends, in part, on the source of the information. If the information was received as part of a patient–client relationship or a university staff member's participation as a clinical supervisor, then professional standards and ethical considerations mandate how this information is to be handled. Gail would need to be treated as any other qualified applicant. If, however, the information was obtained from observations during the interview or from references provided by the student, then a different set of circumstances exists. Unless information received as part of the normal interview process raises questions about Gail's ability to perform the essentials of the program and profession, she needs to be treated as any other qualified applicant. However, once Gail is admitted to the program, she would not be eligible for accommodations unless she requested them as a qualified applicant under ADA.

Case Study 3

Joe has a history of substance abuse. After six years of sobriety, Joe began drinking again, and his supervisor removed him from his field experience. Joe completed an in-house treatment program one month ago and has now asked to be reinstated into the program and wants to return to his former clinical site. Does ADA require that Joe be re-admitted and returned to his previous site?

In determining whether Joe may be re-admitted to a program or site, the institution must consider whether the student is now qualified to carry out the professional duties as well as the wishes of the site. If the student left the site under circumstances that endangered patient or client care or caused negative repercussions for the site, the site will be less likely to consider having the student return. If, on the other hand, the student sought treatment and there were no negative repercussions to patients or clients, the site may view the student's return differently.

As with any placement, the views of the site must be taken into consideration. The conditions under which the student left the site and the impact on the site and its clients will influence the site's decision to allow the student to continue in the placement. The policies of the facility must meet the same requirements of the ADA as the university. The site, however, is not bound by the ADA to accept practicum or intern placements and may simply refuse to be involved as a placement site. As always, the university must weigh the possibility of losing the site as a placement for future students.

Another consideration is any guideline that the university or site may have regarding return of students under these circumstances. If such criteria exist, are they defensible? The program may wish to consult with a group such as the Association of Alcoholism and Other Drug Abuse, which has experience with the criteria used for recovering alcoholics or drug abusers seeking certification in this field. Do the criteria include length of time between recruitment and admission of people to the program? If so, this may serve as a model for a program policy.

In any case, once the university has determined that the student is qualified to return to the program, an appropriate placement must be found for the student. The wishes of the student and the site must be considered in determining the most appropriate place for the continuation of the practicum or internship experiences. Working together, the student, program, and site can arrive at a placement decision that will meet the spirit as well as the letter of the law.

Case Study 4

Pete has a learning disability and has received accommodations throughout his college career. Next semester, Pete will begin his first field placement. Pete has requested that the program not share any of the information on his learning disability with the clinical site.

Does the ADA prohibit you from sharing information regarding Pete's learning disability and needed accommodations? If you do not share this information and there is a lawsuit based on Pete's actions, is the university liable because they did not disclose information about his need for accommodations?

In determining the information that Pete must provide to a placement site, one must consider not only the ADA, but also the agreements between the site and the university. At a minimum, the university needs to discuss with Pete the pros and cons of not requesting accommodations and the consequences to patients and clients of not disclosing any special needs. If, in the judgment of the program, the student would not be able to function on the site without accommodations, then the program must address the issue of whether the student meets the minimal requirement to be a qualified applicant for the program without these accommodations. Although the interests of the students must be safeguarded, the program also has a legal and ethical responsibility to the patients and clients at the practicum or intern site that cannot be ignored. Some programs require the students to determine what they will share with the site and provide no materials to the site beyond those shared by the student. Because there may be legal ramifications if the program shares information as well as if it withholds information, programs should have their legal counsel review the affiliation agreements and program policies regarding self-disclosure as it relates to ADA compliance.

Case Study 5

The Social Work Department requires a field trip in one of the required courses. The plan is to transport the class by bus and then spend two nights in a hotel. The trip will include visits to several facilities that do not have level entrances or elevators. George uses an electric wheelchair for mobility and is therefore unable to use a bus for transportation. In addition, George will need an accessible hotel room. What is the university's responsibility for providing accessible transportation and access to the hotel and sites on the trip? Is the university responsible for providing for or covering the costs of attendant care, or both? Can the university exclude George from participating in the program based on its perception that he cannot participate in this activity? If this activity was sponsored by the Social Work Club instead of being part of the required coursework, would the responsibilities be the same? What is the university's responsibility to ensure that professional club activities are accessible?

The university cannot exclude George from the program based on the perceived inability to participate in this field trip. Perhaps a comparable activity could substitute for participation in this field trip. A preferable solution, however, would be to find a way to include George in this activity. Inclusion in the activity would ensure that George had the same opportunity to benefit from this activity and would include him rather then exclude him from his peers.

All motel facilities arranged through the university should be accessible. It is reasonable for universities to hold their activities in motels that meet basic accessibility requirements. It would be advisable to have George contact the motels directly to ensure that his specific needs can be accommodated.

The university is not responsible for providing attendant care for George while on the field trip. George may welcome the opportunity to discuss options for covering personal care during the trip. Ultimately, it is George's decision on how to meet this need and whether he wishes to involve the university in this process. The university should not assume that it is responsible for meeting this need or that George should be excluded from the trip based on its beliefs about his ability to handle this need.

George needs to be informed of the accessibility issues with each facility to be visited. Together, the program and George may be able to address his accessibility needs and resolve the access issues.

If the university is providing transportation for the other students, then it is also responsible for addressing George's transportation needs. It may not be possible to transport George in the same vehicle as other students. Consideration should, however, be given to other means of transportation. Options could include obtaining the services of a company providing accessible transportation or reimbursing George to provide his transportation using his own vehicle.

With regard to the club sponsoring the activity, if not legally, then ethically the club should adhere to the spirit of ADA. The club may feel that because of its size and limited fiscal resources, it cannot address George's needs. However, one would hope that a student club in the education, allied health, and human services areas would look on this as a problem-solving opportunity and a chance to be inclusionary rather then exclusionary. By working with George, club members will find that the obstacles are not as insurmountable as they might at first seem.

DISCUSSION AND CONCLUSION

To address these concerns, a partnership should be formed that includes the person with the disability, the entity providing the services, and other entities knowledgeable about physical and other accommodations. Accommodations made without input from the person with the disability may not be acceptable or appropriate for that person. The person with the disability is often a valuable ally when determining what type of accommodation is needed. Obtaining input from this person does not mean that his or her solution must be implemented. Someone with a disability is not required to accept an accommodation, service, opportunity, or benefit.

Input from the person with the disability, who is most familiar with his or her abilities, is critical. Equally important is input from the site coordinator, who is most familiar with the policies, procedures, and essential aspects of the site. Also valuable is an expert in the area of rehabilitation and adaptive technology. Assistance from the state division of vocational rehabilitation, from services for blind people, from independent-living centers, and from a specialist in adaptive technology will help the university, the person with the disability, and the site staff better understand the options available for adaptations and potential funding.

A number of federal government agencies are responsible for developing and implementing regulations related to ADA. Educational facilities should have completed a self-evaluation as part of ADA compliance. Consulting this document will provide information on current status of the entity in relation to ADA and any plans to meet the regulation requirements. Many entities will have a person designated to handle ADA questions and compliance issues. This person can be helpful in addressing specific questions regarding ADA compliance and accommodations. This person also may be knowledgeable about agencies and people in the area who can provide technical assistance. Most higher education institutions also have an office dedicated to serving students with disabilities. Professionals from this unit will be able to help provide technical expertise and recommend different accommodations and auxiliary aids. These people also can identify other technical expertise.

Working together, the student, faculty, and sites will be able to find solutions to the issues surrounding practicum or internship placements. These problem-solving activities will better equip all students to work with consumers with disabilities.

REFERENCES

Americans with Disabilities Act of 1990, P.L. 101-336, 104 Stat. 327.
Education for All Handicapped Children Act of 1975, P.L. 94-142, 89 Stat. 773.
Individuals with Disabilities Education Act, P.L. 101-476, 104 Stat. 1142 (1990).
Rehabilitation Act of 1973, P.L. 93-112, 87 Stat. 355.

18 Managing Biculturalism at the Workplace:
A Group Approach

Nan Van Den Bergh

The face of America's work force is changing. The increase in the number of women and people of color in the workplace is particularly significant, because of the shrinking labor pool in the last decade of the 20th century, with 4 to 5 million fewer workers in 1990 than there were in 1980. This phenomenon is based on the "baby bust" outcome of zero population growth trends. Also, during the 1990s the percentage of people of color in the population was expected to grow seven times faster than that of white people. In California, the percentage of white people will decrease from 64 percent to 48 percent by 2010, and in 2020, the majority of entry-level workers will be Hispanic. At that time, English will become the second language for most Californians (Copeland, 1988a). During the 21st century, white people will acquire minority status within the United States because, in part, two-thirds of all global emigration is into this country.

A conceptual framework for considering how to manage diversity is biculturalism. Biculturalism suggests that exposure to several cultures can be additive in that people will maximize their coping mechanisms to be comfortable with both the dominant culture and their own ethnic heritage (Kitano, 1980). To become bicultural, people must engage in a dual socialization process. They acquire values, beliefs, and communication and behavioral styles from their culture of origin as well as from the majority culture. People of color will become bicultural to the extent that they receive crucial information and skills needed for negotiating the mainstream culture along with affirmation of the basic values, beliefs, and behavioral styles of their ethnic culture (de Anda, 1984).

Implications of biculturalism for the workplace are as follows. For people of color to be fully contributing members of an organization, they need to be socialized into the "ways of being" for that workplace. This socialization includes learning both written and unwritten rules for success, such as how to dress appropriately, how to communicate successfully, how to take advantage of career development programs, how to build both professional and personal support networks, and how to establish a mentor relationship. If a person of color is not able to become adequately socialized into a workplace culture (which, for the most part, will reflect mainstream values and beliefs), then sociocultural dissonance can arise. This concept relates

to the stress, strain, and incongruence that can occur for a person attempting to belong to differing cultures (Chau, 1989).

The person experiencing sociocultural dissonance is caught in a dialectical process with two competing demands—maintenance of core
beliefs, values, and behavioral styles contrasted with adopting new
and potentially conflicting attitudes and behaviors. For example, a
person's culture of origin may value deference toward others and de-
liberation in decision making. However, this person may join a work
group that values brainstorming and assertiveness in presenting
ideas. An obvious conflict exists that can deter the employee from being fully productive, but if biculturalism and diversity are valued,
conflict can be averted. First, the work group can explain its communication process and provide coaching as well as support for the employee of color to try out the process. Second, members of the work
group can accommodate the employee of color by specifically drawing out his or her ideas during a brainstorming process.

The need for mutual accommodation and adaptation as a part of
managing diversity underscores the ecological nature of promoting a
bicultural workplace. An ecological process is one in which people are
constantly interacting with their environment. As people are changed
by the contexts in which they live and work, so, too, are those environments altered in a process of continuous, reciprocal adaptation (Gitterman & Shulman, 1986). What the ecological model suggests for promoting biculturalism in the workplace is that vehicles must be created
that can promote ongoing reciprocal adaptation. The use of groups,
both existing entities as well as those created for diversity purposes,
can be excellent vehicles for accommodating workplace biculturalism.

GROUP FOCUS FOR MANAGING WORKPLACE BICULTURALISM

Why are groups valuable in promoting workplace biculturalism and
diversity? Basically, they allow processes to occur that can both aid
the worker and contribute to organizational effectiveness. Groups can
nurture workers' internal resources and strengths so that they can
cope with alienation, adapt to new roles, relate to conflicting values
and norms, and contribute to environmental change (Chau, 1989). For
people of color, participation in groups can serve the dual purposes
of assisting with integration into mainstream society and reinforcing
their ethnic identity and pride. For the organization, groups focusing
on ethnic diversity issues are a way to mobilize ideas, strengths, and
resources to create systems that allow diverse employees the opportunity to make productive contributions.

Groups can have a number of foci that can help both the individual
worker and the organization develop a bicultural perspective.
Groups can assist employees in adapting to the norms, values, and
rules of the workplace culture, so that employees of color understand
how to acquire opportunities and rewards. Also, groups can provide a
network function by encouraging varying ethnic groups to collaborate
and build alliances. Ethnic employee groups can reinforce cultural

pride and identity as well as protect and advocate for ethnic rights (Chau, 1989). In a workplace, all of those foci would be appropriate organizing principles to consider when deliberating the diversity-enhancing purpose of an existing or proposed group.

Guaranteeing Ethnic Group Rights

Within an academic environment, it is not unusual to find groups such as Asian, black, Native American, or Hispanic faculty and staff associations. Usually, the groups serve as "watchdogs" for potential discrimination and are advocates for affirmation action recruitment and retention. Those functions are clearly related to group goals of initiating institutional change and advocating for equal opportunity. Ethnic faculty and staff associations also can undertake research to assess equity in salary and rank and present results to higher-education policymakers to influence institutional personnel policies. Further, such groups have drafted position papers advocating for systemwide initiatives to promote diversity in employment practices, advocating for the inclusion of diversity content in curricula, and calling on local colleges or universities to assert leadership in the community by supporting ethnic group rights.

Such groups can wield real power in protecting ethnic employee rights, as illustrated by the following situations. Recently, a Japanese faculty member was denied tenure at a major U.S. university. Organizations on campus representing Asian members of the academic community advocated on behalf of the assistant professor to the university's president. Ultimately, the faculty member was granted tenure.

In another example, a Jewish faculty association at a major university formed for the primary purpose of assessing the impact of campus events on the quality of Jewish academic community life. The group mobilized around an incident in which the Jewish newspaper's editorial office was set on fire and the editor was threatened. The group established a committee to generate a strategy to influence the university's president to take a stand decrying the incident. At another university, a Jewish faculty group undertook proactive efforts to bring to its campus professors from other countries in which academic freedom was in jeopardy, such as Russia.

Groups also are developing in the private sector to advocate for ethnic employees' concerns. For example, at Equitable Life Assurance, business resource groups meet with the firm's chief executive officer (CEO) to discuss company issues related to both ethnic and female employees. The CEO signs off on recommendations that the groups present that enhance diversity as well as organizational effectiveness. Then, a senior manager is assigned to implement the suggestions. On a quarterly basis, the CEO asks for a progress report on the diversity plans. At Avon, councils representing various ethnic groups regularly provide both information and advice to top management. A senior manager who has the means to "move diversity agendas" within the organization is affiliated with each council. At

Procter & Gamble, multicultural advisory teams continually monitor diversity activity within the firm as well as the extent to which ethnic employees have become acclimated to the corporate culture.

These examples from the private and public sectors suggest the ethnic rights focus that groups can provide in facilitating workplace biculturalism. A common thread throughout the examples is a group goal to curtail discriminatory organizational behavior and provide equality of opportunity. Group tasks were of the advocacy and brokerage nature, facilitating the ecological interchange between ethnic employees' needs and organizational response.

Enhancing Bicultural Adaptation

Ethnic groups in the workplace also can focus on bicultural adaptation by helping ethnic members acclimate to the workplace's majority culture. In providing adaptation functions, the group assists in educational and socialization tasks that teach ethnic employees skills and knowledge requisite for succeeding in the organizational culture. There is historical precedent for the use of groups to assist in ethnic socialization—a early social group work focused on assisting immigrants with their acculturation to American society. Those early efforts were aimed at helping people acclimate to industrialization as well as deterring any sense of social isolation and enhancing people's sense of self-worth (Middleman & Goldberg, 1987).

Groups that aid ethnic employees' adaptation to the workplace are valuable not only to the employees but also to the organization because they help the organization retain valuable employees. An organization loses money if ethnic employees do not stay, because it takes time to recoup the costs of training a new worker and the costs of lost productivity. These costs occur regardless of whether the employee is clerical, managerial, or professional. Hence, with an increasingly diverse work force in the United States, it becomes a bottom-line issue to conceptualize and implement programs that facilitate bicultural adaptation and reduce sociocultural dissonance.

Initiatives have begun to establish groups to assist adaptation. Procter & Gamble conducted a study to determine how long it took for newly hired workers to feel "joined up," and the results indicated that gender and ethnicity were crucial explanatory variables. White men became acclimated most quickly, whereas black women took the longest time to feel "at home" with the company. As a result, an "onboarding" process was developed that included the use of groups, so that new ethnic and female workers could develop a sense of belonging more quickly. Also, a mentoring program was developed to raise the retention rate for black and female managers, and a learning task force was established to determine the best learning experiences for the company's ethnic employees (Copeland, 1988b). Also, at Security Pacific Bank, ethnic networks and support groups were established to encourage both personal and professional growth among the firm's ethnic managers.

Groups of corporate executives have been set up to assist ethnic employee adaptation to the workplace for top-down impact. For example, at Mobil, a special executives' group was created to select women and ethnic employees who have potential to become high achievers in the firm. These people are taken from their staff functions and placed in capacities in which they can learn the oil business from the inside out, so that they can rise to managerial responsibility. A similar process exists at Digital Equipment Corporation. A top management "core group" was established as a safe place for managers to discuss how their feelings and attitudes about gender, racial, and cultural differences affect the company decisions they make (Copeland, 1988b).

These examples from the private sector underscore the fact that enhancing biculturalism in the workplace is a reciprocal process, requiring accommodation on the part of the organization as well as the individual employee. The firms undertook actions requiring the investment of time and resources to optimize ethnic and female employees' participation in the organization. An organization cannot carry on in a "business-as-usual" mode when confronted with diversity; personnel practices may need to be altered, allowing for flextime, maternity leave, and paternity leave; benefits need to be offered that fit various forms of families and types of dependent-care needs; and orientational as well as monitoring systems have to be established that give employees information on rules, norms, and protocols. The payoff from investment in procedures that cause organizational change is greater employee commitment and productivity enhancement.

Within academic communities, ethnic faculty and staff associations can also enhance adaptation. Perhaps the most obvious dual socialization function these groups play for faculty occurs when an academic from another country joins the university. By participating in an ethnic association, the person will begin to acquire knowledge of how the campus operates as well as learn about ethnic resources within the larger community. To this extent, such groups play a key role in facilitating the newcomer's dual socialization both into the academic community and into American culture.

In great part, the development of biculturalism is made possible by creating translator, mediator, and model relationships with ethnic colleagues. The above concepts, defined by de Anda (1984), relate to roles that can be played when assisting ethnic men and women in adopting a dual-socialization perspective. Within an academic context, a translator could be an accomplished ethnic professor who would advise on how to navigate the dual-socialization course to meet the behavioral demands of the academic majority culture. Mediators could be senior ethnic faculty, familiar with institutional policies and procedures, who would provide guidance about the steps to take to meet organizational expectations. A model could be an ethnic colleague, comfortable and successful in using a bicultural-behavioral repertoire, who could help the new faculty member in developing a style compatible with norms of both the ethnic and the majority cultures.

Facilitating Ethnic Consciousness

In promoting ethnic pride and building community, groups can provide consciousness raising for members of both nondominant and the majority cultures in the workplace. Clearly, groups that ease bicultural adaptation would have ethnic pride and consciousness-raising components because their focus is on maintaining one's own cultural roots while adopting attitudes and behaviors consonant with the majority culture. For example, it is common for Hispanic groups on an academic campus to sponsor Cinco de Mayo celebrations. Similarly, Black History Month is usually promoted by the black academic community on university campuses and includes cultural events as well as lectures celebrating black contributions to society. In a related vein, associations representing Jewish employees have advocated for their groups to be able to observe holidays such as Passover and Yom Kippur to maintain cultural traditions. When ethnic associations organize workplace events or observances of their cultural traditions, not only do group members benefit, but the organization also gains by learning more about its employees. There also are obvious payoffs to the institution in terms of enhanced employee morale. Organizational support of ethnic pride celebrations creates a workplace environment in which employees feel valued for their diversity, which has obvious implications for employee loyalty and productivity.

Ethnic mutual-aid and self-help groups serve consciousness-raising and ethnic-pride functions as well as enhance employee adaptation to the workplace. As previously noted, several private-sector firms that have clearly articulated corporate goals aimed at enhancing diversity have encouraged the development of support groups for ethnic employees (Copeland, 1988b). These networks allow the exchange of both instrumental assistance (how to get promoted) and affective support (how to maintain sanity).

Perhaps workplace diversity can most effectively be achieved by encouraging the development of support and mutual-aid groups among ethnic and female employees. A considerable amount of writing and research has been undertaken to define the kind of help that mutual-aid and support systems can provide (Froland, Pancoast, Chapman, & Kinboko, 1981; Gitterman & Shulman, 1986; Gottlieb, 1981; Hirsch, 1981; Lee & Swenson, 1986; Whittaker & Garbarino, 1983). In articulating processes inherent in mutual-aid groups, Gitterman and Shulman (1986) noted several with strong positive implications for enhancing workplace diversity, including sharing information with colleagues and coworkers on organizational politics and resources, providing an opportunity to get support or develop strategy concerning discrimination issues, providing opportunities to solve problems or rehearse how to address a difficult situation, and offering the love and support of "kindred spirits."

Offering mutual-aid and self-help groups for ethnic employees also has preventive implications by providing an environment that could mediate sociocultural dissonance. Adopting a bicultural perspective inherently causes a person to experience periodic crises based on trying to reconcile conflicting or contradictory demands. For example, an ethnic employee coming from a cultural background that values cooperation would experience stress if placed in a work context in which he or she is part of a team that values competition. The employee could either face failing at work or experiencing anxiety and depression from having to behave in a way contradictory to his or her values. By sharing their fears about this conflict within a support group, ethnic employees can receive empathy and some concrete suggestions for managing the situation, all of which can avert a firing or voluntary termination. As Bertha Capen Reynolds (1975), activist and organizational social worker, stated, "It is not hard to take help in a circle in which one feels sure of belonging" (p. 10).

Consciousness-raising activities by ethnic groups at the workplace can have an impact on the larger community. For example, the Latino staff and faculty association of a major university sponsored a speech by then–President George Bush on the political and social implications of the growing Hispanic population in the country. This event was open to the community in an effort to demonstrate the university's commitment to supporting biculturalism and diversity in its own organization and in its service delivery area.

Intergroup Cooperation

Potential for social change exists with interethnic group acceptance and cooperation. If different ethnic groups can pursue joint ventures within an organization, then that camaraderie can be generalized to cooperation within the community at large. This change may be the most exciting challenge of an increasingly diverse work force, because the workplace may become the venue where people learn how to accept differences. Acceptance could occur as people acquire more experience in dealing with people different from themselves. Because of the tendency to stereotype people who are unfamiliar, employees' increased familiarity with diverse people could reduce the propensity to be prejudicial in attitudes and discriminatory in behaviors.

For example, for several years a number of groups had been meeting and working independently on "diversity agendas" related to their role in their organization. At some point these groups began crossing paths and decided they should convene all parties who had been pursuing their own diversity activities. There were several positive outcomes from the initial collaborative meeting of those groups. First, people came to know each other better and acquired a better understanding of each others' roles in the organization. Second, a task force was created to design all diversity training conducted on the campus regardless of who facilitated the learning experience. Hence, an outcome of that venture was the establishment of policy and procedures that helped institutionalize diversity training in the organization.

This example highlights how diversity work can take on the cast of planned change in the organizational development sense. Because resistance is endemic to the change process, the creation of inter-group cooperation by ethnic group networking could ameliorate problems and facilitate goal accomplishment.

PROFESSIONAL ROLES WITH WORKPLACE DIVERSITY GROUPS

Having examined various ways in which workplace groups can support cultural diversity, it is appropriate to discuss the roles human services practitioners can play with those groups. Most social work practitioners in workplace contexts would be providing employee assistance program (EAP) services. An EAP professional could not only engage in organizational development efforts aimed at enhancing workplace biculturalism and diversity but also create important services delivery systems enhancing the EAP, such as the diversity network described below.

As a potential means for assisting ethnic workers with diversity problems, an internal EAP established a "diversity network." The purpose of that services delivery system was to identify peer support and mutual aid for employees experiencing diversity difficulties. The diversity network for ethnic workers provided peer support in the following way. When an ethnic employee came to the EAP professional for assistance, if the person's problem was such that he or she could benefit from speaking to another ethnic worker who had resolved a similar issue, a "peer supporter" was contacted. The peer was asked whether he or she would be willing to meet the EAP client during nonworking hours to discuss the issue. The telephone number of the peer supporter was never given out without his or her previous approval. The two people could then meet over coffee or lunch and share their experiences. This process was used as an adjunct to the professional guidance and counseling provided to the troubled employee by the EAP professional and was never the sole assistance a person received.

All potential peer supporters were provided training as part of the diversity network group experience. People volunteering to be part of the diversity network were taught three core helping skills: (1) empathetic listening, (2) reflection of feelings, and (3) presentation of behavioral alternatives. They were admonished neither to provide specific advice nor to offer platitudes such as "count your blessings."

A self-help and mutual-aid diversity network has obvious win–win potential for both the EAP and the organization's ethnic workers. The EAP and workplace ethnic groups can help each other in additional ways as well. For example, the EAP professional can offer advisory assistance to ethnic work groups by clarifying organizational policies and procedures related to affirmative action and sexual harassment. Similarly, the EAP professional can be a linking agent by identifying resources available to the ethnic group from various organizational units as well as identifying other groups interested in similar goals. The EAP professional also can expand its knowledge of ethnic community resources by collaborating with workplace ethnic groups. This information would then enhance the assistance EAP professionals could provide to ethnic clientele using its services.

CONCLUSION

Groups within the workplace that promote biculturalism can help organizations answer the challenge of managing an increasingly diverse work force. Because the bicultural model is inherently additive, that is, it acknowledges that people can function naturally within both a dominant and an ethnic-heritage culture, promoting biculturalism suggests growth, expansion, and opportunity. Ethnically diverse employees become assets rather than liabilities because they have multiple perspectives that can be used in solving problems.

Enhancing biculturalism in the workplace through groups means providing opportunities for ethnic workers to create mutual-aid and social-support networks as well as establishing groups focused on specific knowledge- and skills-building activities to aid their acclimation to the organizational culture. These offerings will enhance ethnic employees' adaptation to the work force, encourage their pursuit of opportunities, promote cultural pride, enrich the organizational culture, and provide a sense of community and well-being. In addition, the organization will become more flexible in accommodating diversity by allowing greater behavioral repertoires in communication styles as well as problem-solving and decision-making processes. Also, workplace norms on what constitutes success and how to achieve it will need to expand to accommodate the values of sharing, cooperation, and building relationships as opposed to promoting exclusively competition, power, and conquest.

The Chinese symbol for crisis includes two concepts: danger and opportunity. That configuration seems apropos to the reality facing organizations in managing diversity. The danger lies in doing nothing but reacting to problems created by tension, conflict, and terminations. The opportunity exists in actively reaching out to capitalize on differences—seeing them as resources that can enrich the organization's future.

REFERENCES

Chau, K. (1989, April). Sociocultural dissonance among ethnic minority populations. *Social Casework, 70,* pp. 224–230.

Copeland, L. (1988a, June). Making the most of cultural differences. *Personnel, 65,* pp. 52–54, 56, 58–60.

Copeland, L. (1988b, July). Pioneers and champions of change. *Personnel, 65,* pp. 44–49.

de Anda, D. (1984). Bicultural socialization: Factors affecting the minority experience. *Social Work, 29,* 101–105.

Froland, C., Pancoast, D., Chapman, N., & Kinboko, P. (1981). *Helping networks and human services.* Beverly Hills, CA: Sage Publications.

Gitterman, A., & Shulman, L. (1986). The life model, mutual aid and the mediating function. In A. Gitterman & L. Shulman (Eds.), *Mutual aid groups and the life cycle* (pp. 3–22). Itasca, IL: F. E. Peacock.

Gottlieb, B. (1981). Preventive interventions involving social networks and social support. In B. Gottlieb (Ed.), *Social networks and social support* (pp. 201–232). Beverly Hills, CA: Sage Publications.

Hirsch, B. (1981). Social networks and the coping process: Creating personal communities. In B. Gottlieb (Ed.), *Social networks and social support* (pp. 149–170). Beverly Hills, CA: Sage Publications.

Kitano, H. (1980). *Race relations.* Englewood Cliffs, NJ: Prentice Hall.

Lee, J., & Swenson, C. (1986). The concept of mutual aid. In A. Gitterman & L. Shulman (Eds.), *Mutual aid groups and the life cycle* (pp. 361–380). Itasca, IL: F. E. Peacock.

Middleman, R., & Goldberg, G. (1987). Social work practice with groups. In A. Minahan (Ed.-in-Chief), *Encyclopedia of social work* (18th ed., Vol. 2, pp. 714–729). Silver Spring, MD: National Association of Social Workers.

Reynolds, B. C. (1975). *Social work and social living.* Washington, DC: National Association of Social Workers.

Whittaker, J., & Garbarino, J. (1983). *Social support networks.* New York: Aldine Press.

19 The Consultation Circle:
A Model for Team Consultation

Carol F. Kuechler

The *consultation circle* is a structured model and process for giving and receiving feedback on practice-related issues. The goal of using this process is to empower the personal responsibility, self-determination, mutual respect, and problem-solving abilities of workers regardless of their level of professional training. The consultation circle can be used to discern practice issues related to values clarification, case direction or action, clarification of roles and responsibilities, and sorting out ethical dilemmas. As a tool for professional development and team building, it can be used to develop skills in solution-focused problem solving, giving and receiving consultation, and work group interdependence. These expected outcomes of problem-solving skill and, indirectly, professional development are achieved in the context of providing better services to clients (Garrett & Barretta-Herman, 1995; Kaiser, 1997; Kuechler & Barretta-Herman, 1995).

This model is presented in the context of the distinctions made in the literature between supervision and consultation (Barnard & Goodyear, 1992; NASW, 1994). Kaiser (1997) suggested that these distinctions involve the nature of the relationship. She also framed the supervisory relationship as involuntary and "imbued with the power to make decisions or take actions that affect such things as hiring and firing, promotion, salaries" (p. 7). In the case of supervision required for licensure, this also would include the power to affirm one's ability to practice one's profession. The consultative relationship is then characterized as voluntary, allowing the consultee the freedom to ask for and then to accept or reject the advice of a consultant. Although other areas of supervisory and consultative relationships overlap (see, for example, Kaiser, 1997), it is the freedom to choose advice or counsel that is important in the use of the consultation circle.

Providing effective and respectful service to clients is a critical goal of consultation (Kaiser, 1997) and of this model. The structured nature of the consultation circle encourages a focus on problem solving and action. It provides an opportunity for each participant to give input to the consultee without facing judgment. By addressing multiple learning and communication styles, the use of the consultation circle increases the potential for effective integration of multiple ideas into a solution. In a culturally diverse practice environment, its structure and process facilitate the participation of all practitioners regardless of professional status. Although the structure is meant to facilitate egalitarian participation, it is intended to be flexible in individual settings. For example, because the Hmong have no written language, comfort with the model's written component needs to be evaluated based on worker training and assimilation with written English.

BACKGROUND

The consultation circle was inspired by a group problem-solving process developed for parent education groups that emphasized personal responsibility and mutuality in identifying solutions to everyday problems from a perspective of potency (Clarke, 1978, 1981, 1984). Clarke's leader-facilitated model has been modified and expanded to one with three distinct roles that includes all participants of a work group. Rotating the facilitator role highlights the expectation of professional accountability and egalitarian participation in professional settings. A writing component also was incorporated to address the learning-style needs of visual and kinesthetic learners, using a consultation form adapted from a format used by a local family-based services agency (Kuechler & Barretta-Herman, 1995).

The consultation circle was introduced to advanced social work students in an MSW field seminar, who quickly incorporated the process and structure into the seminar as one tool used to get input for field issues, professional identity questions, and the transition from student to employee. Feedback included appreciation of the simple, focused format. One student commented, "That's the first time I've not left with a headache," reflecting student frustration with discussions about cases and field issues that were general, sometimes tangential and, from her frame of reference, not productive in solving the presented concern. Two students who tended to be more vocal and favored "spontaneous discussion" found the structure of the consultation circle frustrating and restrictive. They did, however, acknowledge the need to find ways to meet the needs of colleagues with other styles and interaction preferences.

WORKPLACE TRENDS

The consultation circle is available to organizations and teams dealing with current workplace trends, such as flatter organizational structures, shrinking resources for supervision, and increasing diversity in work teams. Flatter organizational structures have resulted in less time for the traditional educational, clinical, and support functions of supervision and more reliance on accountability through paperwork and participation in self-directed or multidisciplinary work groups. This results in an increased reliance on fellow workers for establishing standards of practice and getting support and guidance in performing the work (Kline & Saunders, 1993; personal communication with C. G. Lyle, senior progam evaluator, Ramsey County Community Human Service Department, St. Paul, November 12, 1996; Munson, 1989; Rieman, 1992).

Agency workers struggling with shrinking supervisory resources, increasingly limited time for mutual problem solving, and the formation of multidisciplinary and multicultural work groups have found this model a useful tool for reinforcing self-determination, mutual respect, group support, and problem solving. For example, the administrative team of a community mental health center recently sponsored an all-day workshop focused on team building. They included a presentation and extended practice application of the consultation circle as another tool to facilitate workers supporting and learning from one another. They chose this tool as a vehicle to address team consultation across cultures, disciplines, and levels of education.

Changing demographics have heightened social work's professional awareness to increasingly diverse issues related to understanding and communicating with clients and among ourselves in supervisory and consultative relationships (see, for example, Berg & Miller, 1992; Broken Nose, 1992; Ewalt, Freeman, Kirk, & Poole, 1996; Kaiser, 1977; Sue, 1981; Tsui & O'Reilly, 1989; Van Den Bergh, 1990). Professionals in agencies working with diverse client populations and multicultural staff have found the model attractive because of its simplicity and flexibility in use for work management issues, client cases, and intraoffice matters (personal communication with C. Erickson, youth and families program manager, Lao Family Community of Minnesota, Inc., St. Paul, December 20, 1996). For example, an Asian American worker reported in a workshop evaluation that the process allowed him to participate verbally and with people who were older in a way that he could not during other group consultation formats. A supervisor in a community-based family support agency commented on how the structure and process facilitated mutual sharing of knowledge and skills between degreed white social workers and indigenous workers from Laos, Cambodia, and Vietnam.

GROUP CONSULTATION

The model promotes participatory consultation in a group format. Authors such as Kadushin (1977) and Rieman (1992) have given considerable attention to the advantages of group consultation. Like other models of group consultation, this one is not meant to address "highly individualized or possibly personalized problems" (Kadushin, 1977, p. 176). These issues would likely be referred to individual supervision. Richard and Rodway (1992) outlined three team consultation processes: (1) group supervision, (2) peer group supervision, and (3) peer consultation team. Common characteristics of the group models they reviewed include "their problem-solving or decision-making function" (p. 85) and the "assistance provided by the group/team in the form of support" (p. 86).

As a stand-alone model, the consultation circle combines characteristics of the peer group supervision and peer consultation teams models outlined by Richard and Rodway (1992). Its distinguishing features are worker autonomy and membership based on equal status

(Kuechler & Barretta-Herman, 1995, 1996). In the realm of decision making, the consultation circle emphasizes autonomous decision making, and in terms of group structure, members are considered as equal in the "floating" of roles. Teams with members of different professional affiliations and levels of training use their ground rules and the ethics of mutual respect to moderate their differences; the model and process facilitate equal participation.

For work groups in which a supervisor is a member, efforts must be made to minimize the inherent authority issues. Even though the consultation circle is based on egalitarian participation and responsibility, an administrative person naturally may be viewed in the "supervisory role" (Kuechler & Barretta-Herman, 1995, 1996; Richard & Rodway, 1992). Authority issues can be addressed through the use of ground rules and discussions clarifying the role of the supervisor during "consultation time" for administrative tasks and for education around legal and agency policy mandates. Examples include specifying the supervisor as a participant in the process; stating that, in the case of legal or ethical issues that might arise in the suggestion process, an intervention will be made before moving on to the next circle without interrupting the presentation; and specifying how and when the supervisor will address learning issues, such as those relevant to new staff or new policies, identified during the process.

EMPOWERMENT AND ETHICS

Gutierrez, GlenMaye, and DeLois (1996), in a multiple-case study of human services organizations, identified collaborative approaches as a key support characteristic of agencies engaged in empowerment practice. Included in collaborative activities were teamwork and peer review activities that led to the establishment of relationships, support systems, and "a sense of safety and a shared philosophy" (p. 70). This context supported risk taking and the development of a shared philosophy with an empowerment perspective. The consultation circle incorporates value orientations of the group and egalitarian approaches in an interactive framework (Ryan & Hendricks, 1989). It is this sense of "we're in this together" that can be fostered by using the consultation circle. Although accountability rests with each worker to choose actions, everyone participating in the process contributes to the work of colleagues.

In a discussion of societal and professional concerns with the ethical behavior of professionals, Kaiser (1997) pointed out the growing body of literature on the ethical implications of the practitioner–client relationship. She suggested that

> If practitioners are to treat their clients with the deepest possible integrity, they must have a place to go where they can carefully and honestly examine their own behavior. . . . If that relationship is not one that is itself guided by ethical principles, supervisees will be unable to use it as a resource for this dimension of their practice. (pp. 7–8)

Without the resolution of the issues of safety and trust in the supervisory (and consultative) relationship, the workers are less likely to act on their power to choose supervision or consultation. Kline and Saunders (1993) identified structure, nurturance, and a comprehensive focus on problem solving as the three elements needed to create a safe learning environment in an organization. Only when these are present in the organizational culture will there be a climate safe for risk taking and critical thinking.

The functioning of a work unit itself requires a number of options for supervision and consultation that address its administrative, educational, and support needs (Garrett & Barretta-Herman, 1995). Although many professions have a tradition of individual supervision, changing services delivery structures, reduced financial resources, and the diversification of work groups challenge professionals to explore options for meeting the needs for supervision, consultation, and professional development (Barretta-Herman, 1993; Kadushin, 1977, 1992; Kuechler & Barretta-Herman, 1995; Rieman, 1992). The consultation circle is one model for meeting the needs of team members.

BENEFITS OF THE PROCESS AND SKILLS DEVELOPMENT

The use of this structured process, with clearly delineated roles for participation and implementation, supports the needs of professionals who hesitate to initiate participation in group settings because of cultural or personality factors. It provides an avenue for those who are reticent to speak up in groups and those for whom quick and assertive participation is not characteristic or not culturally valued. The structure provides a means for expected participation based on belonging to the group rather than on social savvy, speedy responses, or perceived expertise. As a structured method for seeking consultation in a team, the consultation circle honors individual differences in approaches and expertise. Everyone has something to contribute, and with structured interdependence comes permission to ask for and receive consultation.

Implementing the consultation circle as part of the overall structure of working together can facilitate addressing many people's needs in a timely manner. The consultation circle is not a substitute for supervision or administration, and unlike other models of consultation (see, for example, Kadushin, 1977; Rieman, 1992), responsibility for consultation lies with the team members rather than with an expert. The structure provides a focus on potency and solutions or interventions rather than on aimless storytelling, griping, blaming, or helplessness.

Consistent with this focus on problem solving is the opportunity to develop and use skills in asking for consultation. Workers are encouraged to apply their skills in problem identification and the articulation of focused questions when asking for feedback, ideas, and advice. Concomitant skills include partializing and summarizing, often in the face of complex case situations. After listening nonjudgmentally to feedback and discerning a course of action, consultants receive feedback about the resolution of the consultative situation. The structure also encourages the development of skills in giving consultation that is focused and thoughtful, written and verbal.

THE MODEL IN OPERATION

In the consultation circle, all members are considered equal, and decision making rests with the person seeking help. The roles of facilitator, requester, and consultant provide structure for the process. The consultation circle is intended to supplement, not replace, other forms of consultation or supervision. Ground rules, established by each group, determine when and how the model will be implemented in the overall agency structure of administration, support, education, and problem solving. An agreement to use this model for team consultation in the spirit intended is critical to its usefulness.

The consultation circle can be used with as few as three people and with as many as 12. It can be used by administrative teams; work groups that include professional and paraprofessional staff; multidisciplinary teams; and homogenous work groups such as all social workers, all adult services workers, or all psychologists. To implement the consultation circle, three roles are needed: facilitator, requester, and consultant.

Facilitator

This position is usually rotated based on ground rules established by the work group; for example, groups rotate this position by week, month, or topic. The facilitator asks who in the group has consultation needs and, in the context of time allotted for a particular session, decides how much time will be available for each consultee. After reviewing the process and making sure everyone has consultation forms, the facilitator invites the requester to present the case, situation, or problem; facilitates clarification of the question if needed; and guides the feedback process around the circle. At times the facilitator may need to redirect the requester to specify the question being addressed or to listen to suggestions without commenting or evaluation. Sometimes facilitation is needed to focus consultees on giving consultation rather than telling their own stories or discounting the value of their contribution. The facilitator also participates in the consulting role.

Requester

The person asking for consultation presents a clear, succinct statement of the problem or situation; listens without responding to all recommendations; and acknowledges each suggestion with "Thank you." After listening to feedback and reviewing written responses, the requester considers all recommendations and chooses what to implement. To complete the communication feedback loop, the requester reports back to the group about outcomes related to the request.

This dimension of the model empowers the requester to maintain autonomy and responsibility for the situation, the choice of intervention, and implementation. Participants have reported that hearing a variety of options for intervention often stimulates their own creative process and ability to determine an appropriate action to take. Solution-focused actions may be based on a single suggestion, a combination of several ideas, or another alternative identified by the worker.

Consultant

Everyone in the group, including the facilitator, fulfills the role of consultant. After hearing the problem or situation, each consultant writes succinct statements of his or her best suggestion (see the sample consultation form in Figure 19-1). In the circle, each person verbally offers one suggestion. Because all views are valued, it is important that each person contributes regardless of whether his or her idea has been offered by someone else. Some participants may need the encouragement of the facilitator or other members to "say it in your own words." Multiple offerings of the same or similar suggestions may indicate an important dimension of the problem to address. Likewise, a requester may understand different aspects by hearing several versions of a theme.

All consultation forms include the name of the requester and of the consultant in addition to the suggestions; the forms are given to the requester at the end of the circle. The consultant has responsibility for responding directly to requests for consultation, and the written

Figure 19-1
Consultation Circle Consultant Form

Requester _____ Date _____

Consultant _____

Case situation _____

My suggestion is _____

_____

_____

_____

_____

suggestions reinforce clear and focused thinking. For both the requester and the consultant, the written suggestion format also provides the opportunity to follow up at a later time to further discuss a suggestion or ask for clarification. This is important for people who want more process time because the format and process of the consultation circle do not include in-depth discussion of the suggestions offered for consideration. Also, a consultant may not have any suggestions at the time but may think of one later; these suggestions can be written and given to the requester at a later time.

An Example

Following is a sample of two scripted consultation circles prepared as practice circles for instructional use with a diverse group of mental health professionals in a community mental health agency. The examples were developed before the workshop with input from clinical supervisors at the clinic. Workshop attendees then practiced writing their own responses to several prepared situations relevant to their work, followed by situations and responses generated solely by participants.

> *Facilitator:* Would you tell us what you would like us to consult about?
>
> *Requester 1:* I have a Native American family with four children under age six with Child Protection involved. One child is in foster care and has been sexually abused. How do we help mom help her daughter with this recent trauma?
>
> *Facilitator:* Is everyone clear about what [Requester 1] is asking for? [*One or two clarifying questions might occur here. The facilitator will keep questions focused, so this process does not turn into a series of questions that might be appropriate for other types of consultation.*] Okay, let's all take a minute to think about our best suggestion for [Requester 1] and write it down. [*After a pause noting people's progress with writing suggestions, the facilitator invites a beginning.*] Whoever is ready, please start, and then we'll go around the circle from there.
>
> *Consultant 1:* My suggestion is to make sure her daughter has had medical care and that mom is assured that her daughter is medically cared for.
>
> *Requester 1:* Thank you, C1. [*This courtesy, although it can feel awkward at first, reinforces the acknowledgment of the contribution to the requester's need. Including the colleague's name personalizes the interaction.*]
>
> *Consultant 2:* My suggestion is to help mom reach out to her support network.
>
> *Requester 1:* Thank you, C2.

Consultant 3: I pass.

Requester 1: Thank you, C3.

Consultant 4: My suggestion is to do whatever you can to get her daughter in individual therapy as soon as possible.

Requester 1: Thank you, C4.

Consultant 5: My suggestion is to check out any legal remedies and support the mother in pursuing them.

Requester 1: Thank you, C5.

Consultant 6: My suggestion is to get individual therapy for mom.

Requester 1: Thank you, C6.

Facilitator: Does anyone who passed have a suggestion at this time? *[No response]* Okay, please give your consultation forms to [Requester 1]. Does anyone else have a case or situation you'd like consultation on?

Requester 2: I do. I am working with a Southeast Asian family with a gang-involved teenage son. He skips school, and his parents are afraid of him. I am making a home visit tomorrow. What issue do I deal with first?

Facilitator: Is everyone clear about what [Requester] is asking for? Okay, let's all take a minute to think about our best suggestion for [Requester 2] and write it down. *[A pause]* Whoever is ready, please start, and then we'll go around the circle from there.

Consultant 1: My suggestion is to attend to your personal safety on the home visit—take the cell phone and make sure your supervisor knows where and when you're going.

Requester 2: Thank you, C1.

Consultant 2: My suggestion is to support the parents in searching the house for other weapons.

Requester 2: Thank you, C2.

Consultant 3: I pass.

Requester 2: Thank you, C3.

Consultant 4 [Facilitator]: My suggestion is to find out who the child is connected with as an ally who can reach out to him—clan leaders, uncles, other extended family.

Requester 2: Thank you, C4.

Consultant 5: My suggestion is to suggest a parenting group for the parents—those run by the mutual-assistance organizations—to encourage them to do prevention with the younger children in the family.

Requester 2: Thank you, C5.

Facilitator: Does anyone who passed have a suggestion at this time?

Consultant 3: Yes I do. My suggestion is to make sure you're safe and are mentally OK with going out alone, or ask someone to go with you.

Requester 2: Thank you, C3.

Advantages

By structuring and facilitating the responsible, autonomous asking and offering of consultation, the model facilitates obtaining information in more than one way with activities that address multiple learning and communication styles. The worker's personal responsibility, self-determination, mutual respect, and problem-solving abilities are empowered in a team setting. By providing a wide range of options not previously considered, the creative problem-solving process can be nurtured.

Using a structured process facilitates the withholding of judgment of ideas and suggestions offered during the process of delivery; rather, they can be thoughtfully assessed in the worker's own time. Likewise, those who might feel put off or intimidated by observing reactions to others' suggestions or fear evaluation of their ideas as not worthy or stupid are supported in their participation by the structure. An ordered process also supports people speaking in turn, increasing the likelihood that each person and idea will be heard.

The consultation circle structures and facilitates responsibility in asking and offering help. It addresses multiple learning and communication styles to facilitate getting information in more than one way. Writing suggestions forces the clarification of ideas. Signing names reinforces accountability and facilitates following up on ideas the consultee may want to explore further. The structure helps ensure equality, active participation, shared responsibility, and respecting the boundaries of time and process.

Participating in this consultation process can open up the creative problem-solving process by providing a wide range of options not considered previously and can further clarify the problem being addressed. This process can help a worker identify specific themes or directions, such as when several people spontaneously have similar suggestions. Workers in the consultant role often discover solutions to their own problems by participating in the process.

This model reinforces mutual respect, acknowledges individual experience and expertise, and reinforces the value of contributions from diverse perspectives. Because some cultures consider it impolite to "jump into conversations," this process facilitates participation because all members, the vocal and the reticent, are charged with the responsibility to respond both in writing and verbally to requests. Also, the consultation circle helps those who need structure to focus and minimizes free-flowing dialogue not directed to the purpose of giving specific help or consultation.

The consultation circle provides a structure and process that may be particularly useful for students in agencies experimenting with nontraditional work structures, such as self-directed work teams and self-managed work groups, or where staff have a wide variation in knowledge and expertise. It provides an alternative to group supervision and can facilitate the use of peer resources in rural or isolated work settings.

Disadvantages

Those who view structure of any kind as rigid or authoritarian may experience the consultation circle as stifling the free-flowing expression of feelings and constraining processing time to explain or describe the problem and possible solutions. In-depth discussion of an interesting solution is not accommodated within the process.

CONCLUSION

Using this model for team consultation empowers the requester to be in charge of the situation, the offered solutions, and implementation. Often requesters find that hearing a variety of options for intervention or action opens their own creative process to find the solution. They can choose suggestions given, combine suggestions, or identify additional alternatives. The feedback loop is completed when the requester reports to the group about actions taken and the results. The completion of the communication cycle is important to honor all participants and to avoid the "worker who cried 'wolf' syndrome."

Having a structure reinforces mutual respect. In some cultures it is considered impolite to interrupt conversations. For example, the Lakota language has no word for "excuse me" because there is no polite way to interrupt; one must wait for the other person to finish speaking (Broken Nose, 1992). Such knowledge is critical for professionals who have been taught to use interrupting techniques to clarify and direct the conversation.

The consultation structure for the process of offering suggestions facilitates participation by vocal and quiet or culturally influenced group members in a way that evens the playing field. It is also helpful for focusing attention on the requested consultation.

REFERENCES

Barnard, J., & Goodyear, R. (1992). *Fundamentals of clinical supervision*. Boston: Allyn & Bacon.

Barretta-Herman, A. (1993). On the development of a model of supervision for licensed social work practitioners. *Clinical Supervisor, 11*(2), 55–64.

Berg, I. K., & Miller, S. D. (1992). Working with Asian American clients: One person at a time. *Families in Society, 73*, 356–363.

Broken Nose, M. A. (1992). Working with the Oglala Lakota: An outsider's perspective. *Families in Society, 73*, 380–384.

Clarke, J. I. (1978). *Self-esteem: A family affair*. San Francisco: Harper.

Clarke, J. I. (1981). *Self-esteem: A family affair leader guide*. San Francisco: Harper.

Clarke, J. I. (1984). The suggestion circle. *WE, Newsletter for Nurturing Support Groups, 5*(6), 1–3.

Ewalt, P. L., Freeman, E. M., Kirk, S. A., & Poole, D. L. (Eds.). (1996). *Multicultural issues in social work*. Washington, DC: NASW Press.

Garrett, K. J., & Barretta-Herman, A. (1995). Moving from supervision to professional development. *Clinical Supervisor, 13*(2), 97–110.

Gutierrez, L., GlenMaye, L., & DeLois, K. (1996). The organizational context of empowerment practice: Implications for social work administration. In P. L. Ewalt, E. M. Freeman, S. A. Kirk, & D. L. Poole (Eds.), *Multicultural issues in social work* (pp. 60–76). Washington, DC: NASW Press.

Kadushin, A. (1977). *Consultation in social work.* New York: Columbia University Press.

Kadushin, A. (1992). *Supervision in social work* (3rd ed.). New York: Columbia University Press.

Kaiser, T. L. (1997). *Supervisory relationships: Exploring the human element.* Monterey, CA: Brooks/Cole.

Kline, P., & Saunders, B. (1993). *Ten steps to a learning organization.* Arlington, VA: Great Ocean.

Kuechler, C. F., & Barretta-Herman, A. (1995, March). *Empowering student participation in field seminar: Using the consultation circle.* Paper presented at the Annual Program Meeting of the Council on Social Work Education, San Diego.

Kuechler, C. F., & Barretta-Herman, A. (1996, June). *The consultation circle: A model for peer consultation.* Workshop presented at the annual statewide meeting of the National Association of Social Workers–Minnesota Chapter, St. Paul.

Munson, C. (1989). Trends of significance for clinical supervision. *Clinical Supervisor, 7*(4), 1–8.

National Association of Social Workers, Council on the Practice of Clinical Social Work. (1994). *Guidelines for clinical social work supervision.* Washington, DC: Author.

Richard, R., & Rodway, M. R. (1992). The peer consultation group: A problem-solving perspective. *Clinical Supervisor, 10*(1), 83–100.

Rieman, D. W. (1992). *Strategies in social work consultation.* New York: Longman.

Ryan, A. S., & Hendricks, C. O. (1989). Culture and communication: Supervising the Asian and Hispanic social worker. *Clinical Supervisor, 7*(1), 27–40.

Sue, D. W. (1981). *Counseling the culturally different: Theory and practice.* New York: John Wiley & Sons.

Tsui, A. S., & O'Reilly, C. A., III. (1989). Beyond simple demographic effects: The importance of relational demography in superior–subordinate dyads. *Academy of Management Journal, 32*(2), 402–423.

Van Den Bergh, N. (1990). Managing biculturalism at the work place: A group approach. *Social Work with Groups, 13*(4), 71–84.

My gratitude goes to Jean Illsley Clarke and colleagues for the inspiration of the "suggestion circle" and to the students and professionals who have contributed to the ongoing development and clarification of the consultation circle model and process, especially the mental health staff at the Community University Health Care Center. I express my heartfelt appreciation for the support, encouragement, and feedback provided by my colleague Dr. Angeline Barretta-Herman. She has often shared the developmental journey of the consultation circle as a copresenter and facilitator in the presentation of this model for national and local conference workshops and social services agencies. Parts of this text have been included in those presentations.

20 White Racial Identity:
Theory, Research, and Implications for Organizational Contexts

Caryn J. Block and Robert T. Carter

I t is estimated that by the year 2010, one out of every two Americans will be nonwhite (Pear, 1992). In recognition of the impact of these changing demographics, organizations are engaging in efforts to prepare employees to make the transition from a predominantly white to a racially diverse work force. There has been a dramatic increase in programs purporting to improve race relations in organizations over the past five years, and this trend is expected to continue (Williams, 1992). To understand individual behavior in organizations, issues related to the race and culture of employees need to be examined (Bolick & Nestleroth, 1988).

Yet, when race and culture are addressed in organizational contexts, it is primarily nonwhite races and cultures that are the focal point of examination. Most of the current approaches to understanding interracial behavior at work focus on nonwhite employees (Thomas, 1992). Interventions designed to improve interracial situations at work typically make three types of recommendations. The first category has to do with access. It suggests that racism in organizations can be eliminated or reduced by providing visible ethnic group members with more opportunity. Thus, the recommendation is to hire more visible ethnic group members. Affirmative action programs are products of this type of recommendation.

The second type of recommendation has to do with helping individual members in the organization, usually white employees, develop sensitivity to people of color. These types of programs are typically called "sensitivity, diversity, or racism training." The aim of these programs is to train people in organizations in the skills necessary to deal with visible ethnic group people and highlight the existence of stereotypes and the kind of roles stereotypes play in intergroup and organizational interactions, even when people are not aware of them.

The third type of recommendation for remedying racism in organizations is to create situations of exposure or contact with visible ethnic group employees. The exposure strategy involves creating situations in which people of different ethnic groups will actually work together. The idea is that by having similar goals and tasks in the work unit, the contact with one another will help break down racial barriers. If racially different people work together, they can see that they are not that different, and they will then get along with one another. Another objective is to set up work situations so that visible ethnic group members are not working in racially homogenous enclaves—so that the organization does not have some work units filled primarily by black workers and others filled primarily by white workers.

All of these strategies for remedying racism in organizations have one thing in common: They are almost exclusively focused on visible ethnic group people or on training white people to be more aware of their perceptions of visible ethnic group people. Affirmative action programs focus solely on increasing visible ethnic group members' participation in the work force. Sensitivity or diversity training is designed to help organizational members understand the attitudes, beliefs, and experiences of visible ethnic group people. There is little or no focus on the racial and cultural characteristics of the majority of people in the organization. All white people have to do is learn to tolerate and get along with others who are different from them. In this way, racial stereotypes can be altered.

Typically in such training efforts, white men and women are encouraged to explore their ethnic background, whereas people from visible ethnic groups talk about their race. Usually, there is no commensurate emphasis on white peoples' view of themselves as racial beings in existing strategies of remedying racism in organizations. This omission fosters a myth and an inequality that maintains the burden of accommodation on the people of color. The myth that only people of color have and belong to racial groups and white people lack race is implicit in most organizational diversity training programs. The inequality arises because without people of color, the person or organization is thought to have no racial identity.

Everyone has a race, and one's membership in a racial group is determined by his or her skin color. Therefore, it is essential that people in organizations learn to understand how their race and their identification with it influences their behavior, perceptions, and feelings. All people are influenced by racial group memberships, and each of us in our particular racial groups may be different in how we psychologically approach and understand that membership. However, consideration of psychological identification with race is usually not included in most discussions about race and racism. The lack of attention given to understanding the influence of the race and culture of white employees is surprising, given that white employees still make up the majority of the work force in this country (Johnston & Packer, 1987). Moreover, because the important decision-making positions in organizations are still primarily populated by white employees (Bell, 1990), it seems critical to understand how identification with white culture influences the behavior of these decision makers. The influence that senior white managers' racial attitudes can have on the diversity climate of the organization is exemplified by the recent lawsuit that was brought against Texaco by black employees (see later in this chapter).

An implicit assumption made in much of our understanding of the effects of race on individual behavior is that all white decision makers will respond the same way to interracial situations at work. Ignored are psychological characteristics of the person and how these characteristics influence his or her behavior (see Jackson, Sullivan, & Hodge, 1993, for an exception). However, research has demonstrated the importance of individual variation in racial attitudes for understanding behavior in interracial situations (McConahay, 1986). Within racial groups a great deal of variation exists in the extent to which people identify with their own racial group and how they perceive members of other racial groups.

The purpose of this chapter is to examine ways in which identification with white racial group membership and culture influences individual behavior in interracial situations in organizations. A framework that has been used to understand individual differences in identification with white racial group membership and culture is white racial identity theory (Helms, 1990). First, we discuss white racial identity attitude theory and then present two studies examining the effects of white racial identity attitudes in organizational contexts. Finally, white racial identity attitude theory is used to predict and understand different organizational responses in the form of policies and procedures related to race, racism, and diversity.

WHITE RACIAL IDENTITY THEORY

White racial identity theory describes the various ways in which white people identify with their own racial group as well as how that identification affects their view and understanding of other racial groups. The theory posits statuses of racial identity development, which determine people's attitudes and behavior in situations in which their race is salient. The statuses are aspects of personality and are used to process information and guide emotional experiences. Development reflects movement from a less personally differentiated status to a more complex and personal status. The developmental tasks for a person are to abandon racism and develop a positive nonracist white identity (Carter, 1995; Helms, 1990; Helms & Carter, 1990). This is accomplished by movement through five statuses: contact, disintegration, reintegration, pseudoindependent, and autonomy. Contact is characterized by a naive curiosity or trepidation about black people as well as a lack of awareness of being white and the benefits one is entitled to as a white person in the United States. A person at this status is likely to use white standards to judge black people. People at this status have limited contact with black people both socially and at work.

Disintegration is characterized by guilt and anxiety as the person becomes aware of the social implications of race on a personal level. At this status the person realizes that black and white people are not treated equally in many situations. The realization of racial inequities creates a moral dilemma and emotional confusion. To deal with these feelings, a person has several options. He or she can avoid further contact with black people, attempt to change inequitable situations, or look for information that would contradict these feelings of guilt—

information that racism is really not the white person's fault. There is more social support for the latter option, so it often becomes the preferred option and leads to beliefs that white superiority and black inferiority are responsible for the current situation (Helms, 1990). Depending on the course the person at disintegration chooses, he or she may or may not move on to one of the following statuses.

If the person chooses to resolve the issues discussed at the disintegration status by adopting the belief that white people are superior and black people are inferior, he or she will then be at the reintegration status. People in the reintegration status are characterized by the belief that white people are superior to people of color. People at this status are hostile toward black people and positively biased toward white people in either an active or passive way. At this stage the person first consciously acknowledges a white identity (Helms, 1990), reasoning that

> individual and cultural racism are the white person's due because he or she has earned such privileges and preferences. Race-related negative conditions are assumed to result from black people's inferior social, moral and intellectual qualities and thus, it is not unusual to find persons in the Reintegration stage selectively attending to and/or reinterpreting information to conform to societal stereotypes of black people. (p. 60)

The anxiety and guilt from the disintegration status are replaced by feelings of fear or anger toward black people.

When a person begins to define a positive white identity and abandon racism, he or she has reached the pseudoindependent status. At this status a person begins to question the beliefs that white people are superior and black people are inferior and begins to recognize that white people can unwittingly perpetuate racism. This status is characterized by an intellectual acceptance and curiosity about black people. A person at this status would be expected to attempt to help black people by teaching them how to be more like white people and therefore have a better chance of succeeding in white society. Thus, the person at this status still views black culture as dysfunctional and therefore responsible for the creation of institutional and cultural racism.

The final status in approaching a racially transcendent view for whites is autonomy. People at the autonomy status accept racial differences and value cultural diversity. A person at this status no longer attempts to change black people but instead attempts to change white people such that they become aware of how they may unwittingly be perpetuating racism. In this status a person no longer judges other people on the basis of racial group membership; thus, institutional, cultural, and personal racism are abandoned. An individual at this status "actively seeks opportunities to learn from other cultural groups" (Helms, 1990, p. 66).

This process of developing a healthy racial identity has two phases, with the first phase, abandonment of racism, comprising the first three statuses of racial identity development (contact, disintegration, and reintegration) and the second phase, development of a positive non-racist white identity, comprising the last two statuses (pseudoindependence and autonomy).

Helms and Carter (1990) developed a scale to measure white racial identity attitudes, and some supporting evidence has accrued. White racial identity has been demonstrated to be predictive of cultural value orientations (Carter & Helms, 1990), perceived racism (Carter, 1990b), the level of discomfort experienced by therapists and clients in mixed-race counseling sessions (Carter, 1990a, 1995) self-actualization (Tokar & Swanson, 1991), and work values (Carter, Gushue, & Weitzman, 1994).

RESEARCH IN WORKPLACE CONTEXTS

Block, Roberson, and Neuger Study

Some empirical research has been done to determine the influence of white racial identity attitudes on behaviors relevant to workplace contexts. Block, Roberson, and Neuger (1995) examined the influence of white racial identity attitudes of executives on their reactions toward interracial situations in organizations. Ninety-seven white executive MBA candidates employed in managerial positions responded to two questionnaires. Reactions toward interracial situations at work were assessed via four scales. The first scale, Endorsing Principles of Equitable Treatment of the Races in the Workplace, measured the degree to which respondents endorse general principles of racial integration and equitable treatment of the races in the workplace. The second scale, Endorsing Steps of Implementation, measured the degree to which the MBA candidates endorse steps to put the principles of equitable treatment of the races and work force integration into practice. The next scale, Perceptions of Equitable Treatment of the Races in the Workplace, measured perceptions about whether equitable treatment exists among the races in organizations. The last scale, Level of Comfort in Interracial Situations, assessed to what extent participants are comfortable in work settings involving black people.

It was hypothesized, consistent with Helms's two-phase model, that higher level racial identity attitudes (pseudoindependent and autonomy) would be related to more favorable reactions to interracial situations at work and that lower level racial identity attitudes (contact, disintegration, and reintegration) would be associated with unfavorable reactions to interracial situations. As expected, people characterized by high levels of disintegration and reintegration were less likely to support principles of work force integration, were less likely to endorse steps necessary to achieve work force integration, viewed current organizational environments as equitable for black people but inequitable for white people, and were less likely to be comfortable interacting with black men and women in organizational settings. However, people characterized by high levels of autonomy, the highest level of racial identity attitude development, were more likely to endorse principles of work force integration, were more likely to endorse steps necessary to achieve work force integration, viewed current organizational environments as equitable for white employees but inequitable for black employees, and were more likely to be comfortable interacting with black men and women in organizational settings. Furthermore, men and women characterized by high levels of pseudoindependent attitudes were more likely to be comfortable interacting with black people. However, there was no effect of pseudoindependent attitudes on endorsing principles of work force integration, endorsing implementation efforts to achieve work force integration, or viewing the environment as inequitable to black employees. Consistent with the theory, people at this level of racial identity development were further along toward developing a non-racist identity than people characterized by high levels of disintegration and reintegration attitudes, but they still had not developed a nonracist identity to the same extent as men and women characterized by high levels of autonomy attitudes.

The results for contact attitudes were less straightforward. People characterized by high levels of this attitude were more likely to endorse principles of work force integration and their implementation. However, high levels of contact attitudes did not affect participants' perceptions of the fairness of current organizational environments, nor did they influence the level of comfort that individuals' felt about interacting with black men and women in organizational environments.

These findings suggest that much is to be gained by looking at the variation in attitudes within racial groups when trying to predict how white employees will respond to working in interracial situations. All white men and women do not respond in the same way to interracial situations at work. By using white racial identity attitude theory, we gain a more profound understanding of how people react to interracial issues in organizational contexts.

The Block et al. (1995) study is informative about the effects of white racial attitudes on reactions to racial issues in organizational settings, but the data collected were attitudinal in nature. A second study that went beyond the previous study was done to examine the impact of white racial identity attitudes on decisions made in a workplace context (Block & Carter, 1992).

Block and Carter Study

The purpose of this study was to examine the influence of white people's racial identity attitudes on decisions they make regarding the careers of visible ethnic group members. We investigated decisions men and women made concerning employee selection—decisions crucial to the careers of those people being selected. There has been a great deal of research on the effects of race on employee-selection decisions (Cox & Nkomo, 1990). The approach most commonly taken in this type of research is to focus on the race of the applicants. Ignored are characteristics of the individual decision makers and how these characteristics influence their decisions.

Studies of the effects of applicant race on employee-selection decisions have found little evidence that black men and women are evaluated less favorably than white men and women (Haefner, 1977; Rand & Wexley, 1975; Wexley & Nemeroff, 1974). In fact, research has found that white people's evaluations of black applicants are frequently more favorable than their evaluations of equally qualified white applicants when the black applicant has an unexpected favorable characteristic such as a high socioeconomic status (Dienstbier, 1970; Feldman, 1972; Jussim, Coleman, & Lerch, 1987; Smedley & Bayton, 1978) or qualifications for a given job (Mullins, 1982). One explanation frequently given for these findings is that black people who possess favorable characteristics violate the expectations or stereotypes that white people hold for black people. This results in the black person who violates the stereotype being rated more favorably than an equally qualified white person (see Jussim et al., 1987, for a more detailed treatment of this issue).

In one study (Block & Carter, 1992), we provided participants with a job description and a job application and asked them to evaluate the applicant's suitability to fill the position. Half of the participants reviewed a job application with a photograph of a black man attached; the remaining participants reviewed a job application with a photograph of a white man attached.

We hypothesized that white people would evaluate a black applicant more favorably than an equally qualified white applicant because of the stereotypes they hold about black people. We further hypothesized that this tendency for a qualified black applicant to violate a white evaluator's stereotype would be moderated by the evaluator's racial identity development. If this were true, individuals characterized by pseudoindependence and autonomy would not evaluate equally qualified black and white applicants differently. Approaching a truly nonracist perspective, these evaluators would have no reason to evaluate the two applicants differently because their expectations would not be violated by a qualified black applicant. In contrast, people characterized by contact, disintegration, and reintegration attitudes would evaluate the black applicant more favorably than the white applicant because the black applicant's qualifications would violate their stereotypes.

The results of this study replicated the finding that black people with a favorable characteristic are evaluated more favorably than are equivalent white applicants (Carver, Glass, & Katz, 1978; Dienstbier, 1970; Hass, Katz, Rizzo, Bailey, & Eisenstadt, 1991; Jackson et al., 1993; Jussim et al., 1987; Linville & Jones, 1980). Consistent with previous research on the influence of applicant race on employee selection decisions (Mullins, 1982), we found that black applicants were given more favorable hiring recommendations than equally qualified white applicants.

This disparity in recommendations did not occur among people characterized by pseudoindependence or autonomy. Rather, evaluators not characterized by the two highest levels of racial identity development either held more negative stereotypes of black people or felt pressure to respond to this situation in a socially appropriate way. Thus, racial identity attitudes did, in fact, moderate the tendency of white evaluators to rate black applicants more favorably than equivalent white applicants. The results of this study suggest that people who are at higher levels of racial identity attitude development are not operating with the same social stereotypes as people at lower levels.

This study demonstrated that white racial identity attitudes influence individual decisions in organizational contexts. The tendency for white evaluators to rate a black applicant more favorably than an equivalent white applicant, a well-established finding, was shown to be moderated by the racial identity of the evaluator. The finding demonstrated that selection decisions are, in fact, influenced by identification with white culture.

An important issue in interpreting these results is the similarity between the contingencies that operate in actual employee selection decisions and the analog selection decision used in this research. An important difference between actual and simulated hiring decisions is that, in actual hiring decisions, the decision makers are evaluated in terms of the consequences of their decisions whereas, in the simulated hiring decision used in this study, the respondents did not have to worry about the consequences of their evaluations. Therefore, it is important to interpret the results of this study with caution. The results can be used to suggest that organizational decision makers characterized by high levels of white racial identity are likely to make selection decisions that are not influenced by differential stereotypes of qualified black and white applicants, whereas organizational decision makers who are not characterized by high levels of white racial identity are likely to make selection decisions that are influenced by the differential stereotypes held of black and white applicants. However, the way in which holding differential stereotypes of black and white applicants will influence actual selection decisions that have important consequences for the decision maker is still an important question that cannot be answered by the data collected in this study.

Both Studies Taken Together

These two studies taken together empirically demonstrate the importance of examining within-racial-group variation for understanding behavior in interracial situations. The utility of focusing on white people in interracial situations also has been demonstrated. These studies found that identification with white racial group membership and culture influenced the behavior of individuals in the workplace.

IMPLICATIONS FOR UNDERSTANDING ORGANIZATIONAL RESPONSES TO RACE AND DIVERSITY

White racial identity has been described as a psychological orientation toward one's racial group membership. As presented, racial identity is an individual psychological phenomenon; however, the theory has been extended by Helms (1990) to groups and social relationships. We think it is reasonable to apply a theory about individual psychological development to an organization, because individuals form groups, and groups form the primary building blocks of organizations (Thompson & Carter, 1997). Some authors have defined organizations as mechanisms for structuring and directing group action (Thompson & Carter, 1997).

In extending racial identity theory, Helms (1990) hypothesized that group members may form coalitions on the basis of their individual racial identity development. A coalition represents the combined influence on the group of the racial identity attitudes of members who are at the same or similar levels of racial identity development. So if most members of a group or organization are characterized by a predominance of a particular level of racial identity, then the organization or group will take on that racial identity perspective. However, a critical factor in whether a coalition's views will dominate a group or organization is the power held by or attributed to the group members. In this way, organizational leaders who create policies and procedures and who establish the organizational climate can be thought of as representing a racial identity power coalition.

We believe that racial identity has the greatest impact on an organization's culture and its climate relative to race. Most organizations derive their climate and culture from the people who are the leaders and decision makers (Burke & Litwin, 1992). Organizational culture is expressed through the formally and informally held beliefs, values, and assumptions that exist in the organization. Organizational culture, so defined, then determines the norms that develop as well as the appropriate patterns of behavior that arise from these norms. These norms also guide an organization's human resources policies and procedures, socialization process, and policies and practices toward visible ethnic groups.

The important influence that high-level management attitudes have on organizational climate for race and diversity is demonstrated by the recent lawsuit that black employees brought against Texaco. Top-level executives were recorded using extremely racist language while discussing a discrimination lawsuit brought by black employees. The white racial identity attitudes of these top executives did, in fact, influence the organizational climate toward diversity. For example, at Texaco, although there were affirmative action hiring guidelines as mandated by law, no internal audits were performed to ensure these guidelines were being followed. Further, black employees were promoted at a much slower rate than were white employees, with few black employees reaching senior management levels. When compared with other oil companies, black workers at Texaco also were paid less. Finally, many black employees perceived the environment as racially hostile (Eichenwald, 1996). Thus, top management's racial attitudes can have a trickle-down effect in the way in which black employees are treated in an organization. White racial identity attitude theory provides a useful framework for diagnosing the racial attitudes of top management and thus allows for predictions about the race and diversity climate that exists in a given organization.

We argue that organizations can be described in terms of their racial identity development. Moreover, we think that an organization's racial identity perspective will have direct implications for how it develops policies and procedures; how it operates its business; how it deals with visible ethnic group people; and how power and authority are distributed, particularly along ethnic lines. Following is a description of the policies and procedures that would exist in an organization characterized by each status of racial identity.

Contact Organization

Contact is a status of racial identity in which one is unaware of himself or herself and others as members of racial groups. Race is not a salient or meaningful aspect of his or her identity or the identity of visible ethnic group people. An organization characterized by contact attitudes will have organizational policies centered on the notion that race is not a salient feature of people's identity. The "color-blind" approach will be the predominant view of the organization. Therefore, any person, even someone who does come from a diverse racial or cultural group, will be encouraged to leave his or her race and culture at the door. The organization may declare that it will not make decisions based on race, it will focus on workers' or members' merit and qualifications, and it will treat everyone fairly. This type of organization will be an equal opportunity employer because of the belief that all people are the same and should be treated equally. It may have affirmative action polices because of legal responsibilities. Organizational socialization would focus on helping visible ethnic group people fit into the "color-blind" organizational culture. Because no one thinks about race explicitly and stereotypes are not conscious, it is assumed that diversity training is not needed.

Overlooked is the fact that some visible ethnic group people are denied equal access to employment and that they often are treated differently in organizations. The idea held by many executives that a strict meritocracy in and of itself is the hallmark of fairness is exclusionary, even when the organization may have intended the opposite. The contact organization is promoting institutional and cultural racism without being aware that it is doing so.

Managers in such an organization would argue that they do not need diversity or racism training because they do not have stereotypes, they see people as individuals, and they respond to them in that way. In part because they are not conscious of themselves as white, such organizational leaders are not able to acknowledge the extent to which the perceptions that they have of members of visible ethnic groups are influenced by stereotypes that still operate for them in nonapparent ways. For example, they would probably perceive someone who graduated with honors from the University of Michigan as more qualified than someone who graduated with honors from Howard University because of the stereotypes they hold about black colleges being inferior to mainstream universities.

Disintegration Organization

Disintegration is a status of racial identity in which people are aware of being white but are confused and conflicted about what that means for them and for visible ethnic group people. Because of this confusion, they act in contrary and conflicting ways. The organization characterized by disintegration would be confused about how to deal with race. On the one hand, management would feel that it should hire visible ethnic group people and address inequities, which managers acknowledge exist. But the policies would tend to be confused about how to address the inequities. For example, the organization may have an affirmative action program that hires people, but it may fail to do anything else regarding race and diversity because management believes that to do anything else would be to operate in some preferential way toward those who are seen as different. So although the organization is aware of inequities and tries to address them, it does not know what else to do or how to address these inequities in any way other than to hire some people of color. It believes that having an affirmative action program addresses the needs of the visible ethnic group people in the organization, and managers consider themselves enlightened because they are doing this much.

Management of the disintegration organization wants to help members of visible ethnic groups learn how to function effectively in the corporate culture. They may have established an active orientation program. Their policies and procedures are well-meaning, but they also operate under the assumption that visible ethnic group people must make the accommodation, must learn how to function in the white corporate world and, in effect, must give up things that they may value about themselves. Thus, individual, institutional, and cultural racism are represented in these practices.

Reintegration Organization

Reintegration is a status of racial identity in which people idealize their whiteness and believe that all they have achieved was earned, and if others have not achieved, it is because they have not worked hard enough. Organizations characterized by reintegration probably take the position that visible ethnic group people have to make it the same way that everyone else has, and that black people or other visible ethnic group members have not been able to gain access because they do not have what it takes or they have not worked hard enough.

Managers of the organization will hire visible ethnic group members who they think have worked hard enough.

Although organizations at reintegration do not have a policy of hiring visible ethnic group members, this shortcoming is not openly admitted. Instead, these policies are disguised euphemistically by invoking the following logic: "If we hire black people and we give them preferential treatment, then that's reverse discrimination, so we will hire the best people for the job." Therefore, although they may be equal opportunity employers by law and they may have government-mandated affirmative action polices, such organizations will not actively implement them. The only training in place will be basic new-employee orientation with no racial or diversity component. The logic implicit in these procedures is that the privileged status as white men and women in the society is earned, and if black people or people of color lack privilege, it is because they have not earned it and are not worthy of it. This seems to describe the racial identity power coalition at Texaco.

Organizations characterized by different statuses of racial identity create different environments for visible ethnic group members. Some similarities exist between organizations at contact and at reintegration. Reintegration organizations might have similar policies to contact organizations in that their policies will reflect their management's belief that the organization is a meritocracy. However, people would most likely feel treated differently because in a contact organization, the climate would be such that if visible ethnic group people succeed, the organization will reward them, whereas the climate in a reintegration organization would be more hostile. In fact, in a reintegration organization, white people would be comfortable only with black people who essentially deny their blackness, denigrate black people, and take on the view of the majority society, so that a black-identified man or woman would experience it as a hostile environment. In contrast, a contact environment would not be experienced as hostile, just ignorant.

Pseudoindependent Organization

The pseudoindependent status represents intellectual, self-centered, and marginal acceptance and understanding of racial differences. White people with these attitudes do not accept without question social stereotypes about black people or other people of color. They reject racist practices but hold these views on an intellectual level and believe that the answers to addressing these problems lie with the victims. Thus, they look to visible ethnic group people for solutions. Although the organization members feel more comfortable talking about, addressing, and dealing with racial and diversity issues, they use their own world view and their own experience as an ethnic group person as the primary criterion on which to judge black people's experiences. In other words, they still apply their own experiences as the standard, expressing the idea that "I understand what it is to be discriminated against because, as an Italian or as a Greek, that happened to me or to my grandmother." What they are not acknowledging in using that criterion is that in this society they still are more accepted as members of the white group than has been true for people who are not white regardless of their ethnic origins. People in organizations characterized by pseudoindependence tend to look to visible ethnic group people for solutions to the problems of racism and explanations about diversity. At this level, individual racism is rejected, and the person is aware of institutional and cultural racism but has not grasped its subtleties.

Thus, an organization that has these characteristics would have an affirmative action program; it also might have socialization training, but the training would tend to deal with how these people can be helped fit into the organization and culture. In other words, white organization members would go to visible ethnic group people and ask them what should be done to help them function in the organization. They would not believe or see that the core of the problem is not the visible ethnic group members. This perspective results in tension and conflict because the visible ethnic group members feel marginalized, like outsiders, and so do the white people who support the programs. Each group will begin to feel distrustful of the other and will retreat into racially similar settings, and the discussions will eventually end with no real resolutions identified. The pseudoindependent organization, then, is well-meaning and well-intentioned, but it is still unintentionally applying inappropriate criteria, and thus it experiences subtle conflict without understanding why. White people feel inert because they do not know what to do to address the issues and they are not getting the kind of support from black organization members that they think they should receive—after all, they are "just trying to help them." Thus, the sporadic attempts at addressing these issues usually end in failure.

Autonomy Organization

The autonomy status of racial identity development is not based on any form of racism. White people at this level are nonracist and are aware of being white. An organization at this level would be able to build and use the racial differences in the styles, perceptions, and values of its members in the way the organization functions. It would create forums and mechanisms for its members to be who they are and use various perspectives as part of the organization's ability to be flexible and responsive. The organization would have an aggressive affirmative action program and probably have a large mix of people. The organization is able to look at people in different ways and develop different strengths in different employees. It would develop policies and practices that would foster a climate that welcomed different types of people, one that reflected an understanding of who they are and what they need to be productive. Thus, the socialization orientation of this type of organization would include diversity- and race-based training that would be ongoing elements of employee training. The upper management of this type of organization also would be racially diverse, and power in the organization would be reflected in the diversity that the organization values.

CONCLUSION

We have tried to show that white racial identity theory is useful in understanding how organizations may respond to racism and diversity. We have argued that each status of white identity might lead to a different climate and culture that result in distinctly different organizational policies and procedures about race and diversity. We hope that we have demonstrated the usefulness of focusing on white racial identity attitude development as a way of remedying racism and promoting diversity in organizations.

Once we begin to acknowledge that white people have a racial identity and that there are differences among white people regarding that identity, we can identify the variation that exists among white individuals. For instance, it is possible not to be racist. It also is possible that some of the levels of racial identity that are not explicitly racist lead to perceptions, behaviors, and policies that apply and promote societal notions based on racist ideology, even if that is not at all the intention of a particular policy or practice.

We think this emphasis on working with white people regarding race and culture is vital, given how much race divides us as a society and as members in organizations. What happens when one incorporates white racial identity is that he or she now includes all societal groups in the dialogue about racial diversity. To us, it seems easier to discuss something that we all know we share.

REFERENCES

Bell, E. L. (1990). The bicultural life experiences of career-oriented black women. *Journal of Organizational Behavior, 11,* 459–477.

Block, C. J., & Carter, R. T. (1992, August). *The influence of white racial identity on personnel selection decisions.* Paper presented at the meeting of the American Psychological Association, Washington, DC.

Block, C. J., Roberson, L. A., & Neuger, D. A. (1995). White racial identity theory: A framework for understanding reactions toward interracial situations at work. *Journal of Vocational Behavior, 46,* 71–88.

Bolick, C., & Nestleroth, S. (1988). *Opportunity 2000: Creative affirmative action strategies for the changing workforce.* Washington, DC: U.S. Government Printing Office.

Burke, W. W., & Litwin, G. H. (1992). A causal model of organizational performance and change. *Journal of Management, 18,* 532–545.

Carter, R. T. (1990a). Does race or racial identity attitudes influence the counseling process in black and white dyads? In J. E. Helms (Ed.), *Black and white racial identity: Theory, research and practice* (pp. 145–163). Westport, CT: Greenwood Press.

Carter, R. T. (1990b). The relationship between racism and racial identity among white Americans: An exploratory investigation. *Journal of Counseling and Development, 69,* 46–50.

Carter, R. T. (1995). *The influence of race and racial identity in psychotherapy: Toward a racially inclusive model.* New York: John Wiley & Sons.

Carter, R. T., Gushue, G. V., & Weitzman, L. M. (1994). White racial identity development and work values. *Journal of Vocational Behavior, 44,* 185–197.

Carter, R. T., & Helms, J. E. (1990). White racial identity attitudes and cultural values. In J. E. Helms (Ed.), *Black and white racial identity: Theory, research and practice* (pp. 150–218). Westport, CT: Greenwood Press.

Carver, C. S., Glass, D. C., & Katz, I. (1978). Favorable evaluations of blacks and the handicapped: Positive prejudice, unconscious denial, or social desirability? *Journal of Applied Social Psychology, 8,* 97–106.

Cox, T., Jr., & Nkomo, S. M. (1990). Invisible men and women: A status report on race as a variable in organizational behavior research. *Journal of Organizational Behavior, 11,* 419–431.

Dienstbier, R. A. (1970). Positive and negative prejudice: Interaction of prejudice with race and social desirability. *Journal of Personality, 38,* 198–215.

Eichenwald, K. (1996, November 10). The two faces of Texaco. *New York Times,* pp. 1, 10, 11.

Feldman, J. (1972). Stimulus characteristics and subject prejudice as determinants of stereotype attribution. *Journal of Personality and Social Psychology, 21,* 333–340.

Haefner, J. E. (1977). Race, age, sex and competence as factors in employer selection of the disadvantaged. *Journal of Applied Psychology, 62,* 199–202.

Hass, R. G., Katz, I., Rizzo, N., Bailey, J., & Eisenstadt, D. (1991). Cross-racial appraisal as related to attitude ambivalence and cognitive complexity. *Personality and Social Psychology Bulletin, 17,* 83–92.

Helms, J. E. (1990). *Black and white racial identity: Theory, research and practice.* Westport, CT: Greenwood Press.

Helms, J. E., & Carter, R. T. (1990). The development of the white racial identity attitude inventory. In J. E. Helms (Ed.), *Black and white racial identity: Theory, research and practice* (pp. 67–80). Westport, CT: Greenwood Press.

Jackson, L. A., Sullivan, L. A., & Hodge, C. N. (1993). Stereotype effects on attributions, predictions, and evaluations: No two social judgments are quite alike. *Journal of Personality and Social Psychology, 65,* 69–84.

Johnston, W. B., & Packer, A. E. (1987). *Workforce 2000: Work and workers for the 21st century.* Indianapolis: Hudson Institute.

Jussim, L., Coleman, L. M., & Lerch, L. (1987). The nature of stereotypes: A comparison and integration of three theories. *Journal of Personality and Social Psychology, 52,* 536–546.

Linville, P. W., & Jones, E. E. (1980). Polarized appraisals of outgroup members. *Journal of Personality and Social Psychology, 38,* 689–703.

McConahay, J. B. (1986). Modern racism, ambivalence, and the modern racism scale. In J. F. Dovidio & S. L. Gaertner (Eds.), *Prejudice, discrimination, and racism* (pp. 91–126). San Diego: Academic Press.

Mullins, T. W. (1982). Interviewer decisions as a function of applicant race, applicant quality and interviewer prejudice. *Personnel Psychology, 35,* 163–174.

Pear, R. (1992, December 4). Population growth outstrips earlier U.S. census estimates. *New York Times,* pp. A1, D6.

Rand, T. M., & Wexley, K. N. (1975). Demonstration of the effect, "similar to me," in simulated employment interviews. *Psychological Reports, 36,* 535–544.

Smedley, J., & Bayton, J. (1978). Evaluative race–class stereotypes by race and perceived class of subjects. *Journal of Personality and Social Psychology, 30,* 530–535.

Thomas, R. T. (1992). Managing diversity: A conceptual framework. In S. E. Jackson (Ed.), *Diversity in the workplace: Human resources initiatives* (pp. 306–318). New York: Guilford Press.

Thompson, C., & Carter, R. T. (1997). *Racial identity development theory: Applications to individuals, groups and organizations.* Hillsdale, NJ: Lawrence Earlbaum.

Tokar, P. M., & Swanson, J. L. (1991). An investigation of the validity of Helms' (1984) model of white racial identity development. *Journal of Counseling Psychology, 30,* 296–301.

Wexley, K. N., & Nemeroff, W. F. (1974). The effects of racial prejudice, race of appli-
cant, and biographical similarity on interviewer evaluations of job applicants.
Journal of Social and Behavioral Sciences, 20, 66–78.
Williams, L. (1992, December 15). Companies capitalizing on worker diversity. *New
York Times,* pp. D11, D20.

*Portions of this chapter were presented in separate papers by both authors at a
meeting of the American Psychological Association, August 1992,
Washington, DC.*

21

Mentoring and Diversity in Organizations:

Importance of Race and Gender in Work Relationships

David A. Thomas

R esearch is beginning to reveal the complexities of workplace relationships, both superior–subordinate and among peers (Ibarra, 1995; Kram & Isabella, 1985; Thomas & Higgins, 1996). Earlier studies have established that forming supportive relationships in the workplace is positively linked to both job satisfaction and career mobility (Podolny & Baron, 1997; Thomas & Kram, 1988). This finding has led to a new investigative path that examines the external properties and internal dynamics of developmental relationships. Although a range of types of developmental relationships have already been identified, much still remains to be determined about the impact of race and gender on whether, how, and why such relationships form and on how effective, beneficial, and satisfying they are for the parties involved. The studies detailed in this chapter represent an attempt to better understand the dynamics of race in the workplace, particularly with regard to cross-race relationships and career development.

LITERATURE REVIEW

Career and Psychological Support

A developmental relationship provides needed support for the enhancement of a person's career development and organizational experience. It is a relationship in which both parties have considerable knowledge of one another and from which both may potentially benefit (Kram, 1988; Thomas, 1990). Two types of support can emerge from such relationships: career support and psychosocial support. Career support provides performance feedback, coaching, protection, and challenging work assignments and also increases the junior person's share of organizational rewards and resources. Psychosocial support as provided by mentoring relationships in the workplace includes the development and maintenance of self-esteem and professional identity.

Such career-enhancing support can manifest itself in either sponsor–protégé or mentor–protégé relationships. Sponsor–protégé relationships provide exclusive career support for the junior member; mentor–protégé relationships offer both career and psychosocial

support. Although the parties in mentor–protégé relationships generally form closer and more intimate ties than those in sponsor–protégé relationships, both categories can be instrumental in providing the requisite support and resources for the junior party's career development
while simultaneously ensuring high-quality work results, increased
managerial influence, and expanded networks for the senior party.

Developmental Relationships

The analysis of race and gender influences on developmental relationships in the workplace can be conducted on two levels. One involves
an analysis of the external, structural properties of such relationships.
Such external measures include the number of relationships people
tend to have, the amount and type of support the relationships provide, the race and gender of sponsors or mentors and protégés, the location of sponsors and mentors in the organization, the amount of mutuality in the relationships, and the duration of the relationships. The
second approach investigates the effect of race and gender on the interpersonal dynamics involved in such relationships and examines individual approaches to and strategies for dealing with race relations
and racial diversity.

Both levels of study can be conducted through analysis of the experiences of black and white managers in both same-race and cross-
race relationships, all of whom share the same organizational setting.
Such an examination can help determine whether black people and
white people, both men and women, who share the same organizational context have significantly different experiences of participating in developmental relationships.

Early writing about race and careers postulated that ethnic groups,
specifically black people, in predominantly white organizations do
not form developmental relationships (Davis & Watson, 1982;
Karmel, 1984). Studies conducted throughout the 1980s have refuted
this conclusion, but many questions remain unanswered (Ford &
Wells, 1985; Malone, 1981; Murray, 1982). One study addressing these
concerns was conducted at WRL Corporation, a public utility in the
northeastern United States that employs more than 12,000 people.
Survey data were collected from 197 employees, a group that included 35 black men, 51 white men, 53 black women, and 58 white
women. The survey asked the respondents to identify the person or
people who had been most influential in their career development
and then rate each of those people in 11 support categories (Thomas,
1990). The researchers used the responses to assess the frequency and
relational properties of the relationships.

Race, Gender, and Relationship Formation. At WRL Corporation,
white men predominate in the organizational hierarchy in terms of
number and power, a fact that significantly affected the pattern of developmental relationships at the company. Not only did white men
have 91 percent of their developmental relationships with other white

men, but they also constituted the majority of mentors or sponsors for the black men, black women, and white women in the company. This situation is consistent with the proposition that the group with the most power in a given system will be most numerous as sponsors and mentors.

There was, however, substantial evidence that black people and women seek out relationships with members of their own race and gender groups. The number of relationships black people and women formed with people of their own gender and race far exceeded the proportional representation at WRL in any of those groups. For example, although black people make up only 10 percent of the WRL work force, black male protégés had 22 percent of their relationships with other black men. Similarly, 26 percent of the mentors and sponsors for black female protégés were black women.

Seventy percent of black people had at least one developmental relationship with a white employee at WRL. Overall, 34 percent of black men and women had both cross-race and same-race relationships, 36 percent had only cross-race relationships, and 14 percent had exclusively same-race relationships.

Number of Relationships. Although race had no major effect on the number of relationships that people formed, women tended on average to have more developmental relationships than did men. White and black employees did not differ significantly in the average number of developmental relationships reported (2.8 and 2.7, respectively). Black men and black women did differ from one another; black women reported an average of 3.0 relationships, compared with 2.4 for black men.

Location of Relationships. When forming developmental relationships at WRL, all protégés, regardless of race or gender, tended to follow a pattern of horizontal and vertical location: relationships were formed with direct supervisors located in the protégés' departments. Black people, however, tended to have more relationships that deviated from this pattern. Furthermore, a significant percentage of black same-race relationships were with sponsors or mentors who were not their direct supervisors and who were outside their department. This suggests that black employees crossed the typical hierarchical and departmental boundaries at WRL to establish developmental relationships with other black people.

Type of Support. Race had a significant effect on the amount of psychosocial support provided by developmental relationships. Same-race relationships provided considerably greater psychosocial support than did cross-race relationships. This finding reflects primarily the experiences of black men and women at WRL because so few of the cross-race relationships studied involved white protégés.

Whereas race did not have an effect on the amount of career support experienced, gender affected the amount of psychosocial and career support in relationships. Same-gender relationships provided more of both types of support than did cross-gender relationships.

Trust. Race did not seem to affect the amount of trust in cross-race superior–subordinate relationships, but it did have a significant effect in cross-gender relationships. Both cross-race and same-race relationships were found to involve comparable levels of mutuality, but same-gender relationships were experienced as having more mutuality than cross-gender relationships.

Duration of Relationships. Both race and gender influenced the duration of developmental relationships. Cross-race relationships did not last as long, on average, as same-race relationships, but cross-gender relationships tended to last longer than same-gender relationships.

Factors of Cross-Race Relationships

What factors account for the development of some cross-race relationships into the mentor–protégé category, whereas others remain sponsor–protégé? Do both parties in each relationship experience the relationship the same way? A study in which all members of 22 cross-race developmental relationships at WRL were interviewed addressed these and other questions in an attempt to better understand and define the specific influences of race on the interpersonal dynamics of workplace relations (Thomas, 1989, 1993).

The interaction of three factors was found to influence significantly the type of relationship that formed (mentor–protégé or sponsor–protégé) and the effectiveness of the relationship in providing either career or psychosocial support. The first factor was individual perspective on race and the corresponding strategy for dealing with race and racial issues; the second was the actual strategy implementation in the relationship; and the third was the complementarity of the strategies between the two parties involved.

Each person in the study had a strategy preference for managing racial diversity: denial and suppression or direct engagement. The denial-and-suppression strategy entailed a preference for not discussing race openly and for not acknowledging race as an important or influential aspect of relationships. In contrast, the direct-engagement strategy involved a preference for open discussion of racial diversity and its effect on relationships. These strategies correlated with two categories of racial perspective determined in previous research by Hraba and Hoiberg (1983): liberal assimilationism and pluralism. The former involves a belief that as racial subgroups develop the tastes and sensibilities of the majority, race ceases to be a salient dimension of difference (Park, 1950). Under this paradigm, "color blindness" becomes the ideal psychological state (Will, 1990). Because racial difference is viewed as negative and divisive, proponents of this view generally wish to keep the subject of race out of work relationships that they consider positive, finding that the need to acknowledge race in a relationship suggests that there is a problem of some kind. This attitude is congruent with the behavior of those preferring the denial-and-suppression strategy. Pluralism is a belief that people seek to maintain a positive sense of racial identity and connectedness while adopting aspects of the dominant culture that enable them to be effective (Greeley, 1974; Hraba & Hoiberg, 1983). Under the pluralist paradigm, similar to the direct-engagement preference, relationships are facilitated by acknowledging and valuing differences and by the commitment to work against inequalities (Jackson & Holvino, 1988). Examples of both strategies were found among black and white managers and in sponsor–protégé and mentor–protégé relationships.

MODEL OF RACIAL DYNAMICS IN CROSS-RACE DEVELOPMENTAL RELATIONSHIPS

The model developed in this research and depicted in Figure 21-1 focuses on the link between strategies for managing racial differences and the type of relationship that develops. When people join in a cross-race developmental relationship, their racial perspectives may or may not be "complementary"—a term I use to stress the idea of mutually supportive perspectives, as opposed to sameness. African Americans and white Americans arrive at their perspectives out of different racial experiences and therefore may agree on behavioral approaches to cross-racial encounters while having different reasons for their choices. In complementary relationships the parties' racial

Figure 21-1

Racial Dynamics in Cross-Race Developmental Relationships

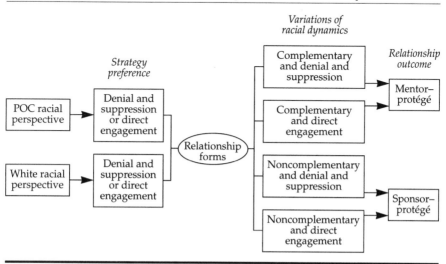

SOURCE: Reprinted from "Racial Dynamics in Cross-Race Developmental Relationships," by David A. Thomas, published in *Administrative Science Quarterly, 38*(2), by permission of *Administrative Science Quarterly.* Copyright © 1993 Cornell University.

NOTE: POC = person of color.

perspectives are mutually supportive, and they prefer the same strategy for managing racial difference. In noncomplementary relationships, the parties have different strategy preferences.

Over time, a recurrent pattern or strategy of responding to race-related aspects of the parties' individual racial experiences and broader race-related dynamics develops. The pattern constitutes a response of either open engagement or a reticence and inhibition that leads to denial and suppression of race-related data in the relationship. The model indicates four possible variations of racial dynamics: (1) complementary racial perspectives and use of the denial-and-suppression strategy, (2) complementary racial perspectives and use of the direct-engagement strategy, (3) noncomplementary racial perspectives and use of the denial-and-suppression strategy, and (4) noncomplementary racial perspectives and direct engagement of race-related issues.

Cross-race relationships are most likely to become mentor–protégé relationships when the parties have complementary racial perspectives and, therefore, similar strategy preferences. Each party is then engaged in a relationship that attends to racial diversity in a manner consistent with his or her preference. The result is that neither party experiences race as a factor that inhibits the development of the relationship and its ability to provide psychosocial support. Noncomplementary relationships can become only sponsor–protégé relationships, in part because the party for whom the enacted strategy is not preferred will feel race is an obstacle to developing a close personal bond.

Eight of the African American protégés interviewed preferred to use the denial-and-suppression strategy in their cross-race developmental relationships. They all found that race had little impact on their relationship, noticed no negative effect of race, did not feel that their mentors or sponsors were prejudiced, and did not feel that the lack of discussion of race was a deficit in the relationship. All of the protégés in this category lacked a strong African American support network. Six of the eight relationships were of the mentor–protégé type. The other two were sponsor–protégé type relationships that provided little psychosocial support.

Fourteen of the white mentors and sponsors preferred the denial-and-suppression strategy. Like the African Americans, they did not feel that race had a significant impact on the relationship with their protégé and did not feel that the lack of discussion about race was a negative factor in the relationship. They viewed race as inconsequential to the dynamics of the relationship and often claimed not to "see" race, observing that race was never a problem between the two parties. The denial-and-suppression preference often was verbalized in the form of stories about others' prejudices as contrasted with the interviewee's personal lack of racial bias. None of the members of this group acknowledged any form of institutional bias, although many spoke of having confronted people in the organization who had made overtly racist comments. Like their African American counterparts, white workers preferring the denial-and-suppression strategy held views similar to the liberal assimilationist perspective of race relations.

Fourteen of the 22 African American protégés demonstrated a preference for the direct-engagement strategy. These employees embraced their racial identity as an integral part of their personal and professional identities and made a conscious effort to develop working relationships with both white and black mentors and sponsors. Most tended to form extensive support networks, including being active members of the organization's African American employee forum. Members of this group who were involved in direct-engagement relationships experienced racial diversity as a positive aspect of the relationship and saw the openness about race and issues of racial diversity as an enhancement of the tie between themselves and their white mentor or sponsor. In contrast, direct-engagement African Americans involved in relationships in which denial and suppression was the implemented strategy found the inability to discuss issues of race to be a limiting factor and a deficit.

White sponsors and mentors who preferred the direct-engagement strategy also found the open discussion of race and race issues to be a positive influence on their cross-race relationships. Several common themes emerged regarding their experience of mentoring or sponsoring African American protégés: they emphasized a need to acknowledge the existence of race-based cultural and perspective differences in organizations, they believed that black people are at a disadvantage with white people because of institutional barriers and white prejudice, they discussed a need to be open about race and proactive about broaching the topic with their protégés, and they acknowledged that cross-race relationships often require considerably more effort from both parties to find common ground and to develop trust.

The model of racial dynamics in developmental relationships in Figure 21-1 suggests that complementarity mediates the relationship between the strategy for managing racial diversity and the type of relationship that develops—whether mentor–protégé or sponsor–protégé. Figure 21-2 illustrates the central proposition of this model and the degree of support found in the study. In cells I and IV, the white and African American parties have the same strategy preferences, and the strategies used are congruent with the preferences. Relationships in these cells are thus complementary, and they tend to become mentor–protégé relationships. In cells II and III, the parties have different strategy preferences and noncomplementary racial perspectives. Under these conditions the relationship appears capable of becoming only a sponsor–protégé relationship, and denial and suppression is the strategy used. Seventeen of 22 relationships fit the model's predictions. Furthermore, none of the five relationships not fitting the model combined noncomplementarity with being a mentor–protégé dyad. Instead, all five were complementary sponsor-protégé relationships. This finding suggests that complementarity is a necessary but insufficient requirement for developing a mentor–

Figure 21-2

Relationship between White and African American Strategy Preferences and Type of Relationship that Develops

	White strategy preferences	
African American strategy preferences	Denial and suppression	Direct engagement
Denial and suppression	Denial and suppression (MPR) $N = 6$	Direct engagement (SPR) $N = 0$
Direct engagement	Denial and suppression (SPR) $N = 6$	Direct engagement (MPR) $N = 5$

SOURCE: Reprinted from "Racial Dynamics in Cross-Race Developmental Relationships," by David A. Thomas, published in *Administrative Science Quarterly, 38(2)*, by permission of *Administrative Science Quarterly.* Copyright © 1993 Cornell University.

NOTE: MPR = mentor–protégé relationship; SPR = sponsor–protégé relationship; N = number of relationships from the study that fit the model's prediction.

protégé relationship. Interestingly, no relationships were found involving a white person whose strategy preference was direct engagement and an African American whose preference was denial and suppression. Therefore, the proposed dynamics of cell II are speculative.

IMPLICATIONS

One important finding was that in all eight of the direct-engagement relationships, the involved parties held complementary views of race relations. No noncomplementary direct-engagement relationships were found. Of the eight complementary direct-engagement relationships, five were mentor–protégé and three were sponsor–protégé. In such relationships, open dialogue about race tends to lead to a greater understanding for both parties. For example, the white mentor or sponsor may gain a new perspective and feel for the power of racial group membership and identity, and the black protégé may come to understand that it is possible to have relationships with white people in which one can show one's "whole self." One consistent pattern in direct-engagement relationships was the proactive nature of the mentor's or sponsor's behavior, particularly as it related to active dialogue about race, including factoring race into discussions of protégé performance and development and also by helping the protégé cope with and neutralize racism in the organizational environment. In direct-engagement relationships, the senior party was consistently the first to broach the topic of race. The fact that some complementary direct-engagement and denial-and-suppression relationships did not develop into mentor–protégé relationships suggests that other influences may factor into the type of relationship that ultimately develops.

These findings suggest that there is no one best way for people to manage racial diversity. Rather, the racial perspectives of the parties are critical. Both direct-engagement and denial-and-suppression relationships exhibited the characteristics of a mentor–protégé relationship. This contradicts a widely held belief that for cross-race relationships to become mentor–protégé relationships, the parties have to be able to discuss issues of race and its influence on the relationship.

Because the strategies appear to have become basic assumptions in the relationships, it is difficult to make definitive claims about how a strategy is negotiated and adopted. There are, however, some clearly observed patterns that provide insights. The strategy chosen was always consistent with the preference of the senior party regardless of the race and gender of the mentor or sponsor and the protégé, reflecting the reality that cross-race developmental relations are embedded in and influenced by the culture of hierarchical group relations in the organization. Some mentors and sponsors said that they chose people to develop who shared their values and agendas, but the African American protégés in noncomplementary relationships consciously used a strategy that did not reflect their preference.

The in-depth exploration of cross-racial mentoring in the WRL Corporation yielded a rich set of findings about the structure and process of cross-race relationships. It also must be acknowledged that more studies of these aspects of relationships are necessary to determine how broadly applicable these results are. A few recent studies have provided some indication that they are generalizable. Ibarra (1995) examined racial influences on network structure and achieved results that support the basic patterns observed in the WRL study. Podolny and Baron (1997) provided data that support the finding that relationships between dissimilar people are likely to provide less psychosocial support than those involving demographically similar people.

Organizational demography constrains the set of employees available to mentor and sponsor junior people. Where the available group of mentors lacks racial and gender diversity, minorities are likely to find relationships with members of the majority. These relationships, however, may provide inadequate levels of psychosocial support and tend not to become close and personal. It is likely, therefore, that black and female employees will cross hierarchical and organizational boundaries to form relationships with similar others to gain psychosocial support and intimacy they need. But crossing these boundaries may not be without cost. Black and female workers may have to spend more time and resources searching out relationships. Furthermore, extra effort is required to maintain two distinct networks of work-related contacts. The cost is less time to devote to work, family, and other career development activities.

Organizations can help with this issue in several ways. One is to make diversifying the gender and racial composition of their management and senior professionals a high priority, in part because it increases the availability of a diverse pool of mentors. I also advocate that organizations support forums, such as employee affinity groups and local professional organizations, that address the needs of racial and gender minorities and facilitate their finding similar others with whom to connect. Managers of black and female employees frequently discourage participation in such groups. The managers are often put off by what they see as the separatism and advocacy of these groups. "Promising and talented individuals should have no need for such an affiliation," they reason. This attitude fails to recognize the benefits that can flow to both the employee and the organization because of such an affiliation. It increases the likelihood that the organization can compensate for deficiencies in the network of developmental relationships available, especially in terms of psychosocial support early in a person's career development.

That cross-race and cross-gender relationships provide less psychosocial support than do same-race and same-gender relationships has tremendous implications for the discussion dynamics and outcomes associated with personnel decisions. It is highly likely that when racial and gender minorities are discussed in personnel meetings, no one at the table will have an intimate relationship and comfort with the person. Jobs that have the most potential for enhancing an employee's career prospects are usually those that are high profile, involve high risk, and bring extra scrutiny on the employee and his or her advocates. In the discussions to make these personnel decisions, the lack of psychosocial connection can make a subtle difference that leads to a negative career outcome for racial or gender minorities. Lack of closeness in the relationships may mean that sponsors would have a lower ceiling for the type of risk they are willing to take on a protégé. It also may limit their ability to persuade others because they cannot provide the decision-making group with a sense of the candidate that allays their anxiety and doubts.

Finally, the research reported here can be used to educate managers about the challenges and complexities race and gender diversity present for developing an effective work force. I have used the findings of these studies in the design and development of mentoring programs, leadership training, orientation for new employees and diversity workshops. In these activities my aim is to increase the awareness of how race and gender influence the formation and unfolding of developmental relationships. It is important, for example, that people be aware of the fact that theirs may not be the only perspective on how best to treat and manage racial difference. Until they are presented with the model in Figure 21-1, people often are unaware of what their perspective is and that their values and behavior may be inconsistent.

CONCLUSION

Since the studies at WRL were conducted, changes in the organizational landscape of U.S. society only reinforce the importance of the findings. The pace at which the work force and client populations of services-providing organizations are diversifying is accelerating. Simultaneously, organizations are removing layers of management, and employment relationships are becoming less stable. This means that where people may once have depended on bureaucratic mechanisms, such as close supervision and stable long-term employment, out of which relationships grew to give the needed instrumental career and psychosocial support, they now will be even more dependent on their organization's abilities to promote the formation of developmental relationships. Increasing work force diversity only complicates this picture and perhaps makes employees from nondominant groups more vulnerable to losing out on this initial source of support.

Organizational and individual efforts to initiate and maintain cross-race and cross-gender developmental relationships offer a major benefit well worth the effort—opportunity to learn about diversity in the context of relationships. Organizations in which cross-race developmental relationships form easily and become sources of learning are more likely to be effective at using their internal diversity to meet client needs (Thomas & Ely, 1996).

REFERENCES

Davis, G., & Watson, G. (1982). *Black life in corporate America.* Garden City, NY: Doubleday.

Ford, D., & Wells, L., Jr. (1985). Upward mobility factors among black public administrators. *Centerboard: Journal of the Center for Human Relations, 3,* 33–48.

Greeley, A. M. (1974). *Ethnicity in the United States: A preliminary reconnaissance.* New York: John Wiley & Sons.

Hraba, J., & Hoiberg, E. (1983). Ideational origins of modern theories of ethnicity: Individual freedom vs. organizational growth. *Sociological Quarterly, 24,* 381–391.

Ibarra, H. (1995). Race, opportunity, and diversity of social circles in managerial networks. *Academy of Management Journal, 38*(3), 673–703.

Jackson, B., & Holvino, E. (1988). Working with multicultural organizations: Matching theory and practice. *Organizational Development Practitioner, 20*(3), 1–13.

Karmel, A. (1984, April). Why blacks still haven't made it on Wall Street. *American Lawyer,* p. 1.

Kram, K. E. (1988). *Mentoring at work* (2nd ed.). Lanham, MD: University Press of America.

Kram, K. E., & Isabella, L. (1985). Mentoring alternatives: The role of peer relationships in career development. *Academy of Management Journal, 28*(1), 110–132.

Malone, B. (1981). *Relationship of black females' mentoring experiences and career satisfaction.* Unpublished doctoral dissertation, University of Cincinnati.

Murray, M. (1982). *The middle years of life of middle-class black men.* Unpublished manuscript, Psychology Department, University of Cincinnati.

Park, R. E. (1950). *Race and culture.* Glencoe, IL: Free Press.

Podolny J. M., & Baron, J. M. (1997). Resources and relationships: Social networks and mobility in the workplace. *American Sociological Review, 62,* 673–693.

Thomas, D. A. (1989). Mentoring and irrationality: The role of racial taboos. *Human Resource Management, 28*, 279–290.

Thomas, D. A. (1990). The impact of race on managers' experiences of developmental relationships. *Journal of Organizational Behavior, 11*, 479–492.

Thomas, D. A. (1993). Racial dynamics in cross-race developmental relationships. *Administrative Science Quarterly, 38*, 169–194.

Thomas, D. A., & Ely, R. J. (1996, September–October). Making differences matter: A new paradigm for managing diversity. *Harvard Business Review, 74*(5), 79–90.

Thomas, D. A., & Higgins, M. (1996). Mentoring and the boundaryless career: Lessons from the minority experience. In M. B. Arthur & D. M. Rousseau (Eds.), *The boundaryless career: A new employment principle for a new organizational era* (pp. 268–281). New York: Oxford University Press.

Thomas, D. A., & Kram, K. E. (1988). Promoting career-enhancing relationships in organizations: The role of the human resource professional. In M. London & E. Mone (Eds.), *Career growth and human resource strategies: The role of the human resource professional in employee development* (pp. 50–66).Westport, CT: Quorum Books.

Will, G. F. (1990, June 18). The journey up from guilt. *Newsweek*, p. 68.

Part VI

EMERGING ISSUES IN THE WORKPLACE

Many unresolved problems (for example, racism, ethnocentrism, sexism, and ableism) are embedded in policies and structures even as we move ahead with implementation of supports for truly diverse workplaces. Old issues intensify as new problems emerge. This is all part of emergent conditions. In this concluding section, we examine several areas that will generate increasing interest as organizational factors, societal interests and demands, and developing research and technology interact with changing population demographics. The first two chapters focus on supports and benefits, particularly the impact of women's roles as caretakers and employees. These chapters present research and theory on issues that are emerging into the discourse on diversity: balancing family concerns with work responsibilities. Many organizations respond to these concerns with benefit packages and leave policies. Not only has little effort gone into tracking the use of these benefits, but little has gone into determining workers' preferences for particular work and family supports by gender, race, or occupational characteristics. Later chapters present history and issues from the perspective of formerly subjugated voices rather than from powerful professional experts.

Lambert addresses organizational benefits and supports in chapter 22. About 600 employees of a manufacturing company responded to questionnaires seeking answers regarding benefits use: how use varied by gender, race, and other demographics and what personal and occupational factors explained workers' use of benefits. Differences were found in use by gender, race, and income. The research supports further inquiry into workplace supports that looks at ethnic and low-skilled employees' satisfaction and use as well as at gender differences.

Rooney investigates employed women's concerns and their perception of how these affect job performance. The fit between employee assistance program (EAP) priorities and employed women's perceptions of priority concerns also are examined in chapter 23. Rooney looks at the social roles and contexts of employed women, particularly women of color. These roles and contexts constantly place women in tension with work responsibilities. This qualitative study identified time and work versus family tensions as issues of greatest concern. However, EAPs ranked substance abuse and mental health as women's greatest concerns. Also, lack of personal time was perceived by the professionals as evidence of low self-esteem, whereas the women considered this a consequence of their multiple roles. Some of the discrepancy between the perceptions of the employed women and those of the professionals can be attributed to differences in perspective and interpretation of events. These differences also underscore the need to take special care to provide women ample opportunity to articulate their concerns and the need for professionals to be aware of their own assumptions and paradigms in encoding what they hear.

Much time and energy has been devoted to the idea of entrepreneurship in general and, more particularly, entrepreneurship among various people of color. African American entrepreneurship has been strongly affected by access to economic means for developing businesses and opportunities as well as economic reality. Herbert deconstructs the notion of entrepreneurship as beyond the reach of African Americans in chapter 24. In fact, entrepreneurship played a significant role in the historical records of African Americans' experience in the United States. Accounts of this entrepreneurship have been lost to history because the dominant group shaped a hegemonic history in its own image. Herbert relates this lost history and then examines current statistics and status of entrepreneurship among African Americans as we move into the 21st century. The real issue, he argues, is how decisions regarding social, educational, and public policy will support small business enterprises and family businesses in the future. Herbert suggests that human services is an area in which diversity issues can be addressed through networking and training for entrepreneurial enterprises. The notion of "kidpreneurs" who learn skills for developing a business can be useful in providing children useful skills to overcome poverty. The benefits in implementing these ideas are far reaching.

Schiele extends this concern for self-help among African Americans and people of color in chapter 25. He argues that the concept of workplace diversity should be extended to include traditional philosophical assumptions of people of African descent (that is, the Afrocentric paradigm) and other people of color and that recommendations for innovation in organizational structure and behavior to support diversity can be postulated from this perspective. He first elucidates the Afrocentric paradigm's assumptions about human beings and then applies them to demonstrate how the structure of the workplace can be altered to elicit positive organizational potential. His argument that diversity can be enhanced if people of color are encouraged to initiate self-help activities is predicated on beliefs in collective identity and spirituality and on beliefs that emotions and reason explain behavior. Schiele argues that using paradigms derived from cultural systems of people of color in general and African Americans specifically relieves cultural oppression through challenging the Eurocentric hegemony and by the affirmation of the "other" cultural values in emerging theory.

   In the 21st century, managers will universally face a variety of new issues. One is how to work with culturally diverse and other populations in the workplace without reducing them to a single dimension. In chapter 26, See examines some of the complex problems experienced by Africans and Asians in U.S. workplaces. Unfortunately, there are no universal theories or criteria available for managing diversity, largely because of the lack of investigation by social scientists until very recently. The chapter concludes with African and Asian immigrants articulating less-than-positive experiences they encountered at work sites. See offers recommendations for humanizing the workplace and celebrating differences.

   In chapter 27, Hong looks at Asian American women in the workplace and the particular issues they encounter. Three problems that can occur in the workplace when the "other" is unfamiliar are (1) stereotypic images, (2) mismatched psychological contracts, and (3) discriminatory treatment. Hong uses a vignette of a Chinese woman passed over for promotion that illustrates all three problems: (1) the stereotypic thinking her superiors used in evaluating her performance, (2) the behaviors she engaged in with the expectation of some reward or recognition versus the ways in which rewards and recognition were actually achieved, and (3) the ways in which the informal systems operated around her with no recognition of her absence. Managers can argue that these subtle issues occur largely because of lack of knowledge that could have modified the stereotypes on which these behaviors were based. The author calls for joint approaches in which both managers and employees are active in understanding the perspective of the other. In this way, the social, cultural, and historical contexts of both parties in an ongoing interaction are present. These ongoing interactions provide social and historical roots for interdependent relationships for the marginalized party as well as for the dominant member of the dyad. This approach can be used for addressing embedded stereotypes of ethnic groups and subgroups.

   Part VI concludes with a macro-level illustration of social oppression of a marginalized group when the hegemony approaches social issues from a binary construction of reality. Differences are perceived as opposites in Western thought as a result of a basic assumption of a singular, logical order in basic truth (Sands & Nuccio, 1992). Thus, if Western medicine, based on the scientific method for developing knowledge, is a valid treatment system, then native healing, based on a different approach to knowledge development, is not valid. This is the situation Ka'opua presents in chapter 28. That chapter examines the cultural clash between native healing and allopathic (Western) medicine in a climate in which Western culture reinforced the hegemony of Western medicine. Native healing was outlawed in Hawaii when the lack of immunity to Western infections introduced by colonists resulted in a high death rate; however, despite allopathic approaches to treatment of Native Hawaiians, their health statistics remain serious. Ka'opua describes barriers to developing culturally compatible models of practice and pluralistic systems of care for a vulnerable population. This chapter describes the deeply embedded cultural and structural factors that strongly support the present hegemony and illustrates a need for serious discourse about system-level change and the more equitable sharing of power with populations whose voices continue to be suppressed in policy and planning.

REFERENCE

Sands, K., & Nuccio, R. G. (1992). Postmodern feminist theory and social work. *Social Work, 37,* 489–494.

22 Workers' Use of Supportive Workplace Policies:

Variations by Gender, Race, and Class-Related Characteristics

Susan J. Lambert

There is growing recognition in the workplace that many employees find it difficult to balance their work and personal roles. There also is increasing awareness that the labor market is changing, with larger proportions of women and people of color making up the work force. Organizations have tended to tackle work and family concerns separately from work force diversity issues; employers often have separate work and family and diversity specialists and programs. But the policy initiatives in these areas often have a common goal—to recognize and respond to individual differences in a way that allows workers to contribute to the organization in unique and productive ways. Introducing a diversity perspective into work and family efforts is likely to facilitate the accomplishment of this goal by helping ensure that work and family programs meet the needs of the composite of workers employed at an organization; workers' preferences for particular work and family supports are likely to vary with their gender, race, and occupational characteristics.

Human resources professionals have long recognized the need to take variations in preference into account when designing workplace programs and policies. Many of them have adopted a constituency approach to human resources management based on the idea that the organization comprises different types of stakeholders who may require different things from it to be both healthy and productive (Tsui & Milkovich, 1987). Yet, assessments of preferences for certain programs and policies are rarely followed by assessments of actual use. This is especially true in the work and family field, in which few data exist as to who actually uses available benefits. The Families and Work Institute's (1993) study of Johnson & Johnson details how participation rates for a variety of workplace supports vary with workers' personal characteristics, but this study looked only at use during a one-year period. Beyond this study, little systematic data exist that track workers' use of different types of policies and programs. Knowing what types of supports different kinds of people use is important information for those striving to tailor programs and policies to meet the needs of a diverse work force.

In this chapter, data from a company with an abundance of work-place supports are used to examine how benefit use varies by work-ers' gender-, race-, and class-related personal and occupational characteristics. Implications for both research and practice are discussed.

DEFINING SUPPORTIVE WORKPLACE POLICIES

Family-responsive policies are usually equated with employer sup-ports for child care, but this definition increasingly is seen as too nar-row. Bailyn (1993) argued that being responsive means devising ways in which people can work without sacrificing their commitments not only to their families but also to their communities. Similarly, Kossek (1989, 1990) advocates providing supports that workers can dip into as their needs and interests change across their life cycle. In keeping with the trend toward expanding definitions of what makes a com-pany responsive, this study focuses on three types of supports: for dependents, for community, and for self.

As described in detail in the "Method" section, supports for chil-dren include onsite child care, a summer day camp, in-home sick-child care, tutoring for school-aged children, and scholarships for post–high school education. Supports for elderly or ill family mem-bers include in-home temporary dependent care and a resource and referral service. Community supports consist of a matching-gifts pro-gram and grants to groups in which workers are actively involved. Supports for workers themselves include reimbursement for tuition, wellness massages, and an on-site fitness center. One characteristic of all of these is that workers have the discretion to use them; participa-tion is not mandatory for anyone.

VARIATIONS IN BENEFIT USE

Many reasons exist for suspecting that proportionately more women than men will use supportive workplace policies when available. To-day's women are characterized as the "sandwich generation," simul-taneously caring for both children and parents. On average, working women continue to do more housework and child care than working men and often are the primary caregivers of ailing or elderly adult relatives (Berardo, Shehan, & Leslie, 1987; England, Levit, & Linsk, 1990; Galinsky, Bond, & Friedman, 1993). Thus, it is not surprising that women find supports for dependents especially attractive (Gold-berg, Greenberger, Koch-Jones, O'Neil, & Hamill, 1989). Previous re-search documents women's disproportionate representation among users of parental-leave policies (Bond, Galinsky, Lord, Staines, & Brown, 1991) and onsite child care (see Berkeley Planning Associates, 1989, and Miller, 1984, for a review of this research).

Indeed, a primary rationale for implementing family-responsive policies in the workplace is to provide some assistance to the increas-ing proportion of women with children who work. Yet, as Friedman (1991) observed, "very little is known about how men and women respond to different corporate initiatives" (p. 95). Although women may use more supports for dependents than men do, proportionately more men than women may use other kinds of supports. For example, because working women's combined family and paid labor consumes greater time than is true of men, men may have more time to spare for recreational and educational activities. Comparing the participation of men and women across supports for dependents, community, and self should provide new insight into how gender roles help shape benefit use in the workplace.

The study of Johnson & Johnson suggested that advantaged workers are the greatest users of supportive workplace policies. Drawing on self-reported data of use during the past year, the study found that employees from higher-income households were more likely to have used all of Johnson & Johnson's family-responsive policies, with the one exception that use of flexible work schedules did not vary by income (Families and Work Institute, 1993). The authors of this study suggested that limited income restricts workers' access to benefits, perhaps because workers are required to share the cost for some supports.

Affordability alone, however, is unlikely to account for variations in the use of benefits by disparate income groups. Differences in income often reflect differences in class, which may shape preferences for types of benefits. Fussell (1983) described the pervasive influence of class on everyday choices and lifestyles. Higher-status workers, such as professionals and managers, may be more likely than lower-status workers, such as operatives and laborers, to use those benefits conveying some prestige. For example, higher-status workers may be more likely than lower-status workers to use an onsite fitness center because it is consistent with the healthy image they may like to portray, even though no fee is charged for participation.

Status also may be related to benefit use because of differences in corresponding job conditions. Most notably, higher-status workers are likely to have more flexible jobs and thus may be better able to take advantage of programs operating at the work site, such as an onsite fitness center. Thus, to assess the extent to which use of benefits favors more advantaged workers, both income and occupational status must be examined.

Moreover, no investigation of variations in benefit use would be complete without considering workers' race and ethnicity; people of color are often among the least advantaged in the workplace (Bell, 1990). Currently, information on benefit use by workers of different races is even rarer than information on variations by gender. Use of supports for dependents, community, and self is likely to depend not only on workers' occupational conditions but also on the extent to which workers from different cultural backgrounds give priority to their families, the larger community, and their own needs for education and recreation (Bell, 1990; Cervantes, 1992; Cervantes & Castro, 1985). This study provides a unique opportunity to investigate how benefit use is related to workers' race, because the sample contains a large proportion of African American, Hispanic, and white workers.

According to the constituency approach to human resources management, it is important to look at how benefit use varies with workers' gender, race, income, and occupational status to get a good sense
of what users "look like." These occupational and personal characteristics are, however, often associated with one another; for example, managers and professionals at the company studied tend to be
white, male, and well paid. Therefore, it also is useful to know which
occupational and personal characteristics are driving different patterns of benefit use, that is, to identify the unique contribution each
makes in explaining the amount and types of benefits workers use.

This study asked two research questions: (1) How does use of supports for dependents, community, and self vary by gender, race, family income, and occupational status? Are women and more-advan-
taged workers overrepresented among the users of workplace
supports? (2) What is the unique contribution of these personal and
occupational characteristics in explaining workers' use of benefits?

METHOD

Study Site and Research Design

The data for this study were collected at Fel-Pro, Inc., an engine-
gasket manufacturing firm in Skokie, Illinois. The family-owned company employs about 2,000 workers; none are unionized. Fel-Pro was
recently named one of the 10 best companies to work for in America
(Levering & Moskowitz, 1993). Fel-Pro employees represent a wide
range of occupations, from assembly-line workers and clerical workers to engineers and managers. The data for this chapter come from
self-administered questionnaires and administrative records. Early
interviews with workers were used to frame the survey, and follow-
up interviews with 30 workers were conducted to explore some of the
survey findings in more depth.

Sample Selection and Response Bias

Questionnaires were distributed to a random sample of 884 Fel-Pro
employees: 667 workers (424 blue-collar workers and 243 white-collar
workers) and 217 supervisors. Nonrespondents were contacted by
telephone and mail to encourage their participation. All respondents
were paid $10 for returning their completed questionnaires; 10 were
randomly chosen to receive a $50 gift certificate from a local grocery
store. These efforts yielded an overall response rate of 67.9 percent
($N = 599$).[1]

To specify the nature of the response bias in the data, we gathered
organizational data on all those selected into the sample, both nonrespondents and respondents. Analyses reveal that respondents and

---

[1]For the purposes of this chapter, respondents were dropped from the analysis if
they were working less than full-time or their questionnaires had large amounts of
missing information, leaving a final sample of 581 respondents.

nonrespondents did not vary in terms of supervisor ratings, disciplinary actions, absenteeism, or job tenure; this is true for both office and factory workers.

The response rates are significantly ($p < 0.01$) different for blue-collar workers in the factory (51.4 percent), white-collar workers in the office (86.4 percent), and supervisors or managers (79.5 percent). Among office workers and supervisors or managers, the response rate does not vary significantly by race or gender. Among factory workers, the response rate for white men is 65.9 percent, whereas the response rates for African American and Hispanic men are only 44.9 percent and 39.4 percent, respectively. Among women working in the factory, Hispanic women have a relatively low response rate (45.7 percent) when compared with white women (64.7 percent) and African American women (68.2 percent). Thus, the external validity of the findings is limited by the fact that the data underrepresent the experiences of blue-collar workers, especially Hispanic men and women and African American men.

The sample selection bias introduced by these differences in response rate also may limit the internal validity of the results (Berk, 1983; Heckman, 1979). The instructions on the questionnaire informed workers that a major goal of the study was to document their experiences with Fel-Pro's fringe benefits. To the extent that response to the survey was related to workers' experiences with benefits, ordinary statistical procedures would not provide a representative picture of workers' experiences with Fel-Pro's benefits unless corrections were made for this response bias.

Analyses

Two techniques were used to adjust the statistics presented in this chapter for the sample selection bias resulting from nonresponse to the survey.[2] First, following procedures recommended by Braver and Bay (1992), a weighting technique was used to adjust the descriptive statistics presented; the weighting factor adjusts for the actual number of respondents so that tests of statistical significance remain unbiased. Second, a probit analysis using maximum likelihood estimation was conducted to construct a hazard rate of nonresponse to the survey; a function of this hazard rate was then included as an additional independent variable in regression analyses (Greene, 1988; Maddala, 1983).

When conducting the regression analyses, I assigned missing data the mean for the relevant independent variable, following procedures described by Cohen and Cohen (1983); for all variables, data are missing on fewer than 10 percent of the cases. As with the descriptive statistics, each case is weighted by the probability of being

---

[2]Readers are invited to contact the author of this chapter for details. Comparisons with administrative data indicate that the corrected data provide a more accurate assessment of benefit use than the uncorrected data would.

selected into the sample. Because of the severe problems that correlated independent variables can create with the estimation of regression coefficients, steps were taken to identify problems with multicollinearity that might render the regression coefficients unstable. The only problem found was that age was correlated with a number of other control variables (seniority and marital and parental status) that together created problematic multicollinearity. Thus, age was excluded from the analyses to yield stable regression estimates and because doing so did not change the substantive results. The highest correlation between the variables included in the reported regression equations was between marital status and family income ($r = 0.46$).

Measures

Benefit Use. The quality of the program, the amount workers have to pay to participate, and the length of time the program had been in operation are important factors in understanding workers' use of different programs and policies. Figure 22-1 describes the supports for dependents, community, and self that were investigated.

Figure 22-1

Supports for Dependents, Community, and Self

Supports for Children

Scholarship for a child—*introduced in 1962*
Employees with at least three years of service are eligible to apply for an academic scholarship for their children who are attending an accredited postsecondary school. Fel-Pro contributes up to $3,000 annually for up to four years with proof of satisfactory completion of each year of school.

Summer day camp for children—*introduced in 1973*
Children of employees are eligible to attend a day camp for nine weeks during the summer. The children must be between ages seven and 15. Transportation to and from the camp is provided by Fel-Pro for $15 per family. The camp programs are managed by trained counselors. About 178 children from various ethnic and economic backgrounds attend the camp each year. Children who once attended the camp often return as camp counselors when they are older.

Onsite child care center—*introduced in 1983*
Full-time employees with children between ages two and six are eligible to use the day care center located in its own building adjacent to Fel-Pro. The center can accommodate about 46 children, who are selected on the basis of employees' seniority. The cost of the day care center is $175 a week, of which employees are required to pay $70 a week. The day care center is staffed with certified teachers in child development, and the center offers a state-licensed kindergarten program.

Tutoring for a child—*introduced in 1983*
Fel-Pro has a contract with a learning center to provide diagnostic testing and individual tutoring to employees' children. Employees are asked to pay a small fee; Fel-Pro pays most of the cost.

(Continued on next page)

Figure 22-1 (continued)

Sick-child care—*introduced in 1988*

Professionally trained caregivers are available for up to five days per year per employee to take care of sick children when their parents have to go to work. The employee only pays $2 per hour, and Fel-Pro subsidizes the rest of the cost. Fel-Pro contracts with a social services agency to provide this service.

Supports for Elderly or Ill Family Members

Emergency care for an adult—*introduced in 1989*

Professionally trained caregivers are available for up to five days per year per employee to adults living in the home of a Fel-Pro employee. The employee is required to pay about $16 per day, which is 25 percent of the total cost.

Eldercare referral service—*introduced in 1990*

Employees who are helping care for an elderly family member can use the eldercare referral service at Fel-Pro to access information on programs in the community that can assist or care for older relatives. Workshops that feature experts who specialize in senior and eldercare issues are regularly provided to Fel-Pro employees as part of the eldercare referral service.

Supports for Community

Better-neighborhood fund—*introduced in 1976*

Fel-Pro makes donations to neighborhood organizations that help improve the quality of life for the communities in which employees live. Any employee actively involved in a community or neighborhood organization can submit to a standing committee of nine Fel-Pro employees a request for a donation (up to $1,500 a year). Community centers, youth clubs, sports teams, senior citizen programs, job training programs, and housing services have received funding.

Matching-gifts program—*introduced in 1982*

Fel-Pro matches dollar-for-dollar full-time employees' contributions to a variety of nonprofit organizations that are eligible under Section 501(c) of the Internal Revenue Service Code. Drug and alcohol treatment programs, food and shelter programs, and day care programs have received matching funds. Excluded are clubs, religious and political organizations, and lobbying groups. The maximum amount of matching contributions is $1,000 a year.

Supports for Self

Tuition reimbursement—*introduced in 1963*

All employees with at least three months of service are eligible for a 100 percent annual tuition refund up to $2,000 for undergraduate studies and up to $5,000 for graduate studies, provided that the courses have been completed with passing grades.

Onsite fitness center—*introduced in 1981*

All employees are eligible to join after they have completed a health screening that includes basic medical tests and have received approval from a physician. The fitness center offers employees a variety of overall fitness, shape-up, relaxation, and stress management programs.

Wellness massage—*introduced in 1990*

All employees who have joined the fitness program have regular access, by appointment, to a wellness body massage by a professional masseur or masseuse. Employees pay for this service themselves.

Fel-Pro provides a number of other benefits in addition to those contained in Figure 22-1, including counseling services and some targeted health promotion programs. Benefits were selected if they clearly fit into the categories of those supports chosen for examination: supports for dependents, community, and self. The target of some policies was unclear; for example, it was impossible to tell whether workers themselves went to counseling sessions or whether only their spouse or child did.

That workers had access to a larger number of supports is taken into consideration when measuring level of benefit use, a variable included in the regression analyses. Respondents indicated on the questionnaire whether they or anyone in their immediate family had ever used each of 20 programs or policies and, if so, whether they had used them in the past year. Level of benefit use is measured by summing the total number of the benefits respondents had used during their tenure at Fel-Pro ($M = 3.2$). Once adjusted for response bias, these self-reported data on program use compares well with statistics available from the company on program participation.

Independent Variables. Information on gender, race, and occupational status comes from organizational records; information on family income comes from the questionnaire.

A total of 38.3 percent of the sample are women. In terms of race, 48.6 percent are white, 29.7 percent are Hispanic, 15.9 percent are African American, and 5.6 are Asian American.

In presenting descriptive statistics, one variable is used to differentiate respondents' occupational status. It distinguishes among workers in management (managers or supervisors, 13.5 percent); high-status workers (professionals or craftspeople, 19.1 percent); middle-status workers (technicians or clerical staff, 12.8 percent); and lower-status workers (operatives or laborers, 54.6 percent). In the regression analyses, two dummy variables differentiate white-collar (39.2 percent) and blue-collar (60.8 percent) workers and managers or supervisors (16.0 percent) from lower-status workers (84.0 percent).

Family income includes the respondent's income from Fel-Pro and the income of a partner, when applicable. For descriptive purposes, respondents' family income was categorized along the following lines: 44.2 percent of respondents had incomes of $35,000 or below, 35.9 percent had family incomes between $35,000 and $60,000, and 18.9 percent had incomes above $60,000. For the multivariate analyses, income is a continuous variable (median = $45,000).

Control Variables. Both seniority and household composition are likely to help explain workers' use and appreciation of benefits beyond that explained by gender, race, family income, and occupational status; these variables are controlled in the regression analyses. Workers' seniority is measured with a continuous variable constructed from information gathered from organizational records ($M = 7.92$ years). Two dummy variables were created to capture whether respondents lived with a partner (70.3 percent) and whether they had any children (72.3 percent); this information came from the questionnaire.

RESULTS

How Use Varied

Contrary to common assumptions, the women did not use more supports for dependents than did men (Table 22-1). A total of 40.6 percent of men, compared with 44.7 percent of women, had used at least one support for a child, a difference that is not statistically significant. This lack of significance was not a result of the averaging of participation rates across individual benefits. There are only two significant differences ($p < 0.05$) in the use of supports for children by men and women: Significantly more women (33.1 percent) than men (25.2 percent) had used the summer day camp, whereas significantly more men (9.1 percent) than women (2.8 percent) had used sick-child

Table 22-1

Benefit Use by Personal and Occupational Characteristics (*N* = 581)

Characteristic	% Using One or More Supports for				Average No. of Benefits	SD
	Child	Adult	Community	Self		
Gender						
Men	40.6	17.8	36.5	48.5	3.22	2.65
Women	44.7	7.5*	38.8	41.8	3.19	2.35
Race						
White	40.0	14.7	39.3	53.1	3.42	3.42
Hispanic	48.7	14.5	36.0	40.3	3.19	3.19
African American	41.8	11.1	31.9	33.6	2.72	2.87
Asian American	26.0	10.9	39.1	47.3*	2.89	2.40
Family income						
≤$35,000	29.8	14.8	26.2	35.3	2.50	2.45
>$35,000 to $60,000	49.0	12.3	42.5	46.3	3.45	2.21
>$60,000	55.5*	11.5	57.2*	73.0*	4.57*	2.85
Occupational status						
Managers or supervisors	58.2	13.3	60.2	73.4	4.69	2.83
Professionals or craftspeople	45.1	16.3	40.5	55.2	3.55	2.30
Technicians or clerical staff	41.9	9.2	38.7	66.0	3.75	2.58
Operatives or laborers	37.0*	14.3	30.0*	30.7*	2.59*	2.29

NOTE: Levels of significance pertain to differences among respondents with different characteristics; that is, comparisons should be made by looking down columns (for example, between men and women who used supports for children or among workers of different races who used supports for adults).

*$p ≤ .01$.

care. Moreover, proportionately more men than women had used supports for elderly or ill family members: 17.8 percent of men, compared with only 7.5 percent of women, reported using either emergency in-home care or the resource and referral service ($p < 0.01$).

Men and women do not vary significantly in their use of supports for community or self. Contrary to the idea that men's lower total workload may enable them to take better advantage of supports for self, the difference in the proportion of men (48.5 percent) and women (41.8 percent) using supports for oneself is not statistically significant, even though the women reported doing about 11 more hours of family work per week than did the men ($p < 0.01$). When looking at the use of individual benefits, however, significantly more men (25.2 percent) than women (16.0 percent) had received a tuition reimbursement ($p < 0.05$).

Workers' overall use of supports for children, adults, and community does not vary significantly by race. There are, however, some significant differences in the use of some individual policies and programs. A total of 15.8 percent of Hispanic workers, followed by 10.8 percent of Asian American workers, 10.0 percent of African American workers, and 8.9 percent of white workers secured tutoring for a child ($p < 0.05$). Similarly, 35.2 percent of Hispanic workers as compared with 29.3 percent of African American workers, 25.8 percent of white workers, and 10.7 percent of Asian American workers had sent at least one child to the summer day camp ($p < 0.05$). Thus, the data suggest that proportionately more Hispanic workers than other workers had used some of the supports for children.

Use of supports for self is more strongly related to workers' race than is true of the other types of supports, with proportionately more white workers than other workers using these supports. A total of 53.1 percent of white workers as compared to 47.3 percent of Asian American workers, 40.3 percent of Hispanic workers, and 33.6 percent of African American workers had used one or more supports for education or recreation. Most notably, significantly ($p < 0.05$) more white workers (29.4 percent) than workers of other races (12.6 percent for Hispanics and 13.5 percent for African Americans) received a tuition reimbursement, although the proportion of Asian American workers who received a tuition reimbursement was comparable to that of white workers (24.6 percent). The only exception to the pattern of white workers using the most supports for self is that significantly ($p < 0.05$, based on paired comparison tests of significance) more Asian American workers (21.1 percent) than other workers had received a wellness massage (11.1 percent of white workers, 4.8 percent of Hispanic workers, and 4.7 percent of African American workers). Workplace massage is a good example of how participation rates for the work force as a whole can obscure the fact that a benefit may be meeting the needs and preferences of a relatively small group of workers, an idea consistent with both the constituency approach to human resources management and a valuing of diversity in the work force. Overall, however, the data suggest that,

compared with their white coworkers, workers of other races and ethnicities made good use of supports for their children but made limited
use of supports for themselves.

The data on occupational status and family income suggest that
workers with more resources use more benefits. The higher workers'
income and status is, the greater is their overall use of supports for
children, community, and self.[3] A few notable exceptions, however,
can be discerned from looking at the use of particular supports.
Workers shared some of the cost for use of the child care center, summer day camp, sick-child care, tutoring, adult emergency care, matching gifts program, and workplace massage. For the majority of the
supports, the higher the workers' family income, the greater the
workers' use; these relationships suggest that higher-income workers can take better advantage of supports requiring a fee. This relationship does not hold, however, when looking at the use of emergency care for children or adults. The relationship between family
income and use of sick-child care is not significant, and the relationship between family income and use of adult emergency care is negative: the lower the workers' income, the greater their use. Thus,
these findings run counter to the idea that lower-income workers can
ill afford to use supports requiring a fee. Instead, these results suggest that sometimes lower-income workers can ill afford not to use a
benefit; workers who used emergency dependent care were those
who could least afford to take time off from work. The fact that, with
the few exceptions noted earlier, workers with higher family incomes used all the supports more, not just those requiring fees, suggests that factors other than money are important in helping explain
the use of workplace supports.

The data suggest that occupational status is one of those other factors. A greater proportion of workers with high occupational status
used supports for self and community than did workers with lower
occupational status. For example, 60.2 percent of managers and supervisors, compared with 30.0 percent of operatives and laborers,
used one or more support for community; 73.4 percent of managers
and supervisors, as compared with 30.7 percent of operatives and laborers, used one or more supports for self.

How Characteristics Explained Use

Multivariate analyses provide better insight into the possibility that
occupational status can help account for workers' benefit use beyond
what can be accounted for by income and other personal and occupational characteristics. The data suggest that women, workers with children age five or younger, and those who had been with the company
for some time were more likely to have used supports for children
(Table 22-2). The only significant factor explaining use of supports for

---

[3]Similar variations were found when looking at the relationship between benefit use
and respondents' educational attainment.

Table 22-2
Relationship between Personal and Occupational Characteristics and Benefit Use (N = 581)

Characteristic	Supports for Children		Supports for Elderly or Ill		Supports for Community		Supports for Self		Total No. of Benefits	
	b	SE	b	SE	b	SE	b	SE	b	SE
Gender (women = 1)	.445*	.216	-.885**	.322	.229	.213	-.349	.212	.188	.234
African American	.521	.309	-.177	.479	.239	.320	.328	.310	.224	.346
Hispanic	.502	.319	-.039	.430	.343	.325	.662*	.323	.395	.338
Supervisor	.405	.289	.149	.396	.450	.285	.671*	.313	.636*	.276
Blue-collar worker	-.442	.342	.125	.462	-.468	.345	-.884**	.344	-.978**	.355
Family income	.0004	.0006	-.0001	.0009	.0005	.0006	.0008	.0006	-.0004	.0006
Control variables										
Seniority	.112**	.016	.022	.019	.083**	.015	.046**	.015	.118**	.015
Has partner	.314	.268	.120	.370	.429	.276	-.067	.269	.066	.290
Has (young) child[a]	.746**	.211	-.494	.332	.186	.252	-.271	.248	.824**	.268
Selection term	.563	.725	.291	.977	-.633	.745	-1.65*	.745	-.564	.902
Constant	-2.38**	.428	-1.13*	.436	-1.53**	.411	.74	.40	2.21**	.434
Model chi-square	105.35**		19.08*		88.19**		113.34**		NA	
% predicted correctly (or R²)	69.22		86.83		67.15		70.46		(23.1)	

NOTES: Logistic regression was used to estimate the models pertaining to the types of benefit use; ordinary least-squares regression was used to estimate the model pertaining to the total number of different benefits workers had used. All results are adjusted for sample selection bias using techniques described in the "Method" section. NA = not applicable.

[a] A dichotomous variable indicating whether respondents had a child five years or younger was used in the model pertaining to use of supports for children; in all other analyses a dichotomous variable distinguishes workers who had children from those who had none.

*p ≤ .05. **p ≤ .01.

adults is gender, with men being more likely than women to use supports for an elderly or ill relative. Only seniority emerged significant in explaining workers' use of supports for community. Thus, these findings suggest that personal characteristics are more strongly associated with use of supports for children, adults, and community than are occupational conditions.

Occupational conditions, however, help explain workers' use of supports for self as well as the total number of benefits workers had used during their tenure at Fel-Pro. Supervisors and white-collar workers were more likely than other workers to have used supports for self and to have used a greater number of benefits, even after taking into consideration other differences in their personal and occupational characteristics. Note, however, that income is unrelated to the type and level of benefit use once these other personal and occupational characteristics have been controlled, suggesting that being advantaged in the workplace is not a matter of money.

It is possible that the causal order between occupational status and use of supports for self is the reverse of the one posited here. For example, it is likely that securing supports for education later results in blue-collar workers becoming white-collar workers and lower-level workers moving into managerial positions. Although there is no way to empirically assess the causal direction between occupational status and benefit use with the current data, looking at use of benefits during the current year helps avoid such problems by relating current benefit use to current occupational status. Bivariate and multivariate analyses incorporating measures of benefit use during the past year yielded similar differences in the use of benefits by blue- and white-collar workers and by supervisors and lower-level workers. Thus, the findings provide support for the idea that workers advantaged in terms of occupational status use more benefits than other workers.

DISCUSSION AND CONCLUSION

This study builds on a diversity perspective to investigate variations in the use of workplace supports for dependents, community, and self by workers who differ in gender-, race-, and class-related personal and occupational conditions. Overall, the data suggest that the company studied at least workers' use of particular types of programs is systematically related to their personal and occupational characteristics. Thus, individual differences must be taken into account if patterns of overall benefit use are to be understood.

Some of the findings run counter to common perceptions of who uses what benefits. The data support the common belief that women benefit more than men from workplace supports only when the focus is limited to supports for children. Proportionately more women than men used the summer day camp and, although not statistically significant, a higher percentage of women used the onsite child care center. The regression analyses indicate that women were overrepresented among users of supports for children in general once other occupational and personal characteristics were controlled. But men and women differed little in their use of other supports.

In fact, one interesting finding is that a greater proportion of men than women had used supports for elderly or ill family members even after controlling for differences in occupational and personal characteristics. Most notably, a high proportion of male operatives and laborers had used emergency care for an adult during the three years this program had been in operation. Subsequent analyses revealed that most of these men were without partners. Thus, emergency care for an adult is of special help to men in lower-status jobs who can least afford to take time off from work and who cannot depend on a wife to share caregiving. This finding substantiates Starrels's (1992) claim that more information is needed on men's support for elder care, because men are often more involved in caring for parents than in caring for children.

Variations in the use of different types of supports by race are both encouraging and worrisome. The good news is that there were few significant differences among workers of different races in terms of their use of supports for children. In fact, significantly more Hispanic workers than other workers had secured tutoring for a child. The utilization rates of both Hispanic and African American workers meet or exceed those of white workers for all supports for children except securing a scholarship for a child. The disquieting news is that significantly fewer Hispanic and African American workers than white and Asian American workers had used supports for self, including the onsite fitness center and tuition reimbursement. Thus, the data suggest that Hispanic and African American workers were able to make good use of supports for their children but that barriers may have existed to limit their use of supports important to their own health and career advancement. Similarly, the use of workplace supports may be class biased; bivariate analyses indicated that the greater the workers' family income and the higher their occupational status, the greater was the workers' use of supports for children, community, and self.

Thus, the results raise concerns that inequities exist in the distribution of family-responsive policies in this company, but where should these concerns reside? Regression analyses examining benefit use suggest that personal characteristics (such as gender, parental status, and seniority) can best account for differences in workers' use of supports for children, adults, and community. On the other hand, occupational status plays a large role in explaining variations in workers' use of supports for self and overall use of benefits beyond that explained by workers' personal characteristics. That race was not related to workers' use of supports for self once occupational conditions were controlled suggests that nonwhite workers' lower use of these supports resulted from their lower representation in white-collar jobs and supervisory positions. Thus, the results suggest that promoting workers' use of benefits is not just a matter of identifying their personal needs but is also a matter of recognizing and perhaps overcoming class-based preferences, inadequate job designs, and barriers to organizational advancement.

These findings hold implications for both research and practice. In terms of research, devising evaluations to assess the full effects of a program is facilitated the more one knows about its users. In the current study, the surprising finding that more men than women used emergency dependent care suggests new questions about the role these supports play in the lives of men. Similarly, the finding that workers advantaged in occupational status used the greatest number of benefits raises questions about how occupational conditions may help explain different patterns of benefit use beyond that explained by differences in income—perhaps by shaping workers' preferences themselves, by regulating workers' access to needed supports, or both. In general, knowing who uses which benefits is likely to suggest questions for study that might never be asked if patterns of program use are assumed but not assessed.

Moreover, data on actual use may provide more accurate predictions of future use than is true of predictions made on the basis of workers' assessments of their likely future behavior; child care consultants have learned that a good proportion of workers who say they would use onsite child care or emergency dependent care do not do so when it is offered. At the least, data on actual use would be an important supplement to the usual data human resources professionals use to construct benefit plans. If studies of benefit use in other organizations show similar patterns, then it may be possible to improve the targeting of benefit packages.

In terms of practice, the study suggests that a diversity perspective can add value to work and family programs by taking advantage of the opportunity such programs present to attend to the needs of historically neglected organizational constituencies such as people of color and women. Moreover, the logic underlying the study reported here reflects the trend toward extending definitions of organizational responsiveness beyond the provision of child care and suggests a change in the way family-responsive policies are rolled out in most organizations. Usually, family-responsive policies are introduced as a separate set of policies for helping workers balance work and family responsibilities. A constituency view of human resources management suggests that it be made clear that the organization is providing something for everyone. Keeping the work force informed of the use of supports that workers may not deem a fringe benefit, let alone a family-friendly policy such as tuition reimbursement, may help minimize the risk that workers will perceive inequities in the distribution of organizational resources. Providing information on use over time instead of the yearly participation rates commonly reported is likely to correct conceptions that only a small group of workers benefit from the organization's policies and programs.

It would be wise to consider this a "best-practices" case study. Few companies, especially those employing such a large proportion of people of color and low-skilled workers, provide so many supports.

Patterns of benefit use are likely to depend on the organizational context in which workplace supports are implemented, a possibility that could not be tested with data from one company.

REFERENCES

Bailyn, L. (1993). *Breaking the mold: Women, men and time in the new corporate world.* New York: Free Press.

Bell, E. L. (1990). The bicultural life experience of career-oriented black women. *Journal of Organizational Behavior, 11,* 459–477.

Berardo, D., Shehan, C., & Leslie, G. (1987). A residue of tradition: Jobs, careers, and spouses' time in housework. *Journal of Marriage and the Family, 49,* 381–390.

Berk, R. A. (1983). An introduction to sample selection bias in sociological data. *American Sociological Review, 48,* 386–398.

Berkeley Planning Associates. (1989). *Employer-supported child care: Measuring and understanding its impacts on the workplace* (Report prepared for the U.S. Department of Labor, Office of Strategic Planning and Policy Development). Washington, DC: Author.

Bond, J., Galinsky, E., Lord, M., Staines, G., & Brown, K. (1991). *Beyond the parental leave debate: The impact of laws in four states.* New York: Families and Work Institute.

Braver, S. L., & Bay, R. C. (1992). Assessing and compensating for self-selection bias (non-representativeness) of the family research sample. *Journal of Marriage and the Family, 54,* 925–939.

Cervantes, R. (1992). Occupational and economic stressors among immigrant and United States–born Hispanics. In S. Knouse, P. Rosenfeld, & A. Culbertson (Eds.), *Hispanics in the workplace* (pp. 120–133). Newbury Park, CA: Sage Publications.

Cervantes, R., & Castro, F. (1985). Stress, coping, and Mexican American mental health: A systematic review. *Hispanic Journal of Behavioral Sciences, 7,* 85–88.

Cohen, J., & Cohen, P. (1983). *Applied multiple regression/correlation analysis for the behavioral sciences* (2nd ed.). Hillsdale, NJ: Lawrence Erlbaum.

England, S., Levit, G., & Linsk, N. (1990). *To work and love: Private and public response to the needs of employed caregivers of the health-impaired elderly* (Project for the Study of Families, Health and Social Policy, Department of Medical Social Work, University of Illinois at Chicago). Chicago: University of Illinois.

Families and Work Institute. (1993). *An evaluation of Johnson & Johnson's work–family initiative.* New York: Author.

Friedman, D. (1991). *Linking work–family issues to the bottom line* (Report No. 962). New York: Conference Board.

Fussell, P. (1983). *Class: A guide through the American status system.* New York: Summit Books.

Galinsky, E., Bond, J., & Friedman, D. (1993). *The changing workforce: Highlights of the national study.* New York: Families and Work Institute.

Goldberg, W., Greenberger, E., Koch-Jones, J., O'Neil, R., & Hamill, S. (1989). Attractiveness of child care and related employer-supported benefits and policies to married and single parents. *Child and Youth Care Quarterly, 18,* 23–37.

Greene, W. (1988). *LIMDEP* (Version 5). New York: William H. Greene.

Heckman, J. J. (1979). Sample selection bias as a specification error. *Econometrica, 47,* 153–161.

Kossek, E. (1989). The acceptance of human resource innovation by multiple constituencies. *Personnel Psychology, 42,* 263–791.

Kossek, E. (1990). Diversity in childcare assistance needs: Employee problems, preferences, and work-related outcomes. *Personnel Psychology, 43,* 769–791.

Levering, R., & Moskowitz, M. (1993). *The 100 best companies to work for.* Garden City, NY: Doubleday/Currency.

Maddala, G. S. (1983). *Limited-dependent and qualitative variables in econometrics.* New York: Cambridge University Press.

Miller, T. I. (1984). The effects of employer-sponsored child care on employee absenteeism, turnover, productivity, recruitment or job satisfaction: What is claimed and what is known. *Personnel Psychology, 37,* 277–289.

Starrels, M. (1992). The evolution of workplace family policy research. *Journal of Family Issues, 13,* 259–278.

Tsui, A., & Milkovich, G. (1987). Personnel department activities: Constituency perspectives and preferences. *Personnel Psychology, 40,* 519–537.

The author thanks the employees of Fel-Pro for their participation in this study. This research was funded by the Fel-Pro/Mecklenburger Foundation and the Lois and Samuel Silberman Fund. A reduced version of this chapter is included in Dorothy Perrin Moore (Ed.), Proceedings of the Academy of Management: Best Papers, 1995. *Madison, WI: Omnipress.*

23 Concerns of Employed Women:
Issues for Employee Assistance Programs

Glenda Dewberry Rooney

Numerous studies have emphasized tensions between family responsibility and employment. The combined responsibility of employment and providing elder care affects the caregivers, many of whom are employed, in turn affecting employee productivity and job performance (Anastas, Gibeau, & Larson, 1990; Brody, Kleban, Johnsen, Hoffman, & Schoonover, 1987; Denton, Love, & Slate, 1990; Gibeau & Anastas, 1989; Kola & Dunkle, 1988; Scharlach & Boyd, 1989). Similarly, concern for children while at work and the adequacy of child care arrangements can predict stress and lower productivity (Fernandez, 1986; Galinsky & Stein, 1990; Googins, 1988; Googins & Burden, 1987; Kammerman & Kahn, 1987; O'Connell & Bloom, 1987; Shellenbarger, 1992). Parental worry about limited or inadequate care choices for older children and their supervision also is a concern (Rooney, 1994). Tensions between family responsibility and employment, along with inflexible workplace policies, are associated with poor job performance, poor morale, and absenteeism (Crouter, 1984; Galinsky, Hughes, & David, 1990; Galinsky & Stein, 1990; Gonyea & Googins, 1992; Googins, 1988; Lambert, 1993; McNeely & Fogarty, 1988; Morgan & Milliken, 1992; Nelson & Couch, 1990; Rodgers, 1992; Stillman & Bowen, 1985).

Elder care, the care of children, and work and family conflicts are generally categorized as gender specific. Although men are involved with and concerned about work and family issues, family role obligations are primarily perceived as within the domain of women (Berado, Shehan, & Leslie, 1987; Burris, 1991; Chambers, 1986; Coverman & Sheley, 1986; Galinsky, Bond, & Friedman, 1993; Moen & Dempster-McClain, 1987; Presser, 1988; Rachlin, 1987; Rextroat & Shehan, 1987; Seccommbe, 1986).

Research that examines specific familial tensions can make significant contributions to the understanding of factors (for example, child care and employment) that influence productivity and job performance. Few studies have linked these concerns with the service provision of employee assistance programs (EAPs), although some connections have been implied. This linkage is particularly advisable in that EAPs function as the organizational response to personal problems that affect employee productivity and performance level. The core technology and organizing principles that shape EAPs in general involve the treatment of mental health or substance abuse concerns (Roman & Blum, 1985, 1988; Spicer, 1987). Focus on structuring EAPs to address these two issues may mean that other employee concerns may not receive systematic program attention.

TRANSFORMATION OF THE WORK FORCE

Demographic data project that the U.S. work force will comprise up to 80 percent women and people of color sometime early in the 21st century (Fullerton, 1987; Hoyt, 1988; Johnston & Packer, 1987; Marshall, 1991; United Way of America, 1988). These data reveal that 65 percent of the female workers will have school-aged children, 80 percent will be of childbearing age, and 90 percent will bear children. Twenty-four percent of female workers will be single parents, 54 percent will be part of dual-wage-earner families, and 44 percent will be adult daughters responsible for the care of an aged parent or other relative (United Way of America, 1988). Given the demographic profile of women and their family gender role expectations, substantive issues will emerge for employed women and work organizations.

The extent to which the profile of women will be affected by membership in other nondominant groups also is an issue. Ethnic and immigrant women will no doubt face work and family tensions perhaps exacerbated by traditional roles within community and family systems (Bell & Williams, 1981; Jaramillo & Zapata, 1987; Kim & Hurh, 1988; Rooney, 1994).

Diversity in ethnic and racial origins should challenge those who seek harmonious relations to learn about social ties and social structures within groups and potential sources of conflict between workers and the organization—its policies and structures (Daft & Lengel, 1984; Katz, 1982; Moreland, 1985; Nelson, 1989; O'Reilly, Caldwell, & Barnett, 1989; O'Reilly & Chatman, 1986; Pfeffer, 1981, 1983; Tsui & O'Reilly, 1989; Van Den Bergh, 1991; Zenger & Lawrence, 1989). Differences need to be identified and acknowledged by organizational leadership as an initial step in reducing conflicts. Group dynamics suggest that networks and social interactions that are crucial to the success of majority employees may not be accessible to nonwhite women and other relatively new organization members. These exclusions may be experienced as a lack of support by women and people of color, thereby adding to their work and family tensions. Recognizing these problems and mutually engaging in some resolution is an organization's next step. Ideally, these steps lead to more group cohesion and ease in social networking, communicating, and reciprocating as a result of recognizing similarities and celebrating differences.

The influx of immigrants from non-Western countries poses yet another challenge in the diversity mix. On the whole, immigrant women, diverse in their own right, are projected to make up 23 percent of new work force entrants (Johnston & Packer, 1987). Some of these women will be educated and have resources; others will not. Regardless of immigrant education level and socioeconomic status, the United States currently does not embrace diversity in language. Use of English as a second language can be a source of tension in social networks, interpersonal transactions, and communications. Indifference to the critical role of language is reflected in societal hostility to those who speak limited English, particularly if the speaker is a person of color. Recently, hostility to the effort of many governmental agencies accommodating people who are not proficient in English led to a congressional proposal to make English the official language of the United States. The expectation that immigrants should assimilate can have deleterious effects, and their ability to contribute their skills to organizational outcomes can be compromised. Pressures to conform to majority cultural requirements may distract from energy given to task performance. It also can precipitate other problems such as a delay in the process of finding one's place in the organization and stress in the family system.

The primary organizational response to the issue of diversity has focused on helping its members learn to value, appreciate, or manage diversity. Thus, workplace efforts to address diversity and multicultural issues in the workplace have tended to focus on appreciating differences between ethnic and racial groups. Although racial and cultural awareness training is helpful, diversity training must include families and significant others as important forces in the lives of organization members.

The argument can be made that awareness of changing demographics in the workplace provides a starting point for recognizing the full range of diversity issues that affect employed women. A link between EAPs and diversity issues is intuitive, given the EAPs' function as an employee benefit; as a human resources and performance mechanism; and, more important, as the organizational response to personal problems. Employee assistance has proved to be an effective mechanism for addressing a variety of employee and family problems, including mental health and substance abuse. The aggregate of needs to be met through EAPs appears to change with the work force. Because women from both the dominant and nondominant cultures will account for a greater percentage of work force growth, issues surrounding their participation and their effects on organizational performance and productivity goals will become an area of increasing interest.

METHOD

Description and Research Questions

The study reported here examined the concerns of employed women and their perception of how the concerns they identified affected their job performance. An implicit hypothesis for this study was that the changing composition of the work force has implications for EAPs. This study asked four research questions:

1. What are the concerns of employed women?

2. To what extent do employed women perceive that their concerns affect or interfere with their job performance?
3. Do the concerns identified by employed women vary by race and marital status?
4. To what extent do existing definitions of personal problems used by EAPs reflect actual experiences as perceived by these women.

The study was exploratory because there were no previous assumptions with regard to type, content, or incidence of concerns that women might identify. For example, the study did not imply a range of concerns for these women or limit them to issues that are common service provisions of EAPs. It was acknowledged that EAPs' functions in work organizations are a critical resource for providing organizational response to and remediation of concerns of employed women, particularly when these concerns affect job performance.

Procedures

Focus group interviews and pre- and postgroup self-administered questionnaires were used to collect data. Questionnaires were administered to corroborate qualitative data and to obtain demographic information. A major strength of the study was the use of focus groups, which allowed participants to define and discuss their priority concerns. The discussions provided for in-depth exploration of concerns, adding depth and contextual elements to data yielded by self-administered questionnaires. Eight focus groups of employed women were interviewed. An additional group of EAP counselors was interviewed separately.

Questionnaires completed by participants before the group discussion allowed the women to identify three priority concerns. This procedure was intended to facilitate participants' thinking about their concerns and about their commitment to participation before the focus group discussion. To minimize the effect of group dynamics on participation, nominal group process ensured that all participants had the opportunity to voice their list of concerns. Concerns identified by the women were recorded and served as the basis for the focused discussion. Using the same process, we asked EAP counselors to identify priority concerns for employed women.

Sample

Forty-eight women in nonsupervisory management positions participated in the study. The random sample of women was drawn from a large public agency. Most of the women ranged in age from 36 to 50. Twelve (25 percent) were people of color (racially diverse people and immigrants). Seventy-three percent had a combined family or household annual income between $25,000 and $75,000. Fifty-three percent had school-aged children. A majority of the women had elderly parents. Nine EAPs participated in the counselors' focus group. They

Table 23-1
Concerns Identified by Employed Women

| | Priority Concern | | |
Group	1	2	3
1	Time	Physical health	Work and family
2	Work and family	Time	Physical health
3	Work and family	Time	Extended family
4	Time	Work and family	Physical health
5	Work and family	Time	Extended family
6	Extended family	Time	Physical health
7	Work and family	Time	Financial
8	Time	Gender inequality	Work and family

were selected because of their role as external contract service provider for the organization where the women were employed.

RESULTS AND DISCUSSION

Concerns of Employed Women

Five concerns emerged as issues of high importance. The women identified time, work and family, physical health, financial issues, and extended family as their chief concerns (Table 23-1). EAP staff perceived work and family tensions as primary concerns for women, followed by relationship and parenting concerns.

The frequency of topics indicated higher interest and an issue's importance. The concerns most frequently mentioned by women in these focus group were time and work and family (Table 23-2).

Although each employed woman's concerns stood alone, the concerns proved to be complex and intermingled with other identified concerns. For example, time, defined as pressures and constraints the women experienced, had implications for work and family. The work and family concern was defined as tensions between the multiple role demands the women filled, such as those of employee, mother, and spouse or partner. These multiple roles were discussed as role overload and strain. These issues also involved time pressures. Partici-

Table 23-2
Frequency with Which Concerns Were Raised in the Groups

Concern	N
Time	67
Work and family	55
Physical health	19
Financial	15
Extended family	13

pants further attached consequences such as effects on physical health, quality of life, and leisure time to concerns about time and work and family.

Parenting concerns about time and work and family conflicts emerged in these discussions. Demands and concerns related to parenting shifted with the age of children. Conflicts between parenting and work remained constant. The women dismissed the notion of "balance" between work and family, instead preferring "juggling" as a more accurate description of their lives. The women agreed that the notion of achieving balance between work and family was not a rational expectation, given that organizational policies tended to disallow rational interface between the two domains. When work responsibilities spilled into family life, spousal response was rarely to fill the void; thus, women did not experience a remission of family responsibilities. Balance, women implied, involved equality and integration. The women also believed that in comparison with their spouses, they were limited in their options when family responsibilities demanded their attention; unlike their spouses, they had to respond. The women felt that family structure, particularly a gender-driven division of labor, and their own conformity to gender expectations governed their lives, further exacerbating the notion of balance.

Affordability, availability, and cost of child care were concerns. The women felt these could be generalized to all employed women with children. They emphasized that finding good child care was a challenge. Once good care was secured, however, they could depend on younger children staying put until they were picked up. Women who had older children discussed the need to broaden child care concerns to include provisions for the supervision of older children and the support these parents needed. The predominant view expressed by the participants was that children reaching a certain age do not suddenly become self-sufficient or self-reliant; rather, their need for structure continues. Concerns and fears expressed for the older children had to do with their potential involvement with violence, juvenile delinquency, teenage pregnancy, and gangs. Times of particular vulnerability include the period just after school, summer vacations, and holidays. Few activities, either public or private, were offered for older children, and many activities that were available were not accessible because of costs or geographical location. These concerns are underreported and understudied in the literature on child care.

Concerns by Race and Marital Status

Of primary concern to all women, regardless of race and marital status, was work and family tensions, time pressures, or constraints related to the management of multiple roles. Elements of time, work, and family tensions expressed by single parents embodied all the dimensions discussed by other women. Issues particular to single parents involved their need to fulfill both male and female roles and to fulfill all family responsibilities. Family responsibility often placed these women at odds with their workplace supervisors and had particular implications for single and single-parent women.

Surprisingly, single women who had never married felt the strains of work and family, especially in the care of older family members. These women reported feeling coerced by both male and female relatives to manage various family responsibilities because they were perceived as having fewer demands on their time. Employers, on the other hand, used the same rationale for asking them to take on additional responsibilities at work to maintain productivity levels or to reduce the burden of their married coworkers. Differential treatment of men and women also was noted. Specifically, supervisors tended to consider men as model employees and were more lenient when men experienced work and family conflicts.

In general, concerns for physical health did not vary by race or marital status. The women felt that they were much more adept than men in managing emotional strain, and thus they were more concerned about and conscious of the physical impact of work. They spoke of progressively debilitating physical symptoms, such as chronic fatigue, daily exhaustion, and decreased energy levels, that affected their functioning. An added dimension of this discussion was raised by the older women. They expressed concern about the constant managing of multiple roles and over time the impact on their quality of life, their diminished stamina or resilience, and their physical health. They perceived the physical problems to be compounded by the normal changes of aging.

Time and work and family demands were discussed as posing particular difficulties for women of color and immigrant women. How time was spent, family obligations, and gender expectations were discussed as embedded in culturally explicit norms or scripts of their families and communities. Family responsibility as discussed by the women involved attending to the needs of a larger, more inclusive family system. Family obligations included acting as a bicultural liaison between relatives and the larger society. For example, for those whose relatives lacked English proficiency, some women had to be available to navigate, negotiate, and interpret almost every interaction their relatives had outside the family. Another issue was the degree to which family members relied on them as high school or college graduates to transact business, instruct them in interactions with institutions, and provide transportation. Women of color reported experiencing added workplace tensions as a result of these obligations. In particular, the women believed that organizations, in their reluctance to recognize nuclear family obligations, were barely sensitive to responsibilities for people generally defined as extended family. Women from the dominant culture, however, spoke of work tensions related to the care of elderly relatives.

Financial concerns emerged as an issue for few women in the study. Half of all women of color cited finances as a primary concern, compared with 31 percent of the white women. Financial issues were a priority concern for 44 percent of the single women who had never married, compared with 63 percent of the divorced women and 23 percent of the married women or women living with a partner. Although there was general consensus that the women were employed outside of the home because of financial necessity, these financial concerns were perhaps the most difficult to summarize thematically. Specifically, the range of concerns dealt with current realities for some women; for others, the nature of financial concerns were in the future or goals to be achieved.

Single and single-parent women whose income was the sole source of support for their families commented on the financial pressures of this position. Several women held second jobs to sustain their families. Single women with or without children reported that their lives were dominated by financial decisions ranging from whether to complete needed car or home repairs to having funds for food, clothing, or school supplies. Surprisingly, single, never-married women expressed concern about their ability to assist financially with the college educations of younger dependent relatives, such as the offspring of their siblings.

Another group of women was concerned about anticipated financial changes or shifts in the economy. Among the other topics of concern raised by the women were organizational downsizing and restructuring. Single women and women of color believed they were the most vulnerable to job loss and felt vulnerable to being forced to leave the job as a result of work and family conflicts. Job loss also was an intense concern for women nearing retirement age regardless of their marital status. They feared loss of benefits, especially health insurance, insufficient money for retirement, and the eventual obligation to care for an elderly parent. These older women also viewed their continued employment and that of their spouse as being vulnerable because of age.

Whereas work and family, time, and physical health were priority concerns for all women regardless of marital status, concerns related to extended family and financial issues varied by race and marital status. An obligation to care for relatives, extended family, and specifically the elderly members was a priority concern expressed by some majority-culture and all non-majority-culture women. Care of elderly relatives was inherent in cultural and community norms with women of color and consistent with gender role expectations related to family and how time was spent.

Impact on Job Performance

Eighty-eight percent of the women and all nine EAPs indicated that the identified concerns had altered their job performance. The focus group discussion further highlighted ways in which job performance was impaired. Decreased morale, decreased enthusiasm, and lack of motivation or creativity were among the issues discussed. A significant number of women indicated that time pressures and work and family tensions precluded them from seeking or accepting job advancements or assuming extra role responsibilities at work. Many of the women also dealt with these tensions by lowering their career aspirations and by viewing their job as having extrinsic rather than intrinsic value. Work and family tensions were also cited as influencing job commitment.

Influences and Modifiers of Job Performance

Although an impact on job performance was perceived, the relationship among the women's identified concerns was discussed as being more complex. Specifically, the extent to which job performance was altered by the identified concerns was influenced or modified by a number of variables: workplace policies and supervisory discretion, the nature of the family situation, and a supportive work environment.

Workplace Policies and Supervisor Discretion. Organizational pressures to keep work and family separate and inflexible work policies in conjunction with how supervisors applied policies were reported as having an adverse impact on job performance. Effects tended to result from the accompanying stress or frustration when family matters were treated as abnormal occurrences. Also, inability to take time off for home or family matters without being judged as slacking off, according to the women, meant the eventual intrusion of unresolved issues on work.

In general, organizational policies were perceived by the women as measures to ensure that their lives were aligned to work requirements. Flexibility was limited to a fixed formula, for example, a four-day workweek. Requests for time off, including taking the allowable time for maternity leave, often negatively influenced performance evaluations and limited future promotional opportunities.

The women perceived female, racial, or ethnic supervisors and managers as being more rigid in their application of workplace policies. The women did not believe that these supervisors should ignore work rules on their behalf, but they did expect that they would understand their concerns.

Despite the tensions, the women perceived female, racial, and ethnic supervisors to be most vulnerable in terms of job security. These supervisors were seen as being scrutinized more intensely than were majority-culture supervisors; their status in the organization was considered more tenuous, their decision making protective, and their continued status contingent on conformity. According to the women, these supervisors were "routinely eaten up by organizations" and their mistakes were "subjected to the organizational billboard." The women perceived this situation as contributing to the reluctance of the supervisors to act outside the organizational culture.

Nature of Family Situation. The extent to which job performance was affected by family matters was dependent on whether the situation was routine, sustained, or at a crisis level. The impact on job performance was minimal in routine matters. A majority of the women reported using planning and schedules that included a number of contingencies to ensure to the extent possible that routine family matters did not interfere with work. Sustained or crisis situations, such as a child's illness or injury or an ill or dying relative, demanded immediate or prolonged responses and were much more likely to result in impaired job performance. An overriding factor was the women's perception that organizations tended to be punitive and undiscriminating in their response regardless of circumstances.

Supportive Work Environment. A supportive work environment was discussed as exerting a positive influence on job performance and well-being. Defined as workplace interactions and friendships, the dynamics of relationships within the workplace were characterized by the women as satisfying social needs and contributing to job performance and productivity levels. Relationships women had with other women were described as vital to productivity. Workplace relationships were likened to interactions that would normally occur in a neighborhood or social group for which the women had little time because they were employed.

Interactions and relationships with coworkers were noted as taking the "edge off situations that may otherwise be devastating." The dominant thought may be summarized by the words of one participant: "You may not spend a great deal of time with someone in the course of the day, [but] it is nice to see a friendly face and to have the continuity of knowing that five days a week you are going to see somebody who cares about what happens to you." Another woman noted, "Interactions with coworkers [are] a part of life, so you do care about what is happening with their kids, what happens to their families, and you do care about whether they are getting enough exercise, or whether they are depressed, whether it is their birthday."

The value of workplace relationships also was realized by women joining together to get the job done. Productivity was enhanced by the synergy and strength resulting from the support of and rapport with colleagues that enabled a work unit to accomplish more, simply because they were aware of each other as people.

Women across focus groups indicated that they understood that work and family demands were incompatible. The two domains could be rendered less so, however, if workplace and public policies were reflective of contemporary realities instead of outmoded images. Women also emphasized that they did not quarrel with organizational measures intended to ensure productivity and that their own productivity goals were consistent with those of the organization. They spoke of taking pride in their work or careers. Productivity became an issue as a result of the nonalignment of work and family and a failure of organizations to understand that flexibility (considered the gift of time) would enhance rather than distract from productivity. Trust also was an issue. In particular, the women wanted supervisors to recognize and support their judgment by not responding in a manner that suggested slacking off. They also wanted recognition for their actions to prevent a particular situation from reaching the point that it interfered with the job.

Issues for EAPs

Participants were asked to rate the extent to which problem categories around which EAP service is organized were issues for them or their family. EAP service categories are organized to respond to marital or family issues, parent–child conflict, emotional problems, relationship issues, alcohol and substance abuse, financial problems, and career and vocational concerns.

Eighty percent of the women indicated that substance abuse was not a concern for themselves or a family member. Concerns or problems that may be categorized as mental health or emotional problems were a concern for 4 percent of the women. These data support information generated from the focus groups, in which women emphasized physical health rather than emotional health as a priority concern.

EAPs responding to the same set of questions indicated substance abuse (55 percent) and mental health (55 percent) at a much higher level than did the women. The differences between the perceptions of women and EAP staff may be accounted for, in part, because EAP staff perceived a stronger clinical relationship between the effects or outcomes of women's concerns and their use of chemicals and the incidence of mental health concerns. Staff also noted that women seen in their practice reported using over-the-counter drugs as remedies for stress-related symptoms. Women may not perceive this as chemical use or abuse.

The differences also may be explained by the fact that women seen in EAP practice are perhaps in a crisis. A challenging reason for the perceived differences is the manner in which concerns are defined by EAPs as a result of educational backgrounds, theoretical orientations, program focus, and the categories required for insurance reimbursement. At the same time, the perception of EAPs that a relationship exists between the concerns of women and substance abuse needs further research.

EAPs in this study knew of the concerns of employed women. For example, work and family concern was identified as a priority by both women and EAP professionals. EAPs noted the increased pressures that women experienced stemming from gender role demands, inflexible workplace policies, supervisory discretion, and differential or unequal treatment of female compared to male employees. Although there was congruence in the identified concerns, the differences in the origin and context of concerns as conceptualized by the women and professionals raise important considerations. Lack of time for self, identified by both groups, illustrates this point. Lack of time for self was by perceived EAPs as an indicator of a lack of self-esteem, poor self-definition, and the inability to set boundaries. In contrast, women perceived their lack of time for self as a natural consequence of their multiple roles, for example, parenting responsibilities that consumed available time after work. Whereas the women perceived the pressures that they faced with respect to time and multiple roles as diminishing the time they had for social interactions and the nurturing of intimate relationships, EAPs rated these issues as priority concerns and attributed them to relational conflicts embedded in family-of-origin issues for which time constraints were symptomatic of larger issues.

Professional bias is suggested but, without further investigation, the extent to which this bias may influence the definition of insufficiencies is not confirmed. Yet, discrepancies in the perceptions of the origins, elements, and ecological base are issues for consideration. The literature also advises caution in making inferences about the perceived nature of individual difficulties (Abramovitz & Epstein, 1983; Berlin & Marsh, 1993; Donovan, 1987; Ramanathan, 1992; Rosen & Livne, 1992; Specht, 1991; Trice & Beyer, 1993). Discrepancies between how people view their concerns and the actual services provided affect program use. In particular, employees may not use or may underuse a service that they feel is unresponsive or lacking in understanding of the concerns that they express.

This study emphasized concerns of employed women, with particular nuances related to cultural expectations for non-dominant-culture women. In general, the concerns identified as priorities for women do not easily fit the mental health model of service currently used by EAPs. Some women and racial and ethnic group members will certainly experience problems that EAPs are able to address with the existing service ideology and resources. Using a clinical framework with racial and ethnic group members will, however, demand some level of cultural competence; an understanding of the psychosocial aspects of human behavior; and recognition of oppression, interpersonal conflicts, and the asymmetrical nature of the helping relationship. The social structure of employing institutions, trust, and interpersonal relationships and dynamics also are of critical importance. Finally, consideration must be given to the role that class, race, gender, and gender role expectations in the family system play in shaping the issues that emerged as concerns identified by women and EAPs.

IMPLICATIONS AND CONCLUSION

It is encouraging that over the past several years human resources and employee assistance literature has raised awareness of work and family tensions. Elder care and child care may be considered facets of family responsibility. Combined efforts of human resources and EAPs to address these issues have included health and wellness seminars; educational materials or classes related to the stresses associated with child care, elder care, and balancing work and family; and information and referral resources. According to the EAPs in this study, most of those attending the seminars or requesting information are women, which reinforces the gender specificity of family responsibilities.

Few women in this study had used the EAP, nor did the majority understand the program to be a resource for the concerns they identified. This lack of use may be related to the fact that work and family concerns, although addressed at some level, are often auxiliary to the services provided by EAPs.

Inquiry into the concerns of employed women has implications for EAPs and their function as the interface between employee problems and productivity. Major issues point to what women value. First and foremost, women emphasized the need for both public and organizational policies that value the family in contrast to those that tout "family values." Women in this study articulated a value for uniformly supportive family policies and for good quality and affordable child care that also addressed the need for care resources for unsupervised older children. They valued flexibility—the opportunity to take time off from work to attend to family matters that they felt prevented the intrusion of these matters on work. Flexible policies uniformly and fairly applied and interaction with coworkers were essential ingredients in promoting employee well-being, commitment, and productivity.

Further research is needed to clarify the extent to which the concerns identified by women in this study may be generalized to a larger group. What has emerged from the data nonetheless is an expansion of the issues that may be conceptualized as affecting job performance. The focus group discussions provided information about how job performance is influenced or modified, including the effects of the manner in which organizations and supervisors respond to family role responsibilities. These data also suggest that in the mix of a more diverse work force, issues related to work and family carry particular nuances specific to age, race, culture, and marital status.

In the development of programs or services in response to work and family concerns, EAPs may need to assume the leadership in articulating the linkages between employee concerns and productivity. This role may involve de-emphasizing the outcomes for which a treatment solution is required. It also would include exerting influence on organizational and public policy, along with the development of organizational and community resources.

EAPs also must position themselves to provide information to employers about employees' needs and concerns. Just as previous data documented the incidence of mental health problems and substance abuse thought to be present in the population at any given time

(Masi, 1984), data are now needed to demonstrate the extent to which a new set of concerns exists for employees. Articulation of employee concerns should include the involvement of women in the identification of their needs and the relationship of these issues to job performance. The women in this study expressed appreciation for the opportunity to define and discuss their concerns.

It would seem that EAPs, having taken an active role in educating managers and supervisors about the effects of mental health problems and substance abuse on performance, are also called to focus attention on the issues of a work force with more women and more people from racial and ethnic subgroups. Although a work force with a greater number of female and ethnic employees may present new challenges for contemporary EAPs, such programs originated in the industrial scheme referred to as "welfare capitalism." Workplace-sponsored welfare services emerged again during World War II, when a significant number of women entered the work force. These earlier schemes may be viewed as mechanisms for dealing with diversity. Specifically, employers faced with a largely immigrant labor pool and, later, with women and people of color, sought ways to enhance productivity through provisions that addressed the conditions that accompanied a diverse work force. Contemporary programs, driven by different social and economic forces, differ from their historical counterparts. The reviewed literature and the results of this study suggest that the United States is entering an era in which the mix of problems that affect job performance may change. The core technology and function of employee assistance may continue, but its focus may need to be expanded so that such programs can address other types of problems as well. The needs of a largely female and ethnic work force are best served by EAPs that offer services along a continuum and are capable of intervening with individuals, families, organizations, and social conditions.

REFERENCES

Abramovitz, M., & Epstein, E. (1983). The politics of privatization: Industrial social work practice and private enterprise. *Social and Urban Review, 16*(1), 13–20.

Anastas, J. W., Gibeau, J. L., & Larson, P. J. (1990). Working families and eldercare: A national perspective in an aging America. *Social Work, 35*, 405–411.

Bell, P. A., & Williams, S. R. (1981). Black women's participation in the labor force. *Free Inquiry in Creative Sociology, 9*(2), 159–161, 164.

Berado, D. H., Shehan, C., & Leslie, G. (1987). A residue of tradition: Jobs, careers and spouse time in housework. *Journal of Marriage and the Family, 49*, 381–390.

Berlin, S. B., & Marsh, J. C. (1993). *Informing practice decisions*. New York: Macmillan.

Brody, E. M., Kleban, M. H., Johnsen, P. T., Hoffman, C., & Schoonover, C. B. (1987). Work status and parent care: A comparison of four groups of women. *Gerontologist, 27*, 201–208.

Burris, B. H. (1991). Employed mothers: The impact of class and marital status on the prioritizing of family and work. *Social Science Quarterly, 72*, 50–66.

Chambers, D. A. (1986). The constraints of work and domestic schedules on women's leisure. *Leisure Studies, 5*, 309–325.

Coverman, S., & Sheley, J. F. (1986). Changes in men's housework and child care time, 1965–1975. *Journal of Marriage and the Family, 48*, 413–422.

Crouter, A. C. (1984). Spillover from family to work: The neglected side of work and family interface. *Human Relations, 37*, 425–442.

Daft, R. L., & Lengel, R. H. (1984). Information richness: A new approach to managerial behavior and organizational design. In B. M. Staw & L. L. Cummings (Eds.), *Research in organizational behavior* (Vol. 6, pp. 191–223). Greenwich, CT: JAI Press.

Denton, K., Love, L. T., & Slate, R. (1990). Eldercare in the 90's: Employee responsibility, employer challenge. *Families in Society, 71*, 349–359.

Donovan, R. (1987). Stress in the workplace: A framework for research and practice. *Social Casework, 68*, 259–266.

Fernandez, J. P. (1986). *Child care and corporate productivity: Resolving family/work conflicts.* Lexington, MA: Lexington Books.

Fullerton, H. N. (1987). Laborforce projections: 1986–2000. *Monthly Labor Review, 110*(9), 19–24.

Galinsky, E., Bond, J., & Friedman, D. (1993). *The changing work force: Highlights of the national study.* New York: Families and Work Institute.

Galinsky, E., Hughes, D., & David, J. (1990). Trends in corporate family supportive policies. *Marriage and Family Review, 15*(3–4), 75–94.

Galinsky, E., & Stein, P. J. (1990). The impact of human resource policies on employees: Balancing work and family life. *Journal of Family Issues, 11*, 368–383.

Gibeau, J. L., & Anastas, J. W. (1989). Breadwinners and caregivers: Interviews with working women. *Journal of Gerontological Social Work, 14*(1–2), 19–40.

Gonyea, J. G., & Googins, B. K. (1992). Linking the world of work and family: Beyond the productivity trap. *Human Resource Management, 31*, 209–226.

Googins, B. K. (1988). The relationship between work and family. *ALMACAN, 18*(9), 20–24.

Googins, B. K., & Burden, D. (1987). Vulnerability of working parents: Balancing work and home roles. *Social Work, 23*, 295–300.

Hoyt, K. B. (1988). The changing work force: A review of projections—1986 to 2000. *Career Development Quarterly, 37*, 31–39.

Jaramillo, P. T., & Zapata, J. T. (1987). Roles and alliances with Mexican American and Anglo families. *Journal of Marriage and the Family, 49*, 727–735.

Johnston, W. B., & Packer, A. H. (1987). *Workforce 2000: Work and workers for the 21st century.* Indianapolis: Hudson Institute.

Kammerman, S., & Kahn, A. J. (1987). *The responsive workplace: Employers and the changing work force.* New York: Columbia University Press.

Katz, R. (1982). The effects of group longevity on project communication and performance. *Administrative Science Quarterly, 27*, 81–104.

Kim, K. C., & Hurh, W. M. (1988). The burden of double roles: Korean wives in the USA. *Ethnic and Racial Studies, 11*, 150–167.

Kola, L. A., & Dunkle, R. E. (1988). Eldercare in the workplace. *Social Casework, 69*, 569–574.

Lambert, S. J. (1993). Workplace policies as social policy. *Social Services Review, 67*, 237–260.

Marshall, R. (1991). *The state of families.* Milwaukee, WI: Family Service America.

Masi, D. A. (1984). *Designing employee assistance programs.* New York: American Management Association.

McNeely, R. L., & Fogarty, B. A. (1988). Balancing parenthood and employment: Factors affecting company receptiveness to family-related innovations in the workplace. *Family Relations, 37*, 189–195.

Moen, P., & Dempster-McClain, D. I. (1987). Employed parents: Role strain, work-time and preferences for working less. *Journal of Marriage and the Family, 49*, 570–590.

Moreland, R. L. (1985). Social categorization and the assimilation of new group members. *Journal of Personality and Social Psychology, 48*, 1173–1190.

Morgan, H., & Milliken, F. J. (1992). Keys to action: Understanding differences in organizations' responsiveness to work and family issues. *Human Resource Management, 31*, 410–422.

Nelson, P. T., & Couch, S. (1990). The corporate perspective on family responsive policy. *Marriage and Family Review, 15*(3–4), 95–113.

Nelson, R. (1989). The strength of strong ties, social networks and intergroup conflict in organizations. *American Management Journal, 32*, 377–401.

O'Connell, M., & Bloom, D. E. (1987). *Juggling jobs and babies: America's child care challenge* (Population Trends in Public Policy). Washington, DC: Population Reference Bureau.

O'Reilly, C. A., III, Caldwell, D., & Barnett, W. (1989). Work group demography, social integration, and turnover. *Administrative Science Quarterly, 34*(1), 21–37.

O'Reilly, C., III, & Chatman, J. (1986). Organizational commitment and psychological attachment: The effects of compliance, identification and internalization on prosocial behavior. *Journal of Applied Psychology, 71*, 492–499.

Pfeffer, J. (1981). Some consequences of organizational demography: Potential impacts on an aging work force and formal organizations. In S. B. Kessler, J. N. Morgan, & V. K. Oppenheimer (Eds.), *Aging: Social change* (pp. 291–321). New York: Academic Press.

Pfeffer, J. (1983). Organizational demography. In L. L. Cummings & B. M. Staw (Eds.), *Research in organizational behavior* (Vol. 5, pp. 299–357). Greenwich, CT: JAI Press.

Presser, H. B. (1988). Shift work and child care among young dual earner American parents. *Journal of Marriage and the Family, 50*, 133–148.

Rachlin, V. C. (1987). Fair vs. equal role relations in dual-career and dual-earner families: Implications for family interventions. *Family Relations, 36*, 187–192.

Ramanathan, C. S. (1992). EAP's response to personal stress and productivity. *Social Work, 37*, 234–239.

Rextroat, C., & Shehan, C. (1987). The family life cycle and spouses' time in housework. *Journal of Marriage and the Family, 49*, 737–750.

Rodgers, C. S. (1992). The flexible workplace: What have we learned. *Human Resource Management, 31*, 183–199.

Roman, P. H., & Blum, T. (1985). The core technology of employee assistance programs. *ALMACAN, 15*(3), 8–19.

Roman, P. H., & Blum, T. (1988). The core technology of employee assistance programs: A reaffirmation. *ALMACAN, 18*(8), 17–22.

Rooney, G. D. (1994). *Employee assistance programs and the changing composition of the work force.* Unpublished dissertation, University of Minnesota, Minneapolis.

Rosen, A., & Livne, S. (1992). Personal versus environmental emphasis in social worker's perceptions of client problems. *Social Service Review, 66*, 85–96.

Scharlach, A. E., & Boyd, S. L. (1989). Caregiving and employment: Results of an employee survey. *Gerontologist, 29*, 383–387.

Seccombe, K. (1986). The effects of the occupational condition upon the division of household labor: An application of Kohn's Theory. *Journal of Marriage and the Family, 48*, 839–848.

Shellenbarger, S. (1992). Lessons from the workplace: How corporate policies and attitudes lag behind workers' changing needs. *Human Resource Management, 31*, 157–168.

Specht, H. A. (1991). Social work and the popular psychotherapies. *Social Service Review, 64*, 345–347.

Spicer, J. (1987). EAP program model and philosophies. In J. Spicer (Ed.), *The EAP solution: Current trends and future issues.* Center City, MN: Hazelden Educational Foundation.

Stillman, F., & Bowen, G. L. (1985). Corporate support mechanism for families: An exploratory study and agenda for research and evaluation. *Evaluation and Program Planning, 8*, 309–314.

Trice, H. M., & Beyer, J. M. (1993). *The cultures of work organizations*. Englewood Cliffs, NJ: Prentice Hall.

Tsui, A. S., & O'Reilly, C. A., III. (1989). Beyond simple demographic effects: The importance of relational demography in superior–subordinate dyads. *Academy of Management Journal, 32*, 420–423.

United Way of America. (1988). *The future world of work*. Alexandria, VA: Author.

Van Den Bergh, N. (1991). Managing biculturalism at the workplace: A group approach. *Journal of Social Work with Groups, 13*(4), 71–84.

Zenger, T. R., & Lawrence, B. S. (1989). Organizational demography: The differential aspects of age and tenure distributions on technical communication. *Academy of Management Journal, 32*, 353–376.

24 African American Entrepreneurship and Work Force Diversity

James I. Herbert

This chapter introduces the concepts of entrepreneurship, small business, family business, and entrepreneurial enterprises as influential variables affecting the whole notion of work force diversity. One rationale for publishing this book is directly linked to the Hudson Institute's report *Workforce 2000* (Johnston & Packer, 1987), which projected that the United States will have an ever-increasing nonwhite work force through the year 2010. With this increased nonwhite participation in the workplace, the need to accommodate ethnic and racial differences will continue.

However, for-profit initiatives will continue to be rooted in economic self-interest and economic self-sufficiency. That is, corporations will continue to make decisions aimed at increasing profits. They must be capable of competing in regional, national, and global markets. One major impediment in this process is the private sector's failure to provide new economic opportunities to unskilled and blue-collar workers, especially when manufacturing employment began its swift decline some 20 years ago.

With this new nonwhite work force, the workplace will not be the same as we now know it. Most jobs and job creations will come from small business, small enterprise, and family businesses, many of which will be owned by women, African Americans, and other ethnic and racial group members. We can assume, and perhaps anticipate, that these new owners of small enterprise will engage in a higher level of sensitivity to the issue of diversity in the workplace. We can anticipate the establishment of a new paradigm, a new mindset, regarding work force diversity.

Private initiatives such as black-owned businesses and family business will not be sufficient by themselves. To affect significantly the issues and the perspectives of diversity in the workplace, small business initiatives must go hand-in-hand with government programs addressing racial, housing, banking, and hiring discrimination. The ultimate objective is the creation of jobs. To achieve this, we must look at changing the nature of work, changing our hiring policies in both the private and the public sectors, and examining our accountability for creating too few jobs.

Corporate America is sizing down and sourcing out. In addition to seeking a diverse work force, most corporations also are looking for

opportunities for business joint ventures. This initiative will be greatly influenced by our national participation in the global economy.
The central question will deal with our readiness for this transition.
Can we develop a new mindset that will lend itself well to our engagement in this new world of work and mainstream economy?

AFRICAN AMERICAN ENTREPRENEURSHIP

Contrary to popular belief, entrepreneurship and self-help are deeply
woven into the African American historical fabric. Even in the historical presence of racism and discrimination, enterprise and entrepreneurship have been commonplace. We need to look at a different
perspective on race and economic stability in American society by
engaging in a comparative approach to the subject of racism and inequality in America.

19th Century

Before the Civil War, many free African Americans made their living
as entrepreneurs. Many of these owners of small businesses were in
communities such as Philadelphia and New York City; Baltimore
was a major center of commerce for African American businesses. It
has been estimated that more than 40 percent of African American
entrepreneurs were former slaves that were purchased out of slavery
by loved ones and relatives (Butler, 1991). African Americans owned
engineering firms, brick factories, and restaurants and monopolized
industries such as tailoring and catering not only in the Northeast
but also in the South. African Americans during this era were a small
business–oriented community operating in an extremely hostile
racial environment.

   The entrepreneurial African American developed a true sense of
the significance of education. W.E.B. DuBois, in *The Philadelphia Negro*
(1899), identified an upper class among African Americans, many of
whom were descendants of entrepreneurs. They established themselves in the Philadelphia business community. In their great classical debate, Booker T. Washington and DuBois advocated different
views of the best course for adjusting to American society as free
people. Washington stressed the development of business enterprise
as the fundamental pattern of adjustment to America (Butler, 1991).
In doing so, Washington advocated the business tradition already established by free African Americans before the Civil War. The National Negro Business League was really an extension of African
American organizations prevalent in communities before the Civil
War. It is ironic that as we approach the 21st century, we are revisit-
ing initiatives that Washington spearheaded a century ago.

   Although Washington advocated compromising civil rights for
white support of African American business enterprise, he argued
that African Americans should concentrate on industrial education
rather than higher education. DuBois, on the other hand, recognized

the importance of business enterprise but has been portrayed by historians as the guardian of civil rights and higher education. Indeed, African Americans did adopt different patterns of adjustment to American society. Under the cloak of racism and discrimination, African Americans concentrated on the development of business enterprise. A key consideration was that Jim Crow segregation restricted African American entrepreneurs to doing business exclusively in the black community. The other significant adjustment consisted of African Americans joining the American work force in the same tradition as other European ethnic groups. Hence, a tremendous migration began from the South to the North, Midwest, and the West Coast in search of jobs. Both types of adjustment were critically important. Those who concentrated on self-help, self-sufficiency, reputation building, and entrepreneurship developed values and traditions much like other racial and ethnic groups.

African American entrepreneurs developed a strong emphasis on education for their children. The children of entrepreneurs are more likely to be professionals in today's society. African Americans who are descendants of generations of entrepreneurs rose from poverty to become second-, third-, and fourth-generation college graduates. This highly educated segment of the African American community has tremendous respect for and allegiance to historically black institutions. A large proportion of this segment of the population has attended and continues to attend African American universities and colleges. Until the 1960s, most black doctors, lawyers, teachers, and preachers were graduates of historically black colleges and universities.

Early 20th Century

Entrepreneurship was a core component of the African American community during the first half of the 20th century. Not only did African Americans develop viable business enterprises, but they also cultivated strong educational and achievement expectations for their offspring. They built important institutions, including churches, colleges, and civic organizations, because of and in spite of the hostilities of Jim Crow segregation. These institutions were instrumental in serving their interests and those of their children and community. Even today, institutions such as the Masons, fraternities and sororities, and churches continue to be cornerstones to the African American community. Like their ancestors, current generations have great respect for the founders of these organizations and the roles these organizations play within the community.

Because of Jim Crow legal segregation during the early 20th century, African American entrepreneurs, no matter what size their business or what industry, were limited to doing business within the African American community. Participation in the American economic mainstream was not allowed. This was the only racial or ethnic group other than Native Americans to be so excluded and isolated by law and by societal dictate from participating in mainstream America (Butler, 1991).

Hence, the civil rights movement of the late 1950s and the 1960s took on a deep significance for the African American community. The preoccupation with obtaining the right to vote and the right to sit at a lunch counter or drink from a public water fountain was profound and costly. It moved African Americans away from their entrepreneurial roots, and they are still paying a price for that transition. Great emphasis was placed on attending college, securing jobs in corporate America, attending integrated schools, owning homes in suburbia, and gaining all the other trappings of the American dream. Consequently, the entrepreneurial spirit and component of African American society were inadvertently ignored. In retrospect, it seems almost strange that there was not the same kind of intensity, focus, or interest in entrepreneurial participation in the American mainstream economy. The few entrepreneurs who did continue their endeavors did so because of post–World War II opportunities. Most of these businesses were within-race focused, for example, publication of African American magazines or newspapers or production of hair care and beauty products exclusively for the African American community. A few African American businesses are currently approaching the potential for cross-generation transfer of ownership and management. Again, these businesses and entrepreneurial efforts are limited primarily to an African American clientele. Two such businesses are the Johnson Publishing Company and Earl G. Graves Ltd. John H. Johnson, chief executive officer (CEO) of Johnson Publishing, the publisher of *Jet* and *Ebony* magazines, is being succeeded by his daughter, Linda Johnson Rice, the company's president. The CEO of *Black Enterprise Magazine*'s parent company, Earl G. Graves, is being succeeded by two of his sons, Earl and John, both of whom are presently part of the company's top leadership.

Late 20th Century

Having won the right to participate in various segments of American society, including the right to vote and the right to attend universities and colleges of their choice, some men and women in the African American community found a renewed interest in business and entrepreneurial opportunities. Among the 25 largest black-owned companies in the United States, six are in the publishing and broadcasting industry, six are in data-processing services, and several are in specialty construction or manufacturing. But of significance here is that 16 of the 25 largest African American companies in the United States started after 1975. There is a growing African American middle class willing to bring its expertise, experience, and resources together to participate in the American economic mainstream. The country is seeing the first wave of African Americans who have the education, skills, and access to capital and who will take some entrepreneurial risk.

According to the most recent U.S. Bureau of the Census statistics, the number of black-owned firms in the country grew by 46 percent between 1987 and 1992, to 621,000 businesses. In comparison, the overall number of U.S. businesses grew by just 26 percent during the same time. The income picture is not as positive, with median household incomes rising from $19,373 in 1970 to $19,533 in 1993, constituting little change. In 1970, 1.7 percent of African American households enjoyed annual incomes in excess of $75,000 a year; by 1993, that number had increased to 5.2 percent. There were 727,000 African Americans enrolled in colleges and universities in 1972; in 1993, that number had doubled to 1.4 million. Nonwhite entrepreneurs are among those in position to take advantage of the downsizing and outsourcing of corporate America. Also, technological innovations have made the cost of doing business more affordable for home-based businesses and sole proprietorships, and 90 percent of all black businesses were in these categories as of 1992. African Americans tend to serve individual consumers rather than other businesses or corporations. Most African American entrepreneurs currently are in skill-service industries, including insurance, real estate, business services, and legal services (Mergenhagen, 1996).

This entrepreneurial reawakening is occurring at the same time that strong opposition to affirmative action is developing in all sectors, public and private, including the academic community. Strong evidence of this onslaught against affirmative action can be seen clearly in the construction industry. The 1980s saw a tremendous growth in African American–owned construction firms in the United States—a rise of 68 percent between 1982 and 1987. However, the number of black-owned construction firms grew only 16 percent between 1987 and 1992. Some of this difference can be attributed to changes in public policy and court rulings during the late 1980s and early 1990s. California Governor Pete Wilson, for example, led the effort to reduce significantly that state's goal for set-aside business opportunities for disadvantaged business enterprise participation in the state's federal highway program. Also, the U.S. Supreme Court ruled that the city of Richmond, Virginia, did not merit a set-aside program because of the lack of documented discrimination (*City of Richmond [VA] v. J. H. Croson Company*, 1989).

Between 1987 and 1992, the receipts of all businesses in the United States rose 67 percent to $3.3 trillion. By contrast, sales by African American businesses rose 63 percent, from $19.8 billion to $32.2 billion. According to the Black Enterprise Industrial Service 100 (1997), these companies' combined sales, in the amount of $7.4 billion, would rank only 174th on the *Fortune 500* list of top American corporations.

Although there is positive movement in African American entrepreneurship, and the number of black-owned businesses is growing faster than average, the businesses remain smaller than average. According to a U.S. Bureau of the Census survey of minority-owned enterprises, between 1987 and 1992, the number of black-owned businesses increased 46 percent, from 424,200 to 620,900 (Litram, 1996).

The total number of U.S. businesses increased 26 percent during the same period, from 13.7 million to 17.3 million. African Americans, who make up 12 percent of the U.S. population, are still underrepresented among business owners. In 1987, African American–owned companies were 3.1 percent of the nation's businesses; in 1992, they were 3.6 percent. African American entrepreneurs are well educated and tend to provide highly skilled services, but their businesses are often run on a part-time basis to accommodate their full-time employment. Consequently, revenues of African American–owned enterprises in general are significantly lower than those of small businesses owned by members of other nonwhite groups. Revenues for African American–owned companies increased 32 percent in inflation-adjusted dollars, from $24 billion in 1987 to $32 billion in 1992. In contrast, sales of all companies increased 35 percent, from $2.5 trillion to $3.3 trillion.

The Future

The proportion of college-educated African Americans will continue to rise as baby boomers and busters replace the older, less-educated generations in prime working ages. This trend will provide a growing population of motivated and knowledgeable potential owners and entrepreneurs. Without a doubt, the future direction of government policies and the issues of job security and participation in a global economy will affect the extent to which African Americans will venture out on their own; these factors will affect all ethnic and racial groups in America.

FACTORS THAT AFFECT ENTREPRENEURSHIP

Education has been a motivating factor for increased African American entrepreneurial activity and initiatives. In 1970, 56 percent of African Americans in the United States ages 25 to 29 had completed at least 12 years of schooling. By 1993, 83 percent were high school graduates. In 1970, just 7 percent of African Americans in their late twenties had four or more years of college; by 1993, 13 percent had college degrees (Mergenhagen, 1996). Apparently, black business owners are highly educated people who have had previous work experience in the corporate world.

Most people believe that businesses employ workers, and to some extent, they do. However, 82 percent of all U.S. businesses had no paid employees in 1992. Among African American businesses, 90 percent had no paid employees. African American business owners, for the most part, are sole proprietors; in 1992, 94 percent were sole proprietors, compared with 85 percent for all business owners (Mergenhagen, 1996).

In addition, most African American enterprises are part-time ventures by people with other employment. African American businesses are more likely to provide supplemental rather than primary income. Because African American firms face unique problems and barriers regarding access to capital and business financing, many test the market before making any major commitment to their entrepreneurial endeavor. Consequently, African Americans frequently pursue their entrepreneurial interest part-time and typically on their own, and thus they tend to attract less capital than the average American company.

The average U.S. business earned $193,000 in 1992 sales, compared with the average African American business at $52,000 in sales. Obviously the lower initial investment of African American firms is directly correlated and responsible for their smaller size. And as we know, having adequate capital not only gives entrepreneurs a solid foundation for stating the business, it also is positively connected with the ability to secure additional funding. According to census data, the profile of the successful African American entrepreneur is that of a college graduate between the ages of 35 and 60 with above average income and a relatively large initial investment (Mergenhagen, 1996).

In one study of 229 of the largest African American businesses (Mergenhagen, 1996), half were identified as Subchapter C corporations, legal entities in which the ownership of the company is in shares of assignable and transferrable stock. In 1993, 53 percent had sales of more than $1,000,000. African American businesses tend to bring in less than average revenue because of the nature of their work. However, African American businesses are usually in the service industry (54 percent in 1992, up from 49 percent in 1987). There is an emerging group of African American enterprises in skill-intensive areas such as business and professional services. In 1987, personal-service companies accounted for 27 percent of African American–owned service firms; by 1992, the portion had declined to 23 percent. Meanwhile, the number of black-owned amusement and recreation firms, as well as firms involved in the film industry, grew at a faster than average rate. The proportion of African American firms providing education and social services also grew during that five-year period. The number of African American owners involved in finance, insurance, and real estate rose slightly faster than all black-owned businesses. The number of companies in manufacturing, agriculture, transportation, public utilities, and wholesale and retail trade industries each increased about a third, whereas the number of African American construction enterprises grew just 18 percent. These statistics refute the historical perception of African American service firms as being typically "mom-and-pop" convenience stores, beauty parlors, and barber shops. Most people start businesses in an industry or economic sector in which they have confidence. Because a growing number of African Americans have college degrees, they are increasingly likely to venture into the entrepreneurial world as providers of highly skilled professional and business services.

IMPLICATIONS AND CONCLUSION

Will African American entrepreneurship, small business enterprises, and family businesses continue their growth in the future? To what extent will changes in affirmative action policy in the public and private sectors affect business growth in various industries? The continuing tendency of corporate America to downsize and outsource will offer a range of opportunities to African American entrepreneurs. In terms of raising adequate capital, an increasing number of African Americans are participating in venture capital activities, putting deals together for other African Americans who wish to start or enlarge their businesses. Will these activities result in an increased opportunity or an improved environment for entrepreneurs to obtain adequate funding? Owning one's own business, being an entrepreneur, is still very much a part of the American dream. African Americans must step up their efforts and do what it takes to achieve that dream.

Now is the time for the human services community to revisit and redress the lack of opportunities for African Americans and to help improve their economic conditions. Assistance with education and job training, for example, has been helpful and somewhat adequate. But human services must interact more directly with both the public and the private sectors. New initiatives must involve new training and skills development in entrepreneurship and changing attitudes toward African American entrepreneurship, small business, and family enterprises.

It is much more common today to read headlines such as "Texaco Looking for Black Business" (1996; Williams, 1992). Corporate America increasingly will be seeking qualified, committed, and competent black businesspeople with whom it can begin trading. The racial woes of Texaco and other corporations with similar issues and problems can be transformed into benefits for new and established black entrepreneurs and communities across the nation. These corporations not only are creating new programs (voluntarily and involuntarily) that will instill racial sensitivity in upwardly mobile employees, but also are simultaneously opening up opportunities for black vendors and entrepreneurs to do business with the company.

African Americans must change their attitudes. They not only must focus on new job opportunities but, most important, must capture the entrepreneurial opportunities as well. These opportunities are almost endless—from operating franchises to becoming suppliers. This full participation in the mainstream American economy will affect human services delivery systems enormously.

As state and federal governments continue the journey toward privatizing certain segments of public service, new entrepreneurial business opportunities will also emerge in the public sector. What will the roles of human services be in these transactions? African Americans deserve adequate representation in these emerging opportunities.

What are some of the effects of family dynamics on the success of the entrepreneur? African American culture encourages a man to support his family by means of a successful career or occupation. His success at making a living influences how he sees himself, and it shapes his relationship with his family. Family involvement and support of the entrepreneur are critical to success. The correlation between healthy, helpful family and spousal relationships and entrepreneurial success is positive (Herbert, 1989).

Racial discrimination controversies at companies such as Texaco, Avis, and Circuit City attest to the struggle of corporate America to adapt to a changing work force. During the past 30 years, corporate America has been pushing for inclusiveness and diversity, mainly through affirmative action initiatives. The issue now is whether the culture of corporate America is prepared for a diverse work force. Most of the predominant cultural values of corporate America began more than a hundred years ago when the work force was much more homogeneous. Today, corporations and organizations of all kinds are struggling with diversity issues. Diversity training arose from a short-term mentality and, hence, remains a short-term solution. To create a culture that will allow substantial progress requires a major paradigm shift, that is, a major change to a new set of rules and values.

This new paradigm would set the stage for the creation of free enterprise and investment in future generations of African American children. Teaching business entrepreneurship to African American children should be a top priority. They should acquire entrepreneurial skills early in life to foster creative thinking and to impart a positive sense of accomplishment through their actions. The uncertainty regarding long-term job stability should be directly correlated with the need to develop entrepreneurial skills. Learning these skills is especially valuable for children who grow up in poverty. The "kidpreneurs" would have the advantage of learning early from their mistakes and would have less to lose if their business fails. They would learn that losing money and having a business fail is not the end of the world. African American children must become aware that they control their own destinies.

REFERENCES

Black Enterprise Industrial Service 100. (1997, June). *Black Enterprise Magazine,* pp. 137–145.

Butler, J. S. (1991). *Entrepreneurships and self-help among black Americans: A reconsideration of race and economics.* Albany: State University of New York Press.

City of Richmond (VA) v. J. A. Croson Company. (1989). 109 S. Ct. 706.

DuBois, W.E.B. (1899). *The Philadelphia negro.* Boston: Ginn.

Herbert, J. I. (1989). *Black male entrepreneurs and adult development.* New York: Praeger.

Johnston, W. B., & Packer, A. H. (1987). *Workforce 2000: Work and workers for the 21st century.* Indianapolis: Hudson Institute.

Litram, L. M. (1996, June 25). The changing face of ownership. *Investor's Business Daily.*

Mergenhagen, P. (1996, June). Black-owned businesses. *American Demographics and Consumer Trends*, pp. 27–33.

Texaco looking for black business. (1996, December 7–13). *Atlanta Voice*, p. 3.

Williams, L. (1992, December 15). Companies capitalizing on worker diversity. *New York Times*, pp. D1, D20.

25 The Afrocentric Paradigm and Workplace Diversity

Jerome H. Schiele

The recent emphasis on diversity in organizations throughout the United States represents a significant step toward greater inclusion of those who have been historically precluded from meaningful participation in the workplace. This emphasis has emerged primarily in response to claims that racism, sexism, and other "isms" have impeded employment and promotion opportunities for historically excluded groups and to demographic projections indicating that people of color will constitute a majority of the U.S. population in the near future (Carnevale & Stone, 1995; Fernandez, 1991; Henderson, 1994). Although the focus on diversifying the racial, ethnic, gender, and other demographic characteristics of the workplace is important, the meaning of workplace diversity needs to be expanded if we truly seek to empower those groups who have been excluded.

One way to expand the concept of workplace diversity is to view the cultural values of excluded groups as foundations on which to develop alternative theoretical assumptions of organizational structure and behavior. Although organizational theorizing appears to embrace diverse ideas, most of these theories are Eurocentric in their philosophical and cultural thrust and thus do not reflect the cultural values of people of color (Schiele, 1990). If values from European American culture can be used to develop theoretical assumptions of organizational structure and behavior, then cultural values from people of color should likewise be used as theoretical foundations for structuring organizations. Also, if the concept of workplace diversity is to expand even further, it should include the need for people of color to establish organizations that are managed and financed by them and that integrate their unique cultural style and traditions.

This chapter expands the concept of workplace diversity by applying traditional philosophical assumptions of people of African descent (that is, the Afrocentric paradigm) to identify recommendations for organizational structure and behavior. The chapter first elucidates the Afrocentric paradigm's assumptions about human beings and then applies them to demonstrate how the structure of the workplace can be altered to elicit positive organizational potentiality. *Positive organizational potentiality* is defined here as an organization's vast capabilities to be inclusive in its conceptions of human worth and in its use of culturally different strategies to become more effective in meeting the complete needs of clientele and staff. Last, this chapter applies the Afrocentric paradigm to suggest that diversity can be enhanced if people of color are encouraged to initiate self-help activities aimed at establishing organizations that reflect their cultural ethos and worldview.

ASSUMPTIONS OF THE AFROCENTRIC PARADIGM

In response to the cultural imposition and universalization of Euro-centric concepts in the social sciences and the general American society, a number of African American social scientists over the past 20 years have codified the cultural values and worldviews of people of African descent into a paradigm for explaining human behavior and solving human and societal problems (see, for example, Akbar, 1976, 1984, 1994; Ani, 1994; Asante, 1988, 1990; Baldwin, 1981, 1985; Baldwin & Hopkins, 1990; Boykin, 1983; Cook & Kono, 1977; Daly, Jennings, Beckett, & Leashore, 1995; Dixon, 1976; Hale-Benson, 1982; Harvey & Coleman, 1997; Hilliard, 1989; Kambon, 1992; Karenga, 1996; Khatib, Akbar, McGee, & Nobles, 1979; Myers, 1988; Nobles, 1980; Schiele, 1994, 1996). A primary assumption of this paradigm—generally referred to as the "Afrocentric," "Africentric," or "African-centered" paradigm—is that despite the colonization and enslavement of people of African descent by both Europeans and Arabs, traditional African philosophical assumptions and values have survived among people of African descent worldwide, including African Americans. Although the proponents of this paradigm acknowledge differences within the African diaspora, they generally believe that there is a common set of values and cultural themes that cuts across the diasporic diversity. These themes highlight a collective, spiritual, and affective worldview and can be said to affirm at least three fundamental assumptions: (1) human beings are perceived collectively, (2) human beings are spiritual, and (3) both affect and reason equally govern human behavior and knowing.

Collective Conception of Human Identity

The first assumption of the Afrocentric paradigm posits human identity as a collective identity (Akbar, 1984, 1994; Asante, 1988, 1990; Mbiti, 1970). The focus and belief found in much of Eurocentric social science that there is an insular entity called the "self" is refuted in Afrocentric theory. Although individual uniqueness is acknowledged, the Afrocentric paradigm maintains that individual identity cannot be separated from one's corporate or collective identity (Akbar, 1984; Boykin & Toms, 1985; Nobles, 1980). In this way, individual identity is viewed not only as a reflection of one's corporate identity but also as a unique way in which the corporate self operates and expresses itself in the person. Because individual identity is seen as a unique expression of a broader collective identity in the Afrocentric paradigm, there is no need to view the unique expression as oppositional to its collective source (Gyekye, 1992a). Moreover, this collective concept of self can foster unity among distinct elements of collective selves, because critical to the Afrocentric paradigm is the notion that all people are created from a similar universal source and thus potentially represent different expressions of the source that is God. In this regard, the Afrocentric paradigm encourages an emphasis on similarity and inclusion rather than on difference and exclusion (Baldwin & Hopkins, 1990), and it contends that social unity among people with different collective selves (that is, cultural identities) can be achieved without cultural uniformity (Asante, 1992; Swigonski, 1996).

Spiritual Foundation of Human Beings

Consistent with the notion of collective identity is the belief that humans not only are material beings, but also are spiritual beings who are infinite in their scope and capacity. The unseen component of human beings is believed to generate greater scope and capacity because the spiritual self is not limited by time and space and, as a result of its capacity for self-extension, is better suited to tap into the vastness of the Creator and the cosmos (Baldwin, 1981; Kambon, 1992). The notion of a spiritual being with vast capabilities supports the belief that when humans acknowledge and tap into the power inherent in spiritual oneness, they tend to behave in ways that are constructive rather than destructive. Behavior is likely to be aimed toward morally affirming practices that accentuate concern for the welfare of the community and humanity. From an Afrocentric perspective, when people perceive themselves exclusively as physical and material beings, this perception not only limits their potential but also restricts their ability to regulate their physical and material desires that, if left unchecked, can influence extreme avarice and human exploitation (Myers, 1988; Schiele, 1996).

Affect and Reason as Equally Important

The Afrocentric paradigm's collective and spiritual view of human beings fosters a multidimensional perspective of human behavior and knowing. Within this paradigm, affect (emotion) and reason are acknowledged as equally important aspects of human behavior and knowing, because affect and reason are two transparent and penetrable sides of the same coin. Both work together and unsubordinately to shape human behavior and knowing (Schiele, 1996).

Although the Afrocentric paradigm recognizes the role of rationality, it conceives rationality differently from its conceptualization in traditional Eurocentric social science. The traditional view of human rationality in Eurocentric social science validates the belief in an unemotional thinker who is analytical and objective (Akbar, 1984, 1994). Within this framework, considerable value is placed on exclusively viewing the world fragmentarily and not allowing observations to be tainted by feelings and opinions, which are seen as separate from and inferior to reason.

The Afrocentric paradigm's concept of rationality underscores the importance of affect and the reliance on holistic logic (Ani, 1994; Bell, 1994). The Afrocentric paradigm contends that acknowledging the significance of affect in human behavior prevents humans from being conceived as mechanistic and sterile beings who invariably behave predictably (Akbar, 1984; Ani, 1994). Moreover, recognizing the importance of affect allows human knowing to be predicated on not only material evidence discerned through the physical senses, but also through extrasensual perception such as psychokinesis, precognition, intuition, and "vibes" (Gyekye, 1995; Kambon, 1992). This affective epistemology also rejects objectivity and replaces it with a positive view of subjectivity that highlights feelings and personal values as intrinsic attributes of people (Asante, 1988; Schiele, 1996).

Holistic logic is based on the assumption that although world elements can appear as parts, it is the whole that should be given the most attention (Bell, 1994; Dixon, 1976). The whole is significant because it unifies the parts, even if they appear oppositional. Holistic logic sees opposites as in conflict and in unity simultaneously (Dzobo, 1992); thus, it handles contradictions better than linear or analytic logic, because it acknowledges the interconnectedness of the most seemingly extreme polarities (Bell, 1994; Kambon, 1992).

AFROCENTRICITY AND POSITIVE POTENTIALITY IN ORGANIZATIONS

Because of the heavy emphasis on rationality (efficiency), competition, and individualism found in Eurocentric organizational theories and models (Daly, 1994; Schiele, 1990; Warfield-Coppock, 1995), the current structure of U.S. organizations can be viewed as limiting positive organizational potentiality. Positive organizational potentiality seeks to preclude the development and maintenance of the overemphasis in Eurocentric organizational models toward efficiency, competition, and individualism. Also, when positive organizational potentiality is maximized, the likelihood of organizations that are multicultural in their demographic makeup practicing cultural oppression is diminished. To structure organizations that are based on Afrocentric assumptions and that can influence greater positive organizational potentiality, the following approaches are advocated: de-emphasize efficiency, focus on collective work and responsibility, use consensus decision making, and incorporate diverse ideas about hiring and performance appraisal.

De-emphasize Efficiency

From an Afrocentric perspective, the overwhelming value placed on efficiency and speed in organizations should be diminished. This perspective does not imply that effectiveness must be compromised, because efficiency and effectiveness are two different organizational entities (Bloom, Fischer, & Orme, 1995). Although some degree of attention to quantitative measures (for example, quickness and speed) is important, its overemphasis can lessen the kind of quality time needed for successful problem solving, change, and goal achievement. In human services organizations, this concept means that an overemphasis on efficiency can bring about hasty solutions and procedures that might not adequately fit the needs of consumers. Because of the priority given to efficiency, consumer needs and problems can be oversimplified so that they "fit" neatly into statistical categories and hasty goal statements.

The focus on efficiency in organizations also implies that humans should and can work mechanistically with little or no error. The Afrocentric paradigm, which recognizes the importance of affect and spontaneity in people's lives, would suggest that mechanistic and error-free assumptions or desires in several Eurocentric organizational models are not only inappropriate but also oppressive. Upholding expectations of people as mechanistic creates an unrealistic standard that can be used to superfluously criticize, reprimand, demote, or fire workers. Also, because the speed at which activities are accomplished is usually a major organizational objective, needs of workers that are external to their expectations to perform efficiently (their socioemotional needs) are generally unmet and are considered secondary. Thus, workers are dehumanized because their worth as human beings is confined to their ability to perform efficiently.

Focus on Collective Work and Responsibility

The concept of collective work and responsibility in the Afrocentric paradigm, known as *ujima,* underscores the importance of unity and collective responsibility in organizational work (Karenga, 1996). This concept flows from the Afrocentric paradigm's concept of spirituality, which accentuates the oneness and interconnectedness of human beings. Thus, the individual organizational member is perceived as a unique manifestation of the collective identity of the organization. To this extent, it is important from an Afrocentric viewpoint to limit internal organizational conflict and competition. To achieve organizational unity, the Afrocentric model recommends the following actions: value the worth and dignity of organizational members equally; limit internal differentiation of work tasks and, when possible, exchange or share tasks; emphasize person-to-person communications more than written communications; and recognize groups more than individual members.

Value Worth and Dignity. Because spirituality also implies morality in Afrocentric thought (Akbar, 1984; Boykin, 1983), the worth and dignity of each organizational member would be equally affirmed in Afrocentric organizations. Worth and dignity of organizational members imply not only the overall self-worth of the member as part of the human family connected to a common universal source, but also the importance of the skill the person brings to the organization and the unique way he or she performs the skill. When organizations focus on the similar origins and spiritual connection of humans, hierarchical schemes of human self-worth that rank order people by their outer (material) qualities such as gender, skin color, and weight are unnecessary. Organizations based on Afrocentric principles also would not value some worker skills over others because the Afrocentric paradigm accentuates the mutual dependency, or interdependency, of worker skills and talents. All skills needed for the effective operation of the organization are considered equally essential. Thus, for example, housekeeping skills, which are often seen as subordinate to others, would be valued just as much as others and even more so because the execution of additional organizational activities are predicated significantly on a sanitary and aesthetically pleasant work milieu.

Limit Differentiation of Work Tasks. Low internal differentiation and exchange of work tasks are important in fostering organizational collectivity and effectiveness (Daly, 1994). High internal differentiation of tasks often leads to the emergence of well-defined organizational subunits that can encourage members to become more committed to the goals and interests of their subdivisions than to the collective goals of the entire organization (Daly, 1982; Selznick, 1948). The exchange of work tasks can prevent the overcommitment to subunit goals and provide organizational members with the opportunity to take on the "skill identity" of another. This exchange can nurture a kind of collective, organizational empathy and respect for diverse tasks that otherwise one would not have.

Emphasize Person-to-Person Communications. Warfield-Coppock (1995) maintained that person-to-person communications would be appropriate in Afrocentric organizations and could facilitate greater organizational harmony among workers because the exchange of ideas would not be filtered through a medium (for example, a memorandum) that could make communications appear impersonal and perfunctory. Person-to-person communication also provides the advantage of observing gestures and facial expressions and listening to someone's voice. In the Afrocentric paradigm, not only is what people say important, but also important is how they express their ideas through the rhythm and tone of their voice and through their body and facial gestures (Akbar, 1976; Asante, 1980). Face-to-face communications also require organizational members who may be at odds with one another to communicate rather than to sustain their animosity through avoidance.

Recognize Groups. Group recognition is encouraged more than individual recognition. Focus on individual achievement alone denies or downplays collective efforts and skills of those involved in helping a person strive. Also, exclusive or primary attention to individual achievement may tend to engender envy among organizational members when they are not equally recognized for their accomplishments.

Use Consensus Decision Making

In traditional African societies, although an elected chief and council of elders served as the governing body of a village, town, or state, there was the practice of eliciting public opinions from any citizen. If disagreement occurred on an issue, the council of elders would listen to arguments until unanimity was obtained (Chazan, 1993; Gyekye, 1992b; Williams, 1987). The goal of these debates was not for one perspective to overcome another, but for opposites to be blurred so that a compromise could be reached (Chazan, 1993; Gyekye, 1992b). Because these discussions could sometimes be extensive, there was less concern for making swift decisions by a few people for the sake of efficiency (Gyekye, 1992b; Williams, 1987).

The emphasis on communalism and consensus in traditional African practice and philosophy encourages organizations to form structures and procedures that elicit the opinions of all organizational members when there is disagreement. This practice can foster not only inclusion but also prudent decision making because the more heads that work together to solve a problem, the greater the likelihood will be of finding a good solution and anticipating contingencies. This conclusion was confirmed by Daly (1994), who found that the use of problem-solving communication, in which ideas are elicited from a variety of workers, can assist organizations in successfully meeting the challenges of a turbulent organizational milieu. Also, the focus on consensus decision making is extended to include the opinions and suggestions of those in the organization's environment. From an Afrocentric perspective, the organization and the environment or community to which it belongs and serves are deemed one, because the concept of organizational survival in the Afrocentric paradigm transcends the boundaries of the organization to include the survival of the environment or community of which the organization is a part (Schiele, 1990).

Although some degree of hierarchy would be expected in Afrocentric organizations, superior–subordinate relationships would be discouraged (Schiele, 1990). Relationships wherein one person is responsible for the actions of others would be seen less as power-imposing relationships and more as compassionate power relationships. Power-imposing relationships in organizations are built on superior–subordinate relationships and on beliefs that workers are prone to indolence and a lack of self-regulation. Compassionate power relationships are based on sincere mutual respect, the belief in worker self-regulation, and the belief that power should be shared.

From an Afrocentric viewpoint, it also is important to realize that for organization members to participate fully in decision-making processes, the stress related to home and child care must be minimized. To do this, the Afrocentric paradigm encourages flexible work hours, provision of child care services at the workplace, and ample family leave and vacation time (Schiele, 1997; Warfield-Coppock,

1995). These strategies may lead to greater perceptions of organizational support among workers. Indeed, when workers perceive that organizations care about their overall well-being, job satisfaction, job performance, and commitment to the organization increases (Daly, 1994; Eisenberger, Fasolo, & Davis-LaMastro, 1990; Witt, 1994).

Incorporate Diverse Ideas about Hiring and Performance Appraisal

To the degree that an organization employs people from culturally diverse backgrounds, the Afrocentric paradigm supports the application of diverse procedures for hiring and performance appraisal. Too often in organizations today, uniform criteria are used to hire and evaluate workers. This practice is usually justified by the need to uphold the values of fairness and meritocracy. However, the ideals of complete fairness and meritocracy are rarely observed in organizational practice (Arvey & Faley, 1988). From an Afrocentric viewpoint, fairness and meritocracy in the American workplace can be viewed as smoke screens to conceal the practice of white supremacy and to promote the universalism of European American (Eurocentric) culture. For this chapter's purpose, *white supremacy* is defined as the individual and institutional intentions and practices of European Americans to ensure their political and economic advantage over people of color. *Eurocentric cultural universalism* can be defined as the belief and projection of European American definitions of reality as historically ubiquitous and culturally global. Both white supremacy and Eurocentric cultural universalism obviate the hiring (inclusion) of people of color in the workplace and, more importantly, preclude additional cultural ideas about hiring and performance appraisal.

From an Afrocentric perspective, inclusion of more people of color in the workplace can be significantly aided by eliminating the hegemony of Eurocentric cultural concepts of hiring and performance appraisal. These concepts reinforce what Eurocentric culture projects to be proper criteria for hiring and performance appraisal. Some examples of these criteria—keeping in mind that many are subtle—are direct eye contact in personal conversations; the pervasive integration of humor in conversations; the acceptance and knowledge of Eurocentric theories of human behavior, development, and service interventions (for example, in mental health and social services organizations); the suppression of affect and bodily gestures in communication; the denial of racism or racial discrimination in organizational activities; the recognition of individual achievement over collective achievement; the familiarity with the English language and specific European American applications of English; and the evaluation of workers primarily on material and specific aspects of their work that tend to conform easily to reductionistic definitions of efficiency and effectiveness.

The Afrocentric paradigm, therefore, advocates more culturally inclusive criteria for hiring and performance appraisal that embrace the cultural values of diverse groups that constitute an organization.

This inclusiveness also extends to those who receive organizational interventions—the clients or consumers. For example, in mental health and social services organizations, rather than exclusively applying Eurocentric standards in hiring that seek to determine the degree to which one affirms and is knowledgeable of Eurocentric theories of human behavior, development, and human services interventions, standards would include knowledge of theories that emerge from different cultural traditions and worldviews. Instead of applicants of color, for instance, being expected to limit knowledge and skills to Eurocentric theories, hiring standards would be developed to tap their degree of familiarity and ability to apply theories of human behavior and human services interventions that emanate from their unique cultural traditions and worldviews.

Likewise, performance appraisals for people of color would be based on knowledge and application of similar kinds of knowledge. Furthermore, because performance appraisals are predicated heavily on accepting and exhibiting organizational norms of language and communication style and because in the United States, these norms validate Eurocentric standards, people of color and others who possess different language and communication styles may be unfairly evaluated. The Afrocentric paradigm recommends that existing workplaces either evaluate people of color on their particular language or communication styles or exclude language and communication skills entirely from the assessment process. Diversification of organizational standards of hiring and performance appraisal, in short, would encourage the cultural pluralism of the workplace, in which there would be complete validation and inclusion of culturally diverse ideas about the structure and activities of organizations. In this way, organizational climates that encourage integration of diverse skills and ideas to address demands of a culturally diverse organizational environment can emerge.

ENHANCING DIVERSITY THROUGH GROUP SELF-HELP

Although the Afrocentric paradigm urges the inclusion of diverse ideas about organizational structure and operation that emanate from culturally excluded and oppressed groups, it also realizes that there is and will be tenacious opposition to complete cultural inclusion. This opposition can stem not only from practical considerations about managing diversity in the workplace but also from efforts to maintain Eurocentric cultural hegemony. To a considerable extent, concerns raised about the difficulty in managing diversity can be interpreted as subterfuge to continue Eurocentric cultural hegemony. From an Afrocentric viewpoint, maintaining this hegemony has less to do with concerns about hiring more culturally excluded and oppressed groups and more to do with concerns about the inclusion of culturally different organizational models that challenge the assumptions of traditional Eurocentric paradigms of organizations.

Because some people will continue to fight against workplace diversity of this kind for the sake of continuing Eurocentric cultural dominance and thus marginalize the legitimacy of using the cultural values of people of color as a foundation for new organizational structures, the Afrocentric paradigm encourages culturally excluded and oppressed groups, especially African Americans and other people of color, to establish and support organizations that are managed and financed by them and that are structured to integrate their unique cultural style and traditions (that is, self-help). Although self-help may sound contrary to the previous discussions about inclusion, the Afrocentric paradigm maintains that the tactic of challenging Eurocentric cultural hegemony is not inconsistent with encouraging people of color to do for themselves (Asante, 1988; Karenga, 1993).

Self-help is important for all groups in the United States and especially for those whose cultural style is most distinct from the European American cultural model. Although similarities in experiences of oppression cut across racial and ethnic groups, there have been significant differences between the ways various European immigrant groups and people of color have been received and treated (Lieberson, 1980; Takaki, 1993). People of color, especially those who were colonized and forced into the United States, have had a more difficult time being included and accepted (Longres, 1995). In part, this exclusion occurred because they were seen as more culturally different (Longres, 1995), which caused them to experience maximum cultural oppression (Blauner, 1972). Because African Americans arguably represent the most extreme and prolonged example of involuntary entry into the United States through slavery, it can be maintained that they have been one of the most dehumanized victims of cultural oppression.

The cultural oppression experienced by people of color whose entry into the United States was forced renders self-help an essential option for these groups for at least three reasons. First, it prevents the group from placing all of its social-change eggs in one basket. Although efforts to challenge the existing European American society to be more inclusive are worthwhile, this strategy depends heavily on the hope that a significant number of European Americans, especially those in power, will radically alter their mindsets and, more important, the institutional structures from which they benefit economically. Although transforming the mindsets of some European Americans is definitely possible, it may not be politically and economically advantageous for European Americans collectively, particularly because many European Americans today are finding it increasingly difficult to find stable employment themselves.

Second, self-help for people of color is important because it is an avenue through which they can eliminate the adverse psychological effects of cultural oppression. Eurocentric cultural oppression has resulted in the pervasive belief that Eurocentric definitions of reality are the only lenses through which reality can be perceived (Ani, 1994;

Kambon, 1992). Eurocentric cultural oppression has been psychologically damaging for both people of European descent and people of color. For people of European descent, it tends to engender a false sense of cultural superiority, whereas for people of color it tends to create a false sense of cultural inferiority (Ani, 1994; Kambon, 1992). Thus, the act of people of color establishing and maintaining their own organizations can be viewed as an essential step in repairing and enhancing their collective self-confidence and self-esteem.

Last, self-help can be seen as a stronger strategy to bring cultural pluralism into complete fruition. Because the United States is based on a capitalist economy, the Afrocentric perspective maintains that a group's political power is significantly related to its degree of economic autonomy. Besides enhancing opportunities for advancing their material interests, the political power generated from economic autonomy would give people of color greater political leverage for promoting their cultural values and worldviews. Thus, Eurocentric cultural hegemony would be eradicated, because people of color would be better able to project and imprint their cultural styles and traditions onto the American landscape. This would influence a more egalitarian distribution of power among diverse cultural groups.

CONCLUSION

The concept of workplace diversity could be substantially broadened if the cultural values of people of color were used to develop additional ideas about organizational structure and behavior. Based on traditional African philosophical assumptions, the Afrocentric paradigm is one mode through which organizations can be conceptualized and structured. It provides a psychological and political justification for groups of color generally, and African Americans specifically, to establish organizations that reflect their cultural ethos. The conceptualization of organizations through the cultural values of people of color and the call for them to establish their own organizations help diversify the workplace and bring cultural pluralism into reality. When the concept of workplace diversity expands and cultural pluralism is brought into fruition, cultural hegemony dissipates. The elimination of cultural hegemony should not be interpreted as a threat but rather as an opportunity for the United States to redeem itself from the persistent plight it has caused those who rightfully have sought economic justice and human affirmation.

REFERENCES

Akbar, N. (1976). Rhythmic patterns in African personality. In L. King, V. Dixon, & W. Nobles (Eds.), *African philosophy: Assumptions and paradigms for research on black people* (pp. 175–189). Los Angeles: Fanon Center Publications.

Akbar, N. (1984). Africentric social sciences for human liberation. *Journal of Black Studies, 14*, 395–414.

Akbar, N. (1994). *Light from ancient Africa.* Tallahassee, FL: Mind Productions.

Ani, M. (1994). *Yurugu: An African-centered critique of European cultural thought and behavior.* Trenton, NJ: Africa World Press.

Arvey, R. D., & Faley, R. H. (1988). *Fairness in selecting employees* (2nd ed.). Reading, MA: Addison-Wesley.

Asante, M. K. (1980). International/intercultural relations. In M. K. Asante & A. Vandi (Eds.), *Contemporary black thought* (pp. 43–58). Beverly Hills, CA: Sage Publications.

Asante, M. K. (1988). *Afrocentricity.* Trenton, NJ: Africa World Press.

Asante, M. K. (1990). *Kemet, Afrocentricity, and knowledge.* Trenton, NJ: Africa World Press.

Asante, M. K. (1992, April). The painful demise of Eurocentrism. *World & I,* pp. 305–317.

Baldwin, J. (1981). Notes on an Africentric theory of black personality. *Western Journal of Black Studies, 5,* 172–179.

Baldwin, J. (1985). Psychological aspects of European cosmology in American society. *Western Journal of Black Studies, 9,* 216–223.

Baldwin, J., & Hopkins, R. (1990). African-American and European-American cultural differences as assessed by the worldviews paradigm: An empirical analysis. *Western Journal of Black Studies, 14,* 38–52.

Bell, Y. R. (1994). A culturally sensitive analysis of black learning style. *Journal of Black Psychology, 20*(1), 47–61.

Blauner, R. (1972). *Racial oppression in America.* New York: Harper & Row.

Bloom, M., Fischer, J., & Orme, J. (1995). *Evaluating practice: Guidelines for the accountable professional* (2nd ed.). Needham Heights, MA: Allyn & Bacon.

Boykin, W. (1983). The academic performance of Afro-American children. In J. Spence (Ed.), *Achievement and achievement motives* (pp. 324–371). San Francisco: Freeman.

Boykin, W., & Toms, F. (1985). Black child socialization: A conceptual framework. In H. P. McAdoo (Ed.), *Black children* (pp. 33–51). Beverly Hills, CA: Sage Publications.

Carnevale, A. P., & Stone, S. C. (1995). *The American mosaic: An in-depth report on the future of diversity at work.* New York: McGraw-Hill.

Chazan, N. (1993). Between liberalism and statism: African political cultures and democracy. In L. Diamond (Ed.), *Political culture and democracy in developing countries* (pp. 67–105). Boulder, CO: Lynne Rienner.

Cook, N., & Kono, S. (1977). Black psychology: The third great tradition. *Journal of Black Psychology, 3*(2), 18–20.

Daly, A. (1982). *The impact of decentralization on organizational effectiveness in an urban county department of social services.* Unpublished doctoral dissertation, University of Michigan, Ann Arbor.

Daly, A. (1994). African American and white managers: A comparison in one agency. *Journal of Community Practice, 1*(1), 57–79.

Daly, A., Jennings, J., Beckett, J., & Leashore, B. (1995). Effective coping strategies of African Americans. *Social Work, 40,* 240–248.

Dixon, V. (1976). World views and research methodology. In L. King, V. Dixon, & W. Nobles (Ed.), *African philosophy: Assumptions and paradigms for research on black persons* (pp. 51–93). Los Angeles: Fanon Center.

Dzobo, N. K. (1992). The image of man in Africa. In K. Wiredu & K. Gyekye (Eds.), *Person and community: Ghanaian philosophical studies* (pp. 123–135). Washington, DC: Council for Research in Values and Philosophy.

Eisenberger, R., Fasolo, P., & Davis-LaMastro, V. (1990). Perceived organizational support and employee diligence, commitment, and innovation. *Journal of Applied Psychology, 75*(1), 51–59.

Fernandez, J. P. (1991). *Managing a diverse work force: Regaining the competitive edge.* Lexington, MA: Lexington Books.

Gyekye, K. (1992a). Person and community in African thought. In K. Wiredu & K. Gyekye (Eds.), *Person and community: Ghanaian philosophical studies* (pp. 101–122). Washington, DC: Council for Research in Values and Philosophy.

Gyekye, K. (1992b). Traditional political ideas: Their relevance to development in contemporary Africa. In K. Wiredu & K. Gyekye (Eds.), *Person and community: Ghanaian philosophical studies* (pp. 241–255). Washington, DC: Council for Research in Values and Philosophy.

Gyekye, K. (1995). An essay on African philosophical thought—The Akan conceptual scheme. In A. G. Mosely (Ed.), *African philosophy: Selected readings* (pp. 339–349). Englewood Cliffs, NJ: Prentice Hall.

Hale-Benson, J. (1982). *Black children: Their roots, culture, and learning styles.* Provo, UT: Brigham Young University Press.

Harvey, A. R., & Coleman, A. (1997). An Afrocentric program for African American males in the juvenile justice system. *Child Welfare, 76,* 197–211.

Henderson, G. (1994). *Cultural diversity in the workplace.* Westport, CT: Quorum Books.

Hilliard, A. G. (1989). Kemetic concepts in education. In I. V. Sertima (Ed.), *Nile Valley civilizations* (pp. 153–162). Atlanta: Morehouse College.

Kambon, K. (1992). *The African personality in America: An African-centered framework.* Tallahassee, FL: Nubian Nation.

Karenga, M. (1993). *Introduction to black studies* (2nd ed.). Los Angeles: University of Sankore Press.

Karenga, M. (1996). The nguzo saba (the seven principles): Their meaning and message. In M. K. Asante & A. S. Abarry (Eds.), *African intellectual heritage* (pp. 543–554). Philadelphia: Temple University Press.

Khatib, S., Akbar, N., McGee, D., & Nobles, W. (1979). Voodoo or IQ: An introduction to African psychology. In W. D. Smith, K. H. Burlew, M. H. Mosley, & W. M. Whitney (Eds.), *Reflections on black psychology* (pp. 61–87). Washington, DC: University Press of America.

Lieberson, S. (1980). *A piece of the pie: Blacks and white immigrants since 1880.* Berkeley: University of California Press.

Longres, J. F. (1995). *Human behavior in the social environment* (2nd ed.). Itasca, IL: F. E. Peacock.

Mbiti, J. (1970). *African religions and philosophy.* Garden City, NY: Anchor Books.

Myers, L. J. (1988). *Understanding an Afrocentric world view: Introduction to an optimal psychology.* Dubuque, IA: Kendall/Hunt.

Nobles, W. W. (1980). African philosophy: Foundations for black psychology. In R. Jones (Ed.), *Black psychology* (3rd ed., pp. 23–35). New York: Harper & Row.

Schiele, J. H. (1990). Organizational theory from an Afrocentric perspective. *Journal of Black Studies, 21*(2), 145–161.

Schiele, J. H. (1994). Afrocentricity as an alternative world view for equality. *Journal of Progressive Human Services, 5*(1), 5–25.

Schiele, J. H. (1996). Afrocentricity: An emerging paradigm in social work practice. *Social Work, 41,* 284–294.

Schiele, J. H. (1997). An Afrocentric perspective on social welfare philosophy and policy. *Journal of Sociology & Social Welfare, 24*(2), 21–39.

Selznick, P. (1948). Foundation for the theory of organization. *American Sociological Review, 13,* 25–35.

Swigonski, M. E. (1996). Challenging privilege through Africentric social work practice. *Social Work, 41,* 153–161.

Takaki, R. (1993). *A different mirror: A history of multicultural America.* Boston: Little, Brown.

Warfield-Coppock, N. (1995). Toward a theory of Afrocentric organizations. *Journal of Black Psychology, 21*(1), 30–48.

Williams, C. (1987). *The destruction of black civilization: Great issues of a race from 4500 B.C. to 2000 A.D.* Chicago: Third World Press.

Witt, L. A. (1994). *Perceptions of organizational support and affectivity as predictors of job satisfaction.* Washington, DC: Federal Aviation Administration, Office of Aviation Medicine.

26 Diversity in the Workplace:
Issues and Concerns of Africans and Asians

Letha A. See

History shows that great economic and social forces flow like a tide over communities only half conscious of that which is befalling them. Wise statesmen foresee what time is thus bringing, and try to shape institutions and mold men's thoughts and purposes in accordance with the change that is silently coming on. The unwise are those who bring nothing constructive to the process, and who greatly imperil the future of mankind by leaving great questions to be fought out between ignorant change on one hand and ignorant opposition to change on the other.

—John Stuart Mill

Mill's eloquence strikes a resounding note. But the most telling part of the statement is that as far back as the 1800s, he correctly predicted many of America's postindustrial work force challenges and the supersonic speed of change that would occur in America's social system in general and in its workplaces in particular. Currently, as we straddle two eras and edge toward the next millennium, workplaces throughout this nation will continue to face formidable change and turbulence of an order unlike any that has occurred in the past (Bell, 1985; Naisbitt, 1982; Toffler, 1990). An in-depth analysis reveals that this impending work force change will be, in part, a result of burgeoning technological sophistication characterized by complex communication systems and from occupational upheaval stemming from increased mechanization and automation (Naisbitt, 1982; Toffler, 1990). This significant change is driven by globalization of the economy and the vigorous and expanding internationalization of business negotiated by individual states in the nation. In this scheme of things, plant closings, firings, takeovers, mergers, downsizing, outsourcing, and restructuring, as well as product obsolescence and modification of production, are causing disorientation of dizzying proportions (Bargal, 1984; Chestang, 1982; Ribner, 1993; Toffler, 1971, 1981, 1990). Unfortunately, the social outcome of these macroforces accounts for systemic disequilibrium, frustration, and bewilderment—partially caused by trade imbalance in the global economy, America's transformation from a creditor to a debtor nation, worker displacement, a thinning and collapsing white middle class, and the emergence of an increasingly angry black underclass (Cose, 1993; Herrnstein & Murray, 1994; Murray, 1984; Wilson, 1987, 1991).

Ostensibly, America faces many serious workplace challenges and opportunities. But a second imponderable also exists, apart from macrosystemic problems—successive waves of Africans, Asians, and other foreign-born groups are entering this country seeking to participate in the world of work. In the 1990s they accounted for half of the work force (Johnston & Packer, 1987). These new multicultural, multiethnic, multiracial workers, many of whom are trained professionals in various scientific disciplines, have the capacity to help stimulate economic growth and ultimately influence the direction of the country's future. On the contrary, they have the power to destroy the foundation of the traditional workplace, halt economic growth, and threaten this country's economic dynamism and its role as the world's superpower (Adler & Bartholomew, 1992; Ehrlich & Garland, 1988; Gardenswartz & Rowe, 1989a, 1989b, 1989c; Gurwitt, 1989; Johnston & Packer, 1987; Linomes, 1993; Nelton, 1988; Schachter, 1988).

The new work force entrants are a conglomeration of diverse groups who exhibit differences in age, ethnic heritage, culture, language, history, gender, religion, spirituality, physical ability, qualities, race, and sexual orientation. Already they have contributed to a new mix of skin colors and have resettled in every region of the country (Fine, 1991; Johnston & Packer, 1987; See, 1996). Clearly, responding to the mix of new people and variations in circumstance with which they are associated requires creative thinking, rapid assessment, and decisive action on the part of the nation's economic, social, and political managers—especially because the flow of migration to this country is irreversible.

A broad objective of this chapter is to describe and analyze troublesome trends, issues, and concerns that are affecting Africans and Asians in America's workplaces. An effort will be made to properly define the dimensions of diversity and to examine the meaning and significance of work. A sequential task is to examine why managers have used assimilation as the prevailing model for incorporating groups such as Africans and Asians into the workplace. Finally, strategies for assisting managers to celebrate difference are presented.

SOCIODEMOGRAPHIC DATA FOR AFRICANS AND ASIANS

Pervasive sociodemographic changes are occurring at a dramatic pace. Asians and Africans are diverse populations representing a sizable number of the immigrants and refugees entering the United States. Demographic evidence reveals that the confluence of legal immigrants admitted to America is close to 1 million per year. The *1992 Statistical Yearbook of the Immigration and Naturalization Service* (U.S. Immigration and Naturalization Service, 1993) reported that 1.9 million newcomers (legal and illegal) entered this nation in 1991, and more than 1.8 million were granted permanent residence. According to Brown and Broderick (1994) and Lum (1996), during the past two decades, two waves of Asian and African immigrants requested entry to the United States. Between waves, the Asian population increased from 1.5 million to 3.5 million (a 126 percent growth rate). At present, Asians constitute 2 percent of the total American population.

Between 1975 and 1993, a total of 1,803,527 refugees were admitted to the United States. Of that number, 1,136,957, or 63 percent, came from East Asia; 84,828, or 5 percent, from the Near East and South Asia; and 40,945, or 2 percent, from Africa. In 1994, the annual ceiling on refugee admissions was 121,000, with the following breakdown of Africans and Asians: Africans, 7,000, and Asians, 45,000 (Lum, 1996; U.S. Bureau of the Census, 1990, 1991a, 1991b, 1991c, 1993). However, between 1965 and 1992, more than 2.25 million people emigrated from Africa to the United States, about 3 percent of the total number of immigrants accepted.

With population and migratory shifts of these subcultures and with their technological competency, they represent a source of potent human resources for workplace needs and work force capabilities. Correspondingly, with the remarkable work ethic both Asians and Africans have developed, predictably they will be the subject of attention of social scientists, futurists, economists, professionals, union watchers, and cinema and electronic media for many years to come.

LITERATURE GAP ON WORKPLACE ISSUES

Despite the spate of attention focused on the demographics of Asians and Africans seeking employment in the United States and notwithstanding the heated rhetoric about the diversity mosaic, no systematic, orderly, or sustained attention has been devoted to a serious study of these groups. Similarly, social science theorists have failed to propose theoretical models, perspectives, paradigms, critical methods, and frameworks with sufficient rigor to explain certain sociocultural and demographic variables caused by changes in the mix of human diversity in the workplace.

Literature reveals that the failure by researchers to devise appropriate theoretical frameworks for studying diverse populations is largely the result of their attempt to use logical positivism and its attendant theoretical and methodological assumptions in formulating theory. However, with new consideration being given to ontological and epistemological assumptions that differ significantly from logical positivism, models for studying diversity in the workplace may soon become a reality (Souflee, 1993). At another level, social science scholars, who engage in a relentless search for truth, have been noticeably inattentive to America's refusal to admit that changing complexions are among the causal factors exacerbating conflicts between newcomers in and out of the workplace (Bach, 1979; See, 1986). A sinister implication drawn by some observers is that our national identity is so fragile that it can absorb diverse and immigrant cultures only by re-contextualizing them as deficient or by pitting one group against another. The implicit assumption is that this nation cannot survive unless it contains only like-looking, like-speaking, like-worshipping people who embrace the same ideology and value system.

At a commencement ceremony at the University of California at San Diego on June 16, 1997, President Bill Clinton, among the most eloquent white politicians on the subject of racial reconciliation since Abraham Lincoln, delivered a powerful address in which he chronicled a constellation of attitudes and behaviors that keeps the races divided and he issued a call to action. His prescription for celebrating diversity in and out of the workplace could open a new national debate on the issue of race and work, an issue that is at the crux of intergroup conflict.

A THEORETICAL FORMULATION FOR EXAMINING WORK FORCE DIVERSITY

Before examining how Africans and Asians are actually adjusting in the workplace, it should be stated that several theoretical frameworks could be used for setting boundaries and examining work force issues. These could include Germain and Gitterman's (1980) life model, Hill's (in press) asset-resilience insights, and Maluccio's (1981) competency-oriented practice. However, general systems theory as a theoretical construct seems to represent a clear, appropriate, noncontroversial frame of reference that addresses how various "systems" (in this context, Africans and Asians) adjust in the American workplace and how various processes enhance the adjustment. Although systems theory is basically a mathematical model adapted from the second law of thermodynamics, it is sufficiently broad for reorientation in a gamut of disciplines from physics and biology to the social sciences and philosophy.

A number of physical and social scientists from related disciplines have alluded to general systems theory as a theoretical model that is applicable to the nature of interaction between groups (Asians and Africans) and found it has great currency in its application (Bredemeier & Stephenson, 1964; Churchman, 1968; Laszlo, 1972; von Bertalanffy, 1968). Specifically, systems in the context of foreign-born people in the work force can be open or closed to interaction with the outside environment and can be linked hierarchically. Systems have inputs and outputs; they can possess states of viable homeostasis or lapse into disequilibrium. Systems are regulated through positive and negative feedback, and causal influences are curvilinear. In other words, change in one part of a system (for example, the entry of Asians and Africans into the workplace) have consequences for other linked systems that, in turn, through feedback, have consequences for the first system. Finally, general systems theory emphasizes equifinality, which suggests that a given effect might be brought about in many different ways (Daly, 1994; Wakefield, 1996).

Viewing the workplace as a total system, it can forcefully be argued that homeostasis can be maintained only when the workplace remains in a state of constancy and is free of destructive conflict or "static." This statement does not mean that conflict should never occur in the workplace, because it often helps crystallize issues and promote growth. But systems are fluid and fragile; thus, tension, infighting, gross disrespect for authority, poor intergroup relations, and widespread dysfunctionality can give rise to disequilibrium and can ultimately lead to seriously low production.

REAL MEANING OF DIVERSITY

To fully appreciate the complexity of restructuring a workplace to reflect diversity, one must understand that this concept merits unique inquiry. "Diversity" is a term that, at first glance, appears simple but cannot be treated as though its meaning were intuitively evident. It has become a "politically correct" buzzword of the late 1980s and has made its way into the American lexicon. Diversity is a knotty concept, largely because it is multifaceted and laden with cultural components and nuances in wording and scope. From a subjective view, diversity denotes not just difference in ethnic background but also involves complex relationships between groups and exemplifies important dimensions of humanness in all members of a species: age, ethnic heritage, gender, physical abilities or qualities, race, sexual orientation, and religious and cultural beliefs (Copeland, 1988a, 1988b; Harris & Morgan, 1987; Loden & Rosener, 1991; Mbiti, 1970). Loden and Rosener (1991) posited that in some workplaces, diversity represents an institutional environment built on the values of fairness, mutual respect, understanding, and cooperation. Therefore, shared goals, rewards, performance standards, operating norms, and vision of the future guide the efforts of every employee and manager. Of late, numerous essays, commentaries, texts, and monographs have defined diversity from various perspectives. As used here, the construct is defined within the context of cultural differences, adjustments, interaction, and interrelatedness among foreign-born participants (Africans and Asians) and American workers.

WORLD OF WORK

The term "work" also has a special meaning here. Numerous efforts have been made in society to define "work" but, like "diversity," it is an elusive term that defies definition. Diverse forms of data indicate that, for foreign-born populations such as Africans and Asians, work is a complex phenomenon with multiple sociological, psychological, and economic dimensions (Borow, 1964). To give the American people a knowledge of the salient uniqueness of work, Elliot Richardson, then-secretary of the U.S. Department of Health, Education, and Welfare, commissioned a study in 1973 titled *Work in America*. The study, conducted by the Upjohn Institute for Employment Research, revealed that the quality of one's life is inextricably connected to the quality of one's work, ideology, life history, and experience.

In reviewing the voluminous literature on work and the workplace, one is struck by the myriad views that are advanced. For example, theologians are interested in the moral dimensions of work;

sociologists see it as a determinant of status; some contemporary critics say work is simply the best way of filling lost time; Calvinist doctrine gave religious sanction to worldly wealth and achievement through work; and Karl Marx described work as a means of fulfilling capitalist exploitation (Levenstein, 1962). For Asians and Africans, one's work transcends hygienic factors and the notion of producing something of value for other people and moves into the rich area of work as a cultural entity. Therefore, work is intertwined with culture. The significance of this perspective rests with the fact that a group's culture (Asian or African) is a major determinant of actions in the workplace (Borow, 1964). Underscoring this sociocultural context, work affirms one's reason for being and establishes a person as part of a cultural group. Levenstein (1962) succinctly summed up *work* as action that is as important to defining one's culture as food is to nourishing one's body.

AFRICANS IN THE AMERICAN WORKPLACE

Writings on immigrant and refugee resettlement have appeared in the literature during the past three decades, capturing the attention of immigration theorists from different fields of study. Yet, few attempts have been made to examine what happens to Africans (mostly immigrants) who join the American labor force (Bryce-LaPorte, 1972; Kamya, 1997; Muir, 1996; Ross-Sheriff, 1995).

Africans have experienced difficulty entering this country because before 1965 American immigration policies excluded them from admission to the United States (Kamya, 1997; Muir, 1996). After 1965, however, a mass of African immigrants fleeing the effects of war, military dictatorship, intolerant government officials, political unrest, and famine requested entry into this country.

Previous refusal to admit Africans to the United States was based on the Immigration Act of 1924, which froze the ethnic composition of aliens "ineligible for citizenship" except for those with a country-of-origin visa allocation (Europeans). Through the years the nation's immigrant admission process went through peaks and valleys (see Figure 26-1), but the 1924 law closed the doors to all third- and fourth-world groups, which included Africans and Asians (see Table 26-1). With the passing of the 1965 Immigration Law and Nationality Act, the U.S. Congress repealed the country-of-origin visa allocation, which shifted immigration away from Western Europe and toward Asia, the Pacific Islands, Latin America, and Africa.

It is easy to visualize Africans as one population, but the continent is quite diverse and comprises many nationalities and ethnicities. In general, however, when America's doors were opened, Africans from many regions made an effort to enter. Unfortunately, Africans did not arrive in this country in a strong economic position, their greatest capital asset being their education. Although well-educated professionals, scientists, and university professors were among the first arrivals after 1965, all were viewed as a burden to taxpayers.

Figure 26-1

Shifts in U.S. Immigration, 1820–1940

THOUSANDS

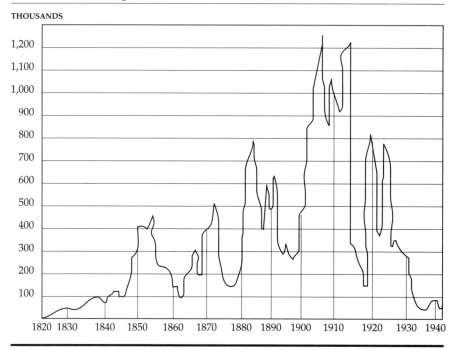

SOURCE: Statistics to 1925 from Jenks, J. O. (1926). *The immigration problem* (6th ed., rev.). New York: Funk & Wagnalls. Statistics after 1925 from Calavita, K. (1980). *A sociological analysis of immigration.* Doctoral dissertation, University of Delaware, Dover.

Employment and Wages

In the logic of "first things first," on entering this country, new African arrivals' priority was to seek employment sufficient to cover need, support a family, and offer a range of intrinsic satisfactions. Unfortunately, in their quest for labor force participation, even well-educated workers became the unwilling monopolists of the worst service-oriented jobs America had to offer.

Africans' efforts to seek employment are fraught with four distinct barriers. First, they are mistaken frequently for black Americans and, unfortunately, in this country skin color (particularly dark skin) is a liability, in that many employers view black people as lazy, shiftless, and poorly educated, and as consumers rather than producers of goods and services (Daniels, Davis, & See, in press). Second, many managers cannot move intellectually beyond what I describe as the "Tarzan Syndrome." Inherent in this perspective is a feeling of intellectual superiority on the part of some white people toward people of color. For example, some managers can be compared to the arrogant white safari hunter in the old B-rated Tarzan movies. He is the self-annointed omnipotent authority who obtains information about the jungle from multiple sources and then lectures about the jungle to

Table 26-1

U.S. Immigration Policy

Policy/Period	Date	Situation
Open-door policy	1800	Open to all immigrants.
Regulation period	1882–1916	Excluded people from the Asiatic zone.
Restriction period	1917–1964	Resulted from Immigration Act of 1917; this era saw literacy testing for immigrants, penalties for violations of contract labor, and quota laws favoring immigration from northern and western Europe.
Liberalization period	1965–1985	The composition of immigration began to change with the arrival of a significant number of Cubans, Haitians, Mexicans, and Asians.
Enforcement period	Post-1985	Followed the era of the historical passage of the Immigration Reform and Control Act of 1986.

native hunters, tribesmen, and warriors who are already masters of the jungle and authorities on its terrain. In America's workplaces, managers have been observed seeking information about black people from other black people and then lecturing the job applicants on what they should know about material in their area of expertise.

A third liability is Africans' efforts to retain native rituals and other religious and secular functions characteristic of their native country. These cultural activities, many of which represent rites of passage, are alien to Americans and are therefore viewed as "pagan." Some managers contend that cultural relics have no place in work sites or, for that matter, in "civilized" society. Taken together, these barriers limit Africans to the most menial jobs in this nation's labor force.

Overriding all these factors is the issue of denying African workers a good salary. Reports from monitoring groups enumerate instances in which Africans highly trained for professional and managerial employment have been denied pay equity because of their color. Obviously, being forced to accept menial jobs means Africans will have low disposable income. Moreover, they will hardly be in a position to share the American dream and will therefore remain on the bottom rung of the socioeconomic ladder.

The complex interconnectedness between low-level employment and low wages for Africans with high educational attainment brings to the fore a truth about America's workplaces: They sacrifice production and squander productive human capital capable of making a contribution to the economic health of this nation just so that they can select and maintain a work force of one skin color.

To gain insight into these and other complex issues, I interviewed a distinguished Nigerian professor at a northeastern university (he preferred to remain anonymous for political reasons). When asked about the educational attainment of Africans, the professor gave the following response:

> I would hazard a guess that Africans are indeed likely to be the most highly educated of all the third- and fourth-world groups. You see, educational opportunities are not the same in the whole of Africa, and naturally some sections provide better schooling than others. As a whole, however, Africans who come to the United States are well educated. In Africa students still receive a British education, and there are still missions that provide educational opportunities. Most students are required to undergo a rigorous level of academic training, which requires a period of apprenticeship. After graduation, students are prepared to immediately enter the global labor marketplace [because] most are multilingual. Africans have reached tremendous heights in education, but in the United States they have been afforded only limited opportunities to make use of their education. Sadly, Africans receive little black support in their efforts to locate good jobs with good pay.

Tensions between Africans and African Americans

The Nigerian professor's remark that African American support was unavailable in the United States to help Africans become gainfully employed sparked a lively discussion. The professor explained:

> As a group, African Americans have given little support to African newcomers inside or outside the workplace, and of course for Africans this has been disappointing, given the outpouring of support received from blacks during the South African revolution where apartheid was overthrown and [Nelson] Mandela became the president of South Africa. In some cases blacks have, on occasion, shown sheer indignation toward Africans in this country and in this city. I believe support has been withheld because blacks fear Africans will work for low wages and subsequently take the few remaining jobs still open to them. I have been here 15 years and have noticed with interest how foreign-born groups have taken jobs that were at one time held by blacks. I cannot say that blacks' fears are unfounded. It is also my view that blacks are skeptical of Africans because of the influence that Englishmen have had in our country. Blacks can never forget that the British are authorities on exploitation and colonization—so it's a matter of trust.

In seeking a solution to the problem of strained relations between Africans and black people and the lack of mutual assistance, the professor made this prediction:

> When Africans move into the American work force (as indeed they will during the 21st century) and as they become victims of oppressive treatment meted out by white women bosses who will replace white men (and predictably will be more oppressive than men), it is my fervent opinion that blacks and Africans will connect in a spirit of brotherhood—as each will need the other in order to survive in the white-women-run workplace.

To gain even deeper insight into the problems Africans face in the American workplace, I held an informal interview with a high-level executive from Nigeria who is currently employed with a *Fortune 500* corporation in Atlanta.

> Although I had attended universities in Ibadan and Lagos in Nigeria, then went to Leeds University (England) and later to Oxford (England), I was still perceived as an African American, and many opportunities for employment were denied me. I was at the bottom level of middle management. I was paid far less than the chaps whose skills were inferior to mine, and for a time it appeared that I would remain in place for the rest of my employment life. The work environment for me was extremely taxing, and unfortunately I could not seem to establish amiable relationships with either African Americans or whites on my team in the corporation. At social gatherings negative comments were expressed about Africans' body hygiene, and other atrocities directed toward me contributed to my self-absorption. Six years passed before I was finally promoted, but in all those years I was engaged in work at a level higher than my immediate rank. What was puzzling is that my supervisor mentioned that I should cast aside all vestiges of African influence (rituals, clothing, language, etc.). You see, at formal gatherings I wore my African attire, and this formal dress seemed to offend my supervisor. As I moved still further up the ladder of the corporation, pressure was imposed on me to write more clearly, speak articulately, and get rid of my British accent.

After listening carefully to this executive, one could argue that assimilation is the prevailing model at *Fortune 500* corporations. Furthermore, it seems to be clearly understood that diversity and multicultural differences are viewed as dysfunctional and hence as a distraction to the corporation. Loden and Rosener (1991) alluded to assimilation as an outdated model for managing diversity and to integration as the future goal. They explained that assimilation is based on the values and assumptions of the dominant group, which are shaped by the values and beliefs of those who founded our society and its powerful institutions—primarily white men of European culture.

Clearly, managers of diversity who are providers of pluralistic leadership must be on the cutting edge of change. Understanding that many foreign-born groups will be among the work force of the year 2000, managers must invest considerable time and effort to become knowledgeable about the cultural nuances of their employees. The pluralistic leader working with Africans must therefore study the history of African civilizations and gain knowledge about great kings, queens, and vast empires. Asante (1996) warned that one must dismiss erroneous information provided by white and black conservative antagonists. He charged these detractors with waging a campaign to discredit the significance of Africans. Indeed, some have all but annexed Egypt to the continent of Europe because of Egypt's historic influence in art, architecture, astronomy, medicine, geometry, mathematics, law, politics, and religion (Bernal, 1987; Lefkowitz, 1992; Schlesinger, 1991; Will, 1996).

In like manner, it may be prudent for pluralistic managers to study the cultural and political complexity of African people, their intratribal differences, rituals, voodoo, perceptions of healing, and the great Mystic schools. Awareness of African culture could be a powerful tool and an extremely useful management strategy for effecting creativity, inclusiveness, and sensitivity toward Africans in the workplace.

ASIANS IN THE AMERICAN WORKPLACE

Brown and Broderick (1994) and Haines (1989) observed that the Asian and Pacific Islander population comprises more than 30 cultures. Of this number, Asians include, but are not limited to, Japanese, Chinese, Koreans, Filipinos, Indochinese (Southeast Asians), Vietnamese, Asian Indians, Thais, Hmong, Indonesians, Pakistanis, Cambodians, and Laotians.

In examining Asian participation in the workplace, as Berg and Jaya (1993) underscored, Japanese, Chinese, Koreans, and Asian Indians are more likely to emigrate to the United States for advanced education, a higher quality of employment, and increased wages than are third- and fourth-world groups. Also, Asians do not suffer the same discrimination and disadvantages that are visited on other racial groups whose skin color is of darker hue. Thus, within the past few years Asians have been welcomed to the American work force because of their high intellectual achievement and scientific and technological excellence.

As previously mentioned, the 1965 Immigration and Nationality Act made it possible for more Asians to enter this country. However, Southeast Asians were admitted to the United States on the basis of a legal agreement. The entry of Southeast Asians into the United States and subsequently into the work force was made possible by government intervention (See, 1986). Congressional reports show that America provided a safe haven, benefits, and employment to Laotians, Vietnamese, and Cambodians who, during the Vietnam War, served as U.S. surrogates and fought the North Vietnamese alongside U.S. troops. After the war, Asians were provided jobs and training necessary for starting a new life in America. After the fall of Saigon, now Ho Chi Minh City, hundreds of Southeast Asians were airlifted by helicopter from the Tan Son Nhut Airport, ferried to America's Sixth Naval Fleet out into the China Sea, and then flown to the United States for resettlement. Wealthy, well-educated Southeast Asians kept many of their resources intact.

Clearly, unlike other immigrant groups, Southeast Asians were provided preparation for entry into U.S. society with the purpose of eventually making them self-supporting. However, with all the assistance received from these Asians in the war effort, Americans still harbored negative feelings toward them because this country lost the war, because Asians have high intellectual ability, and because they are producers in the workplace.

Some theorists have observed that Americans' attitude toward Asians is that they are too alien to be comprehended and too strange ever to be familiar to the American people. This attitude translates into "Asians are different." However, despite the negative comments that have been made about them, Asians have many accomplishments in the American workforce. In fact, their rigorous work ethic has helped earn them the stereotypical label of America's "model minority."

Model-Minority Myth

Considerable controversy has arisen in the academic community between Asian and other scholars over the labeling of Asians as America's "model minority." Inherent in this label is the notion that Asians are quiet, law-abiding, self-sufficient, clean, industrious, hard-working, well-adjusted, but immutably hyphenated Americans who practice thrift and industry and are committed to promoting capitalism and growth in this country. Takaki (1989), one of the most eloquent modern-day writers on Asian life and thought, soundly rejects the labeling of Asians as model minorities. Before taking a position regarding the stereotyping of Asians, he systematically analyzed demographic data using the variables of personal and family income, number of hours worked, number of people in the household who are working, and level of employment. His analysis revealed that Asians are not doing as well as reported and that there is little significant difference in the income of Asians in relation to other groups with different physical features and skin color when all variables are considered.

Takaki (1989), therefore, viewed the label of "model minority" as a cruel myth that exaggerates Asian success. He blames the news media for spreading the myth. That author would likewise assign blame for spreading the model minority myth to Murray (1984) and D'Souza (1995), two radical pundits employed by right-wing think tanks. The two, both of whom have been sternly challenged in matters concerning people of color, have successfully used the plight of people from non-dominant-culture groups of every kind to influence and support racist social policies at the highest levels of government. Takaki believed that the model-minority myth was calculated to systematically use Asians to smear African Americans and other oppressed groups who have been active in challenging the unequal distribution of power and resources in this nation. This labeling has also been used to set an example for other people of color to make them work harder within the workplace. To accomplish this end, Asians are held up as well-adjusted Americans who are helping to promote growth in this country.

Other Asian thinkers contend that the cruel part of establishing this myth is that Asians have come to believe it and have paid a severe price for accepting this false sense of reality. First, by permitting themselves to be viewed as self-righteous and to be placed on a pedestal, Asians have angered African Americans, some white people, and other racial groups, and can therefore expect little or no support from them.

Worse still, the myth has denied Asians much-needed social, medical, and mental health services as well as student loans and stipends. These resources are denied because Asians do not qualify for assistance; they are assumed to have resources. An even greater disservice is that meaningful and effective social services programs designed to help Asians learn English, enter the work force, and brush off the insidious and demoralizing effects of prolonged states of alienation and powerlessness have not been approved (Barth, 1964). All of these important supports were denied because Asians have been too proud to shed the yoke of oppression caused by the cruel myth perpetuated by those who have not had their best interests at heart.

Religious Influence

A number of academics argue that Asians face conflict in the American workplace because of religious beliefs that control every aspect of their lives. Religion is a powerful force in the life of the Asian worker. In general, most Asians follow the cultural ideology of Confucianism, Animism, Buddhism, or Taoism (Osgood, 1951). In the workplace, these religious teachings translate into a doctrine that fosters obedience to authority, rejection of conflict, and rejoicing in harmony, humility, simplicity, alertness, and social relations.

In the workplace, Confucian and Buddhist teachings (subdued self, support of things in their natural states, humility, and silence) seem to be compatible with capitalism. In a capitalist workplace, the status quo is important to production. Thus, for managers concerned about the barrage of challenges that are coming from the rank and file and from other ethnic groups and low-level workers, having a population of workers who are quiet and passive and will not "rock the boat" is advantageous.

Control of Emotions

Attitudes and behaviors of Asians in the workplace collide with the behaviors of Americans and other foreign-born groups. Because of their view of obedience to authority, Asians have been accused of working against their own best interests in defense of capitalism. For example, managers of diversity are accustomed to workers exhibiting considerable "blustering bravado" and engaging in social action such as strikes when management takes an oppositional stand on issues involving workers. On the other hand, Asians, following Confucian, Taoist, or Buddhist teachings, believe that it is more important to ego development for one to regulate emotions, practice self-control, alter private displays, and measure self-expression than to engage in catharsis or the public display of emotion that is generally displayed by Americans (Lum, 1996).

Given this belief system, it is difficult to imagine that in the workplace Asians would take an active role in a strike or any other civil action involving conflict. With a background of information on Asian religious teachings, one would make the assumption that Asians in the workplace would be passive and continue as "silent sufferers," when other groups fight to humanize the workplace (See, 1986, 1996).

Quietness

The Confucian–Taoist teaching compels Asians in the workplace to withhold complaints but at the same time provide proper care and protection to their families. Managers of diversity have always found it advantageous to hear workers express their opinions about their jobs and the general state of an organization. However, they may encounter total silence in their attempts to retrieve information from Asians in the workplace. Not only diversity managers but also black workers have observed with interest how Asians in and out of the workplace keep their secrets until their plans have culminated. What Americans fail to understand, however, is that Taoism suggests that one must practice tranquillity, alertness, and silence, because each of the three is a virtue.

In my research dealing with Southeast Asians, an African American respondent had this to say about Asian silence:

> All I can say is that this set of Southeast Asian refugees will be the undoing of white America. They play a low profile and they don't tell the white man about their plans. That's the only correct way to deal with the businessmen in this country. . . . That's the mistake blacks have made. They talk too damn much—show all their cards. You'd think the middle-class blacks would know better, but they are such braggers they just can't wait to unveil their plans to white folks. These refugees don't say a word, and the next thing you know they have quit jobs working for someone else and up goes a little restaurant, or a little fabric shop, or some little spice shop. I hear that when refugees make money, they don't put it in banks, so the white power structure has no way of keeping a running account of the extent of their resources. I also hear that refugees don't use credit cards, seldom purchase on credit, and pay cash for all their supplies. So, American businessmen don't make no profit from them. They work hard, live frugal lives in large groups, and are not "into" America's show-off. Hell! White businessmen see these refugees as little innocent passer-byers, but soon they'll be able to purchase Madison Avenue because they don't tell their business. (See, 1986, p. 130)

From this narrative, the point to be made is that Asians work hard in the workplace and save their money for realizing greater goals. Their ability not to divulge their plans in the workplace puts them in an enviable position to other racial groups who have not learned to keep their plans secret until they have materialized.

Conflict with Work and Family

Asian men have a deeply held responsibility for the care and protection of their families. Even after Asian executives reach a pinnacle in their work world, they still feel a profound obligation to their families. In discussions with Asian executives and their wives, one problem that surfaced was that of the spouse's travel for the organization.

Asian men seem to be acutely aware that travel is necessary for the realization of upward mobility, but it still poses serious problems in the family.

From informal reports, Asian executives are faced with the difficult task of determining how to balance work and family life. Because compliance with authority and care for one's family are equally important in Confucian–Taoist teachings, Asian workers are caught in a vortex from which there is no escape. Each year, reports abound of Asian executives suffering from severe stress stemming from workplace dilemmas. An educated guess is that corporate travel may be one dilemma that drives Asian executives to purchase their own businesses and move to less stressful environments (Padilla, Wagatsuma, & Lindholm, 1985).

Perception of Women as Managers

Women in America are continuing to enter the work force at record rates. It is projected that by the year 2005, nearly 48 percent of the work force will be women. Women will be working in increasingly professional, high-end jobs (Avery, 1994), and their influence will be felt in all parts of the organization.

However, patriarchy is an accepted phenomenon in Asian culture, and Confucian–Taoist teaching defines specific roles for each person within the Asian society (Harper & Lantz, 1996; Wang, 1980). In her comprehensive writing on Chinese women, Wang (1980) observed, "Confucius taught that the virtue of a woman lay in her being talented, unskilled and ignorant. Too much knowledge would lead to her unsubmissiveness, and submissiveness is the ideal feminine propriety" (p. 98). In addition, in the Asian culture, sons are considered more valuable than daughters.

It can be deduced from the available data that Asian male workers may have difficulty with female authority in the workplace. According to at least one source, if that is true, what may be missed by these workers is that white men will be the minority in the work force by the year 2000 and that black men will continue to be incarcerated and subjected to genocide, so it will be incumbent on women to fill the void (Lester, 1994). Female leadership will be present for many years to come. It follows, therefore, that diversity managers will need to address this problem, which, if not resolved, may reach an emotional pitch that could limit growth so necessary if the nation is to remain a leader of the free world.

STRATEGIES FOR MANAGING DIVERSITY

Managers in the 21st century will be forced to work with diverse groups. The reality is that this will be an awesome responsibility. Although not always familiar with the culture of these new groups, managers still have the responsibility to become knowledgeable. Eight basic strategies can assist in this effort:

1. The workplace should prepare to accommodate diverse people and prepare to weave accommodations for diverse staff into an effective support culture.
2. Cross-functional teams should be established to assist in worker bonding, improve intergroup relations, and build the workplace into a diverse community.
3. Managers must gain knowledge and understanding of the backgrounds and histories of diverse groups that have to work together.
4. Assimilation is no longer the paradigm of choice in work force management; integration and pluralism are the prevailing models because they provide the adaptive flexibility needed in an evolving and diverse work force.
5. Workshops and seminars must be planned to assist both managers and workers in recognizing and eliminating racism, bigotry, and prejudice.
6. Management must strive to ensure effective communication and feedback through participative communication structures, deal effectively with cultural clashes, and establish some means for fit among diverse organizational members and organizational outcomes.
7. A "business-as-usual" mentality must be averted.
8. Organizations must be open to innovation, change, and creativity.

Adhering to these strategies should help managers create a pleasant environment for the work force in 2000—one that is equipped to face the multiple challenges and responsibilities that lie ahead.

IMPLICATIONS FOR POLICY

Demographic data indicate that the United States is experiencing significant change and is fast becoming a more diverse nation. This trend is certain to mean increasing demands to diversify the workplace so that the nation may sustain its competitive edge. The need for greater economic growth and higher productivity can be achieved only if all citizens play a part in this endeavor.

Because so many diverse groups are entering this nation, managers of diversity should be provided with supports to assist in diversity efforts. Also, the federal government should provide tax breaks to workplaces that show good faith in diversifying their work forces. Obviously, legislative enactments and economic incentives alone may not be sufficient to hasten workplace diversity, so this effort must be accomplished through the education of the citizenry and by showcasing organizations that have been exemplary in achieving effective models. These activities would be an incentive for others to help the nation continue positive growth and innovation.

REFERENCES

Adler, N. J., & Bartholomew, S. (1992). Managing globally competent people. *Academy of Management Executives, 6*(3), 52–65.

Avery, C. (1994, June 24). The new worker. *Washington Times*, pp. E6–E7.

Asante, M. (1996, July–August). Ancient truths. *Emerge*, pp. 66–70.

Bach, R. L. (1979, January). *Employment characteristics of Indochina*. Staten Island, NY: Center for Migration Studies.

Bargal, D. (1984). *Social work in the world of work*. Jerusalem: Council of Social Work Schools in Israel.

Barth, C. (1964). *Bitter strength: A history of the Chinese in the United States, 1850–1870.* Cambridge, MA: Harvard University Press.

Bell, D. A. (1985, July 15–22). America's greatest success story: The triumph of Asian-Americans. *New Republic*, pp. 24–26.

Berg, I., & Jaya, A. (1993). Difference and same: Family therapy with Asian-American families. *Journal of Marital and Family Therapy, 19,* 31–38.

Bernal, M. (1987). *Black Athena: The Afro-Asiatic roots of classical civilization* (Vol. 1). London: Free Association Books.

Borow, H. (1964). *Man in a world of work*. Boston: Houghton-Mifflin.

Bredemeier, H. C., & Stephenson, R. M. (1964). *The analysis of social system*. New York: Holt, Rinehart & Winston.

Brown, C., & Broderick, A. (1994). Asian and Pacific Island elders: Issues for social work practice and education. *Social Work, 39,* 252–259.

Bryce-LaPorte, R. S. (1972). Black immigrants: The experience of invisibility and inequality. *Journal of Black Studies, 3*(1), 29–56.

Calavita, K. (1980). *A sociological analysis of immigration*. Doctoral dissertation, University of Delaware, Dover.

Chestang, L. W. (1982). Work, personal change, and human development. In S. H. Akabas & P. A. Kurzman (Eds.), *Work, workers, and work organizations: A view from social work* (pp. 61–89). Englewood Cliffs, NJ: Prentice Hall.

Churchman, C. W. (1968). *The systems approach*. New York: Dell.

Copeland, L. (1988a). Valuing diversity part 1: Making the most of cultural differences at the workplace. *Personnel, 65,* 52–60.

Copeland, L. (1988b). Valuing diversity part 2: Pioneers and champions of change. *Personnel, 65,* 44–49.

Cose, E. (1993). *The rage of the privileged class*. New York: HarperCollins.

Daly, A. (1994). African American and white managers: A comparison in one agency. *Journal of Community Practice, 1,* 57–79.

Daniels, M., Davis, K., & See, L. (in press). The psychology effects of skin color on African Americans. In L. See (Ed.), *Human behavior in the social environment from an African American perspective*. New York: Haworth Press.

D'Souza, D. (1995). *The end of racism*. New York: Free Press.

Ehrlich, E., & Garland, S. B. (1988, September 19). For American business, a new world of workers. *Business Week: Industrial Technical Edition*, pp. 112–120.

Fine, M. G. (1991). New voices in the workplace: Research directions in multicultural communications. *Journal of Business Communications, 28,* 259–275.

Gardenswartz, L., & Rowe, A. (1989a, May 16). The multicultural workforce. *Working World*, p. 16.

Gardenswartz, L., & Rowe, A. (1989b, June 26). The multicultural workforce. *Working World*, p. 34.

Gardenswartz, L., & Rowe, A. (1989c, August 14). The multicultural workforce. *Working World*, p. 20.

Germain, C. B., & Gitterman, A. (1980). *The life model of social work practice*. New York: Columbia University Press.

Gurwitt, R. (1989, August). How we spent the 1980s: A pre-census look at a changing America. *Governing*, pp. 26–33.

Haines, D. W. (1989). Introduction. In D. W. Haines (Ed.), *Refugees as immigrants* (pp. 1–23). Totowa, NJ: Rowman & Littlefield.

Harper, K., & Lantz, J. (1996). *Cross cultural practice with diverse populations*. Chicago: Lyceum Books.

Harris, P. R., & Morgan, R. T. (1987). *Managing differences* (2nd ed.). Houston: Gulf.

Herrnstein, R. J., & Murray, C. (1994). *The bell curve: Intelligence and class structure in American life*. New York: Free Press.

Hill, R. (in press). Enhancing the resilience of African American families. In L. See (Ed.), *Human behavior in the social environment from an African American perspective*. New York: Haworth Press.

Immigration Act, ch. 190, 43 Stat. 153 (May 26, 1924).

Immigration and Nationality Act, P.L. No. 89–236, 79 Stat. 911 to 920 (1965).

Jenks, J. (1926). *The immigration problem* (6th ed., rev.). New York: Funk & Wagnalls.

Johnston, W. B., & Packer, A. E. (1987). *Workforce 2000: Work and workers for the twenty-first century*. Indianapolis: Hudson Institute.

Kamya, H. A. (1997). African immigrants in the United States: The challenge for research and practice. *Social Work, 42,* 154–165.

Laszlo, E. (1972). *The systems view of the world*. New York: George Braziller.

Lefkowitz, M. (1992). *Not out of Africa: How Afrocentrism became an excuse to teach myth as history*. New York: Basic Books.

Lester, J. S. (1994). *The future of white men and other diversity dilemmas*. Berkeley, CA: Conari Press.

Levenstein, A. (1962). *Why people work*. New York: Thomas Y. Crowell.

Linomes, R. G. (1993). The Japanese manager's traumatic entry into the United States: Understanding the American Japanese cultural divide. *Executive, 2*(4), 21–38.

Loden, M., & Rosener, J. (1991). *Workforce America*. Homewood, IL: Richard D. Irwin.

Lum, D. (1996). *Social work practice and people of color*. Monterey, CA: Brooks/Cole.

Maluccio, A. N. (1981). *Promoting competence in clients: A new/old approach to social work practice*. New York: Free Press.

Mbiti, J. S. (1970). *African religions and philosophy*. Garden City, NY: Doubleday.

Muir, C. (1996, October). Workplace readiness for communicating diversity. *Journal of Business Communications, 33,* 475–484.

Murray, C. (1984). *Losing ground: American policy, 1950–1980*. New York: Basic Books.

Naisbitt, J. (1982). *Megatrends*. New York: Warner Books.

Nelton, S. (1988, July). Meet your new work force. *Nation's Business,* pp. 2–7.

Osgood, C. (1951). *The Koreans and their culture*. New York: Ronald Press.

Padilla, A. M., Wagatsuma, Y., & Lindholm, K. (1985). Acculturation and personality as predictors of stress in Japanese and Japanese Americans. *Journal of Social Psychology, 125,* 295–305.

Ribner, D. S. (1993). Crisis in the workplace: The role of the occupational social worker. *Social Work, 38,* 333–337.

Ross-Sheriff, F. (1995). African Americans: Immigrants. In R. L. Edwards (Ed.-in-Chief), *Encyclopedia of social work* (19th ed., Vol. 1, pp. 130–136). Washington, DC: NASW Press.

Schachter, J. (1988, April 17). Firms begin to embrace diversity. *Los Angeles Times,* p. 1.

Schlesinger, A. (1991). *The disuniting of America*. New York: W. W. Norton.

See, L. A. (1986). *Tensions and tangles between Afro-Americans and Southeast Asian refugees*. Atlanta: Wright.

See, L. A. (1996). Should medical social workers take clients' "folk beliefs" into account in practice? Yes. In B. Thyer (Ed.), *Controversial issues in social work practice* (pp. 232–242). Needham Heights, MA: Allyn & Bacon.

Souflee, F. (1993). A metatheoretical framework for social work practice. *Social Work, 38,* 317–331.

Takaki, R. (1989). *Strangers from a different shore*. New York: Penguin Books.

Toffler, A. (1971). *Future shock*. New York: Bantam Books.

Toffler, A. (1981). *The third wave*. New York: Bantam Books.

Toffler, A. (1990). *Power shift*. New York: Bantam Books.

Upjohn Institute for Employment Research. (1973). *Work in America* (Report of a Special Task Force to the Secretary of Health, Education, and Welfare). Cambridge, MA: MIT Press.

Wakefield, J. C. (1996, March). Does social work need the eco-systems perspective? *Social Service Review*, pp. 2–30.

Wang, B.L.C. (1980). Chinese women: The relative influence of ideological revolution, economic growth, and cultural change. In B. Lindsay (Ed.), *Comparative perspectives of third world women* (pp. 96–120). New York: Praeger.

Will, G. F. (1996, February 19). Intellectual segregation. *Newsweek*, p. 78.

Wilson, W. J. (1987). *The truly disadvantaged: The inner city, the underclass, and public policy*. Chicago: University of Chicago Press.

Wilson, W. J. (1991). Studying inner city dislocation. *American Sociological Review, 56*, 1–14.

U.S. Bureau of the Census. (1990). *Statistical abstracts of the United States: 1990. The national data book*. Washington, DC: U.S. Government Printing Office.

U.S. Bureau of the Census. (1991a). *Census Bureau releases counts on specific racial groups* (Press Release CB91-215). Washington, DC: Author.

U.S. Bureau of the Census. (1991b). *The Hispanic population in the United States: March 1990* (Current Population Reports, Series P -20, No. 449). Washington, DC: U.S. Government Printing Office.

U.S. Bureau of the Census. (1991c). *Resident population distribution for the United States regions, and states, by race and Hispanic origin: 1990* (Press Release CB91-100). Washington, DC: Author.

U.S. Bureau of the Census. (1993). *Statistical abstract of the United States: 1993* (113th ed.). Washington, DC: U.S. Government Printing Office.

U.S. Immigration and Naturalization Service. (1993). *1992 statistical yearbook of the Immigration and Naturalization Service*. Washington, DC: U.S. Government Printing Office.

von Bertalanffy, L. (1968). *General systems theory*. New York: George Braziller.

27

Creating Fair Workplaces for Asian American Women:

A Joint-Constructional Approach

Gui-Young Hong

Facing a new work force and re-creating the workplace are inevitable tasks for all 21st-century American organizations. These tasks are precipitated by general changes in the demographic composition of the American work force and driven by the human resources required for successful competition in a global economy (Mirvis, 1992). In the United States, following a 20-year influx of Asian immigrants, the population of Asian Americans has nearly quintupled, from 1.5 million in 1970 to 7.3 million in 1990 (U.S. Bureau of the Census, 1993). By the year 2000, the Asian American population is projected to reach nearly 10 million and constitute about 4 percent of the expected total U.S. population (Patel, 1988).

Based on estimated demographic changes in the U.S. population, a Hudson Institute report predicted that women and ethnic group members would represent about 85 percent of all new workers entering the work force between 1988 and 2000 (Johnston & Packer, 1987). Within this group, the labor force participation of immigrant women surpasses that of native-born women, and Asian American women record among the highest rates of employment among women of any ethnic group (Gardner, Robey, & Smith, 1985; Wong & Hirschman, 1983; Woo, 1985). In 1990, for example, 60 percent of Asian American women participated in the labor force (U.S. Bureau of the Census, 1993), and this figure is expected to increase.

Rapidly changing workplace demographics dictate urgency in preparing all parties for the transition, as unfamiliarity with "different" groups of people is associated with stereotypic perceptions and interactions for managers, between colleagues, and among other employees. In organizational settings, where hierarchically stratified relationships naturally vary along dimensions of status, power, and role, unfamiliarity with members from different groups creates problems in at least three areas: (1) stereotypic images, (2) mismatched psychological contracts, and (3) discriminatory treatment. This chapter will elaborate on potential problems in each of these areas and offer suggestions to ameliorate them, with special attention on Asian American female employees.

CURRENT PROBLEMS

Case of Jessica Chang[1]

Jessica Chang was a second-generation Chinese American who graduated from Cornell University with BS, MS, and PhD degrees in electrical engineering and computer science. She accepted a job as a design engineer at the world's second-largest manufacturer of disk drives for personal computers. During her early years at the company, she was a quick study and soon made suggestions that were later implemented, resulting in a 20-percent manufacturing cost reduction. Jessica's supervisor, however, credited others more than he did her. Because of her quietness, Jessica's contributions were generally underestimated because of a perception that she lacked confidence or understanding. Because Jessica rarely complained, her supervisor thought that she was satisfied with her job.

After five years with the company, Jessica observed that many of her colleagues who had started at the same time or after she did were moving into managerial positions. She wondered why her opportunity to move up did not arise. What Jessica did not know was that her peers were effectively networking and managing up. They belonged to the same churches and outside organizations as their bosses. Their children played together, and many were active in common social groups.

When Jessica scheduled a meeting with her supervisor to discuss her career, her supervisor expressed surprise that she was interested in becoming a manager. He said that she always seemed to be cheerful and happy with her work. In fact, Jessica reminded him of the wife of Dr. Wang, one of his "closest" friends. Apparently, Mrs. Wang was a wonderful cook and mother. When pressed, Jessica's supervisor said that she was not "leaderlike" and needed to be more assertive.

Stereotypes of Asian American Women and Their Consequences

Asian Americans have been described as "model minorities" (Kitano & Sue, 1973; Sue & Frank, 1973; Suzuki, 1995; U.S. Commission on Civil Rights, 1992). This term implies academic and economic success in the United States despite a historically grim past characterized by ideological and institutional discrimination. Examples of such have included restrictive prejudicial naturalization and immigration laws, a host of anti-Asian state and local statutes, and discriminatory employment and business practices (Espiritu, 1996; U.S. Commission on Civil Rights, 1992). In general, the model-minority stereotype conveys overgeneralized and romanticized images of Asian Americans as a "problem-free" group. They do not complain, they easily conform to contextual demands, they do not need social support, they are unaggressive, and they are desensitized to cultural conflict (Atkinson, Morten, & Sue, 1993; Crystal, 1989; Sue & Sue, 1990; Takaki, 1995; U.S. Commission on Civil Rights, 1992).

---

[1]This case should not be taken as representative of problems that all Asian American female employees face. In fact, some Asian American women at managerial levels in various types of organizations have managed their positions in creative, constructive, and successful ways. Case summarized from Chen and Leong (1997).

From the perspective of a perceiver (whether a society, an organization, or a person), the model-minority stereotype serves as a cognitive anchor by providing the perceiver with readily available "representative" heuristic information about the unfamiliar group or group member (Tversky & Kahneman, 1982). In the case of Jessica's supervisor, his use of the model-minority stereotype in place of real knowledge colored his perceptual filters, allowing him to "understand" Jessica's behavior in terms of the stereotype instead of her actual accomplishments. Jessica never complained before talking to him, and he "understood" that she had been always happy. Furthermore, Jessica's apparent attitude and behavior also likely confirmed or provided the supervisor with additional "proof" of the stereotype's verisimilitude. In other words, in dual ways, the problem-free stereotypic image became a reality for the supervisor.

Although Asian Americans, as a group, are extremely diverse (Espiritu, 1996; Min, 1995; Sue, 1994; Uba, 1994), they all generally adhere to Asian cultural values emphasizing hard work, education, compromise, harmony, and adaptation to nature. Consequently, the model-minority stereotype was partially "earned" by Asian groups because of a shared ethos that group members actively cultivated as a route to success in American society (see Woo, 1985, for the relationship between effort and achievement). The model-minority stereotype also can function as a social force by creating additional social expectations that Asian Americans are supposed to meet. Then, because of their value systems, Asian Americans are likely to behave in ways predicted by the model-minority stereotype, but problems arise when the stereotype is used to judge or constrain an individual's achievements (Kim, 1973; Kitano & Sue, 1973; Lee, 1994).

Besides the model-minority stereotype, Asian American women also live with an additional set of gender-related stereotypes. According to these, Asian American women are expected to be domestic, submissive, and passive. These images can lead employers and supervisors to underestimate Asian American women's qualifications for appropriate promotion and performance recognition. For Asian American women, the stereotypic images with which they are viewed may contribute to a doubly thick glass ceiling that impedes their upward career mobility, particularly into management jobs (see Garland, 1991; Mize, 1992; Morrison & Von Glinow, 1990; Solomon, 1990; and Van Velsor, 1987, for the case of women in general).

MISMATCHED PSYCHOLOGICAL CONTRACTS

In the United States, mutual intentions of entering into an employment relationship are expressed in formal, written contracts that specify enforceable rights and obligations between the employer and the employee. After employment, many employees in general and Asian American women in particular come to realize that their workplace expectations are different from those of their employer. Besides the formal contract, expectations in employment relationships, like other relationships, begin, develop, and change over time (Levinson et al., 1966, cited in Morrison, 1994; Spindler, 1994). Often this incongruence results from a mismatch between the "psychological contracts" of the employee and employer.

Psychological contracts refers to "the bundle of unexpressed expectations that exist at the interfaces between humans" (Spindler, 1994, p. 326). Unlike formal (legal) contracts, psychological contracts carry the following five characteristics (Levinson et al., 1966, cited in Morrison, 1994):

1. Expectation is unspoken.
2. Expectation exists before the present employment relationship.
3. Involved parties are interdependent.
4. Optimal psychological distance is expected.
5. Changes occur without formal acknowledgment (dynamic).

The notion of psychological contracts is not new, but it has long been ignored by organizational management. Recently, however, it has received renewed attention, as managers and business leaders have begun to focus on improving management efficiency and have attempted to optimize their human resources in a search for a competitive edge in the global economy.

As business organizations face the realities of multicultural work forces and workplaces, they must familiarize themselves with the different types of psychological contracts that female Asian American employees expect. Markus and Kitayama (1991) characterized Eastern cultures as "interdependent," whereas they described Western cultures as "independent." In most Asian cultures, both rationality as well as emotionality are considered fundamental to human relationships (Kitayama & Markus, 1994). In general, considerations, concern not to hurt other people's feelings, and nonverbal communication skills (knowing or understanding others by reading certain looks or movements) are culturally valued attributes of Asian women. In return for behaving in a socioculturally appropriate way, Asian American female employees may expect to be perceived as "good" and subsequently recognized and rewarded. With unfamiliarity or insensitivity on the part of employers or supervisors, however, the unspoken expectations of female Asian American employees may go unfulfilled because of mismatched psychological contracts between employers and employees. Ultimately, accumulated evidence of mismatch leads only to mutual loss for both.

TREATMENT DISCRIMINATION

Stereotypic images and mismatched psychological contracts entail potentially negative practical consequences for female Asian American employees. With a dearth of research focused specifically on treatment discrimination against Asian American female employees, the literature on treatment discrimination against ethnic groups and women in general will be used to describe an overall picture. Carnevale and

Gainer (1989), for example, reported significant ethnic group discrepancies in rates of training program participation. They found that although white, black, and Hispanic workers constituted 86.0 percent, 9.5 percent, and 5.5 percent of the work force, respectively, their percentage of representation in formal training programs were 92.0 percent, 5.1 percent, and 2.7 percent, respectively. Corresponding results in a study by Greenhaus, Parasuraman, and Warmley (1990) revealed that black employees were less favorably assessed for promotion by their supervisors than were white employees. Ilgen and Youtz (1986) examined factors affecting the evaluation and development of ethnic groups in organizational settings. They identified "absence of mentors," "less interesting and challenging work as a result of being in the outgroup," and "being left out of the informal social networks" (p. 326) as ethnic employees' primary obstacles to advancement.

Unlike the access discrimination that occurs at the hiring stage, treatment discrimination occurring after one is hired is more affected by informal, selectively available social networks in and out of organizational settings. In Jessica's case, the fact that she did not know her peers were effectively networking and managing up through close interpersonal relationships with their boss outside the company implies that she was never invited to the activities.[2] The psychological contract that Jessica established as an employee—the unspoken yet "obvious" or "natural" expectation that her hard work would be recognized and would pay off—was violated by her supervisor. Not only did he fail to promote her as merit would dictate, but he even failed to recognize any ambition on her part.

The consequences of treatment discrimination are beneficial to no party involved. The consequences for the employee range from the obvious (in terms of lost raises and promotions) to the more subtle (such as "relative deprivation"; Crosby, 1982). As Jessica's achievements and performance go unrecognized, she is likely to develop negative emotions and attitudes toward her colleagues and supervisors, and eventually her work performance will be affected. If the negative sentiments are sufficiently strong, they might even cause her to leave the company. The consequences of treatment discrimination for the company, too, are destructive. By failing to recognize the achievements and aspirations of its employees, it stands to lose productivity, creativity, and ultimately the services of talented employees by failing to appreciate differing expectations and cultural backgrounds. Clearly, this treatment would not be an optimal human resources strategy for a company attempting to maximize its human capital and compete successfully in a global economy.

---

[2]Of course, this problem is not unique to Asian American women but also applies to any employees who are not in (or welcome in) the center of the informal groups. Often when this issue comes up between an excluded employee and network insiders, the insiders typically (and with sympathy) deflect responsibility by asking, "Oh, we did not know you wanted to join us" or "Why didn't you ask?" The point that such redirection misses is how one can be expected to request participation in events that one had no way of knowing about in the first place.

ADDRESSING 21ST-CENTURY CHALLENGES: JOINT-CONSTRUCTIONAL APPROACHES

Recognizing and accepting the current problems are the first steps toward meeting the challenges of a multicultural work force. Numerous voices have advocated multiculturalism and multicultural training as ways of facing the new work force in the new workplace (Cox, 1991; Heskin & Heffner, 1987; Mason & Spich, 1987; Mobley & Payne, 1992; Ridley, Mendoza, & Kanitz, 1994; Thiederman, 1990). The associated literature describes detailed multicultural training programs (for example, Mason & Spich, 1987), learning issues (for example, Thiederman, 1990), and potential backlashes (for example, Mobley & Payne, 1992). Here, I would like to introduce the notion of "joint-constructional approaches," a theoretical framework currently unrepresented within the extant multicultural training literature but which could be used to address the three problems discussed above. Whereas standard multicultural training programs are unidirectionally oriented (from a trainer to an employee or manager), a joint-constructional approach assumes the need for adopting an active or multi-influential perspective on both the recipient and the context.

Joint-Constructional Perspectives in Psychology

You can clap only if your two palms simultaneously meet.
                                                                    —Korean proverb

In psychology, joint-constructional perspectives originally grew out of sociogenetic theoretical orientations (Mead, 1934; Valsiner & Van der Veer, 1988; Vygotsky, 1928/1987). These perspectives posit that all human psychological functions—thinking, feeling, and acting—are socioculturally and historically rooted and that they develop through ongoing interactions with the social and cultural contexts in which a person's life is embedded. Joint-constructional (also called "co-constructional"[3]) perspectives assume that both individual agents and their social, cultural, and historical contexts are active members of the ongoing interactions and that, together, they exist in mutually influencing, interdependent relationships (Hong, 1996; Valsiner, 1994). Every person is situated within multiple pre-existing sociocultural contexts into which "rules and resources, organized as properties of social systems" are embedded (Giddens, 1979, p. 66). These rules and resources impel individual members of a society to think, feel, and act toward achievement of socioculturally defined milestones using socioculturally available means. In this sense, sociocultural rules or expectations (for example, the model-minority stereotype, an organizational culture, or multicultural training information) may be regarded as sociocultural forces shaping the form and content

---

[3]Joint construction presented here is developed from Jaan Valsiner's metatheory of "co-constructionism," bearing more practical applications in mind. See Valsiner (1994) for further in-depth, theoretical elaboration of the concept.

of individual actors' thoughts, feelings, and actions. From this perspective, peoples' psychological functioning would be considered a sociocultural product molded by the dominant social forces expressed at a given time within a given context. As people re-express sociocultural rules and expectations in their everyday practices and actions, however, they do not simply replicate the rules and expectations transmitted by extant social forces. Rather, people personalize and transform the rules and expectations as they express them and thereby alter the qualitative nature of the extant social forces of the context in which they are expressed. Consequently, both sociocultural rules and expectations and people simultaneously act as social forces on each other and become each other's social products in a chain of mutually interdependent interactions.

Shattering Stereotype-Related Problems with Joint Constructions

In general, many traditional Asian cultures tend to discourage their members from expressing independence (Triandis, 1994). Women in particular are both individually and collectively rewarded for appearances of being domestic, docile, and submissive (at least on the surface). Asian cultures have developed powerful sociocultural prescripts (for example, myths, folk tales, folk songs, norms, roles, and rituals) that deliver sociocultural messages to people within the culture (Hong, 1997). By simultaneously belonging to two cultural worlds, Asian Americans in general and Asian American women in particular must find interaction methods that permit them to juggle their "appropriate" roles and activities in both cultural worlds. When roles or behaviors appropriate in one world are expressed in the other, the result often ends with confusion or embarrassment for the Asian American (Lee, 1994).

Despite the fact that virtually all Asian American women face the common problem of living in two worlds, Chow (1987) found substantial within-group variation among 161 Asian American women. In American contexts, some Asian American women who were identified as instrumental or androgynous registered higher self-esteem, higher-status jobs, and more job satisfaction than their more traditional peers. Although Chow's study contributed to a more articulated picture of existing diversity among Asian American women as a group, at an individual level her study may have identified some personal factors that contribute to "success." An even more comprehensive picture would require examination of both stereotypes and stereotype-related behaviors that each woman experienced within the organizational cultural of her company and how each differentially reacted to it.

Organizational culture, as a set of "shared values, beliefs, norms, artifacts, and patterns of behavior" (Ott, 1989, p. 1), provides a frame of reference for the way in which individual employees with different statuses and roles in an organization treat one another. It is the social force that pre-exists Asian American women in the workplace. Thus, any stereotype reduction training program that hopes to succeed must include not only managers' and supervisors' correctable behaviors, but also a thorough analysis of the existing organizational culture. These requirements are necessary because individual employees, their managers and supervisors, and organizational culture are all partners in creating the types, forms, and contents of stereotypic attitudes and behaviors that are jointly constructed (and permitted) in the workplace.

First, from a sociogenetic perspective, organizational culture functions as social force, dictating which stereotype-related attitudes and behaviors are considered permissible and which are sanctioned. As social products, managers, supervisors, and fellow employees of female Asian Americans respond to the organizational culture by tempering their expressions and actions (with individual variation) to the "boundaries" established within the organizational culture.

Second, the expressions and actions of managers, supervisors, and colleagues of female Asian American employees (each with their own idiosyncratic characteristics) act as social forces by partially determining the flavor of the everyday work environment and thereby influencing the organizational culture. In this sense, organizational culture is considered a social product of the expressions and actions exhibited by managers, supervisors, and fellow employees.

Third, the reactions of individual female Asian American employees to whatever stereotype-related attitudes and behaviors they encounter in the workplace can play a significant role in altering offensive expressions and actions of managers, supervisors, and colleagues. In this capacity, the Asian American woman herself exerts direct social force on those with whom she most closely interacts and exerts a less-direct impact in setting the boundaries of stereotypic behaviors and attitudes permitted by her company's organizational culture. Of course, individual Asian American women also must be viewed as social products subject to the social forces exerted by the company's organizational context; their fellow employees, supervisors, and managers; and their own internalized ethnic cultural heritage. In short, sociogenetic perspectives would suggest that successful stereotype-reduction programs must consider a wide-ranging, comprehensive set of factors that contribute to tolerance and perpetuation of stereotypic attitudes and behaviors in the workplace as well as address the active roles played by multiple participants in the phenomenon.

Joint-constructional perspectives recognize that each partner who contributes toward determining the stereotype-related attitudes and behaviors in an organization also possesses characteristics, attitudes, and behaviors that can help overcome or circumvent the stereotypes. Focusing, for example, on individual Asian women in the partnership, Lebra (1984) illustrated how strongly imposed and often strongly internalized gender roles deprive Japanese women of many social privileges in the workplace. At the same time, she found that "some Japanese women . . . converted their sex-based disadvantage into resources to promote themselves; inferiority, peripherality, backstage invisibility, or outsider status provided a woman the kind of freedom and opportunity from which a male colleague was barred: new prominent roles were precisely due to a woman's structural inferiority" (p. 304). In Lebra's study, the Japanese women exhibited characteristics congruent with the female Asian stereotypes discussed earlier; nonetheless, some of them used what would typically be considered negative stereotype-related consequences to their own advantage in surmounting the barriers raised by the stereotypes.

Similar opportunities for overcoming stereotypes likewise can be specified for each of the other partners who contribute toward determining stereotype-related attitudes and behaviors in an organization. As a practical consequence, therefore, the opportunities presented by the partners' strengths can be harnessed for overcoming stereotypic attitudes, behaviors, and sequelae. Asian American female employees can be supported and encouraged to informally communicate with their counterparts both within the same company and in other companies to share experiences and strategies for addressing stereotype-related attitudes and behavior in their companies.[4] Organizational training can be structured to capitalize on the partners' joint and active contributions to stereotypes within a company's organizational environment. For example, seminars or workshops can be used to inform female Asian American employees about "hidden" factors in organizational culture that play into advancement and promotion decisions, can help them formulate and carry out strategies for breaking the glass ceiling, and can help them learn to more effectively juggle their lives between their two cultural worlds. Organizational training can be used to alter the attitudes and behavior of managers, supervisors, and fellow employees as well as to eliminate stereotypic attitudes and behavior from the organizational culture of the company. Multicultural awareness and sensitivity programs can be used, for example, to help female Asian American employees and their supervisors and managers better appreciate each other's implicit psychological contracts, can provide a "safe" forum for each to express his or her expectations, and can assist each in recalibrating psychological contracts so that they are more congruent. Also, through joint-constructionally oriented multicultural training, supervisors and managers can be made aware of their own implicit stereotypes and how these can insidiously affect their judgments and evaluations of ethnic employees.

In all of these examples, joint-constructional perspectives suggest that active, experiential training must be used whenever possible to effect more permanent results. It also suggests including Asian American women as active, full, and equal partners in setting training

---

[4]To some degree, electronic forums such as e-mail, listservs, and news groups on the Internet can fill this need (at least for those who have Internet access, the technical savvy, and the computer skills to use them).

session agendas, planning the sessions, and conducting them. Company management can exert significant influence over organizational culture by establishing official company policies at the highest levels that do not tolerate stereotype-related prejudice or discrimination in evaluation, promotion, or treatment and then by exemplifying their policies through their own actions.

CONCLUSION

Joint-constructional perspectives can provide insight on advantages and limitations of current stereotype reduction programs in company workplaces. Through the insights they yield, joint-constructional perspectives can suggest ways of enhancing current programs and guide the development of innovative programs for the future. Ultimately, joint-constructional perspectives may prove a cornerstone in the fight for amelioration of stereotype-related problems in the workplace.

REFERENCES

Atkinson, E. R., Morten, G., & Sue, D. W. (Eds.). (1993). *Counseling American minorities: A cross-cultural perspective* (5th ed.). Dubuque, IA: W. C. Brown.

Carnevale, A. P., & Gainer, I. J. (1989). *The learning enterprise.* Alexandria, VA: American Society for Training and Development.

Chen, S., & Leong, F.T.L. (1997). The case of Jessica Chang. *Career Development Quarterly, 46,* 142–147.

Chow, E. N. (1987). The influence of sex-role identity and occupational attainment on the psychological well-being of Asian American women. *Psychology of Women Quarterly, 11,* 69–82.

Cox, T., Jr. (1991). The multicultural organization. *Executive, 5*(2), 34–47.

Crosby, F. J. (1982). *Relative deprivation and working women.* New York: Oxford University Press.

Crystal, D. (1989). Asian Americans and the myth of the model minority. *Social Casework, 70,* 405–413.

Espiritu, Y. L. (1996). *Asian American women and men.* Newbury Park, CA: Sage Publications.

Gardner, R., Robey, B., & Smith, P. C. (1985). Asian Americans: Growth, change, and diversity. *Population Bulletin, 40*(4).

Garland, S. B. (1991, April 29). Can the Feds bust through the "glass ceiling"? *Business Week,* p. 33.

Giddens, A. (1979). *Central problems in social theory: Action, structure and contradiction in social analysis.* Berkeley: University of California Press.

Greenhaus, J. H., Parasuraman, S., & Warmley, W. M. (1990). Effects of race on organizational experiences, job performance evaluations, and career outcomes. *Academy of Management Journal, 33,* 64–86.

Heskin, A. D., & Heffner, R. A. (1987). Learning about bilingual, multicultural organizing. *Journal of Applied Behavioral Science, 23,* 525–541.

Hong, G. Y. (1996, September). *Virtuousness in marginal identity: Themes of a sonless Korean diving woman's life story.* Paper presented at the Second Conference of Society for Socio-Cultural Research [Vygotsky-Piaget], Geneva.

Hong, G. Y. (1997). Just world beliefs and attributions of causal responsibility among Korean adolescents. *Cross-Cultural Research, 31*(2), 121–136.

Ilgen, D. R., & Youtz, M. A. (1986). Factors affecting the evaluation and development of minorities in organizations. *Research in Personnel and Human Resource Management, 4,* 307–337.

Johnston, W. B., & Packer, A. E. (1987). *Workforce 2000: Work and workers for the 21st century.* Indianapolis: Hudson Institute.

Kim, B.L.C. (1973). Asian Americans: No model minority. *Social Work, 18*(3), 44–53.

Kitano, H.H.L., & Sue, S. (1973). The model minorities. *Journal of Social Issues, 29*(2), 1–9.

Kitayama, S., & Markus, H. (1994). (Eds.). *Emotion and culture: Empirical studies of mutual influence.* Washington, DC: American Psychological Association.

Lebra, T. S. (1984). *Japanese women: Constraint and fulfillment.* Honolulu: University of Hawaii Press.

Lee, S. (1994). Behind the model-minority stereotype: Voices of high- and low-achieving Asian American students. *Anthropology and Education Quarterly, 25,* 413–429.

Markus, H., & Kitayama, S. (1991). Culture and the self: Implications for cognition, emotion, and motivation. *Psychological Review, 98,* 224–253.

Mason, H., & Spich, R. S (1987). *Management: An international perspective.* Homewood, IL: Richard D. Irwin.

Mead, G. H. (1934). *Mind, self, and society.* Chicago: Open Court.

Min, P. G. (Ed.). (1995). *Asian Americans: Contemporary trends and issues.* Newbury Park, CA: Sage Publications.

Mirvis, P. H. (1992). Introduction: The new workforce/The new workplace. *Human Resource Management, 30,* 1–5.

Mize, S. (1992). Shattering the glass ceiling. *Training and Development Journal, 46*(1), 60–62.

Mobley, M., & Payne, T. (1992). Backlash: The challenge to diversity training. *Training and Development Journal, 43*(12), 45–52.

Morrison, A. M., & Von Glinow. M. A. (1990). Women and minorities in management. *American Psychologist, 45,* 200–208.

Morrison, D. E. (1994). Psychological contracts and change. *Human Resource Management, 33,* 353–372.

Ott, J. S. (1989). *The organizational culture perspective.* Chicago: Dorsey Press.

Patel, D. (1988). Asian Americans: A growing force. *Journal of State Government, 61*(2), 71–77.

Ridley, C. R., Mendoza, D. W., & Kanitz, B. E. (1994). Multicultural training: Reexamination, operationalization, and integration. *Counseling Psychologist, 22,* 227–289.

Solomon, C. (1990). Careers under glass. *Personnel Journal, 69*(4), 96–105.

Spindler, G. S. (1994). Psychological contracts in the workplace—A lawyer's view. *Human Resource Management, 33,* 325–333.

Sue, D. W. (1994). Asian-American mental health and help-seeking behavior: Comment on Solberg et al. (1994), Tara and Leong (1994), and Lin (1994). *Journal of Counseling Psychology, 41,* 292–295.

Sue, D. W., & Frank, A. C. (1973). A typological approach to the study of Chinese and Japanese-American college males. *Journal of Social Issues, 29,* 129–148.

Sue, D. W., & Sue, D. (1990). *Counseling the culturally different: Theory and practice* (2nd ed.). New York: John Wiley & Sons.

Suzuki, B. H. (1995). Education and the socialization of Asian Americans: A revisionist analysis of the "model minority" thesis. In D. T. Nakanishi & T. Y. Nishida (Eds.), *The Asian American educational experience: A source book for teachers and students* (pp. 113–132). New York: Routledge.

Takaki, R. (1995). The myth of the "model minority." In D. M. Newman (Ed.), *Sociology: Exploring the architecture of everyday life* (pp. 255–259). Thousand Oaks, CA: Pine Forge Press.

Thiederman, S. (1990). *Bridging cultural barriers for corporate success.* Lexington, MA: Lexington Books.

Triandis, H. C. (1994). *Culture and social behavior.* New York: McGraw-Hill.

Tversky, A., & Kahneman, D. (1982). Judgments of and by representatives. In D. Kahneman, P. Slovic, & A. Tversky (Eds.), *Judgment under uncertainly: Heuristics and biases* (pp. 84–98). New York: Cambridge University Press.

Uba, L. (1994). *Asian Americans: Personality patterns, identity, and mental health.* New York: Guilford Press.

U.S. Bureau of the Census. (1993). *We the American Asians.* Washington, DC: U.S. Government Printing Office.

U.S. Commission on Civil Rights. (1992). *Civil rights issues facing Asian-Americans in the 1990s.* Washington, DC: Author.

Valsiner, J. (1994). Co-constructionism: What is (and is not) in a name. In P. Van Geert & L. Mos (Eds.), *Annals of theoretical psychology* (Vol. 10, pp. 1–15). New York: Plenum Press.

Valsiner, J., & Van der Veer, R. (1988). On the social nature of human cognition: An analysis of the shared intellectual roots of George Herbert Mead and Lev Vygotsky. *Journal for the Theory of Social Behavior, 18,* 117–136.

Van Velsor, E. (1987). *Breaking the glass ceiling: Can women make it to the top in America's largest corporations?* Reading, MA: Addison-Wesley.

Vygotsky, L. S. (1987). Thinking and speech. In R. W. Rieber & A. S. Carton (Eds.), *The collected works of L. S. Vygotsky* (N. Minick, Trans., pp. 39–285). New York: Plenum Press. Originally published in 1928

Wong, M., & Hirschman, C. (1983). Labor force participation and socioeconomic attainment of Asian-American women. *Sociological Perspectives, 26,* 423–446.

Woo, D. (1985). The socioeconomic status of Asian American women in the labor force: An alternative view. *Sociological Perspectives, 28,* 307–338.

I express my sincere appreciation to Stephen Chen and Frederick T. L. Leong for their generosity in allowing me to use the case of Jessica Chang.

28 Hawaiian Health, Native Healing, and Medical Hegemony

Lana Ka'opua

In the 19th century Native Hawaiians were threatened with extinction by foreign infectious diseases (Blaisdell, 1989; Stannard, 1989). The practice of native healing was outlawed, and only allopathic (Western) medicine was legal. However, allopathic medicine was expensive, inaccessible to those living in rural areas, and often culturally unfamiliar to natives (Bushnell, 1993). Native healers of that time, or *kahuna la'au lapa'au*, were faced with a legal and ethical dilemma: Allopathic medicine alone was inadequate to stem the epidemic proportions of Native Hawaiian mortality, yet administering *la'au*, or herbal healing, was illegal (Chun, 1994a). In appealing to the authorities of the time, *kahuna* asked the rhetorical question: "Must we wait in despair?" (Chun, 1994a). The *kahuna* reasoned that the tradition of native healing and the network of healers could provide an important alternative to Western medicine in rendering aid to the ailing population. Native Hawaiians believed that a policy change allowing licensing and regulation of their practice was in order, and they willingly submitted to evaluation of their practice by Western standards.

In the cultural clash between native healing and allopathic medicine, *kahuna* were unable to gain lasting legal recognition. The growing hegemony of Western medicine in Hawaii fostered a climate in which the practice of native healing was systematically discredited. *Kahuna* were unable to gain even a modicum of acceptance in the social mainstream of the dominant Western culture. Indeed, the growing political and economic power of allopathic medicine and its intolerance for any form of perceived competition reflected a larger process of Western political and economic domination in Hawaii. The practice of healing was one of many native traditions deemed inferior and unacceptable by the Western oligarchy (Blaisdell, 1989). From the Western perspective, native medicine was relegated to an inferior position in relation to allopathic medicine. However, many natives did not believe that the traditional healing methods had "failed" them and continued to seek care from *kahuna* (Hunt, 1994). In the culturally intolerant atmosphere of 19th-century Hawaii, many Hawaiian traditions such as native healing were outlawed and forced underground (Bushnell, 1993). In the case of native healing, *kahuna la'au lapa'au* continued to administer care to native help seekers but were careful to stay outside the view of Western law and medicine. The practice of native medicine did not re-emerge into the social mainstream until the 1980s (Bushnell, 1993; Chun, 1994a).

Today the problem of poor health in the Native Hawaiian population remains. Although epidemics of infectious disease are no longer a prevalent cause of death, the health status of Native Hawaiians remains problematic because of the prevalence of chronic illness and other serious health problems (Alu Like, 1985; Look & Braun, 1995; U.S. Office of Technology Assessment [OTA], 1988; Wegner, 1989). In Hawaii, mortality rates for Native Hawaiians have increased, whereas mortality rates for other ethnic groups living in Hawaii have declined (Look & Braun, 1995). In national comparisons, the causes of death among Native Hawaiians and other ethnic groups living there are similar, but there are dramatic differences in the rates of death, even after adjustment for age (Look & Braun, 1995; OTA, 1988). According to the OTA (1988), the overall death rate or rate of mortality from all known causes is 34 percent higher for Native Hawaiians than for the all-races category. Cancer, heart disease, and other preventable conditions are documented as the leading causes of death among Native Hawaiians (Look & Braun, 1995; OTA, 1988).

The problem of poor health among Native Hawaiians is compounded by patterns of low health care and social services use (Alu Like, 1985). Native Hawaiian consumers consistently report discomfort in Western medical settings and have often stated a preference for native healers on the grounds of cultural compatibility. In the past decade Native Hawaiian scholars and health care professionals have increasingly advocated the need for culturally compatible and community-driven strategies, including native healing (Alu Like, 1985; Blaisdell, 1989; Look & Braun, 1995; Mokuau & Matsuoka, 1995).

From a policy perspective, the integration of native healing practices into Western health care systems has been problematic (personal communication with M. N. Chun, Ph.D., cultural consultant, Queen Liliu'okalani Children's Center, Honolulu, June 6, 1996). This chapter will examine three policy documents relevant to the integration of native healing in Western health care systems: (1) *Healthy People—The Surgeon General's Report on Health Promotion and Disease Prevention* (U.S. Department of Health and Human Services, 1979), which has served as the framework for a series of publications dealing with national and state health promotion and disease prevention efforts; (2) *E Ola Mau: The Native Hawaiian Health Needs Study Report* (Alu Like, 1989), a comprehensive study documenting the problem of Hawaiian health from a native perspective; and (3) the 1988 Native Hawaiian Health Care Improvement Act, which legislated the Native Hawaiian health care system. This chapter reviews the conflicting policy goals and action agendas set forth in these documents. It discusses the implications these differences have had on the integration of native healers into health care efforts and explores barriers in the development of culturally compatible models of practice and pluralistic systems of care.

NATIVE HEALING AND ALLOPATHIC MEDICINE

Key terms in the discussion of native healing and allopathic medicine are Native Hawaiians, native healing, native healers, health status, health care, access and acceptability of services, medical hegemony, allopathic medicine, and cultural politics. Native Hawaiians are the descendants of the oceanic voyagers who settled Hawaii and populated the islands before 1778 (Blaisdell, 1989). Native Hawaiians are further classified as either full- or part-Hawaiian. In certain disease categories, morbidity and mortality rates differ significantly between part- and full-Hawaiians. Full-Hawaiians tend to be older and to live in more isolated regions. In general, this group has a poorer health status than that of part-Hawaiians; has reported a reluctance to seek Western medical care; and has expressed a preference for native medicines, native healers, home care, and prayer (Look & Braun, 1995).

Native healing includes methods of healing that predate contact with the West and with allopathic medicine. Before Western contact, the priest–physicians of Hawaii developed diagnoses and treatments for physical and spiritual illnesses as well as injuries to bones and muscles (Bushnell, 1993; Chun, 1994b). In ancient times, *kahuna* were classified by their specializations, which included inducing pregnancy and delivering babies, treating childhood ailments, and treating illnesses of the spirit (Chun, 1994b). In their diagnoses and treatments, all *kahuna,* regardless of specialization, relied on the aid of spirit-guardians and the gods (Bushnell, 1993). Methods of healing might include *la'au,* or administration of medicine; *lomilomi,* or massage; *h'oponopono,* a relational process that resembles group prayer and counseling (Whistler, 1992); or in certain cases, surgical intervention (Bushnell, 1993; Chun, 1994b). These methods might be practiced singly or in various combinations.

The current state of native healing reflects an evolving relationship with Western concepts of healing and spirituality. For example, modern practitioners tend to recognize the Judeo–Christian god in place of the ancestral gods (personal communication with M. N. Chun, June 6, 1996; personal communication with N. Judd, University of Hawaii John A. Burns School of Medicine, Honolulu, June 7, 1996). Regardless of the preference for Hawaiian or Judeo–Christian gods, spirituality is central to the practice of healing. Spirituality is the aspect of native healing that attracts many help seekers. Paradoxically, the spirituality that attracts help seekers also repels Western medicine. Indeed, the epistemological, ontological, and methodological basis of Hawaiian and Western medicines are fundamentally in conflict. One is given here a small glimpse of the difficulty of integrating native medicine into Western health care systems, even those that are targeted toward Native Hawaiians.

Allopathic medicine is synonymous with Western medicine (Bannerman, Burton, & Ch'en, 1983). Scientific materialism guides the theory and practice of allopathic medicine. That which is considered "real" must stand the test of observation and experimental manipulation. That is, all assumptions about what occurs in the world are subject to experimentation and statistical validation. A biomedical paradigm undergirds explanations of cause and effect. "Allopathic hegemony" refers to the dominance of the medical profession and the medical care system in matters related to health and illness. It refers to the professional monopoly of physicians in the domain of health and healing as well as to the profession's dominance over the organization of medical services and the cultural power of medical authority. The term "medicalization of health" is related. The conversion of medical authority into high income, professional autonomy, and other rewards of privilege required the medical profession to gain control over the political economy of health care. This process has involved gaining control over the health care marketplace and all the supporting superstructures related to governance, financing, and policy making (Starr, 1982).

The term "health status" reflects the allopathic paradigm and includes measures of the nature and extent of mortality, morbidity, and disability in populations (U.S. Department of Health and Human Services, 1992). These measures form the basis for comparing health status among groups of people. Although the disparities in health status between Native Hawaiians and the general population in the United States (OTA, 1988) and in Hawaii are well documented (Alu Like, 1985; Look & Braun, 1995), the challenges of decreasing the disparity and, ultimately, creating public policies and programs that maintain health in this population remain.

Thus, health care services are popularly perceived as the treatment of patients' illnesses by physicians (Wegner, 1989). The term "health care" often is used to mean "medical care," specifically treatment of illness and disease. Conrad and Kern (1994) viewed this phenomenon as part of the larger social process called the "medicalization of health." According to Zola (1972), the mid-20th century marked the extension of medicine's jurisdiction into areas of human experience such as childbirth that were not previously viewed as medical problems by Western society. This extension of medicine's domain accelerated the course of medical hegemony. Human life would be increasingly viewed along a sickness–wellness continuum, with an emphasis on individual organic pathology, physiological etiologies, and biomedical interventions (Conrad & Kern, 1994).

Barriers to access and acceptability of medical services have been cited as reasons for the underuse of health care services by Native Hawaiians (Alu Like, 1985; Look & Braun, 1995; Wegner, 1989). "Access" is related to the ease with which consumers of care can get to the service. "Acceptability" refers to the compatibility between services and the beliefs and practices of the consumer (Wegner, 1989).

"Culture" refers to a shared system of beliefs, values preferences, symbols, and ways of behaving (Herberg, 1989). Although it is often associated with a particular ethnic group, as in the Hawaiian culture, culture also has been applied to organizations and professions

(Helman, 1992). In this discussion, the term "cultural politics" refers to the action agenda embodying the values, interests, and loyalties of an organized group. To achieve a particular outcome, information is shaped into strategic argument and diffused in the political process by an organized power base (Stone, 1989).

NATIVE HEALING AND CULTURAL POLITICS

E Ola Mau: The Native Hawaiian Health Needs Study (Alu Like, 1985) is regarded as seminal in the documentation of poor health status and health needs of Native Hawaiians in the 20th century. The Needs Study recognizes that the problem of poor health results partly from the lack of accessible and acceptable health care service and largely from the established relationship between gradients of socioeconomic class and health status. The Needs Study specifically recognizes that the poor health status of Native Hawaiians is related to the low socioeconomic status among them as a group. It recognizes the need to address the problem of poor health at the level of individual patient and practitioner as well as at the macrosystemic level. At the first level, the person and his or her symptoms of physical or mental illness require accessible and acceptable health care intervention. At the second level, the Needs Study emphasizes political action aimed at structural changes.

Through historical account, the Needs Study illustrates how health and disease are produced by Western capitalist society's organization and class-stratified distribution of goods and services. Influenced by the larger body of Native Hawaiian cultural politics and the view that health and disease are socially produced, health status comes to be understood in the context of a larger political agenda to improve the socioeconomic and sociocultural conditions of Native Hawaiians as a group. Control of land, political power, and distribution of wealth are viewed as central to the empowerment of Native Hawaiians. From the perspective of Hawaiian cultural politics, the sociocultural dislocation of the race and the alienation of native people from the land are key factors in their poor health status. Dislocation and land alienation are understood to have profound effects on the physical, mental, and spiritual well-being of Hawaiians.

Obviously, the problems of land alienation and sociocultural dislocation cannot be resolved through medical intervention. Hence, the Needs Study calls for macrosystemic intervention. At this level, health improvement must be addressed through "deliberate political and legislative action" (p. 2). For some of the contributors to the Needs Study, this meant that health is intrinsically linked to Native Hawaiian political and economic sovereignty and the restoration of a land base (Casken, 1995; personal communication with N. Judd, June 7, 1996; Mokuau & Matsuoka, 1995).

Cultural revival is seen as having a large impact on Hawaiian cultural politics. It follows that culturally compatible strategies of healing and helping would be viewed as necessary components of effective services delivery and that Native Hawaiian healing would be seen as an important option in the provision of primary health care services (Alu Like, 1985).

The Needs Study recognizes that native healing methods continue to be practiced throughout Hawaii and that many traditionally oriented Hawaiians continue to trust and seek help from native healers. Furthermore, the Needs Study recognizes that native healing has been historically subjugated to Western allopathic medicine on the grounds of its inferiority. It acknowledges that native practices are generally credible methods of healing and that native healers embody Hawaiian culture and, as such, are cultural treasures (personal communication with N. Judd, June 7, 1996). For these reasons, the Needs Study makes recommendations for the integration of native healing into primary health care for Native Hawaiians. It implicitly presents native healing as a complement to, rather than a substitute for, allopathic medicine.

The Needs Study specifically recommends "that third-party payments for treatment services based on traditional Hawaiian orientation, and practices be legitimized" (Alu Like, 1985, p. 26); "that research be done on Native Hawaiian healers" (p. 26); "that cooperation be fostered between traditional healers and physicians" (p. 29); and "that traditional Hawaiian remedies be incorporated into the care of Native Hawaiians whenever medically feasible" (p. 29). These recommendations reopened discussions of standardization of training, validation of practice effectiveness, legal recognition, licensure, regulation, liability, and vendorship—issues with which native healers had struggled in the 19th and early 20th centuries (Bushnell, 1993; Chun, 1994a). In addition, the issue of remuneration through insurance reimbursement also arose (personal communication with M. N. Chun, June 6, 1996).

The recommendations to legitimize and integrate native healing practices represented the collective efforts of healers, community elders, Native Hawaiian organizations, Hawaiian scholars and health care professionals, and other concerned community members. Following the publication and popular dissemination of the Needs Study, efforts were made to identify native healers and to facilitate the building of an islandwide network of *kahuna* (Agard, 1994; Clark, 1994; personal communication with N. Judd, June 7, 1996).

Concurrently, some architects of the study became stakeholders in the formulation and passage of the 1988 Native Hawaiian Health Care Improvement Act. The legislation intended to give credibility to cultural strengths and existing native health practice. A notable thrust of the legislation was the integration of native healers into a culturally competent, community-driven medical care system for Native Hawaiians. At first glance, the resulting legislation seemed like an antecedent of the Needs Study. However, on closer examination, the final legislation actually subverted the study's intent to create a culturally competent system of care. Only one of the Needs Study's four recommendations regarding native healing is reflected in the Native

Hawaiian Health Care Improvement Act. Recommendation 3.12, related to the incorporation of native healers into the care of Native Hawaiians "whenever medically feasible" (p. 29), is weakly reflected in the public policy to improve Native Hawaiian health. In the act, native healers are grouped with indigenous workers and community outreach workers whose sole charge remains in the domain of health promotion. In actuality, the legislation functions to limit the role and responsibilities of native healers. Furthermore, owing to the centrality of the medical model in the legislation, Western-trained health professionals, including physicians, nurse practitioners, and nurses, are charged with being the primary and essential staff. Healers are implicitly given a secondary place, and their role in the new system is ill defined. From the medical model of health care services, what would be the responsibilities of a kahuna? What could a healer do that would not incur liability? Were the services of the healer expected to compete with those of a Western-trained health care professional? How would the system ensure the competence of the healer? Who would be liable for the healer? Who would pay for the healer's services?

Because these questions could not be resolved, the role of the healer remained ambiguous in the implementation process. This ambiguity is problematic for those implementing the act but advantageous to those whose interests coincide with maintenance of the medical hegemony.

The questions of the medical establishment seemed reasonable, especially because they were couched in the manifest discourse of providing quality patient care. However, the metadiscourse was that of monopoly over the domain of health care services. Indeed, the underlying issues reflected the need to ensure survival of biomedical authority, professional domain, medical monopoly, and the political and legal superstructures that served to maintain medical hegemony. Hence, whereas some stakeholders optimistically argued that healers had legitimacy through legislative mandate (personal communication with N. Judd, June 7, 1996), others were more pragmatic and saw the real challenge of integrating native practices into the medical model of health and the system of medical hegemony and hierarchy (personal communication with M. N. Chun, June 6, 1996).

In the long, heated discussions about integration, the background text involved a realistic appraisal of how much diversity was allowed by the medical hegemony. In the latter part of the 20th century, medical systems outside the United States have taken a more tolerant approach to the use of indigenous healing in health care services. However, integration abroad has involved scientific measurement of indigenous methods, and indigenous healers have been relegated to little more than community health outreach workers and health educators (Stepan, 1983).

In reviewing the implications of integration, Native Hawaiian healers questioned if integration would mean re-creating themselves in the image of allopathic practitioners and scientific empiricism. Would they not have to do this to achieve professional status and all that status entailed in Western medical hegemony? Would the healers even be able to do this? Had not the Native Hawaiian healers of the 19th century attempted such an integration and failed? Even if they were able to do this, would they lose the very essence, indeed the spirit-giving power, of healing? (personal communication with M. N. Chun, June 6, 1996; personal communication with N. Judd, June 7, 1996).

CONFLICTING NOTIONS

Healing

To some healers, the integration into Western health care systems connotated professional stature, financial rewards, and greater access to help seekers (personal communication with M. N. Chun, June 6, 1996). However, healers also could see the disadvantages to integration. Among their concerns, the greatest was that of maintaining integrity to the traditions of native healing.

The concern is well founded. The Western and Hawaiian traditions of healing are fundamentally different in ontology, epistemology, and methodology. In the Western tradition, human illness can be understood as a series of physical and biochemical processes that are observable and open to human manipulation. From the perspective of objective materialism, that which is real can be observed in the physical world. Truth is known through empirical study of cause-and-effect relationships. Once a human phenomenon is verified, it becomes possible to predict and control life processes through mechanical and engineered interventions. Mind and body can be separated, as evidenced in the Western duality of physical and mental health. Furthermore, the scientific paradigm of modern allopathic medicine disavows the metaphysical (Herberg, 1989). The allopathic healer or physician is both scientist and practitioner. The locus of intervention is the individual patient, who agrees to submit to the advice and treatment by the expert. Professionalism entails the maintenance of objectivity. Hence, although a pleasing bedside manner is desirable, the practitioner is trained to err on the side of professional boundary maintenance. From the Native Hawaiian perspective, this approach could translate into an impersonality that is unacceptable in the healing relationship.

By comparison, the Native Hawaiian tradition of healing relies on its ability to express a three-part relationship with God and spirits; to view people as community, extended family, and individuals; and to enlist the healer as an intermediary (Chun, 1991). The Hawaiian term *ola pono* has been roughly equated with the Western concept of health. In the context of Native Hawaiian culture, *ola pono* actually suggests relationships and maintenance of balance in relationships between communities, individual people, the environment, and the spirit forces. According to Blaisdell (1989), *ola pono* entails having sufficient *mana,* or personal power. *Ma'i,* or illness, comes about when *mana* is lost due to a lack of *pono,* or proper behavior with self, others, the spirits, or the forces of nature. In the Native Hawaiian tradition, the power of healing is a gift of spirit. Training in diagnosis and "treatment" of illness symptoms involves lengthy apprenticeship. The ability to heal is maintained by the healer's being *pono* in all the various relationships of life. As a gift of spirit forces, healing is traditionally given without expectation of monetary payment. In fact, to expect payment could prompt the loss of healing power.

In contrasting Western and Native Hawaiian paradigms of healing, it becomes apparent that the Hawaiian system does not readily lend itself to scientific quantification and validation. Thus, evaluating credibility by Western standards is problematic. It follows that at the practice level, Native Hawaiian healing and Western medicine are difficult to integrate.

HEALTH AND DISEASE DETERMINANTS

Why are some people healthy and others not? What determines health and disease in a group of people? Notions of health and disease determinants are key to any discourse on the improvement of health in a population and serve to guide the formal health system in mobilizing its resources to improve health. Two competing notions of disease causation can be found in policies influencing Native Hawaiian health: lifestyle theory and social production theory of health and illness. Lifestyle theory focuses on individual responsibility for choices affecting health status. Social production theory views health as a function of the way in which goods and services are distributed or, more precisely, the limited way in which health and health care are distributed to members of the lower socioeconomic groups (Turshen, 1989).

Competing theories of health and disease causation are reflected in the policy-relevant documents that inform the Native Hawaiian Health Care Improvement Act. The Needs Study (Alu Like, 1985) reflects social production theory. The Needs Study articulates health and disease in the Native Hawaiian population as a function of the way in which society is currently organized. It is reasoned that the health of the race would be more likely to come about when the larger agenda of political and economic well-being of the race is achieved. The premise that poor health in the Native Hawaiian population is related to socioeconomic class comes into direct competition with the lifestyle theory of health and disease as articulated in *Healthy People—The Surgeon General's Report on Health Promotion and Disease Prevention* (U.S. Department of Health and Human Services, 1979). The report frames the problem of poor health among ethnocultural groups and others as a function of individual responsibility: "The health of the nation's citizens can be significantly improved through actions individuals can take themselves . . . often only modest lifestyle changes are needed to substantially reduce risk factors for several diseases" (p. 12). The report emphasizes individual initiative and responsibility and is consonant with classical liberalism, the philosophy that drives the American political economy and the medical model of health (Casken, 1995). Casken explained that "when the stress on individual initiative and responsibility is as strong as it is in the United States, we observe the effect of the successes of the few coming to serve as the justification for the continuation of the stress on individual efforts rather than bringing about policies that change the structure in which individuals operate" (p. 22).

Thus, to become public law, the problem of poor health required a formulation that reflected the biomedical model of health care as well as the principles of classical liberalism. According to Renaud (1975), the state's intervention in health has specific limitations imposed by the contradictory position of the state in capitalist society. Thus, although government may be charged with meeting the health needs produced by industrial capitalism, it must do so in ways that legitimize the capitalist system. Hence, although social reorganization may be the most effective strategy for dealing with the problem of poor health, the nature of the reorganization process destabilizes the system. Alternatively, legislative reforms may be less effective but more desirable because they are less threatening to the political economy of the state (Casken, 1995; Renaud, 1975).

Renaud spoke to the difficulty, perhaps the impossibility, of shifting the explanatory paradigm of U.S. medical hegemony. Indeed, the strength of allopathic medicine and the medicalization of the health care industry is regarded as the most successful and powerful example of classical liberalism (Alford, 1975; Casken, 1995). Given its cultural authority and political and economic power, any attempt to compete with the prevailing interests of the medical hegemony would be necessarily transformed. Such was the process of political accommodation that occurred in the formulation and passage of the Native Hawaiian Health Care Improvement Act. This process of accommodation resulted in legislation that failed to structure cultural diversity into the health care system. After the passage of the act, disappointed stakeholders called it successful in creating another Western system of care, administrative bureaucracy, and Hawaiian tokenism (Casken, 1995).

NO LONGER "WAITING IN DESPAIR"

To define is to mark the limits of inclusion and exclusion. The corollary to this maxim is that those who define, limit. By defining credible practice using Western scientific standards and by linking this view of credibility with public interest, the medical monopoly was able to limit the domain of medicine to Western-trained physicians. In the political process of policy making, it is always the weaker side that is on the defensive and that is called on to explain itself using the parameters set by the stronger side (Stone, 1989). Implicit in asking the question "must we wait in despair" is the need for permission. It implies deference and a willingness to take direction from the superior force.

When *kahuna* of the 19th century sought legal and professional recognition, they accepted the definitional process set forth by the medical oligarchy. Over time, the healers lost in the discourse of legitimacy—it was a set-up. The legitimacy of native healing was predicated on a paradigm of healing that was fundamentally beyond the understanding of Western medicine. The manifest discourse focused on credible patient care based on scientific proof. The metadiscourse was one of maintaining dependence on medical monopoly. As a result, native healers went underground to keep their tradition alive.

In the 1990s the metadiscourse of medical monopoly is couched in more tolerant terms. Nonetheless, the discourse remains the same. As healers in this century began to organize their profession, they were presented with a scenario similar to the one presented their predecessors. Validation by Western standards was the avenue to recognition and integration into the larger health care system. However, the price of integration and legal recognition involved regulation and restriction that threatened the very essence of what it meant to be a traditional healer. If healers were integrated into the health care system, they would come more directly in contact with the dominance of allopathic medicine and the vast organizational system of medical care. Native healers had only to look at international examples of other indigenous healers who chose integration and the pattern of consequences that resulted. In developing countries where integrated systems of healers and allopathic physicians exist, healers are organized into the biomedical structure of health care delivery. The work of the healers is negotiated and supervised by Western medical professionals. Leslie (1983) described the movement to professionalize scientific medicine and how it subverts indigenous traditions of healing:

> Their [Western trained physicians] training with its regular schedule of examinations conditions them to hold professionally correct ideas for thinking about health problems. Confronted with different ideas, they must interpret them in the "correct" terms of their own system. In a show of goodwill they may translated indigenous health concepts and practices into those of modern . . . medicine . . . the most common action is to tolerate traditional medicine by attributing a placebo effect to practices that are otherwise considered harmless. (p. 315)

"No longer waiting in despair" refers to the capacity of modern healers to recast the discourse of integration and legitimacy so that it is consonant with the values and traditions of Native Hawaiian healing. In redefining integration into health care, modern healers have embraced a mission of education to all people, including health care professionals, lay community, Hawaiians, and non-Hawaiians (personal communication with N. Judd, June 7, 1996). *Haumana,* or students in native healing methods, learn to heal themselves as well as others. Lifestyles might change, for indeed the practice of native healing often necessitates a particular relationship with the world (personal communication with N. Judd, June 7, 1996). Education to Western-trained health care professionals has resulted in informal referral networks to native healers (personal communication with M. N. Chun, June 6, 1996; personal communication with N. Judd, June 7, 1996). In reframing integration into the health care system, native healers have begun to develop a parallel system of care that is flourishing and improving on itself through collective study and knowledge-building through consensus. Although legitimization by Western standards is not the goal of native healers' organization, some believe that the process of legitimization of native healing is well underway (personal communication with N. Judd, June 7, 1996).

CONCLUSION

The discourse of diversity in health care systems seems resolved at present, but the daunting challenge to improve Native Hawaiian health remains. The healers' struggle to gain legitimacy in the present health care system focuses attention on the political and economic barriers that can accompany movement toward a more pluralistic system of care. As the United States grows in demographic diversity, the challenge of the upcoming century may be that of understanding critical power relationships and negotiating true cultural diversity in health services.

REFERENCES

Agard, K. K. (1994, January). E ho'omau lomilomi (Perpetuate the practice of Native Hawaiian therapeutic massage). *Ka wai ola o OHA, 11,* 20–21.

Alford, R. R. (1975). *Health care politics: Ideological and interest group barriers to reform.* Chicago: University of Chicago Press.

Alu Like. (1985). *E ola mau: The Native Hawaiian health needs study report.* Honolulu: Native Hawaiian Research Consortium.

Bannerman, R. H., Burton, J., & Ch'en, W. C. (Eds.). (1983). *Traditional medicine and health care coverage.* Geneva: World Health Organization.

Blaisdell, R. K. (1989). Historical and cultural aspects of Native Hawaiian health. In E. L. Wegner (Ed.), *Social process in Hawai'i: The health of Native Hawaiians* (Vol. 32, pp. 1–21). Honolulu: University of Hawaii Press.

Bushnell, O. (1993). *The gifts of civilization—Germs and genocide in Hawai'i.* Honolulu: University of Hawaii Press.

Casken, J. (1995). *Culture and health: The Native Hawaiian Health Care Improvement Act of 1988.* Unpublished doctoral dissertation, University of Hawaii-Manoa.

Chun, M. N. (1991, January). Ola: Seeking cultural perspectives. *Ka wai ola o OHA, 8,* 12–13.

Chun, M. N. (Trans. and Ed.). (1994a). *Must we wait in despair? The 1867 Report of the 'Ahahui La'au Lapa'au of Wailuku, Maui on Native Hawaiian health.* Honolulu: First People's Productions.

Chun, M. N. (Trans. and Ed.). (1994b). *Native Hawaiian medicines.* (Originally published as *Hawaiian herbs of medicinal value*). Honolulu: First People's Productions.

Clark, J. (1994, September). OHA holds Hawaiian massage 'aha: E ho'omau I ka lomilomi. *Ka wai ola o OHA, 11,* 9.

Conrad, P., & Kern, R. (Eds.). (1994). *The sociology of health and illness. Critical perspectives* (4th ed.). New York: St. Martin's Press.

Helman, C. G. (1992). *Culture, health and illness.* Oxford, England: Butterworth-Heineman.

Herberg, P. (1989). Theoretical foundations of transcultural nursing. In J. Boyle & M. Andrews (Eds.), *Transcultural nursing* (pp. 3–65). Glenview, IL: Scott, Foresman.

Hunt, K. (1994). *The Native Hawaiian health care system: Program evaluation.* Honolulu: Papa Ola Lokahi.

Leslie, C. (1983). Policy options in regulating the practice of traditional medicine. In R. H. Bannerman, J. Burton, & W. C. Ch'en (Eds.), *Traditional medicine and health care coverage* (pp. 314–318). Geneva: World Health Organization.

Look, M., & Braun, K. (1995). *A mortality study of the Hawaiian people 1910–1990.* Honolulu: Queen's Health System.

Mokuau, N., & Matsuoka, J. (1995). Turbulence among a native people: Social work practice with Hawaiians. *Social Work, 40,* 465–472.

Native Hawaiian Health Care Improvement Act, P.L. 100-579, 102 Stat. 2916 (1988).

Renaud, M. (1975). On the structural constraints to state intervention in health. *International Journal of Health Services, 5,* 559–571.

Stannard, D. (1989). *Before the horror: The population of Hawai'i on the eve of Western contact.* Honolulu: University of Hawaii Press.

Starr, P. (1982). *The social transformation of medicine.* New York: Basic Books.

Stepan, J. (1983). Patterns of legislation concerning traditional medicine. In R. H. Bannerman, J. Burton, & W. C. Ch'en (Eds.), *Traditional medicine and health care coverage* (pp. 290–313). Geneva: World Health Organization.

Stone, D. (1989). *Policy paradox and political reason.* New York: HarperCollins.

Turshen, M. (1989). *The politics of health.* New Brunswick, NJ: Rutgers University Press.

U.S. Department of Health and Human Services. (1979). *Healthy people: The Surgeon General's report on health promotion and disease prevention* (DHHS Publication No. 79-55071). Washington, DC: Author.

U.S. Department of Health and Human Services. (1992). *Improving minority health statistics.* Washington, DC: Author.

U.S. Office of Technology Assessment. (1988). *Native Hawaiian Health Care Improvement Act—Report to accompany S. 136.* Washington, DC: Author.

Wegner, E. L. (1989). A framework for assessing health needs. In E. L. Wegner (Ed.), *Social process in Hawai'i: The health of Native Hawaiians* (Vol. 32, pp. 32–54). Honolulu: University of Hawaii Press.

Whistler, A. (1992). *Polynesian herbal medicine.* Hong Kong: Everbest.

Zola, E. (1972). Medicine as an institution of social control. *Sociological Review, 20,* 487–504.

Afterword

The intent of this book has been to inform and stimulate those who are interested in diversity in the workplace. There are several comments that may be useful in extending the utility of what has been written here in search of effective frameworks for addressing diversity's multifaceted issues.

First of all, the language we use in discussing diversity issues needs to be defined with intentional clarity to advance the discourse on resolution of its problems. One person's innocent use of some words can be very painful to another person whose history with the same words is different. An example of this point is the word "racist." It is apparent that this word has differential meanings out of the historical experience and understanding of the concept. Although it is a valid word, it is too often used in ways that undermine communication and understanding; "cultural embeddedness" more accurately describes the complexity of issues we seek to convey with the label of "racist." Discourse and research need to reveal and elaborate on how culture and institutions transmit expectations, behaviors, and perceptions if we are to reduce conflict and produce change.

At the same time, the reality of institutional racism can be perceived more objectively as the language moves from implicating individuals to focusing on system dynamics (Sleek, 1997). The issue of *corporate ethnocentrism,* defined by Thomas, Phillips, and Brown (1998) as the propensity in some corporate cultures to favor historically dominant groups while they fail to recognize barriers to other groups (Bell, 1998), is another example of an issue needing sensitive discourse.

A further concern involves the fact that most organizational work is done through teams. Group diversity is considered a positive situation because the challenges generated by global migration as well as by patterns of migration within national and regional boundaries benefit from the dynamics of multiple inputs (Jackson & Ruderman, 1995). Research into group dynamics of diversity in groups is underexplored. McGrath, Berdahl, and Arrow (1995) made a significant contribution to understanding the state of research in this area and offered a model for understanding the complexity of variables in addressing group processes and outcomes (Figure A-1). Their model encompasses a way of looking at varying attributes among group members by using five clusters, each of which defines a particular dimension or type of attitude. The authors also examined the effects of time and changes in participants on group process. Some aspects of these clusters may overlap at a point, but the clusters can differentiate people contextually so that within-group diversity can be observed.

Figure A-1

An Integrative Model for Studying Diversity

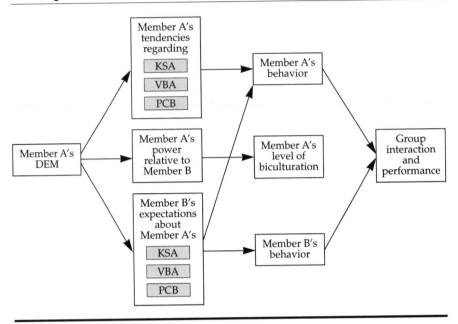

SOURCE: McGrath, J. E., Berdahl, J. L., & Arrow, H. (1995). Trait, expectations, culture, and clout: The dynamics of diversity in work groups. In S. E. Jackson & M. N. Ruderman (Eds.), *Diversity in work teams: Research paradigms for a changing workplace* (p. 26). Washington, DC: American Psychological Association. Copyright © 1995 by the American Psychological Association. Reprinted with permission.

NOTE: DEM = demographic attributes; KSA = task-related knowledge, skills, and abilities; PCB = personality and cognitive behavioral styles; VBA = values, beliefs, and attitudes. The fifth cluster (not shown) is organizational rank, tenure, and occupational specialty.

Diversity has been described as complex and multidimensional. In fact, urban areas that are not only complex but also have intensely diverse populations are frequently described as having problems that defy resolution. The subtext here is that these problems may be too complex for traditional linear models of analysis. A recent development for addressing complex chaotic situations in human services comes out of open systems theory and modeling: chaos theory. Gleick (1987), one of the early writers to approach this highly sophisticated mathematical modeling as a framework for thinking about social science modeling, noted that it defied accepted ways of thinking about the science as it focused on the behavior of complex systems—or looked for order in disorder. Krippner (1994) described *chaos theory* as the science that looks for patterns in nature that are very complex but that have an eloquent beauty at their core. Chaos theory can deepen and simplify understanding of natural processes (the best example is with weather forecasting). What is the relevance here? It also is being used to construct health, ecological, and organizational lifespan models (Hurst, 1995; Krippner, 1994). I suggest that chaos theory is a powerful nonlinear model that can contribute to understanding diversity among organizations and their members and to understanding the complex dynamic interface between organizational members of human services agencies and their diverse constituencies.

This is an exciting time for those interested in finding relevant solutions and applications in research and discovery of new answers in the diversity arena. New tools and strategies are being developed at a rapid pace. Even scholars who may have resisted diversity for various reasons are modifying their views (Shea, 1997). President Bill Clinton encourages dialogue on race as a policy issue, and the conversation lurches onward. As these efforts continue, we grow increasingly aware of our interdependence and our need to accept differences.

REFERENCES

Bell, D. (1998, January 29). At last, Harvard sees the light. *New York Times*, p. A-23.

Gleick, J. (1987). *Chaos: The making of a new science.* New York: Penguin Books.

Hurst, D. K. (1995). *Crisis and renewal: Meeting the challenge of organizational change.* Boston: Harvard Business School Press.

Jackson, S. E., & Ruderman, M. N. (Eds.). (1995). *Diversity in work teams: Research paradigms for the changing workplace.* Washington, DC: American Psychological Association.

Krippner, S. (1994). Humanistic psychology and chaos theory: The third revolution and the third force. *Journal of Humanistic Psychology, 34*(3), 48–61.

McGrath, J. E., Berdahl, J. L., & Arrow, H. (1995). Trait, expectations, culture, and clout: The dynamics of diversity in work groups. In S. E. Jackson & M. N. Ruderman (Eds.), *Diversity in work teams: Research paradigms for a changing workplace* (pp. 17–45). Washington, DC: American Psychological Association.

Shea, C. (1997, April 11). Multiculturalism gains an unlikely supporter: Nathan Glazer, a long-time foe of affirmative action, says he underestimated the significance of race. *Chronicle of Higher Education*, p. A-18.

Sleek, S. (1997). White Americans avoid dialogue on societal racism: Public policy is driven largely by racial stereotypes, experts on racism say. *APA Monitor, 28*(10), 40.

Thomas, K. M., Phillips, L. D., & Brown, S. (1998). Redefining race in the workplace: Insights from ethnic identity theory. *Journal of Black Psychology, 24*(1), 76–92.

Index

A

Activity modes, 196–197
Affirmative action, 335
Affirmative action groups, 265
African American entrepreneurship
  early 20th century, 333–334
  factors affecting, 336–337
  future outlook for, 336, 338–339
  late 20th century, 334–336
  19th century, 332–333
  trends in, 331
African American women
  barriers for, 173
  challenges facing, 169–170
  coping strategies for, 173–174
  credibility and, 171–172
  isolation and, 170
  mentoring opportunities and,
    170–171, 173–174
  values and, 172–173
  workplace studies of, 167–168
African Americans. *See also* People of
  color
  Civil Rights Act of 1964 and, 22
  cultural values of, 196, 197
  deaf, 138–139
  developmental relationships and.
    See Cross-race relationships
  dialectic variation among, 133–135
  increases in business and industry,
    21
  job satisfaction and, 152–154, 162
  organizational behavior and, 198
  tensions between Africans and,
    362–364
  19th-century racism and, 72–73
  time orientation and, 196
Africans
  in American workplace, 359
  employment and wages for, 360–362
  immigration trends for, 355–356
  meaning of work for, 258, 259
  sociodemographic data for, 355–356
  tensions between African Americans
    and, 362–364

Afrocentric paradigm
  assumptions of, 342–344
  consensus decision making use and,
    347–348
  de-emphasis of efficiency and,
    344–345
  diversity enhancement and, 349–351
  focus on collective work and
    responsibility and, 345–346
  hiring and performance appraisal
    and, 348–349
  workplace diversity and, 341–342
Afrocentrism
  criticisms of, 11
  proponents of, 79–80
Age Discrimination in Employment Act
  of 1967, 22
Agricultural workers, 46
Allopathic medicine. *See* Hawaiians
American Indians. *See* Native
  Americans
American Sign Language (ASL)
  as separate language, 65, 132
  use of, 63, 137
American Sign Language interpreters
  during job interviews, 121
  during job recruitment, 118, 124
  role of, 65
  in workplace, 125
Americans with Disabilities Act (ADA)
  of 1990. *See also* Individuals with
    disabilities; *specific disabilities*
  deaf individuals and, 64, 66
  description of, 116, 234–235
  discrimination and, 232–233
  framework for passage of, 116–117
  function of, 20, 56–57, 60, 192, 231
  grievance procedures and, 126
  health benefits and, 127
  impact of Rehabilitation Act of 1973
    and, 233–234
  impact of stereotypes and, 232
  impact on clinical programs and
    sites and, 237–241
  input from person with disability
    and, 241–242

ADA, continued
    job application process and, 118–120,
        128
    job interviews and, 120–122
    job promotion and advancement
        and, 126–127
    job recruitment and, 117–118
    Louis Harris and Associates survey
        prior to passage of, 62
    modifications and accommodations
        associated with, 235–237, 241
    overall personnel policy and,
        127–128
    reasonable accommodation and, 119,
        122–126, 128
    workplace diversity and, 22
Asian American women
    joint constructional perspectives
        and, 378–382
    overview of, 373
    psychological contracts with
        employers and, 375–376
    stereotypes of, 374–375
    treatment discrimination and,
        376–377
Asian Americans
    cultural values of, 193, 197
    job satisfaction and, 154–155
    meaning of work for, 258, 259
    naturalization rate among, 27
    organizational behavior and, 198,
        199
    time orientation and, 196
Asians
    in American workplace, 364–365
    emotional control of, 366–367
    female authority and, 368–369
    immigration data for, 25, 27, 28,
        355–356, 373
    as model minority, 365–366
    religious influences on, 366
    silence and, 367
    sociodemographic data for, 355–356
    work and family conflict for, 367–368
Assimilation
    historical background of, 70–76
    opponents of, 78
    pluralism versus, 73–74
    proponents of, 77–78
Associate deans
    African American women as,
        169–174
    role of, 168–169
Attention deficit hyperactivity disorder
    (ADHD), 125

Augmentative and alternative com-
    munication (AAC), 136, 137, 140
Autonomy organization, 277–278

B

Biculturalism. *See also* Workplace
        diversity
    African Americans and, 166
    code switch, 135
    deaf individuals and, 138
    explanation of, 243
    group focus for managing
        workplace, 244–250
    implications for workplace, 243–244
Bilingual individuals, 137
Bisexuals. *See also* Gay men; Lesbians
    attitudes toward, 104–105
    employer responses to issues related
        to, 110–111
    homophobia and discrimination
        and, 106–110
    role of organization leaders and
        work environment for, 111–114
    sexual identity formation and, 105–106
    state legislation to protect, 110
    in workplace, 104, 192
Black English, 133–135
Black History Month, 248
Blind individuals. *See also* Visually
        impaired individuals
    accommodations for workers with,
        123
    job interviews with, 121
Boorstin, Daniel, 6–8
Brazilians, 218

C

Catholic Church, 8, 9
Central Americans, 218. *See also* Latinos
Cerebral palsy, 57–60
Certified occupational therapist
        assistant (COTA), 60
Changing Relation study (Ford
        Foundation), 32
Child care, 298, 319. *See also* Supportive
        workplace policies
Children
    entrepreneurial skills acquisition for,
        339
    socialization of, 103
    workplace supports for, 298
Circuit City, 339
City of Richmond v. J. H. Croson
        Company, 335

Civil Rights Act of 1964, 56
   employment discrimination and, 22
   impact of, 64
   individuals with disabilities and, 116
Civil rights movement, 334
Climate. *See* Organizational climate
Cognitively disabled individuals, 124,
   237
Collective work, 345–346
Colleges/universities
   ADA and modifications for
      handicapped in, 235–236
   African American women in social
      work, 166–174
   ethnic group associations in, 245
   initiatives to enhance bicultural
      adaptation within, 247–248
   women in, 167–169
Colombians, 222–223
Communication. *See also* Linguistic
      diversity; Multicultural
      communication; Organizational
      communication
   culture and, 200–201, 203
   literature on workplace, 191
   person-to-person, 346
   strategies promoting effective, 223–224
   workplace climate and, 191–192
Communication errors
   case example of, 211–212
   explanation of, 201–202
   recovery from, 207
Comparable-worth policies, 147
Conflict, 221
Consciousness-raising activities, 249
Consultation circle
   background of, 254
   empowerment, ethics, and, 256–257
   explanation of, 253–254
   group consultation and, 255–256
   implementation of, 257–258, 263
   use of, 258–263
   workplace trends and, 254–255
Consultation circle consultant form, 259
Contact organization, 274–275
Credibility, 171–172
Cross-race relationships
   factors of, 284–285
   racial dynamics in developmental,
      285–288
Cuban Americans. *See also* Latinos
   in labor force, 47–48
   power and social distance and, 222
   profile of, 217
   speaking style and, 221

Cultural competence, 42–43
Cultural diversity
   assimilation versus, 73–74
   historical background of American,
      70–76
Cultural homophobia, 107
Cultural politics, 389–392
Cultural separatists, 79
Culture. *See also* Organizational culture
   communication and, 200–201
   dimensions of, 193–197
   of Native Hawaiians, 388–389
   organizational behavior and,
      197–200

D

Deaf individuals. *See also* Hearing-
      impaired individuals
   accommodations for, 124–125
   African Americans as, 138–139
   culture of, 137–138
   employment discrimination and, 61
   job interviews and, 121
   manual sign use and bilingual
      nature of, 137
   as manual sign users, 137
   misconceptions about, 62–63
   profile of, 63
   protections of rights of, 66
   theories of education regarding, 63
   work barriers for, 64–65
Decision making
   Afrocentric paradigm and
      consensus, 347–348
   employee participation in, 160–161
   in human relations organizations,
      181–182
Delegated function, 186–187
Detached experts, 184–187
Developmental relationships
   model of racial dynamics in cross-
      race, 285–288
   race, gender, and relationship
      formation in, 282–283
   trust and, 284
   type of support in, 283–284
Dialects. *See also* Linguistic diversity
   ethnicity and, 135
   explanation of, 133–134
   regional variations in, 134–135
Disabled individuals. *See* Americans
      with Disabilities Act (ADA) of
      1990; Individuals with
      disabilities; *specific disabilities*

Discrimination. *See also* Racism
   in corporations, 339
   against deaf individuals, 64, 65
   in hiring and promoting, 23
   against homosexuals, 106–111. *See also* Bisexuals; Gay men; Lesbians
   against individuals with disabilities, 232–233
   legislation prohibiting workplace, 22, 64, 192, 234–235. *See also* Americans with Disabilities Act (ADA) of 1990
   status and earnings and, 158–160
   treatment, 376–377
Disintegration organization, 275
Diversity. *See also* Cultural diversity; Linguistic diversity; Workplace diversity
   explanation of, 88, 99, 358
   human services system and, 93–98, 192, 193
   strategies for using strengths of, 44
   suppression of, 76
   values of, 98–101
Diversity training, 266
Downsizing, 321

E

Earnings. *See* Income
Earth
   debate over shape of, 6–8
   movement around sun by, 8–10
Ebonics, 133, 134
Economic opportunity, 48
Education. *See also* Colleges/universities; Social work education
   of deaf children, 64
   employee, 43–44
   entrepreneurial skills incorporated into, 339
Education for All Handicapped Children Act. *See* Individuals with Disabilities Education Act (IDEA)
Efficiency, Afrocentric paradigm and, 344–345
Elder care, 314
Emerging change, defined, 67
Emotional control, 366–367
Empathy, 206
Employee assistance programs (EAPs)
   diversity issues and, 316
   enhancing workplace biculturalism through, 250–251
   issues for women and, 324–327
   service provision and, 314–315

   work force composition trends and, 316–318
Employee education, 43–44
Employee recruitment, 117–118
Employees, accommodations for disabled, 56–57
Employment benefits. *See also* Medical insurance; Supportive workplace policies
   ethnicity and, 299–300
   for individuals with disabilities, 127
   job satisfaction and, 151
Employment Non-Discrimination Act, 110
Employment patterns, 32
Employment tests, 119, 128
Empowerment, 256–257
Entrepreneurship, African American
   early 20th century, 333–334
   factors affecting, 336–337
   future outlook for, 336, 338–339
   late 20th century, 334–336
   19th century, 332–333
   trends in, 331
Equitable Life Assurance, 245–246
Ethics, 256–257
Ethnic groups. *See also specific ethnic groups*
   associations protecting rights of, 245–246
   initiatives to enhance adaptation of, 246–248
   joint ventures pursued by, 249–250
   promotion of pride among, 248–249
   in work force, 373
Ethnicity. *See also specific ethnic groups*
   benefit use and, 299–300
   dialectic variation and, 135
   job satisfaction study and, 156–158
European Americans. *See also* White racial identity
   conversational norms among, 220
   cultural values of, 341
   eye contact and, 204
   human relationships and, 196
   individualism and, 216
   organizational behavior and, 198
   power and social distance and, 222
   preferred modes of activity and, 196–197
   speaking style and, 221
   time orientation and, 196
Eye contact
   cultural basis of, 204, 207
   Latinos and, 221

F

Family responsibilities
  Afrocentric paradigm and, 347–348
  Asians and, 367–368
  balancing work and, 314, 319
  female immigrants and, 320
  job performance and, 321–324
  single-parent women and, 319–321
  tensions resulting from work and,
    314–315
Family roles, 51–52
Fel-Pro, Inc., 300–302, 304, 309
Financial issues, for single-parent
    women, 321
First Nations people. *See* Native
    Americans
Flexible work schedules, 299
Free African Society, 72
French, intraorganizational boundaries
    and, 199

G

Garment industry, 30, 50
Gay men
  attitudes toward, 104–105
  employer responses to issues related
    to, 110–111
  homophobia and discrimination
    and, 106–110
  role of organization leaders and
    work environment for, 111–114
  sexual identity formation and,
    105–106
  state legislation to protect, 110
  in workplace, 104, 192
Gender
  job satisfaction study and, 144–145,
    147–152, 156–158. *See also* Job
    satisfaction; Job satisfaction study
  mentoring relationships and, 281–289
  organizational behavior and, 198
  perceptions of communication and,
    218
  professionalism and, 219
  supportive workplace policy use by,
    298–299. *See also* Supportive
    workplace policies
Gender identity
  development of, 103–104
  sexual identity versus, 110
Globalization, 22
Great Interruption, 6–7
Grievance procedures, 126
Group recognition, 346

Group relations perspective
  chancellor–board issues and, 12–14
  nature of, 3–4, 15–16
  reason versus faith and, 9–10
  Tavistock, 4–5

H

Hawaiians
  healing practices and cultural
    politics of, 389–392
  health and disease and, 393–394
  health care conflicts for, 392–393
  integration of health care in, 394–396
  medical traditions of, 387–389
  overview of, 385–386
Health care organizations. *See* Urban
    organizations
*Healthy People—The Surgeon General's
    Report on Health Promotion and
    Disease Prevention* (U.S. Dept. of
    Health and Human Services),
    386, 393
Hearing-impaired individuals. *See also*
    Deaf individuals
  accommodations for, 124–125, 236
  African American, 138–139
Homophobia
  types of, 106–107
  in workplace, 107–110
Homosexuals. *See* Bisexuals; Gay men;
    Lesbians
Human services organizations
  diversity achievement in, 98
  job satisfaction within, 144–162. *See
    also* Job satisfaction; Job
    satisfaction study
  multicultural communication in,
    191–213. *See also* Multicultural
    communication
  role of diversity in, 93–98

I

Identity formation
  gay, lesbian, and bisexual, 105–106
Immigrants
  effects on workplace of, 29–32
  profile of new, 24–29
  undocumented, 27, 30, 46
  work and family responsibilities for
    female, 320
  workplace conflicts and new, 32–33
  workplace diversity and, 21, 22
Immigration
  change in patterns of, 75

Immigration, continued
  Latino, 215
  recent waves of African and Asian,
    355–356, 373
  trends in, 315–316, 360
Immigration Act of 1924, 23, 25
Immigration Act of 1990, 22, 24
Immigration and Nationality Act of
    1952, 23–25
Immigration and Nationality Act of
    1965, 22, 24, 25, 359, 364
Immigration policy
  immigrant flow and, 23–24
  Latinos and, 48
  overview of, 22–25
  shifts in U.S., 361
Immigration Reform and Control Act of
    1986, 22, 24
Inclusionists, 78–79
Income
  of African Americans, 335
  of immigrants, 30
  of single-parent women, 321
Independent living movement, 116–117
Individualism, 199, 216
Individuals with disabilities. *See also*
    Americans with Disabilities Act
    (ADA) of 1990; *specific disabilities*
  discrimination against, 232–233
  grievance procedures for, 126
  health benefits and, 127
  job application process and, 118–120,
    128
  job interviews and, 120–122, 128
  job promotion and advancement for,
    126–127
  overall personnel policy and,
    127–128
  overview of, 56
  policy affecting, 56–57
  profile of deaf individual, 61–66
  profile of individual with cerebral
    palsy, 57–60
  reasonable accommodation and, 119,
    122–126, 128
  stereotypes of, 232
Individuals with Disabilities Education
    Act (IDEA), 232–233
Institutional homophobia, 107
Integrative pluralists
  in America, 82–86
  explanation of, 80–82
Intelligences, multiple, 99
Interpersonal homophobia, 107
Interpretive knowledge, 1–2

Interviews. *See* Job interviews
Intuitive knowledge, 2

J

Japanese
  gender roles and, 381
  personal honor and, 205–206
Job application procedures, 118–120, 128
Job interviews, 120–122, 128
Job performance
  family responsibilities and, 321–322
  family situation and, 323
  work environment and, 323–324
  workplace policies and, 322
Job promotion, 126–127
Job recruitment
  Afrocentric paradigm and, 348–349
  Americans with Disabilities Act and,
    117–129. *See also* Americans with
    Disabilities Act (ADA) of 1990
Job satisfaction
  African Americans and, 152–154, 162
  Asian Americans and, 154–155
  determinants of, 145–148
  importance of, 144
  job dullness/monotony and, 148
  Latinos and, 152, 155–156
  pay and fringe benefits and, 151
  pressures and expectations and,
    149–150
  supervisors, managers, and promo-
    tional opportunities and, 150–151
  use of abilities and, 148–149
Job satisfaction study
  conclusions of, 160–162
  discrimination issues and, 158–160
  findings by gender and, 147–152,
    156–158
  findings by race and ethnicity, 152–159
  purpose and method of, 146
Job searches, 32
Joint-constructional perspectives
  explanation of, 378–379
  stereotype-related problems and,
    379–382

K

Knights of Labor, 72

L

Language barriers. *See also* Linguistic
    diversity
  as source of tension, 316
  in workplace, 219–220

Latinos. *See also specific groups*
    background of, 215
    cultural values of, 196, 197
    demographics related to, 46
    diversity among, 216–218
    English proficiency among, 220
    immigration trends for, 48, 215
    interactive style elements and
      communication with, 220
    job satisfaction and, 152, 155–156
    language barriers in communicating
      with, 219–220
    organizational behavior and, 198, 199
    organizational communication and,
      218–219
    overview of, 45–46
    problem behaviors among male, 52
    profile of, 46–48
    social and power distance variations
      among, 222–223
    strategies to promote effective
      communication with, 223–224
    time orientation and, 196
    work and male, 45, 52–54
    work ethics and family and, 51–52
Learning disabled individuals, 125, 237
Lesbians
    attitudes toward, 104–105
    employer responses to issues related
      to, 110–111
    homophobia and discrimination
      and, 106–110
    role of organization leaders and
      work environment for, 111–114
    sexual identity formation and,
      105–106
    state legislation to protect, 110
    in workplace, 104, 192
Linguistic diversity. *See also* Language
    barriers
    augmentative and alternative
      communicators and, 136–137
    dialects and, 133–134
    ethnicity and, 135
    explanation of, 132–133
    geographic regional and, 134–135
    in organizational settings, 139–140
    sign language users and, 137–139
    trends in, 68, 132, 316
Linkage mechanisms
    delegated function as, 186–187
    detached experts as, 184–187
    opinion leaders as, 187–188
    settlement houses as, 185–186
    voluntary associations as, 186

M

Marital status, 319–321
Medical insurance, 127
Medical practices
    First Nations people and, 37–38
    of Hawaiians, 385–396. *See also*
      Hawaiians
Melting pot theory, 73, 77. *See also*
    Assimilation
Mentoring
    African American women and,
      170–171, 173–174
    career and psychological support in,
      281–282
    cross-race relationships in,
      284–289
    developmental relationships in,
      282–284
    for First Nations employees, 42
Mexican Americans. *See also* Latinos
    as agricultural workers, 46
    English proficiency among, 220
    in labor force, 47–48
    organizational behavior and,
      198–199
    power and social distance and, 222
    profile of, 216–217
Model-minority stereotype
    Asians as, 365–366, 374
    consequences of, 375
Multicultural communication. *See also*
    Communication; Linguistic
    diversity
    case example illustrating problems
      in, 208–213
    communication errors as barriers to,
      201–202
    culture and, 200–201
    dimensions of culture and, 193–197
    elements of improving, 202–208
    importance of, 192–193
    organizational behavior and,
      197–200, 218–219
    strategies to promote effective,
      223–224
Multiculturalism
    academic criticism of, 10–12
    movement of earth around sun and,
      8–10
    New York City education issues and,
      12–14
    shape of earth and, 6–8
    theories of, 3–4, 14–16
Mutual-aid groups, 248–249

N

National Negro Business League, 332
Native Americans
    assimilation of, 40–41, 72
    characteristics of traditionally
        raised, 37–38
    cultural values of, 193, 197
    as employees, 40–44
    ethnic identity issues of, 36–37
    person-to-nature relationship and,
        193
    services delivery to, 41–44
    19th-century attempts to assimilate,
        72
    time orientation and, 196
    urban/transitional, 39–40
Native Hawaiian Health Care
        Improvement Act of 1988, 386,
        390, 391
Native Hawaiians. See Hawaiians
Native healing. See Hawaiians
Naturalization rate, 27–29. See also
        Immigrants
New York City, 12–14
Nonverbal communication, 140, 223.
        See also Eye contact

O

Occupational status, 307–309
Occupational therapy, 58–60
Organizational behavior, 197–200
Organizational climate
    communication and, 191–192
    impact of racial identity on, 273, 274
Organizational communication,
        218–219
Organizational culture
    impact of racial identity on, 273, 274
    organizational behavior and,
        197–200
Organizational structure
    as concern of women, 321
    primary group cooperation and,
        179–180
Organizations. See also Urban
        organizations
    African American owned, 334–339.
        See also African American
        entrepreneurship
    Afrocentricity and positive
        potentiality in, 344–349
    autonomy in, 277–278
    changing nature of, 90–93
    contact attitudes in, 274–275

disintegration in, 275
ethnic group associations in, 245–246
money-centered versus idea-
        centered, 89
office-centered versus decision-
        centered, 91
racial discrimination within, 339
reintegration in, 275–276
remedies for racism in, 265–266
thing-centered versus people-
        centered, 90

P

Passover, 248
People of color. See also African
        Americans; Latinos; Native
        Americans
    cultural values of, 196, 197
    time orientation and, 196
    work and family responsibilities for
        female, 320
    in work force, 243, 315, 316
Performance appraisal, 348–349
Personal homophobia, 107
Personalism, 216
Personnel policies, 127–129
Person-to-nature relationship, 193
Peruvians, 218
Physically disabled individuals,
        122–123, 236–237
Pluralism
    assimilation versus, 73–74
    integrative, 80–86
    separative, 79–80
Populist Party, 72
Positivism, 1
Power, 141
Power distance, 222–223
Pregnancy Discrimination Act of 1978,
        22
Primary groups
    balance between bureaucracies and,
        178–179, 181, 188
    organizational structure and, 179–184
Procter & Gamble, 246–247
Pseudoindependent organization,
        276–277
Psychiatrically disabled individuals,
        125
Psychological contracts, 376
Public policy
    historical background of, 67
    to support workplace diversity,
        369–370
    workplace diversity and, 21–22

Public welfare system, 94
Puerto Rican Americans. *See also* Latinos
  as agricultural workers, 46
  English proficiency among, 220
  historical profile of, 48–51
  in labor force, 48
  profile of, 217–218
Puerto Ricans, 221

Q

Qualitative knowledge, 2

R

Race
  career and psychological support
    and, 281–282
  concerns of employed women by,
    319–321
  developmental relationships and,
    282–284
  job satisfaction study and, 156–158
  mentoring relationships and,
    281–289
  supportive workplace policy use
    and, 299–300. *See also* Supportive
    workplace policies
Racial identity. *See also* White racial
    identity
  autonomy organization and, 277–278
  contact organization and, 274–275
  disintegration organization and, 275
  impact in organizational culture and
    climate of, 273–274
  pseudoindependent organization
    and, 276–277
  reintegration organization and,
    275–276
Racism. *See also* Discrimination; White
    racial identity
  African Americans and 19th century,
    72–73
  remedies for organizational, 265–266
Rationality, 343–344
Reasonable accommodation
  for blind or visually impaired
    workers, 123
  for cognitively disabled workers, 124
  for deaf or hearing impaired
    workers, 124–125
  explanation of, 119, 122
  for learning disabled workers, 125
  personnel polices and, 128–129
  for workers with musculoskeletal
    disabilities, 122–123
  for workers with psychiatric
    disabilities, 125
Refugee Act of 1980, 22, 24
Rehabilitation Act of 1973
  enforcement of, 64
  impact of, 231, 233–234
  individuals with disabilities and, 116
  Section 504, 56, 232–234
Reintegration organization, 275–276
Religious beliefs. *See also* Spiritual
    beliefs
  Asians and, 366
  First Nations people and, 38, 41–42
Responsibility, 345–346

S

Schlesinger, Arthur M., Jr., 10–12, 16, 79,
    80, 82, 85
Self-awareness, cultural, 203–204
Self-help groups
  diversity enhancement through,
    349–351
  promotion of ethnic, 249
Sensitivity training, 266
Separatist groups, 77
Separative pluralists, 79–80
Sephardic Jews, 47
Services delivery, 205
Settlement houses, 185–186
Sexual identity, 103–106
Sexual orientation. *See also* Bisexuals;
    Gay men; Lesbians
  corporate nondiscrimination policies
    regarding, 110–111
  discrimination and, 106–110
Sign language interpreters. *See* Ameri-
    can Sign Language interpreters
Silence
  Asians and, 367
  First Nations people and, 38
Single-parent women, 319–321
Smelting-pot theory, 73, 78
Social work
  licenses and credentials for, 43
  recruiting patterns in, 96–97
  status of, 96
Social work education
  African American women as
    associate deans in, 166–174
  use of technology in, 43
South Americans, 218. *See also* Latinos
Speaking style, 221
Spiritual beliefs. *See also* Religious
    beliefs
  Afrocentric paradigm and, 343

Spiritual beliefs, continued
  First Nations people and, 38, 41–43
  Hawaiian native healing and,
      387–388, 392. *See also* Hawaiians
Stereotypes
  of Asian American women, 374–375
  elimination of, 205–206
  for individuals with disabilities, 232
  joint constructions to shatter,
      379–382
Stress, 52
Subjective knowledge, 2
Supportive workplace policies
  conclusions of use of, 309–312
  design of, 297
  explanation of, 298
  study of use of, 300–309
  variations in use of, 298–300

T

Tavistock theory, 5
TDDs (telecommunication devices for
      deaf people)
  job recruitment and, 118, 127
  in workplace, 125
Team consultation. *See* Consultation
      circle
Technological change, 22
Theories
  of multiculturalism, 3–4, 14–16
  nature of, 3
Time orientation, 196
Treatment discrimination, 376–377
TTs (text telephones)
  job recruitment and, 118, 127
  in workplace, 125
Type 1 communication errors
  case example of, 211, 212
  explanation of, 201–202
  by human services workers, 207
Type 2 communication errors, 202, 212

U

Underemployment, 46
Undocumented immigrants
  effect on native-born workers of, 30
  estimates of, 27
  post–World War II, 46
Unemployment, 46
Unskilled employment, 46
Urban organizations. *See also*
      Organizations
  balance between primary groups
      and, 178–179, 181, 188

linkage mechanisms and, 184–188
organizational structure and,
    179–184
in racially or ethnically changing
    neighborhoods, 176–178, 188–189

V

Vietnam Era Veterans' Readjustment
    Assistance Act of 1972, 22
Visually impaired individuals, 123, 236.
    See also Blind individuals
Voluntary associations, 186
Voluntary sector, 95

W

Welfare reform legislation, 23
White racial identity. *See also* European
    Americans
  autonomy organization and, 277–278
  contact organization and, 274–275
  disintegration organization and, 275
  impact on organizational climate
      and culture and, 273–274
  overview of, 265–267, 278
  pseudoindependent organization
      and, 276–277
  reintegration organization and,
      275–276
  studies on influence on attitudes of,
      269–273
  theory of, 267–269
Women. *See also* Single-parent women
  access to employment for Latino, 51,
      52
  African American associate deans in
      social work education study,
      166–174
  concerns of employed, 318–321
  dual roles for, 52
  in garment industry, 30, 50
  in higher education, 167–169
  job satisfaction study and, 144–145,
      147–152, 156–158, 162
  as managers, 368–369
  organizational behavior and, 198
  supportive workplace policy use by,
      298–299. *See also* Supportive
      workplace policies
  tensions between work and family
      responsibility affecting, 314–315
  in work force, 31, 243, 315–316, 368,
      373
Workforce 2000 (Hudson Institute), 192,
    331

Work force
    changing nature of, 243, 315–316
    immigrants in, 31
    people of color in, 243, 315, 316
    people with disabilities in, 62
    women in, 31, 243, 315–316, 368, 373
Workplace
    communication and climate in,
        191–192
    gay men, lesbians, and bisexuals in,
        104
    impact of immigrants on, 29–32
    influence of white racial identity on,
        269–273
    integration of deaf individuals in,
        64–65
    job performance and environment
        in, 323–324
    management of diversity in, 84–85
    supportive policies in, 322. See also
        Supportive workplace policies
    transformation of, 21–23, 192,
        354–355

Workplace diversity. See also
        Biculturalism; Diversity
    addressing issues of, 54, 316
    effective communication and,
        223–224
    employers and, 36
    English proficiency and, 220
    expansion of concept of, 341–342
    factors accounting for, 88–93
    group focus for managing, 244–250
    interactive style elements and,
        220–221
    language barriers and, 219–220
    literature gap on, 356–357
    social and power distance and,
        222–223
    strategies for management of,
        368–369
    theoretical formulation for
        examination of, 357–358

About the Editor

Alfrieda Daly, PhD, earned her MSW and doctoral degrees at the University of Michigan, Ann Arbor, in the joint program in social work and social sciences. She is presently on the faculty of the School of Social Work at Rutgers, The State University of New Jersey, New Brunswick, where she teaches courses in social policy, management, and human behavior in the social environment. She is a member of the Task Force on Disability and Persons with Disability of the Council on Social Work Education, is a member of Catalyst's Research Advisory Board on Women of Color, and is a consulting editor for the journal *Social Work*.

Dr. Daly's interest in organizational development and change began in New York City during the 1960s, when she rose to management through the ranks of the Department of Human Services. Her experiences there shaped her desire to know and understand dynamic system processes, and she has extended that desire to the study of systems theory and its application to services delivery and organizational effectiveness, poverty and its impact on systems, and social adjustment of people living with chronic illness and disabilities.

About the Contributors

Clayton P. Alderfer, PhD, is a distinguished professor of organizational psychology and the director of the Organizational Psychology Doctoral Program at the Graduate School of Applied and Professional Psychology, Rutgers University, New Brunswick, NJ. Having authored nearly 100 scholarly articles and two books, he is currently the editor of the *Journal of Applied Behavioral Sciences.*

Joyce O. Beckett, MSW, PhD, LCSW, is a professor at the School of Social Work, Virginia Commonwealth University, Richmond. She teaches human behavior, practice theory, and diversity courses and serves on the editorial board of several social work journals.

Caryn J. Block, PhD, is an associate professor of psychology and education, Program in Social-Organizational Psychology, Teachers College, Columbia University, New York. She is known for her work on race and gender issues in organizations, and her publications address the influence of white racial identity in organizational contexts and the influence of gender role stereotypes on perceptions of men and women as managers.

Robert T. Carter, PhD, is an associate professor of psychology and education, Program in Counseling Psychology, Teachers College, Columbia University, New York. He consults on legal and educational issues associated with race and diversity, including desegregation, teacher training, equity in schools, cross-racial adoption, and biracial custody.

Delores Dungee-Anderson, DSW, BCD, is an associate professor at the School of Social Work, Virginia Commonwealth University, Richmond. She is co-owner and president of Rockwood Counseling Associates, PC, a private group clinical practice in Midlothian, VA. Presently a member of the board of directors, she also served as vice president of the American Board of Examiners in Clinical Social Work.

Ernest F. Dunn, MDiv, PhD, is an associate professor and the acting chair of the Department of Africana Studies, Rutgers University, New Brunswick, NJ. His research is in the fields of African and African American linguistics and language development and on the African American experience from religious, folkloric, and historical perspectives.

Richard A. English, PhD, is dean and a professor of social work at Howard University, Washington, DC. With interests in refugees and immigration matters, he helped create the displaced populations program for MSW students at Howard University. He is past president of the Council on Social Work Education.

Humberto E. Fabelo-Alcover, PhD, LCSW, is an assistant professor at the School of Social Work, Virginia Commonwealth University, Richmond. He has extensive clinical experience in assisting refugee and immigration resettlement workers to help Latino and Vietnamese families and individuals.

Ovetta H. Harris, PhD, is an assistant professor in the Department of Communicative Disorders at Howard University, Washington, DC. She recently completed postdoctoral studies in augmentative and alternative communication at Purdue University. She has worked as a certified speech-language pathologist in clinical settings and in the public school system and has supervised in university clinics.

James I. Herbert, PhD, is an associate professor of management at Kennesaw State University's Michael J. Coles College of Business in Georgia. He also directs the Urban Enterprise Initiative, a program designed to stimulate the creation and growth of urban family businesses, in the university's Family Enterprise Center. He is vice president of the Family Firm Institute, an international association for professionals who work with and study family enterprise.

Gui-Young Hong, PhD, is an associate professor in the Department of Psychology at the University of Tennessee at Chattanooga. Her current research efforts are in sociocultural approaches to justice, women's work and lives, and human rights.

Dawn Howard, OTR, is a member of the Colorado Interagency Coordinating Council for Part C of the Individuals with Disabilities Education Act, assisting with the evaluation project. She also is part of a grant researching the results of providing direct funding to people with developmental disabilities. She makes presentations to Denver area schools about growing up with disability.

Jeanette Jennings, PhD, is a professor and director of the Tulane Center on Aging, Research, Education, and Services at the School of Social Work, Tulane University, New Orleans. She teaches courses on policy, and her research interests focus on elderly parents as caregivers and on women in leadership.

Lana Ka'opua, LSW, ACSW, is a clinical social worker with Kokua Kalihi Valley Comprehensive Health Services and a member of the faculty for the Ke Ola o Hawai'i Community Health Partnership, a multidisciplinary training program for health care professionals. She is a doctoral candidate at the School of Social Welfare, University of Hawaii.

Beth D. Kivel, EdD, is an assistant professor, Leisure Services Division, University of Northern Iowa, Cedar Falls. She cofounded and directed Lavender Youth Recreation and Information Center in San Francisco, a social recreational program for lesbian, gay, and bisexual youths, and Camp Lavender Hill, a summer camp program for the children of lesbian, gay, and bisexual parents.

Carol F. Kuechler, MSW, PhD, is an assistant professor at the School of Social Work, College of St. Catherine/University of St. Thomas, St. Paul. She teaches research and supervision. Her research and practice include the use of intentional organizational structure and process to encourage mutual responsibility among administrators, practitioners, and clients.

Susan J. Lambert, PhD, is an associate professor in the School of Social Service Administration at the University of Chicago. She has recently completed a study examining the relationship between family-responsive policies and workers' support for organizational change.

Ruth R. Martin, MSW, PhD, is a professor and associate dean for academic affairs at the University of Connecticut School of Social Work, West Hartford. Her practice background in social welfare policy includes work in family agencies, psychiatric and correctional institutions, and public schools.

Yolanda Mayo-Quiñones, PhD, is a full-time assistant faculty member at the Hunter College School of Social Work, New York City. She has published book chapters and journal articles on Latino families and Latino men in their roles as fathers and heads of households. She is a member of the Committee on Racial, Ethnic, and Cultural Diversity of the Council on Social Work Education.

R. L. McNeely, PhD, JD, is a professor of social welfare at the University of Wisconsin–Milwaukee and a practicing attorney. He has served as an American Council of Education Fellow, as a Research Fellow of the Gerontological Society of America, and is a recipient of Marquette University's Lawyer Scholar Award.

Henry J. Meyer, PhD, was formally trained as a sociologist. He is professor emeritus of social work at the School of Social Work, University of Michigan, Ann Arbor. For almost 30 years at that university he taught courses on complex organizations.

Glenda Dewberry Rooney, MSW, PhD, is an associate professor, Augsburg College, Minneapolis. She teaches practice methods, research, and organizational theory and development courses.

Fariyal Ross-Sheriff, PhD, is a professor and director of the PhD program in social work at Howard University, Washington, DC. Her teaching and research areas include applied research, displaced populations, immigrant adolescents, women, elderly populations, and Muslim families.

Richard O. Salsgiver, MSW, PhD, is an associate professor of social work education at California State University, Fresno. He has been director of diversity programs at that university and the executive director of the California Association of the Physically Handicapped Independent Living Centers in Fresno.

Marty Sapp, EdD, is an associate professor in the Department of Educational Psychology (Counseling Area) at the University of Wisconsin–Milwaukee and a licensed psychologist. He is certified in clinical hypnosis by the American Society of Clinical Hypnosis.

Jerome H. Schiele, DSW, is an associate professor and chair of the PhD program at the Clark Atlanta University School of Social Work in Georgia. His scholarly work has focused on Afrocentric social theory and social work practice, race and gender stratification among social work faculty, and cultural oppression.

Sue Schmitt, EdD, is dean of the School of Education at Seattle University. In addition to serving on national and state peer review panels, she was the principal investigator on a $1.4 million Nation Science Foundation grant to enhance math and science opportunities for Native American children with disabilities.

Michael Schwartz, JD, born deaf, is a lawyer now serving as special assistant to the vice president for the National Technical Institute for the Deaf at the Rochester Institute of Technology (RIT), New York. He also teaches in RIT's criminal justice program and is a member of the National Theater of the Deaf.

Letha A. See, PhD, LCSW, ACSW, is an associate professor of social work at the University of Georgia, Athens. Her research is in the areas of refugee resettlement, women's studies, and social policy. Her writings have appeared in many social work education and social sciences publications.

Karen M. Sowers, PhD, ACSW, is a professor of social work and dean of the College of Social Work at the University of Tennessee in Knoxville. She has considerable experience in management with an emphasis on diversity in the workplace and is widely published in the areas of gender differences, culturally competent practice, and delivery of social services to ethnically diverse groups.

David A. Thomas, PhD, is an associate professor of organizational behavior and human resource management at the Harvard Graduate School of Business Administration. He is a noted authority on mentoring, executive development, and the challenges of creating and effectively managing a diverse work force. He is a member of the Academy of Management, National Training Laboratories, and the International Society for the Psychoanalytic Study of Organizations.

John E. Tropman, PhD, teaches at the University of Michigan, Ann Arbor, in the university's Program in Nonprofit Executive Leadership, in the Organizational Behavior and Human Resources Management Section at the Michigan Business School, and in the Executive Education Program at Michigan and at Carnegie Mellon University in Pittsburgh. He also presents nationwide the popular seminars "Effective Group Decision Making: How to Get as Little Done as You Do Now in Half the Time."

Nan Van Den Bergh, PhD, LCSW, has been involved in social work practice, education, and administration since 1971. As an author and researcher, she has worked within the domains of addictions, feminist practice, mental health, crisis intervention, gay and lesbian issues, and employee assistance services. She is currently editing an anthology on employee assistance programs to be published by Springer Press.

Phyllis Ivory Vroom, PhD, is an associate professor and associate dean at the Wayne State University School of Social Work, Detroit. Her major areas of scholarly interest are social work practice with adolescents, particularly in urban public school settings, and with their families; and school-based interprofessional, parental, and community collaboration on behalf of the academic, social, and behavioral development of early adolescents.

Joel W. Wells, PhD, is a professor of family studies, Department of Design, Family, and Consumer Services, University of Northern Iowa, Cedar Falls. His teaching and research focus on sexual communications, sexual orientation, sexuality education, alternate family lifestyles, and gender roles.

Joyce Z. White, DSW, is a professor and director of the social work program at Methodist College in Fayetteville, NC. She founded the American Indian Social Work Educators' Group and served as its president until 1995. She helped establish an employee assistance program for a large general hospital in Ohio and has extensive practice experience in substance abuse, aging, and family intervention.

Workplace Diversity
Issues and Perspectives

Cover design by The Watermark Design Office

Composed by Christine Cotting,
UpperCase Publication Services,
in Palatino and Lucida Sans

Printed by Boyd Printing Company